RIA's Complete Analysis of the Tax Provisions of the Tax Relief and Health Care Act of 2006

With Code Sections as Amended and Committee Reports

Heres your copy of RIAs industry-leading
Complete Analysis of the Tax Provisions of the
Tax Relief and Health Care Act of 2006.
We appreciate your patronage.

Heres a list of handy reference numbers:

1-800-950-1216 To place an order for this or other publications
1-800-431-9025 If you have questions about a previously placed order or a customer service issue
1-800-742-3348 If you have a question about product content

395 Hudson Street
New York, N.Y. 10014

ria.thomson.com

RIA's Complete Analysis of the Tax Provisions of the Tax Relief and Health Care Act of 2006

THOMSON
RIA

Sue Ellen Sobel, *Supervisor*

Alexis Brown
Adel Faltas
Amelia Massiah
Jennifer Stryshak
Marisa Swanson

Data Analysts

Young Sone
Lisa Alcock

Citator Data Managers

Janie Davis
Ivette Terry

Paralegals

Joann Casanova
Catherine Daleo
Monica Grier
Danny Wang

Indexing

David Thompson, *Manager*

Janet Mazefsky, *Assistant Manager*

Tom Adewolu
Oslin Busby
George Flynn
Linda Lao
Andrea Leal
Irene Richards
Arlene Verderber

Legal Resource Center

Peter Durham, *Manager*

Pierre Calixte
Sandra Crowder
Patricia Link
Edward Mack
Theresa Scherne
Bernadette Stanton
Michael Stanton
Holly Yue

Velma Goodwine-McDermon, *Supervisor*

Charyn Johnson
William Lesesne

Product Development

Todd Gordon, *Director*

Kim Chirls, *Lead Project Manager*

End-User Technical Services

Jose Fiol, *Team Lead*

Steven McGill, *Design Lead*

Eric Bauer
Jay Loyola
Tanya McDonald
Joseph Oliveri
Valencia Singleton

Product Technology

Perry Townes, *Senior Director*

Tim Bills, *Manager*

Jay Liu, *Manager*

John Melazzo, *Manager*

Laurie Mitchell, *Manager*

Gene Wojna, *Manager*

Eileen Wood, *Information Manager*

Daryl Alexander
Ron Bergeron
Tom Bontrager
Geoff Braine
Janice Cheung
Isabel Cimitile
Resa Cirrincione
Sharon Coon
Tracey Cruz
Chris DiGanci
Andy Dreistadt
Tatyana Fersht
Janine Francesca
Sammy Francois
Peggy Frank
Terri Ganssley
Lee Gingello
Anthony Guglielmo
Michelle Harmon
Jay Kwon
Terry LaGoy
Cynthia Lewis
Jackie Lynott
Chris Macano
Alex Maskovyak
David McInerney
Ejelonu Onukogu
Pamela J. Otruba
Michelle Paulin
Genevie Peters
Dan Pirro
Steve Pitamber
Jason Rapaccuiolo
Patricia Reilly
Ruth Russell
Becky Sears
Alfred Sehayek
Jason Shen
Esme Smartt
Pisa Sone
Margaret Taylor
Torrod Taylor
Alana Trafford
Vivian Turner
Dmitriy Viner
Rhonda Waller
Jieping Wang
Dennis Wendell
Ava Williams
Steve Wisniewski
Hongtu Zhang
Teresa Zhang

Content Technology

Brian McNamara, *Director*

Gale Metz, *Director*

Alanna Dixon, *Manager*

David Levine, *Manager*

Christopher Grillo, *Project Manager*

Sergey Arutchev
David Bantel
Bob Bridier
Mary Jo Catlett
Karen de Luna
Nadine Graham
Steven Haber
Chris Jungheim
Stephen Karg
Julie Lu
Darren McNelis
Scott Murphy
William Peake
Tasso Quidera
Luc Quirion
Irina Resnikoff
Derek Sanders
Parin Shah
Linda Wiseman
Chris Yourch

Manufacturing & Fulfillment Services

Rick Bivona, *Director*

Anthony Scribano, *Scheduling and Fulfillment Manager*

Gail Gneiding, *Manufacturing and Outside Composition Manager*

Rachel Hassenbein, *Associate Fulfillment Manager*

John Disposti, *Senior Manufacturing Coordinator*

Greg Miller, *Associate Production Manager*

Enid Skolnik, *Associate Fulfillment Manager*

Bryan Gardner, *Senior Manufacturing Coordinator*

Lourdes Barba
Linda Gottlieb
Chris Harrington
Jennifer Kalison

Table of Contents

¶ 1. Organization of the Book

Organization of RIA's Complete Analysis of the Tax Relief and Health Care Act of 2006

The following sections contain RIA's Complete Analysis of the tax provisions of H.R. 6111, the Tax Relief and Health Care Act of 2006 (generally referred to in the Analysis as the "2006 Tax Relief and Health Care Act"), which was passed by the House on Dec. 8, 2006 and passed by the Senate on Dec. 9, 2006.

Date of enactment. The 2006 Tax Relief and Health Care Act has not yet been signed into law. However, the President's signature is a foregone conclusion. For the date of enactment of the 2006 Tax Relief and Health Care Act (i.e., the date the President signs it into law) and the Public Law number of the 2006 Tax Relief and Health Care Act, please consult the Research Institute of America home site on the Internet at ria.thomson.com.

The sections are (1) the Analysis of the Tax Provisions of the 2006 Tax Relief and Health Care Act, (2) the Code as Amended, (3) Act Sections not Amending Code, (4) Committee Reports, (5) Tables for the Complete Analysis, and (6) Index to the Analysis of the Tax Provisions of the 2006 Tax Relief and Health Care Act.

The tax provisions of the 2006 Tax Relief and Health Care Act are in Division A of the Act, except for two provisions, namely 2006 Tax Relief and Health Care Act §403(Div. C, Title IV) (see ¶ 1606) and 2006 Tax Relief and Health Care Act §408(Div. C, Title IV) (see ¶ 1401), which are so designated because they appear in Title IV of Division C of the Act.

Extenders and changes to tax relief provisions made by the 2006 Tax Relief and Health Care Act include:

• Election to deduct State and local general sales taxes. The Act extends the election to take an itemized deduction for State and local general sales taxes in lieu of the itemized deduction permitted for State and local income taxes to tax years beginning after Dec. 31, 2005 and before Jan. 1, 2008. See ¶ 101.

• Deduction for qualified tuition and related expenses. The Act extends the above-the-line tax deduction for qualified higher education expenses to tax years beginning in 2006 and 2007. See ¶ 102.

• Above-the-line deduction for certain expenses of elementary and secondary school teachers. The Act extends for two years (to expenses paid or incurred in tax years beginning during 2006 and 2007) a $250 above-the-line deduction for teachers and other school professionals for expenses paid or incurred for books, supplies (other than non-athletic supplies for courses of instruction in health or physical education), computer equipment (including related software and services), other equipment, and supplementary materials used by the educator in the classroom. See ¶ 103.

• Election to include combat pay as earned income for purposes of earned income credit. The Act extends for one year (for tax years ending before Jan. 1, 2008) the provision allowing the use of combat pay in earned income for purposes of calculating the earned income tax credit. See ¶ 106.

• Extension and modification of research credit. The Act extends the research credit for qualified amounts paid or incurred in 2006 and 2007, and enhances the credit for portions of tax years that are in 2007 by (1) increasing the rates of the alternative incremental credit; and (2) creating a new alternative simplified credit that does not use a gross receipts factor. See ¶ 201, ¶ 202 and ¶ 203.

• Availability of Medical Savings Accounts (MSAs). The Act allows new contributions through Dec. 31, 2007. See ¶ 307.

• Parity in application of certain limits to mental health benefits. The Act extends for an additional year (through Dec. 31, 2007) the provision that imposes an excise tax when group health plans that provide medical/surgical and mental health benefits impose limits on mental health that are not imposed on health. See ¶ 402.

• Fifteen-year straight-line cost recovery for qualified leasehold improvements and qualified restaurant property. The Act extends the provision shortening the cost recovery of certain leasehold improvements and restaurant property from 39 to 15 years to apply to property placed in service after December 31, 2005, and expires December 31, 2007. See ¶ 503.

• Extension of bonus depreciation for certain qualified Gulf Opportunity Zone property. The Act extends the placed-in-service deadline for certain GO Zone property in specified portions of the GO Zone to qualify for bonus depreciation. The placed in service deadline is extended to Dec. 31, 2010 for nonresidential real property or residential rental property. For that property, only the adjusted basis of such property attributable to manufacture, construction, or production before Jan. 1, 2010 ("progress expenditures") would qualify for bonus depreciation. The placed in service deadline is extended for personal property if substantially all the use of such property is in that building and that personal property is placed in service within 90 days of the date the building is placed in service. The specified portions of the GO Zone to which the provision applies are defined as those portions of the GO Zone that are in a county or parish which is identified as being a county or parish with damage to more than 60 percent of the housing units in the county or parish. See ¶ 504.

• Extension and expansion of expensing of brownfields remediation costs. The Act extends the provision that permits expensing of costs associated with cleaning up hazardous ("brownfield") sites through the end of 2007. It also provides that petroleum products may be treated as hazardous substances and permits the expensing of payments made or incurred during 2006 and 2007 to abate related contamination. See ¶ 505 and ¶ 506.

• Taxable income limit on percentage depletion for oil and natural gas produced from marginal properties. Typically under percentage depletion, a taxpayer cannot deduct more than the income derived from the well in a given year. The Act extends the suspension of this 100% limitation for tax years beginning in 2006 and 2007. See ¶ 507.

• Accelerated depreciation for business property on Indian reservations. The Act extends the special depreciation recovery period that applies to qualified Indian reservation property for two additional years (to qualified Indian reservation property placed in service before Jan. 1, 2008). See ¶ 510.

• Corporate donations of scientific property used for research and of computer technology and equipment. The Act extends the provision that allows an enhanced deduction for contributions of computer equipment software to elementary, secondary, and post-secondary schools to contributions made during tax years beginning after Dec. 31, 2005 and before Jan. 1, 2008. The Act also allows equipment "assembled by" the donor to qualify for the enhanced deduction for tax years beginning after Dec. 31, 2005. See ¶ 602 and ¶ 603.

• Special rule for elections under expired provisions. The Act gives fiscal year taxpayers with tax years ending in 2006, but before the date of enactment of the 2006 Tax Relief and Health Care Act, an opportunity to change elections already made on their originally filed returns to take into account the extension of the provisions that expired at the end of 2005. See ¶ 701.

• Work opportunity tax credit and welfare-to-work credit. The Act extends the WOTC and WTW credits for an additional two years (to include wages paid or incurred for individuals beginning work after Dec. 31, 2005, and before Jan. 1, 2008). For wages paid or incurred for individuals who begin work for the employer after Dec. 31, 2006, the provision combines the two credits, expands eligibility for WOTC by raising the age ceiling for food stamp recipients from 25 to 40, eliminates the WOTC family income restrictions for ex-felons, and extends the paperwork filing deadline from 21 days to 28 days. See ¶ 801 through ¶ 805.

• Indian employment tax credit. The Act extends the Indian employment tax credit for two additional years (through the end of 2007). See ¶ 807.

• Extension and modification of new markets tax credit. The Act extends the new markets tax for one additional year (through the end of 2008), permitting a $3.5 billion maximum annual amount of qualified equity investments. It also requires IRS to prescribe regs to ensure that non-metropolitan counties receive a proportional allocation of qualified entity investments. See ¶ 1001 and ¶ 1002.

• Extension and modification of qualified zone academy bonds (QZABs). The Act allows another $400 million of issuing authority to state and local governments for 2006 and 2007 for QZABs, effective for effective for bonds issued after Dec. 31, 2005 and before Jan. 1, 2008. The Act also adds special rules relating to expenditures and arbitrage and adds a reporting requirement for issuers of QZABs, effective for obligations issued after the date of enactment of the 2006 Tax Relief and Health Care Act. See ¶ 1003 and ¶ 1004.

• Tax incentives for investment in the District of Columbia (DC). The Act extends for two years (through 2007) the first-time homebuyer tax credit and four specific tax benefits available to businesses operating in designated DC enterprise zones (i.e., 20% wage credit; $35,000 of additional small business expensing; tax exempt bonds and zero capital gains for property held five years). See ¶ 1101 through ¶ 1104.

• American Samoa economic development credit. The Act creates a temporary, two year credit for possessions corporations operating in American Samoa. The credit is generally based on the amount of wages paid in American Samoa and depreciation deductions with respect to property located in American Samoa, and is effective for the first two tax years beginning after Dec. 31, 2005 and before Jan. 1, 2008. See ¶ 1303.

• Disclosures of certain tax return information. The Act extends IRS's authority to share information with other agencies for one year for requests made through Dec. 31, 2007. See ¶ 1403, ¶ 1404 and ¶ 1405.

• Authority for undercover operations. The Act extends to Dec. 31, 2007, IRS's authority to use the proceeds from an undercover operation to pay additional expenses incurred in the undercover operation. See ¶ 1412.

Energy tax extenders and provisions include:

• Credit for residential energy efficient property. The Act extends for one year a credit, equal to 30 percent of qualifying expenditures, for purchase for qualified photovoltaic property and solar water heating property used exclusively for purposes other than heating swimming pools and hot tubs. It also provides a 30 percent credit for the purchase of qualified fuel cell power plants and applies to property placed in service before Jan. 1, 2009. See ¶ 105.

• Deduction for energy efficient commercial buildings. The Act extends for one year a deduction for energy efficient commercial buildings that reduce annual energy and power consumption by 50 percent compared to the American Society of Heating, Refrigerating, and Air Conditioning Engineers (ASHRAE) standard. See ¶ 501.

• Special depreciation allowance for cellulosic biomass ethanol plant property. The Act allows for 50 percent accelerated depreciation in the year a new cellulosic biomass ethanol facility is placed in service, if it is placed in service before Jan. 1, 2013. See ¶ 508.

• Credit for new energy efficient homes. The Act extends for one year a credit to eligible contractor for construction of a qualified new energy-efficient home. Under the Act, the credit applies to homes that are purchased before Jan. 1, 2009. See ¶ 901.

• Energy credit. The Act extends for one year a 30 percent business energy credit for purchase of qualified fuel cell power plants for businesses and a 10 percent credit for purchase of qualifying stationary microturbine power plants. It also extends a 30 percent credit for purchase of qualifying solar energy property. Under the Act, the credits apply to periods before Jan. 1, 2009. See ¶ 902.

• Credit for electricity produced from certain renewable resources. The Act extends the placed-in-service date by one year (through Dec. 31, 2008) for qualifying facilities: wind facilities; closed-loop biomass facilities; open loop biomass facilities; geothermal facilities; small irrigation power facilities; landfill gas facilities and trash combustion facilities; and qualified hydropower. See ¶ 903.

• Treatment of coke and coke gas. The Act clarifies that petroleum coke, or pet coke, is not a qualifying product for purposes of the nonconventional production tax credit and eliminates the phase-out of the credit for facilities producing coke or coke gas. See ¶ 904.

• Performance standards for sulfur dioxide removal in advanced coal-based generation technology units designed to use subbituminous coal. The Act establishes an alternative measurement to achieve low sulfur dioxide emissions for advanced coal-based generation technology units designed to use sub-bituminous coal, for the investment tax credits for clean coal facilities established in the 2005 Energy Act. Integrated gasification combined cycle (IGCC) projects get a 20 percent investment tax credit and other advanced coal-based projects that produce electricity get a 15 percent credit. See ¶ 905.

• Credit to holders of clean renewable energy bonds (CREBs). The Act adds additional $400 million to a category of tax credit bond called Clean Renewable Energy Bonds ("CREBs"). CREBs are defined as bond issued by qualified issuer if, in addition to other requirements, 95 percent of proceeds are used to finance capital expenditures incurred for facilities qualifying for tax credit under Code Sec. 45. Qualified issuers include governmental bodies (including Indian tribal governments) and mutual or cooperative electric companies. The provision is effective for bonds issued after Dec. 31, 2006. See ¶ 906.

• Special rule for qualified methanol or ethanol fuel. The Act extends a reduced excise tax rate on methanol or ethanol fuel derived from coal (including peat). See ¶ 1501.

Health Savings Account provisions include:

• One-time distribution from individual retirement plans to fund HSAs. The Act allows those who cannot afford to fully fund an HSA with direct contributions to move IRA money to a more tax-advantaged position. See ¶ 301.

• FSA and HRA terminations to fund HSAs. The Act permits an employer to make a one-time transfer of the balance in an employee's health reimbursement account (HRA) or flexible spending account (FSA) to an HSA. The maximum transfer is the lesser of the HRA or FSA balance on the date of transfer or Sept. 21, 2006. Transfers must be made before Jan. 1, 2012. If a high deductible plan is not maintained for at least 12 months following the transfer, the transferred amount is taxable as ordinary income and subject to a 10% excise tax. Any FSA balance remaining at the end of a year can be used up in the first 2 1/2 months of the following year (if the plan allows). See ¶ 302.

• Repeal of annual deductible limitation on HSA contributions. The Act allows an HSA contribution based on a strict dollar amount that is adjusted for inflation (for 2007: $2,850 for self-only coverage, and $5,650 for family coverage). See ¶ 303.

• Exception to requirement for employers to make comparable health savings account contributions. The Act allows employers to provide additional contributions to lower-paid workers. See ¶ 304.

• Modification of cost-of-living adjustment. The Act requires indexing of HSA limits by June 1 and thus facilitates the preparation of enrollment materials and the making of advance planning. See ¶ 305.

• Contribution limitation not reduced for part-year coverage. The Act allows a full year's contribution to an HSA for partial year's coverage, if the taxpayer maintains the high deductible plan for at least 12 months. Failure to maintain the high deductible coverage for at least 12 months results in a loss of the deduction and a 10% penalty. See ¶ 306.

Other tax provisions include:

• Premiums for mortgage insurance. The Act establishes an itemized deduction for the cost of mortgage insurance on a qualified personal residence. The deduction is phased-out ratably by 10% for each $1,000 by which the taxpayer's AGI exceeds $100,000. Thus, the deduction is unavailable for a taxpayer with an AGI in excess of $110,000. The provision is effective for amounts paid or accrued (and applicable to the period) after Dec. 31, 2006 and before Jan. 1, 2008 for mortgage contracts issued after Dec. 31, 2006. See ¶ 104.

• Exclusion of gain from sale of a principal residence by certain employees of the intelligence community. The Act provides the same residency requirement exclusion offered to military service personnel to intelligence officers, except that it requires that the intelligence officers be stationed overseas. The provision is effective for sales and exchanges after the date of enactment of the 2006 Tax Relief and Health Care Act through Dec. 31, 2010. See ¶ 107.

• Loans to qualified continuing care facilities made permanent. The Act makes permanent the Tax Increase Prevention and Reconciliation Act change that reformed the treatment of loans by seniors to qualified continuing care facilities where they are residents. See ¶ 108.

• Sale of property by judicial officers. The Act extends to Federal judges the ability, currently available to executive branch employees, to elect to defer capital gains on property sold to avoid conflicts of interest to the extent the proceeds are reinvested in other permitted property. The provision is effective for divestitures after the date of enactment of the 2006 Tax Relief and Health Care Act. See ¶ 109.

• Returns required in connection with certain options. Every corporation must report transfers of stock pursuant to a person's exercise of an incentive stock option or a transfer of legal title of a share of stock acquired by the transferor pursuant to the exercise of an option. The Act requires the corporation reporting the transfer to provide a statement to the person named in the information return. The provision is effective for calendar years beginning after the date of enactment of the 2006 Tax Relief and Health Care Act. See ¶ 401.

• Partial expensing for advanced mine safety equipment. The Act provides 50% immediate expensing for qualified underground mine safety equipment (that goes above and beyond current safety equipment requirements), including: (1) communications technology enabling miners to remain in constant contact with an individual above ground; (2) electronic tracking devices that enable an individual above ground to locate miners in the mine at all times; (3) self-contained self-rescue emergency breathing apparatuses carried by the miners and additional oxygen supplies stored in the mine; and (4) mine atmospheric monitoring equipment to measure levels of carbon monoxide, methane, and oxygen in the mine. The provision is effective for costs paid or incurred after the date of enactment of the 2006 Tax Relief and Health Care Act and does not apply to property placed in service after Dec. 31, 2008. See ¶ 509.

• Modification of excise tax on unrelated business taxable income of charitable remainder trusts. The Act replaces the rule taking away the income tax exemption of a charitable remainder trust for any year in which the trust has any unrelated business taxable income, and instead imposes a 100-percent excise tax on the unrelated business taxable income of a charitable remainder trust. See ¶ 601.

• Mine rescue team training tax credit. The Act provides for a credit of up to $10,000 for training of mine rescue team members. This tax incentive is effective for tax years beginning after Dec. 31, 2005, and expires on Dec. 31, 2008. See ¶ 806.

• Credit for prior year minimum tax liability made refundable after period of years. Because the grant of incentive stock options (ISOs), even before exercised, is subject to AMT tax at the value of the stock on the date the option was granted, the allows certain taxpayers who have unused AMT credits to claim a refundable credit at 20% of the long-term unused AMT credits per year (up to $5,000) for the next five years. The refundable credit phases out for higher income taxpayers. The provision is effective for tax years beginning after the date of enactment of the 2006 Tax Relief and Health Care Act and sunsets on Dec. 31, 2012. See ¶ 1201.

• Deduction allowable with respect to income attributable to domestic production activities in Puerto Rico. The Act expands the manufacturing deduction under Code Sec. 199 to activities in Puerto Rico for the first two tax years beginning after Dec. 31, 2005 and before Jan. 1, 2008. See ¶ 1302.

• Tax Court has jurisdiction to review IRS's denial of equitable innocent spouse relief from joint liability. The Tax Court has jurisdiction to review IRS's denial of equitable innocent spouse relief from joint liability, even if no deficiency was asserted against the requestor of relief. The provision is effective for liability for taxes arising or remaining unpaid on or after the date of enactment of the 2006 Tax Relief and Health Care Act. See ¶ 1401.

• Regional income tax agencies treated as States for purposes of confidentiality and disclosure requirements. The Act allows a governmental organization composed of multiple municipalities with an aggregate population in excess of 250,000 to enter into agreements with IRS to receive federal tax information to assist with tax administration. See ¶ 1406.

• Frivolous tax submissions. The Act modifies the IRS-imposed penalty by increasing the amount of the penalty from $500 to $5,000 and by applying it to all taxpayers and to all types of Federal taxes. It also changes the law with respect to certain submissions that raise frivolous arguments or that are intended to delay or impede tax administration. The submissions to which the provision applies are requests for a collection due process hearing, installment agreements, offers-in-compromise, and taxpayer assistance orders. The provision (1) permits IRS to disregard these requests, (2) permits IRS to impose a penalty of up to $5,000 for these requests, unless the taxpayer withdraws the request after being given an opportunity to do so, and (3) requires IRS to publish a list of positions, arguments, requests, and submissions determined to be frivolous. See ¶ 1407 and ¶ 1408.

• Whistleblower reforms. The Act reforms the reward program for individuals who provide information regarding violations of the tax laws to IRS that involve an individual whose gross income exceeds $200,000 for any taxable year subject to such action and that involves tax, penalties, and interest of over $2 million. Generally, the provision establishes a reward floor of 15% and a cap of 30% of the collected proceeds (including penalties, interest, additions to tax and additional amounts) if IRS moves forward with an administrative or judicial action based on information brought to IRS's attention by an individual. The provision allows an above-the-line deduction for attorneys' fees and costs paid by, or on behalf of, the individual in connection with any award for providing information regarding violations of the tax laws, allows the whistleblower to appeal the award determination with the Tax Court, and also creates a Whistleblower Office within IRS to administer the reward program. The provision is effective for information provided on or after the date of enactment of the 2006 Tax Relief and Health Care Act. See ¶ 1409 through ¶ 1411.

• Modification of refunds for kerosene used in aviation. The Act allows tax exempt users of fuel, such as crop dusters and air ambulances, to file for a refund or waive their right to claim the refund to the registered vendor. The provision is effective for kerosene sold before the date of enactment of the 2006 Tax Relief and Health Care Act to ultimate purchasers at a price that included the tax imposed on that fuel and for which the amount of the tax has not been repaid or credited, and for fuel sold on or after the date of enactment of the 2006 Tax Relief and Health Care Act. See ¶ 1502.

• Addition of meningococcal and human papillomavirus vaccines to list of taxable vaccines. The Act adds meningococcal and human papillomavirus vaccines to the list of taxable vaccines for purposes of the Vaccine Injury Compensation Trust Fund. This is effective one month after the date of enactment of the 2006 Tax Relief and Health Care Act. See ¶ 1503.

• Capital gains treatment for certain self-created musical works made permanent. The Act makes permanent the provision that allows a taxpayer to elect to have the sale or exchange of musical compositions or copyrights in musical works created by the taxpayer's personal efforts (or having a basis determined by reference to the basis in the hands of the taxpayer whose personal efforts created the compositions or copyrights) to be treated as the sale or exchange of a capital asset. See ¶ 1601.

• Modification of active business definition under Code Sec. 355 made permanent. The Act makes permanent the rule that simplifies the active trade or business test by looking at all corporations in the distributing corporation's and the distributed subsidiary's respective affiliated group to determine if the active trade or business test is satisfied. See ¶ 1602.

• Use of qualified mortgage bonds to finance residences for veterans without regard to first-time homebuyer requirement. The Act allows veterans to have a second chance at being a first-time homebuyer for purposes of qualifying for mortgages with lower interest costs that are available under state tax-exempt mortgage revenue bond programs. The provision is effective for bonds issued after the date of enactment of the 2006 Tax Relief and Health Care Act and before Jan. 1, 2008. See ¶ 1603.

• Revision of State veterans limit made permanent. The Act makes the Tax Increase Prevention and Reconciliation Act qualified veteran's mortgage bond changes permanent. See ¶ 1604.

• Clarification of taxation of certain settlement funds made permanent. The Act makes permanent the rule that certain escrow accounts or settlement funds established for resolving liability claims under the '80 Comprehensive Environmental Response, Compensation and Liability Act (CERCLA) are to be treated as beneficially owned by the U.S. government and therefore, not subject to Federal income tax. See ¶ 1605.

• Exclusion from gross income for part of the gain from certain conservation sales. The Act creates a new exclusion from gross income for 25 percent of the qualifying gain from conservation sales of qualifying mineral or geothermal interests. The provision is effective for sales occurring on or after date of enactment of the 2006 Tax Relief and Health Care Act. See ¶ 1606.

• Modification of railroad track maintenance credit. The Act changes the definition of qualified railroad track maintenance expenditures for purposes of the credit to include gross expenditures. Under the Act, qualified railroad track maintenance expenditures should be determined without regard to any consideration for such expenditures given by the Class II or Class III railroad which assign the track for purposes of the credit. The provision is effective for tax years beginning after Dec. 31, 2004. See ¶ 1607.

• Reduction in minimum vessel tonnage which qualifies for tonnage tax made permanent. The Act makes permanent the provision that lowers from 10,000 to 6,000 deadweight tons the limitation on vessels qualifying to elect into the tonnage tax regime. See ¶ 1608.

• Great Lakes domestic shipping to not disqualify vessel from tonnage tax. The Act changes the treatment of shipping within the Great Lakes for tax years beginning after the date of enactment of the 2006 Tax Relief and Health Care Act to permit vessel operators in the region to qualify for the tonnage tax regime. See ¶ 1609.

Technical corrections include:

• Look-through treatment of payments between related controlled foreign corporations under the foreign personal holding company rules. The Act conforms the Tax Increase Prevention and Reconciliation Act exception from Subpart F for certain payments between related foreign subsidiaries of U.S. persons to its purpose of allowing U.S. companies to redeploy their active foreign earnings without an additional U.S. tax burden in appropriate circumstances. In order to qualify for this exception from Subpart F, a related party payment must not be attributable to income of the payor that is effectively connected with the conduct of a U.S. trade or business. See ¶ 1301.

• Technical correction regarding authority to exercise reasonable cause and good faith exception. The Act clarifies that the Secretary of the Treasury may delegate his authority to permit interest suspension with respect to interest on tax deficiencies resulting from certain tax shelter transactions where taxpayers have acted reasonably and in good faith. See ¶ 1402.

Contents A complete list of topics discussed, arranged by paragraph title and number begins at ¶ 2 . . . . p. xxi

Analysis of the Tax Provisions. This section includes the analysis of the tax provisions of the 2006 Tax Relief and Health Care Act arranged in topical order. Each analysis paragraph starts with a boldface title. That is followed by a list of the Code and/or ERISA sections substantively affected by the change, the Act section that caused the change, and the generally effective date for the change. Each analysis paragraph discusses the background for the change, the new law change, and the effective date for that change. Analysis paragraphs may include (1) illustrations and observations providing practical insight into the effects of the change, (2) recommendations explaining how to take advantage of opportunities presented by the law change, (3) cautions explaining how to avoid pitfalls created by the law change, and (4) client letters highlighting important law changes. The Analysis of the 2006 Tax Relief and Health Care Act is reproduced at ¶ 100 *et seq.* . . . . p. 1

Client Letters. Client letters are included on the following topics:

- A letter highlighting the 2006 Tax Relief and Health Care Act provisions that affect businesses; and
- A letter highlighting the 2006 Tax Relief and Health Care Act provisions that affect individuals.

The Client Letters begin at ¶ 1701 *et seq.* . . . . p. 227

Code as Amended. All Code sections that were amended, added, repealed, or redesignated by the tax provisions of the 2006 Tax Relief and Health Care Act, appear in Code section order as amended, added, repealed, or redesignated. New matter is shown in italics. Deleted material and effective dates are shown in footnotes. The Code as Amended is reproduced at ¶ 3000 *et seq.* . . . p. 501

Act Sections Not Amending Code. This section reproduces in Act section order, all 2006 Tax Relief and Health Care Act sections, or portions thereof that are tax related but do not amend specific Code sections. The Act Sections Not Amending Code are reproduced at ¶ 4000 *et seq.* . . . . p. 701

Committee Reports. This section reproduces all relevant parts of the Joint Committee on Taxation Technical Explanation of H.R. 6408, The "Tax Relief and Health Care Act of 2006," as introduced in the House on Dec. 7, 2006 (JCX-50-06), 12/7/2006.

> ***observation:*** Through a parliamentary maneuver, the legislative text of H.R. 6408 was incorporated into H.R. 6111.

The relevant Committee Reports for the 2006 Tax Relief and Health Care Act (in this case, JCX-50-06) are reproduced at ¶ 5000 *et seq.* . . . . p. 801

Act Section Cross Reference Table. Arranged in Act section order, this table shows substantive Code section(s) amended, added, affected, repealed by or related to the 2006 Tax Relief and Health Care Act section, the topic involved, the generally effective date of the amendment, the relevant paragraph number for the Analysis and the paragraph where the relevant Committee Reports are reproduced. The table is reproduced at ¶ 6000. . . . . p. 1,001

Code Section Cross Reference Table. Arranged in Code section order, this table shows the 2006 Tax Relief and Health Care Act section(s) that amend, add, affect, repeal or relate to the Code Section, the topic involved, the generally effective date of the amendment, the relevant paragraph number for the Analysis and the paragraph where the relevant Committee Reports are reproduced. The table is reproduced at ¶ 6001. . . . . p. 1,025

Code Sections Amended by Act. Arranged in Code section order, this table shows all changes to the Internal Revenue Code made by the tax provisions of the 2006 Tax Relief and Health Care Act, including conforming amendments. The table is reproduced at ¶ 6002. . . . . p. 1,051

Act Sections Amending Code. Arranged in Act section order, this table shows all changes to the Internal Revenue Code made by the 2006 Tax Relief and Health Care Act, including conforming amendments. The table is reproduced at ¶ 6003. . . . . p. 1,057

Federal Tax Coordinator 2d ¶s Affected by Act. Arranged in FTC 2d¶ order, this table shows the FTC 2d paragraphs that have been affected by the 2006 Tax Relief and Health Care Act. The table is reproduced at ¶ 6004. . . . . p. 1,061

United States Tax Reporter ¶s Affected by Act. Arranged in USTR ¶ order, this table shows the USTR paragraphs that have been affected by the 2006 Tax Relief and Health Care Act. The table is reproduced at ¶ 6005. . . . . p. 1,063

Tax Desk ¶s Affected by Act. Arranged in Tax Desk ¶ order, this table shows the Tax Desk paragraphs that have been affected by the 2006 Tax Relief and Health Care Act. The table is reproduced at ¶ 6006. . . . . p. 1,065

PCA ¶s Affected by Act. Arranged in Pension Analysis ¶ order, this table shows the Pension Analysis paragraphs that have been affected by the 2006 Tax Relief and Health Care Act. The table is reproduced at ¶ 6007. . . . . . . p. 1,067

PE ¶s Affected by Act. Arranged in Pension and Profit Sharing 2d ¶ order, this table shows the Pension and Profit Sharing 2d paragraphs that have been affected by the 2006 Tax Relief and Health Care Act. The table is reproduced at ¶ 6008. . . . . p. 1,069

EP ¶s Affected by Act. Arranged in Estate Planning Analysis ¶ order, this table shows the Estate Planning Analysis paragraphs that have been affected by the 2006 Tax Relief and Health Care Act. The table is reproduced at ¶ 6009. . . . . p. 1,071

Current and Prospective Effective Dates. Arranged in Code section order, this table shows the topic related to a change to each specified Code section made by a Tax Act passed by the 107th, 108th, or the 109th Congress, the current and/or prospective effective date of that change, and the Complete Analysis ¶ in which the topic is or has been analyzed. The table is reproduced at ¶ 6010. . . . . p. 1,073

Index. A detailed index, which directs the reader to the appropriate Analysis paragraph, is reproduced immediately after the aforementioned Tables for the Complete Analysis. . . . . p. 1,301

¶ 2. Contents

¶ 100. Individuals

¶ 101. Election to claim itemized deduction for state and local general sales taxes is retroactively extended from 2005 through 2007

Code Sec. 164(b)(5)(I), as amended by 2006 Tax Relief and Health Care Act § 103(a)

Generally effective: Tax years beginning after Dec. 31, 2005 and before Jan. 1, 2008

Committee Reports, see ¶ 5003

Sec. 501 of the 2004 Jobs Act (Sec. 501, PL 108-357, 10/22/2004) provided taxpayers with an election to take an itemized deduction for state and local general sales taxes instead of an itemized deduction for state and local income taxes, but only for tax years beginning after Dec. 31, 2003 and before Jan. 1, 2006. (FTC 2d/FIN ¶ K-4510 *et seq.*; USTR ¶ 1644.03; TaxDesk ¶ 326,019 *et seq.*)

New Law. The 2006 Tax Relief and Health Care Act allows taxpayers to elect to take an itemized deduction for state and local general sales taxes instead of an itemized deduction for state and local income taxes for tax years beginning before Jan. 1, 2008. (Code Sec. 164(b)(5)(I) as amended by 2006 Tax Relief and Health Care Act §103(a)) In other words, the Act extends for two years the provision allowing taxpayers to elect to deduct state and local sales taxes in lieu of state and local income taxes. (Com Rept, see ¶ 5003)

> ***observation:*** The sales tax deduction allowed by the 2004 Jobs Act—and extended by the 2006 Tax Relief and Health Care Act—resembles the sales tax deduction in effect before the '86 Tax Reform Act. Portions of Reg §1.164-3, which deal with that earlier sales tax deduction, and which have never been rescinded or amended by IRS, may be helpful in interpreting the provisions of the newer sales tax deduction.

☐ **Effective:** Tax years beginning after Dec. 31, 2005 (2006 Tax Relief and Health Care Act §103(b)) and before Jan. 1, 2008. (Code Sec. 164(b)(5)(I))

FTC 2d References are to Federal Tax Coordinator 2d
FIN References are to RIAs Analysis of Federal Taxes: Income
USTR References are to United States Tax Reporter: Income, Estate & Gift, and Excise
PCA References are to Pension Analysis (print & electronic)
PE References are to Pension Explanations (print & electronic)
EP References are to Estate Planning Analysis (print & electronic)

¶ 102. Above-the-line deduction for higher-education expenses is retroactively extended from 2005 through 2007

Code Sec. 222(e), as amended by 2006 Tax Relief and Health Care Act § 101(a)

Code Sec. 222(b)(2)(B), as amended by 2006 Tax Relief and Health Care Act § 101(b)(1)

Generally effective: Tax years beginning after Dec. 31, 2005 and before Jan. 1, 2008

Committee Reports, see ¶ 5001

Under pre-2006 Tax Relief and Health Care Act law, individuals were allowed an above-the-line deduction for higher-education expenses in computing adjusted gross income (AGI). The expenses had to be "qualified tuition and related (QT&R) expenses" paid for the enrollment or attendance of the taxpayer, or his spouse or dependents, at a higher education institution during the year for which the deduction was claimed, or an academic term beginning within the first three months of the next year. Reductions were required for scholarships and other amounts that were taken into account in determining certain other education-related exclusions, deductions, and credits. (See FTC 2d/FIN ¶ A-4470 *et seq.*; USTR ¶ 2224 *et seq.*; TaxDesk ¶ 352,000 *et seq.*)

The deduction was subject to an "applicable dollar amount" limit. For 2005, the maximum deduction was $4,000 for an individual whose AGI as specially computed (modified AGI) didn't exceed $65,000 ($130,000 for a joint return), or $2,000 for an individual whose modified AGI didn't exceed $80,000 ($160,000 for a joint return). The deduction wasn't allowed to an individual whose modified AGI exceeded the relevant $80,000/$160,000 limit. (See FTC 2d/FIN ¶ A-4471; USTR ¶ 2224; TaxDesk ¶ 352,001)

Under pre-2006 Tax Relief and Health Care Act law, the higher-education expense deduction expired after 2005. (FTC 2d/FIN ¶ A-4471; USTR ¶ 2224.01; TaxDesk ¶ 352,001)

New Law. The 2006 Tax Relief and Health Care Act extends the deduction for higher-education expenses for two years (Com Rept, see ¶ 5001) by providing that the deduction doesn't apply in tax years beginning after Dec. 31, 2007 (instead of 2005). (Code Sec. 222(e) as amended by 2006 Tax Relief and Health Care Act §101(a)) Thus, the deduction is available through Dec. 31, 2007. (Com Rept, see ¶ 5001)

> ***observation:*** Under pre-2006 Tax Relief and Health Care Act law, the higher-education expense deduction wasn't available in tax years beginning after 2005. The extension of the higher-education expense

deduction through 2007 means that the deduction is available retroactively, for expenses paid after 2005 (see effective date, below).

"Applicable dollar amount" limits on deduction. The 2006 Tax Relief and Health Care Act provides the following "applicable dollar amount" limits on the higher-education expense deduction for tax years beginning after 2003 (Code Sec. 222(b)(2)(B) as amended by 2006 Tax Relief and Health Care Act §101(b)):

(1) $4,000, for a taxpayer whose modified AGI for the tax year doesn't exceed $65,000 ($130,000 for a joint return) (Code Sec. 222(b)(2)(B)(i));

(2) $2,000, for a taxpayer not described in (1) whose modified AGI for the tax year doesn't exceed $80,000 ($160,000 for a joint return) (Code Sec. 222(b)(2)(B)(ii)); and

(3) zero, for any other taxpayer. (Code Sec. 222(b)(2)(B)(iii))

RIA ***observation:*** The "applicable dollar amounts" that the 2006 Tax Relief and Health Care Act prescribes for 2006 through 2007 are the same as the limits that were in effect for 2005.

RIA ***observation:*** The above maximum AGI amounts are "cutoff" points: there is no phase-out range. Thus, if the taxpayer's AGI is just $1 higher than the applicable dollar amount, his allowable higher-education expense deduction is reduced down to the next level—e.g., $2,000 (instead of $4,000), or even completely eliminated—i.e., zero (instead of $2,000).

RIA ***illustration (1):*** Taxpayer, a single filer, has $65,000 of modified AGI in 2006, and pays QT&R expenses of $5,000 for his enrollment at an eligible higher education institution. Because Taxpayer's AGI for 2006 doesn't exceed $65,000, his maximum higher-education expense deduction for 2006 is $4,000. Taxpayer can deduct $4,000 of the QT&R expenses he paid in 2006, in computing his AGI for the year. He gets no deduction for the remaining $1,000 ($5,000 – $4,000).

RIA ***illustration (2):*** The facts are the same as in *RIA Illustration (1),* except that Taxpayer's modified AGI for 2006 is $65,001. Because Taxpayer's AGI exceeds $65,000, he doesn't qualify for the $4,000 applicable dollar amount; his maximum higher-education expense deduction for 2006 is $2,000 (instead of $4,000). Taxpayer can deduct only $2,000 of the QT&R expenses he paid in 2006, in computing his AGI for the year. He gets no deduction for the remaining $3,000 ($5,000 – $2,000). Thus, the additional $1 of AGI cost Taxpayer a $2,000 deduction.

observation: There is no carryover for unused amounts. Any portion of QT&R expenses that the taxpayer can't deduct in the tax year because of the above-described applicable dollar amount maximums can't be carried over to and deducted in a later tax year.

recommendation: Taxpayers who are close to the cutoff point should carefully review any opportunities to defer income or accelerate other deductions, to reduce their modified AGI in order to preserve their higher-education expense deduction.

recommendation: Because a taxpayer can't claim both the higher education expense deduction and a HOPE or Lifetime Learning credit in the same tax year for the same student (see FTC 2d/FIN ¶ A-4473; USTR ¶ 2224; TaxDesk ¶ 352,003), taxpayers qualifying for both the deduction and a credit for the same individual for a tax year should compare the tax benefits that would result from each. Although in general a credit is more beneficial than a deduction because it results in a dollar-for-dollar reduction in tax liability, the taxpayer's particular situation might warrant choosing the deduction. In making the comparison, the taxpayer should take into account the different phase-out ranges that apply for the credits (see FTC 2d/FIN ¶ A-4517; USTR ¶ 25A4.02; TaxDesk ¶ 568,917) as opposed to above-described applicable dollar amount limits on the deduction, for taxpayers whose AGI exceeds the applicable threshold.

☐ **Effective:** Tax years beginning after Dec. 31, 2005 (2006 Tax Relief and Health Care Act §101(c)), and before Jan. 1, 2008. (Code Sec. 222(e))

observation: In other words, to qualify for the deduction, the expenses must be paid before 2008. But the education for which the expenses are paid doesn't have to take place before 2008. A higher-education expense is deductible for the tax year (assuming it otherwise qualifies) if it's for enrollment or attendance during that year, or for an academic term beginning within the first three months of the next year (see FTC 2d/FIN ¶ A-4471; USTR ¶ 2224; TaxDesk ¶ 352,001). Thus, expenses for an academic term beginning as late as Mar. 31, 2008 can qualify for the above-the-line deduction in 2007 (assuming the expenses otherwise qualify), if the taxpayer pays the expenses before 2008.

recommendation: Under pre-2006 Tax Relief and Health Care Act law, the deduction wasn't available in tax years beginning after 2005. Because the extension makes the deduction available for payments made in tax years beginning after Dec. 31, 2005, it applies retroactively. This means that individuals subject to estimated tax in 2006, who pay qualifying higher-education expenses in 2006, may have already paid their first three installments of estimated tax for 2006 (i.e., the installments due on Apr. 17, July 17, and Oct. 16) without deducting any of those expenses. Individuals in this situation should recompute their required payments for the fourth installment for 2006 (due on Jan. 16, 2007), to account for the retroactive extension of the deduction. (See FTC 2d/FIN ¶ S-5200 *et seq.*; USTR ¶ 66,544; TaxDesk ¶ 571,300 *et seq.*)

¶ 103. Up-to-$250 above-the-line deduction for teachers' out-of-pocket classroom-related expenses is retroactively extended for two years through 2007

Code Sec. 62(a)(2)(D), as amended by 2006 Tax Relief and Health Care Act § 108(a)

Generally effective: Expenses paid or incurred in tax years beginning after Dec. 31, 2005 and before Jan. 1, 2008

Committee Reports, see ¶ 5012

The 2002 Job Creation Act provided "eligible educators"—kindergarten through 12th grade teachers, instructors, counselors, principals, or aides in any elementary or secondary school—an above-the-line deduction of up to $250 for out-of-pocket expenses they paid in connection with books, supplies (other than nonathletic supplies for courses of instruction in health or physical education), computer equipment (including related software and services), other equipment, and supplementary materials used in the classroom. Under pre-2006 Tax Relief and Health Care Act law, this educator expense deduction expired after 2005. (FTC 2d/FIN ¶ A-2611.2; USTR ¶ 624.02; TaxDesk ¶ 560,706.1)

New Law. The 2006 Tax Relief and Health Care Act allows the educator expense deduction for tax years beginning in 2006 or 2007. (Code Sec. 62(a)(2)(D) as amended by 2006 Tax Relief and Health Care Act §108(a)) In other words, the Act extends the educator expense deduction for two years, through Dec. 31, 2007. (Com Rept, see ¶ 5012)

FTC 2d References are to Federal Tax Coordinator 2d
FIN References are to RIAs Analysis of Federal Taxes: Income
USTR References are to United States Tax Reporter: Income, Estate & Gift, and Excise
PCA References are to Pension Analysis (print & electronic)
PE References are to Pension Explanations (print & electronic)
EP References are to Estate Planning Analysis (print & electronic)

> **observation:** In the absence of the educator expense deduction, any unreimbursed expenses paid or incurred by elementary or secondary school teachers in connection with their teaching activities are deductible only as unreimbursed employee business expenses—i.e., as miscellaneous itemized (below-the-line) deductions subject to the 2%-of-adjusted gross income (AGI) floor on miscellaneous itemized deductions. See FTC 2d/FIN ¶s L-3900 *et seq.*, L-4108; USTR ¶ 1624.067; TaxDesk ¶s 351,500 *et seq.*, 561,604.

☐ **Effective:** Expenses paid or incurred in tax years beginning after Dec. 31, 2005 (2006 Tax Relief and Health Care Act §108(b)) and before Jan. 1, 2008. (Code Sec. 62(a)(2)(D))

¶ 104. Deduction is allowed for mortgage insurance premiums paid or incurred with respect to qualified residences in 2007, subject to phaseout based on AGI

Code Sec. 163(h)(3)(E), as amended by 2006 Tax Relief and Health Care Act § 419(a)
Code Sec. 163(h)(4)(E), as amended by 2006 Tax Relief and Health Care Act § 419(b)
Code Sec. 163(h)(4)(F), as amended by 2006 Tax Relief and Health Care Act § 419(b)
Code Sec. 6050H(h), as amended by 2006 Tax Relief and Health Care Act § 419(c)
Generally effective: Amounts paid or accrued after Dec. 31, 2006
Committee Reports, see ¶ 5070

Noncorporate taxpayers aren't allowed any deductions for "personal interest." Personal interest is defined as all interest with specified exceptions. See FTC 2d/FIN ¶ K-5510 *et seq.*; USTR ¶ 1634.054; TaxDesk ¶ 314,001. The exceptions include qualified residence interest—that is, interest paid or accrued on acquisition indebtedness or home equity indebtedness incurred with respect to a qualified residence (i.e., the taxpayer's principal residence or a second residence). (FTC 2d/FIN ¶ K-5470.1 *et seq.*; USTR ¶ 1634.052; TaxDesk ¶ 314,501 *et seq.*)

New Law. Under the 2006 Tax Relief and Health Care Act, and subject to the phaseout rules discussed below, premiums paid or accrued during 2007 (see discussion of effective date rules below) by a taxpayer during the tax year for qualified mortgage insurance (as defined below) in connection with acquisition indebtedness with respect to a qualified residence of the taxpayer are treated as qualified residence interest. (Code Sec. 163(h)(3)(E)(i) as amended by 2006 Tax Relief and Health Care Act §419(a))

observation: The 2006 Tax Relief and Health Care Act requires that, in order to be deductible under the above rule, premiums for qualified mortgage insurance must be paid or accrued in connection with acquisition indebtedness. However, the Act does not make qualified mortgage insurance a category of acquisition indebtedness, but rather makes it a separate category of qualified residence interest. Therefore, qualified mortgage insurance is not subject to the amount limitations on acquisition indebtedness, and does not affect the amount of indebtedness that may qualify as acquisition indebtedness under those limitations, see FTC 2d/FIN ¶ K-5485; USTR ¶ 1634.052; TaxDesk ¶ 314,516.

Phaseout of deduction. Except for married taxpayers filing separate returns, the amount otherwise treated as interest under the new rule discussed above must be reduced (but not below zero) by 10% of the amount of qualified mortgage insurance for each $1,000 (or fraction thereof) that the taxpayer's adjusted gross income (AGI) for the tax year exceeds $100,000. For married taxpayers filing separate returns, the reduction equals 10% of the amount of qualified mortgage insurance for each $500 (or fraction thereof) that the taxpayer's AGI for the tax year exceeds $50,000. (Code Sec. 163(h)(3)(E)(ii))

illustration: For the 2007 tax year, H and W, married taxpayers, pay $2,000 for qualified mortgage insurance. For that tax year, H and W file a joint return that shows AGI of $106,000. As a result, H and W's deduction for qualified mortgage insurance must be reduced by 60% of the otherwise deductible amount—10% for each of the six full $1,000 amounts by which their AGI exceeds $100,000. H and W's deduction for qualified mortgage interest is therefore $800—$2,000 minus $1,200 (i.e., 60% of $2,000).

If H and W's AGI were $106,419, they would have to reduce their deduction for qualified mortgage insurance by 70% of the otherwise deductible amount—10% for each of the six full $1,000 amounts by which their AGI exceeds $100,000, and an additional 10% for the additional fraction of $1,000 ($419) by which their AGI exceeds $100,000.

observation: Under the above phaseout rule, the deduction for qualified mortgage insurance phases out completely for taxpayers other than marrieds filing separate returns when AGI exceeds $109,000. This is because there is a 10% reduction in the otherwise deductible amount, for each $1,000, or fraction of $1,000, by which the taxpayer's AGI ex-

FTC 2d References are to Federal Tax Coordinator 2d
FIN References are to RIAs Analysis of Federal Taxes: Income
USTR References are to United States Tax Reporter: Income, Estate & Gift, and Excise
PCA References are to Pension Analysis (print & electronic)
PE References are to Pension Explanations (print & electronic)
EP References are to Estate Planning Analysis (print & electronic)

ceeds $100,000. For a taxpayer with AGI exceeding $109,000, there are at least nine full $1,000 amounts, and one fraction of $1,000, in excess of $100,000. Each of these results in a 10% reduction, which in turn results in a reduction totaling 100%. Similarly, for married taxpayers filing separate returns, the deduction for qualified mortgage interest phases out completely when AGI exceeds $54,500.

observation: The Joint Committee on Taxation Technical Explanation says that the deduction is not allowed if the taxpayer's AGI exceeds $110,000 ($55,000 for married taxpayers filing separate returns). (Com Rept, see ¶ 5070) That is not fully accurate, as explained in the preceding RIA observation, because of the "or fraction thereof" language. Rather, the phaseout is complete when the taxpayer's AGI exceeds $109,000 ($54,500 for married taxpayers filing separate returns).

Prepaid qualified mortgage insurance premiums deductible only in year to which premium is allocable. Except for amounts paid for qualified mortgage insurance provided by the Veterans Administration (VA) or the Rural Housing Administration (RHA) (see below), any amounts paid by the taxpayer for qualified mortgage insurance that is properly allocable to any mortgage the payment of which extends to periods that are after the close of the tax year in which that amount is paid are chargeable to capital account and must be treated as paid in those periods to which they are allocated. (Code Sec. 163(h)(4)(F) as amended by 2006 Tax Relief and Health Care Act §419(b))

observation: Presumably, this means that where, in Year 1, a taxpayer "prepays" the premiums for qualified mortgage insurance for the entire term of the mortgage (for example, 15 or 30 years), only the portion of the premium payment that is allocable to Year 1 is treated as paid in that year, and therefore, only that portion of the payment is deductible in Year 1 under the new rule (which allows a deduction only for premiums paid or accrued during the 2007 tax year). The portions of the payment that are allocable to Year 2, Year 3, etc., are treated as paid in those later years, and hence are nondeductible in Year 1 under the new rule.

However, no deduction is allowed for the unamortized balance of premiums that have been capitalized under the new rule if the mortgage is satisfied before the end of its term. (Code Sec. 163(h)(4)(F))

observation: That is, where mortgage liabilities are terminated before the end of the mortgage term—for example, because of a sale of the underlying property, or because of a refinancing, or because of an early payment of the entire balance of the mortgage—and the taxpayer has not yet deducted the entire amount of "prepaid" qualified mortgage insurance premiums because of the above capitalization rule, the taxpayer is not allowed to deduct the remainder of those prepaid premiums in the year of termination. This rule may reflect Congress's expectation that, in these types of cases, the mortgage insurer will refund that remainder back to the taxpayer.

The above rules regarding "prepayments" of qualified mortgage insurance premiums do not apply to amounts paid for qualified mortgage insurance provided by the VA or the RHA. (Code Sec. 163(h)(4)(F))

observation: Because the only types of mortgage insurance that qualify as qualified mortgage insurance are provided by the VA, the RHA, the Federal Housing Administration (FHA), and private mortgage insurance, see below, the above prepayment rules apply only to qualified mortgage insurance provided by the FHA and by private mortgage insurance.

Qualified mortgage insurance defined. "Qualified mortgage insurance" means (Code Sec. 163(h)(4)(E) as amended by 2006 Tax Relief and Health Care Act §419(b)):

(1) mortgage insurance provided by VA, the FHA, or the RHA (Code Sec. 163(h)(4)(E)(i)), and

(2) private mortgage insurance (as defined by Sec. 2 of the Homeowners Protection Act of '98 (12 U.S.C. 4901), as in effect on date of enactment). (Code Sec. 163(d)(4)(E)(ii))

Mortgage insurance premium reporting requirements. IRS may prescribe, by regs, that any person who, in the course of a trade or business, receives from any individual premiums for mortgage insurance aggregating $600 or more for any calendar year, must make a return with respect to that individual. The return must be in the form, must be made at the time, and must contain the information, that IRS prescribes. (Code Sec. 6050H(h)(1) as amended by 2006 Tax Relief and Health Care Act §419(c))

For purposes of the above rule, "mortgage insurance" is (Code Sec. 6050H(h)(3)(B) as amended by 2006 Tax Relief and Health Care Act §419(c)):

(1) mortgage insurance provided by the VA, the FHA, or the RHA, and (Code Sec. 6050H(h)(3)(B)(i))

FTC 2d References are to Federal Tax Coordinator 2d
FIN References are to RIAs Analysis of Federal Taxes: Income
USTR References are to United States Tax Reporter: Income, Estate & Gift, and Excise
PCA References are to Pension Analysis (print & electronic)
PE References are to Pension Explanations (print & electronic)
EP References are to Estate Planning Analysis (print & electronic)

(2) private mortgage insurance (as defined by Sec. 2 of the Homeowners Protection Act of '98 (12 U.S.C. 4901), as in effect on date of enactment). (Code Sec. 6050H(h)(3)(B)(ii))

> ***observation:*** In other words, "mortgage insurance" for purposes of the above reporting rules has the same definition as "qualified mortgage insurance" for purposes of the deduction rules discussed above. However, the reporting rules apply regardless of the availability of the deduction (which is available only for mortgage insurance premiums paid during 2007, see discussion of effective date rules below).

Every person required to make a return under the above reporting rules must furnish to each individual with respect to whom a return is made a written statement showing the information IRS prescribes. The written statement must be furnished on or before Jan. 31 of the year following the calendar year for which the return had to be made. (Code Sec. 6050H(h)(2))

In connection with the above reporting rules, rules similar to the rules of Code Sec. 6050H(c) (relating to mortgage reporting requirements of governmental units, see FTC 2d/FIN ¶ S-3901; USTR ¶ 60,50H4; TaxDesk ¶ 814,055) apply. (Code Sec. 6050H(h)(3)(A))

☐ **Effective:** Amounts paid or accrued after Dec. 31, 2006. (2006 Tax Relief and Health Care Act §419(d))

However, the rules treating qualified mortgage insurance premiums as deductible qualified residence interest apply only if the amounts satisfy the following conditions:

. . . the amounts must be paid or accrued before Jan. 1, 2008 (Code Sec. 163(h)(3)(E)(iv)(I));

. . . the amounts may not be properly allocable to any period after Dec. 31, 2007 (Code Sec. 163(h)(3)(E)(iv)(II));

. . . the amounts must be paid or accrued with respect to a mortgage insurance contract issued after Dec. 31, 2006. (Code Sec. 163(h)(3)(E)(iii))

> ***observation:*** In other words, the new rules regarding the deduction of qualified mortgage insurance premiums apply only to premiums paid or accrued in 2007, with respect to mortgage insurance contracts issued no earlier than 2007—regardless of whether the taxpayer uses a calendar-year or a fiscal-year tax year. However, the mortgage insurance reporting requirements apply to all amounts paid or accrued after 2006, and not only to amounts paid or accrued in 2007.

¶ 105. Residential energy efficient property credit is extended for one year, through 2008; solar energy property qualifying for credit is clarified

Code Sec. 25D(g), as amended by 2006 Tax Relief and Health Care Act § 206(a)
Code Sec. 25D(a)(1), as amended by 2006 Tax Relief and Health Care Act § 206(b)(1)
Code Sec. 25D(b)(1)(A), as amended by 2006 Tax Relief and Health Care Act § 206(b)(1)
Code Sec. 25D(e)(4)(A)(i), as amended by 2006 Tax Relief and Health Care Act § 206(b)(1)
Code Sec. 25D(d)(2), as amended by 2006 Tax Relief and Health Care Act § 206(b)(2)
Generally effective: date of enactment
Committee Reports, see ¶ 5036

Individuals are allowed a personal credit for expenditures for residential energy efficient property placed in service after Dec. 31, 2005, and, under pre-2006 Tax Relief and Health Care Act law, before Jan. 1, 2008. (FTC 2d/FIN ¶ A-4781; USTR ¶ 25D4; TaxDesk ¶ 569,561)

The credit for a tax year is equal to the sum of:

(1) 30% of qualified solar water heating property expenditures, up to a maximum credit of $2,000;

(2) 30% of qualified fuel cell property expenditures, up to a maximum credit of $500 for each 0.5 kilowatt of capacity; and

(3) under pre-2006 Tax Relief and Health Care Act law, 30% of qualified photovoltaic property expenditures, up to a maximum credit of $2,000. (FTC 2d/FIN ¶ A-4781; USTR ¶ 25D4; TaxDesk ¶ 569,561)

Under pre-2006 Tax Relief and Health Care Act law, a "qualified photovoltaic property expenditure" meant an expenditure for property that uses solar energy to generate electricity for use in a dwelling unit located in the U.S. and used as a residence by the taxpayer. (FTC 2d/FIN ¶ A-4782; USTR ¶ 25D4; TaxDesk ¶ 569,562)

Allocation rules are provided where a dwelling unit is jointly occupied and used as a residence by two or more individuals. Under those rules, the maxi-

FTC 2d References are to Federal Tax Coordinator 2d
FIN References are to RIAs Analysis of Federal Taxes: Income
USTR References are to United States Tax Reporter: Income, Estate & Gift, and Excise
PCA References are to Pension Analysis (print & electronic)
PE References are to Pension Explanations (print & electronic)
EP References are to Estate Planning Analysis (print & electronic)

mum amount of expenditures taken into account by all the individuals during the calendar year is:

. . . $6,667 for qualified solar water heating property expenditures;

. . . $1,667 for each half kilowatt of capacity of qualified fuel cell property for which qualified fuel cell property expenditures are made; and

. . . under pre-2006 Tax Relief and Health Care Act law, $6,667 for qualified photovoltaic property expenditures. (FTC 2d/FIN ¶ A-4785; USTR ¶ 25D4; TaxDesk ¶ 569,565)

> ***observation:*** Those amounts ($6,667 and $1,667) are the maximum amounts of expenditures that qualify for the credit—30% of $6,667 is $2,000 and 30% of $1,667 is $500.

New Law. The 2006 Tax Relief and Health Care Act extends the residential energy efficient property credit for one year, so that it is now available for property placed in service before Jan. 1, 2009. (Code Sec. 25D(g) as amended by 2006 Tax Relief and Health Care Act §206(a))

Clarification of solar energy property qualifying for credit. The 2006 Tax Relief and Health Care Act also provides that 30% of the amount paid for "qualified solar energy property expenditures," rather than "qualified photovoltaic property expenditures," is eligible for the credit. (Code Sec. 25D(a)(1) as amended by 2006 Tax Relief and Health Care Act §206(b)(1))

The maximum credit for qualified solar energy property expenditures in a tax year is $2,000. (Code Sec. 25D(b)(1)(A) as amended by 2006 Tax Relief and Health Care Act §206(b)(1))

The definition of "qualified solar electric property expenditure" is the same as the definition of "qualified photovoltaic property expenditure" under pre-2006 Tax Relief and Health Care Act law. Thus, it means an expenditure for property that uses solar energy to generate electricity for use in a dwelling unit located in the U.S. and used as a residence by the taxpayer. (Code Sec. 25D(d)(2) as amended by 2006 Tax Relief and Health Care Act §206(b)(2))

This change in terminology is meant to clarify that all property that uses solar energy to generate electricity for use in a dwelling unit qualifies for the credit, not just photovoltaic property. (Com Rept, see ¶ 5036)

> ***observation:*** "Photovoltaic property" refers to solar cells that convert sunlight into electricity.

Where a dwelling unit is jointly occupied and used as a residence by two or more individuals, the maximum amount of qualified solar electric property expenditures (rather than qualified photovoltaic property expenditures) that may be taken into account by all the individuals during the calendar year is $6,667.

(Code Sec. 25D(e)(4)(A)(i) as amended by 2006 Tax Relief and Health Care Act §206(b)(1))

☐ **Effective:** date of enactment. (Com Rept, see ¶ 5036) The residential energy efficient property credit is available for property placed in service before Jan. 1, 2009. (Code Sec. 25D(g))

¶ 106. Election to include combat pay as earned income for purposes of the earned income credit (EIC) is extended through 2007

Code Sec. 32(c)(2)(B)(vi)(II), as amended by 2006 Tax Relief and Health Care Act § 106(a)
Generally effective: Tax years beginning after Dec. 31, 2006
Committee Reports, see ¶ 5010

A taxpayer may elect to treat combat pay excluded from gross income under Code Sec. 112 as earned income in determining both eligibility for the earned income credit (EIC) and the amount of that credit. (FTC 2d/FIN ¶ A-4224.1; USTR ¶ 324.05; TaxDesk ¶ 569,025.1)

Under pre-2006 Tax Relief and Health Care Act law, this election wasn't available in tax years ending after Dec. 31, 2006. (FTC 2d/FIN ¶ A-4224.1; USTR ¶ 324.05; TaxDesk ¶ 569,025.1)

New Law. The 2006 Tax Relief and Health Care Act extends the availability of this election for one year through tax years ending before Jan. 1, 2008. (Code Sec. 32(c)(2)(B)(vi)(II) as amended by 2006 Tax Relief and Health Care Act §106(a))

> ***observation:*** As combat pay is normally excluded from earned income in computing the EIC, if this election were not available, a taxpayer with only combat pay would have no earned income for EIC purposes and would therefore be ineligible for the EIC. The election to treat nontaxable combat pay as earned income for EIC purposes thus permits an otherwise eligible taxpayer to claim the EIC even if he or she doesn't have any other earned income.

☐ **Effective:** Tax years beginning after Dec. 31, 2006. (2006 Tax Relief and Health Care Act §106(b))

FTC 2d References are to Federal Tax Coordinator 2d
FIN References are to RIAs Analysis of Federal Taxes: Income
USTR References are to United States Tax Reporter: Income, Estate & Gift, and Excise
PCA References are to Pension Analysis (print & electronic)
PE References are to Pension Explanations (print & electronic)
EP References are to Estate Planning Analysis (print & electronic)

¶ 107. Up to ten-year suspension of the five-year period for determining whether the principal residence gain exclusion applies is extended to apply to sales or exchanges by employees of the intelligence community before Jan. 1, 2011

Code Sec. 121(d)(9)(A), as amended by 2006 Tax Relief and Health Care Act § 417(a)
Code Sec. 121(d)(9)(C)(iv), as amended by 2006 Tax Relief and Health Care Act § 417(b)
Code Sec. 121(d)(9)(C)(vi), as amended by 2006 Tax Relief and Health Care Act § 417(c)
Generally effective: Sales or exchanges after date of enactment and before Jan. 1, 2011
Committee Reports, see ¶ 5068

A taxpayer generally can exclude up to $250,000 ($500,000 for certain married couples filing joint returns) of gain realized on the sale or exchange of a principal residence. To be eligible for the exclusion, the taxpayer has to have owned the residence and used it as a principal residence for at least two years of the five-year period ending on the date of the sale or exchange. (FTC 2d/FIN ¶ I-4521; USTR ¶ 1214; TaxDesk ¶ 225,701).

A taxpayer who fails to meet the ownership and use requirements for the exclusion by reason of a change of place of employment, health, or unforeseen circumstances may qualify for a reduced exclusion. (See FTC 2d/FIN ¶ I-4540; USTR ¶ 1214.08; TaxDesk ¶ 225,720) The reduced exclusion is an amount equal to:

. . . the amount which bears the same ratio to the dollar limitation (either $250,000 for single taxpayers or $500,000 for certain joint filers, determined without regard to the rules relating to the reduced exclusion), as

. . . the shorter of: (1) the aggregate periods, during the five-year period ending on the date of the sale or exchange, that the property has been owned and used by the taxpayer as the taxpayer's principal residence, or (2) the period after the date of the most recent earlier sale or exchange by the taxpayer to which the exclusion applied and before the date of the sale or exchange, bears to two years. (FTC 2d/FIN ¶ I-4557; USTR ¶ 1214.08; TaxDesk ¶ 225,737)

In the case of a taxpayer who becomes physically or mentally incapable of self-care, and owns and uses a property as his principal residence during the five-year period ending on the date of the sale or exchange for periods aggregating at least one year, then the taxpayer is treated as using the property as the taxpayer's principal residence during any time during the five-year period in which the taxpayer owns the property and resides in any facility (including a nursing home) licensed by a state or political subdivision to care for an individual in the taxpayer's condition. (FTC 2d/FIN ¶ I-4563; USTR ¶ 1214.14; TaxDesk ¶ 225,743)

For purposes of determining whether a sale of an individual's principal residence qualifies for the $250,000/$500,000 exclusion, certain individuals can elect to suspend, for a maximum of ten years, the five-year test period for ownership and use of a principal residence during certain absences due to service in the uniformed services or the U.S. Foreign Service. If the election is made, the five-year period ending on the date of the sale or exchange of a principal residence does not include any period up to ten years during which the taxpayer or the taxpayer's spouse is on qualified official extended duty as a member of the uniformed services or the U.S. Foreign Service. (FTC 2d/FIN ¶ I-4528.1; USTR ¶ 1214.08; TaxDesk ¶ 225,737) "Qualified official extended duty" is any extended duty (defined below) while serving at a duty station which is at least 50 miles from the property or while residing under government orders in government quarters. "Extended duty" is any period of active duty under a call or order to active duty for a period of more than 90 days or for an indefinite period. (FTC 2d/FIN ¶ I-4528.2; USTR ¶ 1214; TaxDesk ¶ 225,708.2)

The up to ten-year suspension also applies to the five-year period that applies for determining the amount of the reduced exclusion under Code Sec. 121(c)(1)(B) (FTC 2d/FIN ¶ I-4557.1; USTR ¶ 1214.08; TaxDesk ¶ 225,737.1) and for purposes of determining use during periods when the individual is in out-of-residence care under Code Sec. 121(d)(7). (FTC 2d/FIN ¶ I-4563.1; USTR ¶ 1214.14; TaxDesk ¶ 225,743.1)

New Law. For purposes of determining whether a sale or exchange of an individual's principal residence qualifies for the $250,000/$500,000 exclusion, the 2006 Tax Relief and Health Care Act provides that, at the election of an individual with respect to a property, the running of the five-year ownership and use period with respect to the property is suspended during any period that the individual or the individual's spouse is serving on qualified official extended duty as: (Code Sec. 121(d)(9)(A) as amended by 2006 Tax Relief and Health Care Act §417(a))

. . . a member of the uniformed services, (Code Sec. 121(d)(9)(A)(i))

. . . a member of the U.S. Foreign Service, or (Code Sec. 121(d)(9)(A)(ii))

. . . *an employee of the intelligence community* (defined below). (Code Sec. 121(d)(9)(A)(iii))

FTC 2d References are to Federal Tax Coordinator 2d
FIN References are to RIAs Analysis of Federal Taxes: Income
USTR References are to United States Tax Reporter: Income, Estate & Gift, and Excise
PCA References are to Pension Analysis (print & electronic)
PE References are to Pension Explanations (print & electronic)
EP References are to Estate Planning Analysis (print & electronic)

observation: Thus, the 2006 Tax Relief and Health Care Act adds another category of individual serving on qualified official extended duty whose five year ownership and use period can be suspended for up to ten years, namely, an employee of the intelligence community.

illustration (1): B, an employee of the intelligence community, works at a duty station in the D.C. metropolitan area. B buys a house in northern Virginia in Year 3 that he uses as his principal residence for three years. For eight years, from Year 6 through Year 14, B serves on qualified official extended duty as an employee of the intelligence community at a new duty station in Brazil. In Year 15, B sells the house in northern Virginia. B did not use the house as his principal residence for two of the five years preceding the sale. However, B may elect to suspend the running of the five-year period of ownership and use of the northern Virginia residence during his eight-year period of service as an employee of the intelligence community in Brazil. If B makes the election, the eight-year period is not counted in determining whether B used the house for two of the five years preceding the sale. Therefore, B can exclude the gain from the sale of the house.

caution: As explained below (see **Effective** below), the sale of B's northern Virginia residence (in illustration (1) above) has to occur before Jan. 1, 2011 in order for any suspension of the five-year period under Code Sec. 121(d)(9) to apply.

observation: If a married individual who qualifies for the suspension and his spouse (who doesn't qualify for the suspension of the five-year period) get a divorce, presumably the suspension would end with respect to the individual's former spouse at the time of the divorce.

observation: If a married individual who qualifies for the suspension dies while on qualified official extended duty and his surviving spouse doesn't independently qualify for the suspension of the five-year period, presumably the suspension would end with respect to the individual's surviving spouse at the time of the individual's death.

Employee of the intelligence community defined. An employee of the intelligence community is an employee (as defined by 5 USC §2105) of: (Code Sec. 121(d)(9)(C)(iv) as amended by 2006 Tax Relief and Health Care Act §417(b))

. . . the Office of the Director of National Intelligence, (Code Sec. 121(d)(9)(C)(iv)(I))

. . . the Central Intelligence Agency (CIA), (Code Sec. 121(d)(9)(C)(iv)(II))

. . . the National Security Agency (NSA), (Code Sec. 121(d)(9)(C)(iv)(III))

. . . the Defense Intelligence Agency, (Code Sec. 121(d)(9)(C)(iv)(IV))

. . . the National Geospatial-Intelligence Agency, (Code Sec. 121(d)(9)(C)(iv)(V))

. . . the National Reconnaissance Office, (Code Sec. 121(d)(9)(C)(iv)(VI))

. . . any other office within the Dept. of Defense for the collection of specialized national intelligence through reconnaissance programs, (Code Sec. 121(d)(9)(C)(iv)(VII))

. . . any of the intelligence elements of the Army, the Navy, the Air Force, the Marine Corps, the Federal Bureau of Investigation (FBI), the Dept. of Treasury, the Dept. of Energy, and the Coast Guard, (Code Sec. 121(d)(9)(C)(iv)(VIII))

. . . the Bureau of Intelligence and Research of the Dept. of State, or (Code Sec. 121(d)(9)(C)(iv)(IX))

. . . any of the elements of the Dept. of Homeland Security concerned with the analyses of foreign intelligence information. (Code Sec. 121(d)(9)(C)(iv)(X))

When an employee of the intelligence community isn't treated as serving on qualified extended duty. An employee of the intelligence community isn't treated as serving on qualified extended duty unless the duty is at a duty station located outside the U.S. (Code Sec. 121(d)(9)(C)(vi) as amended by 2006 Tax Relief and Health Care Act §417(c)) Thus, an employee of the intelligence community has to move from one duty station to another duty station (the "new duty station") and the new duty station has to be located outside the U.S. (Com Rept, see ¶ 5068)

> ***observation:*** Congress probably meant to refer to qualified *official* extended duty in Code Sec. 121(d)(9)(C)(vi), rather than qualified extended duty. Presumably, however, omission of the word "official" does not change the intended result.

> ***observation:*** Thus, to be treated as serving on qualified official extended duty, the new duty station of an employee of the intelligence community has to be outside the U.S. in addition to the requirements that (1) the employee has to be serving at a duty station at least 50 miles from the property or while residing under government orders in government quarters (Code Sec. 121(d)(9)(C)(i)), and (2) the employee has to be serving on "extended duty", i.e. serving a period of active duty under a call or order to active duty for a period of more than 90 days or for an indefinite period (Code Sec. 121(d)(9)(C)(v), as

redesignated by 2006 Tax Relief and Health Care Act §417(b)). If the new duty station is outside the U.S. (as required by Code Sec. 121(d)(9)(C)(vi)), presumably, requirement (1) would be satisfied in most cases.

observation: In some cases, certain employees of the intelligence community might qualify for the ten-year suspension period because they are also members of the uniformed services or members of the U.S. Foreign Service. For example, an employee of one of the intelligence elements of the Army, the Navy, the Air Force, and the Marine Corps (described in Code Sec. 121(d)(9)(C)(iv)(VIII) above) might also qualify for the ten-year suspension rule under Code Sec. 121(d)(9) as a member of the uniformed services as well as an employee of the intelligence community. Similarly, an employee of the Bureau of Intelligence and Research of the Dept. of State (described in Code Sec. 121(d)(9)(C)(iv)(IX) above) might also be a member of the U.S. Foreign Service.

It would generally be more advantageous for those employees to qualify for Code Sec. 121(d)(9) as members of the uniformed services or of the U.S. Foreign Service rather than as employees of the intelligence community because:

(1) the new duty station of an employee of the intelligence community has to be outside the U.S. (provided in Code Sec. 121(d)(9)(C)(vi), discussed above), and

(2) any sale or exchange of a residence by an employee of the intelligence community has to occur before Jan. 1, 2011 in order for any suspension of the five-year period under Code Sec. 121(d)(9) to apply (see **Effective** below).

Any suspension of the five-year period under Code Sec. 121(d)(9) by members of the uniformed services or members of the U.S. Foreign Service isn't subject to the rules described at (1) and (2) above.

How the suspension affects the reduced exclusion. The up to ten-year suspension for employees of the intelligence community (described above) also applies to the five-year period that applies for determining the amount of a reduced exclusion under Code Sec. 121(c)(1)(B) (FTC 2d/FIN ¶ I-4557.1; USTR ¶ 1214.08; TaxDesk ¶ 225,737.1). (Code Sec. 121(d)(9)(A) as amended by 2006 Tax Relief and Health Care Act §417(a))

observation: A sale of a principal residence owned by an employee of the intelligence community would still have to meet the requirements for the reduced exclusion (i.e., the sale is by reason of a change of place of employment, health, or unforeseen circumstances). In most cases, a sale of a principal residence by an employee of the intelligence community on qualified official extended duty (defined above) presumably would be considered a sale by reason of a change in place of employment and thus qualify for the reduced exclusion.

illustration (2): D, a single employee of the CIA, buys a residence in California on Jan. 1, Year 1, and uses it as his principal residence until Dec. 31, Year 1. On Jan, 1, Year 2, D goes on qualified official extended duty in Europe until Dec. 31, Year 8. While on qualified official extended duty, D sells (before Jan. 1, 2011) his California residence for a gain of $300,000 on Jan. 2, Year 8. The sale of D's California residence otherwise qualifies for a reduced exclusion as a sale by reason of a change in D's place of employment. If D has elected to suspend the five-year period and otherwise qualifies for the reduced exclusion, D is eligible to exclude up to $125,000 of his gain (12⁄24 × $250,000) because during the relevant period, D owned and used the residence as a principal residence for one year (or twelve months).

illustration (3): The facts are the same as in illustration (2) except that D is on qualified official extended duty from Jan. 1, Year 2 until Dec. 31, Year 13. After his qualified official extended duty, D doesn't live in the California residence. D sells the California residence on Dec. 31, Year 15 (but before Jan. 1, 2011). Under Code Sec. 121(d)(9)(B) (see above), the maximum period of time that the five-year period can be suspended is ten years (i.e., until Dec. 31, Year 11). The five-year period (as suspended) for determining whether D is entitled to a reduced exclusion includes:

. . . Jan. 1, Year 1 to Dec. 31, Year 1, and

. . . Jan. 1, Year 12 to Dec. 31, Year 15.

D is eligible to exclude up to $125,000 of his gain (12⁄24 × $250,000) because during the relevant five-year period, D owned and used the residence as a principal residence for one year (or twelve months).

caution: As explained below (see **Effective** below), the sales of the residences in illustrations (2) and (3) above) have to occur before Jan. 1, 2011 in order for any suspension of the five-year period under Code Sec. 121(d)(9) to apply to the sales.

How the suspension affects the determination of use during periods of out-of-residence care. The up to ten-year suspension for employees of the intelligence community (described above) also applies to the special rule for determining use during periods when the individual is in out-of-residence care under Code Sec. 121(d)(7) (FTC 2d/FIN ¶ I-4563; USTR ¶ 1214.08; TaxDesk ¶ 225,737). (Code Sec. 121(d)(9)(A))

observation: Thus, if an employee of the intelligence community (who has made an election to suspend the five-year period under Code Sec. 121(d)(9)) becomes physically or mentally incapable of self-care, that individual will be treated as using his residence as a principal residence for any period that he resides in any facility licensed by a state or political subdivision to care for an individual in the taxpayer's condition. To qualify for this rule, the taxpayer has to have owned and used the residence as his principal residence for periods aggregating at least one year during the five-year period ending on the date of the sale.

illustration (4): F, a single employee of the NSA, buys a residence in Maine on Jan. 1, Year 1, and uses it as his principal residence until Dec. 31, Year 1. On Jan, 1, Year 2, F goes on qualified official extended duty in the Philippines until he resigns from the NSA on Dec. 31, Year 6. On Jan. 1, Year 7, F becomes physically incapacitated and is confined to a hospital licensed by a state until Dec. 31, Year 8. After his release from the hospital, F lives in an apartment in Boston. F sells his Maine home on Jan. 1, Year 11 (but before Jan. 1, 2011).

If F has made the election to suspend the five-year period for up to ten years, the rules for determining use during periods when the individual is in out-of-residence care are suspended while F is on qualified official extended duty (i.e., from Jan. 1, Year 2 until Dec. 31, Year 6). Since F owned and used the Maine residence for one year during the five-year period (as suspended) before the sale, F is treated as using the Maine residence while he is in the out-of-residence care under Code Sec. 121(d)(7). Thus, the sale of F's residence is eligible for the exclusion because he owned and used (or is treated as owning and using) the residence as his principal residence during the following periods:

. . . Jan. 1, Year 1 until Dec. 31, Year 1 (the period that F lived in the residence), and

. . . Jan. 1, Year 7 until Dec. 31, Year 8 (the period that F was in the hospital).

Since F is treated as owning and using his home as his principal residence for more than two years in the relevant five-year period, the sale of F's residence is eligible for the up to $250,000 exclusion.

caution: As explained below (see **Effective** below), the sale of the residence in illustration (4) above) has to occur before Jan. 1, 2011 in order for any suspension of the five-year period under Code Sec. 121(d)(9) to apply to the sale.

☐ **Effective:** Sales or exchanges after date of enactment and before Jan. 1, 2011. (2006 Tax Relief and Health Care Act §417(e))

observation: Although Code Sec. 121(d)(9) purports to permit a ten-year suspension of the ownership and use period for employees of the intelligence community meeting the requirements of Code Sec. 121(d)(9), 2006 Tax Relief and Health Care Act §417(e) provides that the provision only applies to sales or exchanges occurring *before* Jan. 1, 2011. Thus, any suspension period that would otherwise apply to employees of the intelligence community meeting the requirements of Code Sec. 121(d)(9) will be less than ten years.

¶ 108. Temporary TIPRA amendments that eliminated the dollar cap on below market loans to qualified continuing care facilities, and that eased other rules, are made permanent

Code Sec. 7872(h)(4), as amended by 2006 Tax Relief and Health Care Act § 425(a)
Generally effective: Calendar years beginning after 2005
Committee Reports, see ¶ 5076

A below-market loan is a loan that has an interest rate below the applicable Federal rate (AFR), or has no interest rate at all. Under the so-called below-market loan rules, loans that lack interest rates or have rates that don't reflect market conditions are recharacterized to reflect the reality of the underlying transaction, by imputing a higher rate of interest. The result of this imputation is that the lender has to include the imputed interest in income, and the borrower, subject to the deduction limits, gets a deduction for the imputed interest. (FTC 2d ¶ J-2901; USTR ¶ 78,724.02; TaxDesk ¶ 155,001)

For calendar years beginning before 2006, loans to *qualified* continuing care facilities were subject to the below-market loan rules. (FTC 2d ¶ J-2917; TaxDesk ¶ 155,020)

FTC 2d References are to Federal Tax Coordinator 2d
FIN References are to RIAs Analysis of Federal Taxes: Income
USTR References are to United States Tax Reporter: Income, Estate & Gift, and Excise
PCA References are to Pension Analysis (print & electronic)
PE References are to Pension Explanations (print & electronic)
EP References are to Estate Planning Analysis (print & electronic)

A special exception existed, however, under which the below-market loan rules didn't apply to any below-market loan made by a lender to a qualified continuing care facility pursuant to a continuing care contract—if the lender (or the lender's spouse) attained age 65 before the close of the year. For the special exception to apply, the aggregate outstanding amount of these loans couldn't exceed $90,000, as adjusted for inflation. This amount was scheduled to be $163,300 for 2006, before the enactment of the Tax Increase Prevention Act ("TIPRA," Sec. 209, PL 109-222, 5/17/2006)). If the exception applied, the individual had no imputed interest attributed to him for the below-market loan.

TIPRA removed the statutory limit on outstanding below-market loans, generally effective for calendar years beginning after 2005. TIPRA provided that the below-market loan rules do not apply for any calendar year to any below-market loan owed by a facility that, on the last day of the year, is a "qualified continuing care facility"—if (i) the loan was made pursuant to a continuing care contract, and if (ii) the lender (or the lender's spouse) reaches age 62 before the end of the year. (FTC 2d ¶ J-2988; USTR ¶ 78,724.201; TaxDesk ¶ 155,056)

Qualified continuing care facility. Under pre-TIPRA law, a qualified continuing-care facility was designed to provide services under continuing care contracts, and had to meet the following conditions: (i) substantially all of the residents of the facility had to be covered by continuing-care contracts; and (ii) substantially all of the facilities used to provide services under a continuing-care contract had to be owned or operated by the borrower (i.e., the continuing-care facility). A qualified continuing-care facility did not include any facility of a type traditionally considered a nursing home. (FTC 2d ¶ J-2990; USTR ¶ 78,724.201; TaxDesk ¶ 155,058)

TIPRA redefined a "qualified continuing care facility" as one or more facilities:

(i) which are designed to provide services under continuing care contracts,

(ii) which include an independent living unit, along with an assisted living or nursing facility, or both, and

(iii) substantially all of the independent living unit residents of which are covered by continuing care contracts.

TIPRA further provided that the term "qualified continuing care facility" did not include any facility which was traditionally considered a nursing home. (FTC 2d ¶ J-2990; USTR ¶ 78,724.201; TaxDesk ¶ 155,058)

Continuing care contract. Under pre-TIPRA law, a "continuing care contract" was defined as a written contract between an individual and a qualified continuing care facility under which:

(A) the individual or individual's spouse may use a qualified continuing care facility for their life or lives,

(B) the individual or individual's spouse—

(i) would first (i) reside in a separate, independent living unit with additional facilities outside the unit for providing meals and other personal care, and (ii) would not require long-term nursing care, and

(ii) would later be provided long-term and skilled nursing care as the health of the individual or individual's spouse required, and

(C) no additional substantial payment was required if the individual or individual's spouse required increased personal care services or long-term and skilled nursing care.

TIPRA modified the definition of "continuing care contract" to provide that such a contract was a written contract between an individual and a qualified continuing care facility under which:

(A) the individual or individual's spouse may use a qualified continuing care facility for their life or lives,

(B) the individual or individual's spouse will be provided with housing, as appropriate for the individual's or spouse's health—

(i) in an independent living unit (with additional available facilities outside the unit for providing meals and other personal care), and

(ii) in an "assisted living facility" or a "nursing facility," as is available in the continuing care facility, and

(C) the individual or individual's spouse will be provided assisted living or nursing care as the health of the individual or spouse requires, and as is available in the continuing care facility. (FTC 2d ¶ J-2991; USTR ¶ 78,724.201; TaxDesk ¶ 155,059)

Sunset for TIPRA changes. Under Code Sec. 7872(h)(4), the TIPRA changes outlined above were not to apply to any calendar year after 2010. In effect, the TIPRA rules governing the application of the below-market loan rules to qualified continuing care facilities were to apply only for a five-year period (2006 through 2010). Thereafter, the previous rules (set out in Code Sec. 7872(g)) were to apply once again.

New Law. The 2006 Tax Relief and Health Care Act makes the TIPRA changes to the rules governing the application of the below-market loan rules to qualified continuing care facilities permanent. (Com Rept, see ¶ 5076) The Act accomplishes this by deleting the Code Sec. 7872(h)(4) sunset provision from

FTC 2d References are to Federal Tax Coordinator 2d
FIN References are to RIAs Analysis of Federal Taxes: Income
USTR References are to United States Tax Reporter: Income, Estate & Gift, and Excise
PCA References are to Pension Analysis (print & electronic)
PE References are to Pension Explanations (print & electronic)
EP References are to Estate Planning Analysis (print & electronic)

the Code. (Code Sec. 7872(h)(4) as amended by 2006 Tax Relief and Health Care Act §425(a))

☐ **Effective:** For calendar years beginning after Dec. 31, 2005—for loans made before, on, or after Dec. 31, 2005. (2006 Tax Relief and Health Care Act §425(b))

> ***observation:*** The 2006 Tax Relief and Health Care Act states that the provision making the above TIPRA changes permanent is "effective as if included in" Sec. 209 of TIPRA. Sec. 209 of TIPRA, in turn, provides that these rules are effective for calendar years beginning after Dec. 31, 2005—for loans made before, on, or after Dec. 31, 2005.

¶ 109. Federal judges can defer gain on conflict-of-interest sales

Code Sec. 1043(b)(1), as amended by 2006 Tax Relief and Health Care Act § 418(a)(1)
Code Sec. 1043(b)(2), as amended by 2006 Tax Relief and Health Care Act § 418(a)(2)
Code Sec. 1043(b)(5)(B), as amended by 2006 Tax Relief and Health Care Act § 418(a)(3)
Code Sec. 1043(b)(6), as amended by 2006 Tax Relief and Health Care Act § 418(b)
Generally effective: Sales after date of enactment
Committee Reports, see ¶ 5069

To comply with the federal government's conflict-of-interest laws, federal officers and employees of the executive branch must divest themselves of financial interests in companies and industries with which they will have dealings. These executive-branch employees (and their spouses, minor or dependent children, and certain trustees) who sell property to avoid conflicts of interest can defer recognition of gain on the sale if:

. . . the taxpayer elects (on Form 8824) to defer the gain,

. . . the property is sold under a certificate of divestiture, and

. . . the taxpayer purchases "permitted property" (U.S. obligations or diversified investment funds approved by the Office of Government Ethics) during the 60-day period beginning on the date of the sale.

Gain is recognized only to the extent the amount realized on the sale of the divested property exceeds the cost of any permitted property purchased by the taxpayer during the 60-day period. (FTC 2d/FIN ¶ I-3804; USTR ¶ 10,434) The basis of the permitted property is reduced by the unrecognized gain. (FTC 2d/FIN ¶ P-1118; USTR ¶ 10,434)

illustration: X, an eligible federal officer, sells stock in a corporation for $30,000 under a certificate of divestiture. The stock has a basis of $15,000. X's realized gain is $15,000. Thirty days after the sale, X buys permitted property for $25,000.

X must recognize $5,000 of gain in the year of sale, because the amount realized, $30,000, exceeds the cost of the permitted property, $25,000, by $5,000. The basis of the permitted property is reduced by the $10,000 of gain that isn't recognized, from $25,000 to $15,000.

observation: The basis reduction means that the gain that is rolled over into permitted property isn't excluded, but merely deferred until the permitted property is disposed of.

Under pre-2006 Tax Relief and Health Care Act law, the nonrecognition rule applied only to officers and employees of the executive branch. (FTC 2d/FIN ¶ I-3805; USTR ¶ 10,434) The sale had to be under a certificate of divestiture from the President or the Director of the Office of Government Ethics. The certificate had to specify the property to be divested and state that divestiture was reasonably necessary to comply with a federal conflict-of-interest statute, regulation, rule, or executive order, or was requested by a congressional committee as a condition of confirmation. (FTC 2d/FIN ¶ I-3806; USTR ¶ 10,434)

New Law. The 2006 Tax Relief and Health Care Act makes sales by federal "judicial officers" (defined below) eligible for nonrecognition treatment. (Code Sec. 1043(b)(1)(A) as amended by 2006 Tax Relief and Health Care Act §418(a)(1)(A))

The sale must be under a certificate of divestiture from the Judicial Conference of the U.S. (or its designee). (Code Sec. 1043(b)(2)(B) as amended by 2006 Tax Relief and Health Care Act §418(a)(2)(B)) The certificate must state that divestiture of specific property is reasonably necessary to comply with a federal conflict-of-interest statute, regulation, rule, or judicial canon, or was requested by a congressional committee as a condition of confirmation. (Code Sec. 1043(b)(2)(A))

observation: The Judicial Conference of the U.S. consists of the Chief Justice of the U.S., the chief judge of each judicial circuit, the chief judge of the Court of International Trade, and a district judge from each judicial circuit. Its main purpose is to set policy on federal court administration.

Judges who qualify for deferral of gain. For this purpose, the term "judicial officer" means the Chief Justice of the U.S., the Associate Justices of the Supreme Court, and the judges of:

. . . the U.S. courts of appeals,

. . . the U.S. district courts, including the district courts in Guam, the Northern Mariana Islands, and the Virgin Islands,

. . . the Court of Appeals for the Federal Circuit,

. . . the Court of International Trade,

. . . the Tax Court,

. . . the Court of Federal Claims,

. . . the Court of Appeals for Veterans Claims,

. . . the U.S. Court of Appeals for the Armed Forces, and

. . . any court created by Act of Congress, the judges of which are entitled to hold office during good behavior. (Code Sec. 1043(b)(6) as amended by 2006 Tax Relief and Health Care Act §418(b))

> ***observation:*** The nonrecognition provision doesn't apply to state court judges.

> ***observation:*** This provision gives federal judges the same ability as executive-branch employees to defer gain on conflict-of-interest sales, thus removing a barrier to the acceptance of judicial appointments by candidates with significant investment portfolios.
>
> Judges can avoid divestiture by recusing (i.e., disqualifying) themselves from cases that involve conflicts of interest. However, if the conflict arises in the course of a complex litigation, it is difficult to transfer the case to another judge who is unfamiliar with the litigation, and divestiture may be the best solution.

> ***observation:*** As is the case with executive-branch employees, the judge must elect deferral and must buy permissible property during the 60-day period beginning on the date of sale.

Spouses, children, and trustees. Spouses and minor or dependent children of judicial officers are covered by the nonrecognition provision if the ownership of property by the spouse or child is attributable to the judicial officer under any federal conflict-of-interest statute, regulation, rule, or judicial canon. (Code Sec. 1043(b)(1)(B))

Similarly, a trustee is covered by the nonrecognition provision with respect to sales of trust property if a judicial officer's spouse or minor or dependent child has a beneficial interest in trust principal or income that is attributable to the judicial officer under any federal conflict-of-interest statute, regulation, rule, or judicial canon. (Code Sec. 1043(b)(5)(B) as amended by 2006 Tax Relief and Health Care Act §418(a)(3))

☐ **Effective:** Sales after date of enactment. (2006 Tax Relief and Health Care Act §418(c))

FTC 2d References are to Federal Tax Coordinator 2d
FIN References are to RIAs Analysis of Federal Taxes: Income
USTR References are to United States Tax Reporter: Income, Estate & Gift, and Excise
PCA References are to Pension Analysis (print & electronic)
PE References are to Pension Explanations (print & electronic)
EP References are to Estate Planning Analysis (print & electronic)

¶ 200. Research Credit

¶ 201. Research credit is extended retroactively to amounts paid or incurred after Dec. 31, 2005 and before Jan. 1, 2008

Code Sec. 41(h)(1)(B), as amended by 2006 Tax Relief and Health Care Act § 104(a)(1)
Code Sec. 45C(b)(1)(D), as amended by 2006 Tax Relief and Health Care Act § 104(a)(2)
Generally effective: Amounts paid or incurred after Dec. 31, 2005
Committee Reports, see ¶ 5004

Under pre-2006 Tax Relief and Health Care Act law, a taxpayer was entitled to a research credit equal to 20% of the amount by which the taxpayer's qualified research expenses paid or incurred before Jan. 1, 2006 exceeded a specific base amount. (FTC 2d/FIN ¶ L-15300; USTR ¶ 414; TaxDesk ¶ 384,001) In addition, a separate university basic research credit was available. (FTC 2d/FIN ¶ L-15500; USTR ¶ 414; TaxDesk ¶ 384,018)

Qualified clinical drug testing expenses are eligible for the orphan drug credit. Expenses eligible for this credit are defined, with certain modifications, by reference to the Code Sec. 41 definition of expenses qualifying for the research credit. For this purpose, under pre-2006 Tax Relief and Health Care Act law, Code Sec. 41 was considered to remain in effect for periods after Dec. 31, 2005. (FTC 2d/FIN ¶ L-15614; USTR ¶ 45C4)

New Law. The 2006 Tax Relief and Health Care Act strikes the Dec. 31, 2005 expiration date of the research credit (including the university basic research credit) and replaces that date with Dec. 31, 2007. (Code Sec. 41(h)(1)(B) as amended by 2006 Tax Relief and Health Care Act §104(a)(1)) Thus, the research credit is extended for two years, i.e., for amounts paid or incurred after Dec. 31, 2005 and before Jan. 1, 2008. (Com Rept, see ¶ 5004)

> ***observation:*** Although the extension is for only two years, i.e., for amounts paid or incurred through Dec. 31, 2007, Congress has in the past similarly extended the research credit for relatively short periods of time.

For changes in the rates of the alternative incremental credit, see ¶ 202.

FTC 2d References are to Federal Tax Coordinator 2d
FIN References are to RIAs Analysis of Federal Taxes: Income
USTR References are to United States Tax Reporter: Income, Estate & Gift, and Excise
PCA References are to Pension Analysis (print & electronic)
PE References are to Pension Explanations (print & electronic)
EP References are to Estate Planning Analysis (print & electronic)

For a new alternative simplified credit for qualified research expenses, see ¶ 203.

Orphan drug credit. For purposes of the orphan drug credit, the research tax credit (Code Sec. 41) is considered to remain in effect for periods after Dec. 31, 2007. (Code Sec. 45C(b)(1)(D) as amended by 2006 Tax Relief and Health Care Act §104(a)(2))

For extensions of the period for making an election for a tax year ending after Dec. 31, 2005 and before date of enactment, which would have expired but for relief provided by the 2006 Tax Relief and Health Care Act, see ¶ 701.

☐ **Effective:** Amounts paid or incurred after Dec. 31, 2005. (2006 Tax Relief and Health Care Act §104(a)(3))

¶ 202. Rates for the elective alternative incremental research credit are increased

Code Sec. 41(c)(4)(A), as amended by 2006 Tax Relief and Health Care Act § 104(b)(1)
Generally effective: Tax years ending after Dec. 31, 2006
Committee Reports, see ¶ 5004

Taxpayers are allowed to elect an alternative incremental research credit regime in lieu of the regular research credit. If a taxpayer elects to be subject to this alternative regime, the taxpayer is assigned a three-tiered fixed-base percentage (that is lower than the fixed-base percentage otherwise applicable) and the credit rate likewise is reduced. Under pre-2006 Tax Relief and Health Care Act law, the alternative credit regime provided a credit of:

. . . 2.65% that applied to the extent that a taxpayer's current-year research expenses exceeded a base amount computed by using a fixed-base percentage of 1% (i.e., the base amount equalled 1% of the taxpayer's average gross receipts for the four preceding tax years) but did not exceed a base amount computed by using a fixed-base percentage of 1.5%.

. . . 3.2% that applied to the extent that a taxpayer's current-year research expenses exceeded a base amount computed by using a fixed-base percentage of 1.5% but did not exceed a base amount computed by using a fixed-base percentage of 2%.

. . . 3.75% that applied to the extent that a taxpayer's current-year research expenses exceeded a base amount computed by using a fixed-base percentage of 2%. (FTC 2d/FIN ¶ L-15302.1; USTR ¶ 414.01; TaxDesk ¶ 384,003)

New Law. The 2006 Tax Relief and Health Care Act increases the credit rates applicable under the alternative incremental research credit. (Com Rept, see ¶ 5004) Specifically, under the alternative credit regime, a credit rate of:

... *3.0%* applies to the extent that a taxpayer's current-year research expenses exceed a base amount computed by using a fixed-base percentage of 1% (i.e., the base amount equals 1% of the taxpayer's average gross receipts for the four preceding tax years) but do not exceed a base amount computed by using a fixed-base percentage of 1.5%. (Code Sec. 41(c)(4)(A)(i) as amended by 2006 Tax Relief and Health Care Act §104(b)(1)(A))

... *4.0%* applies to the extent that a taxpayer's current-year research expenses exceed a base amount computed by using a fixed-base percentage of 1.5% but do not exceed a base amount computed by using a fixed-base percentage of 2%. (Code Sec. 41(c)(4)(A)(ii) as amended by 2006 Tax Relief and Health Care Act §104(b)(1)(B))

... *5.0%* applies to the extent that a taxpayer's current-year research expenses exceed a base amount computed by using a fixed-base percentage of 2%. (Code Sec. 41(c)(4)(A)(iii) as amended by 2006 Tax Relief and Health Care Act §104(b)(1)(C))

For 2006 Tax Relief and Health Care Act retroactive extension of the research credit for two years, i.e., for amounts paid or incurred after Dec. 31, 2005 and before Jan. 1, 2008, see ¶ 201.

> ***observation:*** The higher rates applicable under the alternative incremental research credit are subject to the termination date that generally applies to the research credit, i.e., the credit is not available for amounts paid or incurred after Dec. 31, 2007, see ¶ 201.

For rules coordinating the alternative incremental research credit with the elective alternative simplified credit, see ¶ 203.

☐ **Effective:** Tax years ending after Dec. 31, 2006, except to the extent provided in the transition rule discussed immediately below. (2006 Tax Relief and Health Care Act §104(b)(2))

> ***observation:*** Thus, a calendar year taxpayer uses the rates that applied under pre-2006 Tax Relief and Health Care Act law (described above) to compute the alternative incremental research credit for its tax year ending Dec. 31, 2006. The transition rule that applies to fiscal year taxpayers is described below.

Under the transition rule, a special formula applies for calculating the research credit for a specified transitional tax year for which a taxpayer has

---

FTC 2d References are to Federal Tax Coordinator 2d
FIN References are to RIAs Analysis of Federal Taxes: Income
USTR References are to United States Tax Reporter: Income, Estate & Gift, and Excise
PCA References are to Pension Analysis (print & electronic)
PE References are to Pension Explanations (print & electronic)
EP References are to Estate Planning Analysis (print & electronic)

elected, under Code Sec. 41(c)(4), the alternative incremental research credit. (2006 Tax Relief and Health Care Act §104(b)(3)(A)) For purposes of the transition rule, a specified transitional tax year is any tax year that ends *after* Dec. 31, 2006, and *includes* that date. (2006 Tax Relief and Health Care Act §104(b)(3)(B)(i)) Thus, the transition rule applies to fiscal year 2006-2007 taxpayers. (Com Rept, see ¶ 5004)

Under the special formula, the research credit is equal to the sum of: (2006 Tax Relief and Health Care Act §104(b)(3)(A))

(1) the "applicable 2006 percentage" (defined below) multiplied by the amount of alternative incremental research credit as in effect for tax years ending on Dec. 31, 2006, plus (2006 Tax Relief and Health Care Act §104(b)(3)(A)(i))

(2) the "applicable 2007 percentage" (defined below) multiplied by the amount of alternative incremental research credit as in effect for tax years ending on Jan. 1, 2007. (2006 Tax Relief and Health Care Act §104(b)(3)(A)(ii))

The "applicable 2006 percentage" is the number of days in the specified transitional tax year before Jan. 1, 2007, divided by the number of days in the specified transitional tax year. (2006 Tax Relief and Health Care Act §104(b)(3)(B)(ii))

The "applicable 2007 percentage" is the number of days in the specified transitional tax year after Dec. 31, 2006, divided by the number of days in the specified transitional tax year. (2006 Tax Relief and Health Care Act §104(b)(3)(B)(iii))

The effect of the transition rule is that for fiscal year 2006-2007 taxpayers that have elected the alternative incremental research credit, the amount of the credit is the sum of (1) the credit calculated as if it were extended but without the modifications to the credit rates discussed above, multiplied by the applicable 2006 percentage, and (2) the credit calculated under the modified credit rates discussed above, multiplied by the applicable 2007 percentage. (Com Rept, see ¶ 5004)

¶ 203. Alternative simplified credit can be elected for qualified research expenses

Code Sec. 41(c)(4), 2006 Tax Relief and Health Care Act § 104(c)(2)
Code Sec. 41(c)(5), as amended by 2006 Tax Relief and Health Care Act § 104(c)(1)
Generally effective: Tax years ending after Dec. 31, 2006
Committee Reports, see ¶ 5004

A taxpayer's qualified research expenses in excess of a base amount for the tax year plus basic research payments to a qualified organization qualify the taxpayer for the incremental research credit. The credit is equal to the sum of 20% of the excess of the qualified research expenses for the tax year over the base amount, plus 20% of the basic research payments ("the regular credit"). (FTC 2d/FIN ¶ L-15301; USTR ¶ 414.01; TaxDesk ¶ 384,001) An alternative incremental credit regime is also available. (FTC 2d/FIN ¶ L-15302.1; USTR ¶ 414.01; TaxDesk ¶ 384,003)

For discussion of the 2006 Tax Relief and Health Care Act retroactive extension of the research credit for two years, i.e., for amounts paid or incurred after Dec. 31, 2005 and before Jan. 1, 2008, see ¶ 201.

For discussion of the 2006 Tax Relief and Health Care Act changes to the alternative incremental research credit, see ¶ 202.

New Law. The 2006 Tax Relief and Health Care Act adds a new "alternative simplified credit" for qualified research expenses. A taxpayer can elect a credit (in lieu of the regular credit discussed above) equal to 12% of the excess of the qualified research expenses for the tax year over 50% of the average qualified research expenses for the three tax years preceding the tax year for which the credit is being determined. (Code Sec. 41(c)(5)(A) as amended by 2006 Tax Relief and Health Care Act §104(c)(1))

> ***illustration (1):*** Taxpayer W, a calendar year taxpayer, has $200,000 of qualified research expenses for its 2007 tax year. For the preceding three tax years, W's annual qualified research expenses were $40,000, $50,000, and $90,000, an average of $60,000 per year. W can elect an alternative simplified research credit of $20,400 (.12 × ($200,000 minus $30,000 (50% of $60,000)).

FTC 2d References are to Federal Tax Coordinator 2d
FIN References are to RIAs Analysis of Federal Taxes: Income
USTR References are to United States Tax Reporter: Income, Estate & Gift, and Excise
PCA References are to Pension Analysis (print & electronic)
PE References are to Pension Explanations (print & electronic)
EP References are to Estate Planning Analysis (print & electronic)

illustration (2): Taxpayer X has qualified research expenses of $250,000 in each of four consecutive years. In Year 4, X can elect an alternative simplified research credit of $15,000 (.12 × ($250,000 minus $125,000 (50% of $250,000)).

6% credit for taxpayers that had no qualified research expenses in the three tax years preceding the tax year for which the credit is being determined. If a taxpayer has no qualified research expenses in any one of the three preceding tax years, (Code Sec. 41(c)(5)(B)(i)), the alternative simplified research credit is 6% of the qualified research expenses for the tax year for which the credit is being determined. (Code Sec. 41(c)(5)(B)(ii)) Thus, the rate is reduced to 6% if a taxpayer has no qualified research expenses in any one of the three preceding tax years. (Com Rept, see ¶ 5004)

illustration (3): In Year 4, Taxpayer Y has qualified research expenses of $300,000. Y had no qualified research expenses in Years 1 through 3. For Year 4, Y can elect an alternative simplified research credit of $18,000 (.06 × $300,000).

observation: For taxpayers who can bunch their qualified research expenses in particular years, the 6% credit may be more beneficial than the 12% credit since the 6% credit is not subject to the reduction that applies to the 12% credit.

illustration (4): Taxpayer Z has no qualified research expenses in Years 1, 2, and 3 but expects to have $600,000 of qualified research expenses in Year 4, and $100,000 in Year 5. If Z elects the simplified credit, the credit is $36,000 for Year 4 ($600,000 × .06). For Year 5, the 12% credit would apply but would be zero computed as follows: $100,000 minus $100,000 (50% of $200,000 [the average of the $600,000 of qualified research expenses for Years 2, 3, and 4]).

If Z accelerates the $100,000 of Year 5 qualified research expenses into Year 4 (increasing the Year 4 qualified research expenses to $700,000), the alternative simplified credit for Year 4 would be $42,000 (.06 × $700,000).

observation: Code Sec. 41(c)(5)(B)(i) provides a special rule for a taxpayer who has no qualified research expenses in any of the three preceding tax years. There is no express language explaining whether the three-year rule applies to a start-up company, i.e., one that hasn't been in business for the three preceding tax years.

Effect of the election. An election of the alternative simplified research credit for qualified research expenses applies to the tax year for which it is made and all succeeding tax years unless revoked with IRS's consent. (Code Sec. 41(c)(5)(C))

Coordination with alternative incremental research credit. An election of the alternative *simplified* research credit for qualified research expenses (described immediately above) cannot be made for any tax year to which an election of the alternative *incremental* research credit (see ¶ 202) applies. (Code Sec. 41(c)(5)(C))

An election of the alternative incremental research credit that applies to the tax year that includes Jan. 1, 2007 is treated as revoked with IRS's consent if the taxpayer elects the alternative simplified research credit for the year. (2006 Tax Relief and Health Care Act §104(c)(2)) However, an election of both the alternative incremental credit and the alternative simplified credit is permitted for the specified transitional tax year (i.e., a year ending after Dec. 31, 2006 that includes that date, see "Effective date" below). (2006 Tax Relief and Health Care Act §104(c)(4)(B)(ii)) In that case, the election is treated as revoked for the tax year after the specified transitional tax year. (2006 Tax Relief and Health Care Act §104(c)(4)(B)(iii))

Redesignation. Pre-2006 Tax Relief and Health Care Act Code Sec. 41(c)(5) (providing rules for the consistent treatment of expenses, see FTC 2d/FIN ¶ L-15310.1; USTR ¶ 414.01), and Code Sec. 41(c)(6) (defining gross receipts for purposes of computing the base amount for the research credit, see FTC 2d/FIN ¶ L-15309.1; USTR ¶ 414.01; TaxDesk ¶ 384,016) have been redesignated as Code Sec. 41(c)(6) and Code Sec. 41(c)(7) respectively. (2006 Tax Relief and Health Care Act §104(c)(1))

☐ **Effective:** Tax years ending after Dec. 31, 2006, except to the extent provided in the transition rule discussed immediately below. (2006 Tax Relief and Health Care Act §104(c)(3))

Under the transition rule, a special formula applies for calculating the research credit for a specified transitional tax year for which a taxpayer has elected the alternative simplified credit. (2006 Tax Relief and Health Care Act §104(c)(4)(A)) For purposes of the transition rule, a specified transitional tax year is any tax year that ends *after* Dec. 31, 2006, and *includes* that date. (2006 Tax Relief and Health Care Act §104(c)(4)(B)(i)) Thus, the transition rule applies to fiscal year 2006-2007 taxpayers. (Com Rept, see ¶ 5004)

Under the special formula, the research credit is equal to the sum of: (2006 Tax Relief and Health Care Act §104(c)(4)(A))

FTC 2d References are to Federal Tax Coordinator 2d
FIN References are to RIAs Analysis of Federal Taxes: Income
USTR References are to United States Tax Reporter: Income, Estate & Gift, and Excise
PCA References are to Pension Analysis (print & electronic)
PE References are to Pension Explanations (print & electronic)
EP References are to Estate Planning Analysis (print & electronic)

(1) the "applicable 2006 percentage" (defined below) multiplied by the amount of the research credit as determined for tax years ending on Dec. 31, 2006, plus (2006 Tax Relief and Health Care Act §104(c)(4)(A)(i))

(2) the "applicable 2007 percentage" (defined below) multiplied by the amount of the alternative simplified credit as determined for tax years ending on Jan. 1, 2007. (2006 Tax Relief and Health Care Act §104(c)(4)(A)(ii))

The "applicable 2006 percentage" is the number of days in the specified transitional tax year before Jan. 1, 2007, divided by the number of days in the specified transitional tax year. (2006 Tax Relief and Health Care Act §104(c)(4)(B)(i))

The "applicable 2007 percentage" is the number of days in the specified transitional tax year after Dec. 31, 2006, divided by the number of days in the specified transitional tax year. (2006 Tax Relief and Health Care Act §104(c)(4)(B)(i))

The effect of the transition rule is that for fiscal year 2006-2007 taxpayers that have elected the alternative simplified credit, the amount of the research credit is the sum of (1) the amount of the research credit (including the alternative incremental credit for a taxpayer electing that credit) calculated as if it were extended (see ¶ 201) but not modified, multiplied by the applicable 2006 percentage and (2) the alternative simplified credit, multiplied by the applicable 2007 percentage. (Com Rept, see ¶ 5004)

¶ 300. Health and Medical Savings Accounts

¶ 301. Eligible individuals may elect one-time tax-free rollover of IRA distribution into an HSA

Code Sec. 408(d)(9), as amended by 2006 Tax Relief and Health Care Act § 307(a)
Code Sec. 223(b)(4)(C), as amended by 2006 Tax Relief and Health Care Act § 307(b)
Generally effective: Tax years beginning after Dec. 31, 2006
Committee Reports, see ¶ 5045

Any amount paid or distributed out of an IRA is included in gross income by the payee or distributee under the Code Sec. 72 annuity rules (generally providing for the pro rata inclusion in gross income of income on the contract, and an exclusion for a pro rata return of any after-tax basis). An exception to the rule requiring the inclusion of distributed amounts in income generally is provided for distributed amounts that are rolled over to an eligible retirement plan. A health savings account (HSA) is not an eligible retirement plan. Thus, under pre-2006 Tax Relief and Health Care Act law, a distribution from an HSA could not have been rolled over tax-free to an HSA. (FTC 2d/FIN ¶ H-12253.1; USTR ¶ 4084.03; TaxDesk ¶ 143,003.1; PE ¶ 4084.03)

In general, HSAs are tax-exempt trusts or custodial accounts created exclusively to pay for the qualified medical expenses of the account holder, his spouse, and his dependents. Thus, HSAs provide for the tax-favored treatment for distributions used to pay current medical expenses, as well as tax-favored savings for future medical expenses.

Within limits, an "eligible individual" may deduct contributions to an HSA made by him or on his behalf. Contributions to an HSA made by an eligible individual's employer are excludable from the individual's gross income and employment taxes.

"Eligible individuals" under the HSA rules are individuals who are covered by a "high deductible health plan" and no other health plan that provides coverage for any benefit which is covered under the high deductible health plan. After an individual has reached age 65 and becomes enrolled in Medicare benefits, contributions can't be made to an HSA. Eligible individuals don't include individuals who may be claimed as a dependent on another person's tax return. An

FTC 2d References are to Federal Tax Coordinator 2d
FIN References are to RIAs Analysis of Federal Taxes: Income
USTR References are to United States Tax Reporter: Income, Estate & Gift, and Excise
PCA References are to Pension Analysis (print & electronic)
PE References are to Pension Explanations (print & electronic)
EP References are to Estate Planning Analysis (print & electronic)

individual with "other coverage" in addition to coverage under a high deductible health plan is still eligible for an HSA, if the other coverage is certain "permitted insurance" or "permitted coverage." Health flexible spending accounts (FSAs) and health reimbursement arrangements (HRAs) are health plans that are "other coverage" under the HSA rules.

A "high deductible health plan" is a health plan that, for 2007: (a) has a deductible that is at least $1,100 for self-only coverage, or $2,200 for family coverage, and (b) has an out-of-pocket expense limit of no more than $5,500 for self-only coverage, and $11,000 for family coverage. (FTC 2d/FIN ¶ H-1350 *et seq.*; USTR ¶ 2234; TaxDesk ¶ 289,101 *et seq.*; PE ¶ 2234 *et seq.*)

The limit on deductible contributions to an individual's HSA must be reduced (but not below zero) by the sum of: (A) the aggregate amount paid for the tax year to his Archer medical savings accounts (Archer MSAs), and (B) the aggregate contributions made to his HSAs that are excludable from his gross income for the tax year under Code Sec. 106(d). (FTC 2d/FIN ¶ H-1350.8; USTR ¶ 2234.03; TaxDesk ¶ 289,108; PE ¶ 2234.03)

New Law. Generally, on a once-only basis, an eligible individual can withdraw retirement-type funds from an IRA, and, up to a specified limit, transfer the funds tax-free to another tax-favored account (an HSA) from which to pay future medical expenses. Specifically, if an eligible individual so elects, his gross income for a tax year will not include the amount of a "qualified HSA funding distribution" (an IRA distribution that meets certain requirements, see below), to the extent that the distribution is "otherwise includible in income" (see below). (Code Sec. 408(d)(9)(A) as amended by 2006 Tax Relief and Health Care Act §307(a))

In addition, qualified HSA funding distributions are not subject the Code Sec. 72(t) 10% early withdrawal penalty. (Com Rept, see ¶ 5045)

However, no deduction is allowed for the amount contributed from an IRA to an HSA. (Code Sec. 223(b)(4)(C) as amended by 2006 Tax Relief and Health Care Act §307(b)); (Com Rept, see ¶ 5045)

> ***observation:*** An eligible individual may elect qualified HSA funding distribution treatment for a Roth IRA because, under Code Sec. 408A(a), a Roth IRA is treated in the same manner as a traditional IRA (unless otherwise provided). There is no provision for different treatment of Roth IRAs under Code Sec. 408(d)(9). In addition, Congress referred to the treatment of Roth IRA distributions under the HSA rollover rules, in connection with determining the amount of income rolled over from the Roth IRA (see below).

In determining the extent to which amounts distributed from an IRA would "otherwise be included in income" (see above), the aggregate amount distributed from the IRA is treated as includible in income to the extent of the aggregate amount that would have been includible in income if all amounts from all (of that eligible individual's) individual retirement plans were distributed. (Code Sec. 408(d)(9)(E)) Thus, for a traditional IRA, there is no pro rata distribution of basis. (Com Rept, see ¶ 5045)

> ***observation:*** That is, for amounts in an eligible individual's traditional IRAs, a distribution is treated as coming first from income, for purposes of the rules for rollovers to HSAs, to the extent that the IRAs consisted of amounts that would have been taxable upon distribution.

Proper adjustment must be made in applying the Code Sec. 72 annuity rules to other distributions in the tax year, and in later tax years. (Code Sec. 408(d)(9)(E))

> ***Illustration:*** Taxpayer has an IRA with $51,500, consisting of $10,000 of after-tax contributions, and $41,500 that would have been taxable if the entire $51,500 had been distributed. Assume that Taxpayer decides to roll over $2,500 to an HSA in Year 1. Since the $2,500 amount rolled over is less than the $41,500 of income in the IRA, all of the $2,500 is considered to come from income. After the rollover, assume the IRA earned $1,000 in Year 2, as of May 1. On that day, the IRA had a balance of $50,000 ($51,500 − $2,500 rollover + $1,000 earnings). The amount of income in the IRA as of May 1 of Year 2 is $40,000: ($41,500 − $2,500 rollover of income rolled over + $1,000 of earnings). If Taxpayer receives a withdrawal of $3,000 on May 1 of Year 2, the taxable amount of that Year 2 withdrawal is $2,400: (($40,000 income on the contract ÷ $50,000 account balance) × $3,000 distribution.

Also, as under pre-2006 Tax Relief and Health Care Act law, the determination of the amount included in income is made separately for Roth IRAs and other IRAs. (Com Rept, see ¶ 5045)

"Qualified HSA funding distribution" defined. A "qualified HSA funding distribution" is a distribution from an employee's individual retirement plan (other than a SEP or a SIMPLE IRA plan) to the extent that the distribution is contributed to his HSA in a direct trustee-to-trustee transfer. (Code Sec. 408(d)(9)(B))

Limits on excludable rollovers to HSAs. As discussed below, rollovers from IRAs to HSAs are subject to (a) a maximum dollar limitation, and (b) a one-time only limit on transfers. And the exclusion from income is lost if an individual ceases to be an eligible individual within a "testing period."

Maximum dollar limitation. The amount excluded from gross income under an IRA-to-HSA rollover election cannot exceed the excess of:

(1) the annual Code Sec. 223(b) HSA contribution limit, computed on the basis of the type of coverage under the high deductible health plan covering the individual at the time of the qualified HSA funding distribution, over

(2) for a second qualified HSA funding distribution (in a tax year in which there is a conversion from self-only to family coverage, see below), the amount of the earlier qualified HSA funding distribution. (Code Sec. 408(d)(9)(C)(i))

Thus, the limit applies to the combination of both contributions (in each of the months of self-only and family coverage). (Com Rept, see ¶ 5045)

One-time-only election, which is irrevocable. An individual may make an IRA-to-HSA rollover election only for one "qualified HSA funding distribution" during his lifetime. Once made, an IRA-to-HSA rollover election is irrevocable. (Code Sec. 408(d)(9)(C)(ii)(I))

However, if a qualified HSA funding distribution is made during a month in a tax year during which an individual has self-only coverage under a high deductible health plan as of the first day of the month, then he may elect to make an additional qualified HSA funding distribution during a later month in the same tax year during which he has family coverage under a high deductible health plan as of the first day of that later month. (Code Sec. 408(d)(9)(C)(ii)(II))

Testing period for maintaining "eligible individual" status. If an individual does not remain an "eligible individual" during the "testing period" (see below), then:

(a) the aggregate amount of all IRA rollover contributions to the individual's HSA will be includible in the individual's gross income for the first tax year that includes the first month of the testing period for which the individual is not an eligible individual; and

(b) a 10% additional tax will be imposed on the amount includible in the individual's gross income under item (a) for any tax year. (Code Sec. 408(d)(9)(D)(i)); (Com Rept, see ¶ 5045)

Testing period. The "testing period" is the period: (i) beginning with the month in which the qualified HSA funding distribution is contributed to a HSA, and (ii) ending on the last day of the 12th month following the month in item (i). (Code Sec. 408(d)(9)(D)(iii)).

Exception for disability and death. The imposition of tax, and the 10% addition to tax, based on an individual not remaining an "eligible individual" during the testing period, does *not* apply if the individual ceases to be an eligible individual by reason of the individual's death, or the individual becoming disabled (as provided in Code Sec. 72(m)(7)). (Code Sec. 408(d)(9)(D)(ii)).

Reduction of HSA contribution limit. Under the 2006 Tax Relief and Health Care Act, the limit on an individual's deductible contributions to an HSA for a tax year must be reduced by (in addition to the aggregate amount paid for the tax year to the individual's Archer MSAs and the aggregate HSA contributions that are excludable from his gross income under Code Sec. 106(d)) the aggregate amount of IRA rollover distributions contributed to his HSAs for the tax year (under Code Sec. 408(d)(9)). (Code Sec. 223(b)(4)(C))

☐ **Effective:** Tax years beginning after Dec. 31, 2006. (2006 Tax Relief and Health Care Act §307(c))

¶ 302. One-time rollovers from health FSAs and HRAs into HSAs permitted through 2011

Code Sec. 106(e), as amended by 2006 Tax Relief and Health Care Act § 302(a)
Code Sec. 223(c)(1)(B)(iii), as amended by 2006 Tax Relief and Health Care Act § 302(b)
Generally effective: For distributions on or after date of enactment
Committee Reports, see ¶ 5045

Health flexible spending accounts (health FSAs) and health reimbursement arrangements (HRAs) are used by employers to reimburse medical expenses of their employees (and their spouses and dependents). Health FSAs typically are funded on a salary reduction basis, meaning that employees are given the option to reduce current compensation and instead have the compensation used to reimburse the employee for medical expenses. If the health FSA meets certain requirements, then the compensation that is forgone is not includible in gross income or wages, and reimbursements for medical care from the health FSA are excludable from gross income and wages. Health FSAs are subject to the general requirements relating to cafeteria plans, including a requirement that a cafeteria plan generally may not provide deferred compensation. This requirement often is referred to as the "use-it-or-lose-it rule." IRS allows a grace period not to exceed two and one-half months immediately following the end of the plan

FTC 2d References are to Federal Tax Coordinator 2d
FIN References are to RIAs Analysis of Federal Taxes: Income
USTR References are to United States Tax Reporter: Income, Estate & Gift, and Excise
PCA References are to Pension Analysis (print & electronic)
PE References are to Pension Explanations (print & electronic)
EP References are to Estate Planning Analysis (print & electronic)

year during which unused amounts may be used. (FTC 2d/FIN ¶ H-2461; USTR ¶ 1254.05; TaxDesk ¶ 133,044; PE ¶ 125-4.05)

HRAs operate in a manner similar to health FSAs, in that they are an employer-maintained arrangement that reimburses employees for medical expenses. Some of the rules applicable to HRAs and health FSAs are similar, e.g., the amounts in the arrangements can only be used to reimburse medical expenses and not for other purposes. Some of the rules are different. For example, HRAs cannot be funded on a salary reduction basis and the use-it-or-lose-it rule does not apply. Thus, amounts remaining at the end of the year may be carried forward to be used to reimburse medical expenses in the next year. Reimbursements for insurance covering medical care expenses are allowable reimbursements under an HRA, but not under a health FSA. (FTC 2d/FIN ¶ H-1349.1; USTR ¶ 1054.01; TaxDesk ¶ 289,000; PE ¶ 105-4.01)

Individuals with a high deductible health plan (and no other health plan other than a plan that provides certain permitted coverage) may establish a health savings account (HSA). In general, HSAs provide tax-favored treatment for current medical expenses as well as the ability to save on a tax-favored basis for future medical expenses. HSAs are tax-exempt trusts or custodial accounts created exclusively to pay for the qualified medical expenses of the account holder and his spouse and dependents.

Subject to dollar limits, contributions to an HSA are excludable from income and employment taxes if made by the employer, and are deductible if made by the individual. Earnings on amounts in HSAs are not taxable. Distributions from an HSA for qualified medical expenses are not includible in gross income.

Distributions from an HSA that are not used for qualified medical expenses are includible in gross income and are subject to an additional tax of 10%. The 10% additional tax does not apply if the distribution is made after death, disability, or the individual attains the age of Medicare eligibility (i.e., age 65). (FTC 2d/FIN ¶ H-1350; USTR ¶ 2234; TaxDesk ¶ 289,100; PE ¶ 223-4)

Eligible individuals for HSAs are individuals who are covered by a high deductible health plan, and no other health plan that is not a high deductible health plan and which provides coverage for any benefit which is covered under the high deductible health plan. After an individual has attained age 65 and becomes enrolled in Medicare benefits, contributions cannot be made to an HSA. Eligible individuals do not include individuals who may be claimed as a dependent on another person's tax return. Certain kinds of health care coverage, e.g., long-term care insurance, is disregarded for purposes of determining HSA eligibility. (FTC 2d/FIN ¶ H-1350.3; USTR ¶ 2234.02; TaxDesk ¶ 289,104; PE ¶ 223-4.02)

Before the 2006 Tax Relief and Health Care Act, for purposes of HSA eligibility, there was no provision for disregarding coverage under a health FSA from which a rollover to an HSA had been made.

If an employer makes contributions to employees' HSAs, the employer must make available comparable contributions on behalf of all employees with comparable coverage during the same period. Contributions are considered comparable if they are either of the same amount or the same percentage of the deductible under the plan. If employer contributions do not satisfy the comparability rule during a period, then the employer is subject to an excise tax equal to 35% of the aggregate amount contributed by the employer to HSAs for that period. The comparability rule does not apply to contributions made through a cafeteria plan. (FTC 2d/FIN ¶ H-1350.19; USTR ¶ 49,80G4; TaxDesk ¶ 289,117; PE ¶ 4980G-4)

Before the 2006 Tax Relief and Health Care Act, the comparability rules had no provision for rollovers from health FSAs or HRAs.

An individual who is covered by a high deductible health plan and a health FSA or an HRA generally is not eligible to make contributions to an HSA. But, the individual is eligible to make contributions to an HSA if the health FSA or HRA is: (1) a limited purpose health FSA or HRA; (2) a suspended HRA; (3) a post-deductible health FSA or HRA; or (4) a retirement HRA. An individual participating in a health FSA that allows reimbursements during a grace period is generally not eligible to make contributions to an HSA until the first month following the end of the grace period, even if the individual's health FSA has no unused benefits as of the end of the prior plan year. (FTC 2d/FIN ¶ H-1350.4A, ¶ H-2417.2; TaxDesk ¶ 133,045.2, ¶ 289,104.5)

Amounts can be rolled over from one HSA to another HSA, or from an Archer Medical savings account (MSA) to an HSA (FTC 2d/FIN ¶ H-1350.9; USTR ¶ 2234.05; TaxDesk ¶ 289,109; PE ¶ 223-4.05)

Before the 2006 Tax Relief and Health Care Act, there was no provision for the rollover of amounts from a health FSA, or an HRA, to an HSA.

New Law. The 2006 Tax Relief and Health Care Act allows employers—on a one-time only basis, and for a limited time—to roll over unused health FSA and HRA balances to an HSA. A health FSA or HRA can permit these rollovers (as long as the rollovers satisfy the requirements for a "qualified HSA distribution," defined below) without violating the otherwise applicable requirements for health FSAs and HRAs. (Code Sec. 106(e)(1) as amended by 2006 Tax Relief and Health Care Act §302(a))

A "qualified HSA distribution" is treated as a contribution by an employer to an employee's HSA under Code Sec. 106(d). (Code Sec. 106(e)(5)(A)) Thus, amounts contributed to an HSA under these rules are excludable from the em-

FTC 2d References are to Federal Tax Coordinator 2d
FIN References are to RIAs Analysis of Federal Taxes: Income
USTR References are to United States Tax Reporter: Income, Estate & Gift, and Excise
PCA References are to Pension Analysis (print & electronic)
PE References are to Pension Explanations (print & electronic)
EP References are to Estate Planning Analysis (print & electronic)

ployee's gross income and wages for employment tax purposes. (Com Rept, see ¶ 5045)

Also, a "qualified HSA distribution" is treated as a rollover contribution to an HSA under Code Sec. 223(f)(5). (Code Sec. 106(e)(4)(C)).

> ***observation:*** Thus, a "qualified HSA distribution" would not impact an otherwise qualified individual's ability to make an HSA contribution for the year in which the "qualified HSA distribution" occurs.

Only one "qualified HSA distribution" is allowed with respect to any health FSA or HRA. (Code Sec. 106(e)(2))

> ***observation:*** Thus, qualified HSA distributions are allowed on a one-time only basis. However, it appears that one individual may roll-over amounts from both a health FSA, and from an HRA, if he were to have had balances in both types of account on Sept. 21, 2006 (see below).

Qualified HSA distribution defined. A "qualified HSA distribution" is a distribution from an employee's health FSA or HRA to the extent the distribution:

(1) does not exceed the lesser of the balance in the arrangement:

(a) on Sept. 21, 2006; or

(b) as of the date of the distribution; and

(2) is contributed by the employer directly to his HSA before Jan. 1, 2012. (Code Sec. 106(e)(2))

The balance in the health FSA or HRA as of any date is determined on a cash basis (i.e., expenses incurred that have not been reimbursed as of the date the determination is made are not taken into account). (Com Rept, see ¶ 5045)

Tax on failure to maintain high deductible health plan coverage. The above rules are designed to assist individuals in transferring from another type of health plan to a high deductible health plan. (Com Rept, see ¶ 5045) Thus, if, at any time during the "testing period" (defined below), the employee is not an "eligible individual" (defined below), then:

(i) the amount of the qualified HSA distribution must be includible in the gross income of the employee for the tax year that includes the first month in the testing period for which such employee is not an eligible individual, and

(ii) the income tax on the employee for the tax year is increased by 10% of the amount which is so includible. (Code Sec. 106(e)(3)(A))

> ***observation:*** Thus, there is a 10% penalty tax levied on top of the inclusion in gross income of the rollover amount.

If the employee ceases to be an "eligible individual" because of the employee's death, or because the employee has become disabled (as defined in Code Sec. 72(m)(7)), then the additions to gross income and to the tax, under under items (i) and (ii), above, do not apply. (Code Sec. 106(e)(3)(B))

Testing period defined. The "testing period" means the period beginning with the month in which the qualified HSA distribution is contributed to the HSA, and ending on the last day of the 12th month following that month. (Code Sec. 106(e)(4)(A))

Eligible individual defined. "Eligible individual" has the same meaning as under Code Sec. 223(c)(1) (which requires an individual to maintain coverage under a high deductible health plan in order to make deductible contributions to an HSA). (Code Sec. 106(e)(4)(B))

The pre-Act rule that an individual is not an eligible individual if the individual has coverage under a general purpose health FSA or HRA continues to apply. Thus, for example, if the health FSA or HRA from which the contribution is made is a general purpose health FSA or HRA, and the individual remains eligible under the arrangement after the distribution and contribution, the individual is not an eligible individual. (Com Rept, see ¶ 5045)

> ***Illustration:*** The balance in an individual's health FSA as of Sept. 21, 2006, is $2,000, and the balance in the account as of Jan. 1, 2008 is $3,000. Under the Act, a health FSA will not be considered to violate applicable rules if, as of Jan. 1, 2008, an amount not exceeding $2,000 is distributed from the health FSA and contributed to the HSA. The $2,000 distribution would not be includible in income, and the HSA contribution would not be deductible, and would not count against the annual maximum tax deductible contribution that can be made to the HSA. If the individual ceases to be an eligible individual as of June 1, 2008, the $2,000 contribution amount is included in gross income and subject to a 10% additional tax.
>
> If, instead, the distribution and contribution are made as of June 30, 2008, when the balance in the health FSA (under the qualified HSA distribution limit) would be $1,500, the amount of the distribution and contribution is limited to $1,500. (Com Rept, see ¶ 5045)

Comparability excise tax on qualified HSA distributions. Under the Act, a modified comparability rule applies to qualified HSA distributions. (Com Rept, see ¶ 5045) Generally, the comparability excise tax under Code

Sec. 4980G does not apply to qualified HSA distributions. (Code Sec. 106(e)(5)(B)(i)) However, if a qualified HSA distribution is made to any employee, the failure to offer a qualified HSA distribution to any eligible individual covered under a high deductible health plan of the employer is (notwithstanding Code Sec. 4980G(d), see ¶ 304) treated for excise tax purposes as a failure to meet the comparability requirements. (Code Sec. 106(e)(5)(B)(ii)) Thus, the excise tax applies if all employees who qualify are not given the same opportunity to make the rollover. (Com Rept, see ¶ 5045)

> ***observation:*** Code Sec. 4980G (the excise tax on an employer's failure to make comparable HSA contributions) itself doesn't spell out any tax rate or rules, but refers to the Code Sec. 4980E excise tax for an employer's failure to make comparable contributions to Archer MSAs. Under Code Sec. 4980E, the excise tax is 35% of the aggregate amount contributed by the employer for the tax year. It would seem that the comparability excise tax on qualified HSA distributions (i.e., which are contributions to HSAs) that violate the comparability rule would be 35% of the aggregate amount of qualified HSA distributions for the tax year. In any event, a technical correction is in order to clarify what the excise tax rate is.

FSA coverage disregarded for "eligible individual" definition purposes. For tax years beginning after Dec. 31, 2006, coverage under a health FSA during any period immediately following the end of the health FSA's plan year during which unused benefits or contributions remaining at the end of that plan year may be paid or reimbursed to plan participants for qualified benefit expenses incurred during such period, is disregarded coverage (for purposes of determining who is an eligible individual for HSA purposes) if:

(I) the balance in the FSA at the end of the plan year is zero; or

(II) the individual is making a qualified HSA distribution in an amount equal to the remaining balance in the FSA as of the end of the plan year, in accordance with IRS rules. (Code Sec. 223(c)(1)(B)(iii) §302(b))

> ***Illustration:*** If, as of Dec. 31, 2006, a participant's health FSA balance is zero, coverage under the health FSA during the period from Jan. 1, 2007, until Mar. 15, 2007 (i.e., the "grace period") is disregarded in determining if tax deductible contributions can be made to an HSA for that period. Similarly, if the entire balance in an individual's health FSA as of Dec. 31, 2006, is distributed and contributed to an HSA, coverage during the health FSA grace period is disregarded. (Com Rept, see ¶ 5045)

Congress intended that IRS will provide guidance under this provision with respect to the timing of health FSA distributions contributed to an HSA in order to facilitate such rollovers, and the establishment of HSAs in connection with high deductible plans. For example, it is intended that IRS provide rules under which coverage is disregarded if, before the end of a year, an individual elects high deductible plan coverage, and contributes any remaining FSA balance to an HSA in accordance with the above rules, even if the trustee-to-trustee transfer cannot be completed until the following plan year. Similar rules apply for the general provision allowing amounts from a health FSA or HRA to be contributed to an HSA in order to facilitate such contributions at the beginning of an employee's first year of HSA eligibility.

The Act does not modify the permitted health FSA grace period allowed under existing IRS guidance. (Com Rept, see ¶ 5045)

☐ **Effective:** Generally, for distributions on or after date of enactment. (2006 Tax Relief and Health Care Act §302(c)(1))

The disregarded coverage changes are effective on date of enactment. (2006 Tax Relief and Health Care Act §302(c)(2))

¶ 303. Limit on HSA contributions is no longer restricted by health plan's annual deductible

Code Sec. 223(b)(2), as amended by 2006 Tax Relief and Health Care Act § 303(a)
Generally effective: For tax years beginning after Dec. 31, 2006
Committee Reports, see ¶ 5045

Individuals with a high deductible health plan and no other health plan other than a plan that provides certain permitted coverage may establish a health savings account ("HSA"). In general, HSAs are tax-exempt trusts or custodial accounts created exclusively to pay for the qualified medical expenses of the account holder and his spouse and dependents.

An eligible individual is allowed a limited annual deduction for cash contributions to an HSA made by him or on his behalf. The amount otherwise allowable as a deduction for the tax year can not exceed the sum of the monthly limitations for months during the tax year. Under pre-2006 Tax Relief and Health Care Act law, the monthly limit was:

(A) for an eligible individual who had self-only coverage under a high deductible health plan as of the first day of the month, one-twelfth of the lesser of—

FTC 2d References are to Federal Tax Coordinator 2d
FIN References are to RIAs Analysis of Federal Taxes: Income
USTR References are to United States Tax Reporter: Income, Estate & Gift, and Excise
PCA References are to Pension Analysis (print & electronic)
PE References are to Pension Explanations (print & electronic)
EP References are to Estate Planning Analysis (print & electronic)

(i) the plan's annual deductible for self-only coverage, or

(ii) $2,250, or

(B) for an eligible individual who had family coverage under a high deductible health plan as of the first day of the month, one-twelfth of the lesser of—

(i) the plan's annual deductible for family coverage, or

(ii) $4,500.

These amounts are adjusted for inflation. For 2006, the amount of the maximum highest deductible is $2,700 for self-only coverage, and $5,450 for family coverage. (FTC 2d/FIN ¶ H-1350.7; USTR ¶ 2234.03; TaxDesk ¶ 289,107; PE ¶ 223-4.03)

New Law. The 2006 Tax Relief and Health Care Act eliminates the references to the plan's annual deductible in items (A)(i) and (B)(i), above, and caps the monthly limit strictly in dollar terms: one-twelfth of $2,250 for self-only coverage, and one-twelfth of $4,500 for family coverage. (Code Sec. 223(b)(2) as amended by 2006 Tax Relief and Health Care Act §303(a)(1))

These statutory amounts are adjusted for inflation, as under pre-Act law. For 2007, the dollar limit is $2,850 for self-only coverage, and $5,650 for family coverage. (Com Rept, see ¶ 5045)

> ***observation:*** Thus, the monthly limit for 2007 is:
>
> (A) for an eligible individual who has self-only coverage under a high deductible health plan as of the first day of the month—one-twelfth of $2,850 ($237.50 monthly), or
>
> (B) for an eligible individual who has family coverage under a high deductible health plan as of the first day of the month—one-twelfth of $5,650 ($470.83 monthly).

☐ **Effective:** For tax years beginning after Dec. 31, 2006. (2006 Tax Relief and Health Care Act §303(c))

¶ 304. Employers can make larger HSA contributions for nonhighly compensated employees than for highly compensated employees, without violating comparability rule

Code Sec. 4980G(d), as amended by 2006 Tax Relief and Health Care Act § 306(a)
Generally effective: Tax years beginning after Dec. 31, 2006
Committee Reports, see ¶ 5045

Individuals with a high deductible health plan and no other health plan other than a plan that provides certain permitted coverage may establish a health savings account ("HSA"). In general, HSAs are tax-exempt trusts or custodial accounts created exclusively to pay for the qualified medical expenses of the account holder and his spouse and dependents.

Under rules similar to those under Code Sec. 4980E (relating to Archer medical savings accounts), an employer that chooses to contribute to the HSAs of its employees must make "comparable contributions" to the HSAs of all "comparable participating employees" (i.e., those who are eligible individuals who have the same category of high deductible health plan (HDHP) coverage). "Comparable contributions" are contributions of either: (1) the same amount, or (2) the same percentage of the deductible for eligible participating employees under the plan.

For an employer who makes a contribution to any employee's HSA during a calendar year, a tax is imposed on the employer's failure to make comparable contributions to the HSAs of all comparable participating employees for that calendar year. Accordingly, for purposes of the Code Sec. 4980G excise tax, the testing period for making comparable contributions to employee's HSAs is the calendar year. If an employer's contributions do not satisfy the comparability rule for a calendar year, the employer is subject to an excise tax equal to 35% of the aggregate amount contributed by the employer to HSAs for that period. (FTC 2d/FIN ¶ H-1350.19; USTR ¶ 49,80G4; TaxDesk ¶ 289,117; PE ¶ 4980G-4)

New Law. The 2006 Tax Relief and Health Care Act carves out an exception to the comparability rule enabling employers to make larger HSA contributions for nonhighly compensated employees (non-HCEs) than for "highly compensated employees (HCEs)." (Com Rept, see ¶ 5045)

Specifically, the 2006 Tax Relief and Health Care Act provides that HCEs (as defined in Code Sec. 414(q)) are not treated as "comparable participating employees" for purposes of applying the Code Sec. 4980E comparability rule to an employer's contribution to a non-HCE's HSA. (Code Sec. 4980G(d) as amended by 2006 Tax Relief and Health Care Act §306(a))

> ***observation:*** Thus, an employer may make a smaller HSA contribution for an HCE than for a non-HCE. However, in determining whether an HSA contribution for an HCE satisfies the comparability rule, non-HCEs *may* be comparable participating employees. Thus, a larger con-

FTC 2d References are to Federal Tax Coordinator 2d
FIN References are to RIAs Analysis of Federal Taxes: Income
USTR References are to United States Tax Reporter: Income, Estate & Gift, and Excise
PCA References are to Pension Analysis (print & electronic)
PE References are to Pension Explanations (print & electronic)
EP References are to Estate Planning Analysis (print & electronic)

tribution to an HCE's HSA than to a non-HCE's HSA may violate the comparability rule.

observation: Highly compensated employees are defined under Code Sec. 414(q) to include any employee who—

(1) was a 5% owner at any time during the year or preceding year, or

(2) for the preceding year—

(A) had compensation from the employer in excess of $80,000 (indexed for inflation by IRS), and

(B) if elected by the employer, was in the top-paid group.

(FTC 2d/FIN ¶ H-6702; USTR ¶ 4144.21; TaxDesk ¶ 286,012; PCA ¶ 28,803; PE ¶ 414-4.21)

The comparability rule continues to apply to the contributions made to non-HCEs. Thus, the employer must make available comparable contributions for those non-HCEs with comparable coverage during the same period. (Com Rept, see ¶ 5045)

Illustration: Without violating the rules of Code Sec. 4980G(d), the employer can make a $1,000 contribution to the HSA of each non-HCE without making contributions to the HSA of each HCE. (Com Rept, see ¶ 5045)

☐ **Effective:** For tax years beginning after Dec. 31, 2006. (2006 Tax Relief and Health Care Act §306(b))

¶ 305. Cost-of-living adjustment for HSA and HDHP dollar amounts is modified—tax years beginning after 2007

Code Sec. 223(g)(1), as amended by 2006 Tax Relief and Health Care Act § 304

Generally effective: For adjustments made for tax years beginning after 2007

Committee Reports, see ¶ 5045

Individuals with a high deductible health plan (HDHP) and no other health plan other than a plan that provides certain permitted coverage may establish a health savings account ("HSA"). In general, HSAs are tax-exempt trusts or custodial accounts created exclusively to pay for the qualified medical expenses of the account holder and his spouse and dependents.

The dollar amounts for an HDHP's annual deductible, and the monthly dollar limit for deductible HSA contributions, increase periodically for inflation. The increase is an amount equal to:

(A) the original dollar amount, multiplied by

(B) the cost-of-living adjustment determined under Code Sec. 1(f)(3) for the calendar year in which the tax year begins.

In applying the cost of living adjustment under Code Sec. 1(f)(3), the cost-of-living adjustment for a calendar year is the percentage (if any) by which the consumer price index (CPI) for the preceding calendar year exceeds the CPI for calendar year 1992 (the permanent base year). Under Code Sec. 1(f)(4), the CPI for a calendar year is the average CPI for the 12-month period ending Aug 31. (FTC 2d/FIN ¶ A-1103; USTR ¶ 14.08; TaxDesk ¶ 568,203)

In applying Code Sec. 1(f)(3) to the HSA rules:

. . . for the required dollar amounts for HDHP annual deductibles, the inflation adjustment is determined by substituting "calendar year 2003" for "calendar year 1992," and

. . . for the monthly dollar limit for deductible HSA contributions, the inflation adjustment is determined by substituting "calendar year 1997" for "calendar year 1992." (FTC 2d/FIN ¶ H-1350.14; USTR ¶ 2234.03 ; PE ¶ 223-4.03).

New Law. The Tax Relief and Health Care Act modifies the cost-of-living adjustment that applies under the HSA rules for any tax year beginning after 2007. Specifically, the Code Sec. 1(f)(4) consumer price index (CPI) for a calendar year will have to be determined as of the close of the 12-month period ending on Mar. 31 of the calendar year (rather than Aug. 31) for the purpose of making cost-of-living adjustments for: (1) the Code Sec. 223(b)(2) monthly dollars limit for deductible HSA contributions, and (2) the Code Sec. 223(c)(2)(A) required dollar amounts for HDHP annual deductibles.

IRS will have to publish the adjusted dollar amounts no later than June 1 of the preceding calendar year. (Code Sec. 223(g)(1) as amended by 2006 Tax Relief and Health Care Act §304)

☐ **Effective:** For adjustments made for any tax year beginning after 2007. (2006 Tax Relief and Health Care Act §304)

FTC 2d References are to Federal Tax Coordinator 2d
FIN References are to RIAs Analysis of Federal Taxes: Income
USTR References are to United States Tax Reporter: Income, Estate & Gift, and Excise
PCA References are to Pension Analysis (print & electronic)
PE References are to Pension Explanations (print & electronic)
EP References are to Estate Planning Analysis (print & electronic)

¶ 306. Individuals who establish health savings accounts mid-year can contribute the full-year amount

Code Sec. 223(b)(8), as amended by 2006 Tax Relief and Health Care Act § 305(a)
Generally effective: Tax years beginning after Dec. 31, 2006
Committee Reports, see ¶ 5045

Health savings accounts (HSAs) allow "eligible individuals" to make deductible contributions (subject to the limits described below) that can later be withdrawn tax-free to reimburse the individual (and his spouse and dependents) for out-of-pocket medical expenses. (FTC 2d/FIN ¶ H-1350; USTR ¶ 2234; TaxDesk ¶ 289,100)

"Eligible individuals" are individuals who are covered by a "high deductible health plan" and no other health plan that is not a high deductible health plan, and which provides coverage for any benefit which is covered under the high deductible health plan. After an individual has attained age 65 and becomes enrolled in Medicare benefits, contributions cannot be made to an HSA. Eligible individuals do not include individuals who can be claimed as a dependent on another person's tax return. (FTC 2d/FIN ¶ H-1350.3; USTR ¶ 2234.02; TaxDesk ¶ 289,104)

A "high deductible health plan" is a health plan that (for 2007) has:

. . . a deductible that is at least $1,100 for self-only coverage, and $2,200 for family coverage; and

. . . an out-of-pocket expense limit that is no more than $5,500 for self-only coverage, and $11,000 for family coverage. (FTC 2d/FIN ¶ H-1350.6; USTR ¶ 2234.02; TaxDesk ¶ 289,106)

The amount contributed to an HSA that is otherwise allowable as a deduction for the tax year is subject to a limit under which the deductible amount cannot exceed the sum of the monthly limitations for months during the tax year that the individual is an eligible individual. To calculate the amount of the monthly limitation for any month, see ¶ 303. (FTC 2d/FIN ¶ H-1350.7; USTR ¶ 2234.02; TaxDesk ¶ 289,107)

Under pre-2006 Tax Relief and Health Care Act law, the deductible limit on contributions made to an HSA was reduced for an individual's part-year coverage under a high deductible health plan, since only those months during which the individual was an eligible individual could have been used to calculate his deductible limit for the year.

New Law. The 2006 Tax Relief and Health Care Act eliminates the reduction in the deductible limit for part-year coverage, by allowing eligible individuals who establish an HSA midway through the year to contribute the full-year amount. Specifically, for purposes of calculating the deductible limit on contributions made to an HSA for any tax year, an individual who is an eligible individual during the last month of that tax year is treated:

(1) as having been an eligible individual during *each* of the months in that tax year; and

(2) as having been enrolled, during each of the months the individual is treated as an eligible individual solely by reason of item (1), above, in the same high deductible health plan in which the individual was enrolled for the last month of the tax year. (Code Sec. 223(b)(8)(A) as amended by 2006 Tax Relief and Health Care Act §305(a))

Thus, individuals who become covered under a high deductible health plan in a month *other* than January (and thus become eligible individuals), are allowed to make the *full* deductible contribution for the year. In other words, those individuals can make contributions for months *before* the individual was enrolled in a high deductible health plan. (Com Rept, see ¶ 5045)

> ***observation:*** Thus, individuals who become eligible individuals after January are no longer subject to a reduction in the deductible limit on contributions to an HSA, as provided under pre-2006 Tax Relief and Health Care Act law.

Failure to maintain high deductible health plan coverage. If, at any time during a "testing period" (see below) the individual is *not* an "eligible individual" (except by reason of death or a Code Sec. 72(m)(7) disability), then:

(A) the individual's gross income for the tax year that includes the first month in the testing period for which he is not an eligible individual is increased by the aggregate amount of all of his HSA contributions which could not have been made but for Code Sec. 223(b)(8)(A) (see above); and

(B) a 10% additional tax will be imposed for any tax year on the amount of the increase described in item (A), above.

The "testing period" is the period beginning with the last month of the tax year under Code Sec. 223(b)(8)(A) (see items (1) and (2), above) and ending on the last day of the 12th month following that month. (Code Sec. 223(b)(8)(B))

Thus, if an individual makes contributions as provided under Code Sec. 223(b)(8)(A), and does not remain an eligible individual during the testing period (except by reason of death or disability), then the amount of the contri-

---

FTC 2d References are to Federal Tax Coordinator 2d
FIN References are to RIAs Analysis of Federal Taxes: Income
USTR References are to United States Tax Reporter: Income, Estate & Gift, and Excise
PCA References are to Pension Analysis (print & electronic)
PE References are to Pension Explanations (print & electronic)
EP References are to Estate Planning Analysis (print & electronic)

butions attributable to months preceding the month in which he was an eligible individual which could not have been made but for Code Sec. 223(b)(8)(A) are includible in gross income. The amount is includible in his gross income for the tax year of the first day during the testing period that he is not an eligible individual, and 10% of this amount is imposed as an additional tax for the year. (Com Rept, see ¶ 5045)

> ***Illustration:*** Jill enrolls in a high deductible health plan in December of 2007 and is otherwise an eligible individual in that month. She was not an eligible individual in any other month in 2007. Jill can make HSA contributions as if she had been enrolled in the high deductible health plan for all of 2007. The testing period begins with December of 2007 and ends on November 30, 2008. If Jill ceases to be an eligible individual (e.g., she ceases to be covered under the high deductible health plan) in June 2008, an amount equal to the HSA deduction attributable to treating Jill as an eligible individual for January through November 2007 is included in income in 2008. In addition, 10% of this includible income is added to Jill's tax for 2008. (Com Rept, see ¶ 5045)

☐ **Effective:** Tax years beginning after Dec. 31, 2006. (2006 Tax Relief and Health Care Act §305(b))

¶ 307. Archer MSA program is extended through 2007—trustees' reports for 2005 and 2006 will be timely if made within 90 days of date of enactment

Code Sec. 220(i)(2), as amended by 2006 Tax Relief and Health Care Act § 117(a)
Generally effective: date of enactment
Committee Reports, see ¶ 5021

Archer medical savings accounts (Archer MSAs) provide a tax-favored way to save for and pay medical expenses. Within limits, contributions to an Archer MSA are deductible in determining adjusted gross income if made by an eligible individual, and are excludable from gross income and wages for employment tax purposes if made by the employer of an eligible individual. Earnings on amounts in an Archer MSA are not currently taxable. Distributions from an Archer MSA for medical expenses are not includible in gross income. Archer MSAs are available to employees covered under an employer-sponsored high deductible plan of a small employer and to self-employed individuals covered under a high deductible health plan.

The number of taxpayers benefiting annually from an Archer MSA contribution is limited to a threshold level (generally 750,000 taxpayers). To date, the number of Archer MSAs established has not exceeded the threshold level.

No new Archer MSAs may be established after the close of the "cut-off year." Under pre-2006 Tax Relief and Health Care Act law, the "cut-off year" was defined as the earlier of—

- calendar year 2005, or
- the first calendar year before 2005 for which IRS could have determined that the numerical limitation for the year had been exceeded.

Thus, under pre-2006 Tax Relief and Health Care Act law, no new contributions could be made to Archer MSAs after 2005, except by or on behalf of individuals who previously had Archer MSA contributions, and employees who are employed by a participating employer. (FTC 2d/FIN ¶ H-1342.2; USTR ¶ 2204.02; TaxDesk ¶ 288,101)

Every trustee of an Archer MSA is required to make an annual report to IRS specifying the number of Archer MSAs of which he is trustee, and providing various other information. Under pre-2006 Tax Relief and Health Care Act law, the report for an Archer MSA established by July 1 of any year was due by Aug. 1 of that year. (FTC 2d/FIN ¶ H-1346; USTR ¶ 2204.02)

Under pre-2006 Tax Relief and Health Care Act law, IRS was required to make and publish the determination that a year is a "cut-off year" by Oct. 1 of that year. (FTC 2d/FIN ¶ H-1344.3; USTR ¶ 2204.02; TaxDesk ¶ 288,105)

If IRS determines that the Archer MSA program ends early because the numerical limitation on Archer MSAs has been reached, then an individual who is not covered by a high deductible health plan by the "cut-off date" will be unable to establish an Archer MSA. Under pre-2006 Tax Relief and Health Care Act law, the cut-off date was Oct. 1 of the cut-off year. (FTC 2d/FIN ¶ H-1343.3; USTR ¶ 2204.02)

New Law. The 2006 Tax Relief and Health Care Act extends Archer MSAs through 2007 by amending the definition of "cut-off year" by replacing "2005" with "2007" in each place that "2005" appeared. (Code Sec. 220(i)(2) as amended by 2006 Tax Relief and Health Care Act §117(a))

Reports required from Archer MSA trustees for 2005 or 2006—which, under pre-2006 Tax Relief and Health Care Act law, would have been due on Aug. 1, 2005 or Aug. 1, 2006, respectively—will be treated as timely if made before the end of the 90-day period beginning on date of enactment. (2006 Tax Relief and Health Care Act §117(c)(1))

If IRS determines that either 2005 or 2006 is a cut-off year, then IRS may make and publish that determination—which, under pre-2006 Tax Relief and Health Care Act law, IRS would have been required to do by Oct. 1, 2005 or Oct. 1, 2006, respectively—at any time before the close of the 120-day period beginning on date of enactment. If IRS determines that either 2005 or 2006 is a cut-off year, then the "cut-off date" will be the last day of the 120-day period beginning on date of enactment. (2006 Tax Relief and Health Care Act §117(c)(2))

☐ **Effective:** date of enactment. (Com Rept, see ¶ 5021)

¶ 400. Employee Benefits

¶ 401. Corporations must report to IRS transfers of stock from exercises of incentive stock options or purchases from employee stock purchase plans

Code Sec. 6039(a), as amended by 2006 Tax Relief and Health Care Act § 403(a)
Code Sec. 6039(b), as amended by 2006 Tax Relief and Health Care Act § 403(b)
Code Sec. 6724(d)(1)(B)(xix), as amended by 2006 Tax Relief and Health Care Act § 403(c)(1)
Generally effective: Calendar years beginning after date of enactment
Committee Reports, see ¶ 5053

A corporation that transfers a share of stock to any person when he exercises an incentive stock option (ISO) must furnish that person with a written statement containing information about the transfer. See FTC 2d/FIN ¶ S-3207; USTR ¶ 60,394; TaxDesk ¶ 812,016. A corporation also must furnish a similar statement if it records (or has its agent record) a transfer of stock acquired through the exercise of an option granted under an employee stock purchase plan (ESPP), where the option price is between 85% and 100% of the value of the stock. The statement must be furnished on or before Jan. 31 following the calendar year of the transfer. See FTC 2d/FIN ¶ S-3209; USTR ¶ 60,394; TaxDesk ¶ 812,017.

The Code imposes a penalty for failure to furnish a "payee statement" on time (failure to timely furnish) and for failures to include all the required information on the statement or the inclusion of incorrect information (failure to include correct information). (FTC 2d/FIN ¶ V-1816; USTR ¶ 67,224; TaxDesk ¶ 861,035) The term "payee statement" includes any statement that must be furnished under Code Sec. 6039(a) (information in connection with certain stock options). (FTC 2d/FIN ¶ V-1815; USTR ¶ 67,224; TaxDesk ¶ 861,035)

Under pre-2006 Tax Relief and Health Care Act law, there was no requirement that corporations report to IRS the transfer of stock upon the exercise of ISOs or the purchase of stock in an ESPP. (FTC 2d/FIN ¶ S-3207; USTR ¶ 60,394; TaxDesk ¶ 812,016)

FTC 2d References are to Federal Tax Coordinator 2d
FIN References are to RIAs Analysis of Federal Taxes: Income
USTR References are to United States Tax Reporter: Income, Estate & Gift, and Excise
PCA References are to Pension Analysis (print & electronic)
PE References are to Pension Explanations (print & electronic)
EP References are to Estate Planning Analysis (print & electronic)

New Law. The 2006 Tax Relief and Health Care Act adds a requirement that an employer make an information return with IRS, in addition to providing information to the employee, about the transfer of stock pursuant to the exercise of an incentive stock option, and to certain stock transfers regarding ESPPs. (Com Rept, see ¶ 5053) Thus, under the 2006 Tax Relief and Health Care Act, every corporation has to make a return at the time and in the manner and setting forth the information that IRS prescribes by regs when it: (Code Sec. 6039(a) as amended by 2006 Tax Relief and Health Care Act §403(a))

(1) transfers to any person a share of stock because of that person's exercise of an ISO, or (Code Sec. 6039(a)(1))

(2) records (or has its agent record) a transfer of stock acquired through the exercise of an option granted under an ESPP, where the option price is between 85% and 100% of the value of the stock. (Code Sec. 6039(a)(2))

> ***observation:*** The requirement that corporations report ISO transfers to IRS does not contain a due date for these returns. Presumably, the due date would be Feb. 28, similar to many other information returns.

The 2006 Tax Relief and Health Care Act also amends the pre-2006 Tax Relief and Health Care Act requirement that statements be furnished to persons who exercise ISOs or purchase stock in an ESPP to provide that every corporation making a return to IRS under Code Sec. 6039(a) must furnish (on or before Jan. 31 of the year following the calendar year for which the return to IRS was made) to each person whose name is on the return a written statement setting forth the information IRS requires by regs. (Code Sec. 6039(b) as amended by 2006 Tax Relief and Health Care Act §403(b))

> ***observation:*** The amendment to Code Sec. 6039(b) is not substantive except in that it requires a written statement be sent to any person with respect to whom the corporation has filed an information return with IRS. The requirement that the written statement had to be furnished on or before Jan. 31 was in effect under pre-2006 Tax Relief and Health Care Act law.

Finally, the 2006 Tax Relief and Health Care Act adds to the definition of information returns, for which penalties may be asserted under Code Sec. 6721, returns under Code Sec. 6039(a)—returns required for certain options. (Code Sec. 6724(d)(1)(B)(xix) as amended by 2006 Tax Relief and Health Care Act §403(c)(1))

> ***observation:*** The 2006 Pension Act, Sec. 844(d)(2)(A), PL 109-280, 8/17/2006, added Code Sec. 6724(d)(1)(B)(xix) to the Code and the 2006 Tax Relief and Health Care Act does not redesignate that subsection. Thus, Code Sec. 6724(d)(1)(B)(xix) is now duplicated and a technical correction will be required to fix it.

Redesignations. Pre-2006 Tax Relief and Health Care Act Code Sec. 6039(b) and Code Sec. 6039(c) are redesignated as Code Sec. 6039(c) and Code Sec. 6039(d), respectively. (2006 Tax Relief and Health Care Act §403(b))

☐ **Effective:** Calendar years beginning after date of enactment. (2006 Tax Relief and Health Care Act §403(d))

¶ 402. Mental health parity requirements extended through 2007

Code Sec. 9812(f)(3), as amended by 2006 Tax Relief and Health Care Act § 115(a)
ERISA § 712(f), as amended by 2006 Tax Relief and Health Care Act § 115(b)
Generally effective: date of enactment
Committee Reports, see ¶ 5019

Under the mental health parity rules, group health plans that provide both medical and surgical benefits and mental health benefits cannot impose aggregate lifetime or annual dollar limits on mental health benefits that are not imposed on substantially all medical and surgical benefits. (FTC 2d/FIN ¶ H-1325.46; USTR ¶ 98,124; PE ¶ 98,124)

The Code imposes an excise tax on group health plans that fail to meet these parity requirements. (FTC 2d/FIN ¶ H-1325.34; USTR ¶ 49,80D4; PE ¶ 49,80D4)

Both ERISA and the PHSA contain parallel mental health parity provisions.

Under pre-2006 Tax Relief and Health Care Act law, the Code's mental health parity requirements did not apply to benefits for services furnished:

(1) on or after Sept. 30, 2001 and before Jan. 10, 2002 (as under pre-2004 Working Families Act law);

(2) on or after Jan. 1, 2004 and before Oct. 4, 2004; and

(3) after Dec. 31, 2006.

Thus, under the Code, there are gap periods for services furnished (a) on or after Sept. 30, 2001 and before Jan. 10, 2002, and (b) on or after Jan. 1, 2004 and before Oct. 4, 2004, during which the excise tax does not apply. In contrast, provisions in ERISA and the Public Health Service Act (PHSA) that parallel the Code's mental health parity requirements, and which were scheduled to sunset

FTC 2d References are to Federal Tax Coordinator 2d
FIN References are to RIAs Analysis of Federal Taxes: Income
USTR References are to United States Tax Reporter: Income, Estate & Gift, and Excise
PCA References are to Pension Analysis (print & electronic)
PE References are to Pension Explanations (print & electronic)
EP References are to Estate Planning Analysis (print & electronic)

for benefits for services furnished on or after Dec. 31, 2006, have no gap periods. (FTC 2d/FIN ¶ H-1325.46; USTR ¶ 98,124; PE ¶ 98,124, ¶ ER712-4)

New Law. The 2006 Tax Relief and Health Care Act extends the Code excise tax for failure to comply with the mental health parity requirements through Dec. 31, 2007, an additional year. (Code Sec. 9812(f)(3) as amended by 2006 Tax Relief and Health Care Act §115(a))

> ***observation:*** The Code's excise tax gap periods remain for services furnished (a) on or after Sept. 30, 2001 and before Jan. 10, 2002, and (b) on or after Jan. 1, 2004 and before Oct. 4, 2004.

The parallel provisions in ERISA and PHSA are similarly extended through Dec. 31, 2006, an additional year. (ERISA §712(f) as amended by 2006 Tax Relief and Health Care Act § 115(b)) (PHSA §2705(f) as amended by 2006 Tax Relief and Health Care Act §115(c))

> ***observation:*** The ERISA and PHSA provisions still have no coverage gap periods.

☐ **Effective:** date of enactment. (Com Rept, see ¶ 5019)

¶ 500. Cost Recovery

¶ 501. Deduction for energy efficient commercial building property is extended for one year through Dec. 31, 2008

Code Sec. 179D(h), as amended by 2006 Tax Relief and Health Care Act § 204
Generally effective: date of enactment
Committee Reports, see ¶ 5034

A deduction is allowed in an amount equal to the cost of "energy efficient commercial building property" placed in service during the tax year, see FTC 2d/FIN ¶ L-3170; USTR ¶ 179D4; TaxDesk ¶ 308,100. The maximum deduction for any building for any tax year is the excess (if any) of the product of $1.80, and the square footage of the building, over the aggregate amount of the deduction for the building for all earlier tax years, see FTC 2d/FIN ¶ L-3171; USTR ¶ 179D4; TaxDesk ¶ 308,101. Energy efficient commercial building property is property:

(1) for which depreciation or amortization is allowable,

(2) which is installed on or in a building located in the U.S., and within the scope of Standard 90.1-2001 (of the American Society of Heating, Refrigerating, and Air Conditioning Engineers and the Illuminating Engineering Society of North America),

(3) which is installed as part of the interior lighting systems, the heating, cooling, ventilation, and hot water systems, or the building envelope,

(4) which is certified as being installed as part of a plan designed to reduce the total annual energy and power costs for the interior lighting, heating, cooling, ventilation, and hot water systems of the building by 50% or more in comparison to a reference building that meets the minimum requirements of Standard 90.1-2001, see FTC 2d/FIN ¶ L-3172; USTR ¶ 179D4; TaxDesk ¶ 308,102.

The deduction did not apply for property placed in service after Dec. 31, 2007. (FTC 2d/FIN ¶ L-3171; USTR ¶ 179D4; TaxDesk ¶ 308,101)

New Law. Under the 2006 Tax Relief and Health Care Act, the deduction for energy efficient commercial building property does not apply for property

---

FTC 2d References are to Federal Tax Coordinator 2d
FIN References are to RIAs Analysis of Federal Taxes: Income
USTR References are to United States Tax Reporter: Income, Estate & Gift, and Excise
PCA References are to Pension Analysis (print & electronic)
PE References are to Pension Explanations (print & electronic)
EP References are to Estate Planning Analysis (print & electronic)

placed in service after Dec. 31, 2008. (Code Sec. 179D(h) as amended by 2006 Tax Relief and Health Care Act §204)

> ***observation:*** Thus, the deduction applies for energy efficient commercial building property placed in service during the three-year period between Jan. 1, 2006 and Dec. 31, 2008.

☐ **Effective:** date of enactment. (Com Rept, see ¶ 5034)

¶ 502. Placed-in-service deadline for the treatment of "qualified leasehold improvement property" as 15-year MACRS property is retroactively restored to Jan. 1, 2006 and is extended for two years to Dec. 31, 2007

Code Sec. 168(e)(3)(E)(iv), as amended by 2006 Tax Relief and Health Care Act § 113(a)

Generally effective: Property placed in service after Dec. 31, 2005 and before Jan. 1, 2008

Committee Reports, see ¶ 5017

Under pre-2006 Tax Relief and Health Care Act law, "qualified leasehold improvement property" placed in service after Oct. 22, 2004 and before Jan. 1, 2006 was treated as 15-year MACRS property (the leasehold improvement rule) and, thus, under the general depreciation system (GDS), was depreciated over a period of 15 years. (FTC 2d/FIN ¶ L-8208, ¶ L-8208.1, ¶ L-8210; USTR ¶ 1684.01, ¶ 1684.02; TaxDesk ¶ 266,208, ¶ 266,208.1, ¶ 266,211) Code Sec. 168(b)(3)(G) provides that property that qualified as 15-year MACRS property only because of the leasehold improvement rule had to be depreciated, under the GDS, on the straight-line method. (FTC 2d/FIN ¶ L-8917; USTR ¶ 1684.02; TaxDesk ¶ 267,018) Code Sec. 168(g)(3)(B) provides that, under the alternative depreciation system (ADS), property that qualified as 15-year MACRS property only because of the leasehold improvement rule was depreciated over a 39-year period (FTC 2d/FIN ¶ L-9403; USTR ¶ 1684.03; TaxDesk ¶ 267,503) and, as is generally required for property depreciated under the ADS, under the straight-line method, see FTC 2d/FIN ¶ L-9401; USTR ¶ 1684.03; TaxDesk ¶ 267,501.

"Qualified leasehold improvement property" was any improvement to an interior portion of a building that was nonresidential real property, provided certain requirements were met. The improvement had to be section 1250 property (and thus, generally, a structural component of the building, see FTC 2d/FIN ¶ L-8210; USTR ¶ 1684.02; TaxDesk ¶ 266,211). Also, the improvement had to be made under or pursuant to a lease either by the lessee, sublessee or lessor of that interior building portion, and the portion had to be occupied exclusively by the lessee or sublessee. The improvement had to be placed in service more than three years after the date the building was first placed in service. Qualified leasehold improvement property didn't include any improvement for which the expenditure was attributable to the enlargement of the building, to any elevator or escalator, to any structural component benefiting a common area, or to the internal structural framework of the building. Additionally, if a *lessor* made an improvement that qualified as qualified leasehold improvement property, the improvement didn't qualify as to any later owner of the improvement (the later-owner prohibition). Exceptions to the later-owner prohibition applied in the case of transfers to later owners that were by reason of death or that were certain transfers that qualified for non-recognition treatment, see FTC 2d/FIN ¶s L-8208.1, L-9328; USTR ¶s 1684.02, 1684.0271; TaxDesk ¶s 266,208.1, 269,358.

> ***observation:*** The 15-year depreciation period (39 years for ADS purposes) provided by the leasehold improvement rule was an exception to the general rule that buildings and their structural components are depreciable over 39 years (40 years for ADS purposes), see FTC 2d/FIN ¶s L-8208.1, L-8210, L-9403; USTR ¶s 1684.02, 1684.03; TaxDesk ¶s 266,208.1, 266,211, 267,503.

New Law. The 2006 Tax Relief and Health Care Act extends for two years the treatment of qualified leasehold improvement property as 15-year MACRS property (Com Rept, see ¶ 5017) by providing that 15-year property includes qualified leasehold improvement property placed in service before Jan. 1, 2008. (Code Sec. 168(e)(3)(E)(iv) as amended by 2006 Tax Relief and Health Care Act §113(a))

> ***observation:*** By amending Code Sec. 168(e)(3)(E)(iv), the 2006 Tax Relief and Health Care Act moves the placed-in-service deadline for treating "qualified leasehold improvement property" as 15-year MACRS property from Dec. 31, 2005 to Dec. 31, 2007 and retroactively restores the 15-year treatment for property placed in service before enactment of the 2006 Tax Relief and Health Care Act, but on or after Jan. 1, 2006.

> ***observation:*** Because of cross-references to Code Sec. 168(e)(3)(E)(iv) in Code Sec. 168(b)(3)(G) (see above) and Code Sec. 168(g)(3)(B) (see above), the amendment to Code Sec. 168(e)(3)(E)(iv) also moves the placed-in-service deadline to Dec. 31, 2007 (retroactive to Jan. 1, 2006, see immediately above) for pur-

FTC 2d References are to Federal Tax Coordinator 2d
FIN References are to RIAs Analysis of Federal Taxes: Income
USTR References are to United States Tax Reporter: Income, Estate & Gift, and Excise
PCA References are to Pension Analysis (print & electronic)
PE References are to Pension Explanations (print & electronic)
EP References are to Estate Planning Analysis (print & electronic)

poses of the rules that provide straight-line depreciation under the GDS and a 39-year depreciation period under the ADS for "qualified leasehold improvement property."

illustration (1): T, a lessee and calendar-year taxpayer, places in service "qualified leasehold improvement property" on Apr. 1, 2006. If the ADS doesn't apply, T is allowed to depreciate the property over the period beginning in 2006 (Year 1) and ending in 2020 (Year 16). (Although 15-year property has a depreciation period of 15 years, that 15-year period extends over 16 tax years, not 15, because of the use of the required half-year or mid-quarter convention, see FTC 2d/FIN ¶ L-8702; USTR ¶ 1684.01; TaxDesk ¶ 266,702). Depreciating the property under the straight-line method (and assuming that the property is depreciated under a half-year convention), T is allowed in 2006 a depreciation deduction of 3.33% of the property's basis. (3.33% equals 6.66% [which is the taxpayer's annual depreciation deduction on the straight-line method as applied to property with a recovery period of 15 years] × 1/2 [reflecting the use of a half-year convention].)

illustration (2): The facts are the same as in illustration (1), except that T elects to depreciate the property under the ADS system. T is allowed to depreciate the property over the period beginning in 2006 (Year 1) and ending in 2045 (Year 40). (Although the property has an ADS depreciation period of 39 years, that 39-year period extends over 40 tax years, not 39, because of the use of the required mid-month convention, see FTC 2d/FIN ¶ L-8702; USTR ¶ 1684.01; TaxDesk ¶ 266,702). Depreciating the property under the straight-line method and the mid-month convention, T is allowed in 2006 a depreciation deduction of 1.816% of the property's basis. (1.816% equals 2.564% [which is the taxpayer's annual depreciation deduction on the straight-line method as applied to property with a recovery period of 39 years] × 17/24 [reflecting the use of the mid-month convention for property placed in service, by a calendar-year taxpayer, in the fourth month of the year, see FTC 2d/FIN ¶ L-8713; USTR ¶ 1684.02; TaxDesk ¶ 266,713.])

☐ **Effective:** Property placed in service after Dec. 31, 2005 (2006 Tax Relief and Health Care Act §113(b)) and before Jan. 1, 2008. (Code Sec. 168(e)(3)(E)(iv))

¶503. Placed-in-service deadline for the treatment of "qualified restaurant property" as 15-year MACRS property is retroactively restored to Jan. 1, 2006 and is extended for two years to Dec. 31, 2007

Code Sec. 168(e)(3)(E)(v), as amended by 2006 Tax Relief and Health Care Act § 113(a)

Generally effective: Property placed in service after Dec. 31, 2005 and before Jan. 1, 2008

Committee Reports, see ¶5017

Under pre-2006 Tax Relief and Health Care Act law, "qualified restaurant property" placed in service after Oct. 22, 2004 and before Jan. 1, 2006 was treated as 15-year MACRS property (the restaurant property rule) and, thus, under the general depreciation system (GDS), was depreciated over a period of 15 years. (FTC 2d/FIN ¶L-8208, ¶L-8208.2, ¶L-8210; USTR ¶1684.01, ¶1684.02; TaxDesk ¶266,208, ¶266,208.2, ¶266,211) Code Sec. 168(b)(3)(H) provides that property that qualified as 15-year MACRS property only because of the restaurant property rule had to be depreciated, under the GDS, on the straight-line method. (FTC 2d/FIN ¶L-8917; USTR ¶1684.02; TaxDesk ¶267,018) Code Sec. 168(g)(3)(B) provides that, under the alternative depreciation system (ADS), property that qualified as 15-year MACRS property only because of the restaurant property rule was depreciated over a 39-year period (FTC 2d/FIN ¶L-9403; USTR ¶1684.03; TaxDesk ¶267,503) and, as is generally required for property depreciated under the ADS, under the straight-line method, see FTC 2d/FIN ¶L-9401; USTR ¶1684.03; TaxDesk ¶267,501.

> ***observation:*** The 15-year depreciation period (39 years for ADS purposes) under the restaurant property rule was an exception to the general rule that buildings and their structural components are depreciable over 39 years (40 years for ADS purposes), see FTC 2d/FIN ¶s L-8208.2, L-8210, L-9403; USTR ¶s 1684.02, 1684.03; TaxDesk ¶s 266,208.2, 266,211, 267,503.

New Law. The 2006 Tax Relief and Health Care Act extends for two years the treatment of qualified restaurant property as 15-year MACRS property (Com Rept, see ¶5017) by providing that 15-year property includes qualified restaurant property placed in service before Jan. 1, 2008. (Code Sec. 168(e)(3)(E)(v) as amended by 2006 Tax Relief and Health Care Act §113(a))

FTC 2d References are to Federal Tax Coordinator 2d
FIN References are to RIAs Analysis of Federal Taxes: Income
USTR References are to United States Tax Reporter: Income, Estate & Gift, and Excise
PCA References are to Pension Analysis (print & electronic)
PE References are to Pension Explanations (print & electronic)
EP References are to Estate Planning Analysis (print & electronic)

observation: By amending Code Sec. 168(e)(3)(E)(v), the 2006 Tax Relief and Health Care Act moves the placed-in-service deadline for treating "qualified restaurant property" as 15-year MACRS property from Dec. 31, 2005 to Dec. 31, 2007, and retroactively restores the 15-year treatment for property placed in service before enactment of the 2006 Tax Relief and Health Care Act, but on or after Jan. 1, 2006.

observation: Because of cross-references to Code Sec. 168(e)(3)(E)(v) in Code Sec. 168(b)(3)(H) (above) and Code Sec. 168(g)(3)(B) (above), the amendment to Code Sec. 168(e)(3)(E)(v) also moves the placed-in-service deadline to Dec. 31, 2007 (retroactive to Jan. 1, 2006, see immediately above) for purposes of the rules that provide straight-line depreciation under the GDS and a 39-year depreciation period under the ADS for "qualified restaurant property."

illustration (1): T, a calendar-year taxpayer, places in service "qualified restaurant property" on Apr. 1, 2006. If the ADS doesn't apply, T is allowed to depreciate the property over the period beginning in 2006 (Year 1) and ending in 2021 (Year 16). (Although 15-year property has a depreciation period of 15 years, that 15-year period extends over 16 tax years, not 15, because of the use of the required half-year or mid-quarter convention, see FTC 2d/FIN ¶ L-8702; USTR ¶ 1684.01; TaxDesk ¶ 266,702). Depreciating the property under the straight-line method (and assuming that the property is depreciated under a half-year convention), T is allowed in 2006 a depreciation deduction of 3.33% of the property's basis. (3.33% equals 6.66% [which is the taxpayer's annual depreciation deduction on the straight-line method as applied to property with a recovery period of 15 years] × 1/2 [reflecting the use of a half-year convention].)

illustration (2): The facts are the same as in illustration (1), except that T elects to depreciate the property under the ADS system. T is allowed to depreciate the property over the period beginning in 2006 (Year 1) and ending in 2045 (Year 40). (Although the property has an ADS depreciation period of 39 years, that 39-year period extends over 40 tax years, not 39, because of the use of the required mid-month convention, see FTC 2d/FIN ¶ L-8702; USTR ¶ 1684.01; TaxDesk ¶ 266,702). Depreciating the property under the straight-line method and the mid-month convention, T is allowed in 2006 a depreciation deduction of 1.816% of the property's basis. (1.816% equals 2.564% [which is the taxpayer's annual depreciation deduction on the straight-line method as applied to property with a recovery period of 39 years] × 17/24 [reflecting the use of the mid-month convention for property placed in service, by a calendar-year taxpayer, in the fourth month of the year, see FTC 2d/FIN ¶ L-8713; USTR ¶ 1684.02; TaxDesk ¶ 266,713.])

☐ **Effective:** Property placed in service after Dec. 31, 2005 (2006 Tax Relief and Health Care Act §113(b)) and before Jan. 1, 2008. (Code Sec. 168(e)(3)(E)(v))

¶ 504. Placed-in-service deadline for "qualified Gulf Opportunity Zone property" is for some purposes extended to Dec. 31, 2010 (and to as much as 90 days beyond) for certain property used in highly damaged portions of the GO Zone

Code Sec. 1400N(d)(6), as amended by 2006 Tax Relief and Health Care Act § 120(a)
Code Sec. 1400N(e)(2), as amended by 2006 Tax Relief and Health Care Act § 120(b)
Generally effective: Tax years beginning after Aug. 27, 2005
Committee Reports, see ¶ 5024

The "Gulf Opportunity Zone," also known as the "GO Zone," is the portion of the Hurricane Katrina Disaster area, see FTC 2d/FIN ¶ S-8551; USTR ¶ 14,00M4; TaxDesk ¶ 570,401, determined by the President to warrant individual or individual and public assistance from the federal government under the Robert T. Stafford Disaster Relief and Emergency Assistance Act, PL 100-707, 11/23/88. The GO Zone includes 31 parishes in Louisiana, 49 counties in Mississippi and 11 counties in Alabama, see FTC 2d/FIN ¶ S-8552; USTR ¶ 14,00M4; TaxDesk ¶ 570,402. The 2005 Gulf Opportunity Zone Act provided special tax benefits and incentives with respect to the GO Zone following Hurricane Katrina.

For "qualified Gulf Opportunity Zone property," also referred to as "qualified GO Zone property," see FTC 2d/FIN ¶ L-9337; USTR ¶ 14,00N4.021; TaxDesk ¶ 269,332, there is allowed, unless the taxpayer "elects-out," an additional first-year depreciation deduction ("bonus depreciation") equal to 50% of the adjusted basis of the property, see FTC 2d/FIN ¶ L-9336; USTR ¶ 14,00N4.02; TaxDesk ¶ 269,331. The adjusted basis of the qualified GO Zone property is reduced by the amount of the bonus depreciation before computing the amount otherwise allowable as a depreciation deduction for the tax year and any later tax year, see FTC 2d/FIN ¶ L-9336; USTR ¶ 14,00N4.02; TaxDesk ¶ 269,331.

Also, qualified GO Zone property is exempt from the depreciation adjustments required for purposes of the alternative minimum tax ("AMT"), see FTC 2d/FIN ¶ A-8221; USTR ¶ 14,00N4.02; TaxDesk ¶ 696,514.

Among the requirements for qualifying as qualified GO Zone property is satisfaction of a placed-in-service deadline. Under pre-2006 Tax Relief and Health Care Act law, property described in Code Sec. 168(k)(2)(A)(i) (see below) met the deadline if it was placed in service by the taxpayer before Jan. 1, 2008. "Nonresidential real property" or "residential rental property"—two categories that generally include buildings and their structural components, see FTC 2d/FIN ¶s L-8203, L-8210; USTR ¶ 1684.02; TaxDesk ¶s 266,202, 266,211—met the deadline if it was placed in service by the taxpayer before Jan. 1, 2009. (FTC 2d/FIN ¶ L-9337.7; USTR ¶ 14,00N4.021; TaxDesk ¶ 269,332)

The property (referred to above) described in Code Sec. 168(k)(2)(A)(i), see FTC 2d/FIN ¶ L-9324; USTR ¶ 1684.026; TaxDesk ¶ 269,354, is the following:

. . . property to which Code Sec. 168 (which provides the MACRS rules) applies, and which has a recovery period of 20 years or less (i.e. 3-year, 5-year, 7-year, 10-year, 15-year and 20-year MACRS property), see FTC 2d/FIN ¶ L-8202; USTR ¶ 1684.01; TaxDesk ¶ 266,201;

. . . computer software (as defined in Code Sec. 167(f)(1)(B)) for which a deduction is allowable under Code Sec. 167(a), thus, excluding computer software amortized under Code Sec. 197, see FTC 2d/FIN ¶ L-7935; USTR ¶ 1674.033; TaxDesk ¶ 265,434;

. . . "water utility property"(which is a class of MACRS property defined in Code Sec. 168(e)(5)), see FTC 2d/FIN ¶ L-8209.1; USTR ¶ 1684.01; TaxDesk ¶ 266,210; and

. . . "qualified leasehold improvement property" (certain improvements to buildings made more than three years after the building is placed in service and that are made under a lease, see FTC 2d/FIN ¶ L-9328; USTR ¶ 1684.0271; TaxDesk ¶ 269,358).

For "qualified section 179 Gulf Opportunity Zone property," the expensing in lieu of depreciation allowed under Code Sec. 179 is increased by up to $100,000 per year, see FTC 2d/FIN ¶ L-9996; USTR ¶ 14,00N4.025; TaxDesk ¶ 268,601.

"Qualified section 179 Gulf Opportunity Zone Property" is property that is "section 179 property" as defined in Code Sec. 179(d), see FTC 2d/FIN ¶ L-9922; USTR ¶ 1794.02; TaxDesk ¶ 268,424, and, under pre-2006 Tax Relief and Health Care Act law, was "qualified GO Zone property" determined under the same rules as those used to determine eligibility for the 50% bonus depreciation and AMT relief discussed above. (FTC 2d/FIN ¶ L-9997; USTR ¶ 14,00N4.025; TaxDesk ¶ 268,601)

New Law. The 2006 Tax Relief and Health Care Act provides that the placed-in-service deadlines discussed above don't apply to "specified Gulf Opportunity Zone extension property"(see below). (Code Sec. 1400N(d)(6)(A) as amended by 2006 Tax Relief and Health Care Act §120(a)) However, this rule doesn't apply in determining what is "qualified GO Zone property" for purposes of determining what is "qualified section 179 Gulf Opportunity Zone property." (Code Sec. 1400N(e)(2) as amended by 2006 Tax Relief and Health Care Act §120(b))

> ***observation:*** Thus, the pre-2006 Tax Relief and Health Care Act placed-in-service deadlines no longer apply in determining what is "qualified GO Zone property" for purposes of determining property eligible for the 50% bonus depreciation and AMT relief discussed above (and the deadlines discussed below apply instead). However, the pre-2006 Tax Relief and Health Care Act deadlines do continue to apply in determining what is "qualified GO Zone property" for purposes of determining what is "qualified section 179 Gulf Opportunity Zone property" eligible for up to $100,000 of additional expensing in lieu of depreciation (see above).

"Specified Gulf Opportunity Zone extension property" defined. "Specified Gulf Opportunity Zone extension property" is property— (Code Sec. 1400N(d)(6)(B) as amended by 2006 Tax Relief and Health Care Act §120(a))

. . . substantially all of the use of which is in one or more "specified portions of the GO Zone" (defined below), and (Code Sec. 1400N(d)(6)(B)(i))

. . . which is— (Code Sec. 1400N(d)(6)(B)(ii))

(1) nonresidential rental property or residential rental property that is placed in service by the taxpayer before Jan. 1, 2011 (Code Sec. 1400N(d)(6)(B)(ii)(I)), as limited by the pre-2010 adjusted basis limitation discussed below (Code Sec. 1400N(d)(6)(D)), or (Code Sec. 1400N(d)(6)(B)(ii)(I))

(2) in the case of a taxpayer who places a building described in Code Sec. 1400N(d)(6)(B)(ii)(I) (immediately above) in service before Jan. 1, 2011, property described in Code Sec. 168(k)(2)(A)(i) (see above), if substantially all of the use of that property is in the building and the property is placed in service by the taxpayer not later than 90 days after the building is placed in service. (Code Sec. 1400N(d)(6)(B)(ii)(II))

FTC 2d References are to Federal Tax Coordinator 2d
FIN References are to RIAs Analysis of Federal Taxes: Income
USTR References are to United States Tax Reporter: Income, Estate & Gift, and Excise
PCA References are to Pension Analysis (print & electronic)
PE References are to Pension Explanations (print & electronic)
EP References are to Estate Planning Analysis (print & electronic)

observation: In other words, for "specified Gulf Opportunity Zone extension property," the pre-2006 Tax Relief and Health Care Act placed-in-service deadlines don't apply and, instead, (1) if the "specified Gulf Opportunity Zone extension property" is nonresidential real property or residential rental property (i.e., buildings and their structural components, see above), the property must be placed in service before Jan. 1, 2011 and (2) if the "specified Gulf Opportunity Zone extension property" is software or tangible property, substantially all of the use of which is inside a building that meets the pre-Jan. 1, 2011 deadline, the property must be placed in service no later than 90 days after the building is placed in service.

"Specified portions of the GO Zone" are those portions of the GO Zone that are in any county or parish that is identified by IRS as being a county or parish in which hurricanes occurring during 2005 damaged (in the aggregate) more than 60 percent of the housing units in the county or parish which were occupied (determined according to the 2000 Census). (Code Sec. 1400N(d)(6)(C)) Congress noted that the office of the Federal Coordinator for Gulf Coast Rebuilding of the Dept. of Homeland Security, in cooperation with the Federal Emergency Management Agency, the Small Business Administration and the Dept. of Housing and Urban Development, compiled data to assess the full extent of housing damage due to 2005 Hurricanes Katrina, Rita and Wilma. Congress intended that this data, which was published on Feb. 12, 2006, and is available at www.dhs.gov/xlibrary/assets/GulfCoast_HousingDamageEstimates_021206.pdf, will be used by IRS in identifying counties and parishes that qualify as specified portions of the GO Zone. (Com Rept, see ¶ 5024)

Pre-2010 adjusted basis limitation. For property that qualifies as qualified GO Zone property solely because it is described in Code Sec. 1400N(d)(6)(B)(ii)(I) (see item (1) on the above list), Code Sec. 1400N(d)(1) (which provides the 50% bonus depreciation and corresponding basis reduction for qualified GO Zone property discussed above, see FTC 2d/FIN ¶ L-9336; USTR ¶ 14,00N4.02; TaxDesk ¶ 269,331), applies only to the extent of the adjusted basis attributable to manufacture, construction or production before Jan. 1, 2010. (Code Sec. 1400N(d)(6)(D)) Thus, for nonresidential real property or residential rental property, only the adjusted basis attributable to manufacture, construction or production before Jan. 1, 2010 ("progress expenditures") is eligible for 50% bonus depreciation. (Com Rept, see ¶ 5024)

observation: Code Sec. 1400N(d)(6)(D) states only that Code Sec. 1400N(d)(1) applies only to pre-Jan. 1, 2010 adjusted basis. Thus, read literally, Code Sec. 1400N(d)(6)(D) doesn't provide that Code Sec. 1400N(d)(4) (which provides the AMT exemption discussed above, see FTC 2d/FIN ¶ A-8221; USTR ¶ 14,00N4.02; TaxDesk

¶ 696,514) applies only to pre-Jan. 1, 2010 adjusted basis. Thus, read literally, Code Sec. 1400N(d)(6)(D) doesn't bar the AMT exemption for adjusted basis attributable to manufacture, construction or production in calendar year 2010.

☐ **Effective:** Tax years ending after Aug. 27, 2005. (2006 Tax Relief and Health Care Act §120(c))

observation: 2006 Tax Relief and Health Care Act §120(c) provides that the provision discussed above is effective as if included in 2005 Gulf Opportunity Zone Act §101 (Sec. 101, PL 109-135, 12/21/2005). 2005 Gulf Opportunity Zone Act §101(c)(1) (Sec. 101(c)(1), PL 109-135, 12/21/2005) provides that §101 took effect for tax years ending after Aug. 27, 2005.

¶ 505. Election to expense qualified environmental remediation costs is retroactively restored and is extended for two years to apply to expenditures paid or incurred after Dec. 31, 2005 and before Jan. 1, 2008

Code Sec. 198(h), as amended by 2006 Tax Relief and Health Care Act § 109(a)

Generally effective: Expenditures paid or incurred after Dec. 31, 2005 and before Jan. 1, 2008

Committee Reports, see ¶ 5013

Under pre-2006 Tax Relief and Health Care Act law, Code Sec. 198(h), which allows the election to expense qualified environmental remediation costs (see FTC 2d/FIN ¶ L-6150.1; USTR ¶ 1984; TaxDesk ¶ 268,801), didn't apply to expenditures paid or incurred after Dec. 31, 2005. Thus, eligible expenditures were those paid or incurred before Jan. 1, 2006. (FTC 2d/FIN ¶ L-6150.7; USTR ¶ 1984; TaxDesk ¶ 268,801)

New Law. The 2006 Tax Relief and Health Care Act extends Code Sec. 198(h) for two years (Com Rept, see ¶ 5013), by providing that Code Sec. 198(h) won't apply to expenditures paid or incurred after *Dec. 31, 2007.* (Code Sec. 198(h) as amended by 2006 Tax Relief and Health Care Act §109(a))

FTC 2d References are to Federal Tax Coordinator 2d
FIN References are to RIAs Analysis of Federal Taxes: Income
USTR References are to United States Tax Reporter: Income, Estate & Gift, and Excise
PCA References are to Pension Analysis (print & electronic)
PE References are to Pension Explanations (print & electronic)
EP References are to Estate Planning Analysis (print & electronic)

observation: Thus, the 2006 Tax Relief and Health Care Act retroactively restores the expensing election for qualified environmental remediation costs incurred after Dec. 31, 2005, and extends the expensing election to apply to expenditures paid or incurred before Jan. 1, 2008.

observation: With respect to an earlier version of this legislation, which, in relevant part, contained the same statutory language, Congress said that by lowering the net capital cost of a development project, the expensing of remediation costs promotes the goal of environmental remediation and promotes new investment and employment opportunities. In addition, Congress said that the increased investment in the qualifying areas has spillover effects that are beneficial to the neighboring communities. Therefore, Congress said it is appropriate to extend the provision permitting the expensing of environmental remediation costs.

For expansion of the definition of hazardous substances to include petroleum products for purposes of the environmental remediation cost expensing election, see ¶ 506.

For extension of the period for making an election for a tax year ending after Dec. 31, 2005 and before date of enactment, which would have expired but for relief provided by the 2006 Tax Relief and Health Care Act, see ¶ 701.

☐ **Effective:** Expenditures paid or incurred after Dec. 31, 2005 (2006 Tax Relief and Health Care Act §109(c)) and before Jan. 1, 2008. (Code Sec. 198(h))

¶ 506. Definition of hazardous substances for purposes of expensing election for environmental remediation costs is expanded to include petroleum products

Code Sec. 198(d)(1), as amended by 2006 Tax Relief and Health Care Act § 109(b)
Generally effective: Expenditures paid or incurred after Dec. 31, 2005
Committee Reports, see ¶ 5013

Taxpayers can elect to treat certain environmental remediation expenditures that would otherwise be chargeable to capital as deductible in the year paid or incurred. The expense deduction election applies for both regular and alternative minimum tax (AMT) purposes. The expenditure must be incurred in connection with the abatement or control of hazardous substances at a "qualified contaminated site." A qualified contaminated site ("brownfield") is property held for use in a trade or business, for the production of income, or as inventory and is certified by the appropriate state environmental agency to be an area at or on which there has been a release (or threat of release) or disposal of a hazardous substance. Both urban and rural property may qualify. However, sites that are identified on the national priorities list under the Comprehensive Environmental Response, Compensation, and Liability Act of '80 (CERCLA) cannot qualify. See FTC 2d/FIN ¶ L-6159 *et seq.*; USTR ¶ 1984; TaxDesk ¶ 268,801 *et seq.*

The term "hazardous substance" under Code Sec. 198(d)(1) (for purposes of defining "qualified environmental remediation expenditure," in Code Sec. 198(b), see FTC 2d/FIN ¶ L-6159 *et seq.*; USTR ¶ 1984; TaxDesk ¶ 268,801) means—

. . . any substance which is a hazardous substance as defined in §101(14) of CERCLA, and

. . . any substance designated as a hazardous substance under §102 of CERCLA.

The term "hazardous substance" does not include any substance with respect to which a removal or remedial action is not permitted under §104 of CERCLA, by reason of §104(a)(3) of CERCLA (see FTC 2d/FIN ¶ L-6164; USTR ¶ 1984; TaxDesk ¶ 268,801).

> ***observation:*** Under CERCLA §104(a)(3), the President won't provide for removal or remedial action in response to a release or threat of release:
>
> (1) of a naturally occurring substance in its unaltered form, or altered solely through naturally occurring processes or phenomena, from a location where it is naturally found;
>
> (2) from products which are part of the structure of, and result in exposure within, residential buildings or business or community structures; or
>
> (3) into public or private drinking water supplies due to deterioration of the system through ordinary use.

Thus, under §104(a)(3) of CERCLA, the definition of hazardous substance is subject to additional limitations applicable to asbestos and similar substances within buildings, certain naturally occurring substances such as radon, and certain other substances released into drinking water supplies due to ordinary use. Under pre-2006 Tax Relief and Health Care Act law, with the exception of qualified environmental remediation expenditures paid or incurred after Aug. 27, 2005 in connection with a qualified contaminated site in the Gulf Opportunity

---

Zone (GO Zone), petroleum products were generally not regarded as hazardous substances for purposes of Code Sec. 198. (FTC 2d/FIN ¶ L-6164; USTR ¶ 1984; TaxDesk ¶ 268,801)

New Law. Under the 2006 Tax Relief and Health Care Act, petroleum products as defined in Code Sec. 4612(a)(3) (which defines the term "petroleum product" as including crude oil, see FTC 2d ¶ W-4001; USTR ¶ 46,114) *are* also treated as hazardous substances for purposes of Code Sec. 198(d)(1). (Code Sec. 198(d)(1)(C) as amended by 2006 Tax Relief and Health Care Act §109(b)) Thus, the provision expands the definition of hazardous substances to petroleum products, including crude oil, crude oil condensates and natural gasoline. The exceptions for sites on the national priorities list under CERCLA and for substances with respect to which a removal or remediation is not permitted under §104 of CERCLA, would continue to apply to all hazardous substances (including petroleum products). (Com Rept, see ¶ 5013)

> RIA ***observation:*** Thus, for example, under the 2006 Tax Relief and Health Care Act, the release of crude oil on property not identified on the national priorities list under CERCLA can result in the property being treated as a qualified contaminated site for purposes of Code Sec. 198 whether or not the property is located in the GO Zone. The property would have to be held for use in a trade or business, for the production of income, or as inventory, and be certified by the appropriate state environmental agency as an area at or on which there has been a release (or threat of release) or disposal of a hazardous substance, i.e., crude oil.

> RIA ***observation:*** With respect to an earlier version of this legislation, which contained the same relevant statutory language, Congress said that by lowering the net capital cost of a development project, the expensing of brownfields remediation costs promotes the goal of environmental remediation and promotes new investment and employment opportunities. In addition, the increased investment in the qualifying areas has spillover effects that are beneficial to the neighboring communities. Congress said that similar principles apply with respect to contamination of sites by petroleum products and that therefore it is appropriate to expand the scope of the definition of hazardous substances to include petroleum products.

For an extension of the expensing election for environmental remediation costs, see ¶ 505.

☐ **Effective:** Expenditures paid or incurred after Dec. 31, 2005. (2006 Tax Relief and Health Care Act §109(c))

¶ 507. Suspension of taxable income limitation on percentage depletion from marginal oil and gas wells is retroactively extended for two years to include tax years beginning before Jan. 1, 2008

Code Sec. 613A(c)(6)(H), as amended by 2006 Tax Relief and Health Care Act § 118(a)
Generally effective: Tax years beginning after Dec. 31, 2005 and before Jan. 1, 2008
Committee Reports, see ¶ 5022

Taxpayers are permitted to recover their oil and gas well investments through depletion deductions, which may in certain cases be determined using the percentage depletion method. One limitation that applies in calculating percentage depletion deductions is a restriction that, for oil and gas properties, the amount deducted may not exceed 100% of the taxable income from that property in any year. See FTC 2d/FIN ¶ N-2701; USTR ¶ 6134.009; TaxDesk ¶ 271,001. Special percentage depletion rules apply to oil and gas produced from "marginal" properties. See FTC 2d/FIN ¶ N-2424; USTR ¶ 613A4; TaxDesk ¶ 271,001. Marginal production is defined as domestic crude oil and natural gas production from stripper well property or from heavy oil property. See FTC 2d/FIN ¶ N-2426; USTR ¶ 613A4; TaxDesk ¶ 271,001. One special rule under Pre-2006 Tax Relief and Health Care Act law provided that the 100%-of-taxable-income limitation didn't apply to domestic oil and gas production from marginal properties during tax years beginning after Dec. 31, '97, and before *Jan. 1, 2006.* (FTC 2d/FIN ¶ N-2729; USTR ¶ 613A4, ¶ 6134.009; TaxDesk ¶ 271,001)

New Law. The 2006 Tax Relief and Health Care Act extends the rule suspending the 100%-of-taxable-income limitation with respect to oil and gas production from marginal properties to include any tax year beginning before *Jan. 1, 2008.* (Code Sec. 613A(c)(6)(H) as amended by 2006 Tax Relief and Health Care Act §118(a)) Thus, the 2006 Tax Relief and Health Care Act extends for two years the suspension of the taxable income limitation for marginal production through tax years beginning on or before Dec. 31, 2007. (Com Rept, see ¶ 5022)

> ***observation:*** Thus, the suspension is retroactively extended to apply to calendar years 2006 and 2007 and to fiscal years beginning as late as Dec. 31, 2007.

FTC 2d References are to Federal Tax Coordinator 2d
FIN References are to RIAs Analysis of Federal Taxes: Income
USTR References are to United States Tax Reporter: Income, Estate & Gift, and Excise
PCA References are to Pension Analysis (print & electronic)
PE References are to Pension Explanations (print & electronic)
EP References are to Estate Planning Analysis (print & electronic)

☐ **Effective:** Tax years beginning after Dec. 31, 2005 (2006 Tax Relief and Health Care Act §118(b)) and before Jan. 1, 2008. (Code Sec. 613A(c)(6)(H))

¶ 508. 50% bonus depreciation and AMT relief are allowed for "qualified cellulosic biomass ethanol plant property" purchased after date of enactment and placed in service before Jan. 1, 2013

Code Sec. 168(l), as amended by 2006 Tax Relief and Health Care Act § 209(a)

Generally effective: Property purchased after date of enactment and placed in service before Jan. 1, 2013

Committee Reports, see ¶ 5039

For most tangible property, the depreciation deduction under Code Sec. 167(a) is determined under the modified accelerated cost recovery system (MACRS) provided by Code Sec. 168, see FTC 2d/FIN ¶ L-8101; USTR ¶ 1684; TaxDesk ¶ 266,001.

Certain property depreciated on the 200% declining balance method for regular income tax purposes must be depreciated on the 150% declining balance method for alternative minimum tax purposes (the AMT depreciation adjustment). (FTC 2d/FIN ¶ A-8220; USTR ¶ 564.01; TaxDesk ¶ 696,513)

For most new depreciable tangible property (other than buildings), most new depreciable computer software, and certain new depreciable leasehold improvement property, there was allowed (1) 50% additional depreciation (50% bonus depreciation) in the year that the property was placed in service (with corresponding reductions in basis), see FTC 2d/FIN ¶ L-9311; USTR ¶ 1684.025; TaxDesk ¶ 269,341, and (2) exemption from the AMT depreciation adjustment (AMT exemption), see FTC 2d/FIN ¶ A-8221; USTR ¶ 1684.029; TaxDesk ¶ 696,514, if the property was acquired after May 5, 2003 (but not under a written binding contract in effect before May 6, 2003) and before Jan. 1, 2005 and was placed in service before Jan. 1, 2005 (before Jan. 1, 2006 for certain long-production-period property and aircraft, and as late as Dec. 31, 2006 for certain long-production-period property and aircraft affected by Hurricanes Katrina, Rita, or Wilma), see FTC 2d/FIN ¶ L-9312; USTR ¶ 1684.028; TaxDesk ¶ 269,342.

The 50% bonus depreciation and AMT exemption didn't apply to classes of 50% bonus depreciation for which the taxpayer elected to decline the bonus depreciation and AMT exemption (i.e., make an "election-out"). The election-out had to apply to both the bonus depreciation and the AMT exemption; i.e., a taxpayer couldn't elect-out for one, but not the other, see FTC 2d/FIN ¶s A-8221.1, L-9318; USTR ¶ 1684.0291; TaxDesk ¶s 269,348, 696,514.1. Instead of electing out, a taxpayer could elect, on a class-by-class basis, to claim 30% bonus depreciation instead of the 50% bonus depreciation, see FTC 2d/FIN ¶ L-9317; USTR ¶ 1684.0292; TaxDesk ¶ 269,347.

50% bonus depreciation and an AMT exemption is also available for most depreciable tangible property and depreciable computer software (1) acquired by purchase after Aug. 27, 2005 (but not under a written binding contract in effect before Aug. 28, 2005), (2) first used in the area hardest hit by Hurricane Katrina (the Gulf Opportunity Zone or GO Zone) after Aug. 27, 2005, (3) used substantially all of the time in an active business in the GO Zone and (4) placed in service, under pre-2006 Tax Relief and Health Care Act law, before Jan. 1, 2008 (before Jan. 1, 2009 if the property is a building) (qualified GO Zone property), see FTC 2d/FIN ¶s L-9336, L-9337; USTR ¶s 14,00N4.02, 14,00N4.021; TaxDesk ¶s 269,331, 269,332. For the modification, by the 2006 Tax Relief and Health Care Act, of the placed in service deadlines for certain qualified GO Zone property, see ¶ 504.

The 50% bonus depreciation and AMT exemption don't apply to classes of qualified GO Zone property for which the taxpayer elects to make an election-out. The election-out had to apply to both the bonus depreciation and the AMT exemption; i.e., a taxpayer couldn't elect-out for one, but not the other, see FTC 2d/FIN ¶ L-9338; USTR ¶ 14,00N4.023; TaxDesk ¶ 269,334.

New Law. The 2006 Tax Relief and Health Care Act provides that for "qualified cellulosic biomass ethanol plant property" ("QCBEPP,"as defined below): (Code Sec. 168(l)(1) as amended by 2006 Tax Relief and Health Care Act §209(a))

. . . the depreciation deduction under Code Sec. 167(a) for the tax year in which the property is placed in service includes an allowance equal to 50% of the adjusted basis of the QCBEPP, and (Code Sec. 168(l)(1)(A))

. . . the adjusted basis of the QCBEPP is reduced by the amount of that deduction before computing the amount otherwise allowable as a depreciation deduction for the tax year and any later tax year. (Code Sec. 168(l)(1)(B)) Thus, the basis of the property and the depreciation allowances in the year of purchase and later years are appropriately adjusted to reflect the 50% bonus depreciation. (Com Rept, see ¶ 5039)

> ***illustration (1):*** On Nov. 1, 2007, T, a calendar year taxpayer, acquires and places in service QCBEPP that is 7-year MACRS property (see FTC 2d/FIN ¶ L-8206; USTR ¶ 1684.01; TaxDesk ¶ 266,206), and that costs $20,000,000. Assume that T doesn't make an election to de-

FTC 2d References are to Federal Tax Coordinator 2d
FIN References are to RIAs Analysis of Federal Taxes: Income
USTR References are to United States Tax Reporter: Income, Estate & Gift, and Excise
PCA References are to Pension Analysis (print & electronic)
PE References are to Pension Explanations (print & electronic)
EP References are to Estate Planning Analysis (print & electronic)

cline bonus depreciation (see "Election-out" below). T's bonus depreciation deduction for 2007 is $10,000,000 ($20,000,000 × 50%). Then, assuming that T applies the 200% declining balance method (switching to the straight-line method when that method yields larger deductions, see FTC 2d/FIN ¶ L-8909; USTR ¶ 1684.01; TaxDesk ¶ 267,013), the half-year convention, see FTC 2d/FIN ¶ L-8702; USTR ¶ 1684.01; TaxDesk ¶ 266,702 and the percentages provided by the optional depreciation tables, see FTC 2d/FIN ¶ L-8904; USTR ¶ 1684.01; TaxDesk ¶ 267,008, T's remaining depreciation deductions are as follows: for 2007, $1,429,000 (14.29% of $10,000,000); for 2008, $2,449,000 (24.49% of $10,000,000); for 2009, $1,749,000 (17.49% of $10,000,000); for 2010, $1,249,000 (12.49% of $10,000,000); for 2011, $893,000 (8.93% of $10,000,000); for 2012, $892,000 (8.92% of $10,000,000); for 2013, $893,000 (8.93% of $10,000,000); and for 2014, $446,000 (4.46% of $10,000,000).

observation: The half-year, mid-quarter and mid-month depreciations didn't apply to the bonus depreciation available for 50% bonus depreciation property, see FTC 2d/FIN ¶ L-9311; USTR ¶ 1684.025; TaxDesk ¶ 269,341. Thus, it can be presumed that the conventions don't apply to the bonus depreciation available for QCBEPP.

caution: Although it can be presumed that the depreciation conventions don't apply to the bonus depreciation available for QCBEPP, the conventions do apply to the other first-year depreciation deductions allowed with respect to QCBEPP. Further, the placement of QCBEPP into service during the last quarter of a tax year may sometimes cause the taxpayer to be required to use a mid-quarter convention, rather than a half-year convention, for *all* of the taxpayer's MACRS property (other than buildings and railroad gradings or tunnel bores) placed into service during that tax year, see FTC 2d/FIN ¶ L-8103; USTR ¶ 1684.01; TaxDesk ¶ 266,701.

observation: Amounts "expensed" under the election available under Code Sec. 179 reduce the basis of an asset that is 50% bonus depreciation property before the bonus depreciation is calculated for the asset and before other depreciation is calculated for the asset, see FTC 2d/FIN ¶ L-9311; USTR ¶ 1684.025; TaxDesk ¶ 269,341. Presumably, a similar rule applies to QCBEPP.

The 50% bonus depreciation for QCBEPP is subject to the general rules regarding whether an item is deductible under Code Sec. 162 or subject to capitalization under Code Sec. 263 (the regular capitalization rules, see FTC 2d/FIN ¶ L-5601; USTR ¶ 2634; TaxDesk ¶ 256,201) or Code Sec. 263A (the uniform capitalization, or UNICAP, rules, see FTC 2d/FIN ¶ G-5450; USTR ¶ 263A4; TaxDesk ¶ 456,000). (Com Rept, see ¶ 5039)

> ***observation:*** Rules for calculating bonus depreciation in special situations, or rules for the effect of bonus depreciation under other tax rules, for 50% bonus depreciation property will, presumably, be the same for QCBEPP. For example, the bonus depreciation deduction for QCBEPP presumably won't be reduced for property placed in service in a short tax year, see FTC 2d/FIN ¶ L-9311; USTR ¶ 1684.025; TaxDesk ¶ 269,341. Also, it can be presumed that the 50% bonus depreciation for QCBEPP won't reduce a corporation's "earnings and profits," see FTC 2d/FIN ¶ F-10303; USTR ¶ 3124.04; TaxDesk ¶ 171,022.

QCBEPP defined. QCBEPP is property which satisfies seven specified requirements (which are discussed under the seven italicized subheadings below). (Code Sec. 168(l)(2))

> ***caution:*** There are certain types of property which are ineligible to be qualified property even if they satisfy the seven requirements of the definition of QCBEPP, see "Ineligible property" below.

Requirement that property be depreciable. To be QCBEPP, property must be of a character subject to the allowance for depreciation. (Code Sec. 168(l)(2))

> ***observation:*** Under this rule, *any* depreciable property can qualify for the 50% bonus depreciation available for QCBEPP if the property satisfies the other six requirements discussed below. This rule contrasts with the eligibility rules for 50% bonus depreciation (above), under which whole buildings were ineligible, and structural components of buildings were eligible only if they were qualified leasehold improvements, see FTC 2d/FIN ¶ L-9312; USTR ¶ 1684.028; TaxDesk ¶ 269,342.

Requirement that property be used in the U.S. To be QCBEPP, property must be used in the U.S. (Code Sec. 168(l)(2)(A))

> ***observation:*** Unlike qualified GO Zone property (above), QCBEPP can be used anywhere in the U.S.

Requirement that property must perform a specified function. To be QCBEPP, property must be used *solely* to produce cellulosic biomass ethanol. (Code Sec. 168(l)(2)(A)). For this purpose, cellulosic biomass ethanol is ethanol produced by enzymatic hydrolysis of any lignocellulosic or hemicellulosic matter that is available on a renewable or recurring basis. (Code Sec. 168(l)(3)) For example, lignocellulosic or hemicellulosic matter that is available on a renewable or recurring basis includes bagasse (from sugar cane), corn stalks and switchgrass. (Com Rept, see ¶ 5039)

Original use requirement. To be QCBEPP, the original use of the property must begin with the taxpayer after date of enactment. (Code Sec. 168(l)(2)(B))

Rules similar to the rules in Code Sec. 168(k)(2)(E)(ii) (see the first observation below and illustrations (2) and (3) below) and Code Sec. 168(k)(2)(E)(iii) (see the second observation below and illustrations (4) and (5) below) apply for purposes of Code Sec. 168(l), except that (Code Sec. 168(l)(5)) "date of enactment" is substituted for "Sept. 10, 2001" each place it appears. (Code Sec. 168(l)(5)(A))

> ***observation:*** Applying a rule similar to the rule in Code Sec. 168(k)(2)(E)(ii), modified by Code Sec. 168(l)(5)(A) as discussed above, to Code Sec. 168(l) results in the following rule: if property (1) is originally placed in service after date of enactment by a person, and (2) is sold and leased back by that person within three months after the date that property was originally placed in service, the property is treated as originally placed in service, for purposes of the original use requirement (and the syndication rule discussed below), not earlier than the date on which the property is used under the leaseback (the "sale-leaseback rule"), see FTC 2d/FIN ¶ L-9314 *et seq.*; USTR ¶ 1684.028; TaxDesk ¶ 269,344 *et seq.*

> ***illustration (2):*** On Nov. 1, 2007, X, a calendar year taxpayer, buys a newly manufactured machine from manufacturer M, and begins to use the machine in the production of cellulosic biomass ethanol in the U.S. On Jan. 10, 2008, X sells the machine to Y, which is a company in the equipment leasing business and is a calendar-year taxpayer. Also, on Jan. 10, 2008, X leases the machine back from Y under a lease, the term of which begins on Jan. 10, 2008. X continues to use the machine solely to produce cellulosic biomass ethanol in the U.S. Thus, Jan. 10, 2008 is the date that the machine is first used under the leaseback, and, thus, first satisfies the original use requirement. Therefore, if the machine meets the other requirements for being qualified property, and if Y doesn't make an "election-out" (see below), Y is allowed 50% bonus depreciation for the machine in 2008. X is not allowed 50% bonus depreciation for the machine in either 2007 or 2008.

illustration (3): The facts are the same as in illustration (2), except that (1) X acquires the machine and begins to use it on Dec. 1, 2006, and (2) the sale and leaseback of the machine occurs on Feb. 15, 2007. The sale and leaseback of the machine occurs within the three-month time period required under the sale-leaseback rule. However, the machine fails the requirement, under the sale-leaseback rule, that property be originally placed in service after date of enactment. Thus, Y isn't allowed 50% bonus depreciation for the machine. With respect to X, the machine fails a different requirement, i.e., the requirement in Code Sec. 168(l)(2)(B) (above) that the original use of the machine must begin with the taxpayer after date of enactment. Thus, X also isn't allowed 50% bonus depreciation for the machine.

observation: Applying a rule similar to the rule in Code Sec. 168(k)(2)(E)(iii), modified by Code Sec. 168(l)(5)(A) as discussed above, to Code Sec. 168(l) results in the following rule. If:

(1) property is originally placed in service after date of enactment by the lessor of that property,

(2) the property is sold by the lessor or any later purchaser within three months after the date it is originally placed in service (or, if multiple units of property are subject to the same lease, within three months after the final unit is placed in service, so long as the period between the time the first unit is placed in service and the last unit is placed in service is no more than 12 months), and

(3) the user of the property after the last sale during the three-month period remains the same as when the property was originally placed in service,

the property is treated as originally placed in service by the purchaser not earlier than the date of the last sale (the "syndication rule"), see FTC 2d/FIN ¶ L-9314.1; USTR ¶ 1684.028; TaxDesk ¶ 269,344.1.

illustration (4): Lessor F places Property P in service in the U.S. on Aug. 1, 2007. The lessee of Property P is E who uses the property solely to produce cellulosic biomass ethanol. On Sept. 1, 2007, Lessor F sells Property P to G. On Oct. 1, 2007, G sells Property P to H. E continues to be the lessee of Property P, and continues to use the property in the U.S. solely to produce cellulosic biomass ethanol from Aug.

1, 2007 through Oct. 1, 2007. H is the original user of Property P, and is eligible to claim 50% bonus depreciation for the property.

illustration (5): Lessor B places Property Q in service in the U.S. on June 1, 2007 and Property R in service in the U.S. on Apr. 15, 2008. Properties Q and R are subject to the same lease. The lessee of Properties Q and R is N. On July 1, 2008, Lessor B sells Properties Q and R to C. N continues to be the lessee of Properties Q and R, and continues to use them in the U.S. solely to produce cellulosic biomass ethanol from June 1, 2007 through July 1, 2008. C is the original user of Properties Q and R and is eligible to claim 50% bonus depreciation for the properties.

observation: IRS has issued guidance on the sale-leaseback rule, the syndication rule and other aspects of the original use requirement as applied to 50% bonus depreciation property, see FTC 2d/FIN ¶ L-9314 *et seq.*; USTR ¶ 1684.028; TaxDesk ¶ 269,344 *et seq.* Subject to appropriate modifications to take into account different date requirements, it can be expected that similar guidance will be issued with respect to QCBEPP. Thus, for example, it can be presumed that the costs of reconditioning or rebuilding used property (but not the costs of acquiring the used property) can satisfy the original use test for QCBEPP, see FTC 2d/FIN ¶ L-9314; USTR ¶ 1684.028; TaxDesk ¶ 269,344.

Purchase requirement. To be QCBEPP, property must be acquired by "purchase" (as defined in Code Sec. 179(d)). (Code Sec. 168(l)(2)(C))

observation: Under Code Sec. 179(d), a "purchase" is any acquisition of property *other than* an acquisition (1) from a person related to the taxpayer; (2) from another member of a controlled group of corporations; or (3) in which the basis of the acquiring person in the property is (a) in whole or part, a carryover basis, or (b) determined under Code Sec. 1014(a) (concerning property acquired from a decedent), see FTC 2d/FIN ¶ L-9925; USTR ¶ 1794.02; TaxDesk ¶ 268,427.

Timely acquisition requirement. To be QCBEPP, property must be acquired after date of enactment and no written binding contract for the acquisition can be in effect on or before date of enactment. (Code Sec. 168(l)(2)(C))

observation: IRS has, in regs, issued considerable guidance concerning the timely acquisition requirements for 50% bonus depreciation property. The guidance includes rules concerning what is a binding contract, rules concerning components, rules concerning property manufactured, constructed or produced by or for the taxpayer (see discussion of Code Sec. 168(l)(5) below) and the disqualifying effect of certain actions by persons other than the taxpayer (see discussion of Code Sec. 168(l)(5) below), see FTC 2d/FIN ¶ L-9315 *et seq.*; USTR ¶ 1684.028; TaxDesk ¶ 269,345 *et seq.* Subject to appropriate modifications to take into account different date requirements, it can be expected that similar guidance will be issued with respect to QCBEPP.

A rule similar to the rule in Code Sec. 168(k)(2)(E)(i) applies for purposes of Code Sec. 168(l) except that (Code Sec. 168(l)(5)) "date of enactment" is substituted for "Sept. 10, 2001" (Code Sec. 168(l)(5)(A)) and "Jan. 1, 2013" is substituted for "Jan. 1, 2005." (Code Sec. 168(l)(5)(B)) Thus, property that is manufactured, constructed, or produced by the taxpayer for use by the taxpayer is QCBEPP if the taxpayer begins manufacture, construction or production of the property after date of enactment and the property meets the placed in service requirement (see below), as well as all other requirements. (Com Rept, see ¶ 5039) For purposes of this rule, property that is manufactured, constructed or produced *for* the taxpayer by another person under a contract that is entered into before the manufacture, construction or production of the property is considered to be manufactured, constructed or produced by the taxpayer, see FTC 2d/FIN ¶ L-9315; USTR ¶ 1684.028; TaxDesk ¶ 269,345. (Com Rept, see ¶ 5039)

Rules similar to the rules in Code Sec. 168(k)(2)(E)(iv) apply for purposes of Code Sec. 168(l) except that (Code Sec. 168(l)(5)) "date of enactment" is substituted for "Sept. 10, 2001" (Code Sec. 168(l)(5)(A)) and "QCBEPP" is substituted for "qualified property." (Code Sec. 168(l)(5)(C))

> ***observation:*** Applying rules similar to the rules in Code Sec. 168(k)(2)(E)(iv), modified by Code Sec. 168(l)(5)(A) and Code Sec. 168(l)(5)(C) as discussed above, to Code Sec. 168(l) results in the following rule: QCBEPP doesn't include property if:
>
> (1) the user of the property (as of the date on which the property is originally placed in service), or a person that is related (within the meaning of Code Sec. 267(b) or Code Sec. 707(b)) to the user, or the taxpayer, had a written binding contract in effect for the acquisition of the property at any time on or before date of enactment or
>
> (2) in the case of property manufactured, constructed or produced for the user's or related person's own use, the manufacture, construction or production of the property began at any time on or before Sept. 10, 2001, see FTC 2d/FIN ¶ L-9315.2; USTR ¶ 1684.028; TaxDesk ¶ 269,356.3.

FTC 2d References are to Federal Tax Coordinator 2d
FIN References are to RIAs Analysis of Federal Taxes: Income
USTR References are to United States Tax Reporter: Income, Estate & Gift, and Excise
PCA References are to Pension Analysis (print & electronic)
PE References are to Pension Explanations (print & electronic)
EP References are to Estate Planning Analysis (print & electronic)

illustration (6): R, a person related, within the meaning of Code Sec. 267(b), to Taxpayer Z, entered into a written binding contract to buy machinery on Dec. 1, 2006. On Feb. 1, 2007, before the delivery of the machinery to R, R transferred to Z the rights of R under the contract. Z cannot treat the machinery as QCBEPP.

illustration (7): R, a person related, within the meaning of Code Sec. 267(b), to Taxpayer Z, began construction on Mar. 1, 2006 of a plant consisting of QCBEPP for R's use. On Feb. 1, 2007, before completing construction of the plant, R transfers to Z the partially completed plant. Z isn't allowed to treat the plant as QCBEPP and, thus, isn't allowed 50% bonus depreciation for either any amounts it pays to R for the plant or for any of Z's costs of completing the plant.

Timely placement into service requirement. To be QCBEPP, the property must be placed in service by the taxpayer before Jan. 1, 2013. (Code Sec. 168(l)(2)(D))

Ineligible property. The 2006 Tax Relief and Health Care Act provides for two types of property (described below) that are not eligible to be QCBEPP. (Code Sec. 168(l)(4)) For the election to not treat property as QCBEPP, see "Election-out" below. For the denial of double tax benefits for property subject to the election to expense 50% of the cost of certain refinery property, see "Denial of double benefit" below.

Alternative depreciation system property. QCBEPP doesn't include any property described in Code Sec. 168(k)(2)(D)(i). (Code Sec. 168(l)(4)(A))

observation: Thus, property isn't eligible to be QCBEPP if it is depreciated under the alternative depreciation system (ADS), see FTC 2d/FIN ¶ L-9313; USTR ¶ 1684.028; TaxDesk ¶ 269,343. For discussion of the ADS, see FTC 2d/FIN ¶ L-9401 *et seq.*; USTR ¶ 1684.03; TaxDesk ¶ 267,501 *et seq.*

Presumably, the following rules, which are similar to rules that apply under Code Sec. 168(k)(2)(D)(i) and related regs will apply in determining whether property is excluded from being QCBEPP:

(1) property to which the ADS applies merely because the taxpayer *elected* to apply the ADS isn't barred from being QCBEPP;

(2) property that must be depreciated under the ADS includes property that must be depreciated under the ADS because of *any* Code section that requires use of the ADS—for example, Code Sec. 280F(b) (property that is subject to the ADS because it is "listed property" with limited business use, see FTC 2d/FIN ¶ L-10018; USTR ¶ 280F4; TaxDesk ¶ 267,615). In other words, in determining whether property is

ineligible to be QCBEPP, property that is depreciated under ADS won't be limited to property listed in Code Sec. 168(g)(1).

Tax-exempt bond financed property. QCBEPP doesn't include any property any portion of which is financed with the proceeds of any obligation the interest on which is exempt from tax under Code Sec. 103 (which provides the tax-exemption for the interest on municipal bonds, see FTC 2d/FIN ¶ J-3001 *et seq.*; USTR ¶ 1034 *et seq.*; TaxDesk ¶ 158,001 *et seq.*). (Code Sec. 168(l)(4)(B))

Election-out. For any class of property for any tax year, a taxpayer can elect to not apply Code Sec. 168(l) to all property in that class placed in service during the tax year. (Code Sec. 168(l)(4)(C)) Thus, a taxpayer is allowed to elect out of the 50% bonus depreciation for any class of property for any tax year. (Com Rept, see ¶ 5039)

> ***caution:*** Presumably, as was discussed above with respect to elections-out for 50% bonus depreciation property or for qualified GO Zone property, an election out of bonus depreciation for a class of QCBEPP is, inseparably, an election out of the exemption, discussed below, from the AMT depreciation adjustment.

> ***observation:*** Presumably, the classes of property for which an election-out can be made with respect to QCBEPP will generally track the recovery classes for MACRS property, with separate classifications for computer software or any other non-MACRS property. For the classes of property for which an election-out can be made with respect to 50% bonus depreciation property, see FTC 2d/FIN ¶ L-9318.2; USTR ¶ 1684.0291; TaxDesk ¶ 269,348.2. For the classes of property for which elections-out can be made with respect to qualified GO Zone property, see FTC 2d/FIN ¶ L-9338; USTR ¶ 1400N4.023.

> ***caution:*** The election to claim 30% bonus depreciation, instead of 50% bonus depreciation, that is available for 50% bonus depreciation property (see above), isn't available for QCBEPP.

Alternative minimum tax exemption. Rules similar to the rules in Code Sec. 168(k)(2)(G) (see FTC 2d/FIN ¶ A-8221; USTR ¶ 1684.028; TaxDesk ¶ 696,514) apply for purposes of Code Sec. 168(l). (Code Sec. 168(l)(6)) Thus, 50% bonus depreciation is allowed for both regular tax and AMT purposes, and there is no adjustment to the allowable amount of depreciation for purposes of

---

computing a taxpayer's alternative minimum taxable income for QCBEPP. (Com Rept, see ¶ 5039)

> ***observation:*** Accordingly, for QCBEPP, neither the 50% bonus depreciation allowable for the property nor any of the other depreciation deductions allowable for the property (in the first year or in later years) are subject to adjustment for AMT purposes, see FTC 2d/FIN ¶ A-8221; USTR ¶ 1684.028; TaxDesk ¶ 696,514.

> ***illustration (8):*** The facts are the same as in illustration (1) above. The $10,000,000 of bonus depreciation is fully allowable in 2007 for regular tax and AMT purposes. Also, the other depreciation allowable for regular tax purposes in 2007 or later years is not subject to adjustment for AMT purposes.

Recapture. Rules similar to the rules under Code Sec. 179(d)(10) apply with respect to any QCBEPP that ceases to be QCBEPP. (Code Sec. 168(l)(7)) Thus, recapture rules apply if the QCBEPP ceases to be QCBEPP. (Com Rept, see ¶ 5039)

> ***observation:*** Under the Code Sec. 179(d) recapture rules, the amount recaptured (i.e., treated as ordinary income in the tax year of recapture) is, generally, the excess of (a) the amount deducted as an expense under Code Sec. 179(d) in the year that property is placed in service over (b) the total amount that would have been allowed as depreciation, for the expensed amount, for the tax year of recapture and earlier tax years. For tax years following the year of recapture, the taxpayer's depreciation deductions are generally determined as if no expensing election had been made, see Reg §1.179-1(e) and FTC 2d/FIN ¶ L-9935; USTR ¶ 1794.03; TaxDesk ¶ 268,428. In Notice 2006-77, Sec. 6, 2006-40, the IRS provided rules and examples that adapt the rules of Code Sec. 179(d) to the situation in which there is recapture of the 50% depreciation for qualified GO Zone property because it ceased to be qualified GO Zone property, see FTC 2d/FIN ¶ L-9339; USTR ¶ 14,00N4.024. Presumably, IRS will issue similar rules and examples concerning recapture of the 50% bonus depreciation for QCBEPP.

Denial of double benefit. Code Sec. 168(l)(1) (which provides the 50% bonus depreciation and corresponding basis adjustments for QCBEPP, see above) doesn't apply to any QCBEPP for which an election was made under Code Sec. 179C. (Code Sec. 168(l)(8)) Thus, property for which the taxpayer has elected 50% expensing under Code Sec. 179C isn't eligible for the 50% bonus depreciation available for QCBEPP. (Com Rept, see ¶ 5039)

> ***observation:*** Presumably, the double benefit that Code Sec. 168(l)(8) prohibits might otherwise arise because (1) the expensing available

under Code Sec. 179C applies to certain costs of qualified refinery property, see FTC 2d/FIN ¶ L-3156; USTR ¶ 179C4; TaxDesk ¶ 269,371, (2) a qualified refinery is any U.S. refinery designed for the primary purpose of processing liquid fuel from crude oil or "qualified fuels," see FTC 2d/FIN ¶ L-3157.1; USTR ¶ 179C4; TaxDesk ¶ 269,372, and (3) gas produced *from biomass* is included among the qualified fuels, see FTC 2d/FIN ¶ L-3156; USTR ¶ 45K4.01; TaxDesk ¶ 396,001.

observation: Code Sec. 168(l)(8) states only that Code Sec. 168(l)(1) doesn't apply to property for which an election under Code Sec. 179C is made (Code Sec. 179C property). Thus, read literally, Code Sec. 168(l)(8) doesn't bar the application of Code Sec. 168(l)(6) (see above) to Code Sec. 179C property and thus doesn't bar an AMT exemption for Code Sec. 179C property.

☐ **Effective:** Property placed in service after date of enactment in tax years ending after date of enactment (2006 Tax Relief and Health Care Act §209(b)), but only if the property is (1) acquired by the taxpayer by purchase after date of enactment (and not under a written binding contract for the acquisition in effect on or before date of enactment) (Code Sec. 168(l)(2)(C)) and (2) placed in service by the taxpayer before Jan. 1, 2013. (Code Sec. 168(l)(2)(D))

¶ 509. Taxpayers can elect to expense 50% of the cost of "qualified advanced mine safety equipment property" placed in service after date of enactment and before Jan. 1, 2009

Code Sec. 179E, as added by 2006 Tax Relief and Health Care Act § 404(a)
Code Sec. 263(a)(1)(L), as amended by 2006 Tax Relief and Health Care Act § 404(b)(1)
Code Sec. 312(k)(3)(B), as amended by 2006 Tax Relief and Health Care Act § 404(b)(2)
Code Sec. 1245(a)(2)(C), as amended by 2006 Tax Relief and Health Care Act § 404(b)(3)
Code Sec. 1245(a)(3)(C), as amended by 2006 Tax Relief and Health Care Act § 404(b)(3)
Generally effective: Costs paid or incurred after date of enactment
Committee Reports, see ¶ 5055

FTC 2d References are to Federal Tax Coordinator 2d
FIN References are to RIAs Analysis of Federal Taxes: Income
USTR References are to United States Tax Reporter: Income, Estate & Gift, and Excise
PCA References are to Pension Analysis (print & electronic)
PE References are to Pension Explanations (print & electronic)
EP References are to Estate Planning Analysis (print & electronic)

Generally, an immediate deduction isn't allowed for the capital costs of tangible property used in a trade or business. Instead, those costs are allowed to be recovered through depreciation deductions claimed over a period of years as determined under the Modified Accelerated Cost Recovery System ("MACRS"). Code Sec. 179 permits an election to expense the cost of certain MACRS property used in the active conduct of a trade or business. There are limitations on the amount that can be expensed, see FTC 2d/FIN ¶ L-9901 *et seq.*; USTR ¶ 1794 *et seq.*; TaxDesk ¶ 268,401 *et seq.*

Under pre-2006 Tax Relief and Health Care Act law, there was no special provision that allowed a current expense deduction for the cost of advanced mine safety equipment.

New Law. Under the 2006 Tax Relief and Health Care Act, a taxpayer can elect to treat 50% of the cost of any qualified advanced mine safety equipment property (defined below) as an expense that is not chargeable to capital account. Thus, any cost for which the election is made is allowed as a deduction for the tax year in which the qualified advanced mine safety equipment property is placed in service. (Code Sec. 179E(a) as added by 2006 Tax Relief and Health Care Act §404(a))

> ***observation:*** Under Code Sec. 179, the amount that can be expensed in any tax year is subject to dollar amount limitations and a phase-out rule, see FTC 2d/FIN ¶ L-9901; USTR ¶ 1794; TaxDesk ¶ 268,401, as well as a rule that limits the deductions to the taxpayer's active business taxable income, see FTC 2d/FIN ¶ L-9911; USTR ¶ 1794.01; TaxDesk ¶ 268,415. Unlike Code Sec. 179, Code Sec. 179E doesn't impose any of these limitations.

> ***observation:*** Presumably, as is the case for the expensing election under Code Sec. 179, the expensing election under Code Sec. 179E doesn't give rise to an adjustment or preference for alternative minimum tax (AMT) purposes, see FTC 2d/FIN ¶ A-8222; TaxDesk ¶ 696,515.

No expensing deduction is allowed to any taxpayer for any tax year for qualified advanced mine safety equipment property unless the taxpayer files with IRS a report providing information with respect to the operation of the taxpayer's mines as required by IRS. (Code Sec. 179E(f))

"Qualified advanced mine safety equipment property" defined. Qualified advanced mine safety equipment property is any advanced mine safety equipment property (defined below) for use in any underground mine located in the U.S.: (Code Sec. 179E(c))

. . . the original use of which commences with the taxpayer, and (Code Sec. 179E(c)(1))

. . . which is placed in service by the taxpayer after date of enactment. (Code Sec. 179E(c)(2))

> ***observation:*** Used equipment doesn't qualify as qualified advanced mine safety equipment property.

> ***observation:*** Safety equipment used in above-ground (strip) mining doesn't qualify as qualified advanced mine safety equipment property.

> ***caution:*** Even if the property is placed in service *after* date of enactment (as required by the definition of qualified advanced mine safety equipment property provided in Code Sec. 179E(c)(2) discussed above), the property won't qualify for the expensing deduction under Code Sec. 179E if the taxpayer paid or incurred the costs of the property *before* date of enactment. Code Sec. 179E only applies to costs paid or incurred *after* date of enactment, see **Effective** below.

"Advanced mine safety equipment property." Any one of the following is advanced mine safety equipment property: (Code Sec. 179E(d))

. . . Emergency communication technology or device which is used to allow a miner to maintain constant communication with an individual who is not in the mine. (Code Sec. 179E(d)(1))

. . . Electronic identification and location device which allows an individual who is not in the mine to track at all times the movements and location of miners working in or at the mine. (Code Sec. 179E(d)(2))

. . . Emergency oxygen-generating, self-rescue device which provides oxygen for at least 90 minutes. (Code Sec. 179E(d)(3))

. . . Pre-positioned supplies of oxygen which (in combination with self-rescue devices) can be used to provide each miner on a shift, in the event of an accident or other event which traps the miner in the mine or otherwise necessitates the use of a self-rescue device, the ability to survive for at least 48 hours. (Code Sec. 179E(d)(4))

. . . Comprehensive atmospheric monitoring system which monitors the levels of carbon monoxide, methane, and oxygen that are present in all areas of the mine and which can detect smoke in the case of a fire in the mine. (Code Sec. 179E(d)(5))

How to make the expense election. The election to expense 50% of qualified advanced mine safety equipment property for any tax year is made on the taxpayer's income tax return for the tax year. The election must specify the advanced mine safety equipment property to which the election applies, and is to be made in the manner that IRS may prescribe by regs. (Code Sec. 179E(b)(1)) An election to expense 50% of qualified advanced mine safety equipment property cannot be revoked except with IRS's consent. (Code Sec. 179E(b)(2))

No duplicate expense deduction is allowed. Expensing under Code Sec. 179E is not available for the portion of the cost of any property specified in an election under Code Sec. 179. (Code Sec. 179E(e))

Reduction in basis. The basis of any qualified advanced mine safety equipment property is reduced by the portion of its cost expensed under Code Sec. 179E(a). (Com Rept, see ¶ 5055)

Recapture of amount expensed. The 2006 Tax Relief and Health Care Act amends Code Sec. 1245 (which requires recapture of depreciation and amortization on disposition of depreciable personal property and most depreciable real property other than buildings, see FTC 2d/FIN ¶ I-10101; USTR ¶ 12,454; TaxDesk ¶ 223,102) to provide that, for purposes of Code Sec. 1245, any deduction allowed under Code Sec. 179E is treated as if it were a deduction allowable for amortization (FTC 2d/FIN ¶ I-10204; USTR ¶ 12,454.05; TaxDesk ¶ 223,103). (Code Sec. 1245(a)(2)(C) as amended by 2006 Tax Relief and Health Care Act §404(b)(3))

> ***observation:*** The effect of the amendment to Code Sec. 1245(a)(2)(C) is to provide that, for depreciable property that is subject to Code Sec. 1245, amounts expensed under Code Sec. 179E are subject to recapture under Code Sec. 1245.

The 2006 Tax Relief and Health Care Act also amends Code Sec. 1245 to treat as section 1245 property so much of any real property (that wouldn't otherwise be section 1245 property) which has an adjusted basis in which there are reflected adjustments for amortization under Code Sec. 179E (FTC 2d/FIN ¶ I-10106; USTR ¶ 12,454.01; TaxDesk ¶ 223,105). (Code Sec. 1245(a)(3)(C))

"Regular" capitalization rules don't apply to amounts expensed under Code Sec. 179E. The 2006 Tax Relief and Health Care Act amends Code Sec. 263 (which provides the "regular" capitalization rules (FTC 2d/FIN ¶ L-5601; USTR ¶ 2634; TaxDesk ¶ 256,201)) to provide that the rule that requires capitalization of amounts paid for new buildings (or for permanent improvements or betterments made to increase the value of any property or estate) does *not* apply to expenditures for which a deduction is allowed under Code Sec. 179E (which provides the expense election discussed above). (Code Sec. 263(a)(1)(L) as amended by 2006 Tax Relief and Health Care Act §404(b)(1))

Effect on earnings and profits. For purposes of determining corporate earnings and profits, any amount deductible under Code Sec. 179E is deducted ratably over five tax years (beginning with the tax year for which the amount is deductible under Code Sec. 179E, see FTC 2d/FIN ¶ F-10304; USTR ¶ 3124.04; TaxDesk ¶ 171,023). (Code Sec. 312(k)(3)(B) as amended by 2006 Tax Relief and Health Care Act §404(b)(2))

Termination. The Code Sec. 179E expensing deduction election does not apply to property placed in service after Dec. 31, 2008. (Code Sec. 179E(g))

☐ **Effective:** Costs paid or incurred after date of enactment (2006 Tax Relief and Health Care Act §404(c)) with regard to property placed in service before Jan. 1, 2009. (Code Sec. 179E(g))

¶ 510. Depreciation tax breaks for Indian reservation property are extended retroactively to property placed in service after Dec. 31, 2005 and before Jan. 1, 2008

Code Sec. 168(j)(8), as amended by 2006 Tax Relief and Health Care Act § 112(a)
Generally effective: Property placed in service after Dec. 31, 2005 and before Jan. 1, 2008
Committee Reports, see ¶ 5016

Under pre-2006 Tax Relief and Health Care Act law, shortened depreciation recovery periods could be used for qualified Indian reservation property placed in service before Jan. 1, 2006. (FTC 2d/FIN ¶ L-8806; USTR ¶ 1684.01; TaxDesk ¶ 267,007) For example, property normally depreciable over a 5-year period can be depreciated over a 3-year period if it is qualified Indian reservation property. Also, the depreciation deduction allowed for regular tax purposes with respect to qualified Indian reservation property is also allowed for purposes of the alternative minimum tax (AMT). (See FTC 2d/FIN ¶ L-8806; USTR ¶ 1684.01; TaxDesk ¶ 267,007) Generally, qualified Indian reservation property is MACRS property used predominately in the active conduct of a trade or business on an Indian reservation. (See FTC 2d/FIN ¶ L-8807; USTR ¶ 1684.01; TaxDesk ¶ 267,007)

New Law. The 2006 Tax Relief and Health Care Act extends the expiration date of the shortened depreciation recovery periods for qualified Indian reserva-

---

FTC 2d References are to Federal Tax Coordinator 2d
FIN References are to RIAs Analysis of Federal Taxes: Income
USTR References are to United States Tax Reporter: Income, Estate & Gift, and Excise
PCA References are to Pension Analysis (print & electronic)
PE References are to Pension Explanations (print & electronic)
EP References are to Estate Planning Analysis (print & electronic)

tion property for two years (Com Rept, see ¶ 5016) so that the shortened depreciation recovery periods do *not* apply to property placed in service after Dec. 31, 2007. (Code Sec. 168(j)(8) as amended by 2006 Tax Relief and Health Care Act §112(a))

☐ **Effective:** Property placed in service after Dec. 31, 2005 (2006 Tax Relief and Health Care Act §112(b)) and before Jan. 1, 2008. (Code Sec. 168(j)(8))

> ***observation:*** The effective date of the amendment to Code Sec. 168(j)(8) results in the retroactive extension of the shortened depreciation periods for all property placed in service in 2006 until the expiration of these depreciation tax breaks for property placed in service after Dec. 31, 2007. Therefore, there is no break in the time period for which the depreciation tax breaks apply.

> ***observation:*** As a result of the retroactive restoration of the depreciation tax breaks for Indian reservation property, taxpayers that place property in service after Dec. 31, 2005 and before date of enactment receive the same tax treatment as taxpayers that place property in service on or after date of enactment.

¶ 600. Charitable Provisions

¶ 601. Rules for taxing charitable remainder trusts' UBTI are modified

Code Sec. 664(c), as amended by 2006 Tax Relief and Health Care Act § 424(a)
Generally effective: Tax years beginning after 2006
Committee Reports, see ¶ 5075

Generally, a charitable remainder trust is formed to pay income to one or more noncharitable income beneficiaries, and to pay the entire remainder to charity or use it for a charitable purpose. (FTC 2d ¶ K-3251; USTR ¶ 6644; TaxDesk ¶ 331,629; EP ¶ 41,502)

A charitable remainder annuity trust or charitable remainder unitrust (hereinafter "charitable remainder trust" or "CRT") created after July 31, '69 is exempt from income tax unless it has income that would be unrelated business taxable income (UBTI) during the tax year, if it were an exempt organization.

If the charitable remainder trust has any UBTI for any tax year, the trust is subject to tax for that year, to the full extent of its entire net income and not merely with respect to the UBTI. The taxes imposed on such a nonexempt charitable remainder trust are determined under the rules for complex trusts (trusts that may accumulate income or distribute corpus). (FTC 2d ¶ C-5039; USTR ¶ 6644; TaxDesk ¶ 651,030; EP ¶ 85,640)

New Law. As under pre-2006 Tax Relief and Health Care Act law, the Act provides that a charitable remainder trust is not subject to income tax—except where the trust has UBTI. (Code Sec. 664(c)(1) as amended by 2006 Tax Relief and Health Care Act §424(a))

If a CRT has UBTI (as defined under Code Sec. 512, determined as if part III of subchapter F (i.e., Code Sec. 511 through Code Sec. 515), applied to the trust) for a tax year, an excise tax will be imposed on the trust equal to the amount of the UBTI. (Code Sec. 664(c)(2)(A)) In effect, this amounts to a 100% excise tax on UBTI. (Com Rept, see ¶ 5075)

In effect, this provision replaces the pre-2006 Tax Relief and Health Care Act law rule that removes a charitable remainder trust's income tax exemption for any year in which the trust has any UBTI. Consistent with present law, the tax is treated as paid from corpus. The UBTI is considered income of the trust for

FTC 2d References are to Federal Tax Coordinator 2d
FIN References are to RIAs Analysis of Federal Taxes: Income
USTR References are to United States Tax Reporter: Income, Estate & Gift, and Excise
PCA References are to Pension Analysis (print & electronic)
PE References are to Pension Explanations (print & electronic)
EP References are to Estate Planning Analysis (print & electronic)

purposes of determining the character of the distribution made to the beneficiary. (Com Rept, see ¶ 5075)

The amount of the excise tax imposed must be treated as imposed by chapter 42, except for subchapter E of chapter 42 (i.e., Code Sec. 4940 through Code Sec. 4965, excepting Code Sec. 4961 through Code Sec. 4963). (Code Sec. 664(c)(2)(B))

Thus, consistent with pre-2006 Tax Relief and Health Care Act law, the tax is treated as paid from trust corpus. Further, the UBTI is considered income of the trust for purposes of determining the character of the distribution made to the beneficiary. (Com Rept, see ¶ 5075)

For purposes of the UBTI excise tax provision, the references in Code Sec. 6212(c)(1) to Code Sec. 4940, regarding the restriction on IRS sending further deficiency letters to a taxpayer once a Tax Court petition has been filed, are deemed to include references to Code Sec. 664(c). (Code Sec. 664(c)(2)(C))

☐ **Effective:** For tax years beginning after Dec. 31, 2006. (2006 Tax Relief and Health Care Act §424(b))

¶ 602. Enhanced deduction for qualified computer contributions by corporations is retroactively extended for two years through 2007

Code Sec. 170(e)(6)(G), as amended by 2006 Tax Relief and Health Care Act § 116(a)(1)

Generally effective: Contributions made in tax years beginning after Dec. 31, 2005, and before Jan. 1, 2008

Committee Reports, see ¶ 5020

In general, for a charitable contribution of "ordinary income property," i.e., property any portion of the gain on which wouldn't have been long-term capital gain if sold by the taxpayer at its fair market value (FMV) on the date it was contributed, the amount contributed must be reduced by the portion of gain that wouldn't have been long-term capital gain. (FTC 2d/FIN ¶s K-3160, K-3161; USTR ¶ 1704.42; TaxDesk ¶s 331,609, 331,610)

> ***illustration (1):*** A donor bought stock for $4,000 and contributed it to charity four months later, when it was worth $6,000. Because the $2,000 of appreciation is short-term gain, the donor's charitable deduction is only $4,000.

> ***observation:*** The result under this rule is generally the same as if the donor sold the stock for its $6,000 FMV and contributed the proceeds. Instead of a $4,000 contribution, he would have a $6,000 contribution and $2,000 of short-term capital gain.

However, a C corporation (other than a personal holding company or "service organization") that makes a "qualified computer contribution" of computer technology or equipment (software, computer or peripheral equipment, and fiber optic cable) to educational organizations or public libraries for use in the U.S. for educational purposes related to the donee's purpose or function may claim a deduction equal to the lesser of (a) basis plus half of the property's appreciation, or (b) twice the property's basis. (FTC 2d/FIN ¶ K-3241; USTR ¶ 1704.42; TaxDesk ¶ 331,741)

Under pre-2006 Tax Relief and Health Care Act law, the provisions relating to qualified computer contributions weren't to have applied to contributions made during any tax year beginning after Dec. 31, 2005. (FTC 2d/FIN ¶ K-3241; USTR ¶ 1704.42; TaxDesk ¶ 331,741)

New Law. The 2006 Tax Relief and Health Care Act extends for two years the provisions relating to qualified computer contributions. (Com Rept, see ¶ 5020) Thus, those provisions won't apply to contributions made during any tax year beginning after Dec. 31, 2007. (Code Sec. 170(e)(6)(G) as amended by 2006 Tax Relief and Health Care Act §116(a)(1))

> ***illustration (2):*** In 2006, X Corp, a calendar-year taxpayer, makes a qualified computer contribution to its local high school of computer equipment with a basis of $2,000 and fair market value of $5,000. If the property had been sold on the contribution date, the entire $3,000 gain on the sale ($5,000 FMV – $2,000 basis) would be treated as ordinary income, e.g., because the property was inventory. X's charitable deduction is $3,500, which is the lesser of:
>
> . . . $3,500—i.e., $2,000 (basis of the contributed property), plus $1,500 (one-half of $3,000 appreciation); or
>
> . . . $4,000 (twice the $2,000 basis).

> ***observation:*** In Illustration (2), if the corporation's contribution weren't a qualified computer contribution, its deduction would be limited to its $2,000 basis in the property, under the rules discussed at FTC 2d/FIN ¶ K-3160; USTR ¶ 1704.42; TaxDesk ¶ 331,609.

For expansion of the deduction for qualified computer contributions to include property assembled by the taxpayer, see ¶ 603.

FTC 2d References are to Federal Tax Coordinator 2d
FIN References are to RIAs Analysis of Federal Taxes: Income
USTR References are to United States Tax Reporter: Income, Estate & Gift, and Excise
PCA References are to Pension Analysis (print & electronic)
PE References are to Pension Explanations (print & electronic)
EP References are to Estate Planning Analysis (print & electronic)

☐ **Effective:** Contributions made in tax years beginning after Dec. 31, 2005. (2006 Tax Relief and Health Care Act §116(a)(2)) The provision won't apply for contributions made in tax years beginning after Dec. 31, 2007. (Code Sec. 170(e)(6)(G))

¶ 603. Property assembled by donor qualifies for enhanced deduction for qualified research contributions and qualified computer contributions

Code Sec. 170(e)(4)(B)(ii), as amended by 2006 Tax Relief and Health Care Act § 116(b)(1)(A)
Code Sec. 170(e)(4)(B)(iii), as amended by 2006 Tax Relief and Health Care Act § 116(b)(1)(B)
Code Sec. 170(e)(6)(B)(ii), as amended by 2006 Tax Relief and Health Care Act § 116(b)(2)(A)
Code Sec. 170(e)(6)(D), as amended by 2006 Tax Relief and Health Care Act § 116(b)(2)(B)
Generally effective: Tax years beginning after Dec. 31, 2005
Committee Reports, see ¶ 5020

In general, for a charitable contribution of "ordinary income property," i.e., property any portion of the gain on which wouldn't have been long-term capital gain if sold by the taxpayer at its fair market value (FMV) on the date it was contributed, the amount contributed must be reduced by the portion of gain that wouldn't have been long-term capital gain. (FTC 2d/FIN ¶s K-3160, K-3161; USTR ¶ 1704.42; TaxDesk ¶s 331,609, 331,610)

However, a C corporation (other than a personal holding company or "service organization") that makes a "qualified research contribution" of scientific equipment or apparatus to schools or tax-exempt scientific research organizations for research or experimentation research training, in the U.S., in physical or biological sciences may claim a deduction equal to the lesser of (a) basis plus half of the property's appreciation, or (b) twice the property's basis.

Under pre-2006 Tax Relief and Health Care Act law, the property had to have been constructed by the taxpayer and the contribution had to have been made no later than two years after the date the construction was substantially completed. (FTC 2d/FIN ¶ K-3221; USTR ¶ 1704.42; TaxDesk ¶ 331,721)

A C corporation (other than a personal holding company or "service organization") that makes a "qualified computer contribution" of computer technology or equipment (software, computer or peripheral equipment, and fiber optic cable) to educational organizations or public libraries for use in the U.S. for educational purposes related to the donee's purpose or function may claim a deduction equal to the lesser of (a) basis plus half of the property's appreciation, or (b) twice the property's basis.

Under pre-2006 Tax Relief and Health Care Act law, the contribution had to have been made no later than three years after the date the taxpayer acquired the property, or for property constructed by the taxpayer, the date the construction was substantially completed. For property that was reacquired by the taxpayer that constructed it, the three-year rule was applied by taking into account the date the original construction of the property was substantially completed. Thus, reacquired property had to be contributed within three years of the date the original construction was substantially completed. (FTC 2d/FIN ¶ K-3241; USTR ¶ 1704.42; TaxDesk ¶ 331,741)

New Law. Under the 2006 Tax Relief and Health Care Act, property assembled by the taxpayer is made eligible for the enhanced deductions for qualified research contributions and qualified computer contributions. However, old or used components assembled by the taxpayer into scientific property or computer technology or equipment aren't eligible for the enhanced deductions. (Com Rept, see ¶ 5020)

Qualified research contributions. For qualified research contributions, the 2006 Tax Relief and Health Care Act requires that the property contributed must be constructed *or assembled* by the taxpayer. (Code Sec. 170(e)(4)(B)(ii) as amended by 2006 Tax Relief and Health Care Act §116(b)(1)(A)) The contribution must be made not later than two years after the date the construction *or assembly* of the property is substantially completed. (Code Sec. 170(e)(4)(B)(iii) as amended by 2006 Tax Relief and Health Care Act §116(b)(1)(B))

Qualified computer contributions. For qualified computer contributions, the 2006 Tax Relief and Health Care Act requires that the contribution must be made not later than three years after the date the taxpayer acquired the property, or for property constructed *or assembled* by the taxpayer, the date the construction *or assembling* of the property is substantially completed. (Code Sec. 170(e)(6)(B)(ii) as amended by 2006 Tax Relief and Health Care Act §116(b)(2)(A))

For property that was reacquired by the taxpayer that constructed *or assembled* it, the three-year rule is applied by taking into account the date the original construction *or assembly* of the property was substantially completed. (Code Sec. 170(e)(6)(D) as amended by 2006 Tax Relief and Health Care Act §116(b)(2)(B))

For two-year extension of the deduction for qualified computer contributions, see ¶ 602.

FTC 2d References are to Federal Tax Coordinator 2d
FIN References are to RIAs Analysis of Federal Taxes: Income
USTR References are to United States Tax Reporter: Income, Estate & Gift, and Excise
PCA References are to Pension Analysis (print & electronic)
PE References are to Pension Explanations (print & electronic)
EP References are to Estate Planning Analysis (print & electronic)

☐ **Effective:** Tax years beginning after Dec. 31, 2005. (2006 Tax Relief and Health Care Act §116(b)(3))

¶ 700. Elections Under Retroactively Restored Provisions

¶ 701. Taxpayers with a tax year ending after 2005 have until Apr. 15, 2007 to make elections under expired provisions that are retroactively extended by the 2006 Tax Relief and Health Care Act

Code Sec. 280C(c)(3)(C), 2006 Tax Relief and Health Care Act § 123(a)
Code Sec. 41(c)(4), 2006 Tax Relief and Health Care Act § 123(a)
Code Sec. None, 2006 Tax Relief and Health Care Act § 123(b)
Generally effective: Tax years ending after Dec. 31, 2005 and before date of enactment
Committee Reports, see ¶ 5029

Various elections under different provisions of the Code must be made by a certain date and in a certain manner. (Com Rept, see ¶ 5029) For example, the election under Code Sec. 280C(c)(3) of a reduced credit for increasing research expenditures must be made not later than the time for filing the tax return for the year of the election. (FTC 2d/FIN ¶ L-15308; USTR ¶ 280C4; TaxDesk ¶ 384,019)

> ***observation:*** Thus, the election can't be made on an amended return.

Under Code Sec. 41(c)(4), taxpayers may elect an alternative incremental research credit regime that replaces part of the regular research credit. The election is made by attaching a completed Form 6765 to the taxpayer's timely filed (including extensions) original return for the tax year to which the election applies. An election cannot be made on an amended return. (FTC 2d/FIN ¶ L-15302.1; USTR ¶ 414.01; TaxDesk ¶ 384,003) Under pre-2006 Tax Relief and Health Care Act law, the credit was not available for otherwise qualified research expenses paid or incurred after Dec. 31, 2005. (FTC 2d/FIN ¶ L-15300; USTR ¶ 414; TaxDesk ¶ 384,001)

> ***observation:*** The research credit was extended retroactively by the 2006 Tax Relief and Health Care Act, see ¶ 201.

New Law. The 2006 Tax Relief and Health Care Act provides that, for any tax year ending after Dec. 31, 2005 and before date of enactment, any election

FTC 2d References are to Federal Tax Coordinator 2d
FIN References are to RIAs Analysis of Federal Taxes: Income
USTR References are to United States Tax Reporter: Income, Estate & Gift, and Excise
PCA References are to Pension Analysis (print & electronic)
PE References are to Pension Explanations (print & electronic)
EP References are to Estate Planning Analysis (print & electronic)

under Code Sec. 41(c)(4) or Code Sec. 280C(c)(3)(C) is treated as having been timely made for the tax year if the election is made not later than the later of Apr. 15, 2007 or the time IRS specifies. The election must be made in the manner IRS prescribes. (2006 Tax Relief and Health Care Act §123(a)) Except as IRS provides otherwise, a rule similar to the rule in the preceding sentence applies to elections under any other expired provision of the Code the applicability of which is extended by Title I of the 2006 Tax Relief and Health Care Act. (2006 Tax Relief and Health Care Act §123(b))

> ***observation:*** Title I of the 2006 Tax Relief and Health Care Act provides for the extension of a number of expiring or expired tax provisions.

> ***observation:*** Assuming the 2006 Tax Relief and Health Care Act becomes law before Dec. 31, 2006, this provision will apply only to *fiscal year* taxpayers with tax years ending in 2006, but before date of enactment. These taxpayers have an opportunity to change elections already made on their originally filed returns to take into account the extension of the provisions that expired at the end of 2005.

Thus, an election under Code Sec. 41(c)(4) or Code Sec. 280C(c)(3)(C) or any other expired provisions of the Code that are extended by the 2006 Tax Relief and Health Care Act are treated as timely made if made not later than Apr. 15, 2007 or another time IRS provides. (Com Rept, see ¶ 5029)

☐ **Effective:** date of enactment (Com Rept, see ¶ 5029), but applicable for tax years ending after Dec. 31, 2005 and before date of enactment. (2006 Tax Relief and Health Care Act §123(a))

¶ 800. Employment Tax Credits

¶ 801. Work opportunity credit is retroactively restored to Jan. 1, 2006 and is extended two years to Dec. 31, 2007 for most targeted groups

Code Sec. 51(c)(4)(B), as amended by 2006 Tax Relief and Health Care Act § 105(a)

Generally effective: Individuals who begin work for the employer after Dec. 31, 2005 and before Jan. 1, 2008

Committee Reports, see ¶ 5005

A work opportunity tax credit (WOTC) is available on an elective basis to an employer for a percentage of limited amounts of wages paid or incurred by the employer to individuals who belong to a "targeted group," see FTC 2d/FIN ¶ L-17775; USTR ¶ 514; TaxDesk ¶ 380,700.

Code Sec. 51(c)(4)(B), as in effect before the enactment of the 2006 Tax Relief and Health Care Act, stated that the WOTC wasn't available for wages paid or incurred by an employer to or for an individual who began work for the employer after Dec. 31, 2005. (FTC 2d/FIN ¶ L-17775; USTR ¶ 514; TaxDesk ¶ 380,700)

However, section 201(d) of the 2005 Katrina Tax Relief Act (2005 KETRA) (Sec. 201(d), PL 109-73, 9/23/2005) provides that Code Sec. 51(c)(4)(B) doesn't apply to wages paid or incurred to or for the targeted group that consists of "Hurricane Katrina employees." (FTC 2d/FIN ¶ L-17786.3; USTR ¶ 514; TaxDesk ¶ 380,718) Instead, section 201(b) of 2005 KETRA (Sec. 201(b), PL 109-73, 9/23/2005) defines two classes of Hurricane Katrina Employees, one of which is defined to include certain individuals hired in the period running from Aug. 28, 2005 to Aug. 27, 2007 and one of which is defined to include certain individuals hired in the period running from Aug. 28, 2005 through Dec. 31, 2005, see FTC 2d/FIN ¶ L-17786.3; USTR ¶ 514; TaxDesk ¶ 380,718.

> ***observation:*** Thus, in substance, Code Sec. 51(c)(4)(B) as in effect before the enactment of the 2006 Tax Relief and Health Care Act, provided a WOTC termination date that applied to all targeted groups, other than "Hurricane Katrina employees," while section 201(b) of 2005 KETRA provides separate WOTC termination dates for the two

classes of employees that are included in the "Hurricane Katrina employee" targeted group.

New Law. The 2006 Tax Relief and Health Care Act provides that the term "wages" (for purposes of determining the amount of the WOTC) doesn't include any amount paid or incurred to an individual who begins work for the employer after Dec. 31, 2007. (Code Sec. 51(c)(4)(B) as amended by 2006 Tax Relief and Health Care Act §105(a))

observation: By amending Code Sec. 51(c)(4)(B), the 2006 Tax Relief and Health Care Act moves the hiring deadline for the WOTC from Dec. 31, 2005 to Dec. 31, 2007 and retroactively restores the credit for individuals who began work before enactment of the 2006 Tax Relief and Health Care Act, but on or after Jan. 1, 2006.

observation: Under Code Sec. 51(c)(4)(B), the last day a taxpayer can employ a qualifying individual and be eligible to get a credit for wages paid or incurred to that individual is Dec. 31, 2007. However, subject to applicable percentage and dollar-amount limitations, the credit is, for most targeted groups, available for any eligible wages paid or incurred to that individual for service rendered during the period ending one year after the date that the individual was first employed, even though, for employees hired after Dec. 31, 2006, the last day of the one-year period is after Dec. 31, 2007, see FTC 2d/FIN ¶ L-17783; USTR ¶ 514; TaxDesk ¶ 380,700. Further, for the targeted group consisting of "long-term family assistance recipients," the credit is available, subject to applicable percentage and dollar amount limitations, for any eligible wages paid or incurred to or for the individual for service rendered during the period ending two years after the date that the individual was first employed, even though, for employees hired after Dec. 31, 2005, the last day of the two-year period is after Dec. 31, 2007, see ¶ 805.

observation: Because Code Sec. 51(c)(4)(B) doesn't apply with respect to Hurricane Katrina employees (see above), it can be presumed that the dates in the definitions of the two classes of Hurricane Katrina employees (see above) are unchanged by the amendment of Code Sec. 51(c)(4)(B).

For modification of certain "targeted group" requirements for purposes of the WOTC, see ¶ 803 and ¶ 804.

For relaxation of a filing deadline imposed under the WOTC certification requirements, see ¶ 802.

For the extension of the welfare-to-work credit and for the consolidation of the welfare-to-work credit with the WOTC, see ¶ 805.

For extensions of the period for making an election for a tax year ending after Dec. 31, 2005 and before date of enactment, which would have expired but for relief provided by the 2006 Tax Relief and Health Care Act, see ¶ 701.

☐ **Effective:** Individuals who begin work for the employer after Dec. 31, 2005 (2006 Tax Relief and Health Care Act §105(f)(1)) and before Jan. 1, 2008. (Code Sec. 51(c)(4)(B))

¶ 802. Deadline for submitting paperwork for certification of employees under the work opportunity credit is extended to 28 days after the beginning of work

Code Sec. 51(d)(12)(A)(ii)(II), as amended and redesignated by 2006 Tax Relief and Health Care Act § 105

Generally effective: Individuals who begin work for the employer after Dec. 31, 2006 and before Jan. 1, 2008

Committee Reports, see ¶ 5005

A work opportunity tax credit (WOTC) is available on an elective basis to an employer for a percentage of limited amounts of wages paid or incurred by the employer to or for individuals who belong to a "targeted group," see FTC 2d/FIN ¶ L-17775; USTR ¶ 514; TaxDesk ¶ 380,700.

Additionally, for all but one of the targeted groups, the WOTC is allowed for wages paid to an employee only if the taxpayer obtains a certification, from a state employment security agency (the designated local agency), that the employee is a member of a targeted group (the certification requirement). The exception is that a reasonable evidence requirement applies in lieu of the certification requirement for employees in the targeted group consisting of "Hurricane Katrina employees," see FTC 2d/FIN ¶ L-17784.1; USTR ¶ 514; TaxDesk ¶ 380,708.

The certification requirement further provides that the taxpayer has to either (1) obtain the certification before the employee begins working for the taxpayer or (2) obtain the certification after the employee begins work for the taxpayer, but only if the employer (a) completes a pre-screening notice (on Form 8850) before the employee begins working for the taxpayer and, (b) under pre-2006 Tax Relief and Health Care Act law, not later than 21 days after the employee

FTC 2d References are to Federal Tax Coordinator 2d
FIN References are to RIAs Analysis of Federal Taxes: Income
USTR References are to United States Tax Reporter: Income, Estate & Gift, and Excise
PCA References are to Pension Analysis (print & electronic)
PE References are to Pension Explanations (print & electronic)
EP References are to Estate Planning Analysis (print & electronic)

begins work (the 21-day deadline), submits the notice, signed by the employee and the taxpayer under penalties of perjury, as part of a written request to the agency for certification. (FTC 2d/FIN ¶ L-17784.1; USTR ¶ 514; TaxDesk ¶ 380,708)

New Law. Under the 2006 Tax Relief and Health Care Act, if the taxpayer obtains certification after the employee begins work for the taxpayer, the taxpayer must submit the required pre-screening notice to the designated local agency no later than 28 days after the employee begins work. (Code Sec. 51(d)(13)(A)(ii)(II) as amended and redesignated by 2006 Tax Relief and Health Care Act §105) Thus, the 2006 Tax Relief and Health Care Act changes the 21-day deadline (see above) to a 28-day deadline. (Com Rept, see ¶ 5005)

> ***observation:*** Thus, an employer can satisfy the certification requirement, as amended by the 2006 Tax Relief and Health Care Act, by either (1) obtaining the certification before the employee begins working for the taxpayer or (2) obtaining the certification after the employee begins working for the taxpayer, but only if the employer completes a pre-screening notice (on Form 8850) before the employee begins working for the taxpayer and, not later than 28 days after the employee begins work, submits the notice, signed by the employee and the taxpayer under penalties of perjury, as part of a written request to the agency for certification.

For modification of certain "targeted group" requirements for purposes of the WOTC, see ¶ 803 and ¶ 804.

For the extension of the WOTC, for most targeted groups, to hiring taking place before Jan. 1, 2008, see ¶ 801.

For the consolidation of the welfare-to-work credit with the WOTC, see ¶ 805.

☐ **Effective:** Individuals who begin work for the employer after Dec. 31, 2006 (2006 Tax Relief and Health Care Act §105(f)(2)) and before Jan. 1, 2008. (Code Sec. 51(c)(4)(B) as amended by 2006 Tax Relief and Health Care Act §105(a))

¶ 803. Maximum age of a "qualified food stamp recipient" is increased from 24 to 39 for purposes of the work opportunity credit

Code Sec. 51(d)(8)(A)(i), as amended by 2006 Tax Relief and Health Care Act § 105(c)
Generally effective: Individuals who begin work for the employer after Dec. 31, 2006 and before Jan. 1, 2008
Committee Reports, see ¶ 5005

A work opportunity tax credit (WOTC) is available on an elective basis to an employer for a percentage of first-year wages (subject to a per-employee dollar limitation) paid or incurred by the employer to or for individuals who belong to one of several eligible "targeted groups" (e.g., qualified veterans, qualified ex-felons, high-risk youths), see FTC 2d/FIN ¶ L-17775; USTR ¶ 514; TaxDesk ¶ 380,700.

Under pre-2006 Tax Relief and Health Care Act law, an individual qualified as a member of the targeted group consisting of "qualified food stamp recipients" if the individual had been certified by a designated local agency, see FTC 2d/FIN ¶ L-17784.1; USTR ¶ 514; TaxDesk ¶ 380,708, as (1) being a member of a family that received certain public assistance (the "family assistance requirement"), (2) having attained the age of 18 on the hiring date (the "minimum age requirement") and (3) not having attained the age of 25 on the hiring date (the "maximum age requirement"). (FTC 2d/FIN ¶ L-17786.1; USTR ¶ 514; TaxDesk ¶ 380,716)

New Law. The 2006 Tax Relief and Health Care Act raises, from less than 25 to less than 40, the "maximum age requirement" for being a member of the "targeted group" consisting of "qualified food stamp recipients." (Code Sec. 51(d)(8)(A)(i) as amended by 2006 Tax Relief and Health Care Act §105(c))

> ***observation:*** Thus, under the 2006 Tax Relief and Health Care Act, for purposes of the WOTC, an individual will qualify as a member of the "targeted group" consisting of "qualified food stamp recipients" if he is certified by a designated local agency as (1) having not attained the age of 40 on the hiring date, (2) satisfying the "minimum age requirement" (see above) and (3) satisfying the "family assistance requirement" (see above).

FTC 2d References are to Federal Tax Coordinator 2d
FIN References are to RIAs Analysis of Federal Taxes: Income
USTR References are to United States Tax Reporter: Income, Estate & Gift, and Excise
PCA References are to Pension Analysis (print & electronic)
PE References are to Pension Explanations (print & electronic)
EP References are to Estate Planning Analysis (print & electronic)

illustration: W, who turns 32 during calendar year 2007 and has had his age certified by the designated local agency, is hired by taxpayer T on Apr. 1, 2007. Y is a "qualified food stamp recipient" if he is certified as satisfying the family assistance requirement. Had Y been hired on Dec. 1, 2006, W wouldn't have been eligible to be a "qualified food stamp recipient" (see the effective date below).

For modification of the requirements for the targeted group that consists of "qualified ex-felons," see ¶ 804.

For relaxation of a filing deadline imposed under the WOTC certification requirements, see ¶ 802.

For the extension of the WOTC, for most targeted groups, to hiring taking place before Jan. 1, 2008, see ¶ 801.

For the extension of the welfare-to-work credit and the consolidation of the welfare-to-work credit with the WOTC, see ¶ 805.

☐ **Effective:** Individuals who begin work for the employer after Dec. 31, 2006 (2006 Tax Relief and Health Care Act §105(f)(2)) and before Jan. 1, 2008. (Code Sec. 51(c)(4)(B) as amended by 2006 Tax Relief and Health Care Act §105(a))

¶ 804. The "family low-income requirement" is eliminated for the work opportunity credit group consisting of "qualified ex-felons"

Code Sec. 51(d)(4), as amended by 2006 Tax Relief and Health Care Act § 105(b)
Generally effective: Individuals who begin work for the employer after Dec. 31, 2006 and before Jan. 1, 2008
Committee Reports, see ¶ 5005

A work opportunity tax credit (WOTC) is available on an elective basis to an employer for a percentage of first-year wages (subject to a per-employee dollar limitation) paid or incurred by the employer to or for individuals who belong to one of several eligible "targeted groups" (e.g., qualified veterans, qualified ex-felons, high-risk youths), see FTC 2d/FIN ¶ L-17775; USTR ¶ 514; TaxDesk ¶ 380,700.

Under pre-2006 Tax Relief and Health Care Act law, an individual qualified as a member of the targeted group consisting of "qualified ex-felons" if the individual had been certified by a designated local agency, see FTC 2d/FIN ¶ L-17784.1; USTR ¶ 514; TaxDesk ¶ 380,708, as (1) having been convicted of a felony under any statute of the U.S. or any State and having a hiring date no more than one year after the last date on which that individual was convicted or was released from prison (the "recent felony requirement"), and (2) being a member of a family that had annualized income that was no more than 70% or less of the Bureau of Labor Statistics lower living standard (the "family low-income requirement"). (FTC 2d/FIN ¶ L-17785.2; USTR ¶ 514; TaxDesk ¶ 380,712)

New Law. The 2006 Tax Relief and Health Care Act eliminates the "family low-income requirement" for being a member of the "targeted group" consisting of "qualified ex-felons." (Code Sec. 51(d)(4) as amended by 2006 Tax Relief and Health Care Act §105(b))

> ***observation:*** Thus, under the 2006 Tax Relief and Health Care Act, for purposes of the WOTC, an individual need only be certified by a designated local agency as meeting the "recent felony requirement" (see above) to qualify as a "qualified ex-felon."

> ***illustration:*** X is hired by taxpayer T on Apr. 1, 2007. Even though X is a high-income individual, X is a "qualified ex-felon" if he is certified as satisfying the recent felony requirement. Had X been hired on Dec. 1, 2006, X wouldn't have been eligible to be a "qualified ex-felon" (see the effective date below).

For modification of the requirements for the targeted group that consists of "qualified food stamp recipients," see ¶ 803.

For relaxation of a filing deadline imposed under the WOTC certification requirements, see ¶ 802.

For the extension of the WOTC, for most targeted groups, to hiring taking place before Jan. 1, 2008, see ¶ 801.

For the extension of the welfare-to-work credit and the consolidation of the welfare-to-work credit with the WOTC, see ¶ 805.

☐ **Effective:** Individuals who begin work for the employer after Dec. 31, 2006 (2006 Tax Relief and Health Care Act §105(f)(2)) and before Jan. 1, 2008. (Code Sec. 51(c)(4)(B) as amended by 2006 Tax Relief and Health Care Act §105(a))

FTC 2d References are to Federal Tax Coordinator 2d
FIN References are to RIAs Analysis of Federal Taxes: Income
USTR References are to United States Tax Reporter: Income, Estate & Gift, and Excise
PCA References are to Pension Analysis (print & electronic)
PE References are to Pension Explanations (print & electronic)
EP References are to Estate Planning Analysis (print & electronic)

¶ 805. Welfare-to-work credit is retroactively restored to Jan. 1, 2006 and, after Dec. 31, 2006, is consolidated with the work opportunity credit

Code Sec. 51A(f), as amended by 2006 Tax Relief and Health Care Act § 105(a)

Code Sec. 51(d)(1)(I), as amended by 2006 Tax Relief and Health Care Act § 105(e)(1)

Code Sec. 51(d)(10), as amended by 2006 Tax Relief and Health Care Act § 105(e)(2)

Code Sec. 51(e), as amended by 2006 Tax Relief and Health Care Act § 105(e)(3)

Code Sec. 51A, as repealed by 2006 Tax Relief and Health Care Act § 105(e)(4)(A)

Generally effective: Individuals who begin work for the employer after Dec. 31, 2005 (after Dec. 31, 2006 for credit consolidation and post-consolidation rules) and before Jan. 1, 2008

Committee Reports, see ¶ 5005

Under pre-2006 Tax Relief and Health Care Act law, Code Sec. 51A provided a "welfare-to-work credit" to employers and under Code Sec. 51A(f), as in effect before enactment of the 2006 Tax Relief and Health Care Act, the credit wasn't available with respect to individuals who began work for the employer after Dec. 31, 2005. (FTC 2d/FIN ¶ L-17835 *et seq.*; USTR ¶ 51A4; TaxDesk ¶ 381,300 *et seq.*)

The credit was available on an elective basis to an employer for eligible wages paid or incurred to or for "long-term family assistance recipients" for service rendered during the first two years of employment (FTC 2d/FIN ¶ L-17835; USTR ¶ 51A4; TaxDesk ¶ 381,300) and the maximum credit, per each "long-term family assistance recipient" employed, was $8,500—35% of the first $10,000 of eligible wages for service rendered in the first year of employment plus 50% of the first $10,000 of eligible wages for service rendered in the second year of employment. (FTC 2d/FIN ¶ L-17836; USTR ¶ 51A4; TaxDesk ¶ 381,301) The credit wasn't available for an employee unless the employee was employed at least 180 days for the employer or had completed 400 hours of service for the employer (the welfare-to-work minimum work rule). (FTC 2d/FIN ¶ L-17842; USTR ¶ 51A4; TaxDesk ¶ 381,307)

Under Code Sec. 51 (see ¶ 801), a work opportunity tax credit (WOTC) is available on an elective basis to an employer for an applicable percentage of a limited dollar amount of wages paid or incurred to or for individuals who are certified by a designated local agency, see FTC 2d/FIN ¶ L-17784.1; USTR ¶ 514; TaxDesk ¶ 380,708, as belonging to certain "targeted groups," see FTC 2d/FIN ¶ L-17775; USTR ¶ 514; TaxDesk ¶ 380,700.

Under pre-2006 Tax Relief and Health Care Act law, there were 9 targeted groups (qualified IV-A recipients, qualified veterans, qualified ex-felons, high-risk youths, vocational rehabilitation referrals, qualified summer youth employees, qualified food stamp recipients, qualified SSI recipients and Hurricane Katrina employees). (FTC 2d/FIN ¶ L-17776; USTR ¶ 514; TaxDesk ¶ 380,701) The credit was, for all targeted groups, limited to an applicable percentage of the first $6,000 of "qualified first-year wages" ($3,000 with respect to "qualified summer youth employees"). (FTC 2d/FIN ¶ L-17778; USTR ¶ 514; TaxDesk ¶ 380,700.1) The applicable percentage of "qualified first-year wages" was generally 40% (resulting in a maximum credit of $2,400 (i.e., $6,000 × 40%)), but was 25% for employees who had completed at least 120 hours, but less than 400 hours, of service for the employer (the 25% rule). (FTC 2d/FIN ¶ L-17778; USTR ¶ 514; TaxDesk ¶ 380,700.1) The credit wasn't allowable at all for "qualified first-year wages" for employees who completed less than 120 hours of service for the employer (the WOTC minimum work rule). (FTC 2d/FIN ¶ L-17777; USTR ¶ 514; TaxDesk ¶ 380,700) "Qualified first-year wages" are, with respect to any employee, "qualified wages," see FTC 2d/FIN ¶ L-17783; USTR ¶ 514; TaxDesk ¶ 380,707, attributable to service rendered during the 1-year period beginning with the day the individual begins work for the employer, see FTC 2d/FIN ¶ L-17783; USTR ¶ 514; TaxDesk ¶ 380,707.

Under the WOTC and the welfare-to-work credit, "wages," for purposes of determining eligible wages, were, for most employees, similarly defined (FTC 2d/FIN ¶ L-17783, ¶ L-17840; USTR ¶ 514, ¶ 51A4; TaxDesk ¶ 380,707, ¶ 381,305) except that, for purposes of the welfare-to-work credit, "wages" also included some non-taxable fringe benefits that weren't included in "wages" for purposes of the WOTC (the fringe benefit wage rule). (FTC 2d/FIN ¶ L-17840; USTR ¶ 51A4; TaxDesk ¶ 381,305)

Also, under the WOTC, there was a separate definition of wages that applied to agricultural or railroad employees, and that provided that wages of up to $6,000 per year, for *all* agricultural employees, and $500 per month, for *all* railroad employees, were considered unemployment insurance wages, and, therefore, "wages" (the "WOTC farm and railroad wages rule"). (FTC 2d/FIN ¶ L-17783.2, ¶ L-17840; USTR ¶ 514; TaxDesk ¶ 380,707) Similarly, under the welfare-to-work credit, there was a separate definition, provided under Code Sec. 51A(b)(5)(C), that applied to agricultural or railroad employees. This separate definition provided that, for agricultural employees, wages of up to $10,000 per year, and, for railroad employees, wages of up to $833.33 per month, were considered unemployment insurance wages and, therefore, "wages" (the "welfare-to-work farm and railroad wages rule"). (FTC 2d/FIN ¶ L-17856; USTR ¶ 514A; TaxDesk ¶ 381,315)

An employer wasn't allowed to claim a WOTC with respect to any employee for which the employer claimed a welfare-to-work credit (the coordination rule). (FTC 2d/FIN ¶ L-17856; USTR ¶ 51A4; TaxDesk ¶ 381,311)

New Law. The 2006 Tax Relief and Health Care Act provides that Code Sec. 51A (which provides the welfare-to-work credit, see above) does not apply to an individual who begins work for the employer after Dec. 31, 2007. (Code Sec. 51A(f) as amended by 2006 Tax Relief and Health Care Act §105(a))

> ***observation:*** However, as discussed below, effective for individuals who begin work for the employer after Dec. 31, 2006 (see below), 2006 Tax Relief and Health Care Act §105(e) repeals Code Sec. 51A(f) and amends Code Sec. 51 (which provides the WOTC) to provide that "long-term family assistance recipients" are a targeted group for purposes of the WOTC. Also, 2006 Tax Relief and Health Care Act §105(a), in addition to providing, as discussed above, that Code Sec. 51A doesn't apply to an individual who begins work for the employer after Dec. 31, 2007, also provides that Code Sec. 51 doesn't apply to an individual who begins work for the employer after Dec. 31, 2007 (see ¶ 801). The combined effects of all of these changes are as follows:
>
> . . . the welfare-to-work credit, as provided under Code Sec. 51A and the substantive rules described above, is (1) retroactively restored so that it applies to individuals who begin work for the employer before enactment of the 2006 Tax Relief and Health Care Act, but on or after Jan. 1, 2006, and (2) extended so as to apply to individuals who begin work for the employer before Jan. 1, 2007;
>
> . . . the welfare-to-work credit is provided under Code Sec. 51 as part of the WOTC (and under the substantive rules described below) for individuals who begin work for the employer in calendar year 2007.

> ***observation:*** The last day a taxpayer can employ a qualifying individual (i.e., a long-term family assistance recipient, see below) and be eligible to get a credit for wages paid or incurred to that individual is Dec. 31, 2007. However, the credit is available for eligible wages attributable to service rendered during the period ending two years after the date that the individual was first employed, even though, for employees hired after Dec. 31, 2005, the last day of that two-year period is after Dec. 31, 2007.

Consolidation of the welfare-to-work credit and WOTC. The 2006 Tax Relief and Health Care Act repeals Code Sec. 51A (which provided the welfare-to-work credit) (Code Sec. 51A as repealed by 2006 Tax Relief and Health Care Act §105(e)(4)(A)) and designates "long-term family assistance recipients" (defined below) as a "targeted group" for purposes of the WOTC. (Code Sec. 51(d)(1)(I) as amended by 2006 Tax Relief and Health Care Act §105(e)(1))

> ***observation:*** The designation of "long-term family assistance recipients" as a "targeted group" raises the number of "targeted groups" covered by the WOTC from 9 to 10. For modifications by the 2006 Tax Relief and Health Care Act of rules that apply to certain "targeted groups" other than "long-term family assistance recipients," see ¶ 803 and ¶ 804. For a change by the 2006 Tax Relief and Health Care Act in the WOTC certification requirements, see ¶ 802.

Thus, once the WOTC and the welfare-to-work credit are combined (see the effective date below) (Com Rept, see ¶ 5005), coordination of the two credits is no longer necessary (see discussion of the coordination rule above). (Com Rept, see ¶ 5005)

> ***observation:*** There are some differences between how the post-consolidation WOTC will apply to "long-term family assistance recipients" (i.e., the employee group targeted by the pre-consolidation welfare-to-work credit) and how the pre-consolidation welfare-to-work credit applies to "long-term family assistance recipients."
>
> One difference is that after the consolidation the maximum credit allowed with respect to a "long-term family assistance recipient" is $9,000 (see below), instead of, as discussed above, $8,500.
>
> Additionally, after the consolidation, "wages" paid or incurred to "long-term family assistance recipients" are as defined under the WOTC, see FTC 2d/FIN ¶ L-17783; USTR ¶ 514; TaxDesk ¶ 380,707 and, hence, the fringe benefit wage rule (see above) doesn't apply.
>
> Also, the WOTC minimum work rule (see above), instead of the welfare-to-work minimum work rule (see above), will apply to wages paid to "long-term family assistance recipients," see "Credit amount" below. For how the 25% rule (see above) will apply to wages paid to "long-term family assistance recipients," see the last observation under the heading "Credit amount" below.

Credit amount. With respect to the employment of a "long-term family assistance recipient": (Code Sec. 51(e)(1) as amended by 2006 Tax Relief and Health Care Act §105(e)(3))

. . . the amount of the WOTC for the tax year will include 50% of the "qualified-second year wages" (defined below) for that year, and (Code Sec. 51(e)(1)(A))

. . . instead of applying the $6,000 limit that generally applies to "qualified-first year wages" (see above), the amount of "qualified first-year wages," and the amount of "qualified-second year wages," which may be taken into account for the recipient won't be allowed to exceed $10,000 per year. (Code Sec. 51(e)(1)(B))

"Qualified second-year wages" will be "qualified wages," see FTC 2d/FIN ¶ L-17783; USTR ¶ 514; TaxDesk ¶ 380,707, (Code Sec. 51(e)(2))

. . . that are paid to a "long-term family assistance recipient," and (Code Sec. 51(e)(2)(A))

. . . are attributable to service rendered during the 1-year period beginning on the day after the last day of the 1-year period beginning with the day the individual begins work for the employer. (Code Sec. 51(e)(2)(B))

> ***observation:*** The definition of "qualified second-year wages" is the same as the one that applies under the welfare-to-work credit before its consolidation with the WOTC, see FTC 2d/FIN ¶ L-17838; USTR ¶ 51A4; TaxDesk ¶ 381,303.

Thus, the 2006 Tax Relief and Health Care Act provides that, for "long-term family assistance recipients," the maximum credit with respect to "qualified first-year wages" will be $4,000 (i.e., 40% × $10,000) and the maximum credit with respect to "qualified second-year wages" will be $5,000 (i.e., 50% × $10,000). (Com Rept, see ¶ 5005)

> ***observation:*** Accordingly, the maximum amount of WOTC available with respect to a "long-term family assistance recipient" will be $9,000 ($4,000 plus $5,000), as contrasted with the $8,500 maximum that was available under the welfare-to-work credit. As discussed above, the maximum WOTC generally available for other "targeted groups" is $2,400.

> ***illustration:*** W begins work for T (a cash-basis calendar-year taxpayer) on Dec. 1, 2007. Thus, Dec. 1, 2007 is the day on which the year for measuring qualified first-year wages begins. W earns and T pays to W (a long-term family assistant recipient) $1,000 of wages in Dec. 2007 and $11,000 of wages ($1,000 per month) in the 11 month period beginning Jan. 1, 2008 and ending Nov. 30, 2008. Effective Dec.

1, 2008 (which happens to be the day on which the year for measuring qualified second-year wages begins), T gives W a raise. Thus, W earns and T pays to W $1,200 in Dec. 2008 and $13,200 of wages ($1,200 per month) in the 11 month period beginning Jan. 1, 2009 and ending Nov. 30, 2009. T's WOTC in respect of W, for the tax year ending Dec. 31, 2007, is $400 ($1,000 of qualified first-year wages × 40%). T's WOTC in respect of W, for the tax year ending Dec. 31, 2008, is $4,200—i.e., $3,600 (which is $9,000 of qualified first-year wages × 40%) plus $600 (which is $1,200 of qualified second-year wages × 50%). T's WOTC in respect of W, for the tax year ending Dec. 31, 2009, is $4,400 ($8,800 of qualified second-year wages × 50%).

No credit is allowed for qualified wages paid to employees who work less than 120 hours in the first year of employment. (Com Rept, see ¶ 5005)

"Long-term family assistance recipient" defined. A "long-term family assistance recipient" will be any individual who is certified by the designated local agency (see above): (Code Sec. 51(d)(10) as amended by 2006 Tax Relief and Health Care Act §105(e)(2))

(1) as being a member of a family receiving, for at least the 18-month period ending on the hiring date, assistance under a IV-A program—i.e., a program which provides assistance under a state program funded under Part A of Title IV of the Social Security Act ("Title IV-A assistance," which is, generally, known as "Temporary Assistance for Needy Families" or "TANF," see FTC 2d/FIN ¶ L-17785; USTR ¶ 514; TaxDesk ¶ 380,710), (Code Sec. 51(d)(10)(A))

(2) as being a member of a family receiving Title IV-A assistance for 18 months beginning after Aug. 5, '97, and (Code Sec. 51(d)(10)(B)(i)) as having a hiring date which isn't more than 2 years after the end of the earliest of any of those post-Aug. 5, '97 18-month periods, or (Code Sec. 51(d)(10)(B)(ii))

(3) as being a member of a family which stopped being eligible for Title IV-A assistance because of any limitation imposed by Federal or State law on the maximum period that Title IV-A assistance is payable to a family, and (Code Sec. 51(d)(10)(C)(i)) as having a hiring date which is not more than 2 years after the date the assistance ended. (Code Sec. 51(d)(10)(C)(ii))

observation: The definition of "long-term family assistance recipient" is the same as the definition that applies under the welfare-to-work credit before its consolidation with the WOTC, see FTC 2d/FIN ¶ L-17841; USTR ¶ 51A4; TaxDesk ¶ 381,306.

FTC 2d References are to Federal Tax Coordinator 2d
FIN References are to RIAs Analysis of Federal Taxes: Income
USTR References are to United States Tax Reporter: Income, Estate & Gift, and Excise
PCA References are to Pension Analysis (print & electronic)
PE References are to Pension Explanations (print & electronic)
EP References are to Estate Planning Analysis (print & electronic)

Application of consolidation of credits to agricultural and railway labor. The "WOTC farm and labor wages rule" (see above) will apply, but with the following modifications:

... if a "long-term family assistance recipient" is an agricultural employee (Code Sec. 51(e)(3) as amended by 2006 Tax Relief and Health Care Act §105(e)(3)), wages of up to $10,000 per year will be considered unemployment insurance wages for which a WOTC will be allowed; (Code Sec. 51(e)(3)(A)) and

... if a "long-term family assistance recipient" is a railroad employee (Code Sec. 51(e)(3)), wages of up to $833.33 per month will be considered unemployment insurance wages for which a WOTC will be allowed. (Code Sec. 51(e)(3)(B))

> ***observation:*** The modifications, described immediately above, to the "WOTC farm and railroad wages rule" will coordinate, in the case of an agricultural or railroad employee that is a "long-term family assistance recipient," the amount of monthly wages eligible for WOTC with the $10,000 annual limits on qualified first-year and second-year wages that apply to "long-term family assistance recipients" (see above). The modifications provide, under the consolidated credit, a rule that is similar to the "welfare-to-work farm and railroad wages rule" that exists under the welfare-to-work credit (see above).

Redesignations. Pre-2006 Tax Relief and Health Care Act Code Sec. 51(d)(10), Code Sec. 51(d)(11) and Code Sec. 51(d)(12) are respectively redesignated by the 2006 Tax Relief and Health Care Act as Code Sec. 51(d)(11), Code Sec. 51(d)(12), and Code Sec. 51(d)(13). (2006 Tax Relief and Health Care Act §105(e)(2))

For extensions of the period for making an election for a tax year ending after Dec. 31, 2005 and before date of enactment, which would have expired but for relief provided by the 2006 Tax Relief and Health Care Act, see ¶ 701.

☐ **Effective:** Individuals who begin work for the employer (1) after Dec. 31, 2005 (for changes made by 2006 Tax Relief and Health Care Act §105(a)) (2006 Tax Relief and Health Care Act §105(f)(1)), but after Dec. 31, 2006 (for changes made by 2006 Tax Relief and Health Care Act §105(e)) (2006 Tax Relief and Health Care Act §105(f)(2)) and (2) before Jan. 1, 2008. (Code Sec. 51(c)(4)(B) as amended by 2006 Tax Relief and Health Care Act §105(a)) Thus, the extension of the credit is effective for wages paid or incurred to or for a qualified individual who begins work for the employer after Dec. 31, 2005 and before Jan. 1, 2008, and the consolidation of the welfare-to-work credit with the WOTC and other modifications are effective for wages paid or incurred to or for a qualified individual who begins work for an employer after Dec. 31, 2006 and before Jan. 1, 2008. (Com Rept, see ¶ 5005)

¶ 806. A 20% credit is available for amounts paid or incurred in tax years beginning after Dec. 31, 2005 and before Jan. 1, 2009 for training mine rescue teams

Code Sec. 45N, as added by 2006 Tax Relief and Health Care Act § 405(a)
Code Sec. 38(b)(31), as amended by 2006 Tax Relief and Health Care Act § 405(b)
Code Sec. 280C(e), as amended by 2006 Tax Relief and Health Care Act § 405(c)
Generally effective: Tax years beginning after Dec. 31, 2005 and before Jan. 1, 2009
Committee Reports, see ¶ 5056

The general business credit consists of the alcohol fuel credit; biodiesel, low-sulfur, and renewable diesel fuel credits; nonconventional source fuel credit; renewable electricity credit; advanced nuclear power facility credit; distilled spirits credit; contributions to community development corporations credit; disabled access credit; employer-provided child care credit; employer social security credit; empowerment zone employment credit; renewal community employment credit; enhanced oil recovery credit; incremental research credit; Indian employment credit; marginal well production credit; energy efficient home and appliance credits; small employer pension plan startup cost credit; investment tax credit; railroad track maintenance credit; low-income housing credit; orphan drug credit; new markets tax credit; work opportunity credit; welfare-to-work credit; employee retention credits for employers affected by Hurricanes Katrina, Wilma, or Rita; and Hurricane Katrina credit for employers providing housing to employees. (FTC 2d/FIN ¶ L-15201; USTR ¶ 384; TaxDesk ¶ 380,500) This general business credit is subject to annual limitations (based on tax liabilities) and carrybacks and carryovers that are calculated in a combined manner. (FTC 2d/FIN ¶ L-15209; USTR ¶ 384.02; TaxDesk ¶ 380,509) Under pre-2006 Tax Relief and Health Care Act law, there was no general business credit for the costs of training mine rescue teams. (FTC 2d/FIN ¶ L-15201; USTR ¶ 384; TaxDesk ¶ 380,500) The costs incurred to train employees in the principles, procedures, and techniques of mine rescue, as well as the wages paid employees while they are in training, were generally deductible as ordinary and necessary expenses. (Com Rept, see ¶ 5056)

FTC 2d References are to Federal Tax Coordinator 2d
FIN References are to RIAs Analysis of Federal Taxes: Income
USTR References are to United States Tax Reporter: Income, Estate & Gift, and Excise
PCA References are to Pension Analysis (print & electronic)
PE References are to Pension Explanations (print & electronic)
EP References are to Estate Planning Analysis (print & electronic)

New Law. The 2006 Tax Relief and Health Care Act provides a credit for mine rescue team training. (Code Sec. 45N as added by 2006 Tax Relief and Health Care Act §405(a)) For purposes of Code Sec. 38, the mine rescue team training credit for any "qualified mine rescue team employee" (defined below) of an "eligible employer" (also defined below) for any tax year is an amount equal to the lesser of (Code Sec. 45N(a)):

. . . 20 percent of the amount the taxpayer paid or incurred during the tax year for the training program costs of that qualified mine rescue team employee, including wages of the employee (defined below) while attending the program, (Code Sec. 45N(a)(1)) or

. . . $10,000. (Code Sec. 45N(a)(2))

Qualified mine rescue team employee defined. For purposes of Code Sec. 45N, the term "qualified mine rescue team employee" means, for any tax year, any full-time employee of the taxpayer who is (Code Sec. 45N(b)):

(1) a miner eligible for more than 6 months of the tax year to serve as a mine rescue team member as a result of completing, at a minimum, an initial 20-hour course of instruction as prescribed by the Mine Safety and Health Administration's Office of Educational Policy and Development (Code Sec. 45N(b)(1)), or

(2) a miner eligible for more than 6 months of the tax year to serve as a mine rescue team member by virtue of receiving at least 40 hours of refresher training in that instruction. (Code Sec. 45N(b)(2))

Eligible employer defined. For purposes of Code Sec. 45N, the term "eligible employer" means any taxpayer that employs individuals as miners in underground mines in the U.S. (Code Sec. 45N(c))

Wages defined. For purposes of Code Sec. 45N, the term wages has the meaning given to the term by Code Sec. 3306(b) (determined without regard to any dollar limitation contained in Code Sec. 3306). (Code Sec. 45N(d))

> ***observation:*** Wages as defined by Code Sec. 3306(b) means wages for federal unemployment tax purposes, see FTC 2d/FIN ¶ H-4781; TaxDesk ¶ 551,501.

Termination. Code Sec. 45N does not apply to tax years beginning after Dec. 31, 2008. (Code Sec. 45N(e))

General business credit treatment. The mine rescue team training credit under Code Sec. 45N is part of the Code Sec. 38 general business credit. Specifically, the mine rescue team training credit is included in the current year business credit for purposes of the general business credit. (Code Sec. 38(b)(31) as amended by 2006 Tax Relief and Health Care Act §405(b)) *observation:* This means that the mine rescue team training credit under Code Sec. 45N is subject to the rules that, under Code Sec. 38, will prevent some taxpayers from enjoying full use of the credit to reduce their tax liabilities in the year that the credit is claimed (see FTC 2d/FIN ¶ L-15202; USTR ¶ 384.02; TaxDesk ¶ 380,502).

observation: There are no special carryback or carryforward provisions that apply to the mine rescue team training credit under Code Sec. 45N. Thus, the mine rescue team training credit is subject to the carryback and carryforward periods (one-year carryback and 20-year carryforward, see FTC 2d/FIN ¶ L-15209; USTR ¶ 394.01; TaxDesk ¶ 380,509) that apply to the general business credit.

observation: Unlike many individual credits that comprise the general business credit, the mine rescue team training credit is not a "qualified business credit" under Code Sec. 196(c) (see FTC 2d/FIN ¶ L-15212; USTR ¶ 1964; TaxDesk ¶ 380,510). Thus, a taxpayer probably won't be able to *deduct* any mine rescue team training credits that remain unused at the end of the twenty-year carryforward period under Code Sec. 196.

No double benefit. Under the 2006 Tax Relief and Health Care Act, no deduction is allowed for the portion of expenses that would otherwise have been allowable as a deduction for the tax year that is equal to the amount of the mine rescue team training credit determined for the tax year under Code Sec. 45N. (Code Sec. 280C(e) as amended by 2006 Tax Relief and Health Care Act §405(c))

☐ **Effective:** Tax years beginning after Dec. 31, 2005 (2006 Tax Relief and Health Care Act §405(e)) and before Jan. 1, 2009. (Code Sec. 45N(e) as added by 2006 Tax Relief and Health Care Act §405(a))

¶ 807. Indian employment credit is extended retroactively for tax years beginning after Dec. 31, 2005 and before Jan. 1, 2008

Code Sec. 45A(f), as amended by 2006 Tax Relief and Health Care Act § 111(a)
Generally effective: Tax years beginning after Dec. 31, 2005 and before Jan. 1, 2008
Committee Reports, see ¶ 5015

As an incentive for businesses to be located on Indian reservations, employers were eligible for a credit equal to 20% of the first $20,000 of qualified wages and insurance costs paid to a qualified Indian employee for tax years beginning before Jan. 1, 2006. Thus, the credit terminated for tax years beginning after Dec. 31, 2005. The credit generally applied to services performed on Indian reservations by members of Indian tribes who live on the reservation. (FTC 2d/FIN ¶ L-15671; USTR ¶ 45A4; TaxDesk ¶ 384,039)

New Law. The 2006 Tax Relief and Health Care Act extends the Indian employment credit for two years, through the end of 2007 (Com Rept, see ¶ 5015) so that the credit does *not* apply to tax years beginning after Dec. 31, 2007. (Code Sec. 45A(f) as amended by 2006 Tax Relief and Health Care Act §111(a))

☐ **Effective:** Tax years beginning after Dec. 31, 2005 (2006 Tax Relief and Health Care Act §111(b)) and before Jan. 1, 2008. (Code Sec. 45A(f))

> ***observation:*** The effective date of the amendment to Code Sec. 45A(f) results in the retroactive extension of the credit for wages paid to qualified Indian employees for any tax year beginning after Dec. 31, 2005 and before Jan. 1, 2008. Thus, there is no break in the time period for which the credit applies.

¶ 900. Business Energy Related Credits

¶ 901. Energy efficient home credit for eligible contractors is extended through 2008

Code Sec. 45L(g), as amended by 2006 Tax Relief and Health Care Act § 205

Generally effective: Qualified new energy efficient homes acquired after Dec. 31, 2007 and before Jan. 1, 2009

Committee Reports, see ¶ 5035

An eligible contractor may claim a business credit for each qualified new energy efficient home that the contractor constructs and which is acquired by a person from the contractor for use as a residence. The credit is either $2,000 (for a 50% energy reduction in energy usage) or $1,000 (for a 30% energy reduction in energy usage). Under pre-2006 Tax Relief and Health Care Act law, the credit was only available for qualified new energy efficient homes substantially completed after Dec. 31, 2005, and which were acquired after Dec. 31, 2005 and before Jan. 1, 2008. (FTC 2d/FIN ¶ L-17941, ¶ L-17942; USTR ¶ 45L4; TaxDesk ¶ 569,571, ¶ 569,572)

New Law. The 2006 Tax Relief and Health Care Act extends the credit for one year so that it applies to qualified new energy efficient homes acquired before Jan. 1, 2009. (Code Sec. 45L(g) as amended by 2006 Tax Relief and Health Care Act §205)

☐ **Effective:** Qualified new energy efficient homes acquired after Dec. 31, 2007 and before Jan. 1, 2009. (Code Sec. 45L(g) as amended by 2006 Tax Relief and Health Care Act §205)

FTC 2d References are to Federal Tax Coordinator 2d
FIN References are to RIAs Analysis of Federal Taxes: Income
USTR References are to United States Tax Reporter: Income, Estate & Gift, and Excise
PCA References are to Pension Analysis (print & electronic)
PE References are to Pension Explanations (print & electronic)
EP References are to Estate Planning Analysis (print & electronic)

¶902. Increase in business energy tax credit for solar energy property from 10% to 30% is extended through Dec. 31, 2008, as are the 30% credit for qualified fuel cell property and the 10% credit for qualified microturbine property

Code Sec. 48(a)(2)(A)(i)(II), as amended by 2006 Tax Relief and Health Care Act § 207(1)

Code Sec. 48(a)(3)(A)(ii), as amended by 2006 Tax Relief and Health Care Act § 207(1)

Code Sec. 48(c)(1)(E), as amended by 2006 Tax Relief and Health Care Act § 207(2)

Code Sec. 48(c)(2)(E), as amended by 2006 Tax Relief and Health Care Act § 207(2)

Generally effective: Periods after Dec. 31, 2007 and before Jan. 1, 2009

Committee Reports, see ¶5037

The non-refundable business energy credit for any tax year is the energy percentage of the basis of each energy property placed in service during the tax year. The energy percentage is 30% for (1) qualified fuel cell property; (2) energy property described in Code Sec. 48(a)(3)(A)(i) (equipment using solar energy to generate electricity, to heat or cool (or provide hot water for use in) a structure, or to provide solar process heat, excepting property used to generate energy for the purpose of heating a swimming pool); and (3) energy property described in Code Sec. 48(a)(3)(A)(ii) (equipment that uses solar energy to illuminate the inside of a structure using fiber-optic distributed sunlight). The credit is 10% of the basis of any energy property not listed at (1) through (3), above. Under pre-2006 Tax Relief and Health Care Act law, the 30% credit for solar energy property described at (2) was reduced to 10% for periods after Dec. 31, 2007. In addition, the credit for property described at (1) and (3) was eliminated for periods after Dec. 31, 2007, as described below. (FTC 2d/FIN ¶L-16401; USTR ¶484; TaxDesk ¶381,601)

Energy property not listed at (1) through (3), above, refers to geothermal property and qualified microturbine property. Under pre-2006 Tax Relief and Health Care Act law, the credit for qualified microturbine property was eliminated for periods after Dec. 31, 2007, as described below. (FTC 2d/FIN ¶L-16401; USTR ¶484; TaxDesk ¶381,601)

Energy property means (i) equipment using solar energy to generate electricity, to heat or cool (or provide hot water for use in) a structure, or to provide solar process heat, excepting property used to generate energy for purposes of heating a swimming pool; (ii) equipment that uses solar energy to illuminate the inside of a structure using fiber optic distributed sunlight; (iii) equipment used to produce, distribute, or use energy derived from a geothermal deposit, but only, in case of electricity generated by geothermal power, up to (but not including) the electrical transmission stage; or (iv) qualified fuel cell property or qualified microturbine property. Under pre-2006 Tax Relief and Health Care Act law, solar energy equipment described at (ii) was not energy property for periods after Dec. 31, 2007. In addition, qualified fuel cell property and qualified microturbine property did not qualify for periods after Dec. 31, 2007. (FTC 2d/FIN ¶ L-16402, ¶ L-16436.1, ¶ L-16437.1; USTR ¶ 484; TaxDesk ¶ 381,600, ¶ 381,602)

New Law. The 2006 Tax Relief and Health Care Act extends the 30% credits for solar energy property and qualified fuel cell property and the 10% credit for qualified microturbine property, through Dec. 31, 2008. (Com Rept, see ¶ 5037) Specifically, the 2006 Tax Relief and Health Care Act amends the energy credit so that:

(1) the provisions that allow a 30% credit for (i) equipment using solar energy to generate electricity, to heat or cool (or provide hot water for use in) a structure, or to provide solar process heat, excepting property used to generate energy for purposes of heating a swimming pool; (Code Sec. 48(a)(2)(A)(i)(II) as amended by 2006 Tax Relief and Health Care Act §207(1)) and (ii) equipment that uses solar energy to illuminate the inside of a structure using fiber optic distributed sunlight are extended so that the credit applies for periods ending before Jan. 1, 2009. (Code Sec. 48(a)(3)(A)(ii) as amended by 2006 Tax Relief and Health Care Act §207(1))

(2) the provisions terminating the 30% credit for qualified fuel cell property and the 10% credit for qualified microturbine property are amended so that these credits terminate after Dec. 31, 2008. (Code Sec. 48(c)(1)(E) as amended by 2006 Tax Relief and Health Care Act §207(2)); (Code Sec. 48(c)(2)(E) as amended by 2006 Tax Relief and Health Care Act §207(2))

☐ **Effective:** date of enactment. (Com Rept, see ¶ 5037) The above rules are extended for periods after Dec. 31, 2007 and before Jan. 1, 2009. (Code Sec. 48(a)(2)(A)(i)(II) as amended by 2006 Tax Relief and Health Care Act §207(1))(Code Sec. 48(a)(3)(A)(ii) as amended by 2006 Tax Relief and Health Care Act §207(1))(Code Sec. 48(c)(1)(E) as amended by 2006 Tax Relief and Health Care Act §207(2))(Code Sec. 48(c)(2)(E) as amended by 2006 Tax Relief and Health Care Act §207(2))

FTC 2d References are to Federal Tax Coordinator 2d
FIN References are to RIAs Analysis of Federal Taxes: Income
USTR References are to United States Tax Reporter: Income, Estate & Gift, and Excise
PCA References are to Pension Analysis (print & electronic)
PE References are to Pension Explanations (print & electronic)
EP References are to Estate Planning Analysis (print & electronic)

¶ 903. Placed-in-service date is extended for one year through Dec. 31, 2008 for certain qualified facilities for purposes of the credit for electricity produced from renewable resources

Code Sec. 45(d)(1), as amended by 2006 Tax Relief and Health Care Act § 201

Code Sec. 45(d)(2)(A), as amended by 2006 Tax Relief and Health Care Act § 201

Code Sec. 45(d)(3)(A), as amended by 2006 Tax Relief and Health Care Act § 201

Code Sec. 45(d)(4), as amended by 2006 Tax Relief and Health Care Act § 201

Code Sec. 45(d)(5), as amended by 2006 Tax Relief and Health Care Act § 201

Code Sec. 45(d)(6), as amended by 2006 Tax Relief and Health Care Act § 201

Code Sec. 45(d)(7), as amended by 2006 Tax Relief and Health Care Act § 201

Code Sec. 45(d)(9), as amended by 2006 Tax Relief and Health Care Act § 201

Generally effective: Facilities placed in service after Dec. 31, 2007
Committee Reports, see ¶ 5031

Under pre-2006 Tax Relief and Health Care Act law, the following types of facilities had to be originally placed in service *before* Jan. 1, 2008 in order to be a qualified facility for purposes of the credit for electricity produced from renewable resources: wind, closed-loop biomass, open-loop biomass, geothermal energy, small irrigation power, municipal solid waste, and hydropower facilities.

In addition, in order to be a qualified facility, the facility must be owned by the taxpayer. Wind facilities must be originally placed in service after Dec. 31, '93. Closed-loop biomass facilities, which include facilities in which closed-loop biomass is co-fired with coal, with other biomass, or with both, must be originally placed in service after Dec. 31, '92. Open-loop biomass facilities using agricultural livestock waste nutrients (except for certain poultry waste facilities), geothermal and solar energy facilities, small irrigation power facilities and municipal solid waste facilities, which include landfill gas facilities and trash combustion facilities, all must be originally placed in service after Oct. 22, 2004, and hydropower facilities must be placed in service after Aug. 8, 2005.

In order to be a qualified facility for purposes of the credit, a facility using *solar* energy had to be placed in service before Jan. 1, 2006. (FTC 2d/FIN ¶ L-17771, ¶ L-17771.1, ¶ L-17771.2, ¶ L-17771.3, ¶ L-17771.4, ¶ L-17771.5, ¶ L-

17771.6; USTR ¶ 454.09, ¶ 454.10, ¶ 454.11, ¶ 454.12, ¶ 454.13, ¶ 454.14, ¶ 454.15)

To be a qualified facility for purposes of an alternative credit available for the production of refined coal, a refined coal facility must be placed in service after Oct. 22, 2004 and before Jan. 1, 2009, see FTC 2d/FIN ¶ L-17771.7; USTR ¶ 454.16.

To be a qualified facility for purposes of an alternative credit available for the production of Indian coal, an Indian coal production facility must be placed in service before Jan. 1, 2009, see FTC 2d/FIN ¶ L-17771.8; USTR ¶ 454.17.

New Law. Under the 2006 Tax Relief and Health Care Act, to be qualified facilities for purposes of the credit for electricity produced from renewable resources, facilities using wind, closed-loop biomass, open-loop biomass, geothermal energy, small irrigation power, municipal solid waste (landfill gas and trash combustion), or hydropower to produce electricity must be originally placed in service *before* Jan. 1, 2009. (Code Sec. 45(d)(1) as amended by 2006 Tax Relief and Health Care Act §201) (Code Sec. 45(d)(2)(A) as amended by 2006 Tax Relief and Health Care Act §201) (Code Sec. 45(d)(3)(A) as amended by 2006 Tax Relief and Health Care Act §201) (Code Sec. 45(d)(4) as amended by 2006 Tax Relief and Health Care Act §201) (Code Sec. 45(d)(5) as amended by 2006 Tax Relief and Health Care Act §201) (Code Sec. 45(d)(6) as amended by 2006 Tax Relief and Health Care Act §201) (Code Sec. 45(d)(7) as amended by 2006 Tax Relief and Health Care Act §201) (Code Sec. 45(d)(9) as amended by 2006 Tax Relief and Health Care Act §201)

Thus, the 2006 Tax Relief and Health Care Act extends through Dec. 31, 2008, the period during which certain facilities may be placed in service as qualified facilities for purposes of the electricity production credit. The placed-in-service date extension applies for all qualified facilities except for qualified solar, refined coal, and Indian coal facilities. (Com Rept, see ¶ 5031)

> ***observation:*** The 2006 Tax Relief and Health Care Act extends the placed-in-service date (see below) by one year (through Dec. 31, 2008) for wind facilities, closed-loop biomass facilities (including a facility co-firing the closed-loop biomass with coal, other biomass, or coal and other biomass), open-loop biomass facilities, geothermal energy facilities, small irrigation power facilities, landfill gas facilities, trash combustion facilities, and hydropower. Thus, the date by which these facilities have to be placed in service is the same as that for refined coal and Indian coal production facilities. The 2006 Tax Relief and Health Care

Act does not extend the placed-in-service date for solar energy facilities beyond Dec. 31, 2005.

illustration (1): Taxpayer originally places a small irrigation power facility in service on Jan. 1, 2008. Taxpayer is the owner of the facility. The facility will be a qualified facility for purposes of the credit for electricity produced from renewable resources, since the placed-in-service date was extended through Dec. 31, 2008 for those facilities. If this facility were placed in service on Jan. 1, 2009, it would not be a qualified facility.

illustration (2): Taxpayer owns a solar energy facility and placed it in service on Jan. 1, 2006. The facility is not a qualified facility because the placed-in-service date was not extended beyond Dec. 31, 2005 for solar facilities.

☐ **Effective:** Facilities placed in service after Dec. 31, 2007. (Com Rept, see ¶ 5031)

¶ 904. Nonconventional source production credit for coke and coke gas is not subject to the phase-out limitation, and the credit does not apply to a facility producing coke or coke gas from petroleum-based products

Code Sec. 45K(g)(2), as amended by 2006 Tax Relief and Health Care Act § 211(a)

Code Sec. 45K(g)(1), as amended by 2006 Tax Relief and Health Care Act § 211(b)

Generally effective: Fuel produced and sold after Dec. 31, 2005

Committee Reports, see ¶ 5041

Certain fuels produced in the U.S. from "nonconventional sources" and sold to unrelated parties are eligible for an income tax credit (the nonconventional source production credit) of $3 per barrel-of-oil equivalent (indexed for inflation to $6.56 in 2004 and to $6.79 in 2005). (FTC 2d/FIN ¶ L-17704; USTR ¶ 45K4; TaxDesk ¶ 396,001).

The nonconventional source production credit is part of the general business credit of Code Sec. 38 and is available for certain qualified fuels, which are certain biomass gas and synthetic fuels sold before Jan. 1, 2008 and produced at facilities placed in service before July 1, '98, see FTC 2d/FIN ¶ L-17702; USTR ¶ 45K4.04; TaxDesk ¶ 396,001. The nonconventional source production credit also includes a credit for producing coke or coke gas at qualified facilities, see FTC 2d/FIN ¶ L-17703.3; USTR ¶ 45K4.04; TaxDesk ¶ 396,001.

Code Sec. 45K(b)(1) provides that the nonconventional source production credit is reduced (but not below zero) over a $6 phase-out range as the reference price for oil rises from $23.50 to $29.50 per barrel, adjusted for inflation. (FTC 2d/FIN ¶ L-17710; USTR ¶ 45K4.02; TaxDesk ¶ 396,001) The reference price is IRS's estimate of the annual average wellhead price per barrel for all domestic crude oil, see FTC 2d/FIN ¶ L-17712; USTR ¶ 45K4.02; TaxDesk ¶ 396,001.

For 2004 and 2005, the credit did not phase out because the reference price for those years did not exceed the inflation adjusted threshold price, see FTC 2d/FIN ¶s L-17710, L-17712; USTR ¶s 45K4.02, 298.02(5); TaxDesk ¶ 396,001.

New Law. The 2006 Tax Relief and Health Care Act provides that the phase-out limitations and adjustments provided in Code Sec. 45K(b)(1) do not apply to the production of coke and coke gas. (Code Sec. 45K(g)(2)(D) as amended by 2006 Tax Relief and Health Care Act §211(a)) Thus, the 2006 Tax Relief and Health Care Act repeals the phase-out limitation for coke and coke gas otherwise eligible for a credit under Code Sec. 45K(g). (Com Rept, see ¶ 5041)

> ***observation:*** With the repeal of the phase-out limitation for coke and coke gas, the nonconventional source production credit for the production of coke and coke gas will not be reduced even if the price of oil increases above the phase-out range.

Further, qualifying facilities producing coke or coke gas for purposes of the nonconventional source production credit do not include facilities producing coke or coke gas from petroleum based products. (Code Sec. 45K(g)(1) as amended by 2006 Tax Relief and Health Care Act §211(b))

Congress says that the amendments to Code Sec. 45K(g) do not modify the existing 4,000 barrel-of-oil equivalent per day limitation, see FTC 2d/FIN ¶ L-17706.1; USTR ¶ 45K4.04. (Com Rept, see ¶ 5041)

☐ **Effective:** Fuel produced and sold after Dec. 31, 2005. (2006 Tax Relief and Health Care Act §211(c))

> ***observation:*** The 2006 Tax Relief and Health Care Act provides that the rules discussed above are effective as if included in Sec. 1321 of the 2005 Energy Tax Act. (Sec. 1321, PL 108-58, 8/8/2005). 2005 En-

ergy Tax Act §1321(b) provides that 2005 Energy Tax Act §1321(a) was effective for fuel produced and sold after Dec. 31, 2005.

¶ 905. An alternative low-sulfur standard is met for advanced coal-based generation technology units using subbituminous coal where an emission level of 0.04 pounds or less of SO_2 per million Btu is achieved

Code Sec. 48A(f)(1), as amended by 2006 Tax Relief and Health Care Act § 203(a)
Generally effective: Applications for certification submitted after Oct. 2, 2006
Committee Reports, see ¶ 5033

Pre-2006 Tax Relief and Health Care Act law provides for the "qualifying advanced coal project credit" as a component of the investment credit, see FTC 2d/FIN ¶ L-16450; USTR ¶ 48A4; TaxDesk ¶ 396,100. The credit is available for projects certified by IRS in accordance with Code Sec. 48A(d)(2), in consultation with the Dept. of Energy, using a competitive bidding process.

A qualifying advanced coal project must, among other requirements, use an advanced coal-based generation technology. To be advanced coal-based generation technology, the technology had to be designed to meet the following performance requirements.

Performance characteristic:	Design level for project
SO_2 (percent removal)	99 percent
NO_x (emissions)	0.07 lbs/MMBTU
PM* (emissions)	0.015 lbs/MMBTU
Hg (percent removal)	90 percent

Pre-2006 Tax Relief and Health Care Act law provided no exceptions to these performance requirements. (FTC 2d/FIN ¶ L-16458; USTR ¶ 48A4; TaxDesk ¶ 396,107)

New Law. The 2006 Tax Relief and Health Care Act modifies the 99% SO_2 removal requirement necessary for an electric generation unit to be treated as an advanced coal-based generation technology. (Com Rept, see ¶ 5033) For purposes of the performance requirement for the removal of sulfur dioxide, SO_2, the 2006 Tax Relief and Health Care Act provides an alternative removal design level for units designed for use of feedstock substantially all of which is subbituminous coal. For these units, the removal design level of SO_2 is 99 percent *or*, alternatively, the achievement of an emission level of 0.04 pounds or less of

SO_2 per million Btu, determined on a 30-day average. (Code Sec. 48A(f)(1) as amended by 2006 Tax Relief and Health Care Act §203(a))

> ***observation:*** Thus, units designed for use of feedstock substantially all of which is subbituminous coal can meet the performance requirement for SO_2 by *either* having a 99 percent removal design level *or* achieving an emission level of 0.04 pounds per million Btu or less.

☐ **Effective:** Applications for certification under Code Sec. 48A(d)(2) submitted after Oct. 2, 2006. (2006 Tax Relief and Health Care Act §203(b))

¶ 906. National CREB limitation raised to $1.2 billion; amount allocable to governmental borrowers raised to $750 million; termination date for issuance of CREBs extended through end of 2008

Code Sec. 54(f)(1), as amended by 2006 Tax Relief and Health Care Act § 202(a)(1)
Code Sec. 54(f)(2), as amended by 2006 Tax Relief and Health Care Act § 202(a)(2)
Code Sec. 54(m), as amended by 2006 Tax Relief and Health Care Act § 202(a)(3)
Generally effective: Bonds issued, and allocations or reallocations made after, Dec. 31, 2006
Committee Reports, see ¶ 5032

Taxpayers who hold "clean renewable energy bonds" (CREBs) on specified dates during the year are entitled to a nonrefundable credit equal to a portion of the bond's outstanding face amount. The credit is includable in gross income, and is treated as interest income.

However, under pre-2006 Tax Relief and Health Care Act law, there was a national CREB limitation of $800 million. IRS was required to allocate this amount among qualified projects in the manner that IRS determined appropriate. However, IRS was not permitted to allocate more than $500 million of the national CREB limitation to finance qualified projects of qualified borrowers that were governmental bodies.

Under pre-2006 Tax Relief and Health Care Act law, bonds could not qualify as CREBs if they were issued after Dec. 31, 2007. (FTC 2d/FIN ¶ L-16481 *et seq.*, ¶ L-16494; USTR ¶ 544 *et seq.*; TaxDesk ¶ 384,801 *et seq.*, ¶ 384,810)

New Law. The 2006 Tax Relief and Health Care Act raises the limitation on the amount of CREBs from $800 million to $1.2 billion. (Code Sec. 54(f)(1) as amended by 2006 Tax Relief and Health Care Act §202(a)(1)) In other words, the Act authorizes an additional $400 million of CREBs that may be issued. It is expected that the additional authority will be allocated through a new application process similar to the one set forth in Notice 2005-98, 2005-52 IRB 1211 (see FTC 2d/FIN ¶ L-16481 *et seq.*; TaxDesk ¶ 384,801 *et seq.*). (Com Rept, see ¶ 5032)

Moreover, the Act increases the amount of the national CREB limitation that IRS may allocate to finance qualified projects of qualified borrowers that are governmental bodies from $500 million to $750 million. (Code Sec. 54(f)(2) as amended by 2006 Tax Relief and Health Care Act §202(a)(2)) In other words, the Act increases the maximum amount of CREBs that may be allocated to qualified projects of governmental bodies to $750 million. (Com Rept, see ¶ 5032) (For applicability of this increase to allocations or reallocations after Dec. 31, 2006, see discussion of effective dates below.)

Finally, the Act extends the termination date for the issuance of CREBs to Dec. 31, 2008 (Code Sec. 54(m) as amended by 2006 Tax Relief and Health Care Act §202(a)(3))—that is, it extends the authority to issue CREBs through Dec. 31, 2008. (Com Rept, see ¶ 5032)

☐ **Effective:** For the increase in the amount of the national CREB limitation, and for the extension of the termination date for issuance of CREBs, bonds issued after Dec. 31, 2006. (2006 Tax Relief and Health Care Act §202(b)(1))

For the rules affecting allocations or reallocations of CREBs to finance qualified projects of governmental bodies, allocations or reallocations after Dec. 31, 2006. (2006 Tax Relief and Health Care Act §202(b)(2))

¶ 1000. Economic Development Credits

¶ 1001. $3.5 billion new markets tax credit limitation is extended to include 2008

Code Sec. 45D(f)(1)(D), as amended by 2006 Tax Relief and Health Care Act § 102(a)
Generally effective: date of enactment
Committee Reports, see ¶ 5002

A new markets tax credit is available for qualified equity investments in a qualified community development entity (CDE), see FTC 2d/FIN ¶ L-17921; USTR ¶ 45D4; TaxDesk ¶ 384,701. A qualified equity investment is any equity investment in a CDE for which the CDE has received an allocation from IRS if, among other requirements, the CDE uses substantially all of the cash from the investment to make qualified low-income community investments, see FTC 2d/FIN ¶ L-17924; USTR ¶ 45D4; TaxDesk ¶ 384,703. Under pre-2006 Tax Relief and Health Care Act law, there was a new markets credit limitation for each calendar year, i.e., the maximum annual amount of qualified equity investments for each calendar year was limited as follows:

. . . $1 billion for 2001,

. . . $1.5 billion for 2002 and 2003,

. . . $2 billion for 2004 and 2005, and

. . . $3.5 billion for 2006 and 2007. (FTC 2d/FIN ¶ L-17927; USTR ¶ 45D4; TaxDesk ¶ 384,711)

If the credit limitation for any calendar year exceeds the aggregate amount allocated for that year, the excess is carried over and the limitation for the next calendar year is increased by the amount of the excess, see FTC 2d/FIN ¶ L-17927; USTR ¶ 45D4; TaxDesk ¶ 384,711.

> ***observation:*** Describing these dollar amounts as limitations suggests that there was no dollar limitation for calendar years after 2007. Under pre-2006 Tax Relief and Health Care Act law, it was not clear if that was the intention, or if the intent was to bar qualifying equity investments completely after 2007 subject only to the carryover rule described above.

FTC 2d References are to Federal Tax Coordinator 2d
FIN References are to RIAs Analysis of Federal Taxes: Income
USTR References are to United States Tax Reporter: Income, Estate & Gift, and Excise
PCA References are to Pension Analysis (print & electronic)
PE References are to Pension Explanations (print & electronic)
EP References are to Estate Planning Analysis (print & electronic)

New Law. The 2006 Tax Relief and Health Care Act extends the $3.5 billion limitation (that under pre-2006 Tax Relief and Health Care Act law applied for 2006 and 2007) to 2008. (Code Sec. 45D(f)(1)(D) as amended by 2006 Tax Relief and Health Care Act §102(a)) Thus, for 2008, up to $3.5 billion of qualified equity investments is permitted. (Com Rept, see ¶ 5002)

> ***observation:*** The one-year extension of the $3.5 billion cap does not address the question of whether there is a cap for calendar years after 2008.

☐ **Effective:** date of enactment. (2006 Tax Relief and Health Care Act §102(c))

¶ 1002. New markets tax credit regs are to ensure that non-metropolitan counties receive a proportional allocation of qualified equity investments

Code Sec. 45D(i)(6), as amended by 2006 Tax Relief and Health Care Act § 102(b)
Generally effective: date of enactment
Committee Reports, see ¶ 5002

A new markets tax credit is available for qualified equity investments in a qualified community development entity (CDE), see FTC 2d/FIN ¶ L-17921; USTR ¶ 45D4; TaxDesk ¶ 384,701. A qualified equity investment is any equity investment in a CDE for which the CDE has received an allocation from IRS if, among other requirements, the CDE uses substantially all of the cash from the investment to make qualified low-income community investments, see FTC 2d/FIN ¶ L-17924; USTR ¶ 45D4; TaxDesk ¶ 384,703. For this purpose, a low-income community includes any population census tract with a poverty rate of at least 20%, or

... in the case of a tract not located within a metropolitan area, the median family income for the tract doesn't exceed 80% of statewide median family income (85% if the tract is located within a "high migration rural county"), or

... in the case of a tract located within a metropolitan area, the median family income for the tract doesn't exceed 80% (85% if the tract is located within a "high migration rural county") of the greater of statewide median family income or the metropolitan area median family income.

A high migration rural county is any county that, during the 20-year period ending with the year in which the most recent census was conducted, has a net out-migration of inhabitants from the county of at least 10% of the population of the county at the beginning of the period, see FTC 2d/FIN ¶ L-17926; USTR ¶ 45D4.04; TaxDesk ¶ 384,710.

A group that is a "targeted population" qualifies as a low-income community. A targeted population is defined by reference to 12 USC §4702(20) to mean individuals, or an identifiable group of individuals, including an Indian tribe, who are low-income persons or otherwise lack adequate access to loans or equity investments. For this purpose, "low-income" means:

. . . for a targeted population within a metropolitan area, less than 80% of the area median family income, and

. . . for a targeted population within a non-metropolitan area, less than the greater of 80% of the area median family income or 80% of the statewide non-metropolitan area median family income, see FTC 2d/FIN ¶ L-17926.2; USTR ¶ 45D4.04.

Code Sec. 45D(i) provides that IRS is to issue regs as appropriate to carry out five specific issues under the new markets credit rules, including rules for determining whether an investment meets the "substantially all" requirement for being a qualified equity investment, see FTC 2d/FIN ¶ L-17924.3; USTR ¶ 45D4.05; TaxDesk ¶ 384,707.

New Law. The 2006 Tax Relief and Health Care Act adds another item to the list for which IRS is to issue regs as may be appropriate to carry out the new markets tax credit. Specifically, IRS is to prescribe regs as appropriate that ensure that non-metropolitan counties receive a proportional allocation of qualified equity investments. (Code Sec. 45D(i)(6) as amended by 2006 Tax Relief and Health Care Act §102(b))

☐ **Effective:** date of enactment. (2006 Tax Relief and Health Care Act §102(c))

¶ 1003. Permitted issuance of qualified zone academy bonds of up to $400 million per year is extended retroactively through Dec. 31, 2007

Code Sec. 1397E(e)(1), as amended by 2006 Tax Relief and Health Care Act § 107(a)

Generally effective: Obligations issued after Dec. 31, 2005 and before Jan. 1, 2008

Committee Reports, see ¶ 5011

Under pre-2006 Tax Relief and Health Care Act law, qualified zone academy bonds (QZABs) were authorized to be issued for calendar years '98 through

FTC 2d References are to Federal Tax Coordinator 2d
FIN References are to RIAs Analysis of Federal Taxes: Income
USTR References are to United States Tax Reporter: Income, Estate & Gift, and Excise
PCA References are to Pension Analysis (print & electronic)
PE References are to Pension Explanations (print & electronic)
EP References are to Estate Planning Analysis (print & electronic)

2005, up to an annual limitation of $400 million nationally. Except for carry-overs of unused issuance limitations, the limit was zero after 2005. (FTC 2d/FIN ¶ L-15645.12; USTR ¶ 13,97E4.01; TaxDesk ¶ 384,756)

New Law. The 2006 Tax Relief and Health Care Act extends the authorization of the issuance of QZABs up to the national limitation of $400 million per year retroactively for two years through the end of calendar year 2007. (Code Sec. 1397E(e)(1) as amended by 2006 Tax Relief and Health Care Act §107(a))

> ***observation:*** QZABs have been generally authorized for only one or two-year periods at a time.

The 2006 Tax Relief and Health Care Act also adds new expenditure, reporting, and arbitrage requirements to the QZAB rules, see ¶ 1004.

☐ **Effective:** Obligations issued after Dec. 31, 2005 (2006 Tax Relief and Health Care Act §107(c)(1)) and before Jan. 1, 2008. (Code Sec. 1397E(e)(1) as amended by 2006 Tax Relief and Health Care Act §107(a))

> ***observation:*** Thus, the authorization to issue QZABs up to the national limitation of $400 million per year applies retroactively to the entire 2006 calendar year.

¶ 1004. Qualified zone academy bond issuers must meet new expenditure, arbitrage, and reporting requirements

Code Sec. 1397E(d)(1)(E), as amended by 2006 Tax Relief and Health Care Act § 107(b)(1)(A)
Code Sec. 1397E(f), as amended by 2006 Tax Relief and Health Care Act § 107(b)(1)(B)
Code Sec. 1397E(g), as amended by 2006 Tax Relief and Health Care Act § 107(b)(1)(B)
Code Sec. 1397E(h), as amended by 2006 Tax Relief and Health Care Act § 107(b)(1)(B)
Generally effective: Obligations issued after date of enactment
Committee Reports, see ¶ 5011

Under pre-2006 Tax Relief and Health Care Act law, qualified zone academy bonds (QZABs) were authorized to be issued for calendar years '98 through 2005, up to an annual limitation of $400 million nationally. (FTC 2d/FIN ¶ L-15645.12; USTR ¶ 13,97E4.01; TaxDesk ¶ 384,756)

A QZAB was defined, in part, as any bond issued as part of an issue if 95% or more of the proceeds of the issue were to be used for a qualified purpose of a qualified zone academy established by an eligible local education agency and which the issuer had certified that it had written assurances that the private business contribution requirement would be satisfied for the academy. (FTC 2d/FIN ¶ L-15645.7; USTR ¶ 13,97E4; TaxDesk ¶ 384,757)

The Code has rules that restrict the ability to profit from investment of tax-exempt bond proceeds. With limited exceptions, under these arbitrage rules, profits that are earned outside of permitted periods must be rebated to the federal government. (FTC 2d/FIN ¶ J-3401; USTR ¶ 1484; TaxDesk ¶ 158,013) Under pre-2006 Tax Relief and Health Care Act law, the arbitrage rules that apply to tax-exempt bonds did not apply to QZABs. In addition, issuers were not required to report the issuance of QZABs to IRS. (Com Rept, see ¶ 5011)

The credit for QZABs is available to banks, insurance companies, and other corporations in the business of lending money ("eligible taxpayers"), see FTC 2d/FIN ¶ L-15645.6; USTR ¶ 13,97E4; TaxDesk ¶ 384,750. The credit is nonrefundable and is equal to a percentage of the bonds held by an eligible taxpayer. The credit is in lieu of periodic interest payments, compensates the eligible taxpayer for lending money to the issuer, and functions as payment of interest on the bonds, see FTC 2d/FIN ¶ L-15645.1; USTR ¶ 13,97E4; TaxDesk ¶ 384,753. The $400 million national limit is allocated among the states based on the proportion of each state's population below the poverty line, see FTC 2d/FIN ¶ L-15645.12; USTR ¶ 13,97E4; TaxDesk ¶ 384,756. The bonds must be issued for qualified purposes, which are defined as rehabilitating or repairing the facility in which the academy is located, providing equipment, developing course materials, and training teachers and other school personnel, see FTC 2d/FIN ¶ L-15645.7; USTR ¶ 13,97E4; TaxDesk ¶ 384,751. A qualified zone academy is defined, in part, as a public school or program below the post-secondary level that is designed with business input to better prepare students for college and the workforce. The school itself must be located in an empowerment zone or enterprise community or, if the school isn't in such a zone or community, then, at the time the bonds are issued, there has to be a reasonable expectation that, of students attending the school or program, at least 35% will be eligible for free or reduced-cost lunches under the school lunch program, see FTC 2d/FIN ¶ L-15645.8; USTR ¶ 13,97E4.01; TaxDesk ¶ 384,757.

New Law. The 2006 Tax Relief and Health Care Act adds to the definition of QZABs in Code Sec. 1397E(d)(1) the rule that the issue must meet the following requirements: (Code Sec. 1397E(d)(1)(E) as amended by 2006 Tax Relief and Health Care Act §107(b)(1)(A))

(1) as of the date of issuance of the QZAB, the issuer must reasonably expect the issue to meet certain spending requirements for QZABs. (Code Sec. 1397E(f)) See **Special rules for expenditures,** described below.

(2) the issuer of QZABs must satisfy the arbitrage requirements under Code Sec. 148, see FTC 2d/FIN ¶ J-3401; USTR ¶ 1484; TaxDesk ¶ 158,013, with respect to the proceeds of the issue (see **Arbitrage requirements**, below). (Code Sec. 1397E(g))

(3) issuers of QZABs must submit reports of issuance to IRS similar to those required under Code Sec. 149(e), see FTC 2d/FIN ¶ J-3661; USTR ¶ 1494.04; TaxDesk ¶ 158,015. (Code Sec. 1397E(h)) Those reports will be similar to the information returns required for tax-exempt bonds. (Com Rept, see ¶ 5011)

> ***observation:*** Code Sec. 1397E(f) and Code Sec. 1397E(g) (but not Code Sec. 1397E(h)) both state that an issue is treated as meeting the requirements of this *subsection* if the issue meets the requirements of each of Code Sec. 1397E(f) and Code Sec. 1397E(g), but, in each case, Congress presumably meant this *section,* not this *subsection.* If so, a technical correction will be needed to correct the reference to "subsection."

Special rules for expenditures. An issue is treated as meeting the requirements of Code Sec. 1397E(f) if, as of the date of issuance of the QZAB, the issuer reasonably expects that: (Code Sec. 1397E(f)(1) as amended by 2006 Tax Relief and Health Care Act §107(b)(1)(B))

. . . at least 95% of the proceeds from the sale of the issue will be spent for one or more "qualified purposes" with respect to qualified zone academies within the 5-year period beginning on the date the QZAB was issued; (Code Sec. 1397E(f)(1)(A)) Congress says that in addition to the reasonable expectation of spending, the QZAB issuer must *actually spend* 95 percent or more of the bond proceeds on qualified zone academy property within the 5-year period. (Com Rept, see ¶ 5011) See below for discussion of the rule when less than 95 percent of the proceeds are used to finance qualified zone academy property.

> ***observation:*** The term "qualified purposes" is defined in Code Sec. 1397E(d)(5), see FTC 2d/FIN ¶ L-15645.9; USTR ¶ 13,97E4.01; TaxDesk ¶ 384,757.

. . . a binding commitment with a third party to spend at least 10 percent of the proceeds from the sale of the issue will be incurred within the 6-month period beginning on the date the QZAB was issued; and (Code Sec. 1397E(f)(1)(B))

. . . these purposes will be completed with due diligence and the proceeds from the sale of the issue will be spent with due diligence. (Code Sec. 1397E(f)(1)(C))

If the issuer submits a request before the 5-year period described in Code Sec. 1397E(f)(1)(A) (above) expires, IRS can extend the 5-year period if the issuer establishes that the failure to satisfy the 5-year requirement is due to reasonable cause and the related purposes will continue to proceed with due diligence. (Code Sec. 1397E(f)(2))

> ***observation:*** It is unclear whether Congress intended the term "related purpose" as used in Code Sec. 1397E(f)(2) to have the same meaning as "qualified purpose," which is defined in Code Sec. 1397E(d)(5). IRS may have to issue guidance on the definition of "related purpose."

To the extent that less than 95 percent of the proceeds of the issue are expended by the close of the 5-year period beginning on the date of issuance (or if an extension has been obtained from IRS, under Code Sec. 1397E(f)(2), above, by the close of the extended period), the issuer must redeem all of the nonqualified bonds within 90 days after the end of that period. (Code Sec. 1397E(f)(3)) Thus, to the extent less than 95 percent of the proceeds are used to finance qualified zone academy property during the 5-year spending period, bonds will continue to qualify as QZABs if unspent proceeds are used within 90 days from the end of the 5-year period to redeem any non-qualified bonds. (Com Rept, see ¶ 5011) The amount of the nonqualified bonds required to be redeemed is determined in the same manner as under Code Sec. 142, see FTC 2d/FIN ¶ J-3153.1; USTR ¶ 1424.01. (Code Sec. 1397E(f)(3)) Congress says that this amount of nonqualified bonds is to be determined in the same manner as IRS *regulations* under Code Sec. 142. (Com Rept, see ¶ 5011)

Arbitrage requirements. The arbitrage requirements of Code Sec. 148 that apply to interest-bearing tax-exempt bonds are imposed on QZABs. Principles under Code Sec. 148 and their regs will apply to determine the yield restriction and arbitrage rebate requirements applicable to QZABs. For example, for arbitrage purposes, the yield on an issue of QZABs is computed by taking into account all payments of interest, if any, on the bonds, i.e., whether the bonds are issued at par, premium, or discount. However, for purposes of determining yield, the amount of the credit allowed to a taxpayer holding QZABs is not treated as interest, although the credit amount is treated as interest income to the taxpayer. (Com Rept, see ¶ 5011)

Redesignations. Pre-2006 Tax Relief and Health Care Act Code Secs. 1397E(f), 1397E(g), 1397E(h), and 1397E(i) are redesignated by the 2006 Tax

Relief and Health Care Act as Code Sec. 1397E(i), Code Sec. 1397E(j), Code Sec. 1397E(k), and Code Sec. 1397E(l), respectively. (2006 Tax Relief and Health Care Act §107(b)(1)(B))

For the retroactive extension, through Dec. 31, 2007, by the 2006 Tax Relief and Health Care Act, of authorization to issue QZABs, see ¶ 1003.

☐ **Effective:** Obligations issued after date of enactment under the allocations of the national zone academy bond limitation for calendar years after 2005. (2006 Tax Relief and Health Care Act §107(c)(2)) Thus, the 2006 Tax Relief and Health Care Act provisions imposing arbitrage restrictions, reporting requirements, and spending requirements apply to bonds issued after date of enactment with respect to allocations of the annual aggregate bond cap for calendar years after 2005. (Com Rept, see ¶ 5011)

¶ 1100. Extension of D.C. Tax Incentives

¶ 1101. DC homebuyer credit is retroactively extended for two years to apply to property bought before Jan. 1, 2008

Code Sec. 1400C(i), as amended by 2006 Tax Relief and Health Care Act § 110(d)(1)
Generally effective: Property bought after Dec. 31, 2005 and before Jan. 1, 2008
Committee Reports, see ¶ 5014

An individual who is a first-time homebuyer of a principal residence in the District of Columbia (DC) during any tax year is permitted a credit against income tax liability for the tax year. The amount of the credit is the lesser of $5,000 or the purchase price of the residence. A phaseout of the credit applies based on the homebuyer's modified adjusted gross income. Under pre-2006 Tax Relief and Health Care Act law, the credit was scheduled to expire for residences bought after Dec. 31, *2005.* (FTC 2d/FIN ¶ A-4258; USTR ¶ 14,00C4; TaxDesk ¶ 568,801)

New Law. The 2006 Tax Relief and Health Care Act extends the first-time homebuyer credit for two years. (Com Rept, see ¶ 5014) Specifically, under the 2006 Tax Relief and Health Care Act, the DC homebuyer credit applies to property bought before Jan. 1, *2008.* (Code Sec. 1400C(i) as amended by 2006 Tax Relief and Health Care Act §110(d)(1))

> ***observation:*** Thus, the 2006 Tax Relief and Health Care Act adds two years to the pre-2006 Tax Relief and Health Care Act expiration date of the credit, so that purchases of property as late as Dec. 31, 2007 qualify for the DC homebuyer credit.

☐ **Effective:** Property bought after Dec. 31, 2005 (2006 Tax Relief and Health Care Act §110(d)(2)) and before Jan. 1, 2008. (Code Sec. 1400C(i))

FTC 2d References are to Federal Tax Coordinator 2d
FIN References are to RIAs Analysis of Federal Taxes: Income
USTR References are to United States Tax Reporter: Income, Estate & Gift, and Excise
PCA References are to Pension Analysis (print & electronic)
PE References are to Pension Explanations (print & electronic)
EP References are to Estate Planning Analysis (print & electronic)

¶ 1102. Zero percent capital gains rate for DC Zone assets is retroactively extended for two years to apply to assets acquired before Jan. 1, 2008 and includes gain attributable to periods before Jan. 1, 2013

Code Sec. 1400B(b)(2)(A)(i), as amended by 2006 Tax Relief and Health Care Act § 110(c)(1)
Code Sec. 1400B(b)(3)(A), as amended by 2006 Tax Relief and Health Care Act § 110(c)(1)
Code Sec. 1400B(b)(4)(A)(i), as amended by 2006 Tax Relief and Health Care Act § 110(c)(1)
Code Sec. 1400B(b)(4)(B)(i)(I), as amended by 2006 Tax Relief and Health Care Act § 110(c)(1)
Code Sec. 1400B(e)(2), as amended by 2006 Tax Relief and Health Care Act § 110(c)(2)(A)(i)
Code Sec. 1400B(g)(2), as amended by 2006 Tax Relief and Health Care Act § 110(c)(2)(B)
Generally effective: Acquisitions after Dec. 31, 2005 and before Jan. 1, 2008
Committee Reports, see ¶ 5014

There is an exclusion for "qualified capital gain" (FTC 2d/FIN ¶ I-8751; USTR ¶ 14,00B4; TaxDesk ¶ 246,560) from the sale or exchange of any "DC Zone" asset (FTC 2d/FIN ¶ I-8752; USTR ¶ 14,00B4.01; TaxDesk ¶ 246,552) held for more than five years. A DC Zone asset is defined as DC Zone business stock (FTC 2d/FIN ¶ I-8753; USTR ¶ 14,00B4.01; TaxDesk ¶ 246,553), DC Zone partnership interest (FTC 2d/FIN ¶ I-8754; USTR ¶ 14,00B4.01; TaxDesk ¶ 246,554), DC Zone tangible business property (FTC 2d/FIN ¶ I-8755; USTR ¶ 14,00B4.01; TaxDesk ¶ 246,555), and DC Zone buildings which have been substantially improved (FTC 2d/FIN ¶ I-8756; USTR ¶ 14,00B4.01; TaxDesk ¶ 246,555). Pre-2006 Tax Relief and Health Care Act law provided that to qualify, an asset had to be acquired or improved by the taxpayer before Jan. 1, *2006*. Also, qualified capital gain did not include any gain attributable to periods after Dec. 31, *2010*. (FTC 2d/FIN ¶ I-8751; USTR ¶ 14,00B4; TaxDesk ¶ 245,556)

New Law. The 2006 Tax Relief and Health Care Act extends the zero-percent capital gains rate applicable to capital gains from the sale of certain qualified DC Zone assets for two years. (Com Rept, see ¶ 5014) Specifically, under the 2006 Tax Relief and Health Care Act, the "acquired-or-improved-before" date in the definition of DC Zone assets is extended for two years from Dec. 31, 2005 to Dec. 31, *2007*. Thus, DC Zone business stock has to be acquired by the taxpayer before Jan. 1, *2008* (Code Sec. 1400B(b)(2)(A)(i) as amended by 2006 Tax Relief and Health Care Act §110(c)(1)); a DC Zone partnership interest has to be acquired by the taxpayer before Jan. 1, *2008* (Code Sec.

1400B(b)(3)(A)); DC Zone tangible business property has to be acquired by the taxpayer before Jan. 1, *2008* (Code Sec. 1400B(b)(4)(A)(i)); and DC Zone buildings have to be substantially improved by the taxpayer before Jan. 1, *2008*. (Code Sec. 1400B(b)(4)(B)(i)(I))

> ***observation:*** Thus, the 2006 Tax Relief and Health Care Act adds two years to the time period for acquiring or improving DC Zone assets, so that qualified capital gain attributable to DC Zone assets acquired or improved before Jan. 1, 2008 qualifies for the zero capital gains rate.

> ***observation:*** The two-year retroactive extension of the "acquired or improved before" date corresponds to the two-year extension of the time for which the DC Zone designation applies, see ¶ 1103.

Under the 2006 Tax Relief and Health Care Act, qualified capital gain does not include any gain attributable to periods after Dec. 31, 2012. (Code Sec. 1400B(e)(2) as amended by 2006 Tax Relief and Health Care Act §110(c)(2)(A)(i)) With respect to sales and exchanges of interests in partnerships and S corporations which are DC Zone businesses during substantially all of the period that the taxpayer held the interest or stock, qualified capital gain is determined without regard to any gain attributable to periods after Dec. 31, 2012. (Code Sec. 1400B(g)(2) as amended by 2006 Tax Relief and Health Care Act §110(c)(2)(B))

> ***recommendation:*** If a taxpayer holds a DC Zone asset after Dec. 31, 2012, he should consider having it appraised as of that date so as to be able to demonstrate the amount of gain that is attributable to periods before Jan. 1, 2013, i.e., what gain qualifies for the zero capital gains rate.

☐ **Effective:** The amendments made by 2006 Tax Relief and Health Care Act §110(c)(1) apply to acquisitions after Dec. 31, 2005 (2006 Tax Relief and Health Care Act §110(c)(3)(A)) and before Jan. 1, 2008 (Code Sec. 1400B(b)(2)(A)(i)) (Code Sec. 1400B(b)(3)(A)) (Code Sec. 1400B(b)(4)(A)(i)) The conforming amendments to Code Sec. 1400B(e)(2) and Code Sec. 1400B(g)(2) made by 2006 Tax Relief and Health Care Act §110(c)(2) are effective on date of enactment. (2006 Tax Relief and Health Care Act §110(c)(3)(B))

FTC 2d References are to Federal Tax Coordinator 2d
FIN References are to RIAs Analysis of Federal Taxes: Income
USTR References are to United States Tax Reporter: Income, Estate & Gift, and Excise
PCA References are to Pension Analysis (print & electronic)
PE References are to Pension Explanations (print & electronic)
EP References are to Estate Planning Analysis (print & electronic)

observation: Although 2006 Tax Relief and Health Care Act §110(c)(3)(A) effectively provides that the changes to Code Sec. 1400B(b)(2)(A)(i), Code Sec. 1400B(b)(3)(A), Code Sec. 1400B(b)(4)(A)(i), and Code Sec. 1400B(b)(4)(B)(i)(I) apply to acquisitions after Dec. 31, 2005, the change to Code Sec. 1400B(b)(4)(B)(i)(I) applies to property that is substantially improved by the taxpayer before Jan. 1, 2008.

¶ 1103. DC Enterprise Zone and enterprise community designations are retroactively extended for two years through Dec. 31, 2007

Code Sec. 1400(f)(1), as amended by 2006 Tax Relief and Health Care Act § 110(a)(1)
Code Sec. 1400(f)(2), as amended by 2006 Tax Relief and Health Care Act § 110(a)(1)
Generally effective: Periods beginning after Dec. 31, 2005 and ending before Jan. 1, 2008
Committee Reports, see ¶ 5014

Special tax incentives are available to businesses and individual residents within certain economically depressed census tracts within the District of Columbia (DC). These areas are designated as the "DC Enterprise Zone." Under pre-2006 Tax Relief and Health Care Act law, the DC Enterprise Zone designation applied for the period beginning on Jan. 1, '98 and ending Dec. 31, *2005*. (FTC 2d/FIN ¶ J-3396.4; USTR ¶ 14,004.01) In general, the tax incentives available in connection with the DC Zone were:

. . . a 20% wage credit (FTC 2d/FIN ¶ L-15641; USTR ¶ 14,004.01),

. . . an additional $35,000 of Code Sec. 179 expensing for qualified zone property (FTC 2d/FIN ¶ L-15641; USTR ¶ 14,004.01),

. . . expanded tax-exempt financing for certain zone facilities (FTC 2d/FIN ¶ J-3363; USTR ¶ 14,00A4), and

. . . a zero-percent capital gains rate from the sale of certain qualified DC Zone assets. (FTC 2d/FIN ¶ I-8762; USTR ¶ 14,00B4; TaxDesk ¶ 246,560)

Also, certain census tracts in DC (referred to in Code Sec. 1400(b)(1) as the "applicable DC area") were designated as an enterprise community, under Code Sec. 1391 through Code Sec. 1397D (see FTC 2d/FIN ¶ J-3396.3; USTR ¶ 14,004.01). Under pre-2006 Tax Relief and Health Care Act law, this designation terminated on Dec. 31, 2005. (FTC 2d/FIN ¶ J-3396.5; USTR ¶ 14,004.01)

New Law. The 2006 Tax Relief and Health Care Act provides that the DC Zone designation applies to the period beginning on Jan. 1, '98 and ending on

Dec. 31, *2007*. (Code Sec. 1400(f)(1) as amended by 2006 Tax Relief and Health Care Act §110(a)(1)) As a result of the two-year extension of the designation of the DC Zone (through Dec. 31, 2007), the wage credit and Code Sec. 179 expensing are also extended. (Com Rept, see ¶ 5014)

> ***observation:*** The two-year extension of the period during which the DC Zone designation applies corresponds to the extensions of the periods for:
>
> ... issuing a higher amount of DC Zone bonds, see ¶ 1104.
>
> ... acquiring or improving DC Zone assets for purposes of the zero capital gains rate, see ¶ 1102.

The 2006 Tax Relief and Health Care Act also provides that the designation of certain census tracts within DC (referred to in Code Sec. 1400(b)(1) as the "applicable DC area") as an enterprise community terminates on Dec. 31, 2007. (Code Sec. 1400(f)(2) as amended by 2006 Tax Relief and Health Care Act §110(a)(1))

☐ **Effective:** Periods beginning after Dec. 31, 2005 (2006 Tax Relief and Health Care Act §110(a)(2)) and ending before Jan. 1, 2008. (Code Sec. 1400(f)(1)) (Code Sec. 1400(f)(2))

¶ 1104. Higher tax-exempt enterprise zone facility bond limit for DC Zone bonds is retroactively extended to apply to bonds issued after Dec. 31, 2005 and before Jan. 1, 2008

Code Sec. 1400A(b), as amended by 2006 Tax Relief and Health Care Act § 110(b)(1)

Generally effective: Bonds issued after Dec. 31, 2005 and before Jan. 1, 2008

Committee Reports, see ¶ 5014

Tax-exempt private activity bonds may be issued to finance certain facilities in enterprise zones. For the District of Columbia Enterprise Zone (DC Zone), the amount of outstanding bond proceeds that can be borrowed by a qualified DC Zone business can't exceed $15 million, rather than the $3 million limit otherwise prescribed under Code Sec. 1394(c)(1) for tax-exempt enterprise zone facility bonds (see FTC 2d/FIN ¶ J-3355; USTR ¶ 13,944). Under pre-2006 Tax

FTC 2d References are to Federal Tax Coordinator 2d
FIN References are to RIAs Analysis of Federal Taxes: Income
USTR References are to United States Tax Reporter: Income, Estate & Gift, and Excise
PCA References are to Pension Analysis (print & electronic)
PE References are to Pension Explanations (print & electronic)
EP References are to Estate Planning Analysis (print & electronic)

Relief and Health Care Act law, this rule applied to bonds issued during the period beginning on Jan. 1, '98 and ending on Dec. 31, *2005*. (FTC 2d/FIN ¶ J-3363; USTR ¶ 14,00A4)

New Law. Under the 2006 Tax Relief and Health Care Act, the higher limit on DC Zone bonds is extended to include bonds issued during the period beginning on Jan. 1, '98 and ending on Dec. 31, *2007*. (Code Sec. 1400A(b) as amended by 2006 Tax Relief and Health Care Act §110(b)(1)) Thus, the 2006 Tax Relief and Health Care Act extends the tax-exempt financing authority for two years. (Com Rept, see ¶ 5014)

> ***observation:*** That is, the 2006 Tax Relief and Health Care Act adds two years to the pre-2006 Tax Relief and Health Care Act time period for the issuance of the higher amount of DC Zone bonds, so that bonds issued before Jan. 1, 2008 would be subject to the higher limit.

> ***observation:*** The two-year retroactive extension of the time period for issuance of the higher amount of DC Zone bonds corresponds to the two-year retroactive extension of the time for which the DC Zone designation applies, see ¶ 1103.

☐ **Effective:** Bonds issued after Dec. 31, 2005 (2006 Tax Relief and Health Care Act §110(b)(2)) and before Jan. 1, 2008. (Code Sec. 1400A(b))

¶ 1200. AMT Credits

¶ 1201. Portion of minimum tax credit attributable to years before the third immediately preceding tax year is made refundable

Code Sec. 53(e), as amended by 2006 Tax Relief and Health Care Act § 402(a)

Generally effective: Tax years beginning after date of enactment and before Jan. 1, 2013

Committee Reports, see ¶ 5053

The alternative minimum tax (AMT) applies in a tax year only to the extent it exceeds the taxpayer's regular tax liability for the year. An individual's AMT liability equals the excess (if any) of his tentative minimum tax (i.e., AMT before deducting regular tax) over his regular tax, for the year. (Com Rept, see ¶ 5053)

The AMT is imposed on alternative minimum taxable income (AMTI), which is taxable income increased by certain preference items and adjusted by denying the regular-tax income deferral allowed for certain items ("deferral adjustments"). An individual's AMT that is attributable to deferral adjustments generates a minimum tax credit that the individual can use in a later tax year for which regular tax (reduced by other nonrefundable credits) exceeds tentative minimum tax, to reduce his regular tax for that year. (See FTC 2d/FIN ¶ A-8801 *et seq.*; USTR ¶ 534; TaxDesk ¶ 691,501 *et seq.*)

The minimum tax credit for a tax year equals the excess, if any, of the adjusted net minimum tax (ANMT—i.e., the AMT paid for the year reduced by the amount of AMT that would have arisen without the deferral adjustments, plus certain other amounts) for all earlier post-'86 tax years, over the minimum tax credits taken in those years. (See FTC 2d/FIN ¶ A-8802 *et seq.*; USTR ¶ 534; TaxDesk ¶ 691,502 *et seq.*) Under pre-2006 Tax Relief and Health Care Act law, an individual's minimum tax credit for a tax year was limited by Code Sec. 53(c) to the excess of: (a) the individual's regular tax liability for the tax year to which the credit was being carried, reduced by the sum of his nonrefundable personal credits and business-related income tax credits for the year, over (b) his tentative minimum tax (i.e., AMT before deducting regular tax) for the year. (FTC 2d/FIN ¶ A-8801; USTR ¶ 534; TaxDesk ¶ 691,501)

Under pre-2006 Tax Relief and Health Care Act law, the minimum tax credit was nonrefundable—i.e., any amount in excess of the above-described Code Sec. 53(c) limitation could not be refunded. However, the "excess" could be carried forward (but not back) indefinitely. (FTC 2d/FIN ¶ A-8801; USTR ¶ 534; TaxDesk ¶ 691,501)

One of the deferral adjustments that can generate a minimum tax credit is the AMT adjustment for incentive stock options (ISOs). For regular tax purposes, the exercise of an ISO generally has no tax consequences. The individual isn't taxed on the "bargain element"—i.e., the excess of the stock's fair market value (FMV) on the date of exercise, over the amount paid for the stock. (The individual isn't taxed until he disposes of the stock, when he may have long-term capital gain.) (See FTC 2d/FIN ¶ H-2750; USTR ¶ 4224.01; TaxDesk ¶ 136,001.) But the individual must take the "bargain element" into account, as ordinary income, in computing AMTI (and gets a corresponding basis increase in the stock for AMT purposes). (See FTC 2d/FIN ¶s A-8302, A-8193; USTR ¶s 564.02, 564.01; TaxDesk ¶s 697,002, 695,502.) The AMT adjustment for ISOs is a deferral adjustment and therefore generates a minimum tax credit. The credit may be used to reduce regular tax in the year the stock is sold (Com Rept, see ¶ 5053), but under pre-2006 Tax Relief and Health Care Act law the individual couldn't get a refund for it.

New Law. The 2006 Tax Relief and Health Care Act provides that an individual's minimum tax credit for any tax year beginning before Jan. 1, 2013 can't be less than the "AMT refundable credit amount" (defined below), and makes that amount refundable. (Com Rept, see ¶ 5053)

> ***observation:*** While the statute itself doesn't refer specifically to the AMT ISO adjustment, the legislative history indicates that Congress provided the refundable credit in response to the hardships that resulted from the adjustment. For example, say that an employee exercised ISOs for 10,000 shares of stock at an exercise price of $2 a share, at a time when the stock was worth $100 a share. The exercise wouldn't result in regular tax income, but it would result in AMTI equal to the "bargain element," here $980,000. If the stock price later plummeted to $10, a sale of the stock wouldn't generate enough cash to pay the AMT liability. Although the minimum tax credit was available, its usefulness was curtailed by the Code Sec. 53(c) limitation.
>
> Under the new provision, individuals who become subject to the AMT, or whose AMT liability increases, as a result of exercising ISOs may be entitled to a refundable credit attributable to that AMT liability. However, the new provision doesn't alleviate the AMT burden that results from the ISO exercise.

Specifically, if an individual has a long-term unused minimum tax credit (defined below) for any tax year beginning before Jan. 1, 2013, the amount determined under the Code Sec. 53(c) limitation on the minimum tax credit for the tax year can't be less than the AMT refundable credit amount for that tax year. (Code Sec. 53(e)(1) as amended by 2006 Tax Relief and Health Care Act §402(a)) For refundability, see below.

> ***observation:*** In other words, the minimum tax credit allowable for the tax year is the greater of the AMT refundable credit amount or the amount of the credit otherwise allowable. New Code Sec. 53(e) thus provides a "minimum" minimum tax credit. The limitation prescribed by Code Sec. 53(c) is the maximum credit allowable for the year.

> ***illustration (1):*** Individual B has an AMT refundable credit amount equal to $20,000 for a tax year beginning before 2013. B's otherwise allowable minimum tax credit for the year (i.e., with the Code Sec. 53(c) limitation) is $15,000. B's minimum tax credit for the tax year is $20,000, the amount of the AMT refundable credit amount. Thus, B can reduce her regular tax liability for the tax year by $20,000. Under pre-2006 Tax Relief and Health Care Act law, B's minimum tax credit couldn't exceed $15,000, so she could reduce her regular tax liability by only $15,000.

AMT refundable credit amount defined. For purposes of the above rule, the term "AMT refundable credit amount" means, for any tax year, the amount equal to the greater of (Code Sec. 53(e)(2)(A)):

(1) the lesser of:

(a) $5,000, or

(b) the amount of the "long-term unused minimum tax credit" (defined below) for the tax year (Code Sec. 53(e)(2)(A)(i)),

or

(2) 20% of the amount of the long-term unused minimum tax credit. (Code Sec. 53(e)(2)(A)(ii))

The AMT refundable credit amount is reduced for high-income individuals, see further below.

> ***Illustration (2):*** In 2010, J, an individual, has AGI that results in a regular tax of $45,000, a tentative minimum tax of $40,000, no other credits allowable, and a minimum tax credit (before the Code Sec. 53(c) limitation) of $1.1 million, of which $1 million is a long-term unused mini-

---

FTC 2d References are to Federal Tax Coordinator 2d
FIN References are to RIAs Analysis of Federal Taxes: Income
USTR References are to United States Tax Reporter: Income, Estate & Gift, and Excise
PCA References are to Pension Analysis (print & electronic)
PE References are to Pension Explanations (print & electronic)
EP References are to Estate Planning Analysis (print & electronic)

mum tax credit. J's AMT refundable credit amount for 2010 is $200,000. The $200,000 amount is the greater of:

(i) $5,000—i.e., the lesser of (a) $5,000 or (b) the $1 million long-term unused minimum tax credit, or

(ii) $200,000—i.e., 20% of the $1 million long-term unused minimum tax credit.

(Com Rept, see ¶ 5053)

observation: As described above, an individual's minimum tax credit can't be less than his AMT refundable credit amount. Thus, in *Illustration (2),* J's minimum tax credit for 2010 can't be less than $200,000.

observation: For an individual with no long-term unused minimum tax credit, the AMT refundable credit amount is zero (greater of: [i] lesser of $5,000 or 0, or [ii] 20% × 0). Thus, an individual must have a long-term unused minimum tax credit to be entitled to the "minimum" minimum tax credit provided under this rule.

Reduction for high-income individuals. For an individual whose adjusted gross income (AGI) for any tax year exceeds the threshold amount under Code Sec. 151(d)(3)(C) (i.e., the AGI threshold at which the deduction for personal exemptions phases out, see the Observation below and FTC 2d/FIN ¶ A-3502; USTR ¶ 1514; TaxDesk ¶ 564,401), the AMT refundable credit amount as determined above for that year is reduced by the "applicable percentage" under Code Sec. 151(d)(3)(B) (i.e., the percentage reduction in the personal exemption amount, see the Observation below). (Code Sec. 53(e)(2)(B)(i))

observation: Under the rules for the phaseout of the personal exemption amount, an individual whose AGI for a tax year exceeds an annually-adjusted threshold amount must reduce his personal exemption amount by an "applicable percentage." The applicable percentage (which can't exceed 100%) is 2% for each $2,500 (or fraction thereof)—2% for each $1,250 (or fraction thereof) for married individuals filing separately—by which the individual's AGI exceeds the threshold amount.

observation: The new minimum tax credit rules are in effect for tax years beginning after date of enactment (see below). Because individuals generally use the calendar year as their tax year, the rules will first be effective for individuals for their 2007 tax years. For 2007, the AGI thresholds for the phaseout of the AMT refundable credit amount will be as follows:

. . . $234,600, for married individuals filing jointly and surviving spouses;

. . . $195,550, for heads of households;

. . . $156,400, for unmarried individuals (not surviving spouses); and

. . . $117,300, for married individuals filing separately.

Illustration (3): Assume that in *Illustration (2),* J's AGI for 2010 results in a Code Sec. 151(d)(3)(B) applicable percentage of 50%. J's AMT refundable credit amount for 2010 is $100,000 (20% × $1 million long-term unused minimum tax credit reduced by the 50% applicable percentage). J's minimum tax credit allowable for 2010 is $100,000 (the greater of the AMT refundable credit amount [$100,000] or the amount of the credit otherwise allowable). (Com Rept, see ¶ 5053)

observation: Code Sec. 151(d)(3)(E) provides for reductions in the personal exemption amount phaseout for tax years before 2010. The otherwise applicable phaseout amount is reduced by one-third in 2006 and 2007, by two-thirds in 2008 and 2009, and doesn't apply at all after 2009 (see FTC 2d/FIN ¶ A-3502; USTR ¶ 1514; TaxDesk ¶ 564,401). Although Code Sec. 53(e)(2)(B)(i), which prescribes the phaseout for the AMT refundable credit amount, specifically incorporates the Code Sec. 151(d)(3)(C) AGI threshold amounts and the Code Sec. 151(d)(3)(B) applicable percentages that are used in the phaseout of the personal exemption amounts, it doesn't refer to Code Sec. 151(d)(3)(E) or otherwise incorporate that subsection's reduction rules. Thus, it's not clear whether the AMT refundable credit amount is reduced by the full amount of the otherwise applicable phaseout amount for all tax years beginning before 2013.

For purposes of the AMT refundable credit amount phaseout under Code Sec. 53(e)(2)(B)(i), AGI is determined without regard to:

. . . Code Sec. 911 (foreign earned income exclusion for U.S. citizens or residents living abroad, see FTC 2d ¶ O-1101; USTR ¶ 9114; TaxDesk ¶ 191,001),

. . . Code Sec. 931 (exclusion of income for bona fide residents of American Samoa, see FTC 2d/FIN ¶ O-1430 *et seq.*; USTR ¶ 9314), and

---

. . . Code Sec. 933 (exclusion of income of residents of Puerto Rico, see FTC 2d/FIN ¶ O-1450 *et seq.*; USTR ¶ 9334). (Code Sec. 53(e)(2)(B)(ii))

Long-term unused minimum tax credit defined. For purposes of Code Sec. 53(e), the term "long-term unused minimum tax credit" means, with respect to any tax year, the portion of the minimum tax credit determined under Code Sec. 53(b) (i.e., the excess of the ANMT for all earlier tax years over the minimum tax credit for those years) attributable to the ANMT for tax years before the third tax year immediately preceding the tax year. (Code Sec. 53(e)(3)(A))

> ***observation:*** In other words, the long-term unused minimum tax credit—and, therefore, the AMT refundable credit amount—for a tax year doesn't take into account any minimum tax credit for the three immediately preceding tax years. The minimum tax credit amounts for those three years are allowable under the "regular" minimum tax credit rules. But because the "regular" minimum tax credit is nonrefundable, any unused amounts must be carried over to later tax years, rather than refunded (see below).

For purposes of determining the amount of the long-term unused minimum tax credit, credits are treated as allowed under Code Sec. 53(a) on a first-in, first-out (FIFO) basis. (Code Sec. 53(e)(3)(B))

Thus, the long-term unused minimum tax credit for any tax year means the portion of the minimum tax credit attributable to the ANMT for tax years before the third tax year immediately preceding the tax year (assuming the credits are used on a FIFO basis). (Com Rept, see ¶ 5053)

> ***observation:*** The FIFO requirement precludes taxpayers from using their credits from the immediately preceding three tax years before any credits from earlier years, to increase the amount of unused credits that could qualify as the long-term minimum tax credit and, as a result, increase the amount that can be refunded.

> ***observation:*** Many individuals in the dot.com industry were hit with a huge AMT liability in the '90s as a result of exercising ISOs. The resulting AMT liability meets the "preceding three tax years" requirement for the refundable portion of the minimum tax credit.

Portion of minimum tax credit is refundable. For purposes of the Internal Revenue Code (other than Code Sec. 53), the credit allowed by reason of Code Sec. 53(e) is treated as if it were allowed under subpart C (Code Sec. 31 through Code Sec. 36, relating to the refundable credits). (Code Sec. 53(e)(4)) This means that the additional credit allowable by reason of these rules is refundable (Com Rept, see ¶ 5053)—i.e., the excess of the credit over the taxpayer's tax liability may be refunded (see FTC 2d/FIN ¶ T-5511; USTR ¶ 64,014; TaxDesk ¶ 801,008).

For how the AMT refundable credit affects deficiency computations, see ¶ 1202.

> ***observation:*** For refundable credits, the amount by which the taxpayer's allowable credit for the tax year exceeds his tax liability for the year is treated as an overpayment of tax for the year (see FTC 2d/FIN ¶ T-5511; USTR ¶ 64,014; TaxDesk ¶ 801,008). The taxpayer can get a refund or credit of the overpayment through administrative action (e.g., by filing a refund claim), followed, if necessary, by a refund suit.

> ***observation:*** The "regular" minimum tax credit is nonrefundable. That is, unused amounts can only be carried over; they can't be refunded to the taxpayer. However, the carryover is indefinite (see FTC 2d/FIN ¶ A-8801; USTR ¶ 534; TaxDesk ¶ 691,501).

> ***Illustration (4):*** In 2010, Q, an individual, has AGI that results in a regular tax of $45,000, a tentative minimum tax of $40,000, no other credits allowable, a minimum tax credit (before the Code Sec. 53(c) limitation) of $1.1 million, and an AMT refundable credit amount of $100,000. Q's minimum tax credit allowable for the tax year is $100,000—the greater of the AMT refundable credit amount ($100,000) or the amount of the credit otherwise allowable ($5,000 [$45,000 regular tax – $40,000 tentative minimum tax]). The $5,000 credit allowable without regard to the new rules discussed above is nonrefundable. The additional $95,000 of credit allowable by reason of this provision is treated as a refundable credit. Thus, Q has an overpayment of $55,000 ($45,000 regular tax – $5,000 nonrefundable AMT credit – $95,000 refundable AMT credit). The $55,000 overpayment is allowed as a refund or credit to Q. The remaining $1 million minimum tax credit ($1.1 million – $100,000) is carried forward to future tax years. (Com Rept, see ¶ 5053)

☐ **Effective:** Tax years beginning after date of enactment (2006 Tax Relief and Health Care Act §402(c)) and before Jan. 1, 2013. (Com Rept, see ¶ 5053)

¶ 1202. AMT refundable credit may result in negative amount of tax in deficiency computation

Code Sec. 6211(b)(4)(A), as amended by 2006 Tax Relief and Health Care Act § 402(b)(1)

Generally effective: Tax years beginning after date of enactment

Committee Reports, see ¶ 5053

A deficiency is the amount by which the taxpayer's correct tax liability exceeds: (1) the tax shown on the return, plus (2) the amounts previously assessed (or collected without assessment) as a deficiency, reduced by (3) the amount of any rebate (see FTC 2d/FIN ¶ T-1501 *et seq.*; USTR ¶ 62,114; TaxDesk ¶ 822,501 *et seq.*) In this computation, the amount by which certain refundable credits exceed the tax imposed, or the tax shown on the return, without taking those credits into account, is taken into account as a negative amount of tax. As a result, Tax Court deficiency procedures apply to those credits even though they reduce net tax to zero. Under pre-2006 Tax Relief and Health Care Act law, this treatment applied only to the additional child tax credit (see FTC 2d/FIN ¶ A-4055; USTR ¶ 244.02; TaxDesk ¶ 569,105), the gasoline and special fuel tax credit under Code Sec. 34 (see FTC 2d/FIN ¶ A-4011.1; USTR ¶ 344), and the earned income credit (EIC, see FTC 2d/FIN ¶ A-4201; USTR ¶ 324; TaxDesk ¶ 569,001). (FTC 2d/FIN ¶ T-1505; USTR ¶ 62,114; TaxDesk ¶ 822,501)

New Law. Under new Code Sec. 53(e), a portion of the minimum tax credit—the "AMT refundable credit amount"—is made refundable, see ¶ 1201.

The 2006 Tax Relief and Health Care Act adds the Code Sec. 53(e) AMT refundable credit to the refundable credits that can be taken into account as negative amounts of tax in computing a deficiency. Specifically, any excess of: (a) the sum of the additional child tax credit, the gasoline and special fuel tax credit, the earned income credit (EIC), and the AMT refundable credit over (b) the tax imposed under subtitle A (i.e., income taxes: Code Sec. 1 through Code Sec. 1564), without taking those credits into account, is taken into account as a negative amount of tax. (Code Sec. 6211(b)(4)(A) as amended by 2006 Tax Relief and Health Care Act §402(b)(1))

> ***observation:*** Code Sec. 6211(b)(4)(B) provides that any excess of the sum of the Code Sec. 6211(b)(4)(A) credits over the amount shown as tax on the return, without taking those credits into account, is taken into account as a negative amount of tax. Thus, the AMT refundable credit is also included in this computation so as to result in a negative amount of tax.

> ***observation:*** Because the AMT refundable credit may thus result in a negative amount of tax, it enters into the deficiency computation.

Thus, if the taxpayer receives a refund attributable to the AMT refundable credit, but IRS later determines that the refund was paid in error, the "regular" deficiency procedures will apply. This means IRS may issue to the taxpayer a notice of deficiency (90-day letter, see FTC 2d/FIN ¶ T-2701 *et seq.*; USTR ¶ 62,124; TaxDesk ¶ 831,001 *et seq.*), which entitles the taxpayer to file a petition with the Tax Court within 90 days for redetermination of the deficiency. Absent the "negative amount of tax" treatment, the taxpayer couldn't go to Tax Court to contest IRS's determination. Instead, the taxpayer would have to repay the disputed refund amount, and then sue for a refund in the U.S. district court or the Court of Federal Claims (see FTC 2d/FIN ¶s T-9001, U-4201, U-6004; USTR ¶ 74,224 *et seq.*; TaxDesk ¶ 802,019).

illustration: Taxpayer's return claims an AMT refundable credit of $2,000, and shows a tax liability of $500. The "tax shown on the return" is –$1,500 ($500 tax liability – $2,000 AMT refundable credit). On audit, the entire AMT refundable credit is disallowed, resulting in a balance due of $500. There is a deficiency because the tax shown on the return (-$1,500) is less than the actual tax liability ($500). $1,500 ($2,000 – $500) of the AMT refundable credit is a negative amount of tax. IRS may issue a 90-day letter to the taxpayer for this amount. Taxpayer can file a Tax Court petition to contest IRS's determination.

☐ **Effective:** Tax years beginning after date of enactment. (2006 Tax Relief and Health Care Act §402(c))

FTC 2d References are to Federal Tax Coordinator 2d
FIN References are to RIAs Analysis of Federal Taxes: Income
USTR References are to United States Tax Reporter: Income, Estate & Gift, and Excise
PCA References are to Pension Analysis (print & electronic)
PE References are to Pension Explanations (print & electronic)
EP References are to Estate Planning Analysis (print & electronic)

¶ 1300. Foreign Provisions

¶ 1301. Look-through rule doesn't apply to dividends, interest, rents and royalties received from a CFC which are effectively connected with a U.S. trade or business for tax years beginning before 2009

Code Sec. 954(c)(6)(A), as amended by 2006 Tax Relief and Health Care Act § 426(a)(1)

Generally effective: Tax years of foreign corporations beginning after Dec. 31, 2005 and before Jan. 1, 2009 and tax years of U.S. shareholders with or within which such tax years of foreign corporations end

Committee Reports, see ¶ 5077

Under Subpart F, U.S. persons who are 10% shareholders (U.S. shareholders) of a controlled foreign corporation (CFC) are required to include in income their pro rata share of the CFC's subpart F income whether or not this income is distributed to the shareholders.

Subpart F income includes foreign base company income (FBCI), which in turn includes foreign personal holding income (FPHCI). For subpart F purposes, FPHCI includes dividends, interest, income equivalent to interest (including factoring income), rents and royalties. However, FPHCI does not include dividends and interest from a related corporation organized and operating in the same foreign country in which the CFC is organized, or rents and royalties received by a CFC from a related corporation for the use of property within the country in which the CFC is organized. Nevertheless, interest, rent, and royalty payments do not qualify for this exclusion to the extent that such payments reduce the payor's subpart F income or create (or increase) a deficit which under Code Sec. 952(c) may reduce the subpart F income of the payor or another CFC.

Subpart F income does not include any income items from U.S. sources which are effectively connected with the conduct by a CFC of a U.S. trade or business unless the item is exempt from tax, or is subject to a reduced tax rate under a U.S. treaty. (FTC 2d/FIN ¶s O-2303, O-2401, O-2424, O-2424.1, O-2432, O-2433, O-2439, O-2445; USTR ¶s 9544, 9544.02)

Under the Tax Increase Prevention Act (2005 TIPRA) § 103(b) (Sec. 103(b), PL 109-222, 5/17/2006) dividends, interest (including factoring income which is treated as equivalent to interest), rents, and royalties received or accrued from a

---

FTC 2d References are to Federal Tax Coordinator 2d
FIN References are to RIAs Analysis of Federal Taxes: Income
USTR References are to United States Tax Reporter: Income, Estate & Gift, and Excise
PCA References are to Pension Analysis (print & electronic)
PE References are to Pension Explanations (print & electronic)
EP References are to Estate Planning Analysis (print & electronic)

related CFC were not treated as FPHCI to the extent attributable or properly allocable to non-subpart F income of the related payor CFC (the "TIPRA look-through rule"). IRS was also authorized to issue regs to prevent the abuse of the TIPRA look-through rule. (FTC 2d/FIN ¶ O-2447.2; USTR ¶ 9544.02)

New Law. The 2006 Tax Relief and Health Care Act provides that for a payment from a related CFC to be excluded from FPHCI under the TIPRA look-through rule, the dividends, interest, rents or royalties received or accrued from the related CFC must not be attributable or allocable to either subpart F income or income treated as effectively connected with the conduct of a U.S. trade or business of the related CFC payor. (Code Sec. 954(c)(6)(A) as amended by 2006 Tax Relief and Health Care Act §426(a)(1)(A)) Income effectively connected with the conduct of a U.S. trade or business is referred to below as "ECI."

The provision conforms the TIPRA look-through rule to the rule's purpose of allowing U.S. companies to redeploy their active foreign earnings (i.e., CFC earnings subject to U.S. tax deferral) without an additional tax burden in appropriate circumstances. Absent this change, the TIPRA look-through rule would, for example, have allowed an interest payment made by a CFC that had only ECI (and therefore no subpart F income), to avoid being treated as subpart F income to the recipient CFC even though the payment could be deductible by the payor CFC for U.S. tax purposes. After the change, an interest payment made by a CFC does not qualify under the TIPRA look-through rule to the extent the interest payment is allocated to the CFC's ECI. (Com Rept, see ¶ 5077)

> ***observation:*** The 2006 Tax Relief and Health Care Act does not distinguish between the source, the statutory exemption from taxation or the tax treaty treatment of payments allocated to a related CFC's ECI. Therefore, a CFC that is in the active banking, finance, or similar business, or trades stocks or securities for its own account may have U.S. source and also foreign source income and economic equivalents that may be treated as income effectively connected with a U.S. trade or business. That's because a CFC's foreign source income is treated as ECI only if the CFC has an office or other fixed place of business in the U.S.; the income, gain, or loss is attributable to that U.S. office or other fixed place of business; and the income is one of the following:
>
> - rents and royalties from actively conducting a licensing business;
> - dividends or interest from actively conducting a banking, financing, or similar business in the U.S.;
> - dividends or interest received by a corporation the principal business of which is trading in stocks or securities for its own account; or
> - certain inventory sales attributable to a U.S. sales office. (FTC 2d/FIN ¶ O-10622; USTR ¶s 8644.04, 8644.05)

> ***observation:*** Accordingly, foreign source dividends, interest, rents and their economic equivalents or royalties that are received or accrued from a related CFC will not qualify under the TIPRA look-through rule to the extent attributable to the CFC's active banking, finance, or similar U.S. trade or business, or the income is from the CFC trading stocks or securities for its own account.

> ***observation:*** It appears that the amended TIPRA look-through rule would not apply if: (1) a related CFC pays dividends, interest, rents, or royalties out of income that's treated as ECI under Code Sec. 897 (gain or loss from the disposition of U.S. real property interests (USRPI) treated as ECI (see FTC 2d/FIN ¶ O-10701; USTR ¶ 8974) or (2) a related CFC elects under Code Sec. 882(d)(1) (see FTC 2d/FIN ¶ O-10615; USTR ¶ 8824) to treat all income from U.S. real property as if the taxpayer were engaged in a trade or business within the U.S. and it pays dividends, interest, rents, or royalties out of that income.

The 2006 Tax Relief and Health Care Act also authorizes IRS to issue regs that are necessary or appropriate to prevent abuse of the purpose of the amended TIPRA look-through rule. (Code Sec. 954(c)(6)(A) as amended by 2006 Tax Relief and Health Care Act §426(a)(1)(B)) Congress intends that IRS will issue regs that are necessary or appropriate to carry out the amended TIPRA look-through rule, including regs that prevent (1) the inappropriate use of the amended TIPRA look-through rule to strip income from the U.S. income tax base, and (2) the application of the amended TIPRA look-through rule to interest deemed to arise under certain related party factoring arrangements under Code Sec. 864(d) (see FTC 2d/FIN ¶ O-3201; USTR ¶ 8644.09), or under other transactions the net effect of which is the deduction of a payment, accrual, or loss for U.S. tax purposes without a corresponding increase in the subpart F income of the CFC income recipient, where an increase would have occurred absent the amended TIPRA look-through rule. (Com Rept, see ¶ 5077)

☐ **Effective:** Tax years of foreign corporations beginning after Dec. 31, 2005 and before Jan. 1, 2009, and tax years of U.S. shareholders with or within which the tax years of such foreign corporations end. (2006 Tax Relief and Health Care Act §426(a)(2))

> ***observation:*** The 2006 Tax Relief and Health Care Act § 426(a)(2) provides that the above changes are effective as if included in 2005 TIPRA §103(b) (Sec. 103(b), PL 109-222, 5/17/2006). 2005 TIPRA §

FTC 2d References are to Federal Tax Coordinator 2d
FIN References are to RIAs Analysis of Federal Taxes: Income
USTR References are to United States Tax Reporter: Income, Estate & Gift, and Excise
PCA References are to Pension Analysis (print & electronic)
PE References are to Pension Explanations (print & electronic)
EP References are to Estate Planning Analysis (print & electronic)

103(b) amended Code Sec. 954(c)(6)(B) to provide that the changes made by § 103(b) to Code Sec. 954(c)(6)(A) take effect for tax years of foreign corporations beginning after Dec. 31, 2005 and before Jan. 1, 2009, and tax years of U.S. shareholders with or within which the tax years of such foreign corporations end.

¶ 1302. Domestic production activities deduction extended retroactively to production activities in Puerto Rico for first two tax years beginning after 2005

Code Sec. 199(d)(8), as amended by 2006 Tax Relief and Health Care Act § 401(a)

Generally effective: First two tax years beginning after Dec. 31, 2005 and before Jan. 1, 2008

Committee Reports, see ¶ 5052

Starting with tax years beginning in 2005, Code Sec. 199 (enacted by Sec. 102 of the 2004 Jobs Act (Sec. 102, PL 108-357, 10/22/2004)) allows taxpayers—including sole proprietorships, C corporations, agricultural and horticultural cooperatives, and the owners of interests in pass-thru entities (partnerships, S corporations, estates and trusts)—to claim a deduction (the "domestic production activities deduction" [DPAD]) that is equal to a percentage of the income earned from production activities undertaken in the U.S. Eligible activities include manufacturing, food production, software development, film and music production, production of electricity, natural gas or water, real property construction, and engineering and architectural services performed in connection with real property construction.

The Code Sec. 199 deduction equals the lesser of:

(1) a percentage (3% for tax years beginning in 2006, 6% for tax years beginning in 2007-2009, and 9% in later years) of the smaller of—

(a) the taxpayer's "qualified production activities income" for the tax year, or

(b) the taxpayer's taxable income (modified adjusted gross income, for individual taxpayers), without regard to the Code Sec. 199 deduction, for the tax year.

(2) 50% of the W-2 wages of the employer for the tax year that are allocable to domestic production gross receipts. These wages are the sum of the aggregate amounts that must be included on the Forms W-2 of employees under Code Sec. 6051(a)(3)—i.e., wages subject to withholding under Code Sec. 3401(a)—and Code Sec. 6051(a)(8) (elective deferrals). Under specified circumstances, Code Sec. 3401(a)(8) excludes remuneration paid to U.S. citizens for services performed within Puerto Rico from being treated as wages subject to withhold-

ing. See FTC 2d/FIN ¶ H-4446; USTR ¶ 34,014.23; TaxDesk ¶ 536,017. Under pre-2006 Tax Relief and Health Care Act law, this meant that wages paid to bona fide residents of Puerto Rico weren't treated as W-2 wages for Code Sec. 199 purposes. (Com Rept, see ¶ 5052)

"Qualified production activities income" is equal to "domestic production gross receipts," with specified reductions. Generally, domestic production gross receipts are the taxpayer's gross receipts derived from:

. . . any lease, rental, license, sale, exchange or other disposition ("qualified disposition") of qualifying production property (tangible personal property, computer software, certain sound recordings) that was manufactured, produced, grown or extracted by the taxpayer in whole or in significant part within the U.S.;

. . . any qualified disposition of a qualified film—a film if at least 50% of the total compensation relating to its production is compensation for services performed in the U.S. by actors, production personnel, directors and producers—if the film was produced by the taxpayer;

. . . any qualified disposition of electricity, natural gas, or potable water produced by the taxpayer in the U.S.;

. . . real property construction activities performed in the U.S.; or

. . . engineering or architectural services performed in connection with U.S. real property construction projects.

For purposes of the Code Sec. 199 rules, under pre-2006 Tax Relief and Health Care Act law, the U.S. included only the 50 states, the District of Columbia, the territorial waters of the U.S., and the seabed and subsoil of those submarine areas that are adjacent to the territorial waters of the U.S. Under pre-2006 Tax Relief and Health Care Act law, the U.S. did not include Puerto Rico, or other possessions and territories of the U.S. or the airspace over the U.S. and these areas. (FTC 2d/FIN ¶ L-4325 *et seq.*, ¶ L-4339, ¶ L-4385 *et seq.*, ¶ L-4339; USTR ¶ 1994 *et seq.*; TaxDesk ¶ 307,800 *et seq.*, ¶ 307,803)

New Law. Under the 2006 Tax Relief and Health Care Act, for any taxpayer that has gross receipts from sources within the Commonwealth of Puerto Rico for either of its first two tax years beginning after 2005 (see below), if all of those receipts are taxable for that tax year under either Code Sec. 1 (imposing taxes on individuals, see FTC 2d/FIN ¶ A-1101 *et seq.*; USTR ¶ 14 *et seq.*; TaxDesk ¶ 568,201 *et seq.*, and on estates and trusts, see FTC 2d/FIN ¶ C-1003; USTR ¶ 14.03; TaxDesk ¶s 651,003, 661,003) or Code Sec. 11 (imposing

---

FTC 2d References are to Federal Tax Coordinator 2d
FIN References are to RIAs Analysis of Federal Taxes: Income
USTR References are to United States Tax Reporter: Income, Estate & Gift, and Excise
PCA References are to Pension Analysis (print & electronic)
PE References are to Pension Explanations (print & electronic)
EP References are to Estate Planning Analysis (print & electronic)

taxes on regular corporations, see FTC 2d/FIN ¶ D-1103; USTR ¶ 114.01; TaxDesk ¶ 600,503), then, for purposes of determining the domestic production gross receipts of that taxpayer for that tax year, the term "U.S." includes the Commonwealth of Puerto Rico. (Code Sec. 199(d)(8)(A) as amended by 2006 Tax Relief and Health Care Act §401(a)) In other words, a taxpayer is allowed to treat Puerto Rico as part of the U.S. for purposes of the Code Sec. 199 rules, thus allowing the taxpayer to take into account its Puerto Rico business activity for purposes of calculating its domestic production gross receipts and qualified production activities income, but only if the gross receipts from sources within Puerto Rico are currently taxable for U.S. federal income tax purposes. Consequently, a controlled foreign corporation (CFC, see FTC 2d/FIN ¶ O-2301 *et seq.*; USTR ¶ 9514 *et seq.*) is not eligible for the Code Sec. 199 deduction for its Puerto Rico activities. (Com Rept, see ¶ 5052)

observation: Put another way, if a taxpayer has gross receipts sourced within Puerto Rico that would qualify as domestic production gross receipts if they had been sourced within the U.S. as defined above, the new rule allows those gross receipts to be treated as domestic production gross receipts.

Presumably, a taxpayer's gross receipts from sources within Puerto Rico are determined under the regular sourcing rules of Code Sec. 861 and Code Sec. 862, see FTC 2d/FIN ¶ O-10901 *et seq.*; USTR ¶s 8614 *et seq.*, 8624 *et seq.*; TaxDesk ¶ 633,001 *et seq.*

observation: Under Code Sec. 1, U.S. citizens and residents are generally taxable on their worldwide income, including income arising from gross receipts from sources in Puerto Rico, see FTC 2d/FIN ¶ O-1001 *et seq.*; USTR ¶ 14 *et seq.*; TaxDesk ¶ 190,501 *et seq.* However, any individual (whether or not a U.S. citizen) who is a bona fide resident of Puerto Rico for the entire tax year excludes all income from sources in Puerto Rico, except pay as a U.S. employee. And if a U.S. citizen who has been a bona fide resident of Puerto Rico for at least two years changes his residence from Puerto Rico, he excludes income from Puerto Rican sources (except pay as a U.S. employee) attributable to the period before he moved. See FTC 2d/FIN ¶ O-1451 *et seq.*; USTR ¶ 9314.04.

Under Code Sec. 11, U.S. domestic corporations are also generally taxable on their worldwide income, including income arising from gross receipts from sources in Puerto Rico, see FTC 2d/FIN ¶ O-1006. Foreign corporations engaged in a U.S. trade or business are taxed, also under Code Sec. 11, on their U.S. source income that's effectively connected with the conduct of a U.S. trade or business, see FTC 2d/FIN ¶ O-10602; USTR ¶ 114.02; TaxDesk ¶ 641,001, except for certain specifically excluded items, see FTC 2d/FIN ¶ O-10303 *et seq.*; USTR ¶ 8834; TaxDesk ¶ 644,510 *et seq.*

Where a taxpayer has gross receipts sourced in Puerto Rico that aren't eligible for any of these exclusions, the new rule allows those gross receipts to be treated as domestic production gross receipts that are eligible for the U.S. production activities deduction. But the requirement that all of those gross receipts must be taxable under Code Sec. 1 or Code Sec. 11 would seem to mean that the taxpayer's Puerto Rican operations must be conducted by a branch or division that is *not* separately incorporated "offshore." That requirement would also seem to mean that if any part of the taxpayer's gross receipts are eligible for any of the exclusions from taxability under Code Sec. 1 or Code Sec. 11, then none of the taxpayer's gross receipts sourced in Puerto Rico are eligible for treatment as domestic production gross receipts.

illustration: Through a branch, Taxpayer, a U.S. corporation, produces widgets (tangible personal property) in Puerto Rico, and sells the widgets worldwide. The widgets are qualifying production property. Taxpayer is treated as producing the widgets wholly in Puerto Rico. Taxpayer's receipts from these sales are fully taxable under Code Sec. 11. Therefore, Taxpayer's gross receipts from its widget sales in its tax year beginning in 2006 are domestic production gross receipts.

W-2 wage limitation. Under the 2006 Tax Relief and Health Care Act, for any taxpayer with gross receipts from Puerto Rico that are eligible to be treated as domestic production gross receipts under the above new rule, for purposes of applying the "50%-of-W-2-wages limitation" on the domestic production activities deduction for any tax year, the determination of W-2 wages of that taxpayer is made without regard to any exclusion under Code Sec. 3401(a)(8) for remuneration paid for services performed in Puerto Rico. (Code Sec. 199(d)(8)(B)). This rule allows the taxpayer to take into account wages paid to bona fide residents of Puerto Rico for purposes of calculating the 50%-of-W-2-wages limitation. (Com Rept, see ¶ 5052)

☐ **Effective:** Tax years beginning after Dec. 31, 2005 (2006 Tax Relief and Health Care Act §401(b)), but only for a taxpayer's first two tax years beginning after that date and before Jan. 1, 2008. (Code Sec. 199(d)(8)(C)).

¶ 1303. Possessions tax credit for American Samoa retroactively extended through 2007 for existing claimants

Code Sec. 30A, 2006 Tax Relief and Health Care Act § 119
Generally effective: Tax years beginning after Dec. 31, 2005 and before Jan. 1, 2008
Committee Reports, see ¶ 5023

For tax years beginning before Jan. 1, 2006, a U.S. corporation that was an existing credit claimant could claim the Code Sec. 936 possessions tax credit in lieu of the foreign tax credit for certain possessions trade or business income. Thus, the possessions tax credit expired for existing credit claimants for tax years beginning after Dec. 31, 2005. (FTC 2d/FIN ¶ O-1504; USTR ¶ 9314.06; TaxDesk ¶ 394,500, ¶ 394,501)

In order to claim the credit:

- 80% or more of the corporation's gross income for the preceding 3-year period had to be from the possession, and,
- 75% or more of the corporation's gross income for the same period had to be from the active conduct of a trade or business within the possession. (FTC 2d/FIN ¶ O-1513.1; USTR ¶ 9314.06; TaxDesk ¶ 394,519)

An existing credit claimant generally was a U.S. corporation that was operating a business in a U.S. possession on Oct. 13, '95, and which had an election to use the possessions tax credit in effect on that date. A corporation's status as an existing credit claimant (and the amount of the credit) was determined separately for each possession. (FTC 2d/FIN ¶ O-1502; USTR ¶ 9314.06; TaxDesk ¶ 394,515)

The credit was computed on Form 5735, and generally was equal to the tax on the corporation's income from the active conduct of a business within a possession or from the sale or exchange of substantially all of the assets used in the business (possession business income), subject to the limitations described below. (FTC 2d/FIN ¶ O-1513; USTR ¶ 9314.06; TaxDesk ¶ 394,503)

Existing credit claimants had to limit the credit either to a percentage of the otherwise allowable credit (40% for tax years beginning after '97 (the applicable percentage limitation)) or the amount determined under a formula for economic activity in the possession (the economic activity limitation). (FTC 2d/FIN ¶ O-1517, ¶ O-1519; USTR ¶ 9314.06; TaxDesk ¶ 394,505). The economic activity limitation was equal to the sum of:

- 60% of qualified wages and fringe benefit expenses,

• various percentages of short, medium and long-term depreciable tangible property, and

• if the corporation does not have an election to use the profit split method to determine taxable income in effect, the amount of the qualified possession income taxes allocable to nonsheltered income. (FTC 2d/FIN ¶ O-1518; USTR ¶ 9314.06; TaxDesk ¶ 394,505)

For certain other possessions, but not American Samoa, the amount of income that was eligible for the credit was further limited to the adjusted base period income. (FTC 2d/FIN ¶ O-1605.1; USTR ¶ 9314.06; TaxDesk ¶ 394,507)

> ***observation:*** The credit was available regardless of the amount of tax paid to the government of the possession. The effect of the credit was to exempt possessions income from U.S. tax, except to the extent that the credit-limitation applied. For existing credit claimants relating to Puerto Rico that used the economic-activity-based limit, the credit was determined under Code Sec. 30A, rather than under Code Sec. 936.

No deduction or foreign tax credit was allowed for any possessions or foreign tax paid or accrued on taxable income that was taken into account in computing the possessions tax credit. (FTC 2d/FIN ¶ O-1510; USTR ¶ 9314.06; TaxDesk ¶ 394,510)

> ***observation:*** All other foreign source income of a domestic corporation that made a Code Sec. 936 election was taxed currently (with allowances for the regular foreign tax credit).

New Law. The 2006 Tax Relief and Health Care Act extends the possessions tax credit for American Samoa for the first two tax years of a corporation which begin after Dec. 31, 2005 and before Jan. 1, 2008. (2006 Tax Relief and Health Care Act §119(d)) In other words, a domestic corporation that is an existing credit claimant as to American Samoa and that elected the application of Code Sec. 936 for its last tax year beginning before Jan. 1, 2006, is allowed, for two tax years, a credit based on the economic activity-based limitation rules described above. (Com Rept, see ¶ 5023).

Congress intends that the two-year extension of the credit will provide additional time for the development of a comprehensive, long-term economic policy toward American Samoa. Congress expects that in developing a long-term policy, non-tax policy alternatives should be carefully considered and that long-

FTC 2d References are to Federal Tax Coordinator 2d
FIN References are to RIAs Analysis of Federal Taxes: Income
USTR References are to United States Tax Reporter: Income, Estate & Gift, and Excise
PCA References are to Pension Analysis (print & electronic)
PE References are to Pension Explanations (print & electronic)
EP References are to Estate Planning Analysis (print & electronic)

term policy toward the possessions should take into account the unique circumstances in each possession. (Com Rept, see ¶ 5023)

> ***observation:*** The possessions tax credit for all other possessions is not applicable for tax years beginning after Dec. 31, 2005. This uncodified act section extends the tax credit for American Samoa by overriding the expiration dates that remain in the Internal Revenue Code.

Under the rules extending the credit, for purposes of the Code Sec. 30A credit, a domestic corporation is treated as a qualified corporation if the corporation:

(1) is an existing credit claimant as to American Samoa (2006 Tax Relief and Health Care Act §119(a)(1)), and

(2) elected the application of Code Sec. 936 for its last tax year beginning before Jan. 1, 2006. (2006 Tax Relief and Health Care Act §119(a)(2))

Thus, existing credit claimants that conduct business in American Samoa may claim the credit using the economic-activity-based limitation, but not the percentage limitation. (Com Rept, see ¶ 5023)

Notwithstanding the pre-2006 Tax Relief and Health Care Act limitations described in Code Sec. 30A(a)(1), the amount of the credit for any tax year is the economic-activity-based limitation amount determined under Code Sec. 30A(d), as described above, except that this amount is determined without including the amount of the qualified possession income taxes allocable to nonsheltered income. (2006 Tax Relief and Health Care Act §119(b)(1))

> ***observation:*** Thus, the pre-2006 Tax Relief and Health Care Act adjusted base period income limitation does not apply to taxpayers operating in American Samoa. As described above, the adjusted base period income limitation also did not apply to taxpayers operating in American Samoa under pre-2006 Tax Relief and Health Care Act law.

The credit is, therefore, equal to the sum of the amounts used in computing the corporation's economic activity-based limitation under pre-2006 Tax Relief and Health Care Act law, except that no credit is allowed for the amount of any American Samoa income taxes. (Com Rept, see ¶ 5023)

> ***observation:*** Thus, the amount of the credit is equal to the sum of:
>
> - 60% of qualified wages and fringe benefit expenses, and
> - various percentages of short, medium and long-term depreciable tangible property.

The pre-2006 Tax Relief and Health Care Act rule that a corporation's status as an existing credit claimant (and the amount of the credit) is determined separately for each possession applies so that these rules are applied separately for American Samoa. (2006 Tax Relief and Health Care Act §119(b)(2))

However, the pre-2006 Tax Relief and Health Care Act rule barring a deduction or foreign tax credit for foreign or possessions tax paid or accrued on taxable income that was taken into account in computing the possessions tax credit does not apply for the 2006 Tax Relief and Health Care Act American Samoa tax credit. (2006 Tax Relief and Health Care Act §119(b)(3))

For purposes of the 2006 Tax Relief and Health Care Act American Samoa tax credit, any term which is used in this section which is also used in Code Sec. 30A or Code Sec. 936, has the same meaning given the term by Code Sec. 30A or Code Sec. 936. (2006 Tax Relief and Health Care Act §119(c))

☐ **Effective:** First two tax years of a corporation which begin after Dec. 31, 2005 and before Jan. 1, 2008. (2006 Tax Relief and Health Care Act §119(d)).

¶ 1400. Tax Administration

¶ 1401. Tax Court has jurisdiction to review IRS's denial of equitable innocent spouse relief from joint liability even if no deficiency was asserted against the requestor of relief

Code Sec. 6015(e)(1), as amended by 2006 Tax Relief and Health Care Act § 408(a)(Div. C, Title IV)

Code Sec. 6015(e)(1)(A)(i)(II), as amended by 2006 Tax Relief and Health Care Act § 408(b)(1)(Div. C, Title IV)

Code Sec. 6015(e)(1)(B)(i), as amended by 2006 Tax Relief and Health Care Act § 408(b)(2)(Div. C, Title IV)

Code Sec. 6015(e)(1)(B)(ii), as amended by 2006 Tax Relief and Health Care Act § 408(b)(3)(Div. C, Title IV)

Code Sec. 6015(e)(4), as amended by 2006 Tax Relief and Health Care Act § 408(b)(4)(Div. C, Title IV)

Code Sec. 6015(e)(5), as amended by 2006 Tax Relief and Health Care Act § 408(b)(5)(Div. C, Title IV)

Code Sec. 6015(g)(2), as amended by 2006 Tax Relief and Health Care Act § 408(b)(6)(Div. C, Title IV)

Code Sec. 6015(h)(2), as amended by 2006 Tax Relief and Health Care Act § 408(b)(7)(Div. C, Title IV)

Generally effective: Liability for taxes arising or remaining unpaid on or after date of enactment

Committee Reports, None

Married taxpayers who elect to do so may file joint income tax returns (FTC 2d/FIN ¶ S-1801; USTR ¶ 60,134; TaxDesk ¶ 570,601), but if they do, they become jointly and severally liable for any unpaid tax or deficiency, see FTC 2d/FIN ¶ V-8501; USTR ¶ 60,134.05; TaxDesk ¶ 570,901. Spouses who may have unforthcoming husbands or wives can seek relief from joint and several liability by electing innocent spouse or separate liability relief or requesting equitable relief, see FTC 2d/FIN ¶ V-8500; USTR ¶ 60,154; TaxDesk ¶ 570,900.

Generally, to qualify for innocent spouse relief, there must be an understatement of tax on the return that is attributable to erroneous items of the other spouse and about which the taxpayer *did not know or have reason to know* and it must be inequitable to hold the electing spouse liable, see FTC 2d/FIN ¶ V-

FTC 2d References are to Federal Tax Coordinator 2d
FIN References are to RIAs Analysis of Federal Taxes: Income
USTR References are to United States Tax Reporter: Income, Estate & Gift, and Excise
PCA References are to Pension Analysis (print & electronic)
PE References are to Pension Explanations (print & electronic)
EP References are to Estate Planning Analysis (print & electronic)

8506; USTR ¶ 60,154.01; TaxDesk ¶ 570,904. For separate liability relief, the spouses must be divorced or separated, there must be an understatement of tax attributable to the other spouse, and the electing spouse must not have known about the understatement (i.e., doesn't have actual knowledge), see FTC 2d/FIN ¶ V-8533; USTR ¶ 60,154.02; TaxDesk ¶ 570,933. Finally, taxpayers who don't qualify for innocent spouse or separate liability relief may request equitable relief. Equitable relief is available for taxpayers who can establish that it would be inequitable to hold them liable, but who for some reason don't qualify for the other two types of relief. It is also the only relief available when there is no deficiency or understatement of tax on a return, i.e., when a return shows the correct tax, but not all the tax has been paid, see FTC 2d/FIN ¶ V-8553; USTR ¶ 60,154.04; TaxDesk ¶ 570,953.

If IRS denies a taxpayer's claim for innocent spouse relief or separate liability relief, the taxpayer can file a petition for review of the denial in the Tax Court. The time for filing the petition with the Tax Court is any time after the earlier of the date IRS mails, by certified or registered mail to the taxpayer's last known address, notice of IRS's final determination of relief, or the date which is 6 months after the date the election under Code Sec. 6015(b) or Code Sec. 6015(c) is filed with IRS, and not later than the close of the 90th day after the date IRS mails its notice of determination. (FTC 2d/FIN ¶ U-2148; USTR ¶ 60,154.03)

Whether the Tax Court has jurisdiction to review IRS denials of equitable relief has been the subject of litigation. Under pre-2006 Tax Relief and Health Care Act law, the Eighth and Ninth Circuits had held (and the Tax Court later changed its position and agreed) that the Tax Court had no jurisdiction to review denials of equitable relief in cases in which IRS had not asserted a deficiency against the party that requested relief. See, for example, *Ewing,* (2006, CA9) 97 AFTR 2d 2006-1224, and *Billings,* (2006) 127 TC No. 2. These cases usually involved taxpayers who filed accurate returns but did not pay the tax shown on their return. (FTC 2d/FIN ¶ U-2148.1; USTR ¶ 60,154.04)

Except as otherwise provided under the rules for termination assessments under Code Sec. 6851 or jeopardy assessments under Code Sec. 6861, no levy or court proceeding may be made, begun, or prosecuted against an individual who has made an innocent spouse or separate liability election, to collect any assessment to which the election relates, until the close of the 90-day period during which the individual may file a petition for review or, if a Tax Court petition has been filed, until the Tax Court's decision has become final. (FTC 2d/FIN ¶ U-2149; USTR ¶ 60,154.03)

Notwithstanding the prohibition on suits to restrain levy and assessment, the beginning of a levy or court proceeding during the time it is barred under the rule in the above paragraph may be enjoined by a proceeding in the proper court, including the Tax Court. But the Tax Court can't issue an injunction under this rule unless a timely petition has been filed to determine the effect of the innocent spouse or separate liability election, and then only in respect of the amount of the assessment to which the election relates. Likewise, a motion to restrain assessment or collection or to order refund of an amount collected may be filed with the Tax Court only if a timely petition has been filed with the Tax Court. (FTC 2d/FIN ¶ U-2149; USTR ¶ 60,154.03)

Taxpayers who agree with IRS's determination of innocent spouse or separate liability relief can waive in writing the restrictions on collection of an outstanding assessment (discussed above), whether or not IRS has mailed a notice of a final determination of relief. (FTC 2d/FIN ¶ T-3414; USTR ¶ 60,154.03; TaxDesk ¶ 570,950)

The Tax Court was required to establish rules giving the spouse who filed a joint return but didn't make the innocent spouse or separate liability election (the "non-electing spouse") adequate notice and an opportunity to become a party to a Tax Court proceeding under either the innocent spouse or separate liability election. (FTC 2d/FIN ¶ U-2152; USTR ¶ 60,154.03)

If a decision of a court in any earlier proceeding for the same tax year has become final, determinations made in the final decision are conclusive (i.e., *res judicata*), except with respect to the spouse's qualification for relief under the innocent spouse election or the separate liability election, if that relief wasn't an issue in the earlier proceeding. (FTC 2d/FIN ¶ U-2151; USTR ¶ 60,154.03)

IRS has prescribed regs that provide the opportunity for a spouse to have notice of, and to participate in, any administrative proceeding concerning an innocent spouse election or a separate liability election made by the other spouse. (FTC 2d/FIN ¶ V-8550; USTR ¶ 60,154; TaxDesk ¶ 570,950)

New Law. The 2006 Tax Relief and Health Care Act grants taxpayers the right to petition the Tax Court (and gives the Tax Court jurisdiction) to determine the appropriate relief available to an individual who elects equitable relief under Code Sec. 6015(f). (Code Sec. 6015(e)(1) as amended by 2006 Tax Relief and Health Care Act §408(a)(Div. C, Title IV))

> ***observation:*** The Tax Court review of the equitable innocent spouse relief provision that is being analyzed here appears in Division C of the 2006 Tax Relief and Health Care Act.

> ***observation:*** The 2006 Tax Relief and Health Care Act grants the right of petition discussed above by adding the phrase "or in the case of an individual who requests equitable relief under Code Sec. 6015(f)" after the language, "In the case of an individual against whom a defi-

FTC 2d References are to Federal Tax Coordinator 2d
FIN References are to RIAs Analysis of Federal Taxes: Income
USTR References are to United States Tax Reporter: Income, Estate & Gift, and Excise
PCA References are to Pension Analysis (print & electronic)
PE References are to Pension Explanations (print & electronic)
EP References are to Estate Planning Analysis (print & electronic)

ciency has been asserted," which is the language the Eighth and Ninth Circuits and the Tax Court had cited in concluding that the Tax Court lacked jurisdiction to review IRS denials of equitable relief when no deficiency had been asserted against a taxpayer. Thus, the 2006 Tax Relief and Health Care Act gives the Tax Court jurisdiction to review *all* cases involving IRS's determination of relief from joint and several liability.

Period of limitations for petitioning the Tax Court. Under the 2006 Tax Relief and Health Care Act, the provision governing the time within which an individual must file a petition with the Tax Court also applies in the case of requests for equitable relief under Code Sec. 6015(f). (Code Sec. 6015(e)(1)(A)(i)(II) as amended by 2006 Tax Relief and Health Care Act §408(b)(1)(Div. C, Title IV))

observation: Thus, the period of limitations for petitioning the Tax Court to determine a request for equitable relief under Code Sec. 6015(f) is suspended for 6 months after the claim or request for equitable innocent spouse relief is made and remains pending.

Restriction on collection of an assessment. Under the 2006 Tax Relief and Health Care Act, the provisions requiring restrictions on collection of an assessment until the Tax Court enters a final decision also applies in the case of requests for equitable relief under Code Sec. 6015(f). (Code Sec. 6015(e)(1)(B)(i) as amended by 2006 Tax Relief and Health Care Act §408(b)(2)(Div. C, Title IV)); (Code Sec. 6015(e)(1)(B)(ii) as amended by 2006 Tax Relief and Health Care Act §408(b)(3)(Div. C, Title IV))

Non-requesting spouse as a party to Tax Court proceeding. Under the 2006 Tax Relief and Health Care Act, the provision requiring adequate notice to the non-requesting spouse and an opportunity to become a party to the Tax Court proceeding also applies in the case of requests for equitable relief under Code Sec. 6015(f). (Code Sec. 6015(e)(4) as amended by 2006 Tax Relief and Health Care Act §408(b)(4)(Div. C, Title IV))

Waiver of restriction on collection. Under the 2006 Tax Relief and Health Care Act, the provision permitting the requesting spouse to waive the restriction on collection mentioned above also applies in the case of requests for equitable relief under Code Sec. 6015(f). (Code Sec. 6015(e)(5) as amended by 2006 Tax Relief and Health Care Act §408(b)(5)(Div. C, Title IV))

Application of res judicata in joint liability relief cases. Under the 2006 Tax Relief and Health Care Act, the provision governing the application of *res judicata* in joint liability relief cases also applies in the case of requests for equitable relief under Code Sec. 6015(f). (Code Sec. 6015(g)(2) as amended by 2006 Tax Relief and Health Care Act §408(b)(6)(Div. C, Title IV))

Regs permitting non-requesting spouse to participate in any administrative proceeding. Under the 2006 Tax Relief and Health Care Act, the provision requiring IRS to issue regs requiring the non-requesting spouse to be notified and have the opportunity to participate in any administrative proceeding under Code Sec. 6015 also applies in the case of requests for equitable relief under Code Sec. 6015(f). (Code Sec. 6015(h)(2) as amended by 2006 Tax Relief and Health Care Act §408(b)(7)(Div. C, Title IV))

> ***observation:*** Thus, all of the procedural rules that governed administrative and judicial proceedings that applied to innocent spouse and separate liability claims under pre-2006 Tax Relief and Health Care Act law also apply under the 2006 Tax Relief and Health Care Act to requests for equitable relief.

☐ **Effective:** Liability for taxes arising or remaining unpaid on or after date of enactment (2006 Tax Relief and Health Care Act §408(c)(Div. C, Title IV)).

¶ 1402. IRS's authority to exercise reasonable cause exception from continuation of interest on reportable avoidance transactions and listed transactions, is clarified

Code Sec. 6404(g)(2), 2006 Tax Relief and Health Care Act § 426(b)
Generally effective: For interest accruing on, before, or after Oct. 3, 2004
Committee Reports, see ¶ 5077

Under Code Sec. 6404(g)(1), where a taxpayer files a timely income tax return, IRS must suspend the imposition of interest (and penalties) with respect to any failure relating to that return (with certain exceptions such as those discussed below) if IRS doesn't provide a required notice to the taxpayer within a specified 18-month period (see FTC 2d/FIN ¶s V-1401, V-1601.2; USTR ¶ 64,044; TaxDesk ¶s 837,509, 852,006). An exception to this rule (under Code Sec. 6404(g)(2)), which applies to interest accruing on, before, or after Oct. 3, 2004, provides that there's no suspension of interest (i.e., there's a "continuation of interest") with respect to "reportable avoidance transactions" and "listed transactions" even if IRS provides the required notice (see FTC 2d/FIN ¶ V-1401.1; USTR ¶ 64,044; TaxDesk ¶ 852,006.1).

However, Sec. 903(d)(2)(B) of the 2004 Jobs Act, as amended by Sec. 303(a)(1) of the 2005 Gulf Opportunity Zone Act, provides some special cases

---

FTC 2d References are to Federal Tax Coordinator 2d
FIN References are to RIAs Analysis of Federal Taxes: Income
USTR References are to United States Tax Reporter: Income, Estate & Gift, and Excise
PCA References are to Pension Analysis (print & electronic)
PE References are to Pension Explanations (print & electronic)
EP References are to Estate Planning Analysis (print & electronic)

in which interest may still be suspended with respect to reportable avoidance transactions and listed transactions. Among those special cases, Sec. 903(d)(2)(B)(iii) provides that the Secretary of the Treasury may except from the continuation of interest rules any transaction in which the taxpayer acted reasonably and in good faith. (FTC 2d/FIN ¶ V-1401.1; USTR ¶ 64,044; TaxDesk ¶ 852,006.1) For provisions included in the Code, Code Sec. 7701(a)(11) provides that the term "Secretary of the Treasury" means the Secretary in his non-delegable capacity, and that the term "Secretary" means the Secretary or his delegate. However, because Sec. 903 of the 2004 Jobs Act is not a provision of the Code (Com Rept, see ¶ 5077), these definitions aren't applicable.

New Law. The 2006 Tax Relief and Health Care Act amends Sec. 903(d)(2)(B)(iii) of the 2004 Jobs Act (as modified by the 2005 Gulf Opportunity Zone Act) to provide that the Secretary of the Treasury *or the Secretary's delegate* may except from the continuation of interest rules any transaction in which the taxpayer acted reasonably and in good faith. (2004 Jobs Act § 903(d)(2)(B)(iii) as amended by 2005 Gulf Opportunity Zone Act § 303(a) and 2006 Tax Relief and Health Care Act §426(b)(1)) This change is intended to clarify that the Secretary may delegate authority under Sec. 903 of the 2004 Jobs Act (as modified). (Com Rept, see ¶ 5077)

☐ **Effective:** For interest accruing on, before, or after Oct. 3, 2004. (2006 Tax Relief and Health Care Act §426(b)(2))

> ***observation:*** 2006 Tax Relief and Health Care Act § 426(b)(2) provides that the above-described change is effective as if included in the provision of the 2004 Jobs Act to which the above rules relate. The above rules relate to 2004 Jobs Act § 903(d)(2)(B)(iii) (Sec. 903(d)(2)(B)(iii), PL 108-357, 10/22/2004) as amended by 2005 Gulf Opportunity Zone Act § 303(a)(1) (Sec. 303(a)(1), PL 109-135, 12/21/2005), which, by its terms, is effective for interest accruing on, before, or after Oct. 3, 2004.

¶ 1403. IRS's authority to disclose taxpayer identity information to facilitate combined federal/state employment tax reporting is extended for one year through Dec. 31, 2007

Code Sec. 6103(d)(5)(B), as amended by 2006 Tax Relief and Health Care Act § 122(a)(1)
Generally effective: Disclosures after Dec. 31, 2006 and before Jan. 1, 2008
Committee Reports, see ¶ 5026

IRS is permitted to disclose taxpayer identity information and signatures to any agency, body, or commission of any state to enable IRS to carry out a combined federal/state employment tax reporting program that has been approved by IRS, see FTC 2d/FIN ¶ S-2609; USTR ¶ 61,034.07. Code Sec. 6103(a)(2) (which prohibits disclosure of returns or return information by state officers and employees, see FTC 2d/FIN ¶ S-6200; USTR ¶ 61,034); Code Sec. 6103(p)(4) (which provides that IRS may not disclose any tax information to any agency, body, or commission if the agency does not establish procedures satisfactory to IRS for safeguarding the tax information it receives, see FTC 2d/FIN ¶ S-6411; USTR ¶ 61,034.02); and Code Sec. 7213 and Code Sec. 7213A (which are the provisions imposing federal penalties for unauthorized disclosure and inspection of returns or return information, see FTC 2d/FIN ¶s V-3304, V-3305.1; USTR ¶s 72,134, 72,13A4) do not apply to disclosures or inspections made in the course of carrying out the combined federal/state reporting program, see FTC 2d/FIN ¶ S-2609; USTR ¶ 61,034.07.

Under pre-2006 Tax Relief and Health Care Act law, IRS was authorized to make these disclosures until Dec. 31, 2006. (FTC 2d/FIN ¶ S-2609; USTR ¶ 61,034.07)

New Law. The 2006 Tax Relief and Health Care Act provides that IRS may not make disclosures after Dec. 31, 2007 under the above rules to facilitate combined federal/state employment tax reporting. (Code Sec. 6103(d)(5)(B) as amended by 2006 Tax Relief and Health Care Act §122(a)(1)) Thus, the 2006 Tax Relief and Health Care Act extends for one year the authority for the combined employment tax reporting program (through Dec. 31, 2007). (Com Rept, see ¶ 5026)

FTC 2d References are to Federal Tax Coordinator 2d
FIN References are to RIAs Analysis of Federal Taxes: Income
USTR References are to United States Tax Reporter: Income, Estate & Gift, and Excise
PCA References are to Pension Analysis (print & electronic)
PE References are to Pension Explanations (print & electronic)
EP References are to Estate Planning Analysis (print & electronic)

For a similar one year extension of IRS's authority to disclose return information to the Dept. of Education to monitor income-contingent student loan repayments, see ¶ 1404.

For a similar one year extension of IRS's authority to disclose return information in terrorism and national security investigations, see ¶ 1405.

☐ **Effective:** Disclosures after Dec. 31, 2006 (2006 Tax Relief and Health Care Act §122(a)(2)) and before Jan. 1, 2008. (Code Sec. 6103(d)(5)(B))

¶ 1404. IRS's authority to disclose requested return information to the Dept. of Education to monitor income-contingent student loan repayments is extended for one year for requests made through Dec. 31, 2007

Code Sec. 6103(l)(13)(D), as amended by 2006 Tax Relief and Health Care Act § 122(c)(1)
Generally effective: Requests made after Dec. 31, 2006 and before Jan. 1, 2008
Committee Reports, see ¶ 5028

To carry out a federal direct student loan program that allows loans to be repaid on an income-contingent basis, IRS may disclose to officers and employees of the Dept. of Education who request disclosure in writing return information about a taxpayer who has received an "applicable student loan" and whose loan repayments are based in whole or in part on the taxpayer's income. An "applicable student loan" is (1) a loan made under Part D of Title IV of the Higher Education Act of '65 (the federal direct student loan program) or (2) a loan made under Part B or E of the Higher Education Act of '65 that is in default and has been assigned to the Dept. of Education, see FTC 2d/FIN ¶ S-6356.1; USTR ¶ 61,034.01. The exception that permits disclosure to the Dept. of Education does not apply to contractors hired by the Dept. of Education to administer the income-contingent loan verification program. Thus, when contractors are used, the Dept. of Education obtains taxpayer consents to disclosure under Code Sec. 6103(c) rather than relying on the disclosure exception for the loan verification program. (Com Rept, see ¶ 5028)

The information that may be disclosed includes the taxpayer's name, address, taxpayer identification number, filing status, and adjusted gross income. The Dept. of Education may use the information thus disclosed only for purposes of, and to the extent necessary for, establishing the income-contingent repayment amount for a student loan, see FTC 2d/FIN ¶ S-6356.1; USTR ¶ 61,034.01. Under pre-2006 Tax Relief and Health Care Act law, the authority to disclose this tax information to the Dept. of Education didn't apply to requests for information made after Dec. 31, 2006. (FTC 2d/FIN ¶ S-6356.1; USTR ¶ 61,034.01)

New Law. The 2006 Tax Relief and Health Care Act provides that, for requests for disclosure made after Dec. 31, 2007, IRS may not disclose to the Dept. of Education return information about taxpayers who have received income-contingent student loans. (Code Sec. 6103(l)(13)(D) as amended by 2006 Tax Relief and Health Care Act §122(c)(1)) Thus, the 2006 Tax Relief and Health Care Act extends for one year the authority to disclose return information for purposes of the income-contingent loan repayment program (through Dec. 31, 2007). (Com Rept, see ¶ 5028)

For a similar one year extension of IRS's authority to disclose return information to facilitate combined federal/state employment tax reporting, see ¶ 1403.

For a similar one year extension of IRS's authority to disclose return information in terrorism and national security investigations, see ¶ 1405.

☐ **Effective:** Requests made after Dec. 31, 2006 (2006 Tax Relief and Health Care Act §122(c)(2)) and before Jan. 1, 2008. (Code Sec. 6103(l)(13)(D))

¶ 1405. IRS's authority to disclose tax information in terrorism and national security investigations is extended for one year through Dec. 31, 2007

Code Sec. 6103(i)(3)(C)(iv), as amended by 2006 Tax Relief and Health Care Act § 122(b)(1)
Code Sec. 6103(i)(7)(E), as amended by 2006 Tax Relief and Health Care Act § 122(b)(1)
Generally effective: Disclosures after Dec. 31, 2006 and before Jan. 1, 2008
Committee Reports, see ¶ 5027

IRS is authorized, even if not requested, to disclose in writing return information (other than taxpayer return information) that may be related to a terrorist incident, threat, or activity to the extent necessary to apprise the head of the appropriate federal law enforcement agency responsible for investigating or responding to that terrorist incident, threat or activity (the disclosure-without-request rule). The head of the agency may disclose the return information to officers and employees of the agency to the extent necessary to investigate or respond to the terrorist incident, threat or activity. IRS is also authorized to dis-

FTC 2d References are to Federal Tax Coordinator 2d
FIN References are to RIAs Analysis of Federal Taxes: Income
USTR References are to United States Tax Reporter: Income, Estate & Gift, and Excise
PCA References are to Pension Analysis (print & electronic)
PE References are to Pension Explanations (print & electronic)
EP References are to Estate Planning Analysis (print & electronic)

close returns and taxpayer return information under the disclosure-without-request rule to the Attorney General to the extent necessary for, and solely for use in preparing, an application for ex parte court-ordered disclosure initiated by IRS. The disclosure-without-request rule doesn't apply where disclosure would identify a confidential informant or seriously impair a civil or criminal tax investigation, see FTC 2d/FIN ¶ S-6342.1; USTR ¶ 61,034.07.

Once IRS receives a written request that meets certain requirements, it may disclose return information (other than taxpayer return information) to officers and employees of any federal law enforcement agency who are personally and directly engaged in the response to, or investigation of, any terrorist incident, threat, or activity (the requested disclosure rule). The agencies, and current or former agency officers and employees, are subject to rules that limit the disclosures they can make of information received under the requested disclosure rule. Also, no disclosure can be made under the requested disclosure rule if the disclosure would identify a confidential informant or seriously impair a civil or criminal tax investigation, see FTC 2d/FIN ¶ S-6344.1; USTR ¶ 61,034.07.

The head of any federal law enforcement agency can disclose return information obtained under the requested disclosure rule to officers and employees of any state or local law enforcement agency, but only if that agency is part of a team with the federal law enforcement agency engaged in the response to, or investigation of, a terrorist incident, threat or activity, and the information is disclosed only to officers and employees who are personally and directly engaged in that response or investigation. The information disclosed to officers and employees of law enforcement agencies under the requested disclosure rule can be used only by them in that response or investigation. Officers and employees, and former officers and employees, of state and local law enforcement agencies cannot disclose any return or return information received under this rule, except as authorized by the Code, see FTC 2d/FIN ¶ S-6344.1; USTR ¶ 61,034.07.

Once IRS receives a written request that meets certain requirements, it may disclose return information (other than taxpayer return information) to officers and employees of the Treasury Dept., Justice Dept. and other federal intelligence agencies who are personally and directly engaged in the collection or analysis of intelligence and counterintelligence information or investigation concerning any terrorist incident, threat or activity (the disclosure-to-intelligence-agencies rule). The information disclosed must be used solely by those officers and employees in that investigation, collection or analysis. However, no disclosure can be made if disclosure would identify a confidential informant or seriously impair a civil or criminal tax investigation, see FTC 2d/FIN ¶ S-6344.2; USTR ¶ 61,034.07.

IRS is also permitted to disclose returns and return information under certain ex parte court orders issued with respect to terrorist activity (the ex-parte-order disclosure rule), see FTC 2d/FIN ¶ S-6339.1; USTR ¶ 61,034.07.

As a condition of receiving returns or information under any of the above rules, federal and state agencies must establish procedures satisfactory to IRS to safeguard that information and return it or make it undisclosable when they are finished with it, see FTC 2d/FIN ¶ S-6411; USTR ¶ 61,034.02.

Under pre-2006 Tax Relief and Health Care Act law, no disclosure could be made under any of the above disclosure rules after Dec. 31, 2006. (FTC 2d/FIN ¶ S-6339.1, ¶ S-6342.1, ¶ S-6344.1, ¶ S-6344.2; USTR ¶ 61,034.06)

New Law. The 2006 Tax Relief and Health Care Act provides that IRS may not make disclosures after Dec. 31, 2007 under the disclosure-without-request rule (see above) (Code Sec. 6103(i)(3)(C)(iv) as amended by 2006 Tax Relief and Health Care Act §122(b)(1)) or under the requested disclosure rule, disclosure-to-intelligence-agencies rule or ex-parte-order-disclosure rule (see above). (Code Sec. 6103(i)(7)(E) as amended by 2006 Tax Relief and Health Care Act §122(b)(1)) Thus, the 2006 Tax Relief and Health Care Act extends for one year the terrorist activity disclosure provisions (through Dec. 31, 2007). (Com Rept, see ¶ 5027)

For a similar one year extension of IRS's authority to disclose return information to facilitate combined federal/state employment tax reporting, see ¶ 1403.

For a similar one year extension of IRS's authority to disclose return information to the Dept. of Education to monitor income-contingent student loan repayments, see ¶ 1404.

☐ **Effective:** Disclosures after Dec. 31, 2006 (2006 Tax Relief and Health Care Act §122(b)(2)) and before Jan. 1, 2008. (Code Sec. 6103(i)(3)(C)(iv)) (Code Sec. 6103(i)(7)(E))

¶ 1406. Regional income tax agencies are treated as States for purposes of confidentiality and disclosure of returns and return information

Code Sec. 6103(b)(5), as amended by 2006 Tax Relief and Health Care Act § 421(a)
Code Sec. 6103(d)(6), as amended by 2006 Tax Relief and Health Care Act § 421(b)
Generally effective: Disclosures made after Dec. 31, 2006
Committee Reports, see ¶ 5072

FTC 2d References are to Federal Tax Coordinator 2d
FIN References are to RIAs Analysis of Federal Taxes: Income
USTR References are to United States Tax Reporter: Income, Estate & Gift, and Excise
PCA References are to Pension Analysis (print & electronic)
PE References are to Pension Explanations (print & electronic)
EP References are to Estate Planning Analysis (print & electronic)

Return and return information are confidential and may not be disclosed by government employees or other persons except as specifically authorized by statute (see FTC 2d/FIN ¶ S-6200 *et seq.*; USTR ¶ 61,034 *et seq.*).

One exception to the general rule of confidentiality is the disclosure of tax information to States. Tax officials of a State, on the written request of the principal tax official other than the State Governor can inspect federal tax returns and return information solely for administration of State tax law. Disclosure is made only to the duly authorized representatives of a State agency, body or commission who are designated in the written request for inspection. State officials who receive the return information may disclose it to the agency's contractors, but only for State tax administration purposes. (see FTC 2d/FIN ¶ S-6327; USTR ¶ 61,034.07)

For this purpose, the term "State" under pre-2006 Tax Relief and Health Care Act law, includes the 50 States, the District of Columbia, the Commonwealth of Puerto Rico, the Virgin Islands, the Canal Zone, Guam, American Samoa, and the Commonwealth of the Northern Mariana Islands. State taxing authorities can disclose federal tax information to State auditing agencies for auditing the State taxing authority. In addition, any municipality with a population of over 250,000 that imposes a tax on wages or income and with which IRS has entered into an agreement regarding disclosure is also treated as a State for purposes of applying the confidentiality and disclosure provisions for State tax officials, determining the scope of tax administration, applying the rules governing disclosures in judicial and administrative tax proceedings, and applying the safeguard procedures. (FTC 2d/FIN ¶ S-6201; USTR ¶ 61,034.07)

New Law. The 2006 Tax Relief and Health Care Act broadens the definition of "State" under Code Sec. 6103(b)(5) for purposes of disclosure of tax returns and return information to include a "regional income tax agency" administering the tax laws of municipalities which have a collective population in excess of 250,000. (Com Rept, see ¶ 5072) Specifically, the 2006 Tax Relief and Health Care Act provides that the term "State" for purposes of Code Sec. 6103(a)(2), 6103(b)(4), 6103(d)(1), 6103(h)(4) and 6103(p) (i.e., for purposes of applying the confidentiality and disclosure provisions for State tax officials, determining the scope of tax administration, applying the rules governing disclosures in judicial and administrative tax proceedings, and applying the safeguard procedures (Com Rept, see ¶ 5072)), includes any governmental entity: (Code Sec. 6103(b)(5)(A)(iii) as amended by 2006 Tax Relief and Health Care Act §421(a))

. . . which is formed and operated by a qualified group of municipalities (defined below), and (Code Sec. 6103(b)(5)(A)(iii)(I))

. . . with which IRS in its sole discretion has entered into an agreement regarding disclosure. (Code Sec. 6103(b)(5)(A)(iii)(II))

For purposes of applying Code Sec. 6103(b)(5)(A)(iii) to the Code subsections referred to in Code Sec. 6103(b)(5)(A)(iii), any reference to State law, proceedings or tax returns, as the case may be, are treated as references to the law, proceedings or tax returns of the municipalities that form and operate the governmental entity referred to in Code Sec. 6103(b)(5)(A)(iii). (Code Sec. 6103(b)(5)(B)(ii)) This is so because a regional income tax agency administers the laws of its member municipalities. (Com Rept, see ¶ 5072)

Qualified group of municipalities defined. A qualified group of municipalities, with respect to any governmental entity, is two or more municipalities: (Code Sec. 6103(b)(5)(B)(i))

. . . each of which imposes a tax on income or wages, (Code Sec. 6103(b)(5)(B)(i)(I))

. . . each of which, under the authority of a State statute, administers the laws relating to the imposition of those taxes through that governmental entity, and (Code Sec. 6103(b)(5)(B)(i)(II))

. . . which collectively have a population in excess of 250,000 (as determined under the most recent decennial U.S. census data available. (Code Sec. 6103(b)(5)(B)(i)(III))

Disclosures to contractors or other agents. Notwithstanding any other provision of Code Sec. 6103, no return or return information is to be disclosed to any contractor or other agent of a governmental entity referred to in Code Sec. 6103(b)(5)(A)(iii), unless that governmental entity, to IRS's satisfaction: (Code Sec. 6103(b)(5)(B)(iii))

. . . has requirements in effect that require each contractor or agent that would have access to returns or return information to provide safeguards (within the meaning of Code Sec. 6103(p)(4) (i.e., safeguards required for certain federal and State agencies, bodies, commissions, or officers, as a condition for receiving returns or return information, see FTC 2d/FIN ¶ S-6411; USTR ¶ 61,034.02) to protect the confidentiality of returns or return information; (Code Sec. 6103(b)(5)(B)(iii)(I))

. . . agrees to conduct an on-site review every three years (or a mid-point review for contracts or agreements of less than three years in duration) of each contractor or agent to determine compliance with those requirements; (Code Sec. 6103(b)(5)(B)(iii)(II)) The purpose of the review is to assess the contractor's efforts to safeguard federal tax information. This review is intended to cover secure storage, restricting access, computer security, and other safeguards deemed appropriate by IRS. (Com Rept, see ¶ 5072)

. . . submits the findings of the most recent on-site review conducted under Code Sec. 6103(b)(5)(B)(iii)(II), above, to IRS as part of the report required by Code Sec. 6103(p)(4)(E) (discussed below); and (Code Sec. 6103(b)(5)(B)(iii)(III))

> ***observation:*** Code Sec. 6103(p)(4)(E) (see FTC 2d/FIN ¶ S-6411; USTR ¶ 61,034.02) refers to safeguards requiring governmental agencies, bodies or commissions, the Government Accountability Office (GAO) or the Congressional Budget Office (CBO) to furnish a report to IRS, describing the procedures established and utilized to ensure the confidentiality of returns and return information.

. . . certifies to IRS for the most recent annual period that the contractor or other agent is in compliance with all requirements. (Code Sec. 6103(b)(5)(B)(iii)(IV))

The certification required by Code Sec. 6103(b)(5)(B)(iii)(IV) must include the name and address of each contractor and other agent, a description of the contract or agreement with the contractor or other agent, and the duration of the contract or agreement. The requirements in Code Sec. 6103(b)(5)(B)(iii) regarding disclosures to contractors and other agents don't apply to disclosures under Code Sec. 6103(n) (discussed below) for purposes of federal tax administration, and a rule similar to the rule in Code Sec. 6103(p)(8)(B) (discussed below) applies for purposes of Code Sec. 6103(b)(5)(B)(iii). (Code Sec. 6103(b)(5)(B)(iii)(IV))

> ***observation:*** Disclosures under Code Sec. 6103(n) (see FTC 2d/FIN ¶ S-6324; USTR ¶ 61,034.043) are disclosures to certain other persons to the extent necessary in connection with processing, storage, transmission and reproduction of returns and return information; and programming, maintenance, repair, testing and procurement of equipment, and provision of other services.

> ***observation:*** The rule in Code Sec. 6103(p)(8)(B) (see FTC 2d/FIN ¶ S-6332; USTR ¶ 61,034.07) concerns State law requirements in the area of procedure and recordkeeping, specifically disclosure by a State officer or employee to another officer or employee of that State (or one of its political subdivisions) of a copy of any portion of a federal tax return or information on a federal return that is required to be attached to or included in a State return, if that disclosure is specifically authorized by State law.

2006 Tax Relief and Health Care Act §421 does not alter or affect in any way the right of IRS to conduct safeguard reviews of regional income tax agency contractors or other agents. It also does not affect the right of IRS to approve initially the safeguard language in the contract or agreement and the safeguards in place before any disclosures made in connection with those contracts or agreements. (Com Rept, see ¶ 5072)

Limitation on disclosure to regional income tax agencies. For purposes of Code Sec. 6103(d)(1), inspection by or disclosure to a regional income tax agency (discussed above) must be for the purpose of, and only to the extent necessary in, the administration of the laws of the member municipalities in that entity relating to the imposition of a tax on income or wages. The regional income tax agency cannot redisclose any return or return information received for the above purpose to any member municipality. (Code Sec. 6103(d)(6) as amended by 2006 Tax Relief and Health Care Act §421(b)) This rule does not preclude the entity from disclosing data in a form which cannot be associated with or otherwise identify directly or indirectly a particular taxpayer. (Com Rept, see ¶ 5072)

☐ **Effective:** Disclosures made after Dec. 31, 2006. (2006 Tax Relief and Health Care Act §421(c))

¶ 1407. Penalty for frivolous submissions upped to $5,000, extended to other submissions

Code Sec. 6702, as amended by 2006 Tax Relief and Health Care Act § 407(a)
Generally effective: Submissions made and issues raised after IRS prescribes a list of frivolous positions
Committee Reports, see ¶ 5058

Under pre-2006 Tax Relief and Health Care Act law, a $500 penalty applied to an individual who filed what purported to be an income tax return, but which didn't contain information on which the substantial correctness of the self-assessment could be judged, or which contained information that on its face indicated that the self assessment was substantially incorrect. In either case, the penalty applied only if the filing involved a frivolous position or a desire to delay or impede the administration of the federal tax laws. A position was frivolous if it had no basis in law or in fact. The penalty was in addition to any other penalty provided by law. FTC 2d/FIN ¶ V-2551; USTR ¶ 67,024; TaxDesk ¶ 866,001

New Law. The 2006 Tax Relief and Health Care Act cracks down on taxpayers who file frivolous returns, and who make other kinds of frivolous sub-

FTC 2d References are to Federal Tax Coordinator 2d
FIN References are to RIAs Analysis of Federal Taxes: Income
USTR References are to United States Tax Reporter: Income, Estate & Gift, and Excise
PCA References are to Pension Analysis (print & electronic)
PE References are to Pension Explanations (print & electronic)
EP References are to Estate Planning Analysis (print & electronic)

missions intended to delay or impede IRS, by (a) increasing the $500 penalty to $5,000, and (b) extending it to apply to any tax return required under the Internal Revenue Code (not just income tax returns) and to requests for collection due process hearings, installment agreements, offers-in-compromise, and taxpayer assistance orders. (Code Sec. 6702 as amended by 2006 Tax Relief and Health Care Act §407(a))

> ***observation:*** The new law also gives IRS the power to dismiss out of hand frivolous requests for collection due process hearings, installment agreements, and offers-in-compromise, without having to follow otherwise mandated procedures. See ¶ 1408.

Specifically, the 2006 Tax Relief and Health Care Act imposes a $5,000 penalty (instead of $500) on any person who files what purports to be a tax return required under any provision of the Code if:

(1) the purported return doesn't contain information on which the substantial correctness of the self-assessment may be judged (Code Sec. 6702(a)(1)(A)), or

(2) the purported return contains information indicating on its face that the self-assessment is substantially incorrect (Code Sec. 6702(a)(1)(B)), and

(3) the conduct described in (1) and (2) above is based on a position which IRS has identified as frivolous or reflects a desire to delay or impede the administration of federal tax laws. (Code Sec. 6702(a)(2))

The 2006 Tax Relief and Health Care Act also imposes a $5,000 penalty on any person who submits a "specified frivolous submission." (Code Sec. 6702(b)(1)) A "specified frivolous submission" is a "specified submission" (as defined below) if any portion of the submission is based on a position which IRS has identified as frivolous (as described below), or reflects a desire to delay or impede the administration of federal tax laws. (Code Sec. 6702(b)(2)(A))

The term "specified submission" means:

. . . a request for a hearing under Code Sec. 6320 (relating to notice and opportunity for hearing on filing of notice of lien, see FTC 2d/FIN ¶ V-6007; USTR ¶ 63,204; TaxDesk ¶ 911,008),

. . . a request for hearing under Code Sec. 6330 (relating to notice and opportunity for hearing before levy, see FTC 2d/FIN ¶ V-5263; USTR ¶ 63,304; TaxDesk ¶ 902,513),

. . . an application under Code Sec. 6159 (relating to agreements for payment of tax liability in installments, see FTC 2d/FIN ¶ V-5010; USTR ¶ 61,594; TaxDesk ¶ 901,006),

. . . an application under Code Sec. 7122 (relating to compromises, see FTC 2d/FIN ¶ T-9612; USTR ¶ 71,224.03; TaxDesk ¶ 842,012), or

. . . an application under Code Sec. 7811 (relating to taxpayer assistance orders, see FTC 2d/FIN ¶ T-10206; USTR ¶ 78,114; TaxDesk ¶ 821,025). (Code Sec. 6702(b)(2)(B))

> ***observation:*** It had been reported that IRS has been faced with a significant number of tax filers who file returns and other submissions based on frivolous arguments or who seek to hinder federal tax administration by filing returns and submissions that are patently incorrect. Allowing IRS to assert more substantial penalties for frivolous returns and other submissions will help deter frivolous taxpayer behavior.

After IRS provides a taxpayer with notice that a submission is a specified frivolous submission, the penalty does not apply to that submission if the taxpayer withdraws the submission within 30 days after the notice. (Code Sec. 6702(b)(3))

IRS must make (and periodically revise) a list of positions which it has identified as being frivolous for purposes of the new $5,000 penalty. IRS must not include in this list any position that it determines meets the requirement of Code Sec. 6662(d)(2)(B)(ii)(II), (i.e., the taxpayer's position has a sufficiently reasonable basis so that any understatement attributable the position isn't subject to the accuracy related penalty if there is adequate disclosure, see FTC 2d/FIN ¶ V-2167.1; USTR ¶ 66,624.04; TaxDesk ¶ 863,015). (Code Sec. 6702(c))

A frivolous return or submission penalty may be reduced if IRS determines that the reduction would promote compliance with, and administration of, federal tax law. (Code Sec. 6702(d))

These penalties are in addition to any other penalty provided by law. (Code Sec. 6702(e))

☐ **Effective:** Submissions made and issues raised after IRS first prescribes a list of frivolous positions under Code Sec. 6702(c) (discussed above). (2006 Tax Relief and Health Care Act §407(f))

FTC 2d References are to Federal Tax Coordinator 2d
FIN References are to RIAs Analysis of Federal Taxes: Income
USTR References are to United States Tax Reporter: Income, Estate & Gift, and Excise
PCA References are to Pension Analysis (print & electronic)
PE References are to Pension Explanations (print & electronic)
EP References are to Estate Planning Analysis (print & electronic)

¶ 1408. Frivolous submissions are subject to IRS dismissal

Code Sec. 6320(b)(1), as amended by 2006 Tax Relief and Health Care Act § 407(c)(1)
Code Sec. 6320(c), as amended by 2006 Tax Relief and Health Care Act § 407(c)(2)
Code Sec. 6330(b)(1), as amended by 2006 Tax Relief and Health Care Act § 407(b)(3)
Code Sec. 6330(c)(4), as amended by 2006 Tax Relief and Health Care Act § 407(b)(2)
Code Sec. 6330(g), as amended by 2006 Tax Relief and Health Care Act § 407(b)(1)
Code Sec. 7122(f), as amended by 2006 Tax Relief and Health Care Act § 407(d)
Generally effective: Submissions made and issues raised after IRS prescribes a list of frivolous positions
Committee Reports, see ¶ 5058

Under pre-2006 Tax Relief and Health Care Act law, the Tax Court may impose a penalty of up to $25,000 if a taxpayer has instituted or maintained proceedings primarily for delay or if the taxpayer's position in the proceeding is frivolous or groundless. Other courts may impose a penalty of up to $10,000 for frivolous or groundless positions asserted by a taxpayer in tax cases. FTC 2d/FIN ¶s V-2601, V-2612; USTR ¶ 66,734; TaxDesk ¶ 836,014

New Law. The 2006 Tax Relief and Health Care Act adds a new provision under which IRS may treat any portion of certain requests and applications as if it had never been submitted if IRS determines it is based on a position that IRS has identified as frivolous, or it reflects a desire to delay or impede the administration of Federal tax law, see ¶ 1407. The portion will not be subject to any further administrative or judicial review. (Code Sec. 6330(g) as amended by 2006 Tax Relief and Health Care Act §407(b)(1))

> ***observation:*** In other words, IRS may dismiss any such submission out of hand.

This new provision applies to:

- requests for a hearing under Code Sec. 6330 before a levy is made, see FTC 2d/FIN ¶ V-5263; USTR ¶ 63,304; TaxDesk ¶ 902,513, (Code Sec. 6330(g) as amended by 2006 Tax Relief and Health Care Act §407(b)(1))
- requests for a hearing under Code Sec. 6320 before a lien is filed, see FTC 2d/FIN ¶ V-6007; USTR ¶ 63,204; TaxDesk ¶ 911,008, (Code Sec. 6330(g)); (Code Sec. 6320(c) as amended by 2006 Tax Relief and Health Care Act §407(c)(2))

• applications under Code Sec. 6159 for an agreement to pay taxes in installments, see FTC 2d/FIN ¶ V-5010; USTR ¶ 61,594; TaxDesk ¶ 901,006, (Code Sec. 7122(f) as amended by 2006 Tax Relief and Health Care Act §407(d)) and

• applications under Code Sec. 7122 for an offer-in-compromise, see FTC 2d/FIN ¶ T-9612; USTR ¶ 71,224.03; TaxDesk ¶ 842,012. (Code Sec. 7122(f))

> ***observation:*** Note that there already was a subsection (f) in Code Sec. 7122 before the addition of the subsection (f) discussed above so the new subsection probably should be subsection (g).

> ***observation:*** The new power to dismiss frivolous requests and applications apparently doesn't apply to taxpayer assistance orders. Committee reports on earlier versions of the tax legislation stated that the power of IRS to dismiss frivolous requests and applications applied to requests for a collection due process hearing, installment agreements, offers-in-compromise, and taxpayer assistance orders. But, the reference to taxpayer assistance orders doesn't appear in the Code or in the equivalent language in the Technical Explanation of the 2006 Tax Relief and Health Care Act.

A request for a hearing on the filing of a notice of lien must be in writing and state the grounds for the requested hearing. (Code Sec. 6320(b)(1) as amended by 2006 Tax Relief and Health Care Act §407(c)) Likewise, a request for a hearing before levy must be in writing and state the ground for the requested hearing. (Code Sec. 6330(b)(1) as amended by 2006 Tax Relief and Health Care Act §407(b)(3)) Issues that IRS has identified as frivolous or which reflect a desire to delay or impede the administration of Federal tax law may not be raised in a lien or levy hearing. (Code Sec. 6330(c)(4)(B) as amended by 2006 Tax Relief and Health Care Act §407(b)(2)(D))

> ***observation:*** In addition to dismissal, frivolous submissions may be subject to a new $5,000 penalty, see ¶ 1407.

☐ **Effective:** Submissions made and issues raised after IRS first prescribes a list of frivolous provisions under Code Sec. 6702(c), see ¶ 1407. (2006 Tax Relief and Health Care Act §407(f))

FTC 2d References are to Federal Tax Coordinator 2d
FIN References are to RIAs Analysis of Federal Taxes: Income
USTR References are to United States Tax Reporter: Income, Estate & Gift, and Excise
PCA References are to Pension Analysis (print & electronic)
PE References are to Pension Explanations (print & electronic)
EP References are to Estate Planning Analysis (print & electronic)

¶ 1409. Whistleblower rewards are increased, to maximum of 30% (up from 15%) of collected proceeds, interest, penalties, and additional amounts

Code Sec. 7623(a), as amended by 2006 Tax Relief and Health Care Act § 406(a)(1)(B)
Code Sec. 7623(a), as amended by 2006 Tax Relief and Health Care Act § 406(a)(1)(C)
Code Sec. 7623(b), as amended by 2006 Tax Relief and Health Care Act § 406(a)(1)(D)
Code Sec. 7443A(b)(5), as amended by 2006 Tax Relief and Health Care Act § 406(a)(2)(A)
Generally effective: Information provided on or after date of enactment
Committee Reports, see ¶ 5057

IRS is authorized to pay rewards to informers (known as "whistleblowers"), in the amounts deemed necessary, for: (1) detecting underpayments of tax, and (2) detecting and bringing to trial and punishment persons guilty of violating, or conniving to violate, the tax laws. However, under pre-2006 Tax Relief and Health Care Act law, a reward was payable only if the information provided by the whistleblower resulted in *both* the detection of an underpayment of tax, *and* the detection, trial, and punishment of the guilty person(s). This two-pronged test precluded whistleblower rewards in cases other than criminal tax evasion, for example, in cases of negligence. But Congress had indicated that rewards were payable in civil cases. (FTC 2d/FIN ¶ T-1031; USTR ¶ 76,234; TaxDesk ¶ 444,043)

Whistleblower rewards are paid from the proceeds of amounts collected by reason of the information provided, in an amount based on a percentage of those "collected proceeds." Under pre-2006 Tax Relief and Health Care Act law, the "collected proceeds" included tax, fines, and penalties, but not interest. (FTC 2d/FIN ¶ T-1031; USTR ¶ 76,234; TaxDesk ¶ 444,043)

Under pre-2006 Tax Relief and Health Care Act law, regs provided that the amount of a reward for information about tax law violations represented what IRS deemed to be adequate compensation in the particular case, generally not to exceed 15% of the amounts collected by reason of the information. The reward ceiling was $10 million, and the reward floor was $100. Both the ceiling and the percentages could be increased by special agreement. (FTC 2d/FIN ¶ T-1036; TaxDesk ¶ 444,043)

New Law. The 2006 Tax Relief and Health Care Act reforms the reward program for individuals who provide information regarding violations of the tax laws to IRS. (Com Rept, see ¶ 5057)

The 2006 Tax Relief and Health Care Act substitutes "or" for "and" in the language authorizing the payment of rewards to whistleblowers. Thus, IRS is authorized to pay rewards for information necessary for detecting underpayments of tax, *or* detecting and bringing to trial and punishment persons guilty of violating, or conniving to violate, the tax laws. (Code Sec. 7623(a) as amended by 2006 Tax Relief and Health Care Act §406(a)(1)(B))

> ***observation:*** Under this rule, a reward is payable if the information provided by the whistleblower aids IRS in detecting an underpayment of tax, even if the information doesn't result in the trial and punishment of any persons. In other words, rewards are payable for information leading to the detection of tax underpayments attributable to negligence or other non-criminal causes. This statutory change reflects the views Congress had expressed earlier as to the scope of the reward program.

The 2006 Tax Relief and Health Care Act also deletes the parenthetical phrase "(other than interest)" from the language describing the amounts out of which rewards may be paid to whistleblowers. (Code Sec. 7623(a) as amended by 2006 Tax Relief and Health Care Act §406(a)(1)(C)) That is, the "collected proceeds" include—in addition to the collected tax—penalties, interest, additions to tax, and additional amounts. (Com Rept, see ¶ 5057)

For a discussion of the 2006 Tax Relief and Health Care Act provision establishing an IRS "Whistleblower Office," see ¶ 1411.

Awards to whistleblowers must be at least 15%, but not more than 30%, of the collected proceeds including interest and penalties. If IRS proceeds with any administrative or judicial action (subject to dollar amount thresholds, see below) based on information brought to IRS's attention by an individual (i.e., the "whistleblower"), then the whistleblower will (unless his contribution is less than substantial, see below) receive as an award at least 15%, but not more than 30%, of the collected proceeds (including penalties, interest, additions to tax, and additional amounts) resulting from the action (including any related actions), or from any settlement of the action. (Code Sec. 7623(b)(1) as amended by 2006 Tax Relief and Health Care Act §406(a)(1)(D))

In other words, the 2006 Tax Relief and Health Care Act establishes a reward floor of 15% of the collected proceeds, and caps the available reward at 30% of the collected proceeds. (Com Rept, see ¶ 5057)

> ***observation:*** The 2006 Tax Relief and Health Care Act increases the amount of whistleblower rewards in two ways:

FTC 2d References are to Federal Tax Coordinator 2d
FIN References are to RIAs Analysis of Federal Taxes: Income
USTR References are to United States Tax Reporter: Income, Estate & Gift, and Excise
PCA References are to Pension Analysis (print & electronic)
PE References are to Pension Explanations (print & electronic)
EP References are to Estate Planning Analysis (print & electronic)

(1) the maximum reward percentage is increased to 30% (from 15%), and

(2) the base on which the percentage is applied (i.e., the "collected proceeds") is expanded to include the interest on the amounts collected as a result of the information provided by the whistleblower.

The amount of the award is determined by the "Whistleblower Office" (see ¶ 1411), and depends on the extent to which the whistleblower "substantially contributed" to the administrative or judicial action described above (referred to as the "action"). (Code Sec. 7623(b)(1))

observation: The 2006 Tax Relief and Health Care Act does not define "substantially contributed."

Award is limited to 10% of collected proceeds if the whistleblower's contribution was less than substantial. If the Whistleblower Office determines that the action is based principally on disclosures of specific allegations (*other than* information provided by the whistleblower) resulting from a judicial or administrative hearing, a governmental report, hearing, audit, or investigation, or from the news media, the Whistleblower Office may award whatever amount it considers appropriate, but (except as provided below) not more than 10% of the collected proceeds (including penalties, interest, additions to tax, and additional amounts) resulting from the action (including any related actions), or from any settlement of the action. In determining the amount of the whistleblower's award, the Whistleblower Office must take into account the significance of the whistleblower's information, and the role of the whistleblower and his legal representative (if any) in contributing to the action. (Code Sec. 7623(b)(2)(A))

However, the rule limiting an award to 10% of the collected proceeds does not apply if the information resulting in the initiation of the IRS action was originally provided by the whistleblower. (Code Sec. 7623(b)(2)(B))

IRS may reduce or deny whistleblower award. The Whistleblower Office may appropriately reduce a whistleblower award if it determines that the claim for an award is brought by an individual who planned and initiated the actions that led to the underpayment of tax, or to the violation of (or conniving to violate) the tax laws. If an individual who brings a claim for a whistleblower award is convicted of criminal conduct arising from his role in planning and initiating the actions that led to the underpayment of tax, or to the violation of (or conniving to violate) the tax laws, the Whistleblower Office must deny any award. (Code Sec. 7623(b)(3))

Whistleblower can appeal award determination. The 2006 Tax Relief and Health Care Act permits an individual to appeal the amount of, or the denial of, an award determination. (Com Rept, see ¶ 5057) Any determination of a whistleblower award under Code Sec. 7623(b)(1) (the 15%-30% reward), Code

Sec. 7623(b)(2) (the up-to-10% reward), or Code Sec. 7623(b)(3) (the reduction or denial of the reward) may, within 30 days of the determination, be appealed to the Tax Court. The Tax Court will have exclusive jurisdiction over the matter. (Code Sec. 7623(b)(4))

> ***observation:*** Generally, a taxpayer can't go to Tax Court without first getting a notice of deficiency (90-day letter) from IRS (see FTC 2d/FIN ¶ U-2300 *et seq.*; USTR ¶ 62,134; TaxDesk ¶ 831,009). Code Sec. 7623(b)(4) provides an exception to this general rule. Presumably, the Tax Court's jurisdiction will be limited to matters relating to the award.

Any proceeding under Code Sec. 7623(b)(4) is added to the list of Tax Court proceedings which may be assigned to special trial judges. (Code Sec. 7443A(b)(5) as amended by 2006 Tax Relief and Health Care Act §406(a)(2)(A)) In other words, the Tax Court review of an award determination may be assigned to a special trial judge. (Com Rept, see ¶ 5057)

Actions to which the whistleblower award rules apply; dollar amount thresholds. The whistleblower award rules apply to (Code Sec. 7623(b)(5)):

(1) any action against any taxpayer, but in the case of an individual, only if the individual's gross income exceeds $200,000 for any tax year subject to the action (Code Sec. 7623(b)(5)(A)), and

(2) any action if the tax, penalties, interest, additions to tax, and additional amounts in dispute exceed $2 million. (Code Sec. 7623(b)(5)(B))

Other rules. No contract with IRS is necessary for a whistleblower to receive an award. (Code Sec. 7623(b)(6)(A))

A whistleblower may be represented by counsel. (Code Sec. 7623(b)(6)(B)) For an above-the-line deduction for attorneys' fees and court costs, see ¶ 1410.

No award may be made under Code Sec. 7623(b) based on information submitted to IRS unless the information is submitted under penalty of perjury. (Code Sec. 7623(b)(6)(C))

☐ **Effective:** Information provided on or after date of enactment. (2006 Tax Relief and Health Care Act §406(d))

> ***observation:*** Although the above-described reforms to the whistleblower reward program apply to information provided on or after date of enactment, the underlying conduct—i.e, the underpayments

of tax or tax law violations—may be for an earlier period. However, because a whistleblower award is based on "collected proceeds" (see above), the award will not be available where IRS is barred from proceeding against the person(s) responsible for an underpayment of tax, or the person(s) guilty of violating or conniving to violate the tax laws—for example, because the applicable statutory limitations period has expired.

¶ 1410. Above-the-line deduction is allowed for attorneys' fees and court costs relating to whistleblower rewards

Code Sec. 62(a)(21), as amended by 2006 Tax Relief and Health Care Act § 406(a)(3)
Generally effective: Information provided on or after date of enactment
Committee Reports, see ¶ 5057

IRS pays rewards to individuals (known as "whistleblowers") for providing information regarding tax law violations (see ¶ 1409 and FTC 2d/FIN ¶ T-1030 *et seq.*; USTR ¶ 76,234; TaxDesk ¶ 444,043). A deduction is allowed for attorneys' fees and costs incurred by the whistleblower in connection with these activities, if the fees and costs otherwise qualify as deductible legal expenses (see FTC 2d/FIN ¶ L-2901 *et seq.*; USTR ¶ 1624; TaxDesk ¶ 305,000 *et seq.*). Although certain expenses are specifically allowed as a deduction from gross income (including attorneys' fees and court costs of civil discrimination suits, see FTC 2d/FIN ¶ A-2628; USTR ¶ 624.04; TaxDesk ¶ 560,715.2), an "above-the-line" deduction generally isn't allowed for legal expenses. And pre-2006 Tax Relief and Health Care Act law didn't provide a specific above-the-line deduction for any expenses (including legal expenses) incurred by whistleblowers. (FTC 2d/FIN ¶ A-2601; USTR ¶ 624; TaxDesk ¶ 560,702) Thus, a whistleblower could deduct his whistleblower-related attorneys' fees and court costs (to the extent they were otherwise deductible) only if he itemized his deductions.

Moreover, in most cases, to the extent legal expenses are deductible, they are "miscellaneous itemized deductions" subject to a 2%-of-adjusted gross income (AGI) floor (see FTC 2d/FIN ¶ A-2725 *et seq.*; USTR ¶ 674; TaxDesk ¶ 561,600 *et seq.*) and to the overall limitation on itemized deductions (also known as the "Pease limitation," see FTC 2d/FIN ¶ A-2731; USTR ¶ 684; TaxDesk ¶ 561,801), and aren't deductible at all for alternative minimum tax (AMT) purposes (see FTC 2d/FIN ¶ A-8314; USTR ¶ 564.02; TaxDesk ¶ 697,014).

New Law. The 2006 Tax Relief and Health Care Act reforms the whistleblower reward program (Com Rept, see ¶ 5057) by increasing the amounts paid as rewards (see ¶ 1409), providing for appeals of reward determinations (see ¶ 1409), and establishing a Whistleblower Office within IRS (see ¶ 1411).

In addition, the 2006 Tax Relief and Health Care Act provides an above-the-line deduction for attorneys' fees and costs relating to whistleblower rewards paid for providing information regarding violations of the tax laws. (Com Rept, see ¶ 5057) Specifically, any deduction allowable under Chapter 1 of the Code (Code Sec. 1 through Code Sec. 1400T) for attorneys' fees and court costs paid by, or on behalf of, the taxpayer in connection with any Code Sec. 7623(b) whistleblower reward (see ¶ 1409) is—subject to the limit described below—added to the list of deductible expenses that are deducted from gross income. (Code Sec. 62(a)(21) as amended by 2006 Tax Relief and Health Care Act §406(a)(3))

> ***observation:*** In other word, the deduction for whistleblower attorneys' fees and court costs is an above-the-line deduction from gross income. This means the deduction is available to the whistleblower even if he doesn't itemize his deductions.
>
> Moreover, because the deduction is above-the-line, it's not subject to the 2%-of-AGI floor on miscellaneous itemized deductions or the overall limitation on itemized deductions (the Pease limitation), and it is deductible for AMT purposes.

> ***observation:*** The 2006 Tax Relief and Health Care Act doesn't provide a separate deduction for the whistleblower's attorneys' fees and court costs. The expenses still must qualify as deductible legal expenses (i.e., deductible if they're ordinary and necessary business expenses or nonbusiness expenses for the production of income, but not if they're capital expenditures, personal expenses, or incurred in connection with tax-exempt income, see FTC 2d/FIN ¶ L-2901 *et seq.*; USTR ¶ 1624; TaxDesk ¶ 305,000 *et seq.*).

> ***observation:*** The 2006 Tax Relief and Health Care Act provides for Tax Court appeals of determinations as to the amount or denial of whistleblower rewards (see ¶ 1409). Any otherwise deductible attorneys' fees or court costs incurred in connection with these appeals qualify for the above-the-line deduction.

> ***observation:*** The new Whistleblower Office may ask for additional assistance from the whistleblower or his legal representative (see

FTC 2d References are to Federal Tax Coordinator 2d
FIN References are to RIAs Analysis of Federal Taxes: Income
USTR References are to United States Tax Reporter: Income, Estate & Gift, and Excise
PCA References are to Pension Analysis (print & electronic)
PE References are to Pension Explanations (print & electronic)
EP References are to Estate Planning Analysis (print & electronic)

¶ 1411). The fees paid by the whistleblower to his attorney for providing the requested assistance may qualify for the above-the-line deduction. For the Whistleblower Office's reimbursement of the attorney's costs, see ¶ 1411.

This rule doesn't apply to any deduction in excess of the amount includible in the taxpayer's gross income for the tax year on account of the award. (Code Sec. 62(a)(21)) That is, the amount that may be deducted above-the-line may not exceed this includible amount. (Com Rept, see ¶ 5057)

observation: Although an above-the-line deduction isn't allowed for the "excess" attorneys' fees and court costs, the deduction itself isn't disallowed. That is, the whistleblower still can deduct the excess amounts, but only as miscellaneous itemized deductions. As such, the excess amounts are subject to the 2%-of-AGI floor on miscellaneous itemized deductions and the overall limitation on itemized deductions, and aren't deductible at all for AMT purposes.

The rule limiting the amount of the above-the-line deduction to the reward amount that's includible in the taxpayer's gross income for the tax year applies whether the reward is the result of a suit or agreement, and whether it's paid as a lump sum or periodic payments. (Com Rept, see ¶ 5057)

recommendation: Whistleblowers who incur substantial attorneys' fees and court costs in connection with their rewards should consider opting for a lump sum rather than periodic payments, to maximize their above-the-line deduction. In most cases, the whistleblower will pay the attorneys' fees in a single payment, most likely in the tax year in which the reward is first received. Because the lump-sum payment will be larger than any periodic payment, it will result in a larger includible amount. This, in turn, increases the ceiling on the amount allowed as an above-the-line deduction.

☐ **Effective:** Information provided on or after date of enactment. (2006 Tax Relief and Health Care Act §406(d))

¶ 1411. IRS Whistleblower Office is established to administer whistleblower reward program

Code Sec. 7623, 2006 Tax Relief and Health Care Act § 406(b)
Code Sec. 7623, 2006 Tax Relief and Health Care Act § 406(c)
Generally effective: date of enactment
Committee Reports, see ¶ 5057

IRS is authorized to pay awards to informers (known as "whistleblowers") who provide IRS with information for detecting underpayments of tax, or for detecting and bringing to trial and punishment persons guilty of violating, or conniving to violate, the tax laws. (FTC 2d/FIN ¶ T-1031; USTR ¶ 76,234; TaxDesk ¶ 444,043) The 2006 Tax Relief and Health Care Act increases whistleblower awards, see ¶ 1409.

New Law. The 2006 Tax Relief and Health Care Act provides for the establishment of a "Whistleblower Office" within IRS to administer the whistleblower reward program. (Com Rept, see ¶ 5057)

Specifically, the Secretary of the Treasury is required to issue guidance for the operation of a whistleblower program to be administered in IRS by an office to be known as the "Whistleblower Office." The guidance must be issued no later than 12 months after date of enactment. (2006 Tax Relief and Health Care Act §406(b)(1))

The Whistleblower Office (2006 Tax Relief and Health Care Act §406(b)(1)):

(1) must at all times operate at the direction of the IRS Commissioner, and coordinate and consult with other IRS divisions as directed by the Commissioner (2006 Tax Relief and Health Care Act §406(b)(1)(A)),

(2) must analyze information received from any whistleblower, and either investigate the matter itself or assign it to the appropriate IRS office (2006 Tax Relief and Health Care Act §406(b)(1)(B)), and

(3) in its sole discretion, may ask for additional assistance (see below) from the whistleblower or his legal representative (if any). (2006 Tax Relief and Health Care Act §406(b)(1)(C))

> ***observation:*** The Whistleblower Office must also determine the amount to be awarded to the whistleblower under the rules discussed at ¶ 1409.

FTC 2d References are to Federal Tax Coordinator 2d
FIN References are to RIAs Analysis of Federal Taxes: Income
USTR References are to United States Tax Reporter: Income, Estate & Gift, and Excise
PCA References are to Pension Analysis (print & electronic)
PE References are to Pension Explanations (print & electronic)
EP References are to Estate Planning Analysis (print & electronic)

Congress expects that, to the extent possible, the Treasury guidance will address the recommendations of the Treasury Inspector General for Tax Administration (TIGTA) regarding the informant's reward program, including the recommendations to centralize management of the reward program and to reduce the processing time for claims. (Com Rept, see ¶ 5057) For recommendations from IRS, see below.

Requests for assistance from whistleblower or his legal representative. The above-described guidance must specify that any assistance requested under item (3), above, must be under the direction and control of the Whistleblower Office or the IRS office assigned to investigate the matter under item (1) above. (2006 Tax Relief and Health Care Act §406(b)(2))

To the extent that disclosure of returns or return information is required to render the requested assistance, the disclosure must be made under an IRS tax administration contract (i.e., a contract between IRS and the recipients of the disclosure that permits disclosures of returns and return information for tax administration purposes, see FTC 2d/FIN ¶ S-6324; USTR ¶ 61,034.01). Congress expects that disclosures will be infrequent and will be made only when the assigned task cannot be properly or timely completed without the return information to be disclosed. (Com Rept, see ¶ 5057)

No individual or legal representative whose assistance is requested may, by reason of the request, represent himself as an employee of the federal government. (2006 Tax Relief and Health Care Act §406(b)(2))

The Whistleblower Office may reimburse the costs incurred by any legal representative out of the amount of the reward. (Com Rept, see ¶ 5057)

> ***observation:*** The amount that the whistleblower ultimately receives as a reward is reduced by amounts that the Whistleblower Office pays to his legal representative as a reimbursement for costs incurred.

> ***observation:*** The 2006 Tax Relief and Health Care Act doesn't provide for reimbursement of any costs incurred by the whistleblower. However, the whistleblower is allowed an above-the-line deduction for attorney's fees and court costs (see ¶ 1410).

Annual reports by IRS. Every year, IRS must conduct a study and report to Congress on the use of the whistleblower rules (2006 Tax Relief and Health Care Act §406(c)), including the effectiveness of the whistleblower reward program. (Com Rept, see ¶ 5057) The report must include (2006 Tax Relief and Health Care Act §406(c)):

(1) an analysis of the use of the whistleblower rules during the preceding year and the results of that use (2006 Tax Relief and Health Care Act §406(c)(1)), and

(2) any legislative or administrative recommendations regarding the whistleblower rules and their application. (2006 Tax Relief and Health Care Act §406(c)(2))

☐ **Effective:** date of enactment. (Com Rept, see ¶ 5057)

¶ 1412. IRS's authority to churn income earned from undercover operations is extended through 2007

Code Sec. 7608(c)(6), as amended by 2006 Tax Relief and Health Care Act § 121
Generally effective: date of enactment
Committee Reports, see ¶ 5025

IRS undercover operations may be exempted from otherwise applicable non-tax federal law controlling the use of government funds (which, generally, require that all receipts be deposited into the general fund of the U.S. Treasury, and all expenses be paid out of appropriated funds). (Com Rept, see ¶ 5025) In general, the exemption (i.e., a waiver of the general rules that's made based on IRS's written certification that the actions authorized are necessary for the conduct of the operation) permits IRS to use proceeds from a large undercover operation to pay additional expenses incurred in the operation (e.g., to buy property, lease space, establish or acquire businesses, deposit IRS appropriations and proceeds from the undercover operation, and use the proceeds to offset operation expenses). IRS is thus permitted to "churn" the income earned in an undercover operation to pay additional expenses incurred in the operation. (FTC 2d/FIN ¶ T-1182.1; USTR ¶ 76,084)

Under pre-2006 Tax Relief and Health Care Act law, this authority expired after Dec. 31, 2006. All amounts IRS spent for the undercover operations had to be recovered to the extent possible, and deposited in the U.S. Treasury as miscellaneous receipts, before Jan. 1, 2007. (FTC 2d/FIN ¶ T-1182.1; USTR ¶ 76,084)

New Law. Under the 2006 Tax Relief and Health Care Act, the authority is extended to apply before Jan. 1, 2008. (Code Sec. 7608(c)(6)(B) as amended by 2006 Tax Relief and Health Care Act §121) Thus, the provision extends for one year (through Dec. 31, 2007) IRS's authority to use proceeds from undercover operations to pay additional expenses incurred in conducting undercover operations. (Com Rept, see ¶ 5025)

Before Jan. 1, 2008, IRS has to deposit in the U.S. Treasury, as miscellaneous receipts, any recoveries of amounts spent for undercover operations. (Code Sec. 7608(c)(6))

☐ **Effective:** date of enactment (Com Rept, see ¶ 5025)

¶ 1500. Excise Taxes

¶ 1501. Reduced retail excise tax rates for qualified methanol and qualified ethanol fuels (scheduled to terminate after Sept. 30, 2007) are extended through Dec. 31, 2008

Code Sec. 4041(b)(2)(C)(ii), as amended by 2006 Tax Relief and Health Care Act § 208(b)
Code Sec. 4041(b)(2)(D), as amended by 2006 Tax Relief and Health Care Act § 208(a)
Generally effective: date of enactment
Committee Reports, see ¶ 5038

Qualified methanol and qualified ethanol fuels—i.e., liquid at least 85% of which consists of methanol, ethanol or other alcohol produced from coal (including peat)—are taxed at a reduced excise tax rate on the retail sale for use, or use, of the fuel in a motor vehicle or motorboat.

The reduced rate for qualified methanol fuel is 12.35¢ per gallon—computed as follows: the otherwise applicable 18.3¢ per gallon regular retail excise tax rate under Code Sec. 4041(a)(2) (a) *minus* 6¢ per gallon, and (b) *plus* the Leaking Underground Storage Tank trust fund financing rate ("LUST tax") imposed at a special, reduced rate of .05¢ per gallon.

And the reduced rate for qualified ethanol fuel is 13.25¢ per gallon—computed as follows, the otherwise applicable 18.3¢ per gallon regular retail excise tax rate (a) *minus,* for sales or uses for calendar years 2001 through 2007, 1⁄10 of the Code Sec. 40(h)(2) alcohol fuel credit "blender amount" (i.e., for 2005-2007, 51¢ per gallon) for the calendar year of the sale or use, i.e., for 2005-2007, 5.1¢ per gallon, and (b) *plus* the special .05¢ per gallon LUST tax rate.

Under pre-2006 Tax Relief and Health Care Act law, these reduced rates were scheduled to terminate after Sept. 30, 2007. (FTC 2d ¶ W-1725; USTR Excise Taxes ¶ 40,414)

New Law. The 2006 Tax Relief and Health Care Act extends application of the reduced retail excise tax rates for qualified methanol and ethanol fuels through Dec. 31, 2008. (Com Rept, see ¶ 5038) Specifically:

FTC 2d References are to Federal Tax Coordinator 2d
FIN References are to RIAs Analysis of Federal Taxes: Income
USTR References are to United States Tax Reporter: Income, Estate & Gift, and Excise
PCA References are to Pension Analysis (print & electronic)
PE References are to Pension Explanations (print & electronic)
EP References are to Estate Planning Analysis (print & electronic)

. . . The rules for computing the reduced qualified ethanol fuel tax rate are modified to provide that the reduced rate equals the otherwise applicable 18.3¢ per gallon regular retail excise tax rate (a) minus, for sales or uses for calendar years 2001 through *2008*, 1/10 of the Code Sec. 40(h)(2) alcohol fuel credit blender amount for the calendar year of the sale or use (Code Sec. 4041(b)(2)(C)(ii) as amended by 2006 Tax Relief and Health Care Act §208(b)), and (b) plus the .05¢ per gallon LUST tax rate. (Code Sec. 4041(b)(2)(A))

> ***observation:*** Because the Code Sec. 40(h)(2) alcohol fuel credit blender amount for 2008 is the same 51¢ per gallon rate as in effect for 2005-2007 (see FTC 2d/FIN ¶ L-17501; USTR ¶ 404.02), the reduced rate for qualified ethanol fuel sold or used in calendar year 2008 remains 13.25¢ per gallon (i.e., 18.3¢ per gallon retail tax rate, minus 5.1¢ per gallon, and plus the .05¢ LUST tax rate).

. . . The termination date for the qualified methanol and qualified ethanol reduced retail excise tax rates is changed (from "on and after Oct. 1, 2007") to "on and after Jan. 1, 2009." (Code Sec. 4041(b)(2)(D) as amended by 2006 Tax Relief and Health Care Act §208(a))

> ***observation:*** That is, the 12.35¢ per gallon rate for qualified methanol fuel and the 13.25¢ per gallon rate for qualified ethanol fuel are extended to apply for sales or uses during the period Oct. 1, 2007 through Dec. 31, 2008.

☐ **Effective:** date of enactment (Com Rept, see ¶ 5038)

¶ 1502. Ultimate purchaser of kerosene for exempt aviation use (other than state and local government) may claim excise tax refund itself, for fuel sold after Sept. 30, 2005

Code Sec. 6427(l)(4), as amended by 2006 Tax Relief and Health Care Act § 420(a)
Generally effective: For kerosene sold after Sept. 30, 2005
Committee Reports, see ¶ 5071

Generally, if kerosene on which excise tax has been imposed is used for a "nontaxable use," a refund, in the amount of that tax, may be obtained either by the purchaser, or in specified cases, the kerosene's registered ultimate vendor (see FTC 2d ¶s W-1564.2, W-1739.1, USTR Excise Taxes ¶ 64,274). However, other than in cases of export, tax imposed at the 0.1¢-per-gallon Leaking Underground Storage Tank Trust Fund financing rate (the "LUST tax" rate) , isn't refundable (see FTC 2d ¶ W-1542, USTR Excise Taxes ¶ 64,304).

A "nontaxable use" here is any use that's exempt from the retail excise tax under Code Sec. 4041(a)(1) (other than by reason of the prior imposition of tax), e.g., use on a farm, use in foreign trade, use by a state or local government, or exportation (see FTC 2d ¶ W-1564.2, USTR Excise Taxes ¶ 64,274). Because imposition of the retail excise tax is limited to delivery into the fuel supply tank of a diesel-powered highway vehicle or train, kerosene delivered into an aircraft's fuel supply tank is a nontaxable use for purposes of Code Sec. 4041(a)(1) (see FTC 2d ¶ W-1707.1, USTR Excise Taxes ¶ 40,414). However, if kerosene is removed from a refinery or terminal directly into the fuel tank of an aircraft for use in aviation, in addition to the LUST tax rate, the kerosene is subject to a Code Sec. 4081 removal-at-terminal tax but at the following reduced rates: (i) 4.3¢ per gallon for use in commercial aviation by a registered person, (ii) 21.8¢ per gallon for noncommercial aviation use (see FTC 2d ¶ W-1501.1, USTR Excise Taxes ¶ 40,814), and (iii) 0¢ per gallon for a use that's exempt from the retail tax imposed under Code Sec. 4041(c) on kerosene used in aviation (other than by the prior imposition of tax) (see FTC 2d ¶ W-1515.2, USTR Excise Taxes ¶ 40,824).

If kerosene is taxed at 24.4¢ per gallon (i.e., the 24.3¢ regular kerosene removal-at-terminal tax rate, plus the 0.1¢ per gallon LUST tax rate), but is later used in aviation, a partial refund is available, which operates to reduce the actual tax paid to an amount equal to the reduced rates described above—that is, a refund is available of: 2.5¢ per gallon for taxable use in noncommercial aviation; 20¢ per gallon for use in commercial aviation; or 24.3¢ per gallon if the aviation use is a nontaxable use (other than export, for which a full refund is available) (see FTC 2d ¶ W-1564.2, USTR Excise Taxes ¶ 64,274). For commercial aviation use, the ultimate purchaser of the kerosene may file the refund claim, or it may waive the right to make the claim to the fuel's registered ultimate vendor (see FTC 2d ¶ W-1564.2D, USTR Excise Taxes ¶ 64,274). However, under pre-2006 Tax Relief and Health Care Act law, effective Oct. 1, 2005, the ultimate purchaser of kerosene used in noncommercial aviation (for either a taxable or nontaxable use) was barred from making a refund claim, and instead, the claim could only be made by the registered ultimate vendor of the fuel. (FTC 2d ¶ W-1564.2E; USTR Excise Taxes ¶ 64,274)

Separate, special rules apply for kerosene sold to a state or local government, regardless of whether the kerosene is sold for aviation or other purposes. These rules, generally, require that the registered ultimate vendor make the refund claim on behalf of the state or local government (see FTC 2d ¶ W-1564.2C, USTR Excise Taxes ¶ 64,274).

New Law. Retroactive for kerosene sold after Sept. 30, 2005 (2006 Tax Relief and Health Care Act §420(c)(1)), the 2006 Tax Relief and Heath Care Act generally allows purchasers that use kerosene for an exempt aviation purpose (other than a state or local government), to make a claim for refund of the tax that was paid on the fuel, or waive their right to claim the refund to the registered ultimate vendor of the fuel. As a result, under the provision, crop-dusters, air ambulances, aircraft engaged in foreign trade, and other exempt users may either make the claim for refund of the 24.3¢ per gallon tax themselves or waive that right to their vendors. (Com Rept, see ¶ 5071) For special rules for certain pending claims and farm use, see the end of this article.

Specifically, for kerosene sold after Sept. 30, 2005 (2006 Tax Relief and Health Care Act §420(c)(1)) that's used in aviation, the ultimate purchaser may waive its right to refund (or credit) under Code Sec. 6427(l)(1) (the general rule permitting an ultimate purchaser of kerosene to claim a refund of the Code Sec. 4041 retail or the Code Sec. 4081 removal-at-terminal tax for a later non-taxable use of the fuel) to the ultimate vendor, and IRS will pay that amount to the ultimate vendor, except as otherwise provided below. However, this rule doesn't apply to: (1) kerosene described in Code Sec. 6427(l)(4)(C)(ii) (i.e., kerosene that's used for general noncommercial aviation use, see below); and (2) kerosene sold to a state or local government. (Code Sec. 6427(l)(4)(C)(i) as amended by 2006 Tax Relief and Health Care Act §420(a))

For an ultimate vendor to be permitted to make the refund claim waived by the ultimate purchaser as described above, the ultimate vendor must be registered with IRS (Code Sec. 6427(l)(4)(C)(i)(I)), and must meet the requirements under Code Sec. 6416(a)(1)(A), Code Sec. 6416(a)(1)(B) or Code Sec. 6416(a)(1)(D)—i.e., the vendor must establish that it: (i) hasn't included the tax in the price of the fuel and hasn't collected the tax from the purchaser; (ii) has repaid the tax to the ultimate purchaser; or (iii) has filed with IRS a written consent to allowance of the credit or refund obtained from the ultimate purchaser, see FTC 2d ¶ W-2417; USTR Excise Taxes ¶ 64,164. (Code Sec. 6427(l)(4)(C)(i)(II))

Code Sec. 6427(l)(4)(C)(ii), referenced above, specifically provides that the amount that would be paid under Code Sec. 6427(l)(1) with respect to any kerosene to which Code Sec. 6427(l)(4)(B) applies—i.e., kerosene that's used for general (taxable) noncommercial aviation use, see below—is paid only to the ultimate vendor of the kerosene. This ultimate vendor must also be registered with IRS, and must meet the above-described requirements under Code Sec. 6416(a)(1)(A), Code Sec. 6416(a)(1)(B), or Code Sec. 6416(a)(1)(D). (Code Sec. 6427(l)(4)(C)(ii))

And *Code Sec. 6427(l)(4)(B),* referenced above, limits the amount of refund (or credit) permitted under Code Sec. 6427(l)(1) to 2.5¢ per gallon if the kerosene was taxed at 24.4¢ per gallon (or to 0¢ per gallon, if the kerosene was taxed at 21.9¢ per gallon) where the kerosene is later used in noncommercial aviation, other than any use that's exempt from the retail tax imposed on kerosene used in aviation under Code Sec. 4041(c) (other than by a prior imposition of tax). (Code Sec. 6427(l)(4)(B))

> ***observation:*** Thus, under the provisions of Code Sec. 6427(l)(4)(C)(i), Code Sec. 6427(l)(4)(C)(ii) and Code Sec. 6427(l)(4)(B), taken together, the *ultimate purchaser* of kerosene that's used for a *nontaxable, noncommercial aviation use* may claim a refund (or credit) itself, or may waive that right to the ultimate vendor (who may make the claim if the above-described conditions are met). This refund claim will be for 24.3¢ per gallon.

General noncommercial aviation use (i.e., taxable noncommercial aviation use that's entitled to a refund of only 2.5¢ per gallon, as described under Code Sec. 6427(l)(4)(B) above) remains subject to the exclusive ultimate vendor refund rules. (Com Rept, see ¶ 5071)

In addition, the 2006 Tax Relief and Health Care Act doesn't change the refund rules for kerosene used in commercial aviation, other than to: (i) combine them (in Code Sec. 6427(l)(4)) with the rules for kerosene used in noncommercial aviation, and (ii) clarify that the 4.3¢-per-gallon in tax whether imposed under Code Sec. 4081 *or Code Sec. 4041* isn't refundable (or creditable) (other than where the kerosene is used as supplies for vessels or aircraft within the meaning of Code Sec. 4221(d)(3)). (Code Sec. 6427(l)(4)(A))

Further, the substance of the special rules for state and local governments (Code Sec. 6427(l)(5) as redesignated by 2006 Tax Relief and Health Care Act §420(b)(1)) remains unchanged. (Com Rept, see ¶ 5071)

☐ **Effective:** For kerosene sold after Sept. 30, 2005 (2006 Tax Relief and Health Care Act §420(c)(1)), *subject to the special rules below.*

Special rule for pending refund claims. For kerosene used for an aviation use—other than a general (taxable) noncommercial aviation use described in Code Sec. 6427(l)(4)(C)(ii), or by a state or local government (as described in Code Sec. 6427(l)(5)—that was sold after Sept. 30, 2005, and before date of enactment, the ultimate purchaser is treated as having waived the right to payment under Code Sec. 6427(l)(1) and as having assigned the right to the ulti-

FTC 2d References are to Federal Tax Coordinator 2d
FIN References are to RIAs Analysis of Federal Taxes: Income
USTR References are to United States Tax Reporter: Income, Estate & Gift, and Excise
PCA References are to Pension Analysis (print & electronic)
PE References are to Pension Explanations (print & electronic)
EP References are to Estate Planning Analysis (print & electronic)

mate vendor, if the ultimate vendor has met the requirements of Code Sec. 6416(a)(1)(A), Code Sec. 6416(a)(1)(B), or Code Sec. 6416(a)(1)(D) (described above). (2006 Tax Relief and Health Care Act §420(c)(2)) In other words, for kerosene sold after Sept. 30, 2005 and before date of enactment that's used for an exempt aviation purpose eligible for the above-described waiver rule created by the 2006 Tax Relief and Health Care Act (i.e., kerosene used for a nontaxable, noncommercial aviation use), the ultimate purchaser is treated as having waived the right to payment and assigned that right to the ultimate vendor if the ultimate vendor meets the requirements of Code Sec. 6416(a)(1)(A), Code Sec. 6416(a)(1)(B), or Code Sec. 6416(a)(1)(D). (Com Rept, see ¶ 5071)

Special rule for kerosene purchased after Dec. 31, 2004 and before Oct. 1, 2005 that's used in aviation on a farm for farming purposes. For kerosene used in aviation on a farm for farming purposes (see below) that was purchased after Dec. 31, 2004 and before Oct. 1, 2005, IRS is to pay to the ultimate purchaser (2006 Tax Relief and Health Care Act §420(d)(1)), without interest (Com Rept, see ¶ 5071), an amount equal to the aggregate amount of tax imposed on the fuel under Code Sec. 4041 or Code Sec. 4081, as applicable, reduced by any payment made to the ultimate vendor of the fuel under (former) Code Sec. 6427(l)(5)(C), as in effect the day before the date of enactment of the 2005 Transportation Act (PL 109-59, 8/10/2005) (2006 Tax Relief and Health Care Act §420(d)(1)), i.e., as in effect on Aug. 9, 2005.

For purposes of the special farm use refund rule above, kerosene is treated as used on a farm for farming purposes if the kerosene is used for farming purposes (within the meaning of Code Sec. 6420(c)(3), relating to the refunds for farm use of gasoline) in carrying on a trade or business on a farm situated in the U.S. And for purposes of this definition, rules similar to the special rules of Code Sec. 6420(c)(4) permitting aerial or other applicators to claim the farm use gasoline tax credit apply. (2006 Tax Relief and Health Care Act §420(d)(2))

> ***observation:*** Specifically, Code Sec. 6420(c)(3) (see FTC 2d ¶ W-1546, USTR Excise Taxes ¶ 64,204.01) provides that use is farm use only if it is by the owner, tenant, or operator of a farm:
>
> . . . in connection with cultivating the soil, or raising or harvesting any agricultural or horticultural commodity on the farmer's own farm, including the raising, shearing, feeding, caring for, training, and management of livestock, bees, poultry, fur-bearing animals, and wildlife;
>
> . . . in handling, drying, packing, grading, or storing any agricultural or horticultural commodity in its unmanufactured state; but only if the farmer produced more than one-half the commodity that he so treated during the period for which the credit is claimed;

. . . in connection with the planting, cultivating, caring for or cutting of trees, or the preparation (other than milling) of trees for market, if incidental to farming operations; or

. . . in connection with the operation, management, conservation, improvement, or maintenance of the farm and its tools and equipment.

And Code Sec. 6420(c)(4) (see FTC 2d ¶ W-1543, USTR Excise Taxes ¶ 64,204.01) provides that if the person hired by an owner, operator or tenant to perform the above-described farming operations is an aerial or other applicator of fertilizers or other substances, and that aerial or other applicator is the ultimate purchaser of the gasoline, the aerial or other applicator (and not the owner, operator or tenant) is treated as having used the gasoline on the farm for farming purposes, and is allowed to claim the credit (or refund).

No claim will be allowed under the farm use refund rule above unless the ultimate purchaser files the claim before the date that is three months after date of enactment. (2006 Tax Relief and Health Care Act §420(d)(3))

No amount will be paid under the special farm use refund rule above or Code Sec. 6427(l) with respect to any kerosene described in 2006 Tax Relief and Health Care Act §420(d)(1) above, to the extent that the amount is in excess of the tax imposed on the kerosene under Code Sec. 4041 or Code Sec. 4081. (2006 Tax Relief and Health Care Act §420(d)(4)) That is, duplicate claims (for the farm use) may not be filed under Code Sec. 6427(l). (Com Rept, see ¶ 5071)

For purposes of the special farm use rules, rules similar to the Code Sec. 6427(j) rules applicable to the various refund/credit claims permitted under Code Sec. 6427 apply. (2006 Tax Relief and Health Care Act §420(d)(5))

observation: Thus, for the special farm use refund rules, rules similar to the Code Sec. 6427(j) rules below (see FTC 2d ¶s W-1564.6, W-1739, USTR Excise Taxes ¶ 76,094) will apply:

. . . all provisions of law, including penalties, that apply with respect to the taxes imposed by Code Sec. 4041 and Code Sec. 4081 (to the extent applicable and not inconsistent with the Code Sec. 6427 refund provisions) apply to the refunds/credits provided for under Code Sec. 6427, to the same extent as if the payments were refunds of overpayments of the Code Sec. 4041 or Code Sec. 4081 tax; and

FTC 2d References are to Federal Tax Coordinator 2d
FIN References are to RIAs Analysis of Federal Taxes: Income
USTR References are to United States Tax Reporter: Income, Estate & Gift, and Excise
PCA References are to Pension Analysis (print & electronic)
PE References are to Pension Explanations (print & electronic)
EP References are to Estate Planning Analysis (print & electronic)

... for purposes of ascertaining the correctness of any claim made under Code Sec. 6427, or the correctness of any payment made with respect to that credit/refund claim, IRS has authority under Code Sec. 7602(a)(1), Code Sec. 7602(a)(2), and Code Sec. 7602(a)(3) (relating to examination of books and witnesses) as if the claimant were the person liable for the tax.

¶ 1503. Meningococcal vaccine and human papillomavirus vaccine is subject to 75 cents per dose manufacturers excise tax

Code Sec. 4132(a)(1)(O), as amended by 2006 Tax Relief and Health Care Act § 408(a)
Code Sec. 4132(a)(1)(P), as amended by 2006 Tax Relief and Health Care Act § 408(b)
Generally effective: Sales and uses on or after first day of first month beginning more than four weeks after date of enactment
Committee Reports, see ¶ 5059

An excise tax of 75 cents per dose is imposed on a manufacturer's, producer's, or importer's sale, or use before sale, of taxable vaccines. Where the vaccine consists of a combination of taxable vaccine components, this so-called manufacturers excise tax equals 75 cents times the number of taxable components. (FTC 2d ¶ W-2953, USTR Excise Taxes ¶ 41,314) Under pre-2006 Tax Relief and Health Care Act law, the following commonly prescribed vaccines were taxable vaccines: diphtheria, tetanus, pertussis, measles, mumps, rubella, polio, HIB (haemophilus influenza type B), hepatitis B, varicella (chicken pox), rotavirus gastroenteritis, streptococcus pneumoniae, influenza, and hepatitis A. (FTC 2d ¶ W-2952; USTR Excise Taxes ¶ 41,314)

New Law. The 2006 Tax Relief and Health Care Act adds any meningococcal vaccine (Code Sec. 4132(a)(1)(O) as amended by 2006 Tax Relief and Health Care Act §408(a)) and any vaccine against the human papillomavirus (Code Sec. 4132(a)(1)(P) as amended by 2006 Tax Relief and Health Care Act §408(b)) to the list of vaccines subject to the manufacturers excise tax.

☐ **Effective:** For sales and uses on or after the first day of the first month that begins more than four weeks after date of enactment. (2006 Tax Relief and Health Care Act §408(c)(1))

For sales on or before the effective date for which delivery is made after that date, the delivery date is treated as the sale date. (2006 Tax Relief and Health Care Act §408(c)(2))

¶ 1600. Miscellaneous Provisions

¶ 1601. Capital gain treatment for certain self-created musical works, originally set to expire Dec. 31, 2010, is made permanent

Code Sec. 1221(b)(3), as amended by 2006 Tax Relief and Health Care Act § 412(a)

Generally effective: Sales and exchanges in tax years beginning after May 17, 2006

Committee Reports, see ¶ 5063

The maximum tax rate on the net capital gain income of an individual for tax years beginning in 2006 is 15 percent, see FTC 2d/FIN ¶ I-5110.3; USTR ¶ 14.085; TaxDesk ¶ 223,312. The maximum tax rate on ordinary income of an individual for 2006, however, is 35 percent, see FTC 2d/FIN ¶ A-1102; USTR ¶ 14.08; TaxDesk ¶ 568,202. (Com Rept, see ¶ 5063)

Code Sec. 1221(a)(3) provides that copyrights or literary, musical, or artistic compositions, a letter or memorandum or similar property are not capital assets and also are not capital gain/ordinary loss assets if the taxpayer:

(1) created the copyrights, etc., through his or her own personal efforts, or

(2) in the case of a letter, memorandum, or similar property, was the one for whom the property was prepared or produced, or

(3) owns any property described in (1) or (2), above, whose basis is determined in whole or in part by reference to the basis of the property in the hands of a person who created the property through his personal efforts. See FTC 2d/FIN ¶ I-6601; USTR ¶ 12,214.45; TaxDesk ¶ 252,501.

Another exclusion from the definition of a capital asset is inventory property or property a taxpayer holds primarily for sale in the ordinary course of the taxpayer's trade or business, see FTC 2d/FIN ¶ I-6100; USTR ¶ 12,214.01; TaxDesk ¶ 249,500. (Com Rept, see ¶ 5063)

Under pre-2006 Tax Relief and Health Care Act law, a taxpayer may elect under Code Sec. 1221(b)(3) to treat the sale or exchange *before Jan. 1, 2011* of musical compositions or copyrights in musical works created by the taxpayer's personal efforts (or having a basis determined by reference to the basis in the hands of the taxpayer whose personal efforts created the compositions or copy-

---

FTC 2d References are to Federal Tax Coordinator 2d
FIN References are to RIAs Analysis of Federal Taxes: Income
USTR References are to United States Tax Reporter: Income, Estate & Gift, and Excise
PCA References are to Pension Analysis (print & electronic)
PE References are to Pension Explanations (print & electronic)
EP References are to Estate Planning Analysis (print & electronic)

rights) as the sale or exchange of a capital asset. (Com Rept, see ¶ 5063) Thus, if the taxpayer makes that election, Code Sec. 1221(a)(1) (which excludes from the definition of a capital asset, inventory or property held by the taxpayer primarily for sale to customers in the ordinary course of the taxpayer's trade or business) and Code Sec. 1221(a)(3) (which excludes from the definition of a capital asset, a copyright, literary, musical, or artistic composition, as further defined above) do not apply to sales or exchanges of musical compositions or copyrights in musical works. (FTC 2d/FIN ¶ I-6601; USTR ¶ 12,214.45; TaxDesk ¶ 252,501)

If "ordinary income property" (property any portion of the gain on which wouldn't have been long-term capital gain if the property had been sold by the taxpayer at its fair market value on the date it was contributed) is contributed to a charitable organization, the amount treated as contributed must be reduced by the amount (referred to as ordinary income) which would have been recognized as gain other than long-term capital gain if the property had been sold by the donor at its fair market value at the time of its contribution to the charitable organization, see FTC 2d/FIN ¶ K-3160; USTR ¶ 1704.42; TaxDesk ¶ 331,609. That is, a taxpayer is generally allowed a deduction for the fair market value of property contributed to a charity, except that, if a taxpayer contributes property that would have generated ordinary income (or short-term capital gain), the taxpayer's charitable contribution deduction is limited to the adjusted basis of the property. (Com Rept, see ¶ 5063)

Under pre-2006 Tax Relief and Health Care Act law, Code Sec. 170(e)(1)(A) provided that the amount of any charitable contribution otherwise taken into account as a deduction must be reduced by the amount of gain that would not have been long term capital gain (determined without regard to Code Sec. 1221(b)(3)) if the taxpayer had sold the contributed property at fair market value. The phrase "determined without regard to Code Sec. 1221(b)(3)" ensures that a taxpayer's charitable contribution deduction for a contribution of musical compositions or copyrights in musical works is limited to the adjusted basis of the property whether or not it is property described in Code Sec. 1221(b)(3) for which the capital gain treatment election would be available, see FTC 2d/FIN ¶ K-3160; USTR ¶ 1704.42; TaxDesk ¶ 331,609.

New Law. By striking the phrase, "before Jan. 1, 2011," from Code Sec. 1221(b)(3) (Code Sec. 1221(b)(3) as amended by 2006 Tax Relief and Health Care Act §412(a)), the 2006 Tax Relief and Health Care Act makes permanent the availability of the election under Code Sec. 1221(b)(3) to treat certain sales of musical compositions or copyrights in musical works created by the taxpayer's personal efforts (or having a basis determined by reference to the basis in the hands of the taxpayer whose personal efforts created the compositions or copyrights) as being sales of capital assets and therefore generating capital gain. (Com Rept, see ¶ 5063)

observation: Thus, for example, a composer who sells his or her copyrighted composition in a sale in a tax year beginning after May 17, 2006 will pay tax at the lower rates that apply to capital gain if he or she makes the election under Code Sec. 1221(b)(3). A painter or author, however, will not be eligible for that tax advantage.

The 2006 Tax Relief and Health Care Act also makes permanent the accompanying rule limiting to adjusted basis the amount of a charitable contribution deduction allowed for musical compositions or copyrights in musical works to which a taxpayer has elected the application of Code Sec. 1221(b)(3). (Com Rept, see ¶ 5063)

observation: Although Congress stated that the 2006 Tax Relief and Health Care Act made permanent the accompanying rule limiting the amount of the deduction for a charitable contribution for donated property that was subject to the election to treat it as capital gain property, there was no further amendment to a statute to achieve that objective. Under pre-2006 Tax Relief and Health Care Act law, Code Sec. 170(e)(1)(A) provided that the amount of any charitable contribution otherwise taken into account as a deduction must be reduced by the amount of gain that would not have been long term capital gain (determined without regard to Code Sec. 1221(b)(3)) if the taxpayer had sold the contributed property at fair market value. No amendment was necessary to continue this treatment.

observation: IRS has not yet issued guidance on the manner and time for making the election.

☐ **Effective:** Sales and exchanges in tax years beginning after May 17, 2006. (2006 Tax Relief and Health Care Act §412(b))

2006 Tax Relief and Health Care Act §412(b) provides that the above provision is effective as if included in Tax Increase and Prevention Act §204 (Sec. 204, PL 109-222, 5/17/2006). Under Tax Increase and Prevention Act §204(c) (Sec. 204(c), PL 109-222, 5/17/2006), Tax Increase and Prevention Act §204 is effective for sales and exchanges in tax years beginning after May 17, 2006.

¶ 1602. Code Sec. 355 active trade or business test that treats members of a separate affiliated group as one corporation made permanent

Code Sec. 355(b)(3)(A), as amended by 2006 Tax Relief and Health Care Act § 410(a)

Code Sec. 355(b)(3)(D), as amended by 2006 Tax Relief and Health Care Act § 410(a)

Generally effective: Distributions after May 17, 2006

Committee Reports, see ¶ 5061

One of the requirements for a tax-free Code Sec. 355 corporate division (e.g., a spin-off) in which a distributing corporation (D) distributes a controlling interest in its subsidiary (C) to one or more D shareholders is that immediately after the distribution D and C must each be engaged in the active conduct of a trade or business. This requires D and C to satisfy the Code Sec. 355(b)(2) business test. Under pre-Tax Increase Prevention Act (TIPRA) law, a corporation could only satisfy this test if it first met the following requirements:

(1) it was directly engaged in the active conduct of a trade or business, or

(2) substantially all of its assets consisted of stock and securities of a corporation (or corporations) it controlled immediately after the distribution and the controlled corporation(s) were engaged in the active conduct of a trade or business. (This list is referred to below as the Sec. 355(b)(2)(A) business test).

Under pre-2005 TIPRA law, the Sec. 355(b)(2)(A) business test resulted in applying a more stringent test where D held stock of corporations that were engaged in the active conduct of a trade or business, but was not directly engaged in the active conduct of a trade or business itself than the test that applied where D conducted an active business directly. Thus, a corporate group often had to restructure to satisfy the Sec. 355(b)(2)(A) business test (see Illustration (1) below). 2005 TIPRA addressed this problem for pre-2011 distributions by adding a rule under Code Sec. 355(b)(3) that treated a corporation as satisfying the Sec. 355(b)(2)(A) business test if, and only if, it was engaged in the active conduct of a trade or business and for this purpose treated all members of the corporation's "separate affiliated group" as one corporation. Thus, for pre-2011 distributions, the active trade or business test was applied on a group basis including all members of each separate affiliated group, and, as a practical matter, this replaced the Sec. 355(b)(2)(A) business test in almost all situations.

A corporation's separate affiliated group was the affiliated group that would be described under the 80% vote and value test of Code Sec. 1504(a) if the corporation were the common parent and the Code Sec. 1504(b) exclusions (e.g., for insurance companies and foreign corporations) did not apply. (FTC 2d/FIN ¶ F-4803; USTR ¶ 3554.02; TaxDesk ¶ 237,426.1) (FTC 2d/FIN ¶ E-7601; FTC

2d/FIN ¶ E-7606; FTC 2d/FIN ¶ E-7618; USTR ¶ 15,024.17; TaxDesk ¶ 603,300; TaxDesk ¶ 603,301; TaxDesk ¶ 603,303.)

> ***illustration (1):*** D owns 100% of the stock of C1 and C2, each of which is engaged in the active conduct of a trade or business, and 100% of the stock of C3, which holds the group's investments. D performs headquarters functions for its subsidiaries and is not directly engaged in the active conduct of a trade or business. C3's investments represent more than 25% of D's assets. In Oct. 2006, D decides to spin-off C1. D is engaged in the active conduct of a trade or business, because this requirement is tested for D by treating D, C2 and C3 as one corporation. Under pre-2005 TIPRA law, and for distributions after Dec. 31, 2010, D would have to assume that it didn't satisfy the active trade or business requirement (without restructuring) because it isn't directly engaged in the active conduct of a trade or business and C2 doesn't represent substantially all of its assets.

2005 TIPRA also added a special transition rule for determining the continued qualification under the Sec. 355(b)(2) business test of pre-effective date (i.e., pre-May 18, 2006) distributions as a result of a post-effective date acquisition, disposition or other restructuring that occurred after May 17, 2006 and before Jan. 1, 2011. Under Code Sec. 355(b)(3)(D), this distribution was treated as made on the date of the post-effective date acquisition, disposition or restructuring in applying the 2005 TIPRA amendment that added Code Sec. 355(b)(3). Thus, if D, a holding company, distributed C in a pre-May 18, 2006, distribution in which D satisfied the Sec. 355(b)(2)(A) business test of pre-2005 TIPRA law, D was not treated as violating any requirement that it continue that same qualified structure after the distribution solely because of a restructuring that occurred after May 17, 2006 (and before Jan 1, 2011) if the new structure satisfied the Sec 355(b)(2)(A) business test under Code Sec. 355(b)(3). (FTC 2d/FIN ¶ F-4803; USTR ¶ 3554.02; TaxDesk ¶ 237,426.1)

> ***illustration (2):*** Same facts as illustration (1), except that D distributed C1 in 2004 and before the distribution merged C2 and C3 to satisfy the Sec. 355(b)(2)(A) business test under pre-2005 TIPRA law. After May 17 2006, C3 is again organized as a separate corporation to protect its assets from C2 liabilities. The special transitional rule (above) bars IRS from contending that the merger of C2 and C3 was a transitory step that should be ignored so that D didn't satisfy pre-2005 TIPRA law when it distributed C1.

FTC 2d References are to Federal Tax Coordinator 2d
FIN References are to RIAs Analysis of Federal Taxes: Income
USTR References are to United States Tax Reporter: Income, Estate & Gift, and Excise
PCA References are to Pension Analysis (print & electronic)
PE References are to Pension Explanations (print & electronic)
EP References are to Estate Planning Analysis (print & electronic)

New Law. Under the 2006 Tax Relief and Health Care Act, Code Sec. 355(b)(3) no longer sunsets for post-Dec. 31, 2010, distributions. (Code Sec. 355(b)(3)(A) as amended by 2006 Tax Relief and Health Care Act §410(a)) Consistent with this amendment, the special transition rule applies to all post-May 17, 2006 restructurings. (Code Sec. 355(b)(3)(D) as amended by 2006 Tax Relief and Health Care Act §410(a))

> ***observation:*** The Code Sec. 355(b)(3)(D) amendment is unlikely to affect many transactions, since it would only be relevant if IRS applied the step transaction doctrine to a distribution and an acquisition, distribution or other restructuring separated by more than 3½ years, i.e., a pre-May-18, 2006 distribution and a post-2010 transaction. Thus, practically speaking, this amendment is largely a conforming amendment.

☐ **Effective:** Distributions made after May, 17, 2006. (2006 Tax Relief and Health Care Act §410(b))

2006 Tax Relief and Health Care Act § 410(b) provides that the above amendment is effective as if included in 2005 TIPRA §202 (Sec. 202, PL 109-222, 5/17/2006), which applies to distributions after May 17, 2006. (Code Sec. 355(b)(3)(A)); (Code Sec. 355(b)(3)(D))

¶ 1603. Qualified mortgage bonds can be used to finance mortgages for veterans without regard to first-time homebuyer requirement

Code Sec. 143(d)(2)(D), as amended by 2006 Tax Relief and Health Care Act § 416(a)

Generally effective: Bonds issued after date of enactment, and before Jan. 1, 2008

Committee Reports, see ¶ 5067

Tax-exempt status is available for certain state and local bonds used to finance mortgages. Private activity bonds issued after Aug. 15, '86 that are qualified mortgage bonds or qualified veterans' mortgage bonds are tax-exempt qualified bonds. (FTC 2d/FIN ¶ J-3179; USTR ¶ 1434)

An issue of qualified mortgage bonds must meet a number of requirements, including the "first-time homebuyer requirement" (also known as the "three-year requirement"), under which at least 95% of the net proceeds of the issue must be used to finance the residences of mortgagors who had no present ownership interest in their principal residences during the three-year period ending on the date the mortgage is executed.

> ***observation:*** In other words, during the three-year period ending on the execution date of the mortgage being financed with the proceeds of

a qualified mortgage issue, the mortgagor may not have had any present ownership interest in any principal residence other than the residence being financed with that mortgage.

The first-time homebuyer requirement is treated as satisfied for the proceeds of an issue that are used to provide financing for targeted-area residences, qualified home improvement loans, qualified rehabilitation loans, and financing for land possessed under a contract for deed and the construction of any residence on that land. The requirement is also treated as satisfied by financing provided for certain residences affected by Hurricane Katrina in 2005. (FTC 2d/FIN ¶ J-3187; USTR ¶ 1434.012) Under pre-2006 Tax Relief and Health Care Act law, there was no exception for proceeds used to finance mortgages for veterans.

An issue of qualified mortgage bonds must also meet, among other requirements, limitations on the mortgagor's income (see FTC 2d/FIN ¶ J-3193; USTR ¶ 1434.014) and the residence's purchase price (see FTC 2d/FIN ¶ J-3191; USTR ¶ 1434.013).

Mortgages for veterans can also be financed with qualified veterans' mortgage bonds (see ¶ 1604). Only five states are authorized to issue these bonds. Eligibility for mortgages varies among the states. For bonds issued by Alaska, Oregon, and Wisconsin, the veteran must have:

. . . served on active duty, and

. . . applied for the financing before the date 25 years after the last date on which the veteran left active service.

For bonds issued by California and Texas, the veteran must have:

. . . served on active duty at some time before Jan. 1, '77, and

. . . applied for the financing before the later of: (1) 30 years after the veteran left active service or (2) Jan. 31, '85. (FTC 2d/FIN ¶ J-3182.1; USTR ¶ 1434.019)

New Law. The 2006 Tax Relief and Health Care Act allows qualified mortgage bonds to be issued to finance mortgages for veterans who served in the active military without regard to the first-time homebuyer requirement. Veterans are eligible for this exception without regard to the date they last served on active duty or the date they applied for a loan after leaving active duty. However, a veteran may use this exception only once. (Com Rept, see ¶ 5067)

FTC 2d References are to Federal Tax Coordinator 2d
FIN References are to RIAs Analysis of Federal Taxes: Income
USTR References are to United States Tax Reporter: Income, Estate & Gift, and Excise
PCA References are to Pension Analysis (print & electronic)
PE References are to Pension Explanations (print & electronic)
EP References are to Estate Planning Analysis (print & electronic)

Thus, the 2006 Tax Relief and Health Care Act provides that, for bonds issued after date of enactment, and before Jan. 1, 2008, the first-time homebuyer requirement for qualified mortgage bonds is treated as satisfied for financing of any residence for a veteran (as defined in 38 USC §101), if the veteran hasn't previously qualified for and received financing under this exception. (Code Sec. 143(d)(2)(D) as amended by 2006 Tax Relief and Health Care Act §416(a))

> ***observation:*** Under 38 USC §101, the term "veteran" means a person who served in the active military, naval, or air service, and who was discharged or released under conditions other than dishonorable.

Loans to veterans financed with the proceeds of qualified mortgage bonds must meet the limitations on the mortgagor's income and the residence's purchase price. (Com Rept, see ¶ 5067)

☐ **Effective:** Bonds issued after date of enactment (2006 Tax Relief and Health Care Act §416(b)), and before Jan. 1, 2008. (Code Sec. 143(d)(2)(D))

¶ 1604. $25 million volume limits on qualified veterans' mortgage bonds issued by Alaska, Oregon, and Wisconsin won't sunset after 2010

Code Sec. 143(l)(3)(B), as amended by 2006 Tax Relief and Health Care Act § 411(a)
Generally effective: Allocations of state volume limit after Apr. 5, 2006
Committee Reports, see ¶ 5062

Qualified veterans' mortgage bonds are private activity bonds whose proceeds are used to make mortgage loans to certain veterans. Only states that had issued veterans' mortgage bonds before June 22, '84 are eligible to issue them. Those states are Alaska, California, Oregon, Texas, and Wisconsin.

The Tax Increase Prevention Act (2005 TIPRA, PL 109-222, 5/17/2006) provided new annual state volume limits of $25 million each for Alaska, Oregon, and Wisconsin. The limits are phased in during calendar years 2006–2010. The volume limits for those states are:

. . . $5 million (20% of $25 million) in 2006;

. . . $10 million (40% of $25 million) in 2007;

. . . $15 million (60% of $25 million) in 2008; and

. . . $20 million (80% of $25 million) in 2009.

In 2010, each of the three states can issue the full $25 million of qualified veterans' mortgage bonds. Under pre-2006 Tax Relief and Health Care Act law, the limits for Alaska, Oregon, and Wisconsin were to be reduced to zero for 2011 and thereafter. (FTC 2d/FIN ¶ J-3182; USTR ¶ 1434.019)

Under pre-2005 TIPRA law, mortgage loans made with the proceeds of bonds issued by all five states could be made only to veterans who served on active duty before '77 and who applied for the financing before the date 30 years after the last date on which the veteran left active service. However, for qualified veterans' mortgage bonds issued by Alaska, Oregon, and Wisconsin, 2005 TIPRA repealed the requirement that veterans must have served before '77 and reduced the eligibility period to 25 years (rather than 30 years) following release from military service. (FTC 2d/FIN ¶ J-3182.1; USTR ¶ 1434.019)

> ***observation:*** Before 2005 TIPRA, loans under the qualified veterans' bond program were available to a dwindling number of older veterans. However, 2005 TIPRA expanded the program in Alaska, Oregon, and Wisconsin by making loans available to more recent veterans, including potentially those currently on active duty.

New Law. The 2006 Tax Relief and Health Care Act repeals the sunset after 2010 of the annual state volume limits for Alaska, Oregon, and Wisconsin. (Code Sec. 143(l)(B)(3) as amended by 2006 Tax Relief and Health Care Act §411(a)) The total volume of qualified veterans' mortgage bonds that can be issued in each of those states is $25 million for 2010 and each calendar year thereafter. (Com Rept, see ¶ 5062)

Thus, the provision makes permanent 2005 TIPRA's changes to the state volume limits for qualified veterans' mortgage bonds issued by Alaska, Oregon, and Wisconsin and the definition of an eligible veteran. (Com Rept, see ¶ 5062)

> ***observation:*** The 2006 Tax Relief and Health Care Act makes only one statutory change, repealing the sunset on bonds issued by Alaska, Oregon, and Wisconsin that was in former Code Sec. 143(l)(B)(3)(iv), thus allowing those three states to issue qualified veterans' bonds after 2010. The revised definition of an eligible veteran—i.e., a veteran who served on active duty and applied for the financing before the date 25 years after the last date on which the veteran left active service—will thus apply permanently to bonds issued by the three states.

☐ **Effective:** Allocations of state volume limit after Apr. 5, 2006. (2006 Tax Relief and Health Care Act §411(b)) 2006 Tax Relief and Health Care Act §411(b) provides that the above provision is effective as if included in §203 of 2005 TIPRA (Sec. 203, PL 109-222, 5/17/2006). The above rules relate to 2005 TIPRA §203(b)(1) (Sec. 203(b)(1), PL 109-222, 5/17/2006) which, under 2005

TIPRA §203(b)(2) (Sec. 203(b)(2), PL 109-222, 5/17/2006), is effective for allocations of state volume limit after Apr. 5, 2006.

¶ 1605. Federal tax exemption for settlement funds and escrow accounts established for the sole purpose of resolving CERCLA claims is made permanent

Code Sec. 468B(g)(3), as amended by 2006 Tax Relief and Health Care Act § 409(a)

Generally effective: Accounts and funds established after May 17, 2006

Committee Reports, see ¶ 5060

The cleanup of hazardous waste sites is sometimes funded by environmental "settlement funds" or escrow accounts. These escrow accounts are established in consent decrees between the Environmental Protection Agency (EPA) and the settling parties under the jurisdiction of a federal district court. The EPA uses these accounts to resolve claims against private parties under the Comprehensive Environmental Response, Compensation and Liability Act of '80 (CERCLA). (Com Rept, see ¶ 5060) Certain settlement funds that meet the requirements in Code Sec. 468B(g)(2) and that are established in consent decrees for the sole purpose of resolving claims under CERCLA are treated as beneficially owned by the U.S. government and therefore not subject to federal income tax.

Under pre-2006 Tax Relief and Health Care Act law, the exemption from tax for settlement funds and escrow accounts established solely to resolve CERCLA claims did not apply to accounts or funds established after Dec. 31, 2010. (FTC 2d/FIN ¶ G-2791; USTR ¶ 468B4)

New Law. The treatment of certain settlement funds as beneficially owned by the U.S. government (i.e., funds and accounts established solely to resolve CERCLA claims) and therefore not subject to federal income tax, is permanently extended to funds and accounts established after Dec. 31, 2010. (Com Rept, see ¶ 5060) Technically, this is accomplished by striking pre-2006 Tax Relief and Health Care Act Code Sec. 468B(g)(3), which had provided for the termination date of Code Sec. 468B(g)(2) (the Code paragraph that provides the exemption from tax for these funds and accounts). (Code Sec. 468B(g)(3) as amended by 2006 Tax Relief and Health Care Act §409(a))

> ***observation:*** Thus, funds and accounts established after Dec. 31, 2010 will also qualify for the exemption from federal tax, provided they meet the requirements of Code Sec. 468B(g)(2).

For extension of the period for making an election for a tax year ending after Dec. 31, 2005 and before date of enactment, which would have expired but for relief provided by the 2006 Tax Relief and Health Care Act, see ¶ 701.

☐ **Effective:** Accounts and funds established after May 17, 2006. (2006 Tax Relief and Health Care Act §409(b))

> ***observation:*** 2006 Tax Relief and Health Care Act §409(b) provides that the rules discussed above take effect as if included in Tax Increase Prevention Act §201 (Sec. 201(a), PL 109-222, 5/17/2006), which, under Tax Increase Prevention Act §201(b) (Sec. 201(b), PL 109-222, 5/17/2006), is effective for accounts and funds established after May 17, 2006.

¶ 1606. 25% of qualifying gain from conservation sales of qualifying mineral or geothermal interests excluded from gross income

Code Sec. None, 2006 Tax Relief and Health Care Act § 403(a)(Div. C, Title IV)
Code Sec. None, 2006 Tax Relief and Health Care Act § 403(b)(2)(Div. C, Title IV)
Code Sec. 61, 2006 Tax Relief and Health Care Act § 403(c)(Div. C, Title IV)
Generally effective: Sales on or after date of enactment
Committee Reports, see ¶ 5079

The determination of gross income is the first step in the computation of income tax. Gross income consists of all income, from whatever source derived—including gain from the sale of property—in whatever form realized, whether in money, property or services. However, certain items are specifically excluded from gross income—in some cases by the Code, in some cases by other federal statutes. (FTC 2d/FIN ¶ J-1000 *et seq.*; USTR ¶ 614 *et seq.*; TaxDesk ¶ 101,000 *et seq.*)

New Law. The 2006 Tax Relief and Health Care Act creates a new exclusion from gross income. Under the Act, gross income does not include 25% of the "qualifying gain" from a "conservation sale" of a "qualifying mineral or geothermal interest" (as these terms are defined below). (2006 Tax Relief and Health Care Act §403(c)(1)(Div. C, Title IV)) As explained in detail below, the conservation sale must be made to an eligible entity that intends that the acquired property be used exclusively for qualified conservation purposes in perpetuity. (Eligible entities, defined in detail below, are certain governments,

FTC 2d References are to Federal Tax Coordinator 2d
FIN References are to RIAs Analysis of Federal Taxes: Income
USTR References are to United States Tax Reporter: Income, Estate & Gift, and Excise
PCA References are to Pension Analysis (print & electronic)
PE References are to Pension Explanations (print & electronic)
EP References are to Estate Planning Analysis (print & electronic)

certain government agencies, and certain organizations eligible to receive deductible charitable contributions.) Use of property is not considered to be exclusively for conservation purposes unless the conservation purpose is protected in perpetuity and no surface mining is permitted with respect to the property. (Com Rept, see ¶ 5079)

The exclusion is mandatory if all relevant requirements are satisfied, and a taxpayer need not file an election to take advantage of the exclusion. A taxpayer who transfers qualifying property to a qualified organization may opt out of the 25% exclusion without having to file a formal election with IRS, by choosing not to satisfy one or more of the applicable requirements—for example, by failing to obtain the requisite letter of intent from the qualified organization. (Com Rept, see ¶ 5079)

However, a tax is imposed if the interest is later transferred. See below.

For purposes of the above rule, "qualifying gain" means any gain that would be recognized as long-term capital gain (2006 Tax Relief and Health Care Act §403(c)(2)(Div. C, Title IV))—i.e., gain from the sale or exchange of a capital asset, see FTC 2d/FIN ¶ I-6001 *et seq.*; USTR ¶ 12,214 *et seq.*; TaxDesk ¶ 249,001 *et seq.*, held for more than one year, see FTC 2d/FIN ¶ I-5104; USTR ¶ 12,224.02; TaxDesk ¶ 223,304.

For purposes of the above rule, "conservation sale" means a sale that meets the following three requirements (2006 Tax Relief and Health Care Act §403(c)(3)(Div. C, Title IV)):

(1) The transferee of the qualifying mineral or geothermal interest must be an eligible entity. (2006 Tax Relief and Health Care Act §403(c)(3)(A)(Div. C, Title IV))

(2) At the time of the sale, the transferee must provide the taxpayer with a qualifying letter of intent (as defined below). (2006 Tax Relief and Health Care Act §403(c)(3)(B)(Div. C, Title IV))

(3) The sale is not made under an order of condemnation or eminent domain. (2006 Tax Relief and Health Care Act §403(c)(3)(C)(Div. C, Title IV))

Tax on later transfers. The 2006 Tax Relief and Health Care Act imposes a penalty excise tax if an eligible entity fails to take steps consistent with the protection of conservation purposes. (Com Rept, see ¶ 5079) The tax is imposed on any later transfer by an eligible entity of ownership or possession, whether by sale, exchange, or lease, of an interest acquired directly or indirectly in (2006 Tax Relief and Health Care Act §403(c)(6)(A)(Div. C, Title IV)):

(I) a conservation sale as defined above (2006 Tax Relief and Health Care Act §403(c)(6)(A)(i)(Div. C, Title IV)), or

(II) any of the following transfers (2006 Tax Relief and Health Care Act §403(c)(6)(A)(ii)(Div. C, Title IV))—

(A) a transfer to a transferee that is an eligible entity that provides the transferor, at the time of transfer, a qualifying letter of intent (as defined below) (2006 Tax Relief and Health Care Act §403(c)(6)(D)(i)(Div. C, Title IV));

(B) a transfer to a transferee that is not an eligible entity, if:

. . . it is established to IRS's satisfaction that the transfer of ownership or possession, as the case may be, is consistent with the Code Sec. 170(h)(5) requirement that the transfer be exclusively for conservation purposes and be protected for those purposes in perpetuity (see FTC 2d/FIN ¶ K-3506; USTR ¶ 1704.47; TaxDesk ¶ 331,625), and

. . . the transferee provides the transferor, at the time of transfer, a qualifying letter of intent (2006 Tax Relief and Health Care Act §403(c)(6)(D)(ii)(Div. C, Title IV)); or

(C) tax has previously been paid under the above rules as a result of an earlier transfer of ownership or possession of the same interest. (2006 Tax Relief and Health Care Act §403(c)(6)(D)(iii)(Div. C, Title IV))

The amount of tax imposed under the above rules on any transfer is equal to the sum of (2006 Tax Relief and Health Care Act §403(c)(6)(B)(Div. C, Title IV)):

. . . 20% of the fair market value (determined at the time of the transfer) of the interest whose ownership or possession is transferred (2006 Tax Relief and Health Care Act §403(c)(6)(B)(i)(Div. C, Title IV)), plus

. . . the product of (2006 Tax Relief and Health Care Act §403(c)(6)(B)(ii)(Div. C, Title IV))—

- the highest Code Sec. 11 corporate tax rate (see FTC 2d/FIN ¶ D-1003; USTR ¶ 114.01; TaxDesk ¶ 600,503), times (2006 Tax Relief and Health Care Act §403(c)(6)(B)(ii)(I)(Div. C, Title IV))
- any gain or income realized by the transferor as a result of the transfer. (2006 Tax Relief and Health Care Act §403(c)(6)(B)(ii)(II)(Div. C, Title IV))

The tax imposed by the above rules must be paid by the transferor. (2006 Tax Relief and Health Care Act §403(c)(6)(C)(Div. C, Title IV))

However, the person who would otherwise be liable for any tax imposed by the above rules is relieved of liability for that tax with respect to any transfer if that transfer is among the types of transfers described at (II) above. (2006 Tax Relief and Health Care Act §403(c)(6)(D)(Div. C, Title IV)) In other words:

FTC 2d References are to Federal Tax Coordinator 2d
FIN References are to RIAs Analysis of Federal Taxes: Income
USTR References are to United States Tax Reporter: Income, Estate & Gift, and Excise
PCA References are to Pension Analysis (print & electronic)
PE References are to Pension Explanations (print & electronic)
EP References are to Estate Planning Analysis (print & electronic)

... for a transfer by an eligible entity to another eligible entity, the excise tax does not apply if the transferee provides the transferor a letter of intent at the time of the transfer;

... for a transfer by an eligible entity to a transferee that is not an eligible entity, the excise tax does not apply if it is established to IRS's satisfaction that the transfer is exclusively for conservation purposes and the transferee provides the transferor a letter of intent at the time of the transfer. (Com Rept, see ¶ 5079)

Once a transfer has been subject to the excise tax, the excise tax may not apply to any later transfers. (Com Rept, see ¶ 5079)

For purposes of subtitle F of the Code—that is, the provisions governing procedure and administration, Code Sec. 6001 through Code Sec. 7874—the taxes imposed under the above rules are treated as excise taxes with respect to which subtitle F's deficiency procedures apply. (2006 Tax Relief and Health Care Act §403(c)(6)(E)(Div. C, Title IV)) (For excise taxes subject to the subtitle F deficiency procedures, see FTC 2d/FIN ¶ T-2703; USTR ¶ 62,124; TaxDesk ¶ 831,002; for those deficiency procedures, see FTC 2d/FIN ¶ T-2701 *et seq.*; USTR ¶ 62,124 *et seq.*; TaxDesk ¶ 831,001 *et seq.*)

Reporting requirements. IRS may require any reporting as may be necessary or appropriate to further the purpose that any conservation use of property transferred in a conservation sale be in perpetuity. (2006 Tax Relief and Health Care Act §403(c)(7)(Div. C, Title IV))

Qualifying mineral or geothermal interest defined. For purposes of the above rules, the term "qualifying mineral or geothermal interest" means an interest in any mineral or geothermal deposit located on eligible federal land which constitutes a taxpayer's entire interest in that deposit. (2006 Tax Relief and Health Care Act §403(c)(4)(A)(Div. C, Title IV)) Eligible federal land means the Bureau of Land Management land and the Forest Service land, as generally depicted on the map (2006 Tax Relief and Health Care Act §403(a)(2)(Div. C, Title IV)) entitled "Rocky Mountain Front Mineral Withdrawal Area" dated Dec. 31, 2006 (2006 Tax Relief and Health Care Act §403(a)(4)(Div. C, Title IV)), which must be placed on file and available for inspection in the Office of the Chief of the Forest Service. (2006 Tax Relief and Health Care Act §403(b)(2)(Div. C, Title IV))

More specifically:

... Bureau of Land Management land is Bureau of Land Management land and any federally-owned minerals located south of the Blackfeet Indian Reservation and east of the Lewis and Clark National Forest to the eastern edge of R. 8 W., beginning in T. 29 N. down to and including T. 19 N. and all of T. 18 N., R. 7 W. (2006 Tax Relief and Health Care Act §403(a)(1)(Div. C, Title IV));

. . . Forest Service land is (2006 Tax Relief and Health Care Act §403(a)(3)(Div. C, Title IV))—

- the Forest Service land and any federally-owned minerals located in the Rocky Mountain Division of the Lewis and Clark National Forest, including the approximately 356,111 acres of land made unavailable for leasing by the Aug. 28, '97, Record of Decision for the Lewis and Clark National Forest Oil and Gas Leasing Environmental Impact Statement and that is located from T. 31 N. to T. 16 N. and from R. 13 W. to R. 7 W. (2006 Tax Relief and Health Care Act §403(a)(3)(A)(Div. C, Title IV)), and
- the Forest Service land and any federally-owned minerals located within the Badger Two Medicine area of the Flathead National Forest, including the land located in T. 29 N. from the western edge of R. 16 W. to the eastern edge of R. 13 W. and the land located in T. 28 N., Rs. 13 and 14 W. (2006 Tax Relief and Health Care Act §403(a)(3)(B)(Div. C, Title IV))

For purposes of the definition of "qualifying mineral or geothermal interest" (2006 Tax Relief and Health Care Act §403(c)(4)(B)(Div. C, Title IV)), an interest in any mineral or geothermal deposit is not a taxpayer's entire interest if that interest in that mineral or geothermal deposit was divided in order to avoid the requirements of that definition or the requirements of Code Sec. 170(f)(3)(A) (barring a charitable deduction for contributions of partial interests in property not in trust, see FTC 2d/FIN ¶ K-3440.1 *et seq.*; USTR ¶ 1704.45 *et seq.*; TaxDesk ¶ 331,620). (2006 Tax Relief and Health Care Act §403(c)(4)(B)(i)(Div. C, Title IV)) In other words, an interest in property is not the entire interest of the taxpayer if that interest was divided in an attempt to avoid the requirement that the taxpayer sell the taxpayer's entire interest in the property. (Com Rept, see ¶ 5079)

However, a taxpayer's entire interest in a deposit does not fail to satisfy the requirements of the definition of "qualifying mineral or geothermal interest" solely because the taxpayer has retained an interest in other deposits, even if the other deposits are contiguous with that deposit and were acquired by the taxpayer along with that deposit in a single conveyance. (2006 Tax Relief and Health Care Act §403(c)(4)(B)(ii)(Div. C, Title IV))

Congress intends that the partial interest rules contained in Reg §1.170A-7(a)(2)(i) and generally applicable to charitable contributions of partial interests (see FTC 2d/FIN ¶ K-3474; USTR ¶ 1704.45; TaxDesk ¶ 331,621) be applied similarly for purposes of the new rules discussed above. (Com Rept, see ¶ 5079)

Eligible entity defined. For purposes of the above rules, "eligible entity" means—

(a) a governmental unit referred to in Code Sec. 170(c)(1) (2006 Tax Relief and Health Care Act §403(c)(5)(A)(i)(Div. C, Title IV))—i.e., the U.S., a U.S. state, a U.S. possession, a political subdivision of a state or U.S. possession, or the District of Columbia, see FTC 2d/FIN ¶ K-2899; USTR ¶ 1704.25; TaxDesk ¶ 330,274;

(b) an agency or department of a governmental unit described at (a) above, but only if operated primarily for one or more of the conservation purposes specified in Code Sec. 170(h)(4)(A)(i), Code Sec. 170(h)(4)(A)(ii), or Code Sec. 170(h)(4)(A)(iii) (2006 Tax Relief and Health Care Act §403(c)(5)(A)(i)(Div. C, Title IV)), as follows—

. . . Code Sec. 170(h)(4)(A)(i), the preservation of land areas for outdoor recreation by, or the education of, the general public, see FTC 2d/FIN ¶ K-3508; USTR ¶ 1704.47; TaxDesk ¶ 361,625;

. . . Code Sec. 170(h)(4)(A)(ii), the protection of a relatively natural habitat of fish, wildlife, plants or similar ecosystem, see FTC 2d/FIN ¶ K-3509; USTR ¶ 1704.47; TaxDesk ¶ 361,625;

. . . Code Sec. 170(h)(4)(A)(iii), the preservation of open space (including farmland and forest land) where that preservation will yield a significant public benefit and is for the scenic enjoyment of the general public, or under a clearly delineated federal, state or local governmental conservation policy, see FTC 2d/FIN ¶ K-3510; USTR ¶ 1704.47; TaxDesk ¶ 361,625.
(Com Rept, see ¶ 5079)

(c) an entity that meets both of the following requirements (2006 Tax Relief and Health Care Act §403(c)(5)(A)(ii)(Div. C, Title IV)):

(i) the entity must be described in Code Sec. 170(b)(1)(A)(vi) or Code Sec. 170(h)(3)(B) (2006 Tax Relief and Health Care Act §403(c)(5)(A)(ii)(I)(Div. C, Title IV));

> ***observation:*** Entities described in Code Sec. 170(b)(1)(A)(vi) are domestic charitable, etc. organizations described in Code Sec. 170(c)(2) (see FTC 2d/FIN ¶ K-2862 *et seq.*; USTR ¶ 1704.20 *et seq.*; TaxDesk ¶ 330,269 *et seq.*) that are "publicly supported," see FTC 2d/FIN ¶ K-3756 *et seq.*; USTR ¶ 1704.07 *et seq.*; TaxDesk ¶ 333,005).
>
> Entities described in Code Sec. 170(h)(3)(B) are organizations that meet the Code Sec. 501(c)(3) requirements for exemption from tax as a charitable, etc. organization, see FTC 2d/FIN ¶ D-4101 *et seq.*; USTR ¶ 5014.05 *et seq.*; TaxDesk ¶ 670,601 *et seq.*, and that are "qualified organizations" eligible to receive "qualified conservation contributions," see FTC 2d/FIN ¶ K-3505; USTR ¶ 1704.47; TaxDesk ¶ 331,625.

(ii) the entity must be organized and at all times operated primarily for one or more of the conservation purposes specified in Code Sec. 170(h)(4)(A)(i), Code Sec. 170(h)(4)(A)(ii), or Code Sec. 170(h)(4)(A)(iii) (2006 Tax Relief and Health Care Act §403(c)(5)(A)(ii)(II)(Div. C, Title IV))(see (b) above).

Qualifying letter of intent defined. For purposes of the above rules, the term "qualifying letter of intent" means a written letter of intent which includes the following statement: "The transferee's intent is that this acquisition will serve one or more of the conservation purposes specified in clause (i), (ii), or (iii) of section 170(h)(4)(A) of the Internal Revenue Code of 1986, that the transferee's use of the deposits so acquired will be consistent with section 170(h)(5) of such Code, and that the use of the deposits will continue to be consistent with such section, even if ownership or possession of such deposits is later transferred to another person." (2006 Tax Relief and Health Care Act §403(c)(5)(B)(Div. C, Title IV))

☐ **Effective:** Sales occurring on or after date of enactment. (2006 Tax Relief and Health Care Act §403(d)(2)(Div. C, Title IV))

¶ 1607. Qualified railroad track maintenance expenditures for purposes of the railroad track maintenance credit means "gross" expenditures; definition of expenditures is further modified

Code Sec. 45G(d), as amended by 2006 Tax Relief and Health Care Act § 423(a)
Generally effective: Tax years beginning after Dec. 31, 2004
Committee Reports, see ¶ 5074

A credit is available for 50% of the "qualified railroad track maintenance expenditures" (defined below) paid or incurred by an "eligible taxpayer" (defined below) during the tax year. The credit is available for expenditures paid or incurred during tax years beginning after Dec. 31, 2004 and before Jan. 1, 2008, see FTC 2d/FIN ¶ L-18051; USTR ¶ 45G4; TaxDesk ¶ 380,501.

The credit for any tax year cannot exceed the product of $3,500, multiplied by the sum of:

(1) the number of miles of railroad track owned or leased by the eligible taxpayer as of the close of the tax year; and

FTC 2d References are to Federal Tax Coordinator 2d
FIN References are to RIAs Analysis of Federal Taxes: Income
USTR References are to United States Tax Reporter: Income, Estate & Gift, and Excise
PCA References are to Pension Analysis (print & electronic)
PE References are to Pension Explanations (print & electronic)
EP References are to Estate Planning Analysis (print & electronic)

(2) the number of miles of railroad track assigned for purposes of Code Sec. 45G(b) to the eligible taxpayer by a Class II or Class III railroad (defined below) that owns or leases the railroad track as of the close of the tax year, see FTC 2d/FIN ¶ L-18051; USTR ¶ 45G4.

"Eligible taxpayer" means any Class II or Class III railroad, or any person who transports property using the rail facilities of a Class II or Class III railroad or who furnishes railroad-related property or services to a Class II or Class III railroad, but only with respect to miles of railroad track assigned to that person by the Class II or Class III railroad for purposes of Code Sec. 45G(b), see FTC 2d/FIN ¶ L-18051; USTR ¶ 45G4.

The term "qualified railroad track maintenance expenditures," means expenditures (whether or not otherwise chargeable to capital account) for maintaining railroad track (including roadbed, bridges, and related track structures) owned or leased, as of Jan. 1, 2005, by a Class II or Class III railroad. (FTC 2d/FIN ¶ L-18051; USTR ¶ 45G4; TaxDesk ¶ 380,501)

"Class II or Class III railroad," see FTC 2d/FIN ¶ L-18051; USTR ¶ 45G4, has the same respective meanings for purposes of the railroad track maintenance credit as those used by the Surface Transportation Board.

> ***observation:*** Class II railroads are carriers with annual operating revenues of more than $20 million and less than $250 million. They are also referred to as regional railroads. Class III railroads are carriers with operating revenues of $20 million or less, and all switching and terminal companies regardless of operating revenues. Class III railroads are also called short lines. Thus, the railroad track maintenance credit is designed to help all but the largest railroad carriers.

New Law. The 2006 Tax Relief and Health Care Act modifies the term "qualified railroad track expenditures" used in determining the railroad track maintenance credit for a tax year to mean *gross* expenditures. (Code Sec. 45G(d) as amended by 2006 Tax Relief and Health Care Act §423(a)(1)) Thus, for example, qualified railroad track maintenance expenditures are not reduced by the discount amount in the case of discounted freight shipping rates, the increment in a markup of the price for track materials, or by debt forgiveness. (Com Rept, see ¶ 5074)

> ***observation:*** The 2006 Tax Relief and Health Care Act clarifies that the credit is based on the gross, not net, qualified expenditures, thus permitting a larger credit than if the computation of the credit were limited to the amount of net expenditures.

The 2006 Tax Relief and Health Care Act also adds to the definition of "qualified railroad track expenditures," the provision that the expenditures, for purposes of the computation of the credit, are to be determined without regard to any consideration for those expenditures given by the Class II or Class III railroad that made the assignment of the track. (Code Sec. 45G(d) as amended by 2006 Tax Relief and Health Care Act §423(a)(2))

Thus, cash payments made by the Class II or Class III railroad to the assignee are consideration for the expenditures. Consideration received directly or indirectly from persons other than the Class II or Class III railroad, however, does reduce the amount of qualified railroad track maintenance expenditures. Congress does not intend any inference as to whether or not any such consideration is or is not includable in the assignee's income for federal tax purposes. (Com Rept, see ¶ 5074)

☐ **Effective:** Tax years beginning after Dec. 31, 2004. (2006 Tax Relief and Health Care Act §423(b))

2006 Tax Relief and Health Care Act §423(b) provides that the amendment made by 2006 Tax Relief and Health Care Act §423 takes effect as if included in 2004 Jobs Act §245(a) (Sec. 245(a), PL 108-357, 10/22/2004). 2004 Jobs Act §245(a) (Sec. 245(a), PL 108-357, 10/22/2004) added the Code Sec. 45G railroad track maintenance credit. The credit was made applicable by §245(e) of the 2004 Jobs Act (Sec. 245(e), PL 108-357, 10/22/2004) to tax years beginning after Dec. 31, 2004. (2006 Tax Relief and Health Care Act §423(b))

¶ 1608. 6,000 ton weight minimum for qualifying vessels in alternative tonnage tax regime made permanent

Code Sec. 1355(a)(4), as amended by 2006 Tax Relief and Health Care Act § 413(a)
Generally effective: Tax years beginning after Dec 31, 2005
Committee Reports, see ¶ 5064

Corporations may elect a tonnage tax in lieu of the U.S. corporate income tax on taxable income from international shipping activities. Under this tonnage tax regime, an electing corporation's gross income doesn't include its income from "qualifying shipping activities," which include operating qualifying vessels in U.S. foreign trade. Instead, an electing corporation is subject to tax on qualifying shipping activities only at the maximum corporate income tax rate on its notional shipping income, which is based on the net tonnage of the corporation's qualifying vessels. FTC 2d/FIN ¶s O-11550, O-11551, O-11552; USTR ¶s 13,524, 13,534, 13,544; TaxDesk ¶s 644,600, 644,601

FTC 2d References are to Federal Tax Coordinator 2d
FIN References are to RIAs Analysis of Federal Taxes: Income
USTR References are to United States Tax Reporter: Income, Estate & Gift, and Excise
PCA References are to Pension Analysis (print & electronic)
PE References are to Pension Explanations (print & electronic)
EP References are to Estate Planning Analysis (print & electronic)

Under pre-2006 Tax Relief and Health Care Act law, the weight of a qualifying vessel had to be at least 6,000 deadweight tons, (10,000 deadweight tons for tax years beginning before Jan. 1, 2006, or ending after Dec. 31, 2010). (FTC 2d/FIN ¶ O-11554; USTR ¶ 13,554; TaxDesk ¶ 644,602)

New Law. The 2006 Tax Relief and Health Care Act makes permanent the 6,000 deadweight tonnage minimum for a qualifying vessel that, under pre-2006 Tax Relief and Health Care Act law, was scheduled to sunset for tax years ending after Dec. 31, 2010. (Code Sec. 1355(a)(4) as amended by 2006 Tax Relief and Health Care Act §413(a))

> ***observation:*** This change should allow operators of smaller U.S.-flag vessels to be more competitive after 2010 with operators of larger U.S.-flag vessels and with operators of foreign vessels.

Deadweight measures the lifting capacity of a ship expressed in long tons (2,240 lbs.), including cargo, crew, and consumables such as fuel, lube oil, drinking water, and stores. It is the difference between the number of tons of water a vessel displaces without such items on board and the number of tons it displaces when fully loaded. (Com Rept, see ¶ 5064)

☐ **Effective:** For tax years beginning after Dec. 31, 2005. (2006 Tax Relief and Health Care Act §413(b))

2006 Tax Relief and Health Care Act § 413(b) provides that the amendments made by 2006 Tax Relief and Health Care Act § 413(a) take effect as if included in Tax Increase Prevention Act (2005 TIPRA) §205 (Sec. 205, PL 109-222, 5/17/2006). 2005 TIPRA §205 provides that the amendments made by §205 take effect for tax years beginning after December 31, 2005.

> ***observation:*** The above effective date is also the effective date of the change that originally added the 6,000 deadweight tons minimum. Before that the minimum was 10,000 deadweight tons.

¶ 1609. Great Lakes domestic shipping excepted from general rules on temporary domestic use of vessels for tonnage tax purposes

Code Sec. 1355(g), as amended by 2006 Tax Relief and Health Care Act § 415
Generally effective: Tax years beginning after date of enactment
Committee Reports, see ¶ 5066

A corporation may elect a tonnage tax in lieu of the U.S. corporate income tax on taxable income from international shipping activities. Such a corporation is referred to below as an "electing corporation". Under this tonnage tax regime, an electing corporation's gross income doesn't include its income from "qualifying shipping activities," which include operating qualifying vessels in U.S. foreign trade. Instead, an electing corporation is subject to tax on qualifying shipping activities only at the maximum corporate income tax rate on its notional shipping income, which is based on the net tonnage of the corporation's qualifying vessels. FTC 2d/FIN ¶s O-11550, O-11551, O-11552; USTR ¶s 13,524, 13,534, 13,544; TaxDesk ¶s 644,600, 644,601

A "qualifying vessel" is defined in Code Sec. 1355(a)(4) as a self-propelled (or a combination of self-propelled and non-self-propelled) U.S. flag vessel of not less than 6,000 deadweight tons that is used exclusively in the U.S. foreign trade. Notwithstanding the "exclusively in the U.S. foreign trade" requirement, under the Code Sec. 1355(f) temporary use rules, the temporary use of any qualifying vessel in the U.S. domestic trade (i.e., the transportation of goods or passengers between places in the U.S.) may be disregarded, and treated as the continued use of such vessel in the U.S. foreign trade, if the electing corporation provides timely notice of such temporary use to IRS. However, if a qualifying vessel is operated in the U.S. domestic trade for more than 30 days during the tax year, then no usage in the U.S. domestic trade during such year may be disregarded (and the vessel is thereby disqualified). (FTC 2d/FIN ¶ O-11554, ¶ O-11557; USTR ¶ 13,554; TaxDesk ¶ 644,602, ¶ 644,606)

> ***observation:*** Under pre-2006 Tax Relief and Health Care Act law, the weight of a qualifying vessel had to be at least 6,000 deadweight tons, (10,000 deadweight tons for tax years beginning before Jan. 1, 2006, or ending after Dec. 31, 2010). The 2006 Tax Relief and Health Care Act permanently extends the 6,000 deadweight tons threshold, see ¶ 1608.

New Law. The 2006 Tax Relief and Health Care Act provides that if an electing corporation makes an additional election (at the time and in the manner as IRS may require) to apply the rules discussed below for any tax year to any qualifying vessel which is used in "qualified zone domestic trade" during the tax year, then:

(A) solely for purposes of the definition of a qualifying vessel in Code Sec. 1355(a)(4), that use will be treated as use in U.S. foreign trade (and not as use in U.S. domestic trade), and

---

FTC 2d References are to Federal Tax Coordinator 2d
FIN References are to RIAs Analysis of Federal Taxes: Income
USTR References are to United States Tax Reporter: Income, Estate & Gift, and Excise
PCA References are to Pension Analysis (print & electronic)
PE References are to Pension Explanations (print & electronic)
EP References are to Estate Planning Analysis (print & electronic)

(B) the Code Sec. 1355(f) temporary use rules won't apply with respect to the vessel for the tax year. (Code Sec. 1355(g)(1) as amended by 2006 Tax Relief and Health Care Act §415(a))

Thus, a corporation for which a tonnage tax election is in effect may make a further election for a qualifying vessel used during a tax year in qualified zone domestic trade. This second election is known as the "qualified zone domestic trade election". IRS may specify the time, manner and other conditions for making, maintaining, and terminating a qualified zone domestic trade election. An electing corporation making a qualified zone domestic trade election for a vessel is not required to give notice to IRS of the use of the vessel in qualified zone domestic trade, and an otherwise qualifying vessel does not cease to be a qualifying vessel solely due to that use when the election is in effect, even if that use exceeds 30 days during the tax year. (Com Rept, see ¶ 5066)

For these purposes, the term "qualified zone domestic trade" means the transportation of goods or passengers between places in the qualified zone if that transportation is in the U.S. domestic trade. (Code Sec. 1355(g)(4)(A)) The transportation of goods or passengers between a U.S. port in the qualified zone and a U.S. port outside the qualified zone (in either direction) is U.S. domestic trade that is not qualified zone domestic trade. (Com Rept, see ¶ 5066)

The term "qualified zone" means the Great Lakes Waterway and the St. Lawrence Seaway. (Code Sec. 1355(g)(4)(B)) This area consists of the deep-draft waterways of Lake Superior, Lake Michigan, Lake Huron (including Lake St. Clair), Lake Eire (sic) Erie, and Lake Ontario, connecting deep-draft channels, including the Detroit River, the St. Clair River, the St. Marys River, and the Welland Canal, and the waterway between the port of Sept-Iles, Quebec and Lake Ontario, including all locks, canals, and connecting and contiguous waters that are part of these deep-draft waterways. (Com Rept, see ¶ 5066)

An electing corporation that makes a qualified zone domestic trade election for a qualifying vessel will be treated as using that vessel in qualified zone domestic trade during any period of temporary use in the U.S. domestic trade (other than qualified zone domestic trade) if the electing corporation gives timely notice to IRS stating:

(1) that it temporarily operates or has operated in the U.S. domestic trade (other than qualified zone domestic trade) a qualifying vessel which had been used in the U.S. foreign trade or qualified zone domestic trade, and

(2) its intention to resume operation of the vessel in the U.S. foreign trade or qualified zone domestic trade. (Code Sec. 1355(g)(2)(A))

Notice will be deemed timely if given not later than the due date (including extensions) for the corporation's tax return for the tax year in which the temporary cessation begins. (Code Sec. 1355(g)(2)(B))

The temporary use period under (1) above continues until the earlier of the date of which (a) the electing corporation abandons its intention to resume operating the vessel in the U.S. foreign trade or qualified zone domestic trade, or (b) the electing corporation resumes operating the vessel in the U.S. foreign trade or qualified zone domestic trade. (Code Sec. 1355(g)(2)(C))

The above rules won't apply to any qualifying vessel which is operated in the U.S. domestic trade (other than qualified zone domestic trade) for more than 30 days during the tax year. (Code Sec. 1355(g)(2)(D)) Thus, if a qualifying vessel is operated in the U.S. domestic trade (other than qualified zone domestic trade) for more than 30 days during the tax year, then no usage in the U.S. domestic trade (other than qualified zone domestic trade) during that year may be disregarded (and the vessel is thereby disqualified). Thus, a vessel used for 120 days in the tax year in qualified zone domestic trade and 180 days in the tax year in the U.S. foreign trade is not a qualifying vessel if it is used for over 30 days in the tax year in the U.S. domestic trade that is not qualified zone domestic trade. (Com Rept, see ¶ 5066)

Activities in qualified zone domestic trade are not qualifying shipping activities and, therefore, do not qualify for the tonnage tax regime. (Com Rept, see ¶ 5066) In the case of a qualifying vessel for which a qualified zone domestic trade election is in force, IRS is to prescribe rules for the proper allocation of income, expenses, losses, and deductions between the qualified shipping activities and the other activities of the vessel. (Code Sec. 1355(g)(3)) These rules may include intra-vessel allocation rules that are different than the rules pertaining to allocations of items between qualifying vessels and other vessels. (Com Rept, see ¶ 5066)

☐ **Effective:** For tax years beginning after date of enactment. (2006 Tax Relief and Health Care Act §415(b))

¶ 1700. Client Letters

¶ 1701. Tax provisions affecting individuals in the 2006 Tax Relief and Health Care Act

To the practitioner: You can use the following client letter to provide clients with an overview of the tax provisions affecting individuals in the 2006 Tax Relief and Health Care Act.

Dear client,

The recently passed 2006 Tax Relief and Health Care Act is a wide-ranging measure that preserves a variety of popular tax breaks for families and businesses, extends energy provisions encouraging alternative and renewable energy sources, and includes trade, oil drilling, and Medicare provisions. Here is a look at the key tax provisions in the new law that directly affect individual taxpayers.

Extension and modification of certain tax relief provisions.

The new law extends through 2007, and in certain circumstances modifies, provisions which under prior law either expired at the end of 2005 or would have expired at the end of 2006. These include:

Tuition deduction.

The tax deduction for qualified higher education expenses is extended through 2007. The deduction allows taxpayers to deduct up to $4,000 (depending on their income) of higher education expenses in lieu of claiming the Hope or Lifetime Learning tax credits. The deduction is taken "above-the-line," meaning that it may be claimed by all individual taxpayers regardless of whether they itemize their deductions.

State and local general sales taxes.

The tax break allowing individual taxpayers to elect to take an itemized deduction for state and local general sales taxes in lieu of the itemized deduction permitted for state and local income taxes is extended through 2007. Taxpayers have two options for determining deductible sales tax: (i) actual sales tax paid if receipts are maintained for IRS verification or (ii) approximate sales tax paid as estimated in tables provided by the Secretary of the

Treasury plus sales tax on certain additional items (such as a boat or car) that may be added to the table amount.

Combat pay treated as earned income for purpose of the earned income tax credit.

The rule allowing excluded combat pay to count as income for purposes of calculating the earned income tax credit is extended through 2007.

Deduction for certain expenses of elementary and secondary school teachers.

The tax break permitting elementary and secondary school teachers and certain other school professionals to deduct up to $250 of out-of-pocket costs incurred to purchase books, supplies and other classroom equipment is extended through 2007. The deduction is available to all individual taxpayers regardless of whether they itemize their deductions.

Tax credit for first-time homebuyers in the District of Columbia.

The tax break allowing first-time homebuyers in D.C. to claim a tax credit of up to $5,000 on the purchase price of the home is extended through 2007.

Availability of medical savings accounts.

New contributions to Archer medical savings accounts ("Archer MSAs") may be made through 2007 (instead of through 2005, as under prior law). New contributions may be made after 2007 only by or for individuals who previously had Archer MSAs, and employees who are employed by a participating employer. Individuals may make tax-deductible contributions to an Archer MSA to pay for health care expenses. The distributions are tax-free if used to pay for eligible medical expenses.

Extension of certain expiring energy provisions and other energy provisions.

The new law provides an extension through 2008 of a number of energy provisions that would have expired at the end of 2007 under prior law. For individuals, the most important of these provisions is a one-year extension of the 30% tax credit for the purchase of residential solar water heating, solar electric equipment and fuel cell property through Dec. 31, 2008.

Health savings account provisions.

The new law includes many changes for health savings accounts (HSAs), including: allowing one-time rollovers from health flexible spending accounts (FSAs) and health reimbursement arrangements (HRAs) into HSAs (after the enactment date and before 2012); repeal of the annual plan deductible limit on HSA contributions (after 2006); expanded contributions limit for part year coverage (after 2006); and allowing one-time rollovers from IRAs into HSAs (after 2006).

Other tax relief provisions.

The new law also contains a package of other tax provisions designed to provide additional tax relief and certainty to taxpayers. These include:

Incentive stock option AMT provisions.

For tax years beginning after the enactment date, a new law change allows individuals to take advantage of a refundable credit with respect to certain long-term unused alternative minimum tax (AMT) credits existing before Jan. 1, 2013. The annual credit amount, subject to a phase-out, is the greater of (i) the lesser of $5,000 or the amount of the long-term unused AMT credit, or (ii) 20% of the amount of the long-term unused AMT credit. This provision is designed to help taxpayers who wound up with AMT problems because of their exercise of incentive stock options.

Self-created musical works.

The tax break that was enacted on a temporary basis in 2005 providing capital gains treatment for self-created musical works when these works are sold by the artist is made permanent.

Sale of residences by intelligence officers.

The new law gives non-military intelligence officers stationed abroad the same liberalized home sale exclusion rules available to active military personnel. This change applies to sales of homes after the enactment date of the new law and before Jan. 1, 2011.

Premiums for mortgage insurance.

A new itemized deduction for the cost of premiums for mortgage insurance on a qualified personal residence is established. The deduction is phased-out ratably by 10% for each $1,000 by which the taxpayer's adjusted gross income exceeds $100,000. The new deduction applies for 2007 only.

Loans to qualified continuing care facilities.

The new law makes permanent a provision contained in the Tax Increase Prevention and Reconciliation Act of 2005 that reforms the tax treatment of loans to qualified continuing care facilities.

Frivolous submissions.

The new law increases the penalty for frivolous tax return submissions from $500 to $5,000 and expands the penalty to all taxpayers and all types of federal taxes. This increased penalty also applies to frivolous submissions for lien and levy collection due process, installment agreements, offers-in-compromise, and taxpayer assistance orders.

Please keep in mind that I've described only the highlights of the new law. If you would like more details on any aspect of this legislation, please call me at your earliest convenience.

Very truly yours,

¶ 1702. Business and corporate changes in the 2006 Tax Relief and Health Care Act

To the practitioner: You can use the following client letter to provide clients with an overview of the business and corporate tax provisions in the 2006 Tax Relief and Health Care Act.

Dear client,

The recently passed 2006 Tax Relief and Health Care Act is a wide-ranging measure that preserves a variety of popular tax breaks for families and businesses, extends energy provisions encouraging alternative and renewable energy sources, and includes trade, oil drilling and Medicare provisions, and contains an array of tax provisions with immediate and long-term impact on businesses. Here is a look at the key tax provisions that directly affect business taxpayers.

Extension and modification of certain tax relief provisions.

The new law extends through 2007, and in certain circumstances modifies, provisions which under prior law either expired at the end of 2005 or would have expired at the end of 2006. These include:

Research tax credit.

The research and development (R&D) credit, which expired at the end of 2005 under prior law, is extended to qualified amounts paid or incurred during 2006 and 2007. In addition, for tax years ending after 2006, the new law enhances the credit by (i) increasing the rates of the alternative incremental credit and (ii) creating a new alternative simplified credit that does not use gross receipts as a factor (so that newer businesses can access the credit).

Work opportunity and welfare-to-work tax credits.

The work opportunity tax credit (WOTC), which is a credit for wages paid by employers who hire individuals from certain targeted groups, and the welfare-to-work tax credit (WWTC), which is a credit for wages paid by employers who hire long-term family assistance recipients, are extended in their current form for 2006 and combined in 2007. Modifications of the combined credit include expanded eligibility for the WOTC (raised age ceil-

FTC 2d References are to Federal Tax Coordinator 2d
FIN References are to RIAs Analysis of Federal Taxes: Income
USTR References are to United States Tax Reporter: Income, Estate & Gift, and Excise
PCA References are to Pension Analysis (print & electronic)
PE References are to Pension Explanations (print & electronic)
EP References are to Estate Planning Analysis (print & electronic)

ing for food stamp recipients from 25 to 40), revised eligibility requirements for ex-felons, and extension of the paperwork filing deadline from 21 days to 28 days.

New markets tax credit.

The credit is extended for one year (through the end of 2008), permitting a $3.5 billion maximum annual amount of qualified equity investments.

Qualified zone academy bonds (QZABs).

QZABs are tax credit bonds issued by States or localities principally for school renovation. Bond holders may claim a tax credit against federal income taxes in lieu of receiving interest. The new law extends QZABs for two years and authorizes states to issue up to $400 million of QZABs for 2006 and 2007. The new law also adds special rules relating to expenditures and arbitrage and new information reporting rules.

Brownfield remediation expensing.

Expensing of costs associated with cleaning up hazardous ("brownfield") sites is extended through 2007, and the definition of an eligible contaminated site is expanded to include sites contaminated by petroleum products.

Tax incentives for investment in the District of Columbia.

Three tax benefits available to businesses operating in designated D.C. enterprise zones are extended through 2007— 20% wage credit, $35,000 of additional expensing under Sec. 179, tax-exempt bonds—and zero capital gains for property held five years is extended through 2012 (two year extension).

Indian employment tax credit.

The business tax credit available for employers of qualified employees that work and live on or near an Indian reservation is extended through 2007.

Accelerated depreciation for business property on Indian reservations.

A special depreciation recovery period for qualified Indian reservation property is extended to property placed in service through 2007.

Leasehold and restaurant improvement recovery.

The accelerated writeoff for certain leasehold improvements and restaurant property (depreciation over 15 years instead of 39 years) is extended through 2007.

Enhanced deduction for corporate contributions of computer equipment for educational purposes.

The rule that encourages businesses to contribute computer technology and equipment to schools by allowing an enhanced deduction for such contributions is extended through 2007.

Suspension of 100 percent-of-net income limitation on percentage depletion for oil and gas from marginal wells.

This tax break is extended through 2007.

Economic development credit for American Samoa.

A new temporary 2-year credit for possessions corporations operating in American Samoa is provided. The credit, which is generally based on the amount of wages paid in American Samoa and depreciation deductions with respect to property located in American Samoa, is effective for the first two years beginning after Dec. 31, 2005 and before Jan. 1, 2008.

GO Zone bonus depreciation.

The bonus 50% first-year depreciation break that was included in the Gulf Opportunity Zone Act of 2005 is modified by extending the placed-in-service deadline for certain property used in certain highly damaged areas within the Gulf Opportunity Zone.

Extension of certain expiring energy provisions and other energy provisions.

The new law provides an extension through 2008 of a number of energy provisions that would have expired at the end of 2007 under prior law. It also contains a package of other energy provisions. The changes include:

Credit for electricity produced from certain renewable resources.

The placed-in-service date for facilities qualifying for the renewable electricity production tax credit is extended for one year through Dec. 31, 2008 for certain facilities (e.g., those producing electricity from wind, closed-loop biomass, open-loop biomass, small irrigation, landfill gas, and trash combustion).

Energy credit for certain business purchases.

The 30% business tax credit for the purchase of fuel cell power plants and solar equipment is extended through Dec. 31, 2008.

Credit to holders of clean renewable energy bonds.

The clean renewable energy bond (CREB) program is extended through Dec. 31, 2008 and an additional $400 million of CREB bonding authority is provided.

Special depreciation allowance for cellulosic biomass ethanol plant property.

The new law provides 50% bonus first-year depreciation for new qualified cellulosic ethanol plants placed in service after the date of enactment of the new law and before 2013.

Credit for new energy efficient homes.

The tax credit for builders of new energy efficient homes is extended for one year through Dec. 31, 2008. The credit applies to manufactured homes meeting a 30% energy reduction standard and other homes meeting a 50% standard.

Deduction for energy efficient commercial buildings.

The deduction for energy efficient commercial buildings meeting a 50% energy reduction standard is extended for one year, through Dec. 31, 2008.

Clean coal gasification tax credit.

The tax credits for subbituminous coal gasification projects are modified, effective for applications for certification submitted after Oct. 2, 2006, to ensure that more of these facilities are constructed.

Other tax relief provisions.

The new law also contains a package of other tax provisions designed to provide additional tax relief and certainty to taxpayers. These include:

Manufacturing deduction for U.S. businesses with branches in Puerto Rico.

The new law allows qualifying U.S. businesses operating as branches in Puerto Rico to claim the Sec. 199 domestic manufacturing deduction, effective for the first two years of the taxpayer beginning after 2005 and before 2008.

Mine safety provisions.

The new law provides 50% expensing for certain equipment expenditures related to safety equipment for underground mines located in the United States and provides tax credits for certain mine rescue team training programs, effective for three years through 2008.

Certain provisions made permanent.

A number of provisions that were enacted on a temporary basis by the Tax Increase Prevention and Reconciliation Act of 2005 are made permanent, including:

. . . the provision treating environmental cleanup settlement funds as governmentally-owned (i.e., not subject to tax) if certain standards and requirements are met;

. . . the provision simplifying the application of the active trade or business test to certain corporate distributions by applying this test on an affiliated group basis; and

. . . the provision providing capital gains treatment for self-created musical works when these works are sold by the artist.

Please keep in mind that I've described only the highlights of the most important changes in the new law. Give me a call at your earliest convenience for more details on how you may be affected by this important tax legislation.

Very truly yours,

FTC 2d References are to Federal Tax Coordinator 2d
FIN References are to RIAs Analysis of Federal Taxes: Income
USTR References are to United States Tax Reporter: Income, Estate & Gift, and Excise
PCA References are to Pension Analysis (print & electronic)
PE References are to Pension Explanations (print & electronic)
EP References are to Estate Planning Analysis (print & electronic)

[¶ 3000] Code as Amended

This section reproduces Code as Amended by HR6111, the Tax Relief and Health Care Act of 2006. Code sections appear in order, as amended, added or repealed. New matter is shown in *italics.* All changes and effective dates are shown in the endnotes.

[¶ 3001] Code Sec. 25D. Residential energy efficient property.

(a) Allowance of credit. In the case of an individual, there shall be allowed as a credit against the tax imposed by this chapter for the taxable year an amount equal to the sum of—

(1) 30 percent of the [1]*qualified solar electric property expenditures* made by the taxpayer during such year,

(2) 30 percent of the qualified solar water heating property expenditures made by the taxpayer during such year, and

(3) 30 percent of the qualified fuel cell property expenditures made by the taxpayer during such year.

(b) Limitations.

(1) Maximum credit. The credit allowed under subsection (a) (determined without regard to subsection (c)) for any taxable year shall not exceed—

(A) $2,000 with respect to any [2]*qualified solar electric property expenditures,*

(B) $2,000 with respect to any qualified solar water heating property expenditures, and

(C) $500 with respect to each half kilowatt of capacity of qualified fuel cell property (as defined in section 48(c)(1)) for which qualified fuel cell property expenditures are made.

* * * * * * * * * * * *

(d) Definitions. For purposes of this section—

(1) Qualified solar water heating property expenditure. The term "qualified solar water heating property expenditure" means an expenditure for property to heat water for use in a dwelling unit located in the United States and used as a residence by the taxpayer if at least half of the energy used by such property for such purpose is derived from the sun.

(2)[3] *Qualified solar electric property expenditure.* The term [4]*"qualified solar electric property expenditure"* means an expenditure for property which uses solar energy to generate electricity for use in a dwelling unit located in the United States and used as a residence by the taxpayer.

(3) Qualified fuel cell property expenditure. The term "qualified fuel cell property expenditure" means an expenditure for qualified fuel cell property (as defined in section 48(c)(1)) installed on or in connection with a dwelling unit located in the United States and used as a principal residence (within the meaning of section 121) by the taxpayer.

* * * * * * * * * * * *

(e) Special rules. For purposes of this section—

* * * * * * * * * * * *

(4) Dollar amounts in case of joint occupancy. In the case of any dwelling unit which is jointly occupied and used during any calendar year as a residence by 2 or more individuals the following rules shall apply:

(A) Maximum expenditures. The maximum amount of expenditures which may be taken into account under subsection (a) by all such individuals with respect to such dwelling unit during such calendar year shall be—

(i) $6,667 in the case of any [5]*qualified solar electric property expenditures,*

(ii) $6,667 in the case of any qualified solar water heating property expenditures, and

(iii) $1,667 in the case of each half kilowatt of capacity of qualified fuel cell property (as defined in section 48(c)(1)) for which qualified fuel cell property expenditures are made.

* * * * * * * * * * * * *

(g) Termination. The credit allowed under this section shall not apply to property placed in service after [6]*December 31, 2008.*

[For Analysis, see ¶ 105. For Committee Reports, see ¶ 5036.]

[Endnote Code Sec. 25D]

Matter in *italics* in Code Sec. 25D(a)(1), Code Sec. 25D(b)(1)(A), Code Sec. 25D(d)(2), Code Sec. 25D(e)(4)(A)(i), and Code Sec. 25D(g) was added by Sec. 206(a), (b)(1), (b)(2)(A) and (b)(2)(B) of the Tax Relief and Health Care Act of 2006, HR6111, d.o.e., which struck out:

1. "qualified photovoltaic property expenditures"
2. "qualified photovoltaic property expenditures"
3. "Qualified photovoltaic property expenditure"
4. "qualified photovoltaic property expenditure"
5. "qualified photovoltaic property expenditures"
6. "December 31, 2007"

Effective Date Enacted d.o.e..

[¶ 3002] Code Sec. 32. Earned income.

* * * * * * * * * * * * *

(c) Definitions and special rules. For purposes of this section—

* * * * * * * * * * * * *

(2) Earned income.

(A) The term "earned income" means—

(i) wages, salaries, tips, and other employee compensation, but only if such amounts are includible in gross income for the taxable year, plus

(ii) the amount of the taxpayer's net earnings from self-employment for the taxable year (within the meaning of section 1402(a)), but such net earnings shall be determined with regard to the deduction allowed to the taxpayer by section 164(f).

(B) For purposes of subparagraph (A)—

(i) the earned income of an individual shall be computed without regard to any community property laws,

(ii) no amount received as a pension or annuity shall be taken into account,

(iii) no amount to which section 871(a) applies (relating to income of nonresident alien individuals not connected with United States business) shall be taken into account,

(iv) no amount received for services provided by an individual while the individual is an inmate at a penal institution shall be taken into account,

(v) no amount described in subparagraph (A) received for service performed in work activities as defined in paragraph (4) or (7) of section 407(d) of the Social Security Act to which the taxpayer is assigned under any State program under part A of title IV of such Act shall be taken into account, but only to the extent such amount is subsidized under such State program, and

(vi) in the case of any taxable year ending—

(I) after the date of the enactment of this clause, and

(II) before January 1, [1]*2008,*

a taxpayer may elect to treat amounts excluded from gross income by reason of section 112 as earned income.

* * * * * * * * * * * * *

[For Analysis, see ¶106. For Committee Reports, see ¶5010.]

[Endnote Code Sec. 32]

Matter in *italics* in Code Sec. 32(c)(2)(B)(vi)(II) was added by Sec. 106(a) of the Tax Relief and Health Care Act of 2006, HR6111, d.o.e., which struck out:

1. "2007"

Effective Date (Sec. 106(b), HR6111, d.o.e.) effective for tax. yrs. begin. after 12/31/2006.

[¶3003] Code Sec. 38. General business credit.

* * * * * * * * * * * *

(b) Current year business credit. For purposes of this subpart, the amount of the current year business credit is the sum of the following credits determined for the taxable year:

(1) the investment credit determined under section 46,

(2) the work opportunity credit determined under section 51(a),

(3) the alcohol fuels credit determined under section 40(a),

(4) the research credit determined under section 41(a),

(5) the low-income housing credit determined under section 42(a),

(6) the enhanced oil recovery credit under section 43(a),

(7) in the case of an eligible small business (as defined in section 44(b)), the disabled access credit determined under section 44(a),

(8) the renewable electricity production credit under section 45(a),

(9) the empowerment zone employment credit determined under section 1396(a),

(10) the Indian employment credit as determined under section 45A(a),

(11) the employer social security credit determined under section 45B(a),

(12) the orphan drug credit determined under section 45C(a),

(13) the new markets tax credit determined under section 45D(a),

(14) in the case of an eligible employer (as defined in section 45E(c)), the small employer pension plan startup cost credit determined under section 45E(a),

(15) the employer-provided child care credit determined under section 45F(a),

(16) the railroad track maintenance credit determined under section 45G(a),

(17) the biodiesel fuels credit determined under section 40A(a),

(18) the low sulfur diesel fuel production credit determined under section 45H(a),

(19) the marginal oil and gas well production credit determined under section 45I(a),

(20) the distilled spirits credit determined under section 5011(a),

(21) the advanced nuclear power facility production credit determined under section 45J(a),

(22) the nonconventional source production credit determined under section 45K(a),

(23) the new energy efficient home credit determined under section 45L(a),

(24) the energy efficient appliance credit determined under section 45M(a),

(25) the portion of the alternative motor vehicle credit to which section 30B(g)(1) applies,

(26) the portion of the alternative fuel vehicle refueling property credit to which section 30C(d)(1) applies,

(27) the Hurricane Katrina housing credit determined under section 1400P(b),

(28) the Hurricane Katrina employee retention credit determined under section 1400R(a),

(29) the Hurricane Rita employee retention credit determined under section 1400R(b),[1]

(30) the Hurricane Wilma employee retention credit determined under section 1400R(c)[2], *plus*

[3]*(31) the mine rescue team training credit determined under section 45N(a).*

* * * * * * * * * * * *

[For Analysis, see ¶ 806. For Committee Reports, see ¶ 5056.]

[Endnote Code Sec. 38]

Matter in *italics* in Code Sec. 38(b)(29), Code Sec. 38(b)(30), and Code Sec. 38(b)(31) was added by Sec. 405(b) of the Tax Relief and Health Care Act of 2006, HR6111, d.o.e., which struck out:

1. "and"
2. "."
3. added para. (b)(31)

Effective Date (Sec. 405(e), HR6111, d.o.e.) effective for tax. yrs. begin. after 12/31/2005.

[¶ 3004] Code Sec. 41. Credit for increasing research activities.

* * * * * * * * * * * *

(c) Base amount.

* * * * * * * * * * * *

(4) Election of alternative incremental credit.

(A) In general. At the election of the taxpayer, the credit determined under subsection (a)(1) shall be equal to the sum of—

(i) [1]*3 percent* of so much of the qualified research expenses for the taxable year as exceeds 1 percent of the average described in subsection (c)(1)(B) but does not exceed 1.5 percent of such average,

(ii) [2]*4 percent* of so much of such expenses as exceeds 1.5 percent of such average but does not exceed 2 percent of such average, and

(iii) [3]*5 percent* of so much of such expenses as exceeds 2 percent of such average.

(B) Election. An election under this paragraph shall apply to the taxable year for which made and all succeeding taxable years unless revoked with the consent of the Secretary.

[4]***(5) Election of alternative simplified credit.***

(A) In general. At the election of the taxpayer, the credit determined under subsection (a)(1) shall be equal to 12 percent of so much of the qualified research expenses for the taxable year as exceeds 50 percent of the average qualified research expenses for the 3 taxable years preceding the taxable year for which the credit is being determined.

(B) Special rule in case of no qualified research expenses in any of 3 preceding taxable years.

(i) Taxpayers to which subparagraph applies. The credit under this paragraph shall be determined under this subparagraph if the taxpayer has no qualified research expenses in any one of the 3 taxable years preceding the taxable year for which the credit is being determined.

(ii) Credit rate. The credit determined under this subparagraph shall be equal to 6 percent of the qualified research expenses for the taxable year.

(C) Election. An election under this paragraph shall apply to the taxable year for which made and all succeeding taxable years unless revoked with the consent of the Secretary. An election under this paragraph may not be made for any taxable year to which an election under paragraph (4) applies.

[5]***(6)* Consistent treatment of expenses required.**

(A) In general. Notwithstanding whether the period for filing a claim for credit or refund has expired for any taxable year taken into account in determining the fixed-base percentage, the qualified research expenses taken into account in computing such percentage shall be determined on a basis consistent with the determination of qualified research expenses for the credit year.

(B) Prevention of distortions. The Secretary may prescribe regulations to prevent distortions in calculating a taxpayer's qualified research expenses or gross receipts caused by a change in accounting methods used by such taxpayer between the current year and a year taken into account in computing such taxpayer's fixed-base percentage.

[6]*(7)* **Gross receipts.** For purposes of this subsection, gross receipts for any taxable year shall be reduced by returns and allowances made during the taxable year. In the case of a foreign corporation, there shall be taken into account only gross receipts which are effectively connected with the conduct of a trade or business within the United States, the Commonwealth of Puerto Rico, or any possession of the United States.

* * * * * * * * * * * *

(h) Termination.

(1) In general. This section shall not apply to any amount paid or incurred—

(A) after June 30, 1995, and before July 1, 1996, or

(B) after December 31, [7]*2007.*

(2) Computation of base amount. In the case of any taxable year with respect to which this section applies to a number of days which is less than the total number of days in such taxable year, the base amount with respect to such taxable year shall be the amount which bears the same ratio to the base amount for such year (determined without regard to this paragraph) as the number of days in such taxable year to which this section applies bears to the total number of days in such taxable year.

[For Analysis, see ¶ 201, ¶ 202, ¶ 203, and ¶ 701. For Committee Reports, see ¶ 5004 and ¶ 5029.]

[Endnote Code Sec. 41]

Matter in *italics* in Code Sec. 41(c)(4)(A) was added by Sec. 104(b)(1)(A)-(C) of the Tax Relief and Health Care Act of 2006, HR6111, d.o.e., which struck out:

1. "2.65 percent"
2. "3.2 percent"
3. "3.75 percent"

Effective Date (Sec. 104(b)(2), HR6111, d.o.e.) effective for tax. yrs. end. after 12/31/2006, except as provided in Sec. 104(b)(3), HR6111, which reads as follows:

"(3) Transition rule.

"(A) In general. In the case of a specified transitional taxable year for which an election under section 41(c)(4) of the Internal Revenue Code of 1986 applies, the credit determined under section 41(a)(1) of such Code shall be equal to the sum of—

"(i) the applicable 2006 percentage multiplied by the amount determined under section 41(c)(4)(A) of such Code (as in effect for taxable years ending on December 31, 2006), plus

"(ii) the applicable 2007 percentage multiplied by the amount determined under section 41(c)(4)(A) of such Code (as in effect for taxable years ending on January 1, 2007).

"(B) Definitions. For purposes of subparagraph (A)—

"(i) Specified transitional taxable year. The term 'specified transitional taxable year' means any taxable year which ends after December 31, 2006, and which includes such date.

"(ii) Applicable 2006 percentage. The term 'applicable 2006 percentage' means the number of days in the specified transitional taxable year before January 1, 2007, divided by the number of days in such taxable year.

"(iii) Applicable 2007 percentage. The term 'applicable 2007 percentage' means the number of days in the specified transitional taxable year after December 31, 2006, divided by the number of days in such taxable year."

Matter in *italics* in Code Sec. 41(c)(5), Code Sec. 41(c)(6), and Code Sec. 41(c)(7) was added by Sec. 104(c)(1), HR6111, d.o.e., which struck out:

4. "added para. (c)(5)
5. "(5)"
6. "(6)"

Effective Date (Sec. 104(c)(3), HR6111, d.o.e.) effective for tax. yrs. end. after 12/31/2006, except as provided in Sec. 104(c)(4), HR6111, which reads as follows:

"(4) Transition rule for noncalendar taxable years.

"(A) In general. In the case of a specified transitional taxable year for which an election under section 41(c)(5) of the Internal Revenue Code of 1986 (as added by this subsection) applies, the credit determined under section 41(a)(1) of such Code shall be equal to the sum of—

"(i) the applicable 2006 percentage multiplied by the amount determined under section 41(a)(1) of such Code (as in effect for taxable years ending on December 31, 2006), plus

"(ii) the applicable 2007 percentage multiplied by the amount determined under section 41(c)(5) of such Code (as in effect for taxable years ending on January 1, 2007).

"(B) Definitions and special rules. For purposes of subparagraph (A)-

"(i) Definitions. Terms used in this paragraph which are also used in subsection (b)(3) shall have the respective meanings given such terms in such subsection.

"(ii) Dual elections permitted.

"Elections under paragraphs (4) and (5) of section 41(c) of such Code may both apply for the specified transitional taxable year.

"(iii) Deferral of deemed election revocation. Any election under section 41(c)(4) of the Internal Revenue Code of 1986 treated as revoked under paragraph (2) shall be treated as revoked for the taxable year after the specified transitional taxable year."

Sec. 104(c)(2), HR6111, relating to transition rules, reads as follows:

"(2) Transition rule for deemed revocation of election of alternative incremental credit. In the case of an election under section 41(c)(4) of the Internal Revenue Code of 1986 which applies to the taxable year which includes January 1, 2007, such election shall be treated as revoked with the consent of the Secretary of the Treasury if the taxpayer makes an election under section 41(c)(5) of such Code (as added by this subsection) for such year.

Matter in *italics* in Code Sec. 41(h)(1)(B) was added by Sec. 104(a)(1), HR6111, d.o.e., which struck out:

7. "2005"

Effective Date (Sec. 104(a)(3), HR6111, d.o.e.) effective for amounts paid or incurred after 12/31/2005.

[¶3005] Code Sec. 45. Electricity produced from certain renewable resources, etc.

* * * * * * * * * * * *

(d) Qualified facilities. For purposes of this section—

(1) Wind facility. In the case of a facility using wind to produce electricity, the term "qualified facility" means any facility owned by the taxpayer which is originally placed in service after December 31, 1993, and before [1]*January 1, 2009.*

(2) Closed-loop biomass facility.

(A) In general. In the case of a facility using closed-loop biomass to produce electricity, the term "qualified facility" means any facility—

(i) owned by the taxpayer which is originally placed in service after December 31, 1992, and before [2]*January 1, 2009,* or

(ii) owned by the taxpayer which before [3]*January 1, 2009,* is originally placed in service and modified to use closed-loop biomass to co-fire with coal, with other biomass, or with both, but only if the modification is approved under the Biomass Power for Rural Development Programs or is part of a pilot project of the Commodity Credit Corporation as described in 65 Fed. Reg. 63052.

(B) Special rules. In the case of a qualified facility described in subparagraph (A)(ii)—

(i) the 10-year period referred to in subsection (a) shall be treated as beginning no earlier than the date of the enactment of this clause,

(ii) the amount of the credit determined under subsection (a) with respect to the facility shall be an amount equal to the amount determined without regard to this clause multiplied by the ratio of the thermal content of the closed-loop biomass used in such facility to the thermal content of all fuels used in such facility, and

(iii) if the owner of such facility is not the producer of the electricity, the person eligible for the credit allowable under subsection (a) shall be the lessee or the operator of such facility.

(3) Open-loop biomass facilities.

(A) In general. In the case of a facility using open-loop biomass to produce electricity, the term "qualified facility" means any facility owned by the taxpayer which—

(i) in the case of a facility using agricultural livestock waste nutrients—

(I) is originally placed in service after the date of the enactment of this subclause and before [4]*January 1, 2009,* and

(II) the nameplate capacity rating of which is not less than 150 kilowatts, and

(ii) in the case of any other facility, is originally placed in service before [5]*January 1, 2009.*

(B) Credit eligibility. In the case of any facility described in subparagraph (A), if the owner of such facility is not the producer of the electricity, the person eligible for the credit allowable under subsection (a) shall be the lessee or the operator of such facility.

(4) Geothermal or solar energy facility. In the case of a facility using geothermal or solar energy to produce electricity, the term "qualified facility" means any facility owned by the taxpayer which is originally placed in service after the date of the enactment of this paragraph and before [6]*January 1, 2009* (January 1, 2006, in the case of a facility using solar energy). Such term shall not include any property described in section 48(a)(3) the basis of which is taken into account by the taxpayer for purposes of determining the energy credit under section 48.

(5) Small irrigation power facility. In the case of a facility using small irrigation power to produce electricity, the term "qualified facility" means any facility owned by the taxpayer which is originally placed in service after the date of the enactment of this paragraph and before [7]*January 1, 2009.*

(6) Landfill gas facilities. In the case of a facility producing electricity from gas derived from the biodegradation of municipal solid waste, the term "qualified facility" means any facility owned by the taxpayer which is originally placed in service after the date of the enactment of this paragraph and before [8]*January 1, 2009.*

(7) Trash combustion facilities. In the case of a facility which burns municipal solid waste to produce electricity, the term "qualified facility" means any facility owned by the taxpayer which is originally placed in service after the date of the enactment of this paragraph and before [9]*January 1, 2009.* Such term shall include a new unit placed in service in connection with a facility placed in service on or before the date of the enactment of this paragraph, but only to the extent of the increased amount of electricity produced at the facility by reason of such new unit.

(8) Refined coal production facility. In the case of a facility that produces refined coal, the term "refined coal production facility" means a facility which is placed in service after the date of the enactment of this paragraph and before January 1, 2009.

(9) Qualified hydropower facility. In the case of a facility producing qualified hydroelectric production described in subsection (c)(8), the term "qualified facility" means—

(A) in the case of any facility producing incremental hydropower production, such facility but only to the extent of its incremental hydropower production attributable to efficiency improvements or additions to capacity described in subsection (c)(8)(B) placed in service after the date of the enactment of this paragraph and before [10]*January 1, 2009,* and

(B) any other facility placed in service after the date of the enactment of this paragraph and before [11]*January 1, 2009.*

(C) Credit period. In the case of a qualified facility described in subparagraph (A), the 10-year period referred to in subsection (a) shall be treated as beginning on the date the efficiency improvements or additions to capacity are placed in service.

(10) Indian coal production facility. In the case of a facility that produces Indian coal, the term "Indian coal production facility" means a facility which is placed in service before January 1, 2009.

* * * * * * * * * * * * *

[For Analysis, see ¶ 903. For Committee Reports, see ¶ 5031.]

[Endnote Code Sec. 45]

Matter in *italics* in Code Sec. 45(d) was added by Sec. 201 of the Tax Relief and Health Care Act of 2006, HR6111, d.o.e., which struck out:

1. "January 1, 2008"
2. "January 1, 2008"
3. "January 1, 2008"
4. "January 1, 2008"
5. "January 1, 2008"
6. "January 1, 2008"
7. "January 1, 2008"
8. "January 1, 2008"
9. "January 1, 2008"
10. "January 1, 2008"
11. "January 1, 2008"

Effective Date Enacted d.o.e..

[¶ 3006] Code Sec. 45A. Indian employment credit.

* * * * * * * * * * * * *

(f) Termination. This section shall not apply to taxable years beginning after December 31, [1]*2007.*

[For Analysis, see ¶ 807. For Committee Reports, see ¶ 5015.]

[Endnote Code Sec. 45A]

Matter in *italics* in Code Sec. 45A(f) was added by Sec. 111(a) of the Tax Relief and Health Care Act of 2006, HR6111, d.o.e., which struck out:

1. "2005"

Effective Date (Sec. 111(b), HR6111, d.o.e.) effective for tax. yrs. begin. after 12/31/2005.

[¶ 3007] Code Sec. 45C. Clinical testing expenses for certain drugs for rare diseases or conditions.

* * * * * * * * * * * * *

(b) Qualified clinical testing expenses. For purposes of this section—

(1) Qualified clinical testing expenses.

(A) In general. Except as otherwise provided in this paragraph, the term "qualified clinical testing expenses" means the amounts which are paid or incurred by the taxpayer during the taxable year which would be described in subsection (b) of section 41 if such subsection were applied with the modifications set forth in subparagraph (B).

(B) Modifications. For purposes of subparagraph (A), subsection (b) of section 41 shall be applied—

(i) by substituting "clinical testing" for "qualified research" each place it appears in paragraphs (2) and (3) of such subsection, and

(ii) by substituting "100 percent" for "65 percent" in paragraph (3)(A) of such subsection.

(C) Exclusion for amounts funded by grants, etc. The term "qualified clinical testing expenses" shall not include any amount to the extent such amount is funded by any grant, contract, or otherwise by another person (or any governmental entity).

(D) Special rule. For purposes of this paragraph, section 41 shall be deemed to remain in effect for periods after June 30, 1995, and before July 1, 1996, and periods after December 31, [1]*2007.*

* * * * * * * * * * * * *

[For Analysis, see ¶ 201. For Committee Reports, see ¶ 5004.]

[Endnote Code Sec. 45C]

Matter in *italics* in Code Sec. 45C(b)(1)(D) was added by Sec. 104(a)(2) of the Tax Relief and Health Care Act of 2006, HR6111, d.o.e., which struck out:

1. "2005"

Effective Date (Sec. 104(a)(3), HR6111, d.o.e.) effective for amounts paid or incurred after 12/31/2005.

[¶ 3008] Code Sec. 45D. New markets tax credit.

* * * * * * * * * * * * *

(f) National limitation on amount of investments designated.

(1) In general. There is a new markets tax credit limitation for each calendar year. Such limitation is—

(A) $1,000,000,000 for 2001,
(B) $1,500,000,000 for 2002 and 2003,
(C) $2,000,000,000 for 2004 and 2005, and
(D) $3,500,000,000 for 2006[1], *2007, and 2008.*

(2) Allocation of limitation. The limitation under paragraph (1) shall be allocated by the Secretary among qualified community development entities selected by the Secretary. In making allocations under the preceding sentence, the Secretary shall give priority to any entity—

(A) with a record of having successfully provided capital or technical assistance to disadvantaged businesses or communities, or

(B) which intends to satisfy the requirement under subsection (b)(1)(B) by making qualified low-income community investments in 1 or more businesses in which persons unrelated to such entity (within the meaning of section 267(b) or 707(b)(1)) hold the majority equity interest.

(3) Carryover of unused limitation. If the new markets tax credit limitation for any calendar year exceeds the aggregate amount allocated under paragraph (2) for such year, such limitation for the succeeding calendar year shall be increased by the amount of such excess. No amount may be carried under the preceding sentence to any calendar year after 2014.

* * * * * * * * * * * *

(i) Regulations. The Secretary shall prescribe such regulations as may be appropriate to carry out this section, including regulations—

(1) which limit the credit for investments which are directly or indirectly subsidized by other Federal tax benefits (including the credit under section 42 and the exclusion from gross income under section 103),

(2) which prevent the abuse of the purposes of this section,

(3) which provide rules for determining whether the requirement of subsection (b)(1)(B) is treated as met,

(4) which impose appropriate reporting requirements,[2]

(5) which apply the provisions of this section to newly formed entities[3], *and*

[4]*(6) which ensure that non-metropolitan counties receive a proportional allocation of qualified equity investments.*

[For Analysis, see ¶ 1001 and ¶ 1002. For Committee Reports, see ¶ 5002.]

[Endnote Code Sec. 45D]

Matter in *italics* in Code Sec. 45D(f)(1)(D), Code Sec. 45D(i)(4), Code Sec. 45D(i)(5), and Code Sec. 45D(i)(6) was added by Sec. 102(a) and (b) of the Tax Relief and Health Care Act of 2006, HR6111, d.o.e., which struck out:

1. "and 2007"
2. "and"
3. "."
4. added para. (i)(6)

Effective Date (Sec. 102(c), HR6111, d.o.e.) effective d.o.e..

[¶ 3009] Code Sec. 45G. Railroad track maintenance credit.

* * * * * * * * * * * *

(d) Qualified railroad track maintenance expenditures. For purposes of this section, the term "qualified railroad track maintenance expenditures" means [1]*gross* expenditures (whether or not otherwise chargeable to capital account) for maintaining railroad track (including roadbed, bridges, and related track structures) owned or leased as of January 1, 2005, by a Class II or Class III railroad [2]*(determined without regard to any consideration for such expenditures given by the Class II or Class III railroad which made the assignment of such track).*

* * * * * * * * * * * *

[For Analysis, see ¶ 1607. For Committee Reports, see ¶ 5074.]

[Endnote Code Sec. 45G]

Matter in *italics* in Code Sec. 45G(d) was added by Sec. 423(a)(1) and (2) of the Tax Relief and Health Care Act of 2006, HR6111, d.o.e..

1. added matter in subsec. (d)
2. added matter in subsec. (d)

Effective Date (Sec. 423(b), HR6111, d.o.e.) effective for tax. yrs. begin. after 12/31/2004.

[¶ 3010] Code Sec. 45K.

* * * * * * * * * * * *

Credit for producing fuel from a nonconventional source.

(g) Extension for facilities producing coke or coke gas. Notwithstanding subsection (e)—

(1) In general. In the case of a facility for producing coke or coke gas [1]*(other than from petroleum based products)* which was placed in service before January 1, 1993, or after June 30, 1998, and before January 1, 2010, this section shall apply with respect to coke and coke gas produced in such facility and sold during the period—

(A) beginning on the later of January 1, 2006, or the date that such facility is placed in service, and

(B) ending on the date which is 4 years after the date such period began.

(2) Special rules. In determining the amount of credit allowable under this section solely by reason of this subsection—

(A) Daily limit. The amount of qualified fuels sold during any taxable year which may be taken into account by reason of this subsection with respect to any facility shall not exceed an average barrel-of-oil equivalent of 4,000 barrels per day. Days before the date the facility is placed in service shall not be taken into account in determining such average.

(B) Extension period to commence with unadjusted credit amount. For purposes of applying subsection (b)(2) to the $3 amount in subsection (a), in the case of fuels sold after 2005, subsection (d)(2)(B) shall be applied by substituting "2004" for "1979".

(C) Denial of double benefit. This subsection shall not apply to any facility producing qualified fuels for which a credit was allowed under this section for the taxable year or any preceding taxable year by reason of subsection (f).

[2]*(D) Nonapplication of phaseout. Subsection (b)(1) shall not apply.*

[For Analysis, see ¶ 904. For Committee Reports, see ¶ 5041.]

[Endnote Code Sec. 45K]

Matter in *italics* in Code Sec. 45K(g)(1) and Code Sec. 45K(g)(2)(D) was added by Sec. 211(a) and (b) of the Tax Relief and Health Care Act of 2006, HR6111, d.o.e..

1. added matter in para. (g)(1)
2. added subpara. (g)(2)(D)

Effective Date (Sec. 211(c), HR6111, d.o.e.) effective for fuel produced and sold after 12/31/2005, in tax. yrs. end. after 12/31/2005.

[¶ 3011] Code Sec. 45L. New energy efficient home credit.

* * * * * * * * * * * *

(g) Termination. This section shall not apply to any qualified new energy efficient home acquired after [1]*December 31, 2008.*

[For Analysis, see ¶ 901. For Committee Reports, see ¶ 5035.]

[Endnote Code Sec. 45L]

Matter in *italics* in Code Sec. 45L(g) was added by Sec. 205 of the Tax Relief and Health Care Act of 2006, HR6111, d.o.e., which struck out:

1. "December 31, 2007"

Effective Date Enacted d.o.e..

[¶ 3012] Code Sec.[1] 45N. Mine rescue team training credit.

*(a) **Amount of credit.** For purposes of section 38, the mine rescue team training credit determined under this section with respect to each qualified mine rescue team employee of an eligible employer for any taxable year is an amount equal to the lesser of—*

(1) 20 percent of the amount paid or incurred by the taxpayer during the taxable year with respect to the training program costs of such qualified mine rescue team employee (including wages of such employee while attending such program), or

(2) $10,000.

*(b) **Qualified mine rescue team employee.** For purposes of this section, the term "qualified mine rescue team employee" means with respect to any taxable year any full-time employee of the taxpayer who is—*

(1) a miner eligible for more than 6 months of such taxable year to serve as a mine rescue team member as a result of completing, at a minimum, an initial 20-hour course of instruction as prescribed by the Mine Safety and Health Administration's Office of Educational Policy and Development, or

(2) a miner eligible for more than 6 months of such taxable year to serve as a mine rescue team member by virtue of receiving at least 40 hours of refresher training in such instruction.

*(c) **Eligible employer.** For purposes of this section, the term "eligible employer" means any taxpayer which employs individuals as miners in underground mines in the United States.*

*(d) **Wages.** For purposes of this section, the term "wages" has the meaning given to such term by subsection (b) of section 3306 (determined without regard to any dollar limitation contained in such section).*

*(e) **Termination.** This section shall not apply to taxable years beginning after December 31, 2008.*

[For Analysis, see ¶ 806. For Committee Reports, see ¶ 5056.]

[Endnote Code Sec. 45N]

Code Sec. 45N, in *italics*, was added by Sec. 405(a) of the Tax Relief and Health Care Act of 2006, HR6111, d.o.e..

1. added Code Sec. 45N

Effective Date (Sec. 405(e), HR6111, d.o.e.) effective for tax. yrs. begin. after 12/31/2005.

[¶ 3013] Code Sec. 48. Energy credit.

(a) **Energy credit.**

(1) **In general.** For purposes of section 46, except as provided in paragraphs (1)(B) and (2)(B) of subsection (c), the energy credit for any taxable year is the energy percentage of the basis of each energy property placed in service during such taxable year.

(2) **Energy percentage.**

(A) In general. The energy percentage is—

(i) 30 percent in the case of—

(I) qualified fuel cell property,

(II) energy property described in paragraph (3)(A)(i) but only with respect to periods ending before [1]*January 1, 2009*, and

(III) energy property described in paragraph (3)(A)(ii), and

(ii) in the case of any energy property to which clause (i) does not apply, 10 percent.

(B) Coordination with rehabilitation credit. The energy percentage shall not apply to that portion of the basis of any property which is attributable to qualified rehabilitation expenditures.

(3) Energy property. For purposes of this subpart, the term "energy property" means any property—

(A) which is—

(i) equipment which uses solar energy to generate electricity, to heat or cool (or provide hot water for use in) a structure, or to provide solar process heat, excepting property used to generate energy for the purposes of heating a swimming pool,

(ii) equipment which uses solar energy to illuminate the inside of a structure using fiber-optic distributed sunlight but only with respect to periods ending before [2]*January 1, 2009,*

(iii) equipment used to produce, distribute, or use energy derived from a geothermal deposit (within the meaning of section 613(e)(2)), but only, in the case of electricity generated by geothermal power, up to (but not including) the electrical transmission stage, [or]

(iv) qualified fuel cell property or qualified microturbine property,

* * * * * * * * * * * *

(c) Qualified fuel cell property; qualified microturbine property. For purposes of this subsection—

(1) Qualified fuel cell property.

(A) In general. The term "qualified fuel cell property" means a fuel cell power plant which—

(i) has a nameplate capacity of at least 0.5 kilowatt of electricity using an electrochemical process, and

(ii) has an electricity-only generation efficiency greater than 30 percent.

(B) Limitation. In the case of qualified fuel cell property placed in service during the taxable year, the credit otherwise determined under paragraph (1) for such year with respect to such property shall not exceed an amount equal to $500 for each 0.5 kilowatt of capacity of such property.

(C) Fuel cell power plant. The term "fuel cell power plant" means an integrated system comprised of a fuel cell stack assembly and associated balance of plant components which converts a fuel into electricity using electrochemical means.

(D) Special rule. The first sentence of the matter in subsection (a)(3) which follows subparagraph (D) thereof shall not apply to qualified fuel cell property which is used predominantly in the trade or business of the furnishing or sale of telephone service, telegraph service by means of domestic telegraph operations, or other telegraph services (other than international telegraph services).

(E) Termination. The term "qualified fuel cell property" shall not include any property for any period after [3]*December 31, 2008.*

(2) Qualified microturbine property.

(A) In general. The term "qualified microturbine property" means a stationary microturbine power plant which—

(i) has a nameplate capacity of less than 2,000 kilowatts, and

(ii) has an electricity-only generation efficiency of not less than 26 percent at International Standard Organization conditions.

(B) Limitation. In the case of qualified microturbine property placed in service during the taxable year, the credit otherwise determined under paragraph (1) for such year with respect to such property shall not exceed an amount equal $200 for each kilowatt of capacity of such property.

(C) Stationary microturbine power plant. The term "stationary microturbine power plant" means an integrated system comprised of a gas turbine engine, a combustor, a recuperator or regenerator, a generator or alternator, and associated balance of plant components which converts a fuel into electricity and thermal energy. Such term also includes all secondary components located between the existing infrastructure for fuel delivery and the existing infrastructure for power distribution, including equipment and controls for meeting relevant power standards, such as voltage, frequency, and power factors.

(D) Special rule. The first sentence of the matter in subsection (a)(3) which follows subparagraph (D) thereof shall not apply to qualified microturbine property which is used predominantly in the trade or business of the furnishing or sale of telephone service, telegraph service by means of domestic telegraph operations, or other telegraph services (other than international telegraph services).

(E) Termination. The term "qualified microturbine property" shall not include any property for any period after [4]*December 31, 2008.*

[For Analysis, see ¶ 902. For Committee Reports, see ¶ 5037.]

[Endnote Code Sec. 48]

Matter in *italics* in Code Sec. 48(a)(2)(A)(i)(II), Code Sec. 48(a)(3)(A)(ii), Code Sec. 48(c)(1)(E), and Code Sec. 48(c)(2)(E) was added by Sec. 207 1) and (2) of the Tax Relief and Health Care Act of 2006, HR6111, d.o.e., which struck out:

1. "January 1, 2008"
2. "January 1, 2008"
3. "December 31, 2007"
4. "December 31, 2007"

Effective Date Enacted d.o.e..

[¶ 3014] Code Sec. 48A. Qualifying advanced coal project credit.

* * * * * * * * * * * * *

(f) Advanced coal-based generation technology.

(1) In general. For the purpose of this section, an electric generation unit uses advanced coal-based generation technology if—

(A) the unit—

(i) uses integrated gasification combined cycle technology, or

(ii) except as provided in paragraph (3), has a design net heat rate of 8530 Btu/kWh (40 percent efficiency), and

(B) the unit is designed to meet the performance requirements in the following table:

Performance characteristic:	Design level for project:
SO_2 (percent removal)	99 percent
NO_x (emissions)	0.07 lbs/MMBTU
PM* (emissions)	0.015 lbs/MMBTU
Hg (percent removal)	90 percent

[1]*For purposes of the performance requirement specified for the removal of SO_2 in the table contained in subparagraph (B), the SO_2 removal design level in the case of a unit designed for the use of feedstock substantially all of which is subbituminous coal shall be 99 percent SO_2 removal or the achievement of an emission level of 0.04 pounds or less of SO_2 per million Btu, determined on a 30-day average.*

* * * * * * * * * * * * *

[For Analysis, see ¶ 905. For Committee Reports, see ¶ 5033.]

[Endnote Code Sec. 48A]

Matter in *italics* in Code Sec. 48A(f)(1) was added by Sec. 203(a) of the Tax Relief and Health Care Act of 2006, HR6111, d.o.e..

1. added matter in para. (f)(1)

Effective Date (Sec. 203(b), HR6111, d.o.e.) effective for applications for certification under Code Sec. 48A(d)(2) submitted after 10/2/2006.

[¶3015] Code Sec. 51. Amount of credit.

* * * * * * * * * * * * *

(c) Wages defined. For purposes of this subpart—

(1) In general. Except as otherwise provided in this subsection and subsection (h)(2), the term "wages" has the meaning given to such term by subsection (b) of section 3306 (determined without regard to any dollar limitation contained in such section).

* * * * * * * * * * * * *

(4) Termination. The term "wages" shall not include any amount paid or incurred to an individual who begins work for the employer—

(A) after December 31, 1994, and before October 1, 1996, or

(B) after December 31, [1]*2007.*

(d) Members of targeted groups. For purposes of this subpart—

(1) In general. An individual is a member of a targeted group if such individual is—

(A) a qualified IV-A recipient,

(B) a qualified veteran,

(C) a qualified ex-felon,

(D) a high-risk youth,

(E) a vocational rehabilitation referral,

(F) a qualified summer youth employee,

(G) a qualified food stamp recipient,[2]

(H) a qualified SSI recipient[3]*, or*

[4]*(I) a long-term family assistance recipient.*

* * * * * * * * * * * * *

(4) Qualified ex-felon. The term "qualified ex-felon" means any individual who is certified by the designated local agency—

(A) as having been convicted of a felony under any statute of the United States or any State, [5]*and*

(B) as having a hiring date which is not more than 1 year after the last date on which such individual was so convicted or was released from prison[6].

* * * * * * * * * * * * *

(8) Qualified food stamp recipient.

(A) In general. The term "qualified food stamp recipient" means any individual who is certified by the designated local agency—

(i) as having attained age 18 but not age [7]*40* on the hiring date, and

(ii) as being a member of a family—

(I) receiving assistance under a food stamp program under the Food Stamp Act of 1977 for the 6-month period ending on the hiring date, or

(II) receiving such assistance for at least 3 months of the 5-month period ending on the hiring date, in the case of a member of a family who ceases to be eligible for such assistance under section 6(o) of the Food Stamp Act of 1977.

(B) Participation information. Notwithstanding any other provision of law, the Secretary of the Treasury and the Secretary of Agriculture shall enter into an agreement to provide information to designated local agencies with respect to participation in the food stamp program.

* * * * * * * * * * * * *

[8]*(10)* ***Long-term family assistance recipient.*** *The term "long-term family assistance recipient" means any individual who is certified by the designated local agency—*

(A) as being a member of a family receiving assistance under a IV-A program (as defined in paragraph (2)(B)) for at least the 18-month period ending on the hiring date,

(B) (i) as being a member of a family receiving such assistance for 18 months beginning after August 5, 1997, and

(ii) as having a hiring date which is not more than 2 years after the end of the earliest such 18-month period, or

(C) (i) as being a member of a family which ceased to be eligible for such assistance by reason of any limitation imposed by Federal or State law on the maximum period such assistance is payable to a family, and

(ii) as having a hiring date which is not more than 2 years after the date of such cessation.

[9]*(11)* **Hiring date.** The term "hiring date" means the day the individual is hired by the employer.

[10]*(12)* **Designated local agency.** The term "designated local agency" means a State employment security agency established in accordance with the Act of June 6, 1933, as amended (29 U.S.C. 49-49n).

[11]*(13)* **Special rules for certifications.**

(A) In general. An individual shall not be treated as a member of a targeted group unless—

(i) on or before the day on which such individual begins work for the employer, the employer has received a certification from a designated local agency that such individual is a member of a targeted group, or

(ii) (I) on or before the day the individual is offered employment with the employer, a pre-screening notice is completed by the employer with respect to such individual, and

(II) not later than the [12]*28th day* after the individual begins work for the employer, the employer submits such notice, signed by the employer and the individual under penalties of perjury, to the designated local agency as part of a written request for such a certification from such agency.

For purposes of this paragraph, the term "pre-screening notice" means a document (in such form as the Secretary shall prescribe) which contains information provided by the individual on the basis of which the employer believes that the individual is a member of a targeted group.

(B) Incorrect certifications. If—

(i) an individual has been certified by a designated local agency as a member of a targeted group, and

(ii) such certification is incorrect because it was based on false information provided by such individual,

the certification shall be revoked and wages paid by the employer after the date on which notice of revocation is received by the employer shall not be treated as qualified wages.

(C) Explanation of denial of request. If a designated local agency denies a request for certification of membership in a targeted group, such agency shall provide to the person making such request a written explanation of the reasons for such denial.

[13]***(e) Credit for second-year wages for employment of long-term family assistance recipients.***

(1) ***In general.*** *With respect to the employment of a long-term family assistance recipient—*

(A) the amount of the work opportunity credit determined under this section for the taxable year shall include 50 percent of the qualified second-year wages for such year, and

(B) in lieu of applying subsection (b)(3), the amount of the qualified first-year wages, and the amount of qualified second-year wages, which may be taken into account with respect to such a recipient shall not exceed $10,000 per year.

(2) Qualified second-year wages. *For purposes of this subsection, the term "qualified second-year wages" means qualified wages—*

(A) which are paid to a long-term family assistance recipient, and

(B) which are attributable to service rendered during the 1-year period beginning on the day after the last day of the 1-year period with respect to such recipient determined under subsection (b)(2).

(3) Special rules for agricultural and railway labor. *If such recipient is an employee to whom subparagraph (A) or (B) of subsection (h)(1) applies, rules similar to the rules of such subparagraphs shall apply except that—*

(A) such subparagraph (A) shall be applied by substituting "$10,000" for "$6,000", and

(B) such subparagraph (B) shall be applied by substituting "$833.33" for "$500".

* * * * * * * * * * * *

[For Analysis, see ¶ 801, ¶ 802, ¶ 803, ¶ 804, and ¶ 805. For Committee Reports, see ¶ 5005.]

[Endnote Code Sec. 51]

Matter in *italics* in Code Sec. 51(c)(4)(B) was added by Sec. 105(a) of the Tax Relief and Health Care Act of 2006, HR6111, d.o.e., which struck out:

1. "2005"

Effective Date (Sec. 105(f)(1), HR6111, d.o.e.) effective for individuals who begin work for the employer after 12/31/2005.

Matter in *italics* in Code Sec. 51(d)(1)(G), Code Sec. 51(d)(1)(H), Code Sec. 51(d)(1)(I), Code Sec. 51(d)(4)(A), Code Sec. 51(d)(4)(B), Code Sec. 51(d)(4)(C), Code Sec. 51(d)(8)(A)(i), Code Sec. 51(d)(10), Code Sec. 51(d)(11), Code Sec. 51(d)(12), Code Sec. 51(d)(13), and Code Sec. 51(e) was added by Sec. 105(b), (c), (d), (e)(1), (e)(2), and (e)(3) of the Tax Relief and Health Care Act of 2006, HR6111, d.o.e., which struck out:

2. "or"
3. "."
4. added subpara (d)(1)(I)
5. added matter in subpara. (d)(4)(A)
6. ", and"

"(C) as being a member of a family which had an income during the 6 months immediately preceding the earlier of the month in which such income determination occurs or the month in which the hiring date occurs, which, on an annual basis, would be 70 percent or less of the Bureau of Labor Statistics lower living standard.

"Any determination under subparagraph (C) shall be valid for the 45-day period beginning on the date such determination is made."

7. "25"
8. added para. (d)(10)
9. "(10)"
10. "(11)"
11. "(12)"
12. "21st day"
13. added subsec. 51(e)

Effective Date (Sec. 105(f)(2), HR6111, d.o.e.) effective for individuals who begin work for the employer after 12/31/2006.

[¶ 3016] Code Sec. 51A. Temporary incentives for employing long-term family assistance recipients.

* * * * * * * * * * * *

(f) Termination. This section shall not apply to individuals who begin work for the employer after December 31, [1]*2007.*

[For Analysis, see ¶ 805. For Committee Reports, see ¶ 5005.]

[Endnote Code Sec. 51A]

Matter in *italics*, in Code Sec. 51A(f) was added by Sec. 105(a) of the Tax Relief and Health Care Act of 2006, HR6111, d.o.e., which struck out:

1. "2005"

Effective Date (Sec. 105(f)(1), HR6111, d.o.e.) effective for individuals who begin work for the employer after 12/31/2005.

[¶ 3017] Code Sec. 53. Credit for prior year minimum tax liability.

* * * * * * * * * * * * *

[1]*(e)* ***Special rule for individuals with long-term unused credits.***

(1) ***In general.*** *If an individual has a long-term unused minimum tax credit for any taxable year beginning before January 1, 2013, the amount determined under subsection (c) for such taxable year shall not be less than the AMT refundable credit amount for such taxable year.*

(2) ***AMT refundable credit amount.*** *For purposes of paragraph (1)—*

(A) In general. The term "AMT refundable credit amount" means, with respect to any taxable year, the amount equal to the greater of—

(i) the lesser of—

(I) $5,000, or

(II) the amount of long-term unused minimum tax credit for such taxable year, or

(ii) 20 percent of the amount of such credit.

(B) Phaseout of AMT refundable credit amount.

(i) In general. In the case of an individual whose adjusted gross income for any taxable year exceeds the threshold amount (within the meaning of section 151(d)(3)(C)), the AMT refundable credit amount determined under subparagraph (A) for such taxable year shall be reduced by the applicable percentage (within the meaning of section 151(d)(3)(B)).

(ii) Adjusted gross income. For purposes of clause (i), adjusted gross income shall be determined without regard to sections 911, 931, and 933.

(3) ***Long-term unused minimum tax credit.***

(A) In general. For purposes of this subsection, the term "long-term" unused minimum tax credit' means, with respect to any taxable year, the portion of the minimum tax credit determined under subsection (b) attributable to the adjusted net minimum tax for taxable years before the 3rd taxable year immediately preceding such taxable year.

(B) First-in, first-out ordering rule. For purposes of subparagraph (A), credits shall be treated as allowed under subsection (a) on a first-in, first-out basis.

(4) ***Credit refundable.*** *For purposes of this title (other than this section), the credit allowed by reason of this subsection shall be treated as if it were allowed under subpart C.*

[For Analysis, see ¶ 1201. For Committee Reports, see ¶ 5053.]

[Endnote Code Sec. 53]

Code Sec. 53(e), in *italics*, was added by Sec. 402(a) of the Tax Relief and Health Care Act of 2006, HR6111, d.o.e..

1. added subsec. (e)

Effective Date (Sec. 402(c), HR6111, d.o.e.) effective for tax. yrs. begin. after d.o.e..

[¶3018] Code Sec. 54. Credit to holders of clean renewable energy bonds.

* * * * * * * * * * * *

(f) Limitation on amount of bonds designated.

(1) National limitation. There is a national clean renewable energy bond limitation of [1] *$1,200,000,000.*

(2) Allocation by Secretary. The Secretary shall allocate the amount described in paragraph (1) among qualified projects in such manner as the Secretary determines appropriate, except that the Secretary may not allocate more than [2]*$750,000,000* of the national clean renewable energy bond limitation to finance qualified projects of qualified borrowers which are governmental bodies.

* * * * * * * * * * * *

(l) Other definitions and special rules. For purposes of this section—

(1) Bond. The term "bond" includes any obligation.

(2) Pooled financing bond. The term "pooled financing bond" shall have the meaning given such term by section 149(f)(6)(A).

(3) Partnership; S corporation; and other pass-thru entities.

(A) In general. Under regulations prescribed by the Secretary, in the case of a partnership, trust, S corporation, or other pass-thru entity, rules similar to the rules of section 41(g) shall apply with respect to the credit allowable under subsection (a).

(B) No basis adjustment. In the case of a bond held by a partnership or an S corporation, rules similar to the rules under [3]*section 1397E(l)* shall apply.

* * * * * * * * * * * *

(6) Reporting. Issuers of clean renewable energy bonds shall submit reports similar to the reports required under section 149(e).

(m) Termination. This section shall not apply with respect to any bond issued after [4]*December 31, 2008.*

[For Analysis, see ¶906. For Committee Reports, see ¶5032.]

[Endnote Code Sec. 54]

Matter in *italics* in Code Sec. 54(f)(1) was added by Sec. 202(a)(1) of the Tax Relief and Health Care Act of 2006, HR6111, d.o.e., which struck out:

1. "$800,000,000"

Effective Date (Sec. 202(b)(1), HR6111, d.o.e.) effective for bonds issued after 12/31/2006.

Matter in *italics* in Code Sec. 54(f)(2) was added by Sec. 202(a)(2), HR6111, d.o.e., which struck out:

2. "$500,000,000"

Effective Date (Sec. 202(b)(2), HR6111, d.o.e.) effective for allocations or reallocations after 12/31/2006.

Matter in *italics* in Code Sec. 54(l)(3)(B) was added by Sec. 107(b)(2), HR6111, d.o.e., which struck out:

3. "section 1397E(i)"

Effective Date (Sec. 107(c)(2), HR6111, d.o.e) effective for obligations issued after d.o.e. for allocations of the national zone academy bond limitation for calendar years after 2005.

Matter in *italics* in Code Sec. 54(m) was added by Sec. 202(a)(3), HR6111,d.o.e., which struck out:

4. "December 31, 2007'

Effective Date (Sec. 202(b)(1), HR6111, d.o.e.) effective for bonds issued after 12/31/2006.

[¶3019] Code Sec. 62. Adjusted gross income defined.

(a) General rule. For purposes of this subtitle, the term "adjusted gross income" means, in the case of an individual, gross income minus the following deductions:

(1) Trade and business deductions. The deductions allowed by this chapter (other than by part VII of this subchapter) which are attributable to a trade or business carried on by the taxpayer, if such trade or business does not consist of the performance of services by the taxpayer as an employee.

(2) **Certain trade and business deductions of employees.**

(A) Reimbursed expenses of employees. The deductions allowed by part VI (section 161 and following) which consist of expenses paid or incurred by the taxpayer, in connection with the performance by him of services as an employee, under a reimbursement or other expense allowance arrangement with his employer. The fact that the reimbursement may be provided by a third party shall not be determinative of whether or not the preceding sentence applies.

(B) Certain expenses of performing artists. The deductions allowed by section 162 which consist of expenses paid or incurred by a qualified performing artist in connection with the performances by him of services in the performing arts as an employee.

(C) Certain expenses of officials. The deductions allowed by section 162 which consist of expenses paid or incurred with respect to services performed by an official as an employee of a State or a political subdivision thereof in a position compensated in whole or in part on a fee basis.

(D) Certain expenses of elementary and secondary school teachers. In the case of taxable years beginning during 2002, 2003, 2004, [1]*2005, 2006, or 2007*, the deductions allowed by section 162 which consist of expenses, not in excess of $250, paid or incurred by an eligible educator in connection with books, supplies (other than nonathletic supplies for courses of instruction in health or physical education), computer equipment (including related software and services) and other equipment, and supplementary materials used by the eligible educator in the classroom.

(E) Certain expenses of members of reserve components of the Armed Forces of the United States. The deductions allowed by section 162 which consist of expenses, determined at a rate not in excess of the rates for travel expenses (including per diem in lieu of subsistence) authorized for employees of agencies under subchapter I of chapter 57 of title 5, United States Code, paid or incurred by the taxpayer in connection with the performance of services by such taxpayer as a member of a reserve component of the Armed Forces of the United States for any period during which such individual is more than 100 miles away from home in connection with such services.

* * * * * * * * * * * *

[2]***(21) Attorneys fees relating to awards to whistleblowers.*** *Any deduction allowable under this chapter for attorney fees and court costs paid by, or on behalf of, the taxpayer in connection with any award under section 7623(b) (relating to awards to whistleblowers). The preceding sentence shall not apply to any deduction in excess of the amount includible in the taxpayer's gross income for the taxable year on account of such award.*

Nothing in this section shall permit the same item to be deducted more than once.

* * * * * * * * * * * *

[For Analysis, see ¶ 103 and ¶ 1410. For Committee Reports, see ¶ 5012 and ¶ 5057.]

[Endnote Code Sec. 62]

Matter in *italics* in Code Sec. 62(a)(2)(D) was added by Sec. 108(a) of the Tax Relief and Health Care Act of 2006, HR6111, d.o.e., which struck out:

1. "or 2005"

Effective Date (Sec. 108(b), HR6111, d.o.e.) effective for tax. yrs. begin. after 12/31/2005.

Code Sec. 62(a)(21), in *italics*, was added by Sec. 406(a)(3), HR6111, d.o.e..

2. added para. (a)(21)

Effective Date (Sec. 406(d), HR6111, d.o.e.) effective for information provided on or after d.o.e..

[¶ 3020] Code Sec. 106. Contributions by employer to accident and health plans.

* * * * * * * * * * * * *

[1]*(e) **FSA and HRA terminations to fund HSAs.***

*(1) **In general.** A plan shall not fail to be treated as a health flexible spending arrangement or health reimbursement arrangement under this section or section 105 merely because such plan provides for a qualified HSA distribution.*

*(2) **Qualified HSA distribution.** The term "qualified HSA distribution" means a distribution from a health flexible spending arrangement or health reimbursement arrangement to the extent that such distribution—*

(A) does not exceed the lesser of the balance in such arrangement on September 21, 2006, or as of the date of such distribution, and

(B) is contributed by the employer directly to the health savings account of the employee before January 1, 2012.

Such term shall not include more than 1 distribution with respect to any arrangement.

*(3) **Additional tax for failure to maintain high deductible health plan coverage.***

(A) In general. If, at any time during the testing period, the employee is not an eligible individual, then the amount of the qualified HSA distribution—

(i) shall be includible in the gross in-come of the employee for the taxable year in which occurs the first month in the testing period for which such employee is not an eligible individual, and

(ii) the tax imposed by this chapter for such taxable year on the employee shall be increased by 10 percent of the amount which is so includible.

(B) Exception for disability or death. Clauses (i) and (ii) of subparagraph (A) shall not apply if the employee ceases to be an eligible individual by reason of the death of the employee or the employee becoming disabled (within the meaning of (m)(7)section 72(m)(7)).

*(4) **Definition and special rules.** For purposes of this subsection—*

(A) Testing period. The term "testing period" means the period beginning with the month in which the qualified HSA distribution is contributed to the health savings account and ending on the last day of the 12th month following such month.

(B) Eligible individual. The term "eligible individual" has the meaning given such term by section 223(c)(1).

(C) Treatment as rollover contribution. A qualified HSA distribution shall be treated as a rollover contribution described in section 223(f)(5).

*(5) **Tax treatment relating to distributions.** For purposes of this title—*

(A) In general. A qualified HSA distribution shall be treated as a payment described in subsection (d).

(B) Comparability excise tax.

(i) In general. Except as provided in clause (ii), section 4980G shall not apply to qualified HSA distributions.

(ii) Failure to offer too all employees. In the case of a qualified HSA distribution to any employee, the failure to offer such distribution to any eligible individual covered under a high deductible health plan of the employer shall (notwithstanding section 4980G(d)) be treated for purposes of section 4980G as a failure to meet the requirements of section 4980G(b).

[For Analysis, see ¶ 302. For Committee Reports, see ¶ 5045.]

[Endnote Code Sec. 106]

Code Sec. 106(e), in *italics*, was added by Sec. 302(a) of the Tax Relief and Health Care Act of 2006, HR6111, d.o.e..

1. added subsec. (e)

Effective Date (Sec. 302(c)(1), HR6111, d.o.e.) effective for distributions made on or after d.o.e..

[¶ 3021] Code Sec. 121. Exclusion of gain from sale of principal residence.

* * * * * * * * * * * *

(d) Special rules.

* * * * * * * * * * * *

(9) [1]***Uniformed services, foreign service, and intelligence community.***

(A) In general. At the election of an individual with respect to a property, the running of the 5-year period described in subsections (a) and (c)(1)(B) and paragraph (7) of this subsection with respect to such property shall be suspended during any period that such individual or such individual's spouse is serving on qualified official extended [2]*duty—*

(i) as a member of the uniformed services,

(ii) as a member of the Foreign Service of the United States, or

(iii) as an employee of the intelligence community.

(B) Maximum period of suspension. The 5-year period described in subsection (a) shall not be extended more than 10 years by reason of subparagraph (A).

(C) Qualified official extended duty. For purposes of this paragraph—

(i) In general. The term "qualified official extended duty" means any extended duty while serving at a duty station which is at least 50 miles from such property or while residing under Government orders in Government quarters.

(ii) Uniformed services. The term "uniformed services" has the meaning given such term by section 101(a)(5) of title 10, United States Code, as in effect on the date of the enactment of this paragraph.

(iii) Foreign Service of the United States. The term "member of the Foreign Service of the United States" has the meaning given the term "member of the Service" by paragraph (1), (2), (3), (4), or (5) of section 103 of the Foreign Service Act of 1980, as in effect on the date of the enactment of this paragraph. [3]

[3]*(iv) Employee of intelligence community. The term "employee of the intelligence community" means an employee (as defined by section 2105 of title 5, United States Code) of—*

(I) the Office of the Director of National Intelligence,

(II) the Central Intelligence Agency,

(III) the National Security Agency,

(IV) the Defense Intelligence Agency,

(V) the National Geospatial-Intelligence Agency,

(VI) the National Reconnaissance Office,

(VII) any other office within the Department of Defense for the collection of specialized national intelligence through reconnaissance programs,

(VIII) any of the intelligence elements of the Army, the Navy, the Air Force, the Marine Corps, the Federal Bureau of Investigation, the Department of Treasury, the Department of Energy, and the Coast Guard,

(IX) the Bureau of Intelligence and Research of the Department of State, or

(X) any of the elements of the Department of Homeland Security concerned with the analyses of foreign intelligence information. [4]

[4]*(v)* Extended duty. The term "extended duty" means any period of active duty pursuant to a call or order to such duty for a period in excess of 90 days or for an indefinite period.

[5]*(vi) Special rule relating to intelligence community. An employee of the intelligence community shall not be treated as serving on qualified extended duty unless such duty is at a duty station located outside the United States.*

(D) Special rules relating to election.

(i) Election limited to 1 property at a time. An election under subparagraph (A) with respect to any property may not be made if such an election is in effect with respect to any other property.

(ii) Revocation of election. An election under subparagraph (A) may be revoked at any time.

* * * * * * * * * * * *

[For Analysis, see ¶ 107. For Committee Reports, see ¶ 5068.]

[Endnote Code Sec. 121]

Matter in *italics* in Code Sec. 121(d)(9), Code Sec. 121(d)(9)(A), Code Sec. 121(d)(9)(C)(iv), Code Sec. 121(d)(9)(C)(v) and Code Sec. 121(d)(9)(C)(vi) was added by Sec. 417(a)-(d) of the Tax Relief and Health Care Act of 2006, HR6111, d.o.e., which struck out:

1. "Members of uniformed services and foreign service."
2. "duty as a member of the uniformed services or of the Foreign Service of the United States."
3. added clause (d)(9)(C)(iv)
4. "(iv)"
5. added clause(d)(9)(C)(vi)

Effective Date (Sec. 417(e), HR6111, d.o.e.) effective for sales or exchanges after d.o.e. and before 1/1/2011.

[¶ 3022] Code Sec. 143. Mortgage revenue bonds: qualified mortgage bond and qualified veterans' mortgage bond.

* * * * * * * * * * * *

(d) 3-year requirement.

(1) In general. An issue meets the requirements of this subsection only if 95 percent or more of the net proceeds of such issue are used to finance the residences of mortgagors who had no present ownership interest in their principal residences at any time during the 3-year period ending on the date their mortgage is executed.

(2) Exceptions. For purposes of paragraph (1), the proceeds of an issue which are used to provide—

(A) financing with respect to targeted area residences,

(B) qualified home improvement loans and qualified rehabilitation loans, [1]

(C) financing with respect to land described in subsection (i)(1)(C) and the construction of any residence thereon, [2]*and*

[3]*(D) in the case of bonds issued after the date of the enactment of this subparagraph and before January 1, 2008, financing of any residence for a veteran (as defined in section 101 of title 38, United States Code), if such veteran has not previously qualified for and received such financing by reason of this subparagraph,*

shall be treated as used as described in paragraph (1).

(3) Mortgagor's interest in residence being financed. For purposes of paragraph (1), a mortgagor's interest in the residence with respect to which the financing is being provided shall not be taken into account.

* * * * * * * * * * * *

(l) Additional requirements for qualified veterans' mortgage bonds.

* * * * * * * * * * * *

(3) Volume limitation.

* * * * * * * * * * * *

(B) State veterans limit.

(i) In general. In the case of any State to which clause (ii) does not apply, the State veterans limit for any calendar year is the amount equal to—

(I) the aggregate amount of qualified veterans bonds issued by such State during the period beginning on January 1, 1979, and ending on June 22, 1984 (not including the amount of any qualified veterans bond issued by such State during the calendar year (or portion thereof) in such period for which the amount of such bonds so issued was the lowest), divided by

(II) the number (not to exceed 5) of calendar years after 1979 and before 1985 during which the State issued qualified veterans bonds (determined by only taking into account bonds issued on or before June 22, 1984).

(ii) Alaska, Oregon, and Wisconsin. In the case of the following States, the State veterans limit for any calendar year is the amount equal to—

(I) $25,000,000 for the State of Alaska,

(II) $25,000,000 for the State of Oregon, and

(III) $25,000,000 for the State of Wisconsin.

(iii) Phasein. In the case of calendar years beginning before 2010, clause (ii) shall be applied by substituting for each of the dollar amounts therein an amount equal to the applicable percentage of such dollar amount. For purposes of the preceding sentence, the applicable percentage shall be determined in accordance with the following table:

For Calendar Year:	Applicable percentage is:
2006	20 percent
2007	40 percent
2008	60 percent
2009	80 percent.

4

[For Analysis, see ¶ 1603 and ¶ 1604. For Committee Reports, see ¶ 5062 and ¶ 5067.]

[Endnote Code Sec. 143]

Matter in Code Sec. 143(d)(2)(B) was deleted by Sec. 416(a) Tax Relief and Health Care Act of 2006, HR6111, d.o.e., which struck out:

1. "and"

Matter in *italics* in Code Sec. 143(d)(2)(C) was added by Sec. 416(a), HR6111, d.o.e..

2. added matter in subpara. (d)(2)(C)

Code Sec. 143(d)(2)(D), in *italics*, was added by Sec. 416(a), HR6111, d.o.e..

3. added subpara. (d)(2)(D)

Effective Date (Sec. 416(b), HR6111, d.o.e.) effective for bonds issued after d.o.e..

Code Sec. 143(l)(3)(B)(iv) was deleted by Sec. 411(a), HR6111, d.o.e., which struck out:

4. "(iv) Termination. The State veterans limit for the States specified in clause (ii) for any calendar year after 2010 is zero."

Effective Date (Sec. 411(b), HR6111, d.o.e.) effective for allocations of State volume limit after 4/5/2006.

[¶ 3023] Code Sec. 163. Interest.

* * * * * * * * * * * *

(h) Disallowance of deduction for personal interest.

* * * * * * * * * * * *

(3) Qualified residence interest. For purposes of this subsection—

(A) In general. The term "qualified residence interest" means any interest which is paid or accrued during the taxable year on—

(i) acquisition indebtedness with respect to any qualified residence of the taxpayer, or

(ii) home equity indebtedness with respect to any qualified residence of the taxpayer.

For purposes of the preceding sentence, the determination of whether any property is a qualified residence of the taxpayer shall be made as of the time the interest is accrued.

(B) Acquisition indebtedness.

(i) In general. The term "acquisition indebtedness" means any indebtedness which—

(I) is incurred in acquiring, constructing, or substantially improving any qualified residence of the taxpayer, and

(II) is secured by such residence.

Such term also includes any indebtedness secured by such residence resulting from the refinancing of indebtedness meeting the requirements of the preceding sentence (or this sentence); but only to the extent the amount of the indebtedness resulting from such refinancing does not exceed the amount of the refinanced indebtedness.

(ii) $1,000,000 Limitation. The aggregate amount treated as acquisition indebtedness for any period shall not exceed $1,000,000 ($500,000 in the case of a married individual filing a separate return).

(C) Home equity indebtedness.

(i) In general. The term "home equity indebtedness" means any indebtedness (other than acquisition indebtedness) secured by a qualified residence to the extent the aggregate amount of such indebtedness does not exceed—

(I) the fair market value of such qualified residence, reduced by

(II) the amount of acquisition indebtedness with respect to such residence.

(ii) Limitation. The aggregate amount treated as home equity indebtedness for any period shall not exceed $100,000 ($50,000 in the case of a separate return by a married individual).

(D) Treatment of indebtedness incurred on or before October 13, 1987.

(i) In general. In the case of any pre-October 13, 1987, indebtedness—

(I) such indebtedness shall be treated as acquisition indebtedness, and

(II) the limitation of subparagraph (B)(ii) shall not apply.

(ii) Reduction in $1,000,000 limitation. The limitation of subparagraph (B)(ii) shall be reduced (but not below zero) by the aggregate amount of outstanding pre-October 13, 1987, indebtedness.

(iii) Pre-October 13, 1987, indebtedness. The term "pre-October 13, 1987, indebtedness" means—

(I) any indebtedness which was incurred on or before October 13, 1987, and which was secured by a qualified residence on October 13, 1987, and at all times thereafter before the interest is paid or accrued, or

(II) any indebtedness which is secured by the qualified residence and was incurred after October 13, 1987, to refinance indebtedness described in subclause (I) (or refinanced indebtedness meeting the requirements of this subclause) to the extent (immediately after the refinancing) the principal amount of the indebtedness resulting from the refinancing does not exceed the principal amount of the refinanced indebtedness (immediately before the refinancing).

(iv) Limitation on period of refinancing. Subclause (II) of clause (iii) shall not apply to any indebtedness after—

(I) the expiration of the term of the indebtedness described in clause (iii)(I), or

(II) if the principal of the indebtedness described in clause (iii)(I) is not amortized over its term, the expiration of the term of the 1st refinancing of such indebtedness (or if earlier, the date which is 30 years after the date of such 1st refinancing).

[1]*(E) Mortgage insurance premiums treated as interest.*

(i) In general. Premiums paid or accrued for qualified mortgage insurance by a taxpayer during the taxable year in connection with acquisition indebtedness with respect to a qualified residence of the taxpayer shall be treated for purposes of this section as interest which is qualified residence interest.

(ii) Phaseout. The amount otherwise treated as interest under clause (i) shall be reduced (but not below zero) by 10 percent of such amount for each $1,000 ($500 in the case of a married individual filing a separate return) (or fraction thereof) that the taxpayer's adjusted gross income for the taxable year exceeds $100,000 ($50,000 in the case of a married individual filing a separate return).

(iii) Limitation. Clause (i) shall not apply with respect to any mortgage insurance contracts issued before January 1, 2007.

(iv) Termination. Clause (i) shall not apply to amounts—

(I) paid or accrued after December 31, 2007, or

(II) properly allocable to any period after such date.

(4) Other definitions and special rules. For purposes of this subsection—

(A) Qualified residence.

(i) In general. The term "qualified residence" means—

(I) the principal residence (within the meaning of section 121) of the taxpayer, and

(II) 1 other residence of the taxpayer which is selected by the taxpayer for purposes of this subsection for the taxable year and which is used by the taxpayer as a residence (within the meaning of section 280A(d)(1)).

(ii) Married individuals filing separate returns. If a married couple does not file a joint return for the taxable year—

(I) such couple shall be treated as 1 taxpayer for purposes of clause (i), and

(II) each individual shall be entitled to take into account 1 residence unless both individuals consent in writing to 1 individual taking into account the principal residence and 1 other residence.

(iii) Residence not rented. For purposes of clause (i)(II), notwithstanding section 280A(d)(1), if the taxpayer does not rent a dwelling unit at any time during a taxable year, such unit may be treated as a residence for such taxable year.

(B) Special rule for cooperative housing corporations. Any indebtedness secured by stock held by the taxpayer as a tenant-stockholder (as defined in section 216) in a cooperative housing corporation (as so defined) shall be treated as secured by the house or apartment which the taxpayer is entitled to occupy as such a tenant-stockholder. If stock described in the preceding sentence may not be used to secure indebtedness, indebtedness shall be treated as so secured if the taxpayer establishes to the satisfaction of the Secretary that such indebtedness was incurred to acquire such stock.

(C) Unenforceable security interests. Indebtedness shall not fail to be treated as secured by any property solely because, under any applicable State or local homestead or other debtor protection law in effect on August 16, 1986, the security interest is ineffective or the enforceability of the security interest is restricted.

(D) Special rules for estates and trusts. For purposes of determining whether any interest paid or accrued by an estate or trust is qualified residence interest, any residence held by such estate or trust shall be treated as a qualified residence of such estate or trust if such estate or trust establishes that such residence is a qualified residence of a beneficiary who has a present interest in such estate or trust or an interest in the residuary of such estate or trust.

[2]*(E) Qualified mortgage insurance. The term "qualified mortgage insurance" means—*

(i) mortgage insurance provided by the Veterans Administration, the Federal Housing Administration, or the Rural Housing Administration, and

(ii) private mortgage insurance (as defined by section 2 of the Homeowners Protection Act of 1998 (12 U.S.C. 4901), as in effect on the date of the enactment of this subparagraph).

(F) Special rules for prepaid qualified mortgage insurance. Any amount paid by the taxpayer for qualified mortgage insurance that is properly allocable to any mortgage the payment of which extends to periods that are after the close of the taxable year in which such amount is paid shall be chargeable to capital account and shall be treated as paid in such periods to which so allocated. No deduction shall be allowed for the unamortized balance of such account if such mortgage is satisfied before the end of its term. The preceding sentences shall not apply to amounts paid for qualified mortgage insurance provided by the Veterans Administration or the Rural Housing Administration.

(5) Phase-in of limitation. In the case of any taxable year beginning in calendar years 1987 through 1990, the amount of interest with respect to which a deduction is disallowed under this subsection shall be equal to the applicable percentage (within the meaning of subsection (d)(6)(B)) of the amount which (but for this paragraph) would have been so disallowed.

* * * * * * * * * * * *

[For Analysis, see ¶ 104. For Committee Reports, see ¶ 5070.]

[Endnote Code Sec. 163]

Code Sec. 163(h)(3)(E), Code Sec. 163(h)(4)(E), and Code Sec. 163(h)(4)(F), in *italics,* were added by Sec. 419(a) and (b) of the Tax Relief and Health Care Act of 2006, HR6111, d.o.e.

1. added subpara. (h)(3)(E)
2. added subparas. (h)(4)(E) and (F)

Effective Date (Sec. 419(d), HR6111, d.o.e.) effective for amounts paid or accrued after 12/31/2006.

[¶ 3024] Code Sec. 164. Taxes.

* * * * * * * * * * * *

(b) Definitions and special rules. For purposes of this section—

* * * * * * * * * * * *

(5) General sales taxes. For purposes of subsection (a)—

(A) Election to deduct State and local sales taxes in lieu of State and local income taxes. At the election of the taxpayer for the taxable year, subsection (a) shall be applied—

(i) without regard to the reference to State and local income taxes, and

(ii) as if State and local general sales taxes were referred to in a paragraph thereof.

(B) Definition of general sales tax. The term "general sales tax" means a tax imposed at one rate with respect to the sale at retail of a broad range of classes of items.

(C) Special rules for food, etc. In the case of items of food, clothing, medical supplies, and motor vehicles—

(i) the fact that the tax does not apply with respect to some or all of such items shall not be taken into account in determining whether the tax applies with respect to a broad range of classes of items, and

(ii) the fact that the rate of tax applicable with respect to some or all of such items is lower than the general rate of tax shall not be taken into account in determining whether the tax is imposed at one rate.

(D) Items taxed at different rates. Except in the case of a lower rate of tax applicable with respect to an item described in subparagraph (C), no deduction shall be allowed under this paragraph for any general sales tax imposed with respect to an item at a rate other than the general rate of tax.

(E) Compensating use taxes. A compensating use tax with respect to an item shall be treated as a general sales tax. For purposes of the preceding sentence, the term "compensating use tax" means, with respect to any item, a tax which—

(i) is imposed on the use, storage, or consumption of such item, and

(ii) is complementary to a general sales tax, but only if a deduction is allowable under this paragraph with respect to items sold at retail in the taxing jurisdiction which are similar to such item.

(F) Special rule for motor vehicles. In the case of motor vehicles, if the rate of tax exceeds the general rate, such excess shall be disregarded and the general rate shall be treated as the rate of tax.

(G) Separately stated general sales taxes. If the amount of any general sales tax is separately stated, then, to the extent that the amount so stated is paid by the consumer (other than in connection with the consumer's trade or business) to the seller, such amount shall be treated as a tax imposed on, and paid by, such consumer.

(H) Amount of deduction may be determined under tables.

(i) In general. At the election of the taxpayer for the taxable year, the amount of the deduction allowed under this paragraph for such year shall be—

(I) the amount determined under this paragraph (without regard to this subparagraph) with respect to motor vehicles, boats, and other items specified by the Secretary, and

(II) the amount determined under tables prescribed by the Secretary with respect to items to which subclause (I) does not apply.

(ii) Requirements for tables. The tables prescribed under clause (i)—

(I) shall reflect the provisions of this paragraph,

(II) shall be based on the average consumption by taxpayers on a State-by-State basis (as determined by the Secretary) of items to which clause (i)(I) does not apply, taking into account filing status, number of dependents, adjusted gross income, and rates of State and local general sales taxation, and

(III) need only be determined with respect to adjusted gross incomes up to the applicable amount (as determined under section 68(b)).

(I) Application of paragraph. This paragraph shall apply to taxable years beginning after December 31, 2003, and before January 1, [1]*2008.*

* * * * * * * * * * * * *

[For Analysis, see ¶ 101. For Committee Reports, see ¶ 5003.]

[Endnote Code Sec. 164]

Matter in *italics* in Code Sec. 164(b)(5)(I) was added by Sec. 103(a) of the Tax Relief and Health Care Act of 2006, HR6111, d.o.e., which struck out:

1. "2006"

Effective Date (Sec. 103(b), HR6111, d.o.e.) effective for tax. yrs. begin. after 12/31/2005.

[¶ 3025] Code Sec. 168. Accelerated cost recovery system.

* * * * * * * * * * * * *

(e) **Classification of property.** For purposes of this section—

(1) **In general.** Except as otherwise provided in this subsection, property shall be classified under the following table:

Property shall be treated as:	If such property has a class life (in years) of:
3-year property	4 or less
5-year property	More than 4 but less than 10
7-year property	10 or more but less than 16
10-year property	16 or more but less than 20
15-year property	20 or more but less than 25
20-year property	25 or more.

(2) **Residential rental or nonresidential real property.**

(A) Residential rental property.

(i) Residential rental property. The term "residential rental property" means any building or structure if 80 percent or more of the gross rental income from such building or structure for the taxable year is rental income from dwelling units.

(ii) Definitions. For purposes of clause (i)—

(I) the term "dwelling unit" means a house or apartment used to provide living accommodations in a building or structure, but does not include a unit in a hotel, motel, or other establishment more than one-half of the units in which are used on a transient basis, and

(II) if any portion of the building or structure is occupied by the taxpayer, the gross rental income from such building or structure shall include the rental value of the portion so occupied.

(B) Nonresidential real property. The term "nonresidential real property" means section 1250 property which is not—

(i) residential rental property, or

(ii) property with a class life of less than 27.5 years.

(3) Classification of certain property.

(A) 3-year property. The term "3-year property" includes—

(i) any race horse which is more than 2 years old at the time it is placed in service,

(ii) any horse other than a race horse which is more than 12 years old at the time it is placed in service, and

(iii) any qualified rent-to-own property.

(B) 5-year property. The term "5-year property" includes—

(i) any automobile or light general purpose truck,

(ii) any semi-conductor manufacturing equipment,

(iii) any computer-based telephone central office switching equipment,

(iv) any qualified technological equipment,

(v) any section 1245 property used in connection with research and experimentation, and

(vi) any property which—

(I) is described in subparagraph (A) of section 48(a)(3) (or would be so described if "solar or wind energy" were substituted for "solar energy" in clause (i) thereof and the last sentence of such section did not apply to such subparagraph),

(II) is described in paragraph (15) of section 48(l) (as in effect on the day before the date of the enactment [11/5/90] of the Revenue Reconciliation Act of 1990) and is a qualifying small power production facility within the meaning of section 3(17)(C) of the Federal Power Act (16 U.S.C. 796(17)(C)), as in effect on September 1, 1986, or

(III) is described in section 48(l)(3)(A)(ix) (as in effect on the date before the date of the enactment of the Revenue Reconciliation Act of 1990).

Nothing in any provision of law shall be construed to treat property as not being described in clause (vi)(I)(or the corresponding provisions of prior law) by reason of being public utility property (within the meaning of section 48(a)(3)).

(C) 7-year property. The term "7-year property" includes—

(i) any railroad track and

(ii) any motorsports entertainment complex,

(iii) any Alaska natural gas pipeline,

(iv) any natural gas gathering line the original use of which commences with the taxpayer after April 11, 2005, and

(v) any property which—

(I) does not have a class life, and

(II) is not otherwise classified under paragraph (2) or this paragraph.

(D) 10-year property. The term "10-year property" includes—

(i) any single purpose agricultural or horticultural structure (within the meaning of subsection (i)(13)), and

(ii) any tree or vine bearing fruit or nuts.

(E) 15-year property. The term "15-year property" includes—

(i) any municipal wastewater treatment plant,

(ii) any telephone distribution plant and comparable equipment used for 2-way exchange of voice and data communications,

(iii) any section 1250 property which is a retail motor fuels outlet (whether or not food or other convenience items are sold at the outlet),

(iv) any qualified leasehold improvement property placed in service before January 1, [1]*2008,*

(v) any qualified restaurant property placed in service before January 1, [2]*2008,*

(vi) initial clearing and grading land improvements with respect to gas utility property,

(vii) any section 1245 property (as defined in section 1245(a)(3)) used in the transmission at 69 or more kilovolts of electricity for sale and the original use of which commences with the taxpayer after April 11, 2005, and

(viii) any natural gas distribution line the original use of which commences with the taxpayer after April 11, 2005, and which is placed in service before January 1, 2011.

(F) 20-year property. The term "20-year property" means initial clearing and grading land improvements with respect to any electric utility transmission and distribution plant.

* * * * * * * * * * * *

(j) Property on Indian reservations.

(1) In general. For purposes of subsection (a), the applicable recovery period for qualified Indian reservation property shall be determined in accordance with the table contained in paragraph (2) in lieu of the table contained in subsection (c).

* * * * * * * * * * * *

(8) Termination. This subsection shall not apply to property placed in service after December 31, [3]*2007.*

* * * * * * * * * * * *

[4]***(l) Special allowance for cellulosic biomass ethanol plant property.***

(1) Additional allowance. *In the case of any qualified cellulosic biomass ethanol plant property—*

(A) the depreciation deduction provided by section 167(a) for the taxable year in which such property is placed in service shall include an allowance equal to 50 percent of the adjusted basis of such property, and

(B) the adjusted basis of such property shall be reduced by the amount of such deduction before computing the amount otherwise allowable as a depreciation deduction under this chapter for such taxable year and any subsequent taxable year.

(2) Qualified cellulosic biomass ethanol plant property. *The term "qualified cellulosic biomass ethanol plant property" means property of a character subject to the allowance for depreciation—*

(A) which is used in the United States solely to produce cellulosic biomass ethanol,

(B) the original use of which commences with the taxpayer after the date of the enactment of this subsection,

(C) which is acquired by the taxpayer by purchase (as defined in section 179(d)) after the date of the enactment of this subsection, but only if no written binding contract for the acquisition was in effect on or before the date of the enactment of this subsection, and

(D) which is placed in service by the taxpayer before January 1, 2013.

(3) Cellulosic biomass ethanol. *For purposes of this subsection, the term "cellulosic biomass ethanol" means ethanol produced by enzymatic hydrolysis of any lignocellulosic or hemicellulosic matter that is available on a renewable or recurring basis.*

(4) Exceptions.

(A) Alternative depreciation property. Such term shall not include any property described in section 168(k)(2)(D)(i).

(B) Tax-exempt bond-financed property. Such term shall not include any property any portion of which is financed with the proceeds of any obligation the interest on which is exempt from tax under section 103.

(C) Election out. If a taxpayer makes an election under this subparagraph with respect to any class of property for any taxable year, this subsection shall not apply to all property in such class placed in service during such taxable year.

(5) Special rules. *For purposes of this subsection, rules similar to the rules of subparagraph (E) of section 168(k)(2) shall apply, except that such subparagraph shall be applied—*

(A) by substituting "the date of the enactment of subsection (l)" for "September 10, 2001" each place it appears therein,

(B) by substituting "January 1, 2013" for "January 1, 2005" in clause (i) thereof, and

(C) by substituting "qualified cellulosic biomass ethanol plant property" for "qualified property" in clause (iv) thereof.

(6) ***Allowance against alternative minimum tax.*** *For purposes of this subsection, rules similar to the rules of section 168(k)(2)(G) shall apply.*

(7) ***Recapture.*** *For purposes of this subsection, rules similar to the rules under section 179(d)(10) shall apply with respect to any qualified cellulosic biomass ethanol plant property which ceases to be qualified cellulosic biomass ethanol plant property.*

(8) ***Denial of double benefit.*** *Paragraph (1) shall not apply to any qualified cellulosic biomass ethanol plant property with respect to which an election has been made under section 179C (relating to election to expense certain refineries).*

[For Analysis, see ¶ 502, ¶ 503, ¶ 508, and ¶ 510. For Committee Reports, see ¶ 5016, ¶ 5017 and ¶ 5039]

[Endnote Code Sec. 168]

Matter in *italics* in Code Sec. 168(e)(3)(E)(iv) and Code Sec. 168(e)(3)(E)(v) was added by Sec. 113(a) of the Tax Relief and Health Care Act of 2006, HR6111, d.o.e., which struck out:

1. "2006"
2. "2006"

Effective Date (Sec. 113(b), HR6111, d.o.e.) effective for property placed in service after 12/31/2005.

Matter in *italics* in Code Sec. 168(j)(8) was added by Sec. 112(a), HR6111, d.o.e., which struck out:

3. "2005"

Effective Date (Sec. 112(b), HR6111, d.o.e.) effective for property placed in service after 12/31/2005.

Code Sec. 168(l), in *italics*, was added by Sec. 209(a), HR6111, d.o.e..

4. added subsec. (l)

Effective Date (Sec. 209(b), HR6111, d.o.e.) effective for property placed in service after the d.o.e. in tax. yrs. end. after d.o.e..

[¶ 3026] Code Sec. 170. Charitable, etc., contributions and gifts.

* * * * * * * * * * * * *

(e) Certain contributions of ordinary income and capital gain property.

* * * * * * * * * * * * *

(4) Special rule for contributions of scientific property used for research.

(A) Limit on reduction. In the case of a qualified research contribution, the reduction under paragraph (1)(A) shall be no greater than the amount determined under paragraph (3)(B).

(B) Qualified research contributions. For purposes of this paragraph, the term "qualified research contribution" means a charitable contribution by a corporation of tangible personal property described in paragraph (1) of section 1221(a), but only if—

(i) the contribution is to an organization described in subparagraph (A) or subparagraph (B) of section 41(e)(6),

(ii) the property is constructed [1]*or assembled* by the taxpayer,

(iii) the contribution is made not later than 2 years after the date the construction [2]*or assembly* of the property is substantially completed,

(iv) the original use of the property is by the donee,

(v) the property is scientific equipment or apparatus substantially all of the use of which by the donee is for research or experimentation (within the meaning of section 174), or for research training, in the United States in physical or biological sciences,

(vi) the property is not transferred by the donee in exchange for money, other property, or services, and

(vii) the taxpayer receives from the donee a written statement representing that its use and disposition of the property will be in accordance with the provisions of clauses (v) and (vi).

(C) Construction of property by taxpayer. For purposes of this paragraph, property shall be treated as constructed by the taxpayer only if the cost of the parts used in the construction of such property (other than parts manufactured by the taxpayer or a related person) do not exceed 50 percent of the taxpayer's basis in such property.

(D) Corporation. For purposes of this paragraph, the term "corporation" shall not include

(i) an S corporation,

(ii) a personal holding company (as defined in section 542), and

(iii) a service organization (as defined in section 414(m)(3)).

* * * * * * * * * * * * *

(6) Special rule for contributions of computer technology and equipment for educational purposes.

(A) Limit on reduction. In the case of a qualified computer contribution, the reduction under paragraph (1)(A) shall be no greater than the amount determined under paragraph (3)(B).

(B) Qualified computer contribution. For purposes of this paragraph, the term "qualified computer contribution" means a charitable contribution by a corporation of any computer technology or equipment, but only if —

(i) the contribution is to—

(I) an educational organization described in subsection (b)(1)(A)(ii),

(II) an entity described in section 501(c)(3) and exempt from tax under section 501(a) other than an entity described in subclause (I)) that is organized primarily for purposes of supporting elementary and secondary education, or

(III) a public library (within the meaning of section 213(1)(A) of the Library Services and Technology Act (20 U.S.C. 9122(1)(A)), as in effect on the date of the enactment [12/21/2000] of the Community Renewal Tax Relief Act of 2000), established and maintained by an entity described in subsection (c)(1),

(ii) the contribution is made not later than 3 years after the date the taxpayer acquired the property (or in the case of property constructed [3]*or assembled* by the taxpayer, the date the construction [4]*or assembling* of the property is substantially completed),

(iii) the original use of the property is by the donor or the donee,

(iv) substantially all of the use of the property by the donee is for use within the United States for educational purposes that are related to the purpose or function of the donee,

(v) the property is not transferred by the donee in exchange for money, other property, or services, except for shipping, installation and transfer costs,

(vi) the property will fit productively into the donee's education plan,

(vii) the donee's use and disposition of the property will be in accordance with the provisions of clauses (iv) and (v), and

(viii) the property meets such standards, if any, as the Secretary may prescribe by regulation to assure that the property meets minimum functionality and suitability standards for educational purposes.

(C) Contribution to private foundation. A contribution by a corporation of any computer technology or equipment to a private foundation (as defined in section 509) shall be treated as a qualified computer contribution for purposes of this paragraph if—

(i) the contribution to the private foundation satisfies the requirements of clauses (ii) and (v) of subparagraph (B), and

(ii) within 30 days after such contribution, the private foundation—

(I) contributes the property to a donee described in clause (i) of subparagraph (B) that satisfies the requirements of clauses (iv) through (vii) of subparagraph (B), and

(II) notifies the donor of such contribution.

(D) Donations of property reacquired by manufacturer. In the case of property which is reacquired by the person who constructed [5]*or assembled* the property—

(i) subparagraph (B)(ii) shall be applied to a contribution of such property by such person by taking into account the date that the original construction of the property was substantially completed, and

(ii) subparagraph (B)(iii) shall not apply to such contribution.

(E) Special rule relating to construction of property. For the purposes of this paragraph, the rules of paragraph (4)(C) shall apply.

(F) Definitions. For the purposes of this paragraph—

(i) Computer technology or equipment. The term "computer technology or equipment" means computer software (as defined by section 197(e)(3)(B)), computer or peripheral equipment (as defined by section 168(i)(2)(B)), and fiber optic cable related to computer use.

(ii) Corporation. The term "corporation" has the meaning given to such term by paragraph (4)(D).

(G) Termination. This paragraph shall not apply to any contribution made during any taxable year beginning after December 31, [6]*2007.*

* * * * * * * * * * * *

[For Analysis, see ¶ 602 and ¶ 603. For Committee Reports, see ¶ 5020.]

[Endnote Code Sec. 170]

Matter in *italics* in Code Sec. 170(e)(4)(B)(ii), Code Sec. 170(e)(4)(B)(iii), Code Sec. 170(e)(6)(B)(ii), and Code Sec. 170(e)(6)(D) was added by Sec. 116(a)(1), (b)(1)(A)-(B), and (b)(2)(A)-(B), of the Tax Relief and Health Care Act of 2006, HR6111, d.o.e..

1. added matter in clause (e)(4)(B)(ii)
2. added matter in clause (e)(4)(B)(iii)
3. added matter in clause (e)(6)(B)(ii)
4. added matter in clause (e)(6)(B)(ii)
5. added matter in subpara. (e)(6)(D)

Effective Date (Sec. 116(b)(3), HR6111, d.o.e.) effective for tax. yrs. begin. after 12/31/2005.

Matter in *italics* in Code Sec. 170(e)(6)(G) was added by Sec. 116(a)(1), HR6111, d.o.e., which struck out:

5. "2005"

Effective Date (Sec. 116(a)(2), HR6111, d.o.e.) effective for contributions made in tax. yrs. begin. after 12/31/2005.

[¶ 3027] Code Sec. 179D. Energy efficient commercial buildings deduction.

* * * * * * * * * * * *

(h) Termination. This section shall not apply with respect to property placed in service after [1]*December 31, 2008.*

[For Analysis, see ¶ 501. For Committee Reports, see ¶ 5034.]

[Endnote Code Sec. 179D]

Matter in *italics* in Code Sec. 179D(h) was added by Sec. 204 of the Tax Relief and Health Care Act of 2006, HR6111, d.o.e., which struck out:

1."December 31, 2007"

Effective Date Enacted d.o.e..

[¶ 3028] Code Sec.[1] 179E. Election to expense advanced mine safety equipment.

(a) Treatment as expenses. *A taxpayer may elect to treat 50 percent of the cost of any qualified advanced mine safety equipment property as an expense which is not chargeable to* *capital account. Any cost so treated shall be allowed as a deduction for the taxable year in which the qualified advanced mine safety equipment property is placed in service.*

(b) Election.

***(1) In general.** An election under this section for any taxable year shall be made on the taxpayer's return of the tax imposed by this chapter for the taxable year. Such election shall specify the advanced mine safety equipment property to which the election applies and shall be made in such manner as the Secretary may by regulations prescribe.*

***(2) Election irrevocable.** Any election made under this section may not be revoked except with the consent of the Secretary.*

***(c) Qualified advanced mine safety equipment property.** For purposes of this section, the term "qualified advanced mine safety equipment property" means any advanced mine safety equipment property for use in any underground mine located in the United States—*

(1) the original use of which commences with the taxpayer, and

(2) which is placed in service by the taxpayer after the date of the enactment of this section.

***(d) Advanced mine safety equipment property.** For purposes of this section, the term "advanced mine safety equipment property" means any of the following:*

(1) Emergency communication technology or device which is used to allow a miner to maintain constant communication with an individual who is not in the mine.

(2) Electronic identification and location device which allows an individual who is not in the mine to track at all times the movements and location of miners working in or at the mine.

(3) Emergency oxygen-generating, self-rescue device which provides oxygen for at least 90 minutes.

(4) Pre-positioned supplies of oxygen which (in combination with self-rescue devices) can be used to provide each miner on a shift, in the event of an accident or other event which traps the miner in the mine or otherwise necessitates the use of such a self rescue device, the ability to survive for at least 48 hours.

(5) Comprehensive atmospheric monitoring system which monitors the levels of carbon monoxide, methane, and oxygen that are present in all areas of the mine and which can detect smoke in the case of a fire in a mine.

***(e) Coordination with section 179.** No expenditures shall be taken into account under subsection (a) with respect to the portion of the cost of any property specified in an election under section 179.*

***(f) Reporting.** No deduction shall be allowed under subsection (a) to any taxpayer for any taxable year unless such taxpayer files with the Secretary a report containing such information with respect to the operation of the mines of the taxpayer as the Secretary shall require.*

***(g) Termination.** This section shall not apply to property placed in service after December 31, 2008.*

[For Analysis, see ¶ 509. For Committee Reports, see ¶ 5055.]

[Endnote Code Sec. 179E]

Code Sec. 179E, in *italics*, was added by Sec. 404(a) of the Tax Relief and Health Care Act of 2006, HR6111, d.o.e..

1. added Code Sec. 179E

Effective Date (Sec. 404(c), HR6111, d.o.e.) effective for costs paid or incurred after d.o.e..

[¶ 3029] Code Sec. 198. Expensing of environmental remediation costs.

* * * * * * * * * * * * *

(d) Hazardous substance. For purposes of this section—

(1) In general. The term "hazardous substance" means—

(A) any substance which is a hazardous substance as defined in section 101(14) of the Comprehensive Environmental Response, Compensation, and Liability Act of 1980,[1]

(B) any substance which is designated as a hazardous substance under section 102 of such Act[2], *and*

[3]*(C) any petroleum product (as defined in section 4612(a)(3)).*

(2) Exception. Such term shall not include any substance with respect to which a removal or remedial action is not permitted under section 104 of such Act by reason of subsection (a)(3) thereof.

* * * * * * * * * * * * *

(h) Termination. This section shall not apply to expenditures paid or incurred after December 31, [4]*2007.*

[For Analysis, see ¶ 505 and ¶ 506. For Committee Reports, see ¶ 5013.]

[Endnote Code Sec. 198]

Matter in *italics* in Code Sec. 198(d)(1)(A), Code Sec. 198(d)(1)(B), Code Sec. 198(d)(1)(C), and Code Sec. 198(h) was added by Sec. 109(a) and (b) of the Tax Relief and Health Care Act of 2006, HR6111, d.o.e., which struck out:

1. " and"
2. "."
3. added subpara. (d)(1)(C)
4. "2005"

Effective Date (Sec. 109(c), HR6111, d.o.e.) effective for expenditures paid or incurred after 12/31/2005.

[¶ 3030] Code Sec. 199. Income attributable to domestic production activities.

* * * * * * * * * * * * *

(d) Definitions and special rules.

* * * * * * * * * * * * *

[1]***(8) Treatment of activities in Puerto Rico.***

(A) In general. In the case of any taxpayer with gross receipts for any taxable year from sources within the Commonwealth of Puerto Rico, if all of such receipts are taxable under section 1 or 11 for such taxable year, then for purposes of determining the domestic production gross receipts of such taxpayer for such taxable year under subsection (c)(4), the term "United States" shall include the Common-wealth of Puerto Rico.

(B) Special rule for applying wage limitation. In the case of any taxpayer described in subparagraph (A), for purposes of applying the limitation under subsection (b) for any taxable year, the determination of W-60 wages of such taxpayer shall be made without regard to any exclusion under section 3401(a)(8) for remuneration paid for services performed in Puerto Rico.

(C) Termination. This paragraph shall apply only with respect to the first 2 taxable years of the taxpayer beginning after December 31, 2005, and before January 1, 2008.

[2]***(9)* Regulations.** The Secretary shall prescribe such regulations as are necessary to carry out the purposes of this section, including regulations which prevent more than 1 taxpayer from being allowed a deduction under this section with respect to any activity described in subsection (c)(4)(A)(i).

[For Analysis, see ¶ 1302. For Committee Reports, see ¶ 5052.]

[Endnote Code Sec. 199]

Matter in *italics* in Code Sec. 199(d)(8) and Code Sec. 199(d)(9) was added by Sec. 401(a) of the Tax Relief and Health Care Act of 2006, HR6111, d.o.e., which struck out:

1. added para. (d)(8)
2. "(9)"

Effective Date (Sec. 401(b), HR6111, d.o.e.) effective for tax. yrs. begin. after 12/31/2005.

[¶ 3031] Code Sec. 220. Archer MSAs.

* * * * * * * * * * * * *

(i) Limitation on number of taxpayers having Archer MSAs.

(1) In general. Except as provided in paragraph (5), no individual shall be treated as an eligible individual for any taxable year beginning after the cut-off year unless—

(A) such individual was an active MSA participant for any taxable year ending on or before the close of the cut-off year, or

(B) such individual first became an active MSA participant for a taxable year ending after the cut-off year by reason of coverage under a high deductible health plan of an MSA-participating employer.

(2) Cut-off year. For purposes of paragraph (1), the term "cut-off year" means the earlier of—

(A) calendar year [1]*2007,* or

(B) the first calendar year before [2]*2007* for which the Secretary determines under subsection (j) that the numerical limitation for such year has been exceeded.

(3) Active MSA participant. For purposes of this subsection—

(A) In general. The term "active MSA participant" means, with respect to any taxable year, any individual who is the account holder of any Archer MSA into which any contribution was made which was excludable from gross income under section 106(b), or allowable as a deduction under this section, for such taxable year.

(B) Special rule for cut-off years before [3]*2007.* In the case of a cut-off year before [4]*2007*—

(i) an individual shall not be treated as an eligible individual for any month of such year or an active MSA participant under paragraph (1)(A) unless such individual is, on or before the cut-off date, covered under a high deductible health plan, and

(ii) an employer shall not be treated as an MSA-participating employer unless the employer, on or before the cut-off date, offered coverage under a high deductible health plan to any employee.

(C) Cut-off date. For purposes of subparagraph (B)—

(i) In general. Except as otherwise provided in this subparagraph, the cut-off date is October 1 of the cut-off year.

(ii) Employees with enrollment periods after October 1. In the case of an individual described in subclause (I) of subsection (c)(1)(A)(iii), if the regularly scheduled enrollment period for health plans of the individual's employer occurs during the last 3 months of the cut-off year, the cut-off date is December 31 of the cut-off year.

(iii) Self-employed individuals. In the case of an individual described in subclause (II) of subsection (c)(1)(A)(iii), the cut-off date is November 1 of the cut-off year.

(iv) Special rules for 1997. If 1997 is a cut-off year by reason of subsection (j)(1)(A)—

(I) each of the cut-off dates under clauses (i) and (iii) shall be 1 month earlier than the date determined without regard to this clause, and

(II) clause (ii) shall be applied by substituting "4 months" for "3 months".

* * * * * * * * * * * * *

(j) Determination of whether numerical limits are exceeded.

(1) Determination of whether limit exceeded for 1997. The numerical limitation for 1997 is exceeded if, based on the reports required under paragraph (4), the number of Archer MSAs established as of—

(A) April 30, 1997, exceeds 375,000, or

(B) June 30, 1997, exceeds 525,000.

(2) Determination of whether limit exceeded for 1998, 1999, 2001, 2002, [5]*2004, 2005, or 2006.*

(A) In general. The numerical limitation for 1998, 1999, 2001, 2002, [6]*2004, 2005, or 2006* is exceeded if the sum of—

(i) the number of MSA returns filed on or before April 15 of such calendar year for taxable years ending with or within the preceding calendar year, plus

(ii) the Secretary's estimate (determined on the basis of the returns described in clause (i)) of the number of MSA returns for such taxable years which will be filed after such date,

exceeds 750,000 (600,000 in the case of 1998). For purposes of the preceding sentence, the term "MSA return" means any return on which any exclusion is claimed under section 106(b) or any deduction is claimed under this section.

(B) Alternative computation of limitation. The numerical limitation for 1998, 1999, 2001, 2002, [7]*2004, 2005, or 2006* is also exceeded if the sum of—

(i) 90 percent of the sum determined under subparagraph (A) for such calendar year, plus

(ii) the product of 2.5 and the number of Archer MSAs established during the portion of such year preceding July 1 (based on the reports required under paragraph (4)) for taxable years beginning in such year,

exceeds 750,000.

(C) No limitation for 2000 or 2003. The numerical limitation shall not apply for 2000 or 2003.

(3) Previously uninsured individuals not included in determination.

(A) In general. The determination of whether any calendar year is a cut-off year shall be made by not counting the Archer MSA of any previously uninsured individual.

(B) Previously uninsured individual. For purposes of this subsection, the term "previously uninsured individual" means, with respect to any Archer MSA, any individual who had no health plan coverage (other than coverage referred to in subsection (c)(1)(B)) at any time during the 6-month period before the date such individual's coverage under the high deductible health plan commences.

(4) Reporting by MSA trustees.

(A) In general. Not later than August 1 of 1997, 1998, 1999, 2001, 2002, [8]*2004, 2005, and 2006* each person who is the trustee of an Archer MSA established before July 1 of such calendar year shall make a report to the Secretary (in such form and manner as the Secretary shall specify) which specifies—

(i) the number of Archer MSAs established before such July 1 (for taxable years beginning in such calendar year) of which such person is the trustee,

(ii) the name and TIN of the account holder of each such account, and

(iii) the number of such accounts which are accounts of previously uninsured individuals.

(B) Additional report for 1997. Not later than June 1, 1997, each person who is the trustee of an Archer MSA established before May 1, 1997, shall make an additional report described in subparagraph (A) but only with respect to accounts established before May 1, 1997.

(C) Penalty for failure to file report. The penalty provided in section 6693(a) shall apply to any report required by this paragraph, except that—

(i) such section shall be applied by substituting "$25" for "$50", and

(ii) the maximum penalty imposed on any trustee shall not exceed $5,000.

(D) Aggregation of accounts. To the extent practical, in determining the number of Archer MSAs on the basis of the reports under this paragraph, all Archer MSAs of an individual shall be treated as 1 account and all accounts of individuals who are married to each other shall be treated as 1 account.

(5) Date of making determinations. Any determination under this subsection that a calendar year is a cut-off year shall be made by the Secretary and shall be published not later than October 1 of such year.

[For Analysis, see ¶ 307. For Committee Reports, see ¶ 5021.]

[Endnote Code Sec. 220]

Matter in *italics* in Code Sec. 220(i)(2), Code Sec. 220(i)(3)(B), Code Sec. 220(j)(2), and Code Sec. 220(j)(4)(A) was added by Sec. 117(a), (b)(1)(A), (b)(1)(B), and (b)(2) of the Tax Relief and Health Care Act of 2006, HR6111, d.o.e., which struck out:

1. "2005"
2. "2005"
3. "2005"
4. "2005"
5. "or 2004"
6. "or 2004"
7. "or 2004"
8. "and 2004"

Effective Date Enacted d.o.e..

Sec. 117(c) of HR6111, provides:

"(c) Time for filing reports, etc.

"(1) The report required by section 220(j)(4) of the Internal Revenue Code of 1986 to be made on August 1, 2005, or August 1, 2006, as the case may be, shall be treated as timely if made before the close of the 90-day period beginning on the date of the enactment of this Act.

"(2) The determination and publication required by section 220(j)(5) of such Code with respect to calendar year 2005 or calendar year 2006, as the case may be, shall be treated as timely if made before the close of the 120-day period beginning on the date of the enactment of this Act. If the determination under the preceding sentence is that 2005 or 2006 is a cut-off year under section 220(i) of such Code, the cut-off date under such section 220(i) shall be the last day of such 120-day period."

[¶ 3032] Code Sec. 222. Qualified tuition and related expenses.

* * * * * * * * * * * *

(b) Dollar limitations.

(1) In general. The amount allowed as a deduction under subsection (a) with respect to the taxpayer for any taxable year shall not exceed the applicable dollar limit.

(2) Applicable dollar limit.

(A) 2002 and 2003. In the case of a taxable year beginning in 2002 or 2003, the applicable dollar limit shall be equal to—

(i) in the case of a taxpayer whose adjusted gross income for the taxable year does not exceed $65,000 ($130,000 in the case of a joint return), $3,000, and—

(ii) in the case of any other taxpayer, zero.

(B) [1]*After 2003.* In the case of [2]*any taxable year beginning after 2003,* the applicable dollar amount shall be equal to—

(i) in the case of a taxpayer whose adjusted gross income for the taxable year does not exceed $65,000 ($130,000 in the case of a joint return), $4,000,

(ii) in the case of a taxpayer not described in clause (i) whose adjusted gross income for the taxable year does not exceed $80,000 ($160,000 in the case of a joint return), $2,000, and

(iii) in the case of any other taxpayer, zero.

(C) Adjusted gross income. For purposes of this paragraph, adjusted gross income shall be determined—

(i) without regard to this section and sections 199, 911, 931, and 933, and

(ii) after application of sections 86, 135, 137, 219, 221, and 469.

* * * * * * * * * * * *

(e) Termination. This section shall not apply to taxable years beginning after December 31, [3]*2007.*

[For Analysis, see ¶ 102. For Committee Reports, see ¶ 5001.]

[Endnote Code Sec. 222]

Matter in *italics* in Code Sec. 222(b)(2)(B) and Code Sec. 222(e) was added by Sec. 101(a), (b)(1)-(2) of the Tax Relief and Health Care Act of 2006, HR6111, d.o.e., which struck out:

1. "2004 and 2005"
2. "a taxable year beginning in 2004 or 2005"
3. "2005"

Effective Date (Sec. 101(c), HR6111, d.o.e.) effective for tax. yrs. begin. after 12/31/2005.

[¶ 3033] Code Sec. 223. Health savings accounts.

* * * * * * * * * * * *

(b) Limitations.

(1) In general. The amount allowable as a deduction under subsection (a) to an individual for the taxable year shall not exceed the sum of the monthly limitations for months during such taxable year that the individual is an eligible individual.

(2) Monthly limitation. The monthly limitation for any month is 1⁄12 of—

(A) in the case of an eligible individual who has self-only coverage under a high deductible health plan as of the first day of such month, [1]*$2,250.*

(i) the annual deductible under such coverage, or

(ii) $2,250, or

(B) in the case of an eligible individual who has family coverage under a high deductible health plan as of the first day of such month, [2]*$4,500.*

(i) the annual deductible under such coverage, or

(ii) $4,500.

* * * * * * * * * * * *

(4) Coordination with other contributions. The limitation which would (but for this paragraph) apply under this subsection to an individual for any taxable year shall be reduced (but not below zero) by the sum of—

(A) the aggregate amount paid for such taxable year to Archer MSAs of such individual, [3]

(B) the aggregate amount contributed to health savings accounts of such individual which is excludable from the taxpayer's gross income for such taxable year under section 106(d) (and such amount shall not be allowed as a deduction under subsection (a))[4], *and,*

[5]*(C) the aggregate amount contributed to health savings accounts of such individual for such taxable year under section 408(d)(9) (and such amount shall not be allowed as a deduction under subsection (a)).*

Subparagraph (A) shall not apply with respect to any individual to whom paragraph (5) applies.

* * * * * * * * * * * *

[6]***(8) Increase in limit for individuals becoming eligible individuals after the beginning of the year.***

(A) In general. For purposes of computing the limitation under paragraph (1) for any taxable year, an individual who is an eligible individual during the last month of such taxable year shall be treated—

(i) as having been an eligible individual during each of the months in such taxable year, and

(ii) as having been enrolled, during each of the months such individual is treated as an eligible individual solely by reason of clause (i), in the same high deductible health plan in which the individual was enrolled for the last month of such taxable year.

(B) Failure to maintain high deductible health plan coverage.

(i) In general. If, at any time during the testing period, the individual is not an eligible individual, then—

(I) gross income of the individual for the taxable year in which occurs the first month in the testing period for which such individual is not an eligible individual is

increased by the aggregate amount of all contributions to the health savings account of the individual which could not have been made but for subparagraph (A), and

(II) the tax imposed by this chapter for any taxable year on the individual shall be increased by 10 percent of the amount of such increase.

(ii) Exception for disability or death. Subclauses (I) and (II) of clause (i) shall not apply if the individual ceased to be an eligible individual by reason of the death of the individual or the individual becoming disabled (within the meaning of section 72(m)(7)).

(iii) Testing period. The term "testing period" means the period beginning with the last month of the taxable year referred to in subparagraph (A) and ending on the last day of the 12th month following such month.

(c) Definitions and special rules. For purposes of this section—

(1) Eligible individual.

(A) In general. The term "eligible individual" means, with respect to any month, any individual if—

(i) such individual is covered under a high deductible health plan as of the 1st day of such month, and

(ii) such individual is not, while covered under a high deductible health plan, covered under any health plan—

(I) which is not a high deductible health plan, and

(II) which provides coverage for any benefit which is covered under the high deductible health plan.

(B) Certain coverage disregarded. Subparagraph (A)(ii) shall be applied without regard to—

(i) coverage for any benefit provided by permitted insurance, [7]

(ii) coverage (whether through insurance or otherwise) for accidents, disability, dental care, vision care, or long-term care[8], *and,*

[9]*(iii) for taxable years beginning after December 31, 2006, coverage under a health flexible spending arrangement during any period immediately following the end of a plan year of such arrangement during which unused benefits or contributions remaining at the end of such plan year may be paid or reimbursed to plan participants for qualified benefit expenses incurred during such period if—*

(I) the balance in such arrangement at the end of such plan year is zero, or

(II) the individual is making a qualified HSA distribution (as defined in section 106(e)) in an amount equal to the remaining balance in such arrangement as of the end of such plan year, in accordance with rules prescribed by the Secretary.

* * * * * * * * * * * *

(d) Health savings account. For purposes of this section—

(1) In general. The term "health savings account" means a trust created or organized in the United States as a health savings account exclusively for the purpose of paying the qualified medical expenses of the account beneficiary, but only if the written governing instrument creating the trust meets the following requirements:

(A) Except in the case of a rollover contribution described in subsection (f)(5) or section 220(f)(5), no contribution will be accepted—

(i) unless it is in cash, or

(ii) to the extent such contribution, when added to previous contributions to the trust for the calendar year, exceeds the sum of—

(I) the dollar amount in effect under [10]*subsection (b)(2)(B),* and

(II) the dollar amount in effect under subsection (b)(3)(B).

(B) The trustee is a bank (as defined in section 408(n)), an insurance company (as defined in section 816), or another person who demonstrates to the satisfaction of the Secretary that the manner in which such person will administer the trust will be consistent with the requirements of this section.

(C) No part of the trust assets will be invested in life insurance contracts.

(D) The assets of the trust will not be commingled with other property except in a common trust fund or common investment fund.

(E) The interest of an individual in the balance in his account is nonforfeitable.

* * * * * * * * * * * *

(g) Cost-of-living adjustment.

(1) In general. Each dollar amount in subsections (b)(2) and (c)(2)(A) shall be increased by an amount equal to—

(A) such dollar amount, multiplied by

(B) the cost-of-living adjustment determined under section 1(f)(3) for the calendar year in which such taxable year begins determined by substituting for "calendar year 1992" in subparagraph (B) thereof—

(i) except as provided in clause (ii), "calendar year 1997", and

(ii) in the case of each dollar amount in subsection (c)(2)(A), "calendar year 2003".

[11]*In the case of adjustments made for any taxable year beginning after 2007, section 1(f)(4) shall be applied for purposes of this paragraph by substituting "March 31" for "August 31", and the Secretary shall publish the adjusted amounts under subsections (b)(2) and (c)(2)(A) for taxable years beginning in any calendar year no later than June 1 of the preceding calendar year.*

(2) Rounding. If any increase under paragraph (1) is not a multiple of $50, such increase shall be rounded to the nearest multiple of $50.

* * * * * * * * * * * * *

[For Analysis, see ¶ 301, ¶ 302, ¶ 303, ¶ 305, and ¶ 306. For Committee Reports, see ¶ 5045.]

[Endnote Code Sec. 223]

Matter in *italics* in Code Sec. 223(b)(2)(A) and Code Sec. 223(b)(2)(B) was added by Sec. 303(a)(1)-(2) of the Tax Relief and Health Care Act of 2006, HR6111, d.o.e., which struck out:

1. "the lesser of—"
2. "the lesser of—"

Effective Date (Sec. 303(c), HR6111, d.o.e.) effective for tax. yrs. begin. after 12/31/2006.

Matter in Code Sec. 223(b)(4)(A), Code Sec. 223(b)(4)(B), and Code Sec. 223(b)(4)(C) was added by Sec. 307(b), HR6111, d.o.e., which struck out:

3. "and"
4. "."
5. added subpara. (b)(4)(C)

Effective Date (Sec. 307(c), HR6111, d.o.e.) effective for tax. yrs. begin. after 12/31/2006.

Code Sec. 223(b)(8), in *italics*, was added by Sec. 305(a), HR6111, d.o.e..

6. added para. (b)(8)

Effective Date (Sec. 305(b), HR6111, d.o.e.) effective for tax. yrs. begin. after 12/31/2006.

Matter in *italics* in Code Sec. 223(c)(1)(B)(i), Code Sec. 223(c)(1)(B)(ii), and Code Sec. 223(c)(1)(B)(iii) was added by Sec. 302(b), HR6111, d.o.e., which struck out:

7. "and"
8. "."
9. added clause (c)(1)(B)(iii)

Effective Date (Sec. 302(c)(2), HR6111, d.o.e.) effective d.o.e..

Matter in *italics* in Code Sec. 223(d)(1)(A)(ii)(I), was added by Sec. 303(b), HR6111, d.o.e., which struck out:

10. "subsection (b)(2)(B)(ii)"

Effective Date (Sec. 303(c), HR6111, d.o.e.) effective for tax. yrs. begin. after 12/31/2006.

Matter in *italics* in Code Sec. 223(g)(1), was added by Sec. 304, HR6111, d.o.e..

11. added matter in para. (g)(1)

Effective Date (Sec. 307(c), HR6111, d.o.e.) Enacted d.o.e..

[¶ 3034] Code Sec. 263. Capital expenditures.

(a) General rule. No deduction shall be allowed for—

(1) Any amount paid out for new buildings or for permanent improvements or betterments made to increase the value of any property or estate. This paragraph shall not apply to—

* * * * * * * * * * * *

(J) expenditures for which a deduction is allowed under section 179C,[1]

(K) expenditures for which a deduction is allowed under section 179D[2], *or*

[3]*(L) expenditures for which a deduction is allowed under section 179E.*

(2) Any amount expended in restoring property or in making good the exhaustion thereof for which an allowance is or has been made.

* * * * * * * * * * * *

[For Analysis, see ¶ 509. For Committee Reports, see ¶ 5055.]

[Endnote Code Sec. 263]

Matter in *italics* in Code Sec. 263(a)(1)(J), Code Sec. 263(a)(1)(K), and Code Sec. 263(a)(1)(L) was added by Sec. 404(b)(1) of the Tax Relief and Health Care Act of 2006, HR6111, d.o.e., which struck out:

1. "or"
2. "."
3. added subpara. (a)(1)(L)

Effective Date (Sec. 404(c), HR6111, d.o.e.) effective for costs paid or incurred after d.o.e..

[¶ 3035] Code Sec. 280C. Certain expenses for which credits are allowable.

* * * * * * * * * * * *

[1]***(e) Mine rescue team training credit.*** *No deduction shall be allowed for that portion of the expenses otherwise allowable as a deduction for the taxable year which is equal to the amount of the credit determined for the taxable year under section 45N(a).*

[For Analysis, see ¶ 701 and ¶ 806. For Committee Reports, see ¶ 5029 and ¶ 5056.]

[Endnote Code Sec. 280C]

Code Sec. 280C(e), in *italics*, was added by Sec. 405(c) of the Tax Relief and Health Care Act of 2006, HR6111, d.o.e..

1. added subsec. (e)

Effective Date (Sec. 405(e), HR6111, d.o.e.) effective for tax. yrs. begin. after 12/31/2005.

[¶ 3036] Code Sec. 312. Effect on earnings and profits.

* * * * * * * * * * * *

(k) Effect of depreciation on earnings and profits.

* * * * * * * * * * * *

(3) Exception for tangible property.

(A) In general. Except as provided in subparagraph (B), in the case of tangible property to which section 168 applies, the adjustment to earnings and profits for depreciation for any taxable year shall be determined under the alternative depreciation system (within the meaning of section 168(g)(2)).

(B) Treatment of amounts deductible under section 179, 179A, 179B, 179C, [1]*179D, or 179E.* For purposes of computing the earnings and profits of a corporation, any amount deductible under section 179, 179A, 179B, 179C, [2]*179D, or 179E* shall be allowed as a deduction ratably over the period of 5 taxable years (beginning with the taxable year for which such amount is deductible under section 179, 179A, 179B, 179C, [3]*179D, or 179E,* as the case may be).

* * * * * * * * * * * *

[For Analysis, see ¶509. For Committee Reports, see ¶5055.]

[Endnote Code Sec. 312]

Matter in *italics* in Code Sec. 312(k)(3)(B) was added by Sec. 404(b)(2) of the Tax Relief and Health Care Act of 2006, HR6111, d.o.e., which struck out:

1. "or 179D"
2. "or 179D"
3. "or 179D"

Effective Date (Sec. 404(c), HR6111, d.o.e.) effective for costs paid or incurred after d.o.e..

[¶3037] Code Sec. 355. Distribution of stock and securities of a controlled corporation.

* * * * * * * * * * * *

(b) Requirements as to active business.

* * * * * * * * * * * *

(3) Special rule relating to active business requirement.

(A) In general. In the case of any distribution made after the date of the enactment of this paragraph,[1] a corporation shall be treated as meeting the requirement of paragraph (2)(A) if and only if such corporation is engaged in the active conduct of a trade or business.

(B) Affiliated group rule. For purposes of subparagraph (A), all members of such corporation's separate affiliated group shall be treated as one corporation. For purposes of the preceding sentence, a corporation's separate affiliated group is the affiliated group which would be determined under section 1504(a) if such corporation were the common parent and section 1504(b) did not apply.

(C) Transition rule. Subparagraph (A) shall not apply to any distribution pursuant to a transaction which is—

(i) made pursuant to an agreement which was binding on the date of the enactment of this paragraph and at all times thereafter,

(ii) described in a ruling request submitted to the Internal Revenue Service on or before such date, or

(iii) described on or before such date in a public announcement or in a filing with the Securities and Exchange Commission.

The preceding sentence shall not apply if the distributing corporation elects not to have such sentence apply to distributions of such corporation. Any such election, once made, shall be irrevocable.

(D) Special rule for certain pre-enactment distributions. For purposes of determining the continued qualification under paragraph (2)(A) of distributions made on or before the date of the enactment of this paragraph as a result of an acquisition, disposition, or other restructuring after such date[2], such distribution shall be treated as made on the date of such acquisition, disposition, or restructuring for purposes of applying subparagraphs (A) through (C) of this paragraph.

* * * * * * * * * * * *

[For Analysis, see ¶1602. For Committee Reports, see ¶5061.]

[Endnote Code Sec. 355]

Matter in *italics* in Code Sec. 355(b)(3)(A) and Code Sec. 355(b)(3)(D) was added by Sec. 410(a) of the Tax Relief and Health Care Act of 2006, HR6111, d.o.e., which struck out:

1. "and on or before December 31, 2010"
2. "and on or before December 31, 2010"

Effective Date (Sec. 410(b), HR6111, d.o.e.) effective 5/17/2006.

[¶ 3038] Code Sec. 408. Individual retirement accounts.

* * * * * * * * * * * *

(d) Tax treatment of distributions.

* * * * * * * * * * * *

[1]***(9) Distribution for health savings account funding.***

(A) In general. In the case of an individual who is an eligible individual (as defined in section 223(c)) and who elects the application of this paragraph for a taxable year, gross income of the individual for the taxable year does not include a qualified HSA funding distribution to the extent such distribution is otherwise includible in gross income.

(B) Qualified HSA funding distribution. For purposes of this paragraph, the term "qualified HSA funding distribution" means a distribution from an individual retirement plan (other than a plan described in subsection (k) or (p)) of the employee to the extent that such distribution is contributed to the health savings account of the individual in a direct trustee-to-trustee transfer.

(C) Limitations.

(i) Maximum dollar limitation. The amount excluded from gross income by subparagraph (A) shall not exceed the excess of—

(I) the annual limitation under section 223(b) computed on the basis of the type of coverage under the high deductible health plan covering the individual at the time of the qualified HSA funding distribution, over

(II) in the case of a distribution described in clause (ii)(II), the amount of the earlier qualified HSA funding distribution.

(ii) One-time transfer.

(I) In general. Except as provided in subclause (II), an individual may make an election under subparagraph (A) only for one qualified HSA funding distribution during the lifetime of the individual. Such an election, once made, shall be irrevocable.

(II) Conversion from self-only to family coverage. If a qualified HSA funding distribution is made during a month in a taxable year during which an individual has self-only coverage under a high deductible health plan as of the first day of the month, the individual may elect to make an additional qualified HSA funding distribution during a subsequent month in such taxable year during which the individual has family coverage under a high deductible health plan as of the first day of the subsequent month.

(D) Failure to maintain high deductible health plan coverage.

(i) In general. If, at any time during the testing period, the individual is not an eligible individual, then the aggregate amount of all contributions to the health savings account of the individual made under subparagraph (A)—

(l) shall be includible in the gross income of the individual for the taxable year in which occurs the first month in the testing period for which such individual is not an eligible individual, and

(ll) the tax imposed by this chapter for any taxable year on the individual shall be increased by 10 percent of the amount which is so includible.

(ii) Exception for disability or death. Subclauses (I) and (II) of clause (i) shall not apply if the individual ceased to be an eligible individual by reason of the death of the individual or the individual becoming disabled (within the meaning of section 72(m)(7)).

(iii) Testing period. The term "testing period" means the period beginning with the month in which the qualified HSA funding distribution is contributed to a health savings account and ending on the last day of the 12th month following such month.

(E) Application of section 72. Notwithstanding section 72, in determining the extent to which an amount is treated as otherwise includible in gross income for purposes of subparagraph (A), the aggregate amount distributed from an individual retirement plan shall be treated as includible in gross income to the extent that such amount does not exceed the aggregate amount which would have been so includible if all amounts from all individual retirement plans were distributed. Proper adjustments shall be made in applying section 72 to other distributions in such taxable year and subsequent taxable years.

* * * * * * * * * * * *

[For Analysis, see ¶ 301. For Committee Reports, see ¶ 5045.]

[Endnote Code Sec. 408]

Code Sec. 408(d)(9), in *italics*, was added by Sec. 307(a) of the Tax Relief and Health Care Act of 2006, HR6111, d.o.e..

1. added para. (d)(9)

Effective Date (Sec. 307(c), HR6111, d.o.e.) effective for tax. yrs. begin. after 12/31/2006.

[¶ 3039] Code Sec. 468B. Special rules for designated settlement funds.

* * * * * * * * * * * *

(g) Clarification of taxation of certain funds.

(1) In general. Except as provided in paragraph (2), nothing in any provision of law shall be construed as providing that an escrow account, settlement fund, or similar fund is not subject to current income tax. The Secretary shall prescribe regulations providing for the taxation of any such account or fund whether as a grantor trust or otherwise.

(2) Exemption from tax for certain settlement funds. An escrow account, settlement fund, or similar fund shall be treated as beneficially owned by the United States and shall be exempt from taxation under this subtitle if—

(A) it is established pursuant to a consent decree entered by a judge of a United States District Court,

(B) it is created for the receipt of settlement payments as directed by a government entity for the sole purpose of resolving or satisfying one or more claims asserting liability under the Comprehensive Environmental Response, Compensation, and Liability Act of 1980,

(C) the authority and control over the expenditure of funds therein (including the expenditure of contributions thereto and any net earnings thereon) is with such government entity, and

(D) upon termination, any remaining funds will be disbursed to such government entity for use in accordance with applicable law.

For purposes of this paragraph, the term "government entity" means the United States, any State or political subdivision thereof, the District of Columbia, any possession of the United States, and any agency or instrumentality of any of the foregoing.

[1]***(3) Repealed.***

[For Analysis, see ¶ 1605. For Committee Reports, see ¶ 5060.]

[Endnote Code Sec. 468B]

Matter in *italics* in Code Sec. 468B(g)(3) was added by Sec. 409(a) of the Tax Relief and Health Care Act of 2006, HR6111, d.o.e., which struck out:

1. "(3) Termination.

"Paragraph (2) shall not apply to accounts and funds established after December 31, 2010."

Effective Date (Sec. 409(b), HR6111, d.o.e.) effective for accounts and funds established after 5/17/2006.

[¶3040] Code Sec. 613A. Limitations on percentage depletion in case of oil and gas wells.

* * * * * * * * * * * * *

(c) Exemption for independent producers and royalty owners.

* * * * * * * * * * * * *

(6) Oil and natural gas produced from marginal properties.

(A) In general. Except as provided in subsection (d) and subparagraph (B), the allowance for depletion under section 611 shall be computed in accordance with section 613 with respect to—

(i) so much of the taxpayer's average daily marginal production of domestic crude oil as does not exceed the taxpayer's depletable oil quantity (determined without regard to paragraph (3)(A)(ii)), and

(ii) so much of the taxpayer's average daily marginal production of domestic natural gas as does not exceed the taxpayer's depletable natural gas quantity (determined without regard to paragraph (3)(A)(ii)),

and the applicable percentage shall be deemed to be specified in subsection (b) of section 613 for purposes of subsection (a) of that section.

(B) Election to have paragraph apply to pro rata portion of marginal production. If the taxpayer elects to have this subparagraph apply for any taxable year, the rules of subparagraph (A) shall apply to the average daily marginal production of domestic crude oil or domestic natural gas of the taxpayer to which paragraph (1) would have applied without regard to this paragraph.

(C) Applicable percentage. For purposes of subparagraph (A), the term "applicable percentage" means the percentage (not greater than 25 percent) equal to the sum of—

(i) 15 percent, plus

(ii) 1 percentage point for each whole dollar by which $20 exceeds the reference price for crude oil for the calendar year preceding the calendar year in which the taxable year begins.

For purposes of this paragraph, the term "reference price" means, with respect to any calendar year, the reference price determined for such calendar year under section 45K(d)(2)(C).

(D) Marginal production. The term "marginal production" means domestic crude oil or domestic natural gas which is produced during any taxable year from a property which—

(i) is a stripper well property for the calendar year in which the taxable year begins, or

(ii) is a property substantially all of the production of which during such calendar year is heavy oil.

(E) Stripper well property. For purposes of this paragraph, the term "stripper well property" means, with respect to any calendar year, any property with respect to which the amount determined by dividing—

(i) the average daily production of domestic crude oil and domestic natural gas from producing wells on such property for such calendar year, by

(ii) the number of such wells,

is 15 barrel equivalents or less.

(F) Heavy Oil. For purposes of this paragraph, the term "heavy oil" means domestic crude oil produced from any property if such crude oil had a weighted average gravity of 20 degrees API or less (corrected to 60 degrees Fahrenheit).

(G) Average daily marginal production. For purposes of this subsection—

(i) the taxpayer's average daily marginal production of domestic crude oil or natural gas for any taxable year shall be determined by dividing the taxpayer's aggregate marginal production of domestic crude oil or natural gas, as the case may be, during the taxable year by the number of days in such taxable year, and

(ii) in the case of a taxpayer holding a partial interest in the production from any property (including any interest held in any partnership), such taxpayer's production shall be considered to be that amount of such production determined by multiplying the total production of such property by the taxpayer's percentage participation in the revenues from such property.

(H) Temporary suspension of taxable income limit with respect to marginal production. The second sentence of subsection (a) of section 613 shall not apply to so much of the allowance for depletion as is determined under subparagraph (A) for any taxable year beginning after December 31, 1997, and before January 1, [1]*2008.*

* * * * * * * * * * * *

[For Analysis, see ¶ 507. For Committee Reports, see ¶ 5022.]

[Endnote Code Sec. 613A]

Matter in *italics* in Code Sec. 613A(c)(6)(H) was added by Sec. 118(a) of the Tax Relief and Health Care Act of 2006, HR6111, d.o.e., which struck out:

1. "2006"

Effective Date (Sec. 118(b), HR6111, d.o.e.) effective for tax. yrs. begin. after 12/31/2005.

[¶ 3041] Code Sec. 664. Charitable remainder trusts.

* * * * * * * * * * * *

[1]***(c) Taxation of trusts.***

(1) Income tax. *A charitable remainder annuity trust and a charitable remainder unitrust shall, for any taxable year, not be subject to any tax imposed by this subtitle.*

(2) Excise tax.

(A) In general. In the case of a charitable remainder annuity trust or a charitable remainder unitrust which has unrelated business taxable income (within the meaning of section 512, determined as if part III of subchapter F applied to such trust) for a taxable year, there is hereby imposed on such trust or unitrust an excise tax equal to the amount of such unrelated business taxable income.

(B) Certain rules to apply. The tax imposed by subparagraph (A) shall be treated as imposed by chapter 42 for purposes of this title other than subchapter E of chapter 42.

(C) Tax court proceedings. For purposes of this paragraph, the references in section 6212(c)(1) to section 4940 shall be deemed to include references to this paragraph.

* * * * * * * * * * * *

[For Analysis, see ¶ 601. For Committee Reports, see ¶ 5075.]

[Endnote Code Sec. 664]

Code Sec. 664(c), in *italics*, was added by Sec. 424(a) of the Tax Relief and Health Care Act of 2006, HR6111, d.o.e., which struck out:

1. "(c) Exemption from income taxes.

"A charitable remainder annuity trust and a charitable remainder unitrust shall, for any taxable year, not be subject to any tax imposed by this subtitle, unless such trust, for such year, has unrelated business taxable income (within the meaning of section 512, determined as if part III of subchapter F applied to such trust)."

Effective Date (Sec. 424(b), HR6111, d.o.e.) effective for tax. yrs. begin. after 12/31/2005.

[¶ 3042] Code Sec. 954. Foreign base company income.

* * * * * * * * * * * *

(c) Foreign personal holding company income.

* * * * * * * * * * * *

(6) Look-thru rule for related controlled foreign corporations.

(A) In general. For purposes of this subsection, dividends, interest, rents, and royalties received or accrued from a controlled foreign corporation which is a related person shall not be treated as foreign personal holding company income to the extent attributable or properly allocable (determined under rules similar to the rules of subparagraphs (C) and (D) of section 904(d)(3)) to income of the related person [1]*which is neither subpart F income nor income treated as effectively connected with the conduct of a trade or business in the United States.* For purposes of this subparagraph, interest shall include factoring income which is treated as income equivalent to interest for purposes of paragraph (1)(E). [2]*The Secretary shall prescribe such regulations as may be necessary or appropriate to carry out this paragraph, including such regulations as may be necessary or appropriate to prevent the abuse of the purposes of this paragraph.*

(B) Application. Subparagraph (A) shall apply to taxable years of foreign corporations beginning after December 31, 2005, and before January 1, 2009, and to taxable years of United States shareholders with or within which such taxable years of foreign corporations end.

* * * * * * * * * * * *

[For Analysis, see ¶ 1301. For Committee Reports, see ¶ 5077.]

[Endnote Code Sec. 954]

Matter in *italics* in Code Sec. 954(c)(6)(A) was added by Sec. 426(a)(1)(A) and (B) of the Tax Relief and Health Care Act of 2006, HR6111, d.o.e., which struck out:

1. "which is not subpart F income"
2. "The Secretary shall prescribe such regulations as may be appropriate to prevent the abuse of the purposes of this paragraph."

Effective Date (Sec. 426(a)(2), HR6111, d.o.e.) effective for tax. yrs. of foreign corporations begin. after 12/31/2005, and for tax. yrs. of United States shareholders with or within which such tax. yrs. of foreign corporations end.

[¶ 3043] Code Sec. 1043. Sale of property to comply with conflict-of-interest requirements.

* * * * * * * * * * * *

(b) Definitions. For purposes of this section—

(1) Eligible person. The term "eligible person" means—

(A) an officer or employee of the executive branch[1]*, or a judicial officer,* of the Federal Government, but does not mean a special Government employee as defined in section 202 of title 18, United States Code, and

(B) any spouse or minor or dependent child whose ownership of any property is attributable under any statute, regulation, rule, [2]*judicial canon,* or executive order referred to in paragraph (2) to a person referred to in subparagraph (A).

(2) Certificate of divestiture. The term "certificate of divestiture" means any written determination—

(A) that states that divestiture of specific property is reasonably necessary to comply with any Federal conflict of interest statute, regulation, rule, [3]*judicial canon,* or executive order (including section 208 of title 18, United States Code), or requested by a congressional committee as a condition of confirmation,

(B) that has been issued by the President or the Director of the Office of Government Ethics, [4]*in the case of executive branch officers or employees, or by the Judicial Conference of the United States (or its designee), in the case of judicial officers,* and

(C) that identifies the specific property to be divested.

(3) **Permitted property.** The term "permitted property" means any obligation of the United States or any diversified investment fund approved by regulations issued by the Office of Government Ethics.

(4) **Purchase.** The taxpayer shall be considered to have purchased any permitted property if, but for subsection (c), the unadjusted basis of such property would be its cost within the meaning of section 1012.

(5) **Special rule for trusts.** For purposes of this section, the trustee of a trust shall be treated as an eligible person with respect to property which is held in the trust if—

(A) any person referred to in paragraph (1)(A) has a beneficial interest in the principal or income of the trust, or

(B) any person referred to in paragraph (1)(B) has a beneficial interest in the principal or income of the trust and such interest is attributable under any statute, regulation, rule, [5]*judicial canon,* or executive order referred to in paragraph (2) to a person referred to in paragraph (1)(A).

[6]***(6) Judicial officer.*** *The term "judicial officer" means the Chief Justice of the United States, the Associate Justices of the Supreme Court, and the judges of the United States courts of appeals, United States district courts, including the district courts in Guam, the Northern Mariana Islands, and the Virgin Islands, Court of Appeals for the Federal Circuit, Court of International Trade, Tax Court, Court of Federal Claims, Court of Appeals for Veterans Claims, United States Court of Appeals for the Armed Forces, and any court created by Act of Congress, the judges of which are entitled to hold office during good behavior.*

* * * * * * * * * * * * *

[For Analysis, see ¶109. For Committee Reports, see ¶5069.]

[Endnote Code Sec. 1043]

Matter in *italics* in Code Sec. 1043(b)(1)(A), Code Sec. 1043(b)(1)(B), Code Sec. 1043(b)(2)(A), Code Sec. 1043(b)(2)(B), Code Sec. 1043(b)(5)(B), and Code Sec. 1043(b)(6) was added by Sec. 418(a)(1)(A)-(B), (a)(2)(A)-(B), (a)(3), and (b) of the Tax Relief and Health Care Act of 2006, HR6111, d.o.e.

1. added matter in subpara. (b)(1)(A)
2. added matter in subpara. (b)(1)(B)
3. added matter in subpara. (b)(2)(A)
4. added matter in subpara. (b)(2)(B)
5. added matter in subpara. (b)(5)(B)
6. added para. (b)(6)

Effective Date (Sec. 418(c), HR6111, d.o.e.) effective for sales after d.o.e.

[¶3044] Code Sec. 1221. Capital asset defined.

* * * * * * * * * * * * *

(b) Definitions and special rules.

* * * * * * * * * * * * *

(3) **Sale or exchange of self-created musical works.** At the election of the taxpayer, paragraphs (1) and (3) of subsection (a) shall not apply to musical compositions or copyrights in musical works sold or exchanged[1] by a taxpayer described in subsection (a)(3).

* * * * * * * * * * * * *

[For Analysis, see ¶1601. For Committee Reports, see ¶5063.]

[Endnote Code Sec. 1221]

Matter in Code Sec. 1221(b)(3) was deleted by Sec. 412(a) of the Tax Relief and Health Care Act of 2006, HR6111, d.o.e., which struck out:

1. "before January 1, 2011,"

Effective Date (Sec. 412(b), HR6111, d.o.e.) effective for sales and exchanges in tax yrs. begin. after 5/17/2006.

[¶ 3045] Code Sec. 1245. Gain from dispositions of certain depreciable property.

(a) General rule.

(1) Ordinary income. Except as otherwise provided in this section, if section 1245 property is disposed of the amount by which the lower of—

(A) the recomputed basis of the property, or

(B)

(i) in the case of a sale, exchange, or involuntary conversion, the amount realized, or

(ii) in the case of any other disposition, the fair market value of such property,

exceeds the adjusted basis of such property shall be treated as ordinary income. Such gain shall be recognized notwithstanding any other provision of this subtitle.

(2) Recomputed basis. For purposes of this section—

(A) In general. The term "recomputed basis" means, with respect to any property, its adjusted basis recomputed by adding thereto all adjustments reflected in such adjusted basis on account of deductions (whether in respect of the same or other property) allowed or allowable to the taxpayer or to any other person for depreciation or amortization.

(B) Taxpayer may establish amount allowed. For purposes of subparagraph (A), if the taxpayer can establish by adequate records or other sufficient evidence that the amount allowed for depreciation or amortization for any period was less than the amount allowable, the amount added for such period shall be the amount allowed.

(C) Certain deductions treated as amortization. Any deduction allowable under section 179, 179A, 179B, 181, 179C, 179D, [1]*179E,* 190, 193, or 194 shall be treated as if it were a deduction allowable for amortization.

(3) Section 1245 property. For purposes of this section, the term "section 1245 property" means any property which is or has been property of a character subject to the allowance for depreciation provided in section 167 and is either—

(A) personal property,

(B) other property (not including a building or its structural components) but only if such other property is tangible and has an adjusted basis in which there are reflected adjustments described in paragraph (2) for a period in which such property (or other property)—

(i) was used as an integral part of manufacturing, production, or extraction or of furnishing transportation, communications, electrical energy, gas, water, or sewage disposal services,

(ii) constituted a research facility used in connection with any of the activities referred to in clause (i), or

(iii) constituted a facility used in connection with any of the activities referred to in clause (i) for the bulk storage of fungible commodities (including commodities in a liquid or gaseous state),

(C) so much of any real property (other than any property described in subparagraph (B)) which has an adjusted basis in which there are reflected adjustments for amortization under section 169, 179, 179A, 179B, 179C, 179D, [2]*179E,* 185, 188 (as in effect before its repeal by the Revenue Reconciliation Act of 1990), 190, 193, or 194[,]

(D) a single purpose agricultural or horticultural structure (as defined in section 168(i)(13)),

(E) a storage facility (not including a building or its structural components) used in connection with the distribution of petroleum or any primary product of petroleum, or

(F) any railroad grading or tunnel bore (as defined in section 168(e)(4)).

* * * * * * * * * * * * *

[For Analysis, see ¶ 509. For Committee Reports, see ¶ 5055.]

[Endnote Code Sec. 1245]

Matter in *italics* in Code Sec. 1245(a)(2)(C) and Code Sec. 1245(a)(3)(C) was added by Sec. 404(b)(3) of the Tax Relief and Health Care Act of 2006, HR6111, d.o.e..

1. added matter in subpara. (a)(2)(C)
2. added matter in subpara. (a)(3)(C)

Effective Date (Sec. 404(c), HR6111, d.o.e.) effective for costs paid or incurred after d.o.e..

[¶ 3046] Code Sec. 1355. Definitions and special rules.

(a) Definitions. For purposes of this subchapter—

* * * * * * * * * * * *

(4) Qualifying vessel. The term "qualifying vessel" means a self-propelled (or a combination self-propelled and non-self-propelled) United States flag vessel of not less than [1]*6,000* deadweight tons used exclusively in the United States foreign trade during the period that the election under this subchapter is in effect.

* * * * * * * * * * * *

[2]***(g) Great Lakes domestic shipping to not disqualify vessel.***

(1) In general. *If the electing corporation elects (at such time and in such manner as the Secretary may require) to apply this subsection for any taxable year to any qualifying vessel which is used in qualified zone domestic trade during the taxable year—*

(A) solely for purposes of subsection (a)(4), such use shall be treated as use in United States foreign trade (and not as use in United States domestic trade), and

(B) subsection (f) shall not apply with respect to such vessel for such taxable year.

(2) Effect of temporarily operating vessel in United States domestic trade. *In the case of a qualifying vessel to which this subsection applies—*

(A) In general. An electing corporation shall be treated as using such vessel in qualified zone domestic trade during any period of temporary use in the United States domestic trade (other than qualified zone domestic trade) if the electing corporation gives timely notice to the Secretary stating—

(i) that it temporarily operates or has operated in the United States domestic trade (other than qualified zone domestic trade) a qualifying vessel which had been used in the United States foreign trade or qualified zone domestic trade, and

(ii) its intention to resume operation of the vessel in the United States foreign trade or qualified zone domestic trade.

(B) Notice. Notice shall be deemed timely if given not later than the due date (including extensions) for the corporation's tax return for the taxable year in which the temporary cessation begins.

(C) Period disregard in effect. The period of temporary use under subparagraph (A) continues until the earlier of the date of which

(i) the electing corporation abandons its intention to resume operations of the vessel in the United States foreign trade or qualified zone domestic trade, or

(ii) the electing corporation resumes operation of the vessel in the United States foreign trade or qualified zone domestic trade.

(D) No disregard if domestic trade use exceeds 30 days. Subparagraph (A) shall not apply to any qualifying vessel which is operated in the United States domestic trade (other than qualified zone domestic trade) for more than 30 days during the taxable year.

(3) Allocation of income and deductions to qualifying shipping activities. *In the case of a qualifying vessel to which this subsection applies, the Secretary shall prescribe rules for the proper allocation of income, expenses, losses, and deductions between the qualified shipping activities and the other activities of such vessel.*

(4) Qualified zone domestic trade. *For purposes of this subsection—*

(A) In general. The term "qualified zone domestic trade" means the transportation of goods or passengers between places in the qualified zone if such transportation is in the United States domestic trade.

(B) Qualified zone. The term "qualified zone" means the Great Lakes Waterway and the St. Lawrence Seaway.

[3]***(h)*** **Regulations.** The Secretary shall prescribe such regulations as may be necessary or appropriate to carry out the purposes of this section.

[For Analysis, see ¶ 1608 and ¶ 1609. For Committee Reports, see ¶ 5064 and ¶ 5066.]

[Endnote Code Sec. 1355]

Matter in *italics* in Code Sec. 1355(a)(4) was added by Sec. 413(a) of the Tax Relief and Health Care Act of 2006, HR6111, d.o.e., which struck out:

1. "10,000 (6,000, in the case of taxable years beginning after December 31, 2005, and ending before January 1, 2011)"

Effective Date (Sec. 413(b), HR6111, d.o.e.) effective for tax. yrs. begin. after 12/31/2005.

Matter in *italics* in Code Sec. 1355(g) and Code Sec. 1355(h) was added by Sec. 415(a), HR6111, d.o.e., which struck out:

2. added subsec. (g)
3. "(g)"

Effective Date (Sec. 415(b), HR6111, d.o.e.) effective for tax. yrs. begin. after d.o.e..

[¶ 3047] Code Sec. 1397E. Credit to holders of qualified zone academy bonds.

* * * * * * * * * * * *

(d) Qualified zone academy bond. For purposes of this section—

(1) In general. The term "qualified zone academy bond" means any bond issued as part of an issue if—

(A) 95 percent or more of the proceeds of such issue are to be used for a qualified purpose with respect to a qualified zone academy established by an eligible local education agency,

(B) the bond is issued by a State or local government within the jurisdiction of which such academy is located,

(C) the issuer—

(i) designates such bond for purposes of this section,

(ii) certifies that it has written assurances that the private business contribution requirement of paragraph (2) will be met with respect to such academy, and

(iii) certifies that it has the written approval of the eligible local education agency for such bond issuance,[1]

(D) the term of each bond which is part of such issue does not exceed the maximum term permitted under paragraph (3)[2] *and,*

[3]*(E) the issue meets the requirements of subsections (f), (g), and (h).*

* * * * * * * * * * * *

(e) Limitation on amount of bonds designated.

(1) National limitation. There is a national zone academy bond limitation for each calendar year. Such limitation is $400,000,000 for 1998, 1999, 2000, 2001, 2002, 2003, 2004, [4]*2005, 2006, and 2007* and, except as provided in paragraph (4), zero thereafter.

* * * * * * * * * * * *

[5]***(f) Special rules relating to expenditures.***

(1) In general. *An issue shall be treated as meeting the requirements of this subsection if, as of the date of issuance, the issuer reasonably expects—*

(A) at least 95 percent of the proceeds from the sale of the issue are to be spent for 1 or more qualified purposes with respect to qualified zone academies within the 5-year period beginning on the date of issuance of the qualified zone academy bond,

(B) a binding commitment with a third party to spend at least 10 percent of the proceeds from the sale of the issue will be incurred within the 6-month period beginning on the date of issuance of the qualified zone academy bond, and

(C) such purposes will be completed with due diligence and the proceeds from the sale of the issue will be spent with due diligence.

(2) Extension of period. *Upon submission of a request prior to the expiration of the period described in paragraph (1)(A), the Secretary may extend such period if the issuer establishes that the failure to satisfy the 5-year requirement is due to reasonable cause and the related purposes will continue to proceed with due diligence.*

(3) Failure to spend required amount of bond proceeds within 5 years. *To the extent that less than 95 percent of the proceeds of such issue are expended by the close of the 5-year period beginning on the date of issuance (or if an extension has been obtained under paragraph (2), by the close of the extended period), the issuer shall redeem all of the nonqualified bonds within 90 days after the end of such period. For purposes of this paragraph, the amount of the nonqualified bonds required to be redeemed shall be determined in the same manner as under section 142*

(g) Special rules relating to arbitrage. *An issue shall be treated as meeting the requirements of this subsection if the issuer satisfies the arbitrage requirements of section 148 with respect to proceeds of the issue.*

(h) Reporting. *Issuers of qualified academy zone bonds shall submit reports similar to the reports required under section 149(e).*

[6]***(i)*** **Other definitions.** For purposes of this section—

(1) Credit allowance date. The term "credit allowance date" means, with respect to any issue, the last day of the 1-year period beginning on the date of issuance of such issue and the last day of each successive 1-year period thereafter.

(2) Bond. The term "bond" includes any obligation.

(3) State. The term "State" includes the District of Columbia and any possession of the United States.

[7]***(j)*** **Credit included in gross income.** Gross income includes the amount of the credit allowed to the taxpayer under this section (determined without regard to subsection (c)).

[8]***(k)*** **Credit treated as nonrefundable bondholder credit.** For purposes of this title, the credit allowed by this section shall be treated as a credit allowable under subpart H of part IV of subchapter A of this chapter.

[9]***(l)*** **S corporations.** In the case of a qualified zone academy bond held by an S corporation which is an eligible taxpayer—

(1) each shareholder shall take into account such shareholder's pro rata share of the credit, and

(2) no basis adjustments to the stock of the corporation shall be made under section 1367 on account of this section.

[For Analysis, see ¶ 1003 and ¶ 1004. For Committee Reports, see ¶ 5011.]

[Endnote Code Sec. 1397E]

Matter in *italics* in Code Sec. 1397E(d)(1)(C)(iii), Code Sec. 1397E(d)(1)(D), and Code Sec. 1397E(d)(1)(E) was added by Sec. 107(b)(1)(A) of the Tax Relief and Health Care Act of 2006, HR6111, d.o.e., which struck out:

1. "and"
2. "."
3. added subpara. (d)(1)(E)

Effective Date (Sec. 107(c)(2), HR6111, d.o.e.) effective for obligations issued after d.o.e. for allocations of the national zone academy bond limitation for calendar yrs. after 2005.

Matter in *italics* in Code Sec. 1397E(e)(1) was added by Sec. 107(a), HR6111, d.o.e., which struck out:

4. "and 2005"

Effective Date (Sec. 107(c)(1), HR6111, d.o.e.) effective for obligations issued after 12/31/2005.

Matter in *italics* in Code Sec. 1397E(f), Code Sec. 1397E(g), Code Sec. 1397E(h), Code Sec. 1397E(i), Code Sec. 1397E(j), Code Sec. 1397E(k) and Code Sec. 1397E(l), was added by Sec. 107(b)(1)(B), HR6111, d.o.e., which struck out:

5. added subsecs. (f), (g) and (h)
6. "(f)"
7. "(g)"
8. "(h)"
9. "(i)"

Effective Date (Sec. 107(c)(2), HR6111, d.o.e.) effective for obligations issued after d.o.e. for allocations of the national zone academy bond limitation for calendar yrs. after 2005.

[¶ 3048] Code Sec. 1400. Establishment of DC Zone.

* * * * * * * * * * * *

(f) Time for which designation applicable.

(1) In general. The designation made by subsection (a) shall apply for the period beginning on January 1, 1998, and ending on December 31, [1]*2007.*

(2) Coordination with DC enterprise community designated under subchapter U. The designation under subchapter U of the census tracts referred to in subsection (b)(1) as an enterprise community shall terminate on December 31, [2]*2007.*

[For Analysis, see ¶ 1103. For Committee Reports, see ¶ 5014.]

[Endnote Code Sec. 1400]

Matter in *italics* in Code Sec. 1400(f) was added by Sec. 110(a)(1) of the Tax Relief and Health Care Act of 2006, HR6111, d.o.e., which struck out:

1. "2005"
2. "2005"

Effective Date (Sec. 110(a)(2), HR6111, d.o.e.) effective for periods begin. after 12/31/2005.

[¶ 3049] Code Sec. 1400A. Tax-exempt economic development bonds.

* * * * * * * * * * * *

(b) Period of applicability. This section shall apply to bonds issued during the period beginning on January 1, 1998, and ending on December 31, [1]*2007.*

[Endnote Code Sec. 1400A]

Matter in *italics* in Code Sec. 1400A(b) was added by Sec. 110(b)(1) of the Tax Relief and Health Care Act of 2006, HR6111, d.o.e., which struck out:

1. "2005"

Effective Date (Sec. 110(b)(2), HR6111, d.o.e.) effective for bonds issued after 12/31/2005.

[¶ 3050] Code Sec. 1400B. Zero percent capital gains rate.

* * * * * * * * * * * *

(b) DC Zone asset. For purposes of this section—

(1) In general. The term "DC Zone asset" means—

(A) any DC Zone business stock,

(B) any DC Zone partnership interest, and

(C) any DC Zone business property.

(2) DC Zone business stock.

(A) In general. The term "DC Zone business stock" means any stock in a domestic corporation which is originally issued after December 31, 1997, if—

(i) such stock is acquired by the taxpayer, before January 1, [1]*2008,* at its original issue (directly or through an underwriter) solely in exchange for cash,

(ii) as of the time such stock was issued, such corporation was a DC Zone business (or, in the case of a new corporation, such corporation was being organized for purposes of being a DC Zone business), and

(iii) during substantially all of the taxpayer's holding period for such stock, such corporation qualified as a DC Zone business.

(B) Redemptions. A rule similar to the rule of section 1202(c)(3) shall apply for purposes of this paragraph.

(3) DC Zone partnership interest. The term "DC Zone partnership interest" means any capital or profits interest in a domestic partnership which is originally issued after December 31, 1997, if—

(A) such interest is acquired by the taxpayer, before January 1, [2]*2008*, from the partnership solely in exchange for cash,

(B) as of the time such interest was acquired, such partnership was a DC Zone business (or, in the case of a new partnership, such partnership was being organized for purposes of being a DC Zone business), and

(C) during substantially all of the taxpayer's holding period for such interest, such partnership qualified as a DC Zone business.

A rule similar to the rule of paragraph (2)(B) shall apply for purposes of this paragraph.

(4) DC Zone business property.

(A) In general. The term "DC Zone business property" means tangible property if—

(i) such property was acquired by the taxpayer by purchase (as defined in section 179(d)(2)) after December 31, 1997, and before January 1, [3]*2008*,

(ii) the original use of such property in the DC Zone commences with the taxpayer, and

(iii) during substantially all of the taxpayer's holding period for such property, substantially all of the use of such property was in a DC Zone business of the taxpayer.

(B) Special rule for buildings which are substantially improved.

(i) In general. The requirements of clauses (i) and (ii) of subparagraph (A) shall be treated as met with respect to—

(I) property which is substantially improved by the taxpayer before January 1, [4]*2008*, and

(II) any land on which such property is located.

(ii) Substantial improvement. For purposes of clause (i), property shall be treated as substantially improved by the taxpayer only if, during any 24-month period beginning after December 31, 1997, additions to basis with respect to such property in the hands of the taxpayer exceed the greater of—

(I) an amount equal to the adjusted basis of such property at the beginning of such 24-month period in the hands of the taxpayer, or

(II) $5,000.

(5) Treatment of DC Zone termination. The termination of the designation of the DC Zone shall be disregarded for purposes of determining whether any property is a DC Zone asset.

(6) Treatment of subsequent purchasers, etc. The term "DC Zone asset" includes any property which would be a DC Zone asset but for paragraph (2)(A)(i), (3)(A), or (4)(A)(i) or (ii) in the hands of the taxpayer if such property was a DC Zone asset in the hands of a prior holder.

(7) 5-year safe harbor. If any property ceases to be a DC Zone asset by reason of paragraph (2)(A)(iii), (3)(C), or (4)(A)(iii) after the 5-year period beginning on the date the taxpayer acquired such property, such property shall continue to be treated as meeting the requirements of such paragraph; except that the amount of gain to which subsection (a) applies on any sale or exchange of such property shall not exceed the amount which would be qualified capital gain had such property been sold on the date of such cessation.

* * * * * * * * * * * *

(e) Other definitions and special rules. For purposes of this section—

(1) Qualified capital gain. Except as otherwise provided in this subsection, the term "qualified capital gain" means any gain recognized on the sale or exchange of—

(A) a capital asset, or

(B) property used in the trade or business (as defined in section 1231(b)).

(2) Gain before 1998 or after [5]*2012* not qualified. The term "qualified capital gain" shall not include any gain attributable to periods before January 1, 1998, or after December 31, [6]*2012.*

* * * * * * * * * * * *

(g) Sales and exchanges of interests in partnerships and S corporations which are DC Zone businesses. In the case of the sale or exchange of an interest in a partnership, or of stock in an S corporation, which was a DC Zone business during substantially all of the period the taxpayer held such interest or stock, the amount of qualified capital gain shall be determined without regard to—

(1) any gain which is attributable to real property, or an intangible asset, which is not an integral part of a DC Zone business, and

(2) any gain attributable to periods before January 1, 1998, or after December 31, [7]*2012.*

[Endnote Code Sec. 1400B]

Matter in *italics* in Code Sec. 1400B(b) was added by Sec. 110(c)(1) of the Tax Relief and Health Care Act of 2006, HR6111, d.o.e., which struck out:

1. "2006"
2. "2006"
3. "2006"
4. "2006"

Effective Date (Sec. 110(c)(3)(A), HR6111, d.o.e.) effective for acquisitions after 12/31/2005.

Matter in *italics* in Code Sec. 1400B(e)(2), and Code Sec. 1400B(g)(2) was added by Sec. 110(c)(2)(A)(i)-(ii) and (c)(2)(B), HR6111, d.o.e., which struck out:

5. "2010"
6. "2010"
7. "2010"

Effective Date (Sec. 110(c)(3)(B), HR6111, d.o.e.) effective d.o.e..

[¶ 3051] Code Sec. 1400C. First-time homebuyer credit for District of Columbia.

* * * * * * * * * * * *

(i) Application of section. This section shall apply to property purchased after August 4, 1997, and before January 1, [1]*2008.*

[Endnote Code Sec. 1400C]

Matter in *italics* in Code Sec. 1400C(i) was added by Sec. 110(d)(1) of the Tax Relief and Health Care Act of 2006, HR6111, d.o.e., which struck out:

1. "2006"

Effective Date (Sec. 110(d)(2), HR6111, d.o.e.) effective for property purchased after 12/31/2005.

[¶ 3052] Code Sec. 1400F. Renewal community capital gain.

* * * * * * * * * * * *

(d) Certain rules to apply. For purposes of this section, rules similar to the rules of paragraphs (5), (6), and (7) of subsection (b), and subsections (f) and (g), of section 1400B shall apply; except that for such purposes section 1400B(g)(2) shall be applied by substituting "January 1, 2002" for "January 1, 1998" and "December 31, 2014" for "December 31, [1]*2012*".

* * * * * * * * * * * *

[Endnote Code Sec. 1400F]

Matter in *italics* in Code Sec. 1400F(d) was added by Sec. 110(c)(2)(C) of the Tax Relief and Health Care Act of 2006, HR6111, d.o.e., which struck out:

1. "2010"

Effective Date (Sec. 110(c)(3)(B), HR6111, d.o.e.) effective d.o.e..

[¶ 3053] Code Sec. 1400N. Tax benefits for Gulf Opportunity Zone.

* * * * * * * * * * * *

(d) Special allowance for certain property acquired on or after August 28, 2005.

* * * * * * * * * * * *

[1]***(6) Extension for certain property.***

(A) In general. In the case of any specified Gulf Opportunity Zone extension property, paragraph (2)(A) shall be applied without regard to clause (v) thereof.

(B) Specified Gulf Opportunity Zone extension property. For purposes of this paragraph, the term "specified Gulf Opportunity Zone extension property" means property—

(i) substantially all of the use of which is in one or more specified portions of the GO Zone, and

(ii) which is—

(I) nonresidential real property or residential rental property which is placed in service by the taxpayer on or before December 31, 2010, or

(II) in the case of a taxpayer who places a building described in subclause (I) in service on or before December 31, 2010, property described in section 168(k)(2)(A)(i) if substantially all of the use of such property is in such building and such property is placed in service by the taxpayer not later than 90 days after such building is placed in service.

(C) Specified portions of the GO Zone. For purposes of this paragraph, the term "specified portions of the GO Zone" means those portions of the GO Zone which are in any county or parish which is identified by the Secretary as being a county or parish in which hurricanes occurring during 2005 damaged (in the aggregate) more than 60 percent of the housing units in such county or parish which were occupied (determined according to the 2000 Census).

(D) Only pre-January 1, 2010, basis of real property eligible for additional allowance. In the case of property which is qualified Gulf Opportunity Zone property solely by reason of subparagraph (B)(ii)(I), paragraph (1) shall apply only to the extent of the adjusted basis thereof attributable to manufacture, construction, or production before January 1, 2010.

(e) Increase in expensing under section 179.

* * * * * * * * * * * *

(2) Qualified section 179 Gulf Opportunity Zone property. For purposes of this subsection, the term "qualified section 179 Gulf Opportunity Zone property" means section 179 property (as defined in section 179(d)) which is qualified Gulf Opportunity Zone property (as defined in subsection (d)(2) [2]*without regard to subsection (d)(6)*).

* * * * * * * * * * * *

(l) Credit to holders of Gulf tax credit bonds.

* * * * * * * * * * * *

(7) Other definitions and special rules. For purposes of this subsection—

(A) Bond. The term "bond" includes any obligation.

(B) Partnership; S corporation; and other pass-thru entities.

(i) In general. Under regulations prescribed by the Secretary, in the case of a partnership, trust, S corporation, or other pass-thru entity, rules similar to the rules of section 41(g) shall apply with respect to the credit allowable under paragraph (1).

(ii) No basis adjustment. In the case of a bond held by a partnership or an S corporation, rules similar to the rules under [3]*section 1397E(l)* shall apply.

(C) Bonds held by regulated investment companies. If any Gulf tax credit bond is held by a regulated investment company, the credit determined under paragraph (1) shall be allowed to shareholders of such company under procedures prescribed by the Secretary.

(D) Reporting. Issuers of Gulf tax credit bonds shall submit reports similar to the reports required under section 149(e).

(E) Credit treated as nonrefundable bondholder credit. For purposes of this title, the credit allowed by this subsection shall be treated as a credit allowable under subpart H of part IV of subchapter A of this chapter.

* * * * * * * * * * * *

[Endnote Code Sec. 1400N]

Code Sec. 1400N(d)(6), and matter in *italics* in Code Sec. 1400N(e)(2) was added by Sec. 120(a)-(b) of the Tax Relief and Health Care Act of 2006, HR6111, d.o.e..

1. added para (d)(6).

2. added matter in para. (e)(2).

Effective Date (Sec. 120(c), HR6111, d.o.e.) effective as if included in Sec. 101 of the Gulf Opportunity Zone Act of 2005, P.L. 109-135, which provides:

"(1) In general. Except as provided in paragraph (2), the amendments made by this section shall apply to taxable years ending on or after August 28, 2005.

"(2) Carrybacks. Subsections (i)(2), (j), and (k) of section 1400N of the Internal Revenue Code of 1986 (as added by this section) shall apply to losses arising in such taxable years."

Matter in *italics* in Code Sec. 1400N(l)(7)(B)(ii) was added by Sec. 107(b)(2), HR6111, d.o.e., which struck out:

3. "section 1397E(i)"

Effective Date (Sec. 107(c)(2), HR6111, d.o.e.) effective for obligations issued after d.o.e. for allocations of the national zone academy bond limitation for calendar years after 2005.

[¶ 3054] Code Sec. 4041. Imposition of tax.

* * * * * * * * * * * *

(b) Exemption for off-highway business use; reduction in tax for qualified methanol and ethanol fuel.

(1) Exemption for off-highway business use.

(A) In general. No tax shall be imposed by subsection (a) on liquids sold for use or used in an off-highway business use.

(B) Tax where other use. If a liquid on which no tax was imposed by reason of subparagraph (A) is used otherwise than in an off-highway business use, a tax shall be imposed by paragraph (1)(B), (2)(B), or (3)(A)(ii) of subsection (a) (whichever is appropriate) and by the corresponding provision of subsection (d)(1) (if any).

(C) Off-highway business use defined. For purposes of this subsection, the term "off-highway business use" has the meaning given to such term by section 6421(e)(2); except that such term shall not, for purposes of this subsection (a)(1), include use in a diesel-powered train.

(2) Qualified methanol and ethanol fuel.

(A) In general. In the case of any qualified methanol or ethanol fuel—

(i) the rate applicable under subsection (a)(2) shall be the applicable blender rate per gallon less than the otherwise applicable rate (6 cents per gallon in the case of a mixture none of the alcohol in which consists of ethanol), and

(ii) subsection (d)(1) shall be applied by substituting "0.05 cent" for "0.1 cent" with respect to the sales and uses to which clause (i) applies.

(B) [1]*Qualfied methanol and ethanol fuel produced from coal.* The term "qualified methanol or ethanol fuel" means any liquid at least 85 percent of which consists of methanol, ethanol, or other alcohol produced from coal (including peat).

(C) Applicable blender rate. For purposes of subparagraph (A)(i), the applicable blender rate is—

(i) except as provided in clause (ii), 5.4 cents, and

(ii) for sales or uses during calendar years 2001 through [2]*2008,* 1⁄10 of the blender amount applicable under section 40(h)(2) for the calendar year in which the sale or use occurs.

(D) Termination. On and after [3]*January 1, 2009,* subparagraph (A) shall not apply.

* * * * * * * * * * * *

[For Analysis, see ¶ 1507. For Committee Reports, see ¶ 5038.]

[Endnote Code Sec. 4041]

Matter in *italics* in Code Sec. 4041(b)(2)(B), Code Sec. 4041(b)(2)(C)(ii), and Code Sec. 4041(b)(2)(D) was added by Sec. 208(a), (b) and (c) of the Tax Relief and Health Care Act of 2006, HR6111, d.o.e., which struck out:

1. "Qualified methanol or ethanol fuel"
2. "2007"
3. "October 1, 2007"

Effective Date enacted d.o.e..

[¶ 3055] Code Sec. 4082. Exemptions for diesel fuel and kerosene.

* * * * * * * * * * * *

(d) Additional exceptions to dyeing requirements for kerosene.

(1) Use for non-fuel feedstock purposes. Subsection (a)(2) shall not apply to kerosene—

(A) received by pipeline or vessel for use by the person receiving the kerosene in the manufacture or production of any substance (other than gasoline, diesel fuel, or special fuels referred to in section 4041), or

(B) to the extent provided in regulations, removed or entered—

(i) for such a use by the person removing or entering the kerosene, or

(ii) for resale by such person for such a use by the purchaser,

but only if the person receiving, removing, or entering the kerosene and such purchaser (if any) are registered under section 4101 with respect to the tax imposed by section 4081.

(2) Wholesale distributors. To the extent provided in regulations, subsection (a)(2) shall not apply to kerosene received by a wholesale distributor of kerosene if such distributor—

(A) is registered under section 4101 with respect to the tax imposed by section 4081 on kerosene, and

(B) sells kerosene exclusively to ultimate vendors described in [1]*section 6427(l)(5)(B)* with respect to kerosene.

* * * * * * * * * * * *

[Endnote Code Sec. 4082]

Matter in *italics* in Code Sec. 4082(d)(2)(B) was added by Sec. 420(b)(2) of the Tax Relief and Health Care Act of 2006, HR6111, d.o.e., which struck out:

1. "6427(l)(6)(B)"

Effective Date (Sec. 420(c), HR6111, d.o.e.) effective for kerosene sold after 9/30/2005.

[¶ 3056] Code Sec. 4132. Definitions and special rules.

(a) Definitions relating to taxable vaccines. For purposes of this subchapter—

(1) Taxable vaccine. The term "taxable vaccine" means any of the following vaccines which are manufactured or produced in the United States or entered into the United States for consumption, use, or warehousing:

* * * * * * * * * * * *

[1]*(O) Any meningococcal vaccine.*

[2]*(P) Any vaccine against the human papillomavirus.*

* * * * * * * * * * * *

[For Analysis, see ¶ 1503. For Committee Reports, see ¶ 5059.]

[Endnote Code Sec. 4132]

Code Sec. 4132(a)(1)(O) and Code Sec. 4132(a)(1)(P), in *italics*, were added by Sec. 408(a) and (b) of the Tax Relief and Health Care Act of 2006, HR6111, d.o.e., which struck out:

1. added subpara. (a)(1)(O)
2. added subpara. (a)(1)(P)

Effective Date (Sec. 408(c), HR6111, d.o.e.) effective for sales and uses on or after the first day of the first month which begins more than 4 weeks after d.o.e., except as provided in Sec. 408(c)(2), HR6111, which reads as follows:

"(2) Deliveries. For purposes of paragraph (1) and section 4131 of the Internal Revenue Code of 1986, in the case of sales on or before the effective date described in such paragraph for which delivery is made after such date, the delivery date shall be considered the sale date.

[¶ 3057] Code Sec. 4980G. Failure of employer to make comparable health savings account contributions.

* * * * * * * * * * * *

[1]***(d) Exception.*** *For purposes of applying section 4980E to a contribution to a health savings account of an employee who is not a highly compensated employee (as defined in section 414(q)), highly compensated employees shall not be treated as comparable participating employees.*

[For Analysis, see ¶ 304. For Committee Reports, see ¶ 5045.]

[Endnote Code Sec. 4980G]

Code Sec. 4980G(d), in *italics*, was added by Sec. 306(a) of the Tax Relief and Health Care Act of 2006, HR6111, d.o.e., which struck out:

1. added subsec. (d).

Effective Date (Sec. 306(b), HR6111, d.o.e.) effective for tax. yrs. begin. after 12/31/2006.

[¶ 3058] Code Sec. 5388. Designation of wines.

* * * * * * * * * * * *

(c) Use of semi-generic designations.

* * * * * * * * * * * *

[1]***(3) Special rule for use of certain semi-generic designations.***

(A) In general. In the case of any wine to which this paragraph applies—

(i) paragraph (1) shall not apply,

(ii) in the case of wine of the European Community, designations referred to in subparagraph (C)(i) may be used for such wine only if the requirement of subparagraph (B)(ii) is met, and

(iii) in the case any other wine bearing a brand name, or brand name and fanciful name, semi-generic designations may be used for such wine only if the requirements of clauses (i), (ii), and (iii) of subparagraph (B) are met.

(B) Requirements.

(i) The requirement of this clause is met if there appears in direct conjunction with the semi-generic designation an appropriate appellation of origin disclosing the origin of the wine.

(ii) The requirement of this clause is met if the wine conforms to the standard of identity, if any, for such wine contained in the regulations under this section or, if there is no such standard, to the trade understanding of such class or type.

(iii) The requirement of this clause is met if the person, or its successor in interest, using the semi-generic designation held a Certificate of Label Approval or Certificate of Exemption from Label Approval issued by the Secretary for a wine label bearing such brand name, or brand name and fanciful name, before March 10, 2006, on which such semi-generic designation appeared.

(C) Wines to which paragraph applies.

(i) In general. Except as provided in clause (ii), this paragraph shall apply to any grape wine which is designated as Burgundy, Claret, Chablis, Champagne, Chianti, Malaga, Marsala, Madeira, Moselle, Port, Retsina, Rhine Wine or Hock, Sauterne, Haut Sauterne, Sherry, or Tokay.

(ii) Exception. This paragraph shall not apply to wine which—

(I) contains less than 7 percent or more than 24 percent alcohol by volume,

(II) is intended for sale outside the United States, or

(III) does not bear a brand name.

[Endnote Code Sec. 5388]

Code Sec. 5388(c)(3), in *italics,* was added by Sec. 422(a) of the Tax Relief and Health Care Act of 2006, HR6111, d.o.e..

1. added para. (c)(3)

Effective Date (Sec. 422(b), HR6111, d.o.e.) effective for wine imported or bottled in the U.S. on or after d.o.e..

[¶ 3059] Code Sec. 5754. Restriction on importation of previously exported tobacco products.

* * * * * * * * * * * * *

(c) Cross references.

(1) For exception to this section for personal use, see [1]*section 5761(d).*

(2) For civil penalties related to violations of this section, see section 5761(c).

(3) For a criminal penalty applicable to any violation of this section, see section 5762(b).

(4) For forfeiture provisions related to violations of this section, see section 5761(c).

[Endnote Code Sec. 5754]

Matter in *italics* in Code Sec. 5754(c)(1) was added by Sec. 401(f)(2)(B) of the Tax Relief and Health Care Act of 2006, HR6111, which struck out:

1. "section 5761(c)"

Effective Date (Sec. 401(g), HR6111, d.o.e.) effective for goods entered, or withdrawn from warehouse for consumption, on or after the 15th day after d.o.e..

[¶ 3060] Code Sec. 5761. Civil penalties.

* * * * * * * * * * * * *

(c) Sale of tobacco products and cigarette papers and tubes for export. Except as provided in subsections (b) and (d) of section 5704—

(1) every person who sells, relands, or receives within the jurisdiction of the United States any tobacco products or cigarette papers or tubes which have been labeled or shipped for exportation under this chapter,

(2) every person who sells or receives such relanded tobacco products or cigarette papers or tubes, and

(3) every person who aids or abets in such selling, relanding, or receiving,

shall, in addition to the tax and any other penalty provided in this title, be liable for a penalty equal to the greater of $1,000 or 5 times the amount of the tax imposed by this chapter. All tobacco products and cigarette papers and tubes relanded within the jurisdiction of the United States shall be forfeited to the United States and destroyed. All vessels, vehicles, and aircraft used in such relanding or in removing such products, papers, and tubes from the place where relanded, shall be forfeited to the United States.[1]

[2]***(d) Personal use quantities.***

(1) ***In general.*** *No quantity of tobacco products other than the quantity referred to in paragraph (2) may be relanded or received as a personal use quantity.*

(2) ***Exception for personal use quantity.*** *Subsection (c) and section 5754 shall not apply to any person who relands or receives tobacco products in the quantity allowed entry free of tax and duty under chapter 98 of the Harmonized Tariff Schedule of the United States, and such person may voluntarily relinquish to the Secretary at the time of entry any excess of such quantity without incurring the penalty under subsection (c).*

(3) ***Special rule for delivery sales.***

(A) In general. Paragraph (2) shall not apply to any tobacco product sold in connection with a delivery sale.

(B) Delivery sale. For purposes of subparagraph (A), the term "delivery sale" means any sale of a tobacco product to a consumer if—

(i) the consumer submits the order for such sale by means of a telephone or other method of voice transmission, mail, or the Internet or other online service, or the seller is otherwise not in the physical presence of the buyer when the request for purchase or order is made, or

(ii) the tobacco product is delivered by use of a common carrier, private delivery service, or the mail, or the seller is not in the physical presence of the buyer when the buyer obtains personal possession of the tobacco product.

[3]*(e)* **Applicability of section 6665.** The penalties imposed by subsections (b) and (c) shall be assessed, collected, and paid in the same manner as taxes, as provided in section 6665(a).

[4]*(f)* **Cross references.** For penalty for failure to make deposits or for overstatement of deposits, see section 6656.

[Endnote Code Sec. 5761]

Matter in *italics* in Code Sec. 5761(c), Code Sec. 5761(d), Code Sec. 5761(e), and Code Sec. 5761(f) was added by Secs. 401(f)(1) and (f)(2)(A) of the Tax Relief and Health Care Act of 2006, HR6111, d.o.e., which struck out:

1. "This subsection and section 5754 shall not apply to any person who relands or receives tobacco products in the quantity allowed entry free of tax and duty under subchapter IV of chapter 98 of the Harmonized Tariff Schedule of the United States. No quantity of tobacco products other than the quantity referred to in the preceding sentence may be relanded or received as a personal use quantity."
2. "added para. (d)
3. "(d)"
4. "(e)"

Effective Date (Sec. 401(g), HR6111, d.o.e.) effective for goods entered, or withdrawn from warehouse for consumption, on or after the 15th day after d.o.e..

[¶3061] Code Sec. 6015. Relief from joint and several liability on joint return.

* * * * * * * * * * * *

(e) Petition for review by tax court.

(1) In general. In the case of an individual against whom a deficiency has been asserted and who elects to have subsection (b) or (c) apply [1], *or in the case of an individual who requests equitable relief under subsection (f)*—

(A) In general. In addition to any other remedy provided by law, the individual may petition the Tax Court (and the Tax Court shall have jurisdiction) to determine the appropriate relief available to the individual under this section if such petition is filed—

(i) at any time after the earlier of—

(I) the date the Secretary mails, by certified or registered mail to the taxpayer's last known address, notice of the Secretary's final determination of relief available to the individual, or

(II) the date which is 6 months after the date such election is filed [2]*or request is made* with the Secretary, and

(ii) not later than the close of the 90th day after the date described in clause (i)(I).

(B) Restrictions applicable to collection of assessment.

(i) In general. Except as otherwise provided in section 6851 or 6861, no levy or proceeding in court shall be made, begun, or prosecuted against the individual making an election under subsection (b) or (c) [3]*or requesting equitable relief under subsection (f)* for collection of any assessment to which such election [4]*or request* relates until the close of the 90th day referred to in subparagraph (A)(ii), or, if a petition has been filed with the Tax Court under subparagraph (A), until the decision of the Tax Court has become final. Rules similar to the rules of section 7485 shall apply with respect to the collection of such assessment.

(ii) Authority to enjoin collection actions. Notwithstanding the provisions of section 7421(a), the beginning of such levy or proceeding during the time the prohibition under clause (i) is in force may be enjoined by a proceeding in the proper court, including the Tax Court. The Tax Court shall have no jurisdiction under this subparagraph to enjoin any action or proceeding unless a timely petition has been filed under subparagraph (A) and then only in respect of the amount of the assessment to which the election under subsection (b) or (c) relates [5]*or to which the request under subsection (f) relates.*

(2) Suspension of running of period of limitations. The running of the period of limitations in section 6502 on the collection of the assessment to which the petition under paragraph (1)(A) relates shall be suspended—

(A) for the period during which the Secretary is prohibited by paragraph (1)(B) from collecting by levy or a proceeding in court and for 60 days thereafter, and

(B) if a waiver under paragraph (5) is made, from the date the claim for relief was filed until 60 days after the waiver is filed with the Secretary.

(3) Limitation on Tax Court jurisdiction. If a suit for refund is begun by either individual filing the joint return pursuant to section 6532—

(A) The Tax Court shall lose jurisdiction of the individual's action under this section to whatever extent jurisdiction is acquired by the district court or the United States Court of Federal Claims over the taxable years that are the subject of the suit for refund, and

(B) the court acquiring jurisdiction shall have jurisdiction over the petition filed under this subsection.

(4) Notice to other spouse. The Tax Court shall establish rules which provide the individual filing a joint return but not making the election under subsection (b) or (c) [6]*or the request for equitable relief under subsection (f)* with adequate notice and an opportunity to become a party to a proceeding under either such subsection.

(5) Waiver. An individual who elects the application of subsection (b) or (c) [7]*or who requests equitable relief under subsection (f)* (and who agrees with the Secretary's determination of relief) may waive in writing at any time the restrictions in paragraph (1)(B) with respect to collection of the outstanding assessment (whether or not a notice of the Secretary's final determination of relief has been mailed).

* * * * * * * * * * * * *

(g) Credits and refunds.

(1) In general. Except as provided in paragraphs (2) and (3), notwithstanding any other law or rule of law (other than section 6511, 6512(b), 7121, or 7122), credit or refund shall be allowed or made to the extent attributable to the application of this section.

(2) Res judicata. In the case of any election under subsection (b) or (c) [8]*or of any request for equitable relief under subsection (f),* if a decision of a court in any prior proceeding for the same taxable year has become final, such decision shall be conclusive except with respect to the qualification of the individual for relief which was not an issue in such proceeding. The exception contained in the preceding sentence shall not apply if the court determines that the individual participated meaningfully in such prior proceeding.

(3) Credit and refund not allowed under subsection (c). No credit or refund shall be allowed as a result of an election under subsection (c).

(h) Regulations. The Secretary shall prescribe such regulations as are necessary to carry out the provisions of this section, including—

(1) regulations providing methods for allocation of items other than the methods under subsection (d)(3); and

(2) regulations providing the opportunity for an individual to have notice of, and an opportunity to participate in, any administrative proceeding with respect to an election made under subsection (b) or (c) [9]*or a request for equitable relief made under subsection (f)* by the other individual filing the joint return.

[For Analysis, see ¶ 1401.]

[Endnote Code Sec. 6015]

Matter in *italics* in Code Sec. 6015(e)(1), Code Sec. 6015(e)(1)(A)(i)(II), Code Sec. 6015(e)(1)(B)(i), Code Sec. 6015(e)(1)(B)(ii), Code Sec. 6015(e)(4), Code Sec. 6015(e)(5), Code Sec. 6015(g)(2) and Code Sec. 6015(h)(2) was added by Sec. 408(a), (b)(1), (b)(2)(A)-(B) and (b)(3)-(7) of the Tax Relief and Health Care Act of 2006, HR6111, d.o.e..

1. added matter in para. (e)(1)
2. added matter in subclause (e)(1)(A)(i)(II)
3. added matter in clause (e)(1)(B)(i)
4. added matter in clause (e)(1)(B)(i)
5. added matter in clause (e)(1)(B)(ii)
6. added matter in para. (e)(4)
7. added matter in para (e)(5)
8. added matter in para. (g)(2)
9. added matter in para. (h)(2)

Effective Date (Sec. 408(c), HR6111, d.o.e.) effective for liability for taxes arising or remaining unpaid on or after d.o.e..

[¶ 3062] Code Sec. 6039. [1]***Returns* required in connection with certain options.**

(a) [2]***Requirement of reporting.*** Every corporation—

(1) which in any calendar year transfers to any person a share of stock pursuant to such person's exercise of an incentive stock option, or

(2) which in any calendar year records (or has by its agent recorded) a transfer of the legal title of a share of stock acquired by the transferor pursuant to his exercise of an option described in section 423(c) (relating to special rule where option price is between 85 percent and 100 percent of value of stock), [3]*shall, for such calendar year, make a return at such time and in such manner, and setting forth such information, as the Secretary may by regulations prescribe.*

[4]***(b) Statements to be furnished to persons with respect to whom information is reported.*** *Every corporation making a return under subsection (a) shall furnish to each person whose name is set forth in such return a written statement setting forth such information as*

the Secretary may by regulations prescribe. The written statement required under the preceding sentence shall be furnished to such person on or before January 31 of the year following the calendar year for which the return under subsection (a) was made.

[5]*(c)* **Special rules.** For purposes of this section—

(1) Treatment by employer to be determinative. Any option which the corporation treats as an incentive stock option or an option granted under an employee stock purchase plan shall be deemed to be such an option.

(2) Subsection (a)(2) applies only to first transfer described therein. A statement is required by reason of a transfer described in subsection (a)(2) of a share only with respect to the first transfer of such share by the person who exercised the option.

(3) Identification of stock. Any corporation which transfers any share of stock pursuant to the exercise of any option described in subsection (a)(2) shall identify such stock in a manner adequate to carry out the purposes of this section.

[6]***(d)*** **Cross references.** For definition of—

(1) the term "incentive stock option" see section 422(b), and

(2) the term "employee stock purchase plan" see section 423(b).

[For Analysis, see ¶ 401. For Committee Reports, see ¶ 5053.]

[Endnote Code Sec. 6039]

Matter in *italics* in Code Sec. 6039, Code Sec. 6039(a), Code Sec. 6039(b), Code Sec. 6039(c) and Code Sec. 6039(d) was added by Sec. 403(a), (b), (c)(3) and (c)(4) of the Tax Relief and Health Care Act of 2006, HR6111, d.o.e., which struck out:

1. "Information"
2. "Furnishing of information"
3. "shall (on or before January 31 of the following calendar year) furnish to such person a written statement in such manner and setting forth such information as the Secretary may by regulations prescribe."
4. added subsec. (b)
5. "(b)"
6. "(c)"

Effective Date (Sec. 403(d), HR6111, d.o.e.) effective for calendar yrs. begin. after d.o.e..

[¶ 3063] Code Sec. 6050H. Returns relating to mortgage interest received in trade or business from individuals.

* * * * * * * * * * * *

[1]***(h) Returns relating to mortgage insurance premiums.***

(1) In general. *The Secretary may prescribe, by regulations, that any person who, in the course of a trade or business, receives from any individual premiums for mortgage insurance aggregating $600 or more for any calendar year, shall make a return with respect to each such individual. Such return shall be in such form, shall be made at such time, and shall contain such information as the Secretary may prescribe.*

(2) Statement to be furnished to individuals with respect to whom information is required. *Every person required to make a return under paragraph (1) shall furnish to each individual with respect to whom a return is made a written statement showing such information as the Secretary may prescribe. Such written statement shall be furnished on or before January 31 of the year following the calendar year for which the return under paragraph (1) was required to be made.*

(3) Special rules. *For purposes of this subsection—*

(A) rules similar to the rules of subsection (c) shall apply, and

(B) the term "mortgage insurance" means—

(i) mortgage insurance provided by the Veterans Administration, the Federal Housing Administration, or the Rural Housing Administration, and

(ii) private mortgage insurance (as defined by section 2 of the Homeowners Protection Act of 1998 (12 U.S.C. 4901), as in effect on the date of the enactment of this subsection).

[For Analysis, see ¶ 104. For Committee Reports, see ¶ 5070.]

[Endnote Code Sec. 6050H]

Code Sec. 6050H(h), in *italics*, was added by Sec. 419(c) of the Tax Relief and Health Care Act of 2006, HR6111, d.o.e., which struck out:

1. added subsec. (h)

Effective Date (Sec. 419(d), HR6111, d.o.e.) effective for amounts paid or accrued after 12/31/2006.

[¶ 3064] Code Sec. 6103. Confidentiality and disclosure of returns and return information.

* * * * * * * * * * * *

(b) Definitions. For purposes of this section—

* * * * * * * * * * * *

[1]***(5) State.***

(A) In general. The term "State" means—

(i) any of the 50 States, the District of Columbia, the Commonwealth of Puerto Rico, the Virgin Islands, the Canal Zone, Guam, American Samoa, and the Commonwealth of the Northern Mariana Islands,

(ii) for purposes of subsections (a)(2), (b)(4), (d)(1), (h)(4), and (p), any municipality—

(I) with a population in excess of 250,000 (as determined under the most recent decennial United States census data available),

(II) which imposes a tax on income or wages, and

(III) with which the Secretary (in his sole discretion) has entered into an agreement regarding disclosure, and

(iii) for purposes of subsections (a)(2), (b)(4), (d)(1), (h)(4), and (p), any governmental entity—

(I) which is formed and operated by a qualified group of municipalities, and

(II) with which the Secretary (in his sole discretion) has entered into an agreement regarding disclosure.

(B) Regional income tax agencies. For purposes of subparagraph (A)(iii)—

(i) Qualified group of municipalities. The term "qualified group of municipalities" means, with respect to any governmental entity, 2 or more municipalities—

(I) each of which imposes a tax on income or wages,

(II) each of which, under the authority of a State statute, administers the laws relating to the imposition of such taxes through such entity, and

(III) which collectively have a population in excess of 250,000 (as determined under the most recent decennial United States census data available).

(ii) References to state law, etc. For purposes of applying subparagraph (A)(iii) to the subsections referred to in such subparagraph, any reference in such subsections to State law, proceedings, or tax returns shall be treated as references to the law, proceedings, or tax returns, as the case may be, of the municipalities which form and operate the governmental entity referred to in such subparagraph.

(iii) Disclosure to contractors and other agents. Notwithstanding any other provision of this section, no return or return information shall be disclosed to any contractor or other agent of a governmental entity referred to in subparagraph (A)(iii) unless such entity, to the satisfaction of the Secretary—

(I) has requirements in effect which require each such contractor or other agent which would have access to returns or return information to provide safeguards (within the meaning of subsection (p)(4)) to protect the confidentiality of such returns or return information,

(II) agrees to conduct an on-site review every 3 years (or a mid-point review in the case of contracts or agreements of less than 3 years in duration) of each contractor or other agent to determine compliance with such requirements,

(III) submits the findings of the most recent review conducted under subclause (II) to the Secretary as part of the report required by subsection (p)(4)(E), and

(IV) certifies to the Secretary for the most recent annual period that such contractor or other agent is in compliance with all such requirements.

The certification required by subclause (IV) shall include the name and address of each contractor and other agent, a description of the contract or agreement with such contractor or other agent, and the duration of such contract or agreement. The requirements of this clause shall not apply to disclosures pursuant to subsection (n) for purposes of Federal tax administration and a rule similar to the rule of subsection (p)(8)(B) shall apply for purposes of this clause.

* * * * * * * * * * * *

(d) Disclosure to State tax officials and State and local law enforcement agencies.

* * * * * * * * * * * *

(5) Disclosure for combined employment tax reporting.

(A) In general. The Secretary may disclose taxpayer identity information and signatures to any agency, body, or commission of any State for the purpose of carrying out with such agency, body, or commission a combined Federal and State employment tax reporting program approved by the Secretary. Subsections (a)(2) and (p)(4) and sections 7213 and 7213A shall not apply with respect to disclosures or inspections made pursuant to this paragraph.

(B) Termination. The Secretary may not make any disclosure under this paragraph after December 31, [2]*2007.*

[3]***(6) Limitation on disclosure regarding regional income tax agencies treated as states.*** *For purposes of paragraph (1), inspection by or disclosure to an entity described in subsection (b)(5)(A)(iii) shall be for the purpose of, and only to the extent necessary in, the administration of the laws of the member municipalities in such entity relating to the imposition of a tax on income or wages. Such entity may not redisclose any return or return information received pursuant to paragraph (1) to any such member municipality.*

* * * * * * * * * * * *

(i) Disclosure to Federal officers or employees for administration of Federal laws not relating to tax administration.

(3) Disclosure of return information to apprise appropriate officials of criminal or terrorist activities or emergency circumstances.

* * * * * * * * * * * *

(C) Terrorist activities, etc.

(i) In general. Except as provided in paragraph (6), the Secretary may disclose in writing return information (other than taxpayer return information) that may be related to a terrorist incident, threat, or activity to the extent necessary to apprise the head of the appropriate Federal law enforcement agency responsible for investigating or responding to such terrorist incident, threat, or activity. The head of the agency may disclose such return information to officers and employees of such agency to the extent necessary to investigate or respond to such terrorist incident, threat, or activity.

(ii) Disclosure to the Department of Justice. Returns and taxpayer return information may also be disclosed to the Attorney General under clause (i) to the extent necessary for, and solely for use in preparing, an application under paragraph (7)(D).

(iii) Taxpayer identity. For purposes of this subparagraph, a taxpayer's identity shall not be treated as taxpayer return information.

(iv) Termination. No disclosure may be made under this subparagraph after December 31, [4]*2007.*

* * * * * * * * * * * *

(7) Disclosure upon request of information relating to terrorist activities, etc.

(A) Disclosure to law enforcement agencies.

(i) In general. Except as provided in paragraph (6), upon receipt by the Secretary of a written request which meets the requirements of clause (iii), the Secretary may disclose return information (other than taxpayer return information) to officers and employees of any Federal law enforcement agency who are personally and directly engaged in the response to or investigation of any terrorist incident, threat, or activity.

(ii) Disclosure to State and local law enforcement agencies. The head of any Federal law enforcement agency may disclose return information obtained under clause (i) to officers and employees of any State or local law enforcement agency but only if such agency is part of a team with the Federal law enforcement agency in such response or investigation and such information is disclosed only to officers and employees who are personally and directly engaged in such response or investigation.

(iii) Requirements. A request meets the requirements of this clause if—

(I) the request is made by the head of any Federal law enforcement agency (or his delegate) involved in the response to or investigation of any terrorist incident, threat, or activity, and

(II) the request sets forth the specific reason or reasons why such disclosure may be relevant to a terrorist incident, threat, or activity.

(iv) Limitation on use of information. Information disclosed under this subparagraph shall be solely for the use of the officers and employees to whom such information is disclosed in such response or investigation.

(v) Taxpayer identity. For purposes of this subparagraph, a taxpayer's identity shall not be treated as taxpayer return information.

(B) Disclosure to intelligence agencies.

(i) In general. Except as provided in paragraph (6), upon receipt by the Secretary of a written request which meets the requirements of clause (ii), the Secretary may disclose return information (other than taxpayer return information) to those officers and employees of the Department of Justice, the Department of the Treasury, and other Federal intelligence agencies who are personally and directly engaged in the collection or analysis of intelligence and counterintelligence information or investigation concerning any terrorist incident, threat, or activity. For purposes of the preceding sentence, the information disclosed under the preceding sentence shall be solely for the use of such officers and employees in such investigation, collection, or analysis.

(ii) Requirements. A request meets the requirements of this subparagraph if the request—

(I) is made by an individual described in clause (iii), and

(II) sets forth the specific reason or reasons why such disclosure may be relevant to a terrorist incident, threat, or activity.

(iii) Requesting individuals. An individual described in this subparagraph is an individual—

(I) who is an officer or employee of the Department of Justice or the Department of the Treasury who is appointed by the President with the advice and consent of the Senate or who is the Director of the United States Secret Service, and

(II) who is responsible for the collection and analysis of intelligence and counterintelligence information concerning any terrorist incident, threat, or activity.

(iv) Taxpayer identity. For purposes of this subparagraph, a taxpayer's identity shall not be treated as taxpayer return information.

(C) Disclosure under ex parte orders.

(i) In general. Except as provided in paragraph (6), any return or return information with respect to any specified taxable period or periods shall, pursuant to and upon the grant of an ex parte order by a Federal district court judge or magistrate under clause (ii), be open (but only to the extent necessary as provided in such order) to inspection by, or disclosure to, officers and employees of any Federal law enforcement agency or Federal intelligence agency who are personally and directly engaged in any investigation, response to, or analysis of intelligence and counterintelligence information concerning any terrorist incident, threat, or activity. Return or return information opened to inspection or disclosure pursuant to the preceding sentence shall be solely for the use of such officers and employees in the investigation, response, or analysis, and in any judicial, administrative, or grand jury proceedings, pertaining to such terrorist incident, threat, or activity.

(ii) Application for order. The Attorney General, the Deputy Attorney General, the Associate Attorney General, any Assistant Attorney General, or any United States attorney may authorize an application to a Federal district court judge or magistrate for the order referred to in clause (i). Upon such application, such judge or magistrate may grant such order if he determines on the basis of the facts submitted by the applicant that—

(I) there is reasonable cause to believe, based upon information believed to be reliable, that the return or return information may be relevant to a matter relating to such terrorist incident, threat, or activity, and

(II) the return or return information is sought exclusively for use in a Federal investigation, analysis, or proceeding concerning any terrorist incident, threat, or activity.

(D) Special rule for ex parte disclosure by the IRS.

(i) In general. Except as provided in paragraph (6), the Secretary may authorize an application to a Federal district court judge or magistrate for the order referred to in subparagraph (C)(i). Upon such application, such judge or magistrate may grant such order if he determines on the basis of the facts submitted by the applicant that the requirements of subparagraph (C)(ii)(I) are met.

(ii) Limitation on use of information. Information disclosed under clause (i)—

(I) may be disclosed only to the extent necessary to apprise the head of the appropriate Federal law enforcement agency responsible for investigating or responding to a terrorist incident, threat, or activity, and

(II) shall be solely for use in a Federal investigation, analysis, or proceeding concerning any terrorist incident, threat, or activity.

The head of such Federal agency may disclose such information to officers and employees of such agency to the extent necessary to investigate or respond to such terrorist incident, threat, or activity.

(E) Termination. No disclosure may be made under this paragraph after December 31, [5]*2007.*

* * * * * * * * * * * *

(l) Disclosure of returns and return information for purposes other than tax administration.

* * * * * * * * * * * *

(13) Disclosure of return information to carry out income contingent repayment of student loans.

(A) In general. The Secretary may, upon written request from the Secretary of Education, disclose to officers and employees of the Department of Education return information with respect to a taxpayer who has received an applicable student loan and whose loan repayment amounts are based in whole or in part on the taxpayer's income. Such return information shall be limited to—

(i) taxpayer identity information with respect to such taxpayer,

(ii) the filing status of such taxpayer, and

(iii) the adjusted gross income of such taxpayer.

(B) Restriction on use of disclosed information. Return information disclosed under subparagraph (A) may be used by officers and employees of the Department of Education only for the purposes of, and to the extent necessary in, establishing the appropriate income contingent repayment amount for an applicable student loan.

(C) Applicable student loan. For purposes of this paragraph, the term "applicable student loan" means—

(i) any loan made under the program authorized under part D of title IV of the Higher Education Act of 1965, and

(ii) any loan made under part B or E of title IV of the Higher Education Act of 1965 which is in default and has been assigned to the Department of Education.

(D) Termination. This paragraph shall not apply to any request made after December 31, [6]*2007.*

* * * * * * * * * * * *

[For Analysis, see ¶ 1403, ¶ 1404, ¶ 1405, and ¶ 1406. For Committee Reports, see ¶ 5026, ¶ 5027, ¶ 5028, and ¶ 5072.]

[Endnote Code Sec. 6103]

Matter in *italics* in Code Sec. 6103(b)(5) was added by Sec. 421(a) of the Tax Relief and Health Care Act of 2006, HR6111, d.o.e., which struck out:

1. "(5) State. The term 'State' means—

"(A) any of the 50 States, the District of Columbia, the Commonwealth of Puerto Rico, the Virgin Islands, the Canal Zone, Guam, American Samoa, and the Commonwealth of the Northern Mariana Islands, and

"(B) for purposes of subsections (a)(2), (b)(4), (d)(1), (h)(4), and (p) any municipality—

"(i) with a population in excess of 250,000 (as determined under the most recent decennial United States census data available),

"(ii) which imposes a tax on income or wages, and

"(iii) with which the Secretary (in his sole discretion) has entered into an agreement regarding disclosure."

Effective Date (Sec. 421(c), HR6111, d.o.e.) effective for disclosures made after 12/31/2006.

Matter in *italics* in Code Sec. 6103(d)(5)(B) was added by Sec. 122(a)(1), HR6111, d.o.e., which struck out:

2. "2006"

Effective Date (Sec. 122(a)(2), HR6111, d.o.e.) effective for disclosures made after 12/31/2006.

Matter in *italics* in Code Sec. 6103(d)(6) was added by Sec. 421(b), HR6111, d.o.e.

3. added para. (d)(6).

Effective Date (Sec. 421(c), HR6111, d.o.e.) effective for disclosures made after 12/31/2006.

Matter in *italics* in Code Sec. 6103(i)(3)(C)(iv) and Code Sec. 6103(i)(7)(E) was added by Sec. 122(b)(1), HR6111, d.o.e., which struck out:

4. "2006"

5. "2006"

Effective Date (Sec. 122(b)(2), HR6111, d.o.e.) effective for disclosures made after 12/31/2006.

Matter in *italics* in Code Sec. 6103(l)(13)(D) was added by Sec. 122(c)(1), HR6111, d.o.e., which struck out:

6. "2006"

Effective Date (Sec. 122(c)(2), HR6111, d.o.e.) effective for requests made after 12/31/2006.

[¶ 3065] Code Sec. 6211. Definition of a deficiency.

* * * * * * * * * * * *

(b) Rules for application of subsection (a). For purposes of this section—

(1) The tax imposed by Subtitle A and the tax shown on the return shall both be determined without regard to payments on account of estimated tax, without regard to the credit under section 31, without regard to the credit under section 33, and without regard to any credits resulting from the collection of amounts assessed under section 6851 or 6852 (relating to termination assessments).

(2) The term "rebate" means so much of an abatement, credit, refund, or other repayment, as was made on the ground that the tax imposed by subtitle A or B or chapter 41, 42, 43, or 44 was less than the excess of the amount specified in subsection (a)(1) over the rebates previously made.

(3) The computation by the Secretary, pursuant to section 6014, of the tax imposed by chapter 1 shall be considered as having been made by the taxpayer and the tax so computed considered as shown by the taxpayer upon his return.

(4) For purposes of subsection (a)—

(A) any excess of the sum of the credits allowable under sections 24(d), 32, [1]*34, and 53(e)* over the tax imposed by subtitle A (determined without regard to such credits), and

(B) any excess of the sum of such credits as shown by the taxpayer on his return over the amount shown as the tax by the taxpayer on such return (determined without regard to such credits),

shall be taken into account as negative amounts of tax.

* * * * * * * * * * * * *

[For Analysis, see ¶ 1202. For Committee Reports, see ¶ 5053.]

[Endnote Code Sec. 6211]

Matter in *italics* in Code Sec. 6211(b)(4)(A) was added by Sec. 402(b)(1) of the Tax Relief and Health Care Act of 2006, HR6111, d.o.e., which struck out:

1. "and 34"

Effective Date (Sec. 402(c), HR6111, d.o.e.) effective for tax. yrs. begin. after d.o.e..

[¶ 3066] Code Sec. 6320. Notice and opportunity for hearing upon filing of notice of lien.

* * * * * * * * * * * * *

(b) Right to fair hearing.

(1) In general. If the person requests a hearing [1]*in writing under subsection (a)(3)(B) and states the grounds for the requested hearing*, such hearing shall be held by the Internal Revenue Service Office of Appeals.

* * * * * * * * * * * * *

(c) Conduct of hearing; review; suspensions. For purposes of this section, subsections (c), (d) (other than paragraph (2)(B) thereof), [2]*(e), and (g)* of section 6330 shall apply.

[For Analysis, see ¶ 1408. For Committee Reports, see ¶ 5058.]

[Endnote Code Sec. 6320]

Matter in *italics* in Code Sec. 6320(b)(1) and Code Sec. 6320(c) was added by Secs. 407(c)(1) and (2) of Tax Relief and Health Care Act of 2006, HR6111, d.o.e., which struck out:

1. "under subsection (a)(3)(B)"
2. "and (e)"

Effective Date (Sec. 407(f), HR6111, d.o.e.) effective for submissions made and issues raised after the date on which the Secretary first prescribes a list under Code Sec. 6702(c), as amended by Sec. 407(a), HR6111.

[¶ 3067] Code Sec. 6330. Notice and opportunity for hearing before levy.

* * * * * * * * * * * * *

(b) Right to fair hearing.

(1) In general. If the person requests a hearing [1]*in writing under subsection (a)(3)(B) and states the grounds for the requested hearing*, such hearing shall be held by the Internal Revenue Service Office of Appeals.

* * * * * * * * * * * * *

(c) Matters considered at hearing. In the case of any hearing conducted under this section—

* * * * * * * * * * * * *

(4) Certain issues precluded. An issue may not be raised at the hearing if—

(A)

[2]*(i)* the issue was raised and considered at a previous hearing under section 6320 or in any other previous administrative or judicial proceeding; and

[3]*(ii)* the person seeking to raise the issue participated meaningfully in such hearing or proceeding[4]*; or*

[5]*(B) the issue meets the requirement of clause (i) or (ii) of section 6702(b)(2)(A).*

This paragraph shall not apply to any issue with respect to which subsection (d)(2)(B) applies.

* * * * * * * * * * * *

[6]***(g) Frivolous requests for hearing, etc.*** *Notwithstanding any other provision of this section, if the Secretary determines that any portion of a request for a hearing under this section or section 6320 meets the requirement of clause (i) or (ii) of section 6702(b)(2)(A), then the Secretary may treat such portion as if it were never submitted and such portion shall not be subject to any further administrative or judicial review.*

[For Analysis, see ¶ 1408. For Committee Reports, see ¶ 5058.]

[Endnote Code Sec. 6330]

Matter in *italics* in Code Sec. 6330(b)(1), Code Sec. 6330(c)(4)(A)(i), Code Sec. 6330(c)(4)(A)(ii), Code Sec. 6330(c)(4)(B), and Code Sec. 6330(g) was added by Sec. 407(b)(1), (b)(2) and (b)(3) of the Tax Relief and Health Care Act of 2006, d.o.e., which struck out:

1. "under subsection (a)(3)(B)"
2. "(A)"
3. "(B)"
4. "."
5. added subpara. (c)(4)(B)
6. added subsec. (g)

Effective Date (Sec. 407(f), HR6111, d.o.e.) effective for submissions made and issues raised after the date on which the Secretary first prescribes a list under Code Sec. 6702(c), as amended by Sec. 407(a) of this Act.

[¶ 3068] Code Sec. 6427. Fuels not used for taxable purposes.

* * * * * * * * * * * *

(i) Time for filing claims; period covered.

* * * * * * * * * * * *

(4) Special rule for vendor refunds.

(A) In general. A claim may be filed under subsections (b)(4) and [1]*paragraph (4)(C), or (5),* of subsection (l) by any person with respect to fuel sold by such person for any period—

(i) for which $200 or more ($100 or more in the case of kerosene) is payable under [2]*paragraph (4)(C), or (5),* of subsection (l), and

(ii) which is not less than 1 week.

Notwithstanding subsection (l)(1), paragraph (3)(B) shall apply to claims filed under subsections (b)(4), [3]*(l)(4)(C)(ii), and (l)(5).*

(B) Time for filing claim. No claim filed under this paragraph shall be allowed unless filed on or before the last day of the first quarter following the earliest quarter included in the claim.

* * * * * * * * * * * *

(l) Nontaxable uses of diesel fuel, and kerosene.

(1) In general. Except as otherwise provided in this subsection and in subsection (k), if any diesel fuel or kerosene on which tax has been imposed by section 4041 or 4081 is used by any person in a nontaxable use, the Secretary shall pay (without interest) to the ultimate purchaser of such fuel an amount equal to the aggregate amount of tax imposed on such fuel under section 4041 or 4081, as the case may be, reduced by any payment made to the ultimate vendor under [4]*paragraph (4)(C)(i).*

(2) Nontaxable use. For purposes of this subsection, the term "nontaxable use" means any use which is exempt from the tax imposed by section 4041(a)(1) other than by reason of a prior imposition of tax.

(3) Refund of certain taxes on fuel used in diesel-powered trains. For purposes of this subsection, the term "nontaxable use" includes fuel used in a diesel-powered train. The preceding sentence shall not apply with respect to—

(A) the Leaking Underground Storage Tank Trust Fund financing rate under sections 4041 and 4081, and

(B) so much of the rate specified in section 4081(a)(2)(A) as does not exceed the rate applicable under section 4041(a)(1)(C)(ii).

The preceding sentence shall not apply in the case of fuel sold for exclusive use by a State or any political subdivision thereof.

[5]***(4) Refunds for kerosene used in aviation.***

(A) Kerosene used in commercial aviation. In the case of kerosene used in commercial aviation (as defined in section 4083(b)) (other than supplies for vessels or aircraft within the meaning of section 4221(d)(3)), paragraph (1) shall not apply to so much of the tax imposed by section 4041 or 4081, as the case may be, as is attributable to—

(i) the Leaking Underground Storage Tank Trust Fund financing rate imposed by such section, and

(ii) so much of the rate of tax specified in section 4041(c) or 4081(a)(2)(A)(iii), as the case may be, as does not exceed 4.3 cents per gallon.

(B) Kerosene used in noncommercial aviation. In the case of kerosene used in aviation that is not commercial aviation (as so defined) (other than any use which is exempt from the tax imposed by section 4041(c) other than by reason of a prior imposition of tax), paragraph (1) shall not apply to—

(i) any tax imposed by subsection (c) or (d)(2) of section 4041, and

(ii) so much of the tax imposed by section 4081 as is attributable to—

(I) the Leaking Underground Storage Tank Trust Fund financing rate imposed by such section, and

(II) so much of the rate of tax specified in section 4081(a)(2)(A)(iii) as does not exceed the rate specified in section 4081(a)(2)(C)(ii).

(C) Payments to ultimate, registered vendor.

(i) In general. With respect to any kerosene used in aviation (other than kerosene described in clause (ii) or kerosene to which paragraph (5) applies), if the ultimate purchaser of such kerosene waives (at such time and in such form and manner as the Secretary shall prescribe) the right to payment under paragraph (1) and assigns such right to the ultimate vendor, then the Secretary shall pay the amount which would be paid under paragraph (1) to such ultimate vendor, but only if such ultimate vendor—

(I) is registered under section 4101, and

(II) meets the requirements of subparagraph (A), (B), or (D) of section 6416(a)(1).

(ii) Payments for kerosene used in noncommercial aviation. The amount which would be paid under paragraph (1) with respect to any kerosene to which subparagraph (B) applies shall be paid only to the ultimate vendor of such kerosene. A payment shall be made to such vendor if such vendor—

(I) is registered under section 4101, and

(II) meets the requirements of subparagraph (A), (B), or (D) of section 6416(a)(1).

[6]***(5)*** **Registered vendors to administer claims for refund of diesel fuel or kerosene sold to state and local governments.**

(A) In general. Paragraph (1) shall not apply to diesel fuel or kerosene used by a State of local government.

(B) Sales of kerosene not for use in motor fuel. Paragraph (1) shall not apply to kerosene (other than kerosene used in aviation) sold by a vendor—

(i) for any use if such sale is from a pump which (as determined under regulations prescribed by the Secretary) is not suitable for use in fueling any diesel-powered highway vehicle or train, or

(ii) to the extent provided by the Secretary, for blending with heating oil to be used during periods of extreme or unseasonable cold.

(C) Payment to ultimate, registered, vendor. Except as provided in subparagraph (D), the amount which would (but for subparagraph (A) or (B)) have been paid under paragraph (1) with respect to any fuel shall be paid to the ultimate vendor of such fuel, if such vendor—

(i) is registered under section 4101, and

(ii) meets the requirements of subparagraph (A), (B), or (D) of section 6416(a)(1).

(D) Credit card issuer. For purposes of this paragraph, if the purchase of any fuel described in subparagraph (A) (determined without regard to the registration status of the ultimate vendor) is made by means of a credit card issued to the ultimate purchaser, the Secretary shall pay to the person extending the credit to the ultimate purchaser the amount which would have been paid under paragraph (1) (but for subparagraph (A)), but only if such person meets the requirements of clauses (i), (ii), and (iii) of section 6416(a)(4)(B). If such clause (i), (ii), or (iii) is not met by such person extending the credit to the ultimate purchaser, then such person shall collect an amount equal to the tax from the ultimate purchaser and only such ultimate purchaser may claim such amount.

* * * * * * * * * * * *

[For Analysis, see ¶ 1502. For Committee Reports, see ¶ 5071.]

[Endnote Code Sec. 6427]

Matter in *italics* in Code Sec. 6427(i)(4)(A), Code Sec. 6427(l)(1), and Code Sec. 6427(l)(5) was added by Sec. 420(a), (b)(1), (b)(3)(A)-(B), and (b)(4) of the Tax Relief and Health Care Act of 2006, HR6111, d.o.e., which struck out:

1. "paragraph (4)(B), (5), or (6)"
2. "paragraph (4)(B), (5), or (6)"
3. "(l)(5), and (l)(6)"
4. "paragraph (4)(B)"
5. "(4) Refunds for kerosene used in commercial aviation.

"(A) No refund of certain taxes on fuel used in commercial aviation. In the case of kerosene used in commercial aviation (as defined in section 4083(b)) (other than supplies for vessels or aircraft within the meaning of section 4221(d)(3)), paragraph (1) shall not apply to so much of the tax imposed by section 4081 as is attributable to

"(i) the Leaking Underground Storage Tank Trust Fund financing rate imposed by such section, and

"(ii) so much of the rate of tax specified in section 4081(a)(2)(iii) as does not exceed 4.3 cents per gallon.

"(B) Payment to ultimate, registered vendor. With respect to kerosene used in commercial aviation as described in subparagraph (A) , if the ultimate purchaser of such kerosene waives (at such time and in such form and manner as the Secretary shall prescribe) the right to payment under paragraph (1) and assigns such right to the ultimate vendor, then the Secretary shall pay the amount which would be paid under paragraph

"(1) to such ultimate vendor, but only if such ultimate vendor

"(i) is registered under section 4101 , and

"(ii) meets the requirements of subparagraph (A), (B), or (D) of section 6416(a)(1) ."

"(5) Refunds for kerosene used in noncommercial aviation.

"(A) In general. In the case of kerosene used in aviation not described in paragraph (4)(A) (other than any use which is exempt from the tax imposed by section 4041(c) other than by reason of a prior imposition of tax), paragraph (1) shall not apply to so much of the tax imposed by section 4081 as is attributable to

"(i) the Leaking Underground Storage Tank Trust Fund financing rate imposed by such section, and

"(ii) so much of the rate of tax specified in section 4081(a)(2)(A)(iii) as does not exceed the rate specified in section 4081(a)(2)(C)(ii).

"(B) Payment to ultimate, registered vendor. The amount which would be paid under paragraph (1) with respect to any kerosene shall be paid only to the ultimate vendor of such kerosene. A payment shall be made to such vendor if such vendor

"(i)is registered under section 4101, and

"(ii) meets the requirements of subparagraph (A)), (B) , or (D) of section 6416(a)(1)."

6. "(6)"

Effective Date (Sec. 420(c), HR6111, d.o.e., effective for kerosene sold after 9/30/2005, except as provided in Sec. 420(c)(2), HR6111, which reads as follows:

"(2) Special rule for pending claims. In the case of kerosene sold for use in aviation (other than kerosene to which section 6427(l)(4)(C)(ii) of the Internal Revenue Code of 1986 (as added by subsection (a)) applies or kerosene to which section 6427(l)(5) of such Code (as redesignated by subsection (b)) applies) after September 30, 2005, and before the date of the enactment of this Act, the ultimate purchaser shall be treated as having waived the right to payment under section 6427(l)(1) of such Code and as having assigned such right to the ultimate vendor if such ultimate vendor has met the requirements of subparagraph (A), (B), or (D) of section 6416(a)(1) of such Code."

[¶ 3069] ***Code Sec.[1] 6702.*** ***Frivolous tax submissions.***

(a) Civil penalty for frivolous tax returns. *A person shall pay a penalty of $5,000 if—*

(1) such person files what purports to be a return of a tax imposed by this title but which—

(A) does not contain information on which the substantial correctness of the self-assessment may be judged, or

(B) contains information that on its face indicates that the self-assessment is substantially incorrect, and

(2) the conduct referred to in paragraph (1)—

(A) is based on a position which the Secretary has identified as frivolous under subsection (c), or

(B) reflects a desire to delay or impede the administration of Federal tax laws.

(b) Civil penalty for specified frivolous submissions.

(1) Imposition of penalty. *Except as provided in paragraph (3), any person who submits a specified frivolous submission shall pay a penalty of $5,000.*

(2) Specified frivolous submission. *For purposes of this section—*

(A) Specified Frivolous Submission. The term "specified frivolous submission" means a specified submission if any portion of such submission—

(i) is based on a position which the Secretary has identified as frivolous under subsection (c), or

(ii) reflects a desire to delay or impede the administration of Federal tax laws.

(B) Specified submission. The term "specified submission" means—

(i) a request for a hearing under—

(I) section 6320 (relating to notice and opportunity for hearing upon filing of notice of lien), or

(II) section 6330 (relating to notice and opportunity for hearing before levy), and

(ii) an application under—

(I) section 6159 (relating to agreements for payment of tax liability in installments),

(II) section 7122 (relating to compromises), or

(III) section 7811 (relating to taxpayer assistance orders).

(3) Opportunity to withdraw submission. *If the Secretary provides a person with notice that a submission is a specified frivolous submission and such person withdraws such submission within 30 days after such notice, the penalty imposed under paragraph (1) shall not apply with respect to such submission.*

(c) Listing of frivolous positions. *The Secretary shall prescribe (and periodically revise) a list of positions which the Secretary has identified as being frivolous for purposes of this subsection. The Secretary shall not include in such list any position that the Secretary determines meets the requirement of section 6662(d)(2)(B)(ii)(II).*

(d) Reduction of Penalty. *The Secretary may reduce the amount of any penalty imposed under this section if the Secretary determines that such reduction would promote compliance with and administration of the Federal tax laws.*

(e) Penalties in addition to other penalties. *The penalties imposed by this section shall be in addition to any other penalty provided by law.*

[For Analysis, see ¶ 1407. For Committee Reports, see ¶ 5058.]

[Endnote Code Sec. 6702]

Matter in *italics* in Code Sec. 6702 was added by Sec. 407(a) of the Tax Relief and Health Care Act of 2006, HR6111, d.o.e., which struck out:

1. "Sec. 6702. Frivolous income tax return.

"(a) Civil penalty. If—
"(1) any individual files what purports to be a return of the tax imposed by subtitle A but which—
"(A) does not contain information on which the substantial correctness of the self-assessment may be judged, or
"(B) contains information that on its face indicates that the self-assessment is substantially incorrect; and
"(2) the conduct referred to in paragraph (1) is due to—
"(A) a position which is frivolous, or
"(B) a desire (which appears on the purported return) to delay or impede the administration of Federal income tax laws,
then such individual shall pay a penalty of $500.
"(b) Penalty in addition to other penalties. The penalty imposed by subsection (a) shall be in addition to any other penalty provided by law."
Effective Date (Sec. 407(f), HR6111, d.o.e.) effective for submissions made and issues raised after the date on which the Secretary first prescribes a list under Code Sec. 6702(c), as amended by Sec. 407(a), HR6111.

[¶ 3070] Code Sec. 6724. Waiver; definitions and special rules.

* * * * * * * * * * * * *

(d) Definitions. For purposes of this part—

(1) Information return. The term "information return" means—

* * * * * * * * * * * * *

(B) any return required by—

(i) section 6041A(a) or (b) (relating to returns of direct sellers),

(ii) section 6043A(a) (relating to returns relating to taxable mergers and acquisitions),

(iii) section 6045(a) or (d) (relating to returns of brokers),

(iv) section 6050H(a) (relating to mortgage interest received in trade or business from individuals),

(v) section 6050I(a) or (g)(1) (relating to cash received in trade or business, etc.),

(vi) section 6050J(a) (relating to foreclosures and abandonments of security),

(vii) section 6050K(a) (relating to exchanges of certain partnership interests),

(viii) section 6050L(a) (relating to returns relating to certain dispositions of donated property),

(ix) section 6050P (relating to returns relating to the cancellation of indebtedness by certain financial entities),

(x) section 6050Q (relating to certain long-term care benefits),

(xi) section 6050S (relating to returns relating to payments for qualified tuition and related expenses),

(xii) section 6050T (relating to returns relating to credit for health insurance costs of eligible individuals),

(xiii) section 6052(a) (relating to reporting payment of wages in the form of group [term] life insurance),

(xiv) section 6053(c)(1) (relating to reporting with respect to certain tips),

(xv) subsection (b) or (e) of section 1060 (relating to reporting requirements of transferors and transferees in certain asset acquisitions),

(xvi) section 4101(d) (relating to information reporting with respect to fuels taxes),

(xvii) subparagraph (C) of section 338(h)(10) (relating to information required to be furnished to the Secretary in case of elective recognition of gain or loss), [1]

(xviii) section 264(f)(5)(A)(iv) (relating to reporting with respect to certain life insurance and annuity contracts), [2]*or*

[3]*(xix) section 6039(a) (relating to returns required with respect to certain options), and*

(2) Payee statement. The term "payee statement" means any statement required to be furnished under—

(A) section 6031(b) or (c), 6034A, or 6037(b) (relating to statements furnished by certain pass-thru entities),

(B) [4]*section 6039(b)* (relating to information required in connection with certain options),

(C) section 6041(d) (relating to information at source),

(D) section 6041A(e) (relating to returns regarding payments of remuneration for services and direct sales),

(E) section 6042(c) (relating to returns regarding payments of dividends and corporate earnings and profits),

(F) subsections (b) and (d) of section 6043A (relating to returns relating to taxable mergers and acquisitions).[,]

(G) section 6044(e) (relating to returns regarding payments of patronage dividends),

(H) section 6045(b) or (d) (relating to returns of brokers),

(I) section 6049(c) (relating to returns regarding payments of interest),

(J) section 6050A(b) (relating to reporting requirements of certain fishing boat operators),

(K) section 6050H(d) (relating to returns relating to mortgage interest received in trade or business from individuals),

(L) section 6050I(e) or paragraph (4) or (5) of section 6050I(g) (relating to cash received in trade or business, etc.),

(M) section 6050J(e) (relating to returns relating to foreclosures and abandonments of security),

(N) section 6050K(b) (relating to returns relating to exchanges of certain partnership interests),

(O) section 6050L(c) (relating to returns relating to certain dispositions of donated property),

(P) section 6050N(b) (relating to returns regarding payments of royalties),

(Q) section 6050P(d) (relating to returns relating to the cancellation of indebtedness by certain financial entities),

(R) section 6050Q(b) (relating to certain long-term care benefits),

(S) section 6050R(c) (relating to returns relating to certain purchases of fish),

(T) section 6051 (relating to receipts for employees),

(U) section 6052(b) (relating to returns regarding payment of wages in the form of group-term life insurance),

(V) section 6053(b) or (c) (relating to reports of tips),

(W) section 6048(b)(1)(B) (relating to foreign trust reporting requirements),

(X) section 408(i)(relating to reports with respect to individual retirement plans) to any person other than the Secretary with respect to the amount of payments made to such person,

(Y) section 6047(d) (relating to reports by plan administrators) to any person other than the Secretary with respect to the amount of payments made to such person,

(Z) section 6050S (relating to returns relating to qualified tuition and related expenses),

[For Analysis, see ¶ 401. For Committee Reports, see ¶ 5053.]

[Endnote Code Sec. 6724]

Matter in *italics* in Code Sec. 6724(d)(1)(B)(xvii), Code Sec. 6724(d)(1)(B)(xviii), Code Sec. 6724(d)(1)(B)(xix), and Code Sec. 6724(d)(2)(B) was added by Sec. 403(c)(1) and (2) of the Tax Relief and Health Care Act of 2006, d.o.e., which struck out:

1. "or"
2. "and"
3. added clause (d)(1)(B)(xix)
4. "section 6039(a)"

Effective Date (Sec. 403(d), HR6111, d.o.e.) effective for calendar yrs. begin. after d.o.e..

[¶ 3071] Code Sec. 7122. Compromises.

* * * * * * * * * * * *

(f) Deemed acceptance of offer not rejected within certain period. Any offer-in-compromise submitted under this section shall be deemed to be accepted by the Secretary if such offer is not rejected by the Secretary before the date which is 24 months after the date of the submission of such offer. For purposes of the preceding sentence, any period during which any tax liability which is the subject of such offer-in-compromise is in dispute in any judicial proceeding shall not be taken into account in determining the expiration of the 24-month period.

[1]*(f [(g)]) **Frivolous submissions, etc.** Notwithstanding any other provision of this section, if the Secretary determines that any portion of an application for an offer-in-compromise or installment agreement submitted under this section or section 6159 meets the requirement of clause (i) or (ii) of section 6702(b)(2)(A), then the Secretary may treat such portion as if it were never submitted and such portion shall not be subject to any further administrative or judicial review.*

[For Analysis, see ¶ 1408. For Committee Reports, see ¶ 5058.]

[Endnote Code Sec. 7122]

Code Sec. 7122(f) [sic (g)], in *italics,* was added by Sec. 407(d) of the Tax Relief and Health Care Act of 2006, HR6111, d.o.e..

1. added subsec. (f) [sic (g)]

Effective Date (Sec. 407(f), HR6111, d.o.e.) effective for submissions made and issues raised after the date on which the Secretary first prescribes a list under Code Sec. 6702(c), as amended by Sec. 407(a), HR6111.

[¶ 3072] Code Sec. 7443A. Special trial judges.

* * * * * * * * * * * *

(b) Proceedings which may be assigned to special trial judges. The chief judge may assign—

(1) any declaratory judgment proceeding,

(2) any proceeding under section 7463,

(3) any proceeding where neither the amount of the deficiency placed in dispute (within the meaning of section 7463) nor the amount of any claimed overpayment exceeds $50,000,

(4) any proceeding under section 6320 or 6330,

(5) any proceeding under section 7436(c), [1]

[2]***(6)** any proceeding under section 7623(b)(4), and*

[3]***(7)*** any other proceeding which the chief judge may designate, to be heard by the special trial judges of the court.

(c) Authority to make court decision. The court may authorize a special trial judge to make the decision of the court with respect to any proceeding described in paragraph (1), (2), (3), (4), [4]*(5), or (6)* of subsection (b), subject to such conditions and review as the court may provide.

* * * * * * * * * * * *

[For Analysis, see ¶ 1409. For Committee Reports, see ¶ 5057.]

[Endnote Code Sec. 7443A]

Matter in *italics* in Code Sec. 7443A(b)(5), Code Sec. 7443A(b)(6), Code Sec. 7443A(b)(7), and Code Sec. 7443A(c) was added by Sec. 406(a)(2)(A) and (B) of the Tax Relief and Health Care Act of 2006, HR6111, d.o.e., which struck out:

1. "and"
2. added para. (b)(6)
3. "(6)"
4. "or (5)"

Effective Date (Sec. 406(d), HR6111, d.o.e.) effective for information provided on or after d.o.e..

[¶ 3073] Code Sec. 7608. Authority of internal revenue enforcement officers.

* * * * * * * * * * * *

(c) Rules relating to undercover operations.

* * * * * * * * * * * *

(6) Application of section. The provisions of this subsection—

(A) shall apply after November 17, 1988, and before January 1, 1990, and

(B) shall apply after the date of the enactment of this paragraph and before January 1, [1]*2008.*

All amounts expended pursuant to this subsection during the period described in subparagraph (B) shall be recovered to the extent possible, and deposited in the Treasury of the United States as miscellaneous receipts, before January 1, [2]*2008.*

[For Analysis, see ¶ 1412. For Committee Reports, see ¶ 5025.]

[Endnote Code Sec. 7608]

Matter in *italics* in Code Sec. 7608(c)(6) was added by Sec. 121 of the Tax Relief and Health Care Act of 2006, HR6111, d.o.e., which struck out:

1. "2007"
2. "2007"

Effective Date Enacted d.o.e..

[¶ 3074] Code Sec. 7623. Expenses of detection of underpayments and fraud, etc.

[1]***(a) In general.*** *The Secretary* , under regulations prescribed by the Secretary, is authorized to pay such sums as he deems necessary for—

(1) detecting underpayments of tax, [2]*or*

(2) detecting and bringing to trial and punishment persons guilty of violating the internal revenue laws or conniving at the same,

in cases where such expenses are not otherwise provided for by law. Any amount payable under the preceding sentence shall be paid from the proceeds of amounts [3] collected by reason of the information provided, and any amount so collected shall be available for such payments.

[4]***(b) Awards to Whistleblowers.***

(1) In general. *If the Secretary proceeds with any administrative or judicial action described in subsection (a) based on information brought to the Secretary's attention by an individual, such individual shall, subject to paragraph (2), receive as an award at least 15 percent but not more than 30 percent of the collected proceeds (including penalties, interest, additions to tax, and additional amounts) resulting from the action (including any related actions) or from any settlement in response to such action. The determination of the amount of such award by the Whistleblower Office shall depend upon the extent to which the individual substantially contributed to such action.*

(2) Award in case of less substantial contribution.

(A) In general. In the event the action described in paragraph (1) is one which the Whistleblower Office determines to be based principally on disclosures of specific allegations (other than information provided by the individual described in paragraph (1)) resulting from a judicial or administrative hearing, from a governmental report, hearing, audit, or investigation, or from the news media, the Whistleblower Office may award such sums as it considers appropriate, but in no case more than 10 percent of the collected proceeds (including penalties, interest, additions to tax, and additional amounts) resulting from the action (including any related actions) or from any settlement in re-

sponse to such action, taking into account the significance of the individual's information and the role of such individual and any legal representative of such individual in contributing to such action.

(B) Nonapplication of paragraph where individual is original source of information. Subparagraph (A) shall not apply if the information resulting in the initiation of the action described in paragraph (1) was originally provided by the individual described in paragraph (1).

(3) Reduction in or denial of award. *If the Whistleblower Office determines that the claim for an award under paragraph (1) or (2) is brought by an individual who planned and initiated the actions that led to the underpayment of tax or actions described in subsection (a)(2), then the Whistleblower Office may appropriately reduce such award. If such individual is convicted of criminal conduct arising from the role described in the preceding sentence, the Whistleblower Office shall deny any award.*

(4) Appeal of award determination. *Any determination regarding an award under paragraph (1), (2), or (3) may, within 30 days of such determination, be appealed to the Tax Court (and the Tax Court shall have jurisdiction with respect to such matter).*

(5) Application of this subsection. *This subsection shall apply with respect to any action—*

(A) against any taxpayer, but in the case of any individual, only if such individual's gross income exceeds $200,000 for any taxable year subject to such action, and

(B) if the tax, penalties, interest, additions to tax, and additional amounts in dispute exceed $2,000,000.

(6) Additional rules.

(A) No contract necessary. No contract with the Internal Revenue Service is necessary for any individual to receive an award under this subsection.

(B) Representation. Any individual described in paragraph (1) or (2) may be represented by counsel.

(C) Submission of information. No award may be made under this subsection based on information submitted to the Secretary unless such information is submitted under penalty of perjury.

[For Analysis, see ¶ 1409 and ¶ 1411. For Committee Reports, see ¶ 5057.]

[Endnote Code Sec. 7623]

Matter in *italics*, in Code Sec. 7623 was added by Sec. 406(a)(1)(A)-(D) of the Tax Relief and Health Care Act of 2006, HR6111, d.o.e., which struck out:

1. "The Secretary"
2. "and"
3. "(other than interest)"
4. added subsec. (b)

Effective Date (Sec. 406(d), HR6111, d.o.e.) effective for information provided on or after d.o.e..

[¶ 3075] Code Sec. 7652. Shipments to the United States.

* * * * * * * * * * * *

(f) Limitation on cover over of tax on distilled spirits. For purposes of this section, with respect to taxes imposed under section 5001 or this section on distilled spirits, the amount covered into the treasuries of Puerto Rico and the Virgin Islands shall not exceed the lesser of the rate of—

(1) $10.50 ($13.25 in the case of distilled spirits brought into the United States after June 30, 1999, and before January 1, [1]*2008*), or

(2) the tax imposed under section 5001(a)(1), on each proof gallon.

* * * * * * * * * * * *

[Endnote Code Sec. 7652]

Matter in *italics* in Code Sec. 7652(f)(1) was added by Sec. 114(a) of the Tax Relief and Health Care Act of 2006, HR6111, d.o.e., which struck out:

1. "2006"

Effective Date (Sec. 114(b), HR6111, d.o.e.) effective for articles brought into the U.S. after 12/31/2005.

[¶ 3076] Code Sec. 7872. Treatment of loans with below-market interest rates.

* * * * * * * * * * * *

(h) Exception for loans to qualified continuing care facilities.

(1) In general. This section shall not apply for any calendar year to any below-market loan owed by a facility which on the last day of such year is a qualified continuing care facility, if such loan was made pursuant to a continuing care contract and if the lender (or the lender's spouse) attains age 62 before the close of such year.

(2) Continuing care contract. For purposes of this section, the term "continuing care contract" means a written contract between an individual and a qualified continuing care facility under which—

(A) the individual or individual's spouse may use a qualified continuing care facility for their life or lives,

(B) the individual or individual's spouse will be provided with housing, as appropriate for the health of such individual or individual's spouse—

(i) in an independent living unit (which has additional available facilities outside such unit for the provision of meals and other personal care), and

(ii) in an assisted living facility or a nursing facility, as is available in the continuing care facility, and

(C) the individual or individual's spouse will be provided assisted living or nursing care as the health of such individual or individual's spouse requires, and as is available in the continuing care facility.

The Secretary shall issue guidance which limits such term to contracts which provide only facilities, care, and services described in this paragraph.

(3) Qualified continuing care facility.

(A) In general. For purposes of this section, the term "qualified continuing care facility" means 1 or more facilities—

(i) which are designed to provide services under continuing care contracts,

(ii) which include an independent living unit, plus an assisted living or nursing facility, or both, and

(iii) substantially all of the independent living unit residents of which are covered by continuing care contracts.

(B) Nursing homes excluded. The term "qualified continuing care facility" shall not include any facility which is of a type which is traditionally considered a nursing home.

[1]***(4) Repealed.***

* * * * * * * * * * * *

[For Analysis, see ¶ 108. For Committee Reports, see ¶ 5076.]

[Endnote Code Sec. 7872]

Matter in *italics* in Code Sec. 7872(h)(4) was added by Sec. 425(a) of the Tax Relief and Health Care Act of 2006, HR6111, d.o.e., which struck out:

1. "(4) Termination.

"This subsection shall not apply to any calendar year after 2010."

Effective Date (Sec. 425(b), HR6111, d.o.e.) effective for calendar yrs. begin. after 12/31/2005, for loans made before, on, or after 12/31/2005.

[¶ 3077] Code Sec. 9502. Airport and Airway Trust Fund.

* * * * * * * * * * * * *

(d) Expenditures from Airport and Airway Trust Fund.

(2) Transfers from Airport and Airway Trust Fund on account of certain refunds. The Secretary of the Treasury shall pay from time to time from the Airport and Airway Trust Fund into the general fund of the Treasury amounts equivalent to the amounts paid after August 31, 1982, in respect of fuel used in aircraft, under section 6420 (relating to amounts paid in respect of gasoline used on farms, 6421 (relating to amounts paid in respect of gasoline used for certain nonhighway purposes), or 6427 (relating to fuels not used for taxable purposes) (other than subsections (l)(4) [1] thereof).

(3) Transfers from the Airport and Airway Trust Fund on account of certain section 34 credits. The Secretary of the Treasury shall pay from time to time from the Airport and Airway Trust Fund into the general fund of the Treasury amounts equivalent to the credits allowed under section 34 (other than payments made by reason of paragraph (4) [2] of section 6427(l)) with respect to fuel used after August 31, 1982. Such amounts shall be transferred on the basis of estimates by the Secretary of the Treasury, and proper adjustments shall be made in amounts subsequently transferred to the extent prior estimates were in excess of or less than the credits allowed.

* * * * * * * * * * * * *

[Endnote Code Sec. 9502]

Matter in Code Sec. 9502(d)(2) and Code Sec. 9502(d)(3) was deleted by Sec. 420(b)(5)(A)-(B) of the Tax Relief and Health Care Act of 2006, HR6111, d.o.e..

1. "and (l)(5)"
2. "or (5)"

Effective Date (Sec. 420(c), HR6111, d.o.e.) effective for kerosene sold after 9/30/2005, except as provided by Sec. 420(c)(2), HR6111, which reads as follows:

"(2) Special rule for pending claims. In the case of kerosene sold for use in aviation (other than kerosene to which section 6427(l)(4)(C)(ii) of the Internal Revenue Code of 1986 (as added by subsection (a)) applies or kerosene to which section 6427(l)(5) of such Code (as redesignated by subsection (b)) applies) after September 30, 2005, and before the date of the enactment of this Act, the ultimate purchaser shall be treated as having waived the right to payment under section 6427(l)(1) of such Code and as having assigned such right to the ultimate vendor if such ultimate vendor has met the requirements of subparagraph (A), (B), or (D) of section 6416(a)(1) of such Code."

[¶ 3078] Code Sec. 9503. Highway Trust Fund.

* * * * * * * * * * * * *

(c) Expenditures from Highway Trust Fund.

* * * * * * * * * * * * *

(7 [sic 6]) Transfers from the trust fund for certain aviation fuel taxes. The Secretary shall pay at least monthly from the Highway Trust Fund into the Airport and Airway Trust Fund amounts (as determined by the Secretary) equivalent to the taxes received on or after October 1, 2005, and before October 1, 2011, under section 4081 with respect to so much of the rate of tax as does not exceed—

[1]*(A) 4.3 cents per gallon of kerosene subject to section 6427(l)(4)(A) with respect to which a payment has been made by the Secretary under section 6427(l), and*

(B) 21.8 cents per gallon of kerosene subject to section 6427(l)(4)(B) with respect to which a payment has been made by the Secretary under section 6427(l).

Transfers under the preceding sentence shall be made on the basis of estimates by the Secretary, and proper adjustments shall be made in the amounts subsequently transferred to the extent prior estimates were in excess of or less than the amounts required to be transferred. Any amount allowed as a credit under section 34 by reason of paragraph (4) [2] of section 6427(l) shall be treated for purposes of subparagraphs (A) and (B) as a payment made by the Secretary under such paragraph.

* * * * * * * * * * * * *

[Endnote Code Sec. 9503]

Matter in *italics* in Code Sec. 9503(c)(7), Code Sec. 9503(c)(7)(A), and Code Sec. 9503(c)(7)(B) was added by Sec. 420(b)(6)(A)-(B) of the Tax Relief and Health Care Act of 2006, HR6111, d.o.e., which struck out:

1. "(A) 4.3 cents per gallon of kerosene with respect to which a payment has been made by the Secretary under section 6427(l)(4), and"

"(B) 21.8 cents per gallon of kerosene with respect to which a payment has been made by the Secretary under section 6427(l)(5)."

2. "or (5)"

Effective Date (Sec. 420(c), HR6111, d.o.e.) effective for kerosene sold after 9/30/2005. Sec. 402(c)(2), HR6111, provides:

"(2) Special rule for pending claims. In the case of kerosene sold for use in aviation (other than kerosene to which section 6427(l)(4)(C)(ii) of the Internal Revenue Code of 1986 (as added by subsection (a)) applies or kerosene to which section 6427(l)(5) of such Code (as redesignated by subsection (b)) applies) after September 30, 2005, and before the date of the enactment of this Act, the ultimate purchaser shall be treated as having waived the right to payment under section 6427(l)(1) of such Code and as having assigned such right to the ultimate vendor if such ultimate vendor has met the requirements of subparagraph (A), (B), or (D) of section 6416(a)(1) of such Code."

[¶ 3079] Code Sec. 9508. Leaking Underground Storage Tank Trust Fund.

* * * * * * * * * * * * *

(c) Expenditures. Amounts in the Leaking Underground Storage Tank Trust Fund shall be available, as provided in appropriation Acts, only for purposes of making expenditures to carry out [1]*sections 9003(h), 9003(i), 9003(j), 9004(f), 9005(c), 9010, 9011, 9012, and 9013* of the Solid Waste Disposal Act as in effect on the date of the enactment of the [2]*Public Law 109-168.*

* * * * * * * * * * * * *

[Endnote Code Sec. 9508]

Matter in *italics* in Code Sec. 9508(c) was added by Sec. 210(a)(1) and (2) of the Tax Relief and Health Care Act of 2006, HR6111, d.o.e., which struck out:

1. "section 9003(h)"
2. "Superfund Amendments and Reauthorization Act of 1986"

Effective Date (Sec. 210(c), HR6111, d.o.e.) effective d.o.e..

[¶ 3080] Code Sec. 9701. Definitions of general applicability.

* * * * * * * * * * * * *

(c) Terms relating to operators. For purposes of this section—

* * * * * * * * * * * * *

[1]***(8) Successor in interest.***

(A) Safe harbor. The term "successor in interest" shall not include any person who—

(i) is an unrelated person to an eligible seller described in subparagraph (C); and

(ii) purchases for fair market value assets, or all of the stock, of a related person to such seller, in a bona fide, arm's length sale.

(B) Unrelated person. The term "unrelated person" means a purchaser who does not bear a relationship to the eligible seller described in section 267(b).

(C) Eligible seller. For purposes of this paragraph, the term "eligible seller" means an assigned operator described in section 9704(j)(2) or a related person to such assigned operator.

* * * * * * * * * * * *

[Endnote Code Sec. 9701]

Code Sec. 9701(c)(8), in *italics*, was added by Sec. 211(d) of the Tax Relief and Health Care Act of 2006, HR6111, d.o.e..

1. added para. (c)(8)

Effective Date (Sec. 211(e), HR6111, d.o.e.) effective for transactions after d.o.e..

[¶ 3081] Code Sec. 9702. Establishment of the United Mine Workers of America Combined Benefit Fund.

* * * * * * * * * * * *

[1]***(b) Board of trustees.***

(1) In general. *For purposes of subsection (a), the board of trustees for the Combined Fund shall be appointed as follows:*

(A) 2 individuals who represent employers in the coal mining industry shall be designated by the BCOA;

(B) 2 individuals designated by the United Mine Workers of America; and

(C) 3 individuals selected by the individuals appointed under subparagraphs (A) and (B).

(2) Successor trustees. *Any successor trustee shall be appointed in the same manner as the trustee being succeeded. The plan establishing the Combined Fund shall provide for the removal of trustees.*

(3) Special rule. *If the BCOA ceases to exist, any trustee or successor under paragraph (1)(A) shall be designated by the 3 employers who were members of the BCOA on the enactment date and who have been assigned the greatest number of eligible beneficiaries under section 9706.*

* * * * * * * * * * * *

[Endnote Code Sec. 9702]

Matter in *italics*, in Code Sec. 9702(b) was added by Sec. 213(a) of the Tax Relief and Health Care Act of 2006, HR6111, d.o.e., which struck out:

1. "(b) Board of trustees.

"(1) In general. For purposes of subsection (a), the board of trustees for the Combined Fund shall be appointed as follows:

"(A) one individual who represents employers in the coal mining industry shall be designated by the BCOA;

"(B) one individual shall be designated by the three employers, other than 1988 agreement operators, who have been assigned the greatest number of eligible beneficiaries under section 9706;

"(C) two individuals designated by the United Mine Workers of America; and

"(D) three persons selected by the persons appointed under subparagraphs (A), (B), and (C).

"(2) Successor trustees. Any successor trustee shall be appointed in the same manner as the trustee being succeeded. The plan establishing the Combined Fund shall provide for the removal of trustees.

"(3) Special rules.

"(A) BCOA. If the BCOA ceases to exist, any trustee or successor under paragraph (1)(A) shall be designated by the 3 employers who were members of the BCOA on the enactment date and who have been assigned the greatest number of eligible beneficiaries under section 9706.

"(B) Former signatories. The initial trustee under paragraph (1)(B) shall be designated by the 3 employers, other than 1988 agreement operators, which the records of the 1950 UMWA Benefit Plan and 1974 UMWA Benefit Plan indicate have the greatest number of eligible beneficiaries as of the enactment date, and such trustee and any successor shall serve until November 1, 1993."

Effective Date Enacted d.o.e..

[¶ 3082] Code Sec. 9704. Liability of assigned operators.

* * * * * * * * * * * *

[1]***(d) Unassigned beneficiaries premium.***

(1) Plan years ending on or before September 30, 2006. *For plan years ending on or before September 30, 2006, the unassigned beneficiaries premium for any assigned operator shall be equal to the applicable percentage of the product of the per beneficiary premium for the plan year multiplied by the number of eligible beneficiaries who are not assigned under section 9706 to any person for such plan year.*

(2) Plan years beginning on or after October 1, 2006.

(A) In general. For plan years beginning on or after October 1, 2006, subject to subparagraph (B), there shall be no unassigned beneficiaries premium, and benefit costs with respect to eligible beneficiaries who are not assigned under section 9706 to any person for any such plan year shall be paid from amounts transferred under section 9705(b).

(B) Inadequate transfers. If, for any plan year beginning on or after October 1, 2006, the amounts transferred under section 9705(b) are less than the amounts required to be transferred to the Combined Fund under subsection (h)(2)(A) or (i) of section 402 of the Surface Mining Control and Reclamation Act of 1977 (30 U.S.C. 1232)), then the unassigned beneficiaries premium for any assigned operator shall be equal to the operator's applicable percentage of the amount required to be so transferred which was not so transferred.

(e) Premium accounts; adjustments.

(1) Accounts. The trustees of the Combined Fund shall establish and maintain 3 separate accounts for each of the premiums described in subsections (b), (c), and (d). Such accounts shall be credited with the premiums received [2]*and amounts transferred under section 9705(b)* and debited with expenditures allocable to such premiums.

(2) Allocations.

(A) Administrative expenses. Administrative costs for any plan year shall be allocated to premium accounts under paragraph (1) on the basis of expenditures (other than administrative costs) from such accounts during the preceding plan year.

(B) Interest. Interest shall be allocated to the account established for health benefit premiums.

(3) Shortfalls and surpluses.

(A) In general. Except as provided in subparagraph (B), if, for any plan year, there is a shortfall or surplus in any premium account, the premium for the following plan year for each assigned operator shall be proportionately reduced or increased, whichever is applicable, by the amount of such shortfall or surplus. [3]*Amounts credited to an account from amounts transferred under section 9705(b) shall not be taken into account in determining whether there is a surplus in the account for purposes of this paragraph.*

(B) Exception. Subparagraph (A) shall not apply to any surplus in the health benefit premium account or the unassigned beneficiaries premium account which is attributable to—

(i) the excess of the premiums credited to such account for a plan year over the benefits (and administrative costs) debited to such account for the plan year, but such excess shall only be available for purposes of the carryover described in section 9703(b)(2)(C)(ii) (relating to carryovers of premiums not used to provide benefits), or

(ii) interest credited under paragraph (2)(B) for the plan year or any preceding plan year.

(C) No authority for increased payments. Nothing in this paragraph shall be construed to allow expenditures for health care benefits for any plan year in excess of the limit under section 9703(b)(2).

(f) Applicable percentage. For purposes of this section—

(1) In general. The term "applicable percentage" means, with respect to any assigned operator, the percentage determined by dividing the number of eligible beneficiaries assigned under section 9706 to such operator by the total number of beneficiaries assigned under section 9706 to all such operators (determined on the basis of assignments as of October 1, 1993).

(2) Annual adjustments. In the case of any plan year beginning on or after October 1, 1994, the applicable percentage for any assigned operator shall be redetermined under paragraph (1) by making the following changes to the assignments as of October 1, 1993:

(A) Such assignments shall be modified to reflect any changes during the period beginning October 1, 1993, and ending on the last day of the preceding plan year pursuant to the appeals process under section 9706(f).

(B) The total number of assigned eligible beneficiaries shall be reduced by the eligible beneficiaries of assigned operators which (and all related persons with respect to which) had ceased business (within the meaning of section 9701(c)(6)) during the period described in subparagraph (A).

[4]*(C) In the case of plan years beginning on or after October 1, 2007, the total number of assigned eligible beneficiaries shall be reduced by the eligible beneficiaries whose assignments have been revoked under section 9706(h).*

* * * * * * * * * * * * *

[5]***(j) Prepayment of premium liability.***

(1) In general. *If—*

(A) a payment meeting the requirements of paragraph (3) is made to the Combined Fund by or on behalf of—

(i) any assigned operator to which this subsection applies, or

(ii) any related person to any assigned operator described in clause (i), and

(B) the common parent of the controlled group of corporations described in paragraph (2)(B) is jointly and severally liable for any premium under this section which (but for this subsection) would be required to be paid by the assigned operator or related person, then such common parent (and no other person) shall be liable for such premium.

(2) Assigned operators to which subsection applies.

(A) In general. This subsection shall apply to any assigned operator if—

(i) the assigned operator (or a related person to the assigned operator)—

(I) made contributions to the 1950 UMWA Benefit Plan and the 1974 UMWA Benefit Plan for employment during the period covered by the 1988 agreement; and

(II) is not a 1988 agreement operator,

(ii) the assigned operator (and all related persons to the assigned operator) are not actively engaged in the production of coal as of July 1, 2005, and

(iii) the assigned operator was, as of July 20, 1992, a member of a controlled group of corporations described in subparagraph (B).

(B) Controlled group of corporations. A controlled group of corporations is described in this subparagraph if the common parent of such group is a corporation the shares of which are publicly traded on a United States exchange.

(C) Coordination with repeal of assignments. A person shall not fail to be treated as an assigned operator to which this subsection applies solely because the person ceases to be an assigned operator by reason of section 9706(h)(1) if the person otherwise meets the requirements of this subsection and is liable for the payment of premiums under section 9706(h)(3).

(D) Controlled group. For purposes of this subsection, the term "controlled group of corporations" has the meaning given such term by section 52(a).

(3) Requirements. *A payment meets the requirements of this paragraph if—*

(A) the amount of the payment is not less than the present value of the total premium liability under this chapter with respect to the Combined Fund of the assigned operators

or related persons described in paragraph (1) or their assignees, as determined by the operator's or related person's enrolled actuary (as defined in section 7701(a)(35)) using actuarial methods and assumptions each of which is reasonable and which are reasonable in the aggregate, as determined by such enrolled actuary;

(B) such enrolled actuary files with the Secretary of Labor a signed actuarial report containing—

(i) the date of the actuarial valuation applicable to the report; and

(ii) a statement by the enrolled actuary signing the report that, to the best of the actuary's knowledge, the report is complete and accurate and that in the actuary's opinion the actuarial assumptions used are in the aggregate reasonably related to the experience of the operator and to reasonable expectations; and

(C) 90 calendar days have elapsed after the report required by subparagraph (B) is filed with the Secretary of Labor, and the Secretary of Labor has not notified the assigned operator in writing that the requirements of this paragraph have not been satisfied.

(4) ***Use of prepayment.*** *The Combined Fund shall—*

(A) establish and maintain an account for each assigned operator or related person by, or on whose behalf, a payment described in paragraph (3) was made,

(B) credit such account with such payment (and any earnings thereon), and

(C) use all amounts in such account exclusively to pay premiums that would (but for this subsection) be required to be paid by the assigned operator.

Upon termination of the obligations for the premium liability of any assigned operator or related person for which such account is maintained, all funds remaining in such account (and earnings thereon) shall be refunded to such person as may be designated by the common parent described in paragraph (1)(B).

[Endnote Code Sec. 9704]

Matter in *italics*, in Code Sec. 9704(d), Code Sec. 9704(e)(1), Code Sec. 9704(e)(3)(A), and Code Sec. 9704(f)(2)(C) was added by Sec. 212(a)(2)(A), (a)(2)(B)(i)-(ii) and (a)(2)(C) of the Tax Relief and Health Care Act of 2006, HR6111, d.o.e., which struck out:

1. "(d) Unassigned beneficiaries premium. The unassigned beneficiaries premium for any plan year for any assigned operator shall be equal to the applicable percentage of the product of the per beneficiary premium for the plan year multiplied by the number of eligible beneficiaries who are not assigned under section 9706 to any person for such plan year."

2. added matter in para. (e)(1)

3. added matter at the end of subpara. (e)(3)(A)

4. added subpara. (f)(2)(C)

Effective Date (Sec. 212(a)(4), HR6111, d.o.e.) effective for plan years of the Combined Fund beginning after 9/30/2006.

Code Sec. 9704(j), in *italics*, was added by Sec. 211(a), HR6111, d.o.e..

5. added subsec. (j)

Effective Date (Sec. 211(e), HR6111, d.o.e.) effective d.o.e..

[¶ 3083] Code Sec. 9705. Transfers.

* * * * * * * * * * * *

(b) Transfers [1].

(1) In general. The Combined Fund shall include any amount transferred to the Fund under [2]*subsections (h) and (i) of section 402* of the Surface Mining Control and Reclamation Act of 1977 (30 U.S.C. 1232(h)).

[3]*(2)* ***Use of funds.*** *Any amount transferred under paragraph (1) for any fiscal year shall be used to pay benefits and administrative costs of beneficiaries of the Combined*

Fund or for such other purposes as are specifically provided in the Acts described in paragraph (1).

[Endnote Code Sec. 9705]

Matter in *italics*, in Code Sec. 9705(b) was added by Sec. 212(a)(1)(A)-(C) of the Tax Relief and Health Care Act of 2006, HR6111, d.o.e., which struck out:

1. "From Abandoned Mine Rreclamation Fund."
2. "section 402(h)"
3. "(2) Use of funds. Any amount transferred under paragraph (1) for any fiscal year shall be used to proportionately reduce the unassigned beneficiary premium under section 9704(a)(3) of each assigned operator for the plan year in which transferred."

Effective Date (Sec. 212(a)(4), HR6111, d.o.e.) effective for plan years of the Combined Fund beginning after 9/30/2006.

[¶ 3084] Code Sec. 9706. Assignment of eligible beneficiaries.

* * * * * * * * * * * *

[1]***(h) Assignments as of October 1, 2007.***

(1) In general. *Subject to the premium obligation set forth in paragraph (3), the Commissioner of Social Security shall—*

(A) revoke all assignments to persons other than 1988 agreement operators for purposes of assessing premiums for plan years beginning on and after October 1, 2007; and

(B) make no further assignments to persons other than 1988 agreement operators, except that no individual who becomes an unassigned beneficiary by reason of subparagraph (A) may be assigned to a 1988 agreement operator.

(2) Reassignment upon purchase. *This subsection shall not be construed to prohibit the reassignment under subsection (b)(2) of an eligible beneficiary.*

(3) Liability of persons during three fiscal years beginning on and after October 1, 2007. *In the case of each of the fiscal years beginning on October 1, 2007, 2008, and 2009, each person other than a 1988 agreement operator shall pay to the Combined Fund the following percentage of the amount of annual premiums that such person would otherwise be required to pay under section 9704(a), determined on the basis of assignments in effect without regard to the revocation of assignments under paragraph (1)(A):*

(A) For the fiscal year beginning on October 1, 2007, 55 percent.

(B) For the fiscal year beginning on October 1, 2008, 40 percent.

(C) For the fiscal year beginning on October 1, 2009, 15 percent.

[Endnote Code Sec. 9706]

Code Sec. 9706(h), in *italics*, was added by 212(a)(3) of the Tax Relief and Health Care Act of 2006, HR6111, d.o.e..

1. added subsec. (h)

Effective Date (Sec. 212(a)(4), HR6111, d.o.e.) effective for plan years of the Combined Fund beginning after 9/30/2006.

[¶ 3085] Code Sec. 9707. Failure to pay premium.

[1]***(a) Failures to pay.***

(1) Premiums for eligible beneficiaries. *There is hereby imposed a penalty on the failure of any assigned operator to pay any premum required to be paid under section 9704 with respect to any eligible beneficiary.*

(2) Contributions required under the mining laws. *There is hereby imposed a penalty on the failure of any person to make a contribution required under section 402(h)(5)(B)(ii) of the Surface Mining Control and Reclamation Act of 1977 to a plan referred to in section 402(h)(2)(C) of such Act. For purposes of applying this section, each such required monthly contribution for the hours worked of any individual shall be treated* *as if it were a premium required to be paid under section 9704 with respect to an eligible beneficiary.*

* * * * * * * * * * * *

[Endnote Code Sec. 9707]

Matter in *italics*, in Code Sec. 9707(a) was added by Sec. 213(b)(1) of the Tax Relief and Health Care Act of 2006, HR6111, d.o.e, which struck out:

1. "(a) General rule. There is hereby imposed a penalty on the failure of any assigned operator to pay any premium required to be paid under section 9704 with respect to any eligible beneficiary."

Effective Date Enacted d.o.e..

[¶3086] Code Sec. 9711. Continued obligations of individual employer plans.

* * * * * * * * * * * *

[1]***(c) Joint and several liability of related persons.***

(1) In general. *Except as provided in paragraph (2), each related person of a last signatory operator to which subsection (a) or (b) applies shall be jointly and severally liable with the last signatory operator for the provision of health care coverage described in subsection (a) or (b).*

(2) Liability limited if security provided. *If—*

(A) security meeting the requirements of paragraph (3) is provided by or on behalf of—

(i) any last signatory operator which is an assigned operator described in section 9704(j)(2), or

(ii) any related person to any last signatory operator described in clause (i), and

(B) the common parent of the controlled group of corporations described in section 9704(j)(2)(B) is jointly and severally liable for the provision of health care under this section which, but for this paragraph, would be required to be provided by the last signatory operator or related person,

then, as of the date the security is provided, such common parent (and no other person) shall be liable for the provision of health care under this section which the last signatory operator or related person would otherwise be required to provide. Security may be provided under this paragraph without regard to whether a payment was made under section 9704(j).

(3) Security. *Security meets the requirements of this paragraph if—*

(A) the security—

(i) is in the form of a bond, letter of credit, or cash escrow,

(ii) is provided to the trustees of the 1992 UMWA Benefit Plan solely for the purpose of paying premiums for beneficiaries who would be described in section 9712(b)(2)(B) if the requirements of this section were not met by the last signatory operator, and

(iii) is in an amount equal to 1 year of liability of the last signatory operator under this section, determined by using the average cost of such operator's liability during the prior 3 calendar years;

(B) the security is in addition to any other security required under any other provision of this title; and

(C) the security remains in place for 5 years.

(4) Refunds of security. *The remaining amount of any security provided under this subsection (and earnings thereon) shall be refunded to the last signatory operator as of the earlier of—*

(A) the termination of the obligations of the last signatory operator under this section, or

(B) the end of the 5-year period described in paragraph (4)(C).

* * * * * * * * * * * *

[Endnote Code Sec. 9711]

Code Sec. 9711(c), in *italics*, was added by Sec. 211(b) of the Tax Relief and Health Care Act of 2006, HR6111, d.o.e., which struck out:

1. "(c) Joint and several liability of related persons. Each related person of a last signatory operator to which subsection (a) or (b) applies shall be jointly and severally liable with the last signatory operator for the provision of health care coverage described in subsection (a) or (b)."

Effective Date (Sec. 211(e), HR6111, d.o.e.) effective for transactions after d.o.e..

[¶ 3087] Code Sec. 9712. Establishment and coverage of 1992 UMWA benefit plan.

(a) Creation of plan.

* * * * * * * * * * * *

[1] ***(3) Transfers under other federal statutes.***

(A) In general. The 1992 UMWA Benefit Plan shall include any amount transferred to the plan under subsections (h) and (i) of section 402 of the Surface Mining Control and Reclamation Act of 1977 (30 U.S.C. 1232).

(B) Use of funds. Any amount transferred under subparagraph (A) for any fiscal year shall be used to provide the health benefits described in subsection (c) with respect to any beneficiary for whom no monthly per beneficiary premium is paid pursuant to paragraph (1)(A) or (3) of subsection (d).

[2] ***(4) Special rule for 1993 plan.***

(A) In general. The plan described in section 402(h)(2)(C) of the Surface Mining Control and Reclamation Act of 1977 (30 U.S.C. 1232(h)(2)(C)) shall include any amount transferred to the plan under subsections (h) and (i) of the Surface Mining Control and Reclamation Act of 1977 (30 U.S.C. 1232).

(B) Use of funds. Any amount transferred under subparagraph (A) for any fiscal year shall be used to provide the health benefits described in section 402(h)(2)(C)(i) of the Surface Mining Control and Reclamation Act of 1977 (30 U.S.C. 1232(h)(2)(C)(i)) to individuals described in section 402(h)(2)(C) of such Act (30 U.S.C. 1232(h)(2)(C)).

* * * * * * * * * * * *

(d) Guarantee of benefits.

[3] ***(1) In general.*** *All 1988 last signatory operators shall be responsible for financing the benefits described in subsection (c) by meeting the following requirements in accordance with the contribution requirements established in the 1992 UMWA Benefit Plan:*

(A) The payment of a monthly per beneficiary premium by each 1988 last signatory operator for each eligible beneficiary of such operator who is described in subsection (b)(2) and who is receiving benefits under the 1992 UMWA benefit plan.

(B) The provision of a security (in the form of a bond, letter of credit, or cash escrow) in an amount equal to a portion of the projected future cost to the 1992 UMWA Benefit Plan of providing health benefits for eligible and potentially eligible beneficiaries attributable to the 1988 last signatory operator.

(C) If the amounts transferred under subsection (a)(3) are less than the amounts required to be transferred to the 1992 UMWA Benefit Plan under subsections (h) and (i) of section 402 of the Surface Mining Control and Reclamation Act of 1977 (30 U.S.C. 1232), the payment of an additional backstop premium by each 1988 last signatory operator which is equal to such operator's share of the amounts required to be so transferred but which were not so transferred, determined on the basis of the number of eligible and potentially eligible beneficiaries attributable to the operator.

(2) **Adjustments.** The 1992 UMWA Benefit Plan shall provide for—

(A) annual adjustments of the per beneficiary premium to cover changes in the cost of providing benefits to eligible beneficiaries, and

(B) adjustments as necessary to the annual [4]*backstop* premium to reflect changes in the cost of providing benefits to eligible beneficiaries for whom per beneficiary premiums are not paid.

(3) **Additional liability.** Any last signatory operator who is not a 1988 last signatory operator shall pay the monthly per beneficiary premium under [5]*paragraph (1)(A)* for each eligible beneficiary described in such paragraph attributable to that operator.

(4) **Joint and several liability.** A 1988 last signatory operator or last signatory operator described in paragraph (3), and any related person to any such operator, shall be jointly and severally liable with such operator for any amount required to be paid by such operator under this section. [6]*The provisions of section 9711(c)(2) shall apply to any last signatory operator described in such section (without regard to whether security is provided under such section, a payment is made under section 9704(j), or both) and if security meeting the requirements of section 9711(c)(3) is provided, the common parent described in section 9711(c)(2)(B) shall be exclusively responsible for any liability for premiums under this section which, but for this sentence, would be required to be paid by the last signatory operator or any related person.*

(5) **Deductibility.** Any premium required by this section shall be deductible without regard to any limitation on deductibility based on the prefunding of health benefits.

(6) **1988 last signatory operator.** For purposes of this section, the term "1988 last signatory operator" means a last signatory operator which is a 1988 agreement operator.

[Endnote Code Sec. 9712]

Code Sec. 9712(a)(3) and Code Sec. 9712(a)(4), in *italics*, were added by Sec. 212(b)(1) of the Tax Relief and Health Care Act of 2006, HR6111, d.o.e..

1. added para. (a)(3)
2. added para. (a)(4)

Effective Date Enacted d.o.e..

Matter in *italics*, in Code Sec. 9712(d)(1), Code Sec. 9712(d)(2)(B), and Code Sec. 9712(d)(3) was added by Sec. 212(b)(2)(A) and (B)(i) and (ii), HR6111, d.o.e., which struck out:

3. "(1) In general. All 1988 last signatory operators shall be responsible for financing the benefits described in subsection (c), in accordance with contribution requirements established in the 1992 UMWA Benefit Plan. Such contribution requirements, which shall be applied uniformly to each 1988 last signatory operator, on the basis of the number of eligible and potentially eligible beneficiaries attributable to each operator, shall include:

"(A) the payment of an annual prefunding premium for all eligible and potentially eligible beneficiaries attributable to a 1988 last signatory operator,

"(B) the payment of a monthly per beneficiary premium by each 1988 last signatory operator for each eligible beneficiary of such operator who is described in subsection (b)(2) and who is receiving benefits under the 1992 UMWA Benefit Plan, and

"(C) the provision of security (in the form of a bond, letter of credit or cash escrow) in an amount equal to a portion of the projected future cost to the 1992 UMWA Benefit Plan of providing health benefits for eligible and potentially eligible beneficiaries attributable to the 1988 last signatory operator. If a 1988 last signatory operator is unable to provide the security required, the 1992 UMWA Benefit Plan shall require the operator to pay an annual prefunding premium that is greater than the premium otherwise applicable."

4. "prefunding"
5. "paragraph (1)(B)"

Effective Date (Sec. 212(b)(2)(C), HR6111, d.o.e.) effective for fiscal yrs. begin. on or after 10/1/2010.

Matter in *italics*, in Code Sec. 9712(d)(4) was added by Sec. 211(c), HR6111, d.o.e..

6. added matter at the end of para. (d)(4)

Effective Date (Sec. 211(e), HR6111, d.o.e.) effective d.o.e..

[¶3088] ***Code Sec.[1] 9721. Civil enforcement.***

The provisions of section 4301 of the Employee Retirement Income Security Act of 1974 shall apply, in the same manner as any claim arising out of an obligation to pay withdrawal liability under subtitle E of title IV of such Act, to any claim—

(1) arising out of an obligation to pay any amount required to be paid by this chapter; or

(2) arising out of an obligation to pay any amount required by section 402(h)(5)(B)(ii) of the Surface Mining Control and Reclamation Act of 1977 (30 U.S.C. 1232(h)(5)(B)(ii)).

[Endnote Code Sec. 9721]

Code Sec. 9721, in *italics,* was added by Sec. 213(b)(2) of the Tax Relief and Health Care Act of 2006, HR6111, d.o.e., which struck out:

1. "Sec. 9721. Civil enforcement. The provisions of section 4301 of the Employee Retirement Income Security Act of 1974 shall apply to any claim arising out of an obligation to pay any amount required to be paid by this chapter in the same manner as any claim arising out of an obligation to pay withdrawal liability under subtitle E of title IV of such Act. For purposes of the preceding sentence, a signatory operator and related persons shall be treated in the same manner as employers."

Effective Date Enacted d.o.e..

[¶ 3089] Code Sec. 9812. Parity in the application of certain limits to mental health benefits.

* * * * * * * * * * * *

(f) Application of section. This section shall not apply to benefits for services furnished—

(1) on or after September 30, 2001, and before January 10, 2002,

(2) on or after January 1, 2004, and before the date of the enactment of the Working Families Tax Relief Act of 2004, and

(3) after December 31, [1]*2007.*

[For Analysis, see ¶ 402. For Committee Reports, see ¶ 5053.]

[Endnote Code Sec. 9812]

Matter in *italics* in Code Sec. 9812(f)(3) was added by Sec. 115(a) of the Tax Relief and Health Care Act of 2006, HR6111, d.o.e, which struck out:

1. "2006"

Effective Date Enacted d.o.e..

Tax Relief and Health Care Act of 2006

One Hundred Ninth Congress

2nd Session

HR6111

[¶4000] Act sections for the Tax Provisions of the Tax Relief and Health Care Act of 2006, HR6111, or portions thereof, that do not amend specific Internal Revenue Code sections follow. Sections of the Internal Revenue Code as amended are reproduced at *Code as Amended.*

[¶4001] Sec. 1. SHORT TITLE, ETC.

(a) SHORT TITLE. This Act may be cited as the "Tax Relief and Health Care Act of 2006".

(b) TABLE OF CONTENTS. The table of contents for this Act is as follows:

Sec. 381. Findings.

Sec. 382. Availability of special account.

Subtitle I—Amendments to the Lincoln County Conservation, Recreation, and Development Act of 2004

Sec. 391. Disposition of proceeds.

Subtitle J—All American Canal Projects

Sec. 395. All American Canal Lining Project.

Sec. 396. Regulated storage water facility.

Sec. 397. Application of law.

TITLE IV—OTHER PROVISIONS

Sec. 401. Tobacco personal use quantity exception to not apply to delivery sales.

Sec. 402. Ethanol Tariff Schedule.

Sec. 403. Withdrawal of certain Federal land and interests in certain Federal land from location, entry, and patent under the mining laws and disposition under the mineral and geothermal leasing laws.

Sec. 404. Continuing eligibility for certain students under District of Columbia School Choice Program.

Sec. 405. Study on Establishing Uniform National Database on Elder Abuse.

Sec. 406. Temporary duty reductions for certain cotton shirting fabric.

Sec. 407. Cotton Trust Fund.

Sec. 408. Tax court review of requests for equitable relief from joint and several liability.

DIVISION A— EXTENSION AND EXPANSION OF CERTAIN TAX RELIEF PROVISIONS, AND OTHER TAX PROVISIONS

[¶4002] Sec. 100. REFERENCE. Except as otherwise expressly provided, whenever in this division an amendment or repeal is expressed in terms of an amendment to, or repeal of, a section or other provision, the reference shall be considered to be made to a section or other provision of the Internal Revenue Code of 1986.

TITLE I— EXTENSION AND MODIFICATION OF CERTAIN PROVISIONS

[¶4003] Sec. 101. DEDUCTION FOR QUALIFIED TUITION AND RELATED EXPENSES.

****

(c) EFFECTIVE DATE. The amendments made by this section shall apply to taxable years beginning after December 31, 2005.

[¶4004] Sec. 102. EXTENSION AND MODIFICATION OF NEW MARKETS TAX CREDIT.

****

(c) EFFECTIVE DATE. The amendments made by this section shall take effect on the date of the enactment of this Act.

[¶4005] Sec. 103. ELECTION TO DEDUCT STATE AND LOCAL GENERAL SALES TAXES.

(b) EFFECTIVE DATE. The amendments made by this section shall apply to taxable years beginning after December 31, 2005.

[¶4006] Sec. 104. EXTENSION AND MODIFICATION OF RESEARCH CREDIT.

(a) EXTENSION.

****

(3) EFFECTIVE DATE. The amendments made by this subsection shall apply to amounts paid or incurred after December 31, 2005.

(b) INCREASE IN RATES OF ALTERNATIVE INCREMENTAL CREDIT.

****

(2) EFFECTIVE DATE. Except as provided in paragraph (3), the amendments made by this subsection shall apply to taxable years ending after December 31, 2006.

(3) TRANSITION RULE.

****

(B)DEFINITIONS. For purposes of subparagraph (A)—

(i) SPECIFIED TRANSITIONAL TAXABLE YEAR.—The term "specified transitional taxable year" means any taxable year which ends after December 31, 2006, and which includes such date.

(ii) APPLICABLE 2006 PERCENTAGE.— The term "applicable 2006 percentage" means the number of days in the specified transitional taxable year before January 1, 2007, divided by the number of days in such taxable year.

(iii) APPLICABLE 2007 PERCENTAGE.—The term "applicable 2007 percent-age" means the number of days in the specified transitional taxable year after December 31, 2006, divided by the number of days in such taxable year.

(c) ALTERNATIVE SIMPLIFIED CREDIT FOR QUALIFIED RESEARCH EXPENSES.

****

(3) EFFECTIVE DATE. Except as provided in paragraph (4), the amendments made by this subsection shall apply to taxable years ending after December 31, 2006.

****

[¶4007] Sec. 105. WORK OPPORTUNITY TAX CREDIT AND WELFARE TO-WORK CREDIT.

****

(f) EFFECTIVE DATES.

(1) IN GENERAL. Except as provided in paragraph (2), the amendments made by this section shall apply to individuals who begin work for the employer after December 31, 2005.

(2) CONSOLIDATION. The amendments made by subsections (b), (c), (d), and (e) shall apply to individuals who begin work for the employer after December 31, 2006.

[¶4008] Sec. 106. ELECTION TO INCLUDE COMBAT PAY AS EARNED INCOME FOR PURPOSES OF EARNED INCOME CREDIT.

****

(b) EFFECTIVE DATE. The amendment made by this section shall apply to taxable years beginning after December 31, 2006.

[¶4009] Sec. 107. EXTENSION AND MODIFICATION OF QUALIFIED ZONE ACADEMY BONDS.

****

(c) EFFECTIVE DATES.

(1) EXTENSION. The amendment made by subsection (a) shall apply to obligations issued after December 31, 2005.

(2) SPECIAL RULES. The amendments made by subsection (b) shall apply to obligations issued after the date of the enactment of this Act pursuant to allocations of the national zone academy bond limitation for calendar years after 2005.

[¶4010] Sec. 108. ABOVE-THE-LINE DEDUCTION FOR CERTAIN EXPENSES OF ELEMENTARY AND SECONDARY SCHOOL TEACHERS.

****

(b) EFFECTIVE DATE. The amendment made by this section shall apply to taxable years beginning after December 31, 2005.

[¶4011] Sec. 109. EXTENSION AND EXPANSION OF EXPENSING OF BROWNFIELDS REMEDIATION COSTS.

****

(c) EFFECTIVE DATE. The amendments made by this section shall apply to expenditures paid or incurred after December 31, 2005.

[¶4012] Sec. 110. TAX INCENTIVES FOR INVESTMENT IN THE DISTRICT OF COLUMBIA.

(a) DESIGNATION OF ZONE.

****

(2) EFFECTIVE DATE. The amendments made by this subsection shall apply to periods beginning after December 31, 2005.

(b) TAX-EXEMPT ECONOMIC DEVELOPMENT BONDS.

****

(2) EFFECTIVE DATE. The amendment made by this subsection shall apply to bonds issued after December 31, 2005.

(c) ZERO PERCENT CAPITAL GAINS RATE.

****

(3) EFFECTIVE DATES.

(A) EXTENSION. The amendments made by paragraph (1) shall apply to acquisitions after December 31, 2005.

(B) CONFORMING AMENDMENTS. The amendments made by paragraph (2) shall take effect on the date of the enactment of this Act.

(d) FIRST-TIME HOMEBUYER CREDIT.

****

(2) EFFECTIVE DATE. The amendment made by this subsection shall apply to property purchased after December 31, 2005.

[¶4013] Sec. 111. INDIAN EMPLOYMENT TAX CREDIT.

****

(b) EFFECTIVE DATE. The amendment made by this section shall apply to taxable years beginning after December 31, 2005.

[¶4014] Sec. 112. ACCELERATED DEPRECIATION FOR BUSINESS PROPERTY ON INDIAN RESERVATIONS.

****

(b) EFFECTIVE DATE. The amendment made by this section shall apply to property placed in service after December 31, 2005.

[¶4015] Sec. 113. FIFTEEN-YEAR STRAIGHT-LINE COST RECOVERY FOR QUALIFIED LEASEHOLD IMPROVEMENTS AND QUALIFIED RESTAURANT PROPERTY.

****

(b) EFFECTIVE DATE. The amendments made by subsection (a) shall apply to property placed in service after December 31, 2005.

[¶ 4016] Sec. 114. COVER OVER OF TAX ON DISTILLED SPIRITS.

****

(b) EFFECTIVE DATE. The amendment made by subsection (a) shall apply to articles brought into the United States after December 31, 2005.

[¶ 4017] Sec. 116. CORPORATE DONATIONS OF SCIENTIFIC PROPERTY USED FOR RESEARCH AND OF COMPUTER TECHNOLOGY AND EQUIPMENT.

(a) EXTENSION OF COMPUTER TECHNOLOGY AND EQUIPMENT DONATION.

****

(2) EFFECTIVE DATE. The amendment made by paragraph (1) shall apply to contributions made in taxable years beginning after December 31, 2005.

(b) EXPANSION OF CHARITABLE CONTRIBUTION ALLOWED FOR SCIENTIFIC PROPERTY USED FOR RESEARCH AND FOR COMPUTER TECHNOLOGY AND EQUIPMENT USED FOR EDUCATIONAL PURPOSES.

****

(3) EFFECTIVE DATE. The amendments made by this subsection shall apply to taxable years beginning after December 31, 2005.

[¶ 4018] Sec. 117. AVAILABILITY OF MEDICAL SAVINGS ACCOUNTS.

****

(c) TIME FOR FILING REPORTS, ETC.

(1) The report required by section 220(j)(4) of the Internal Revenue Code of 1986 to be made on August 1, 2005, or August 1, 2006, as the case may be, shall be treated as timely if made before the close of the 90-day period beginning on the date of the enactment of this Act.

(2) The determination and publication required by section 220(j)(5) of such Code with respect to calendar year 2005 or calendar year 2006, as the case may be, shall be treated as timely if made before the close of the 120-day period beginning on the date of the enactment of this Act. If the determination under the preceding sentence is that 2005 or 2006 is a cut-off year under section 220(i) of such Code, the cut-off date under such section 220(i) shall be the last day of such 120-day period.

[¶ 4019] Sec. 118. TAXABLE INCOME LIMIT ON PERCENTAGE DEPLETION FOR OIL AND NATURAL GAS PRODUCED FROM MARGINAL PROPERTIES.

****

(b) EFFECTIVE DATE. The amendment made by subsection (a) shall apply to taxable years beginning after December 31, 2005.

[¶ 4020] Sec. 120. EXTENSION OF BONUS DEPRECIATION FOR CERTAIN QUALIFIED GULF OPPORTUNITY ZONE PROPERTY.

****

(c) EFFECTIVE DATE. The amendments made by this section shall take effect as if included in section 101 of the Gulf Opportunity Zone Act of 2005.

[¶ 4021] Sec. 122. DISCLOSURES OF CERTAIN TAX RETURN INFORMATION.

(a) DISCLOSURES TO FACILITATE COMBINED EMPLOYMENT TAX REPORTING.

****

(2) **EFFECTIVE DATE.** The amendment made by paragraph (1) shall apply to disclosures after December 31, 2006.

(b) DISCLOSURES RELATING TO TERRORIST ACTIVITIES.

****

(2) **EFFECTIVE DATE.** The amendments made by paragraph (1) shall apply to disclosures after December 31, 2006.

(c) DISCLOSURES RELATING TO STUDENT LOANS.

****

(2) **EFFECTIVE DATE.** The amendment made by paragraph (1) shall apply to requests made after December 31, 2006.

[¶ 4022] Sec. 123. SPECIAL RULE FOR ELECTIONS UNDER EXPIRED PROVISIONS.

****

(b) OTHER ELECTIONS. Except as otherwise provided by such Secretary or designee, a rule similar to the rule of subsection (a) shall apply with respect to elections under any other expired provision of the Internal Revenue Code of 1986 the applicability of which is extended by reason of the amendments made by this title.

TITLE II— ENERGY TAX PROVISIONS

[¶ 4023] Sec. 202. CREDIT TO HOLDERS OF CLEAN RENEWABLE ENERGY BONDS.

****

(b) EFFECTIVE DATES.

(1) **IN GENERAL.** The amendments made by paragraphs (1) and (3) of subsection (a) shall apply to bonds issued after December 31, 2006.

(2) **ALLOCATIONS.** The amendment made by subsection (a)(2) shall apply to allocations or reallocations after December 31, 2006.

[¶ 4024] Sec. 203. PERFORMANCE STANDARDS FOR SULFUR DIOXIDE REMOVAL IN ADVANCED COAL-BASED GENERATION TECHNOLOGY UNITS DESIGNED TO USE SUBBITUMINOUS COAL.

****

(b) EFFECTIVE DATE. The amendment made by this section shall take apply with respect to applications for certification under section 48A(d)(2) of the Internal Revenue Code of 1986 submitted after October 2, 2006.

[¶ 4025] Sec. 209. SPECIAL DEPRECIATION ALLOWANCE FOR CELLULOSIC BIOMASS ETHANOL PLANT PROPERTY.

****

(b) EFFECTIVE DATE. The amendment made by this section shall apply to property placed in service after the date of the enactment of this Act in taxable years ending after such date.

[¶ 4026] Sec. 210. EXPENDITURES PERMITTED FROM THE LEAKING UNDERGROUND STORAGE TANK TRUST FUND.

****

(c) EFFECTIVE DATE. The amendments made by this section shall take effect on the date of the enactment of this Act.

[¶4027] Sec. 211. TREATMENT OF COKE AND COKE GAS.

****

(c) EFFECTIVE DATE. The amendments made by this section shall take effect as if included in section 1321 of the Energy Policy Act of 2005.

TITLE III— HEALTH SAVINGS ACCOUNTS

[¶4028] Sec. 301. SHORT TITLE. This title may be cited as the "Health Opportunity Patient Empowerment Act of 2006".

[¶4029] Sec. 302. FSA AND HRA TERMINATIONS TO FUND HSAS.

****

(c) APPLICATION OF SECTION.

(1) SUBSECTION (a). The amendment made by subsection (a) shall apply to distributions on or after the date of the enactment of this Act.

(2) SUBSECTION (b). The amendment made by subsection (b) shall take effect on the date of the enactment of this Act.

[¶4030] Sec. 303. REPEAL OF ANNUAL DEDUCTIBLE LIMITATION ON HSA CONTRIBUTIONS.

****

(c) EFFECTIVE DATE. The amendments made by this section shall apply to taxable years beginning after December 31, 2006.

[¶4031] Sec. 305. CONTRIBUTION LIMITATION NOT REDUCED FOR PART-YEAR COVERAGE.

****

(b) EFFECTIVE DATE. The amendments made by this section shall apply to taxable years beginning after December 31, 2006.

[¶4032] Sec. 306. EXCEPTION TO REQUIREMENT FOR EMPLOYERS TO MAKE COMPARABLE HEALTH SAVINGS ACCOUNT CONTRIBUTIONS.

****

(b) EFFECTIVE DATE. The amendment made by this section shall apply to taxable years beginning after December 31, 2006.

[¶4033] Sec. 307. ONE-TIME DISTRIBUTION FROM INDIVIDUAL RETIREMENT PLANS TO FUND HSAS.

****

(c) EFFECTIVE DATE. The amendments made by this section shall apply to taxable years beginning after December 31, 2006.

TITLE IV— OTHER PROVISIONS

[¶4034] Sec. 401. DEDUCTION ALLOWABLE WITH RESPECT TO INCOME ATTRIBUTABLE TO DOMESTIC PRODUCTION ACTIVITIES IN PUERTO RICO.

****

(b) EFFECTIVE DATE. The amendments made by subsection (a) shall apply to taxable years beginning after December 31, 2005.

[¶4035] Sec. 402. CREDIT FOR PRIOR YEAR MINIMUM TAX LIABILITY MADE REFUNDABLE AFTER PERIOD OF YEARS.

****

(c) **EFFECTIVE DATE.** The amendments made by this section shall apply to taxable years beginning after the date of the enactment of this Act.

[¶4036] Sec. 403. RETURNS REQUIRED IN CONNECTION WITH CERTAIN OPTIONS.

****

(d) **EFFECTIVE DATE.** The amendments made by this section shall apply to calendar years beginning after the date of the enactment of this Act.

[¶4037] Sec. 404. PARTIAL EXPENSING FOR ADVANCED MINE SAFETY EQUIPMENT.

****

(c) **EFFECTIVE DATE.** The amendments made by this section shall apply to costs paid or incurred after the date of the enactment of this Act.

[¶4038] Sec. 405. MINE RESCUE TEAM TRAINING TAX CREDIT.

****

(e) **EFFECTIVE DATE.** The amendments made by this section shall apply to taxable years beginning after December 31, 2005.

[¶4039] Sec. 406. WHISTLEBLOWER REFORMS.

****

(d) **EFFECTIVE DATE.** The amendments made by subsection (a) shall apply to information provided on or after the date of the enactment of this Act.

[¶4040] Sec. 407. FRIVOLOUS TAX SUBMISSIONS.

****

(f) **EFFECTIVE DATE.** The amendments made by this section shall apply to submissions made and issues raised after the date on which the Secretary first prescribes a list under section 6702(c) of the Internal Revenue Code of 1986, as amended by subsection (a).

[¶4041] Sec. 408. ADDITION OF MENINGOCOCCAL AND HUMAN PAPILLOMAVIRUS VACCINES TO LIST OF TAXABLE VACCINES.

****

(c) **EFFECTIVE DATE.**

(1) **SALES, ETC.** The amendments made by this section shall apply to sales and uses on or after the first day of the first month which begins more than 4 weeks after the date of the enactment of this Act.

(2) **DELIVERIES.** For purposes of paragraph (1) and section 4131 of the Internal Revenue Code of 1986, in the case of sales on or before the effective date described in such paragraph for which delivery is made after such date, the delivery date shall be considered the sale date.

[¶4042] Sec. 409. CLARIFICATION OF TAXATION OF CERTAIN SETTLEMENT FUNDS MADE PERMANENT.

****

(b) EFFECTIVE DATE. The amendment made by this section shall take effect as if included in section 201 of the Tax Increase Prevention and Reconciliation Act of 2005.

[¶ 4043] Sec. 410. MODIFICATION OF ACTIVE BUSINESS DEFINITION UNDER SECTION 355 MADE PERMANENT.

****

(b) EFFECTIVE DATE. The amendments made by this section shall take effect as if included in section 202 of the Tax Increase Prevention and Reconciliation Act of 2005.

[¶ 4044] Sec. 411. REVISION OF STATE VETERANS LIMIT MADE PERMANENT.

****

(b) EFFECTIVE DATE. The amendment made by this section shall take effect as if included in section 203 of the Tax Increase Prevention and Reconciliation Act of 2005.

[¶ 4045] Sec. 412. CAPITAL GAINS TREATMENT FOR CERTAIN SELF-CREATED MUSICAL WORKS MADE PERMANENT.

****

(b) EFFECTIVE DATE. The amendment made by this section shall take effect as if included in section 204 of the Tax Increase Prevention and Reconciliation Act of 2005.

[¶ 4046] Sec. 413. REDUCTION IN MINIMUM VESSEL TONNAGE WHICH QUALIFIES FOR TONNAGE TAX MADE PERMANENT.

****

(b) EFFECTIVE DATE. The amendment made by this section shall take effect as if included in section 205 of the Tax Increase Prevention and Reconciliation Act of 2005.

[¶ 4047] Sec. 414. MODIFICATION OF SPECIAL ARBITRAGE RULE FOR CERTAIN FUNDS MADE PERMANENT.

****

(b) EFFECTIVE DATE. The amendment made by this section shall take effect as if included in section 206 of the Tax Increase Prevention and Reconciliation Act of 2005.

[¶ 4048] Sec. 415. GREAT LAKES DOMESTIC SHIPPING TO NOT DISQUALIFY VESSEL FROM TONNAGE TAX.

****

(b) EFFECTIVE DATE. The amendments made by this section shall apply to taxable years beginning after the date of the enactment of this Act.

[¶ 4049] Sec. 416. USE OF QUALIFIED MORTGAGE BONDS TO FINANCE RESIDENCES FOR VETERANS WITHOUT REGARD TO FIRST-TIME HOMEBUYER REQUIREMENT.

****

(b) EFFECTIVE DATE. The amendments made by this section shall apply to bonds issued after the date of the enactment of this Act.

[¶ 4050] Sec. 417. EXCLUSION OF GAIN FROM SALE OF A PRINCIPAL RESIDENCE BY CERTAIN EMPLOYEES OF THE INTELLIGENCE COMMUNITY.

****

(e) EFFECTIVE DATE. The amendments made by this section shall apply to sales or exchanges after the date of the enactment of this Act and before January 1, 2011.

[¶ 4051] Sec. 418. SALE OF PROPERTY BY JUDICIAL OFFICERS.

****

(c) EFFECTIVE DATE. The amendments made by this section shall apply to sales after the date of enactment of this Act.

[¶ 4052] Sec. 419. PREMIUMS FOR MORTGAGE INSURANCE.

****

(d) EFFECTIVE DATE. The amendments made by this section shall apply to amounts paid or accrued after December 31, 2006.

[¶ 4053] Sec. 420. MODIFICATION OF REFUNDS FOR KEROSENE USED IN AVIATION.

****

(c) EFFECTIVE DATE.

(1) IN GENERAL. The amendments made by this section shall apply to kerosene sold after September 30, 2005.

(2) SPECIAL RULE FOR PENDING CLAIMS. In the case of kerosene sold for use in aviation (other than kerosene to which section 6427(l)(4)(C)(ii) of the Internal Revenue Code of 1986 (as added by subsection (a)) applies or kerosene to which section 6427(l)(5) of such Code (as redesignated by subsection (b)) applies) after September 30, 2005, and before the date of the enactment of this Act, the ultimate purchaser shall be treated as having waived the right to payment under section 6427(l)(1) of such Code and as having assigned such right to the ultimate vendor if such ultimate vendor has met the requirements of subparagraph (A), (B), or (D) of section 6416(a)(1) of such Code.

(d) SPECIAL RULE FOR KEROSENE USED IN AVIATION ON A FARM FOR FARMING PURPOSES.

(1) REFUNDS FOR PURCHASES AFTER DECEMBER 31, 2004, AND BEFORE OCTOBER 1, 2005. The Secretary of the Treasury shall pay to the ultimate purchaser of any kerosene which is used in aviation on a farm for farming purposes and which was purchased after December 31, 2004, and before October 1, 2005, an amount equal to the aggregate amount of tax imposed on such fuel under section 4041 or 4081 of the Internal Revenue Code of 1986, as the case may be, reduced by any payment to the ultimate vendor under section 6427(l)(5)(C) of such Code (as in effect on the day before the date of the enactment of the Safe, Accountable, Flexible, Efficient Transportation Equity Act: a Legacy for Users).

(2) USE ON A FARM FOR FARMING PURPOSES. For purposes of paragraph (1), kerosene shall be treated as used on a farm for farming purposes if such kerosene is used for farming purposes (within the meaning of section 6420(c)(3) of the Internal Revenue Code of 1986) in carrying on a trade or business on a farm situated in the United States. For purposes of the preceding sentence, rules similar to the rules of section 6420(c)(4) of such Code shall apply.

(3) TIME FOR FILING CLAIMS. No claim shall be allowed under paragraph (1) unless the ultimate purchaser files such claim before the date that is 3 months after the date of the enactment of this Act.

(4) NO DOUBLE BENEFIT. No amount shall be paid under paragraph (1) or section 6427(l) of the Internal Revenue Code of 1986 with respect to any kerosene described in paragraph (1) to the extent that such amount is in excess of the tax imposed on such kerosene under section 4041 or 4081 of such Code, as the case may be.

(5) APPLICABLE LAWS. For purposes of this subsection, rules similar to the rules of section 6427(j) of the Internal Revenue Code of 1986 shall apply.

[¶ 4054] Sec. 421. REGIONAL INCOME TAX AGENCIES TREATED AS STATES FOR PURPOSES OF CONFIDENTIALITY AND DISCLOSURE REQUIREMENTS.

****

(c) EFFECTIVE DATE. The amendments made by this section shall apply to disclosures made after December 31, 2006.

[¶ 4055] Sec. 422. DESIGNATION OF WINES BY SEMI-GENERIC NAMES.

****

(b) EFFECTIVE DATE. The amendments made by this section shall apply to wine imported or bottled in the United States on or after the date of enactment of this Act.

[¶ 4056] Sec. 423. MODIFICATION OF RAILROAD TRACK MAINTENANCE CREDIT.

****

(b) EFFECTIVE DATE. The amendment made by this section shall take effect as if included in the amendment made by section 245(a) of the American Jobs Creation Act of 2004.

[¶ 4057] Sec. 424. MODIFICATION OF EXCISE TAX ON UNRELATED BUSINESS TAXABLE INCOME OF CHARITABLE REMAINDER TRUSTS.

****

(b) EFFECTIVE DATE. The amendment made by this section shall apply to taxable years beginning after December 31, 2006.

[¶ 4058] Sec. 425. LOANS TO QUALIFIED CONTINUING CARE FACILITIES MADE PERMANENT.

****

(b) EFFECTIVE DATE. The amendment made by this section shall take effect as if included in section 209 of the Tax Increase Prevention and Reconciliation Act of 2005.

[¶ 4059] Sec. 426. TECHNICAL CORRECTIONS.

(a) TECHNICAL CORRECTIONS RELATING TO LOOK-THROUGH TREATMENT OF PAYMENTS BETWEEN RELATED CONTROLLED FOREIGN CORPORATIONS UNDER THE FOREIGN PERSONAL HOLDING COMPANY RULES

****

(2) EFFECTIVE DATE. The amendments made by this subsection shall take effect as if included in section 103(b) of the Tax Increase Prevention and Reconciliation Act of 2005.

(b) TECHNICAL CORRECTION REGARDING AUTHORITY TO EXERCISE REASONABLE CAUSE AND GOOD FAITH EXCEPTION.

****

(2) EFFECTIVE DATE. The amendment made by this subsection shall take effect as if included in the provisions of the American Jobs Creation Act of 2004 to which it relates.

DIVISION C— OTHER PROVISIONS.

TITLE I— GULF OF MEXICO ENERGY SECURITY.

[¶ 4060] Sec. 101. SHORT TITLE. This title may be cited as the "Gulf of Mexico Energy Security Act of 2006".

****

Subtitle B— Coal Industry Retiree Health Benefit Act

[¶4061] Sec. 211. CERTAIN RELATED PERSONS AND SUCCESSORS IN INTEREST RELIEVED OF LIABILITY IF PREMIUMS PREPAID.

****

(e) EFFECTIVE DATE. The amendments made by this section shall take effect on the date of the enactment of this Act, except that the amendment made by subsection (d) shall apply to transactions after the date of the enactment of this Act.

[¶4062] Sec. 212. TRANSFERS TO FUNDS; PREMIUM RELIEF.

(a) COMBINED FUND.

****

(4) EFFECTIVE DATE. The amendments made by this subsection shall apply to plan years of the Combined Fund beginning after September 30, 2006.

(b) 1992 UMWA BENEFIT AND OTHER PLANS.

****

(2) PREMIUM ADJUSTMENTS.

****

(C) EFFECTIVE DATE. The amendments made by this paragraph shall apply to fiscal years beginning on or after October 1, 2010.

TITLE IV— OTHER PROVISIONS

[¶4063] Sec. 401. TOBACCO PERSONAL USE QUANTITY EXCEPTION TO NOT APPLY TO DELIVERY SALES.

****

(g) EFFECTIVE DATE. The amendments made by this section shall apply with respect to goods entered, or withdrawn from warehouse for consumption, on or after the 15th day after the date of the enactment of this Act.

[¶4064] Sec. 408. TAX COURT REVIEW OF REQUESTS FOR EQUITABLE RELIEF FROM JOINT AND SEVERAL LIABILITY.

****

(c) EFFECTIVE DATE. The amendments made by this section shall apply with respect to liability for taxes arising or remaining unpaid on or after the date of the enactment of this Act.

[¶ 5000] Joint Committee on Taxation Technical Explanation Accompanying the Tax Relief and Health Care Act of 2006

This section, in ¶ 5001 through ¶ 5079, reproduces all relevant parts of the Joint Committee on Taxation Technical Explanation of H.R. 6408, the "Tax Relief and Health Care Act of 2006," as introduced in the House on Dec. 7, 2006 (JCX-50-06, 12/7/2006). Through a parliamentary maneuver, the legislative text of H.R. 6408 was incorporated into H.R. 6111, the "Tax Relief and Health Care Act of 2006," which was passed by the House on Dec. 8, 2006 and the Senate on Dec. 9, 2006.

[¶ 5001] Section 101. Deduction for qualified tuition and related expenses.

(Code Sec. 222)

[Joint Committee on Taxation Report — JCX-50-06]

Present Law

An individual is allowed an above-the-line deduction for qualified tuition and related expenses for higher education paid by the individual during the taxable year. Qualified tuition and related expenses include tuition and fees required for the enrollment or attendance of the taxpayer, the taxpayer's spouse, or any dependent of the taxpayer with respect to whom the taxpayer may claim a personal exemption, at an eligible institution of higher education for courses of instruction of such individual at such institution. Charges and fees associated with meals, lodging, insurance, transportation, and similar personal, living, or family expenses are not eligible for the deduction. The expenses of education involving sports, games, or hobbies are not qualified tuition and related expenses unless this education is part of the student's degree program.

The amount of qualified tuition and related expenses must be reduced by certain scholarships, educational assistance allowances, and other amounts paid for the benefit of such individual, and by the amount of such expenses taken into account for purposes of determining any exclusion from gross income of: (1) income from certain United States Savings Bonds used to pay higher education tuition and fees; and (2) income from a Coverdell education savings account. Additionally, such expenses must be reduced by the earnings portion (but not the return of principal) of distributions from a qualified tuition program if an exclusion under section 529 is claimed with respect to expenses otherwise deductible under section 222. No deduction is allowed for any expense for which a deduction is otherwise allowed or with respect to an individual for whom a Hope credit or Lifetime Learning credit is elected for such taxable year.

The expenses must be in connection with enrollment at an institution of higher education during the taxable year, or with an academic term beginning during the taxable year or during the first three months of the next taxable year. The deduction is not available for tuition and related expenses paid for elementary or secondary education.

For taxable years beginning in 2004 and 2005, the maximum deduction is $4,000 for an individual whose adjusted gross income for the taxable year does not exceed $65,000 ($130,000 in the case of a joint return), or $2,000 for other individuals whose adjusted gross income does not exceed $80,000 ($160,000 in the case of a joint return). No deduction is allowed for an individual whose adjusted gross income exceeds the relevant adjusted gross income limitations, for a married individual who does not file a joint return, or for an individual with respect to whom a personal exemption deduction may be claimed by another taxpayer for the taxable year. The deduction is not available for taxable years beginning after December 31, 2005.

Explanation of Provision

The provision extends the tuition deduction for two years, through December 31, 2007.

Effective Date

The provision is effective for taxable years beginning after December 31, 2005.

[¶5002] Section 102. Extension and modification of new markets tax credit.

(Code Sec. 45D)

[Joint Committee on Taxation Report — JCX-50-06]

Present Law

Section 45D provides a new markets tax credit for qualified equity investments made to acquire stock in a corporation, or a capital interest in a partnership, that is a qualified community development entity ("CDE").[4] The amount of the credit allowable to the investor (either the original purchaser or a subsequent holder) is (1) a five-percent credit for the year in which the equity interest is purchased from the CDE and for each of the following two years, and (2) a six-percent credit for each of the following four years. The credit is determined by applying the applicable percentage (five or six percent) to the amount paid to the CDE for the investment at its original issue, and is available for a taxable year to the taxpayer who holds the qualified equity investment on the date of the initial investment or on the respective anniversary date that occurs during the taxable year. The credit is recaptured if at any time during the seven-year period that begins on the date of the original issue of the investment the entity ceases to be a qualified CDE, the proceeds of the investment cease to be used as required, or the equity investment is redeemed.

A qualified CDE is any domestic corporation or partnership: (1) whose primary mission is serving or providing investment capital for low-income communities or low-income persons; (2) that maintains accountability to residents of low-income communities by their representation on any governing board of or any advisory board to the CDE; and (3) that is certified by the Secretary as being a qualified CDE. A qualified equity investment means stock (other than nonqualified preferred stock as defined in sec. 351(g)(2)) in a corporation or a capital interest in a partnership that is acquired directly from a CDE for cash, and includes an investment of a subsequent purchaser if such investment was a qualified equity investment in the hands of the prior holder. Substantially all of the investment proceeds must be used by the CDE to make qualified low-income community investments. For this purpose, qualified low-income community investments include: (1) capital or equity investments in, or loans to, qualified active low-income community businesses; (2) certain financial counseling and other services to businesses and residents in low-income communities; (3) the purchase from another CDE of any loan made by such entity that is a qualified low-income community investment; or (4) an equity investment in, or loan to, another CDE.

A "low-income community" is a population census tract with either (1) a poverty rate of at least 20 percent or (2) median family income which does not exceed 80 percent of the greater of metropolitan area median family income or statewide median family income (for a non-metropolitan census tract, does not exceed 80 percent of statewide median family income). In the case of a population census tract located within a high migration rural county, low-income is defined by reference to 85 percent (rather than 80 percent) of statewide median family income. For this purpose, a high migration rural

4. Section 45D was added by section 121(a) of the Community Renewal Tax Relief Act of 2000, Pub. L. No. 106-554 (December 21, 2000).

county is any county that, during the 20-year period ending with the year in which the most recent census was conducted, has a net out-migration of inhabitants from the county of at least 10 percent of the population of the county at the beginning of such period.

The Secretary has the authority to designate "targeted populations" as low-income communities for purposes of the new markets tax credit. For this purpose, a "targeted population" is defined by reference to section 103(20) of the Riegle Community Development and Regulatory Improvement Act of 1994 (12 U.S.C. 4702(20)) to mean individuals, or an identifiable group of individuals, including an Indian tribe, who (A) are low-income persons; or (B) otherwise lack adequate access to loans or equity investments. Under such Act, "low-income" means (1) for a targeted population within a metropolitan area, less than 80 percent of the area median family income; and (2) for a targeted population within a non-metropolitan area, less than the greater of 80 percent of the area median family income or 80 percent of the statewide non-metropolitan area median family income.[5] Under such Act, a targeted population is not required to be within any census tract. In addition, a population census tract with a population of less than 2,000 is treated as a low-income community for purposes of the credit if such tract is within an empowerment zone, the designation of which is in effect under section 1391, and is contiguous to one or more low-income communities.

A qualified active low-income community business is defined as a business that satisfies, with respect to a taxable year, the following requirements: (1) at least 50 percent of the total gross income of the business is derived from the active conduct of trade or business activities in any low-income community; (2) a substantial portion of the tangible property of such business is used in a low-income community; (3) a substantial portion of the services performed for such business by its employees is performed in a low-income community; and (4) less than five percent of the average of the aggregate unadjusted bases of the property of such business is attributable to certain financial property or to certain collectibles.

The maximum annual amount of qualified equity investments is capped at $2.0 billion per year for calendar years 2004 and 2005, and at $3.5 billion per year for calendar years 2006 and 2007.

Explanation of Provision

The provision extends the new markets tax credit through 2008, permitting up to $3.5 billion in qualified equity investments for that calendar year. The provision also requires that the Secretary prescribe regulations to ensure that non-metropolitan counties receive a proportional allocation of qualified equity investments.

Effective Date

The provision is effective on the date of enactment.

[¶5003] Section 103. Election to deduct State and local general sales taxes.

(Code Sec. 164)

[Joint Committee on Taxation Report — JCX-50-06]

Present Law

For purposes of determining regular tax liability, an itemized deduction is permitted for certain State and local taxes paid, including individual income taxes, real property taxes, and personal property taxes. The itemized deduction is not permitted for purposes of determining a taxpayer's alternative minimum taxable income. For taxable years beginning in 2004 and 2005, at the election of the taxpayer, an itemized deduction may be

5. 12 U.S.C. 4702(17) defines "low-income" for purposes of 12 U.S.C. 4702(20).

taken for State and local general sales taxes in lieu of the itemized deduction provided under present law for State and local income taxes. As is the case for State and local income taxes, the itemized deduction for State and local general sales taxes is not permitted for purposes of determining a taxpayer's alternative minimum taxable income. Taxpayers have two options with respect to the determination of the sales tax deduction amount. Taxpayers may deduct the total amount of general State and local sales taxes paid by accumulating receipts showing general sales taxes paid. Alternatively, taxpayers may use tables created by the Secretary of the Treasury that show the allowable deduction. The tables are based on average consumption by taxpayers on a State-by-State basis taking into account number of dependents, modified adjusted gross income and rates of State and local general sales taxation. Taxpayers who live in more than one jurisdiction during the tax year are required to pro-rate the table amounts based on the time they live in each jurisdiction. Taxpayers who use the tables created by the Secretary may, in addition to the table amounts, deduct eligible general sales taxes paid with respect to the purchase of motor vehicles, boats and other items specified by the Secretary. Sales taxes for items that may be added to the tables are not reflected in the tables themselves.

The term "general sales tax" means a tax imposed at one rate with respect to the sale at retail of a broad range of classes of items. However, in the case of items of food, clothing, medical supplies, and motor vehicles, the fact that the tax does not apply with respect to some or all of such items is not taken into account in determining whether the tax applies with respect to a broad range of classes of items, and the fact that the rate of tax applicable with respect to some or all of such items is lower than the general rate of tax is not taken into account in determining whether the tax is imposed at one rate. Except in the case of a lower rate of tax applicable with respect to food, clothing, medical supplies, or motor vehicles, no deduction is allowed for any general sales tax imposed with respect to an item at a rate other than the general rate of tax. However, in the case of motor vehicles, if the rate of tax exceeds the general rate, such excess shall be disregarded and the general rate is treated as the rate of tax.

A compensating use tax with respect to an item is treated as a general sales tax, provided such tax is complementary to a general sales tax and a deduction for sales taxes is allowable with respect to items sold at retail in the taxing jurisdiction that are similar to such item.

Explanation of Provision

The present-law provision allowing taxpayers to elect to deduct State and local sales taxes in lieu of State and local income taxes is extended for two years (through December 31, 2007).

Effective Date

The provision applies to taxable years beginning after December 31, 2005.

[¶5004] Section 104. Extension and modification of research credit.

(Code Sec. 41)

[Joint Committee on Taxation Report — JCX-50-06]

Present Law

General rule

Prior to January 1, 2006, a taxpayer could claim a research credit equal to 20 percent of the amount by which the taxpayer's qualified research expenses for a taxable year exceeded its base amount for that year.[6] Thus, the research credit was generally available with respect to incremental increases in qualified research.

A 20-percent research tax credit was also available with respect to the excess of (1) 100 percent of corporate cash expenses (including grants or contributions) paid for basic research conducted by universities (and certain nonprofit scientific research organizations) over (2) the sum of (a) the greater of two minimum basic research floors plus (b) an amount reflecting any decrease in nonresearch giving to universities by the corporation as compared to such giving during a fixed-base period, as adjusted for inflation. This separate credit computation was commonly referred to as the university basic research credit (see sec. 41(e)).

Finally, a research credit was available for a taxpayer's expenditures on research undertaken by an energy research consortium. This separate credit computation was commonly referred to as the energy research credit. Unlike the other research credits, the energy research credit applied to all qualified expenditures, not just those in excess of a base amount.

The research credit, including the university basic research credit and the energy research credit, expired on December 31, 2005.

Computation of allowable credit

Except for energy research payments and certain university basic research payments made by corporations, the research tax credit applied only to the extent that the taxpayer's qualified research expenses for the current taxable year exceeded its base amount. The base amount for the current year generally was computed by multiplying the taxpayer's fixed-base percentage by the average amount of the taxpayer's gross receipts for the four preceding years. If a taxpayer both incurred qualified research expenses and had gross receipts during each of at least three years from 1984 through 1988, then its fixed-base percentage was the ratio that its total qualified research expenses for the 1984-1988 period bore to its total gross receipts for that period (subject to a maximum fixed-base percentage of 16 percent). All other taxpayers (so-called start-up firms) were assigned a fixed-base percentage of three percent.[7]

In computing the credit, a taxpayer's base amount could not be less than 50 percent of its current-year qualified research expenses.

To prevent artificial increases in research expenditures by shifting expenditures among commonly controlled or otherwise related entities, a special aggregation rule provided that all members of the same controlled group of corporations were treated as a single taxpayer (sec. 41(f)(1)). Under regulations prescribed by the Secretary, special rules applied for computing the credit when a major portion of a trade or business (or unit thereof) changed hands, under which qualified research expenses and gross receipts for periods prior to the change of ownership of a trade or business were treated as transferred with the trade or business that gave rise to those expenses and receipts for purposes of recomputing a taxpayer's fixed-base percentage (sec. 41(f)(3)).

6. Sec. 41.
7. The Small Business Job Protection Act of 1996 expanded the definition of start-up firms under section 41(c)(3)(B)(i) to include any firm if the first taxable year in which such firm had both gross receipts and qualified research expenses began after 1983. A special rule (enacted in 1993) was designed to gradually recompute a start-up firm's fixed-base percentage based on its actual research experience. Under this special rule, a start-up firm would be assigned a fixed-base percentage of three percent for each of its first five taxable years after 1993 in which it incurs qualified research expenses. In the event that the research credit is extended beyond its expiration date, a start-up firm's fixed-base percentage for its sixth through tenth taxable years after 1993 in which it incurs qualified research expenses will be a phased-in ratio based on its actual research experience. For all subsequent taxable years, the taxpayer's fixed-base percentage will be its actual ratio of qualified research expenses to gross receipts for any five years selected by the taxpayer from its fifth through tenth taxable years after 1993 (sec. 41(c)(3)(B)).

Alternative incremental research credit regime

Taxpayers were allowed to elect an alternative incremental research credit regime.[8] If a taxpayer elected to be subject to this alternative regime, the taxpayer was assigned a three-tiered fixed-base percentage (that was lower than the fixed-base percentage otherwise applicable) and the credit rate likewise was reduced. Under the alternative incremental credit regime, a credit rate of 2.65 percent applied to the extent that a taxpayer's current-year research expenses exceeded a base amount computed by using a fixed-base percentage of one percent (i.e., the base amount equaled one percent of the taxpayer's average gross receipts for the four preceding years) but did not exceed a base amount computed by using a fixed-base percentage of 1.5 percent. A credit rate of 3.2 percent applied to the extent that a taxpayer's current-year research expenses exceeded a base amount computed by using a fixed-base percentage of 1.5 percent but did not exceed a base amount computed by using a fixed-base percentage of two percent. A credit rate of 3.75 percent applied to the extent that a taxpayer's current-year research expenses exceeded a base amount computed by using a fixed-base percentage of two percent. An election to be subject to this alternative incremental credit regime could be made for any taxable year beginning after June 30, 1996, and such an election applied to that taxable year and all subsequent years unless revoked with the consent of the Secretary of the Treasury.

Eligible expenses

Qualified research expenses eligible for the research tax credit consisted of: (1) in-house expenses of the taxpayer for wages and supplies attributable to qualified research; (2) certain time-sharing costs for computer use in qualified research; and (3) 65 percent of amounts paid or incurred by the taxpayer to certain other persons for qualified research conducted on the taxpayer's behalf (so-called contract research expenses).[9] Notwithstanding the limitation for contract research expenses, qualified research expenses included 100 percent of amounts paid or incurred by the taxpayer to an eligible small business, university, or Federal laboratory for qualified energy research.

To be eligible for the credit, the research did not only have to satisfy the requirements of present-law section 174 (described below) but also had to be undertaken for the purpose of discovering information that is technological in nature, the application of which was intended to be useful in the development of a new or improved business component of the taxpayer, and substantially all of the activities of which had to constitute elements of a process of experimentation for functional aspects, performance, reliability, or quality of a business component. Research did not qualify for the credit if substantially all of the activities related to style, taste, cosmetic, or seasonal design factors (sec. 41(d)(3)). In addition, research did not qualify for the credit: (1) if conducted after the beginning of commercial production of the business component; (2) if related to the adaptation of an existing business component to a particular customer's requirements; (3) if related to the duplication of an existing business component from a physical examination of the component itself or certain other information; or (4) if related to certain efficiency surveys, management function or technique, market research, market testing, or market development, routine data collection or routine quality control (sec. 41(d)(4)). Research did not qualify for the credit if it was conducted outside the United States, Puerto Rico, or any U.S. possession.

---

8. Sec. 41(c)(4).
9. Under a special rule, 75 percent of amounts paid to a research consortium for qualified research were treated as qualified research expenses eligible for the research credit (rather than 65 percent under the general rule under section 41(b)(3) governing contract research expenses) if (1) such research consortium was a tax-exempt organization that is described in section 501(c)(3) (other than a private foundation) or section 501(c)(6) and was organized and operated primarily to conduct scientific research, and (2) such qualified research was conducted by the consortium on behalf of the taxpayer and one or more persons not related to the taxpayer. Sec. 41(b)(3)(C).

Relation to deduction

Under section 174, taxpayers may elect to deduct currently the amount of certain research or experimental expenditures paid or incurred in connection with a trade or business, notwithstanding the general rule that business expenses to develop or create an asset that has a useful life extending beyond the current year must be capitalized.[10] While the research credit was in effect, however, deductions allowed to a taxpayer under section 174 (or any other section) were reduced by an amount equal to 100 percent of the taxpayer's research tax credit determined for the taxable year (Sec. 280C(c)). Taxpayers could alternatively elect to claim a reduced research tax credit amount (13 percent) under section 41 in lieu of reducing deductions otherwise allowed (sec. 280C(c)(3)).

Explanation of Provision

The provision extends the research credit two years (for amounts paid or incurred after December 31, 2005, and before January 1, 2008).

The provision also modifies the research credit for taxable years ending after December 31, 2006, subject to the general termination provision applicable to the credit.

The provision increases the rates of the alternative incremental credit: (1) a credit rate of three percent (rather than 2.65 percent) applies to the extent that a taxpayer's current-year research expenses exceed a base amount computed by using a fixed-base percentage of one percent (i.e., the base amount equals one percent of the taxpayer's average gross receipts for the four preceding years) but do not exceed a base amount computed by using a fixed-base percentage of 1.5 percent; (2) a credit rate of four percent (rather than 3.2 percent) applies to the extent that a taxpayer's current-year research expenses exceed a base amount computed by using a fixed-base percentage of 1.5 percent but do not exceed a base amount computed by using a fixed-base percentage of two percent; and (3) a credit rate of five percent (rather than 3.75 percent) applies to the extent that a taxpayer's current-year research expenses exceed a base amount computed by using a fixed-base percentage of two percent.

The provision also creates, at the election of the taxpayer, an alternative simplified credit for qualified research expenses. The alternative simplified research is equal to 12 percent of qualified research expenses that exceed 50 percent of the average qualified research expenses for the three preceding taxable years. The rate is reduced to 6 percent if a taxpayer has no qualified research expenses in any one of the three preceding taxable years.

An election to use the alternative simplified credit applies to all succeeding taxable years unless revoked with the consent of the Secretary. An election to use the alternative simplified credit may not be made for any taxable year for which an election to use the alternative incremental credit is in effect. A transition rule applies which permits a taxpayer to elect to use the alternative simplified credit in lieu of the alternative incremental credit if such election is made during the taxable year which includes January 1, 2007. The transition rule only applies to the taxable year which includes that date.

Effective Date

The extension of the research credit applies to amounts paid or incurred after December 31, 2005. The modification of the alternative incremental credit and the addition of the alternative simplified credit are effective for taxable years ending after December 31, 2006.

Special transitional rules apply to fiscal year 2006-2007 taxpayers. In the case of a taxpayer electing the alternative incremental credit, the amount of the credit is the sum of (1) the credit calculated as if it were extended but not modified multiplied by a frac-

10. Taxpayers may elect 10-year amortization of certain research expenditures allowable as a deduction under section 174(a). Secs. 174(f)(2) and 59(e).

tion the numerator of which is the number of days in the taxable year before January 1, 2007, and the denominator of which is the total number of days in the taxable year and (2) the credit calculated under the provision as amended multiplied by a fraction the numerator of which is the number of days in the taxable year after December 31, 2006, and the denominator of which is the total number of days in the taxable year.

In the case of a taxpayer electing the new alternative simplified credit, the amount of the credit under section 41(a)(1) for the taxable year is the sum of (1) the credit that would be determined under section 41(a)(1) (including the alternative incremental credit for a taxpayer electing that credit) if it were extended but not modified multiplied by a fraction the numerator of which is the number of days in the taxable year before January 1, 2007, and the denominator of which is the total number of days in the taxable year and (2) the alternative simplified credit determined for the year multiplied by a fraction the numerator of which is the number of days in the taxable year after December 31, 2006, and the denominator of which is the total number of days in the taxable year.

[¶5005] Section 105. Work opportunity tax credit and welfare-to-work credit.

(Code Sec. 51, 51A)

[Joint Committee on Taxation Report — JCX-50-06]

Present Law

Work opportunity tax credit

Targeted groups eligible for the credit

The work opportunity tax credit is available on an elective basis for employers hiring individuals from one or more of eight targeted groups. The eight targeted groups are: (1) certain families eligible to receive benefits under the Temporary Assistance for Needy Families Program; (2) high-risk youth; (3) qualified ex-felons; (4) vocational rehabilitation referrals; (5) qualified summer youth employees; (6) qualified veterans; (7) families receiving food stamps; and (8) persons receiving certain Supplemental Security Income (SSI) benefits.

A high-risk youth is an individual aged 18 but not aged 25 on the hiring date who is certified by a designated local agency as having a principal place of abode within an empowerment zone, enterprise community, or renewal community. The credit is not available if such youth's principal place of abode ceases to be within an empowerment zone, enterprise community, or renewal community.

A qualified ex-felon is an individual certified by a designated local agency as: (1) having been convicted of a felony under State or Federal law; (2) being a member of an economically disadvantaged family; and (3) having a hiring date within one year of release from prison or conviction.

A food stamp recipient is an individual aged 18 but not aged 25 on the hiring date certified by a designated local agency as being a member of a family either currently or recently receiving assistance under an eligible food stamp program.

Qualified wages

Generally, qualified wages are defined as cash wages paid by the employer to a member of a targeted group. The employer's deduction for wages is reduced by the amount of the credit.

Calculation of the credit

The credit equals 40 percent (25 percent for employment of 400 hours or less) of qualified first-year wages. Generally, qualified first-year wages are qualified wages (not in excess of $6,000) attributable to service rendered by a member of a targeted group during the one-year period beginning with the day the individual began work for the employer. Therefore, the maximum credit per employee is $2,400 (40 percent of the first $6,000 of qualified first-year wages). With respect to qualified summer youth employees, the maximum credit is $1,200 (40 percent of the first $3,000 of qualified first-year wages).

Certification rules

An individual is not treated as a member of a targeted group unless: (1) on or before the day on which an individual begins work for an employer, the employer has received a certification from a designated local agency that such individual is a member of a targeted group; or (2) on or before the day an individual is offered employment with the employer, a pre-screening notice is completed by the employer with respect to such individual, and not later than the 21st day after the individual begins work for the employer, the employer submits such notice, signed by the employer and the individual under penalties of perjury, to the designated local agency as part of a written request for certification.

Minimum employment period

No credit is allowed for qualified wages paid to employees who work less than 120 hours in the first year of employment.

Coordination of the work opportunity tax credit and the welfare-to-work tax credit

An employer cannot claim the work opportunity tax credit with respect to wages of any employee on which the employer claims the welfare-to-work tax credit.

Other rules

The work opportunity tax credit is not allowed for wages paid to a relative or dependent of the taxpayer. Similarly wages paid to replacement workers during a strike or lockout are not eligible for the work opportunity tax credit. Wages paid to any employee during any period for which the employer received on-the-job training program payments with respect to that employee are not eligible for the work opportunity tax credit. The work opportunity tax credit generally is not allowed for wages paid to individuals who had previously been employed by the employer. In addition, many other technical rules apply.

Expiration

The work opportunity tax credit is not available for individuals who begin work for an employer after December 31, 2005.

Welfare-to-work tax credit

Targeted group eligible for the credit

The welfare-to-work tax credit is available on an elective basis to employers of qualified long-term family assistance recipients. Qualified long-term family assistance recipients are: (1) members of a family that have received family assistance for at least 18 consecutive months ending on the hiring date; (2) members of a family that have received such family assistance for a total of at least 18 months (whether or not consecutive) after August 5, 1997 (the date of enactment of the welfare-to-work tax credit) if they are hired within 2 years after the date that the 18-month total is reached; and (3) members of a family who are no longer eligible for family assistance because of either Federal or State time limits, if they are hired within 2 years after the Federal or State time limits made the family ineligible for family assistance.

Qualified wages

Qualified wages for purposes of the welfare-to-work tax credit are defined more broadly than the work opportunity tax credit. Unlike the definition of wages for the work opportunity tax credit which includes simply cash wages, the definition of wages for the welfare-to-work tax credit includes cash wages paid to an employee plus amounts paid by the employer for: (1) educational assistance excludable under a section 127 program (or that would be excludable but for the expiration of sec. 127); (2) health plan coverage for the employee, but not more than the applicable premium defined under section 4980B(f)(4); and (3) dependent care assistance excludable under section 129. The employer's deduction for wages is reduced by the amount of the credit.

Calculation of the credit

The welfare-to-work tax credit is available on an elective basis to employers of qualified long-term family assistance recipients during the first two years of employment. The maximum credit is 35 percent of the first $10,000 of qualified first-year wages and 50 percent of the first $10,000 of qualified second-year wages. Qualified first-year wages are defined as qualified wages (not in excess of $10,000) attributable to service rendered by a member of the targeted group during the one-year period beginning with the day the individual began work for the employer. Qualified second-year wages are defined as qualified wages (not in excess of $10,000) attributable to service rendered by a member of the targeted group during the one-year period beginning immediately after the first year of that individual's employment for the employer. The maximum credit is $8,500 per qualified employee.

Certification rules

An individual is not treated as a member of the targeted group unless: (1) on or before the day on which an individual begins work for an employer, the employer has received a certification from a designated local agency that such individual is a member of the targeted group; or (2) on or before the day an individual is offered employment with the employer, a pre-screening notice is completed by the employer with respect to such individual, and not later than the 21st day after the individual begins work for the employer, the employer submits such notice, signed by the employer and the individual under penalties of perjury, to the designated local agency as part of a written request for certification.

Minimum employment period

No credit is allowed for qualified wages paid to a member of the targeted group unless the number they work is at least 400 hours or 180 days in the first year of employment.

Coordination of the work opportunity tax credit and the welfare-to-work tax credit

An employer cannot claim the work opportunity tax credit with respect to wages of any employee on which the employer claims the welfare-to-work tax credit.

Other rules

The welfare-to-work tax credit incorporates directly or by reference many of these other rules contained on the work opportunity tax credit.

Expiration

The welfare-to-work credit is not available for individuals who begin work for an employer after December 31, 2005.

Explanation of Provision

First year of extension

The provision extends the work opportunity tax credit and welfare-to-work tax credits for one year without modification, respectively (for qualified individuals who begin work for an employer after December 31, 2005 and before January 1, 2007).

Second year of extension

In general

The provision then combines and extends the two credits for a second year (for qualified individuals who begin work for an employer after December 31, 2006 and before January 1, 2008).

Targeted groups eligible for the combined credit

The combined credit is available on an elective basis for employers hiring individuals from one or more of all nine targeted groups. The nine targeted groups are the present-law eight groups with the addition of the welfare-to-work credit/long-term family assistance recipient as the ninth targeted group.

The provision repeals the requirement that a qualified ex-felon be an individual certified as a member of an economically disadvantaged family.

The provision raises the age limit for the food stamp recipient category to include individuals aged 18 but not aged 40 on the hiring date.

Qualified wages

Qualified first-year wages for the eight work opportunity tax credit categories remain capped at $6,000 ($3,000 for qualified summer youth employees). No credit is allowed for second-year wages. In the case of long-term family assistance recipients, the cap is $10,000 for both qualified first-year wages and qualified second-year wages. The combined credit follows the work opportunity tax credit definition of wages which does not include amounts paid by the employer for: (1) educational assistance excludable under a section 127 program (or that would be excludable but for the expiration of sec. 127); (2) health plan coverage for the employee, but not more than the applicable premium defined under section 4980B(f)(4); and (3) dependent care assistance excludable under section 129. For all targeted groups, the employer's deduction for wages is reduced by the amount of the credit.

Calculation of the credit

First-year wages.—For the eight work opportunity tax credit categories, the credit equals 40 percent (25 percent for employment of 400 hours or less) of qualified first-year wages. Generally, qualified first-year wages are qualified wages (not in excess of $6,000) attributable to service rendered by a member of a targeted group during the one-year period beginning with the day the individual began work for the employer. Therefore, the maximum credit per employee for members of any of the eight work opportunity tax credit targeted groups generally is $2,400 (40 percent of the first $6,000 of qualified first-year wages). With respect to qualified summer youth employees, the maximum credit remains $1,200 (40 percent of the first $3,000 of qualified first-year wages). For the welfare-to-work/long-term family assistance recipients, the maximum credit equals $4,000 per employee (40 percent of $10,000 of wages).

Second year wages.—In the case of long-term family assistance recipients the maximum credit is $5,000 (50 percent of the first $10,000 of qualified second-year wages).

Certification rules

The provision changes the present-law 21-day requirement to 28 days.

Minimum employment period

No credit is allowed for qualified wages paid to employees who work less than 120 hours in the first year of employment.

Coordination of the work opportunity tax credit and the welfare-to-work tax credit

Coordination is no longer necessary once the two credits are combined.

Effective Date

Generally, the extension of the credits is effective for wages paid or incurred to a qualified individual who begins work for an employer after December 31, 2005, and before January 1, 2008. The consolidation of the credits and other modifications are effective for wages paid or incurred to a qualified individual who begins work for an employer after December 31, 2006, and before January 1, 2008.

[¶5010] Section 106. Election to include combat pay as earned income for purposes of earned income credit.

(Code Sec. 32)

[Joint Committee on Taxation Report — JCX-50-06]

Present Law

In general

Subject to certain limitations, military compensation earned by members of the Armed Forces while serving in a combat zone may be excluded from gross income. In addition, for up to two years following service in a combat zone, military personnel may also exclude compensation earned while hospitalized from wounds, disease, or injuries incurred while serving in the zone.

Child credit

Combat pay that is otherwise excluded from gross income under section 112 is treated as earned income which is taken into account in computing taxable income for purposes of calculating the refundable portion of the child credit.

Earned income credit

Any taxpayer may elect to treat combat pay that is otherwise excluded from gross income under section 112 as earned income for purposes of the earned income credit. This election is available with respect to any taxable year ending after the date of enactment and before January 1, 2007.

Explanation of Provision

The provision extends for one year (through December 31, 2007) the availability of the election to treat combat pay that is otherwise excluded from gross income under section 112 as earned income for purposes of the earned income credit.

Effective Date

The provision is effective in taxable years beginning after December 31, 2006.

[¶5011] Section 107. Extension and modification of qualified zone academy bonds.

(Code Sec. 1397E)

[Joint Committee on Taxation Report — JCX-50-06]

Present Law

Tax-exempt bonds

Interest on State and local governmental bonds generally is excluded from gross income for Federal income tax purposes if the proceeds of the bonds are used to finance direct activities of these governmental units or if the bonds are repaid with revenues of these governmental units. Activities that can be financed with these tax-exempt bonds include the financing of public schools.

An issuer must file with the IRS certain information in order for a bond issue to be tax-exempt.[11] Generally, this information return is required to be filed no later the 15th day of the second month after the close of the calendar quarter in which the bonds were issued.

Qualified zone academy bonds

As an alternative to traditional tax-exempt bonds, the Code permits three types of tax-credit bonds. States and local governments have the authority to issue qualified zone academy bonds ("QZABS"), clean renewable energy bonds ("CREBS"), and "Gulf tax credit bonds."[12] In lieu of tax-exempt interest, these bonds entitle eligible holders to a tax credit.

QZABs are defined as any bond issued by a State or local government, provided that: (1) at least 95 percent of the proceeds are used for the purpose of renovating, providing equipment to, developing course materials for use at, or training teachers and other school personnel in a "qualified zone academy" ("qualified zone academy property") and (2) private entities have promised to contribute to the qualified zone academy certain equipment, technical assistance or training, employee services, or other property or services with a value equal to at least 10 percent of the bond proceeds.

A school is a "qualified zone academy" if: (1) the school is a public school that provides education and training below the college level, (2) the school operates a special academic program in cooperation with businesses to enhance the academic curriculum and increase graduation and employment rates, and (3) either (a) the school is located in an empowerment zone or enterprise community designated under the Code or (b) it is reasonably expected that at least 35 percent of the students at the school will be eligible for free or reduced-cost lunches under the school lunch program established under the National School Lunch Act.

A total of $400 million of QZABs may be issued annually in calendar years 1998 through 2005. The $400 million aggregate bond cap is allocated each year to the States according to their respective populations of individuals below the poverty line. Each State, in turn, allocates the issuance authority to qualified zone academies within such State.

Financial institutions (banks, insurance companies, and corporations in the business of lending money) are the only taxpayers eligible to hold QZABs. An eligible taxpayer holding a QZAB on the credit allowance date is entitled to a credit. The credit is an amount equal to a credit rate multiplied by the face amount of the bond. The credit is

11. Sec. 149(e).
12. Secs. 1397E, 54, and 1400N(l), respectively.

includable in gross income (as if it were a taxable interest payment on the bond), and may be claimed against regular income tax and AMT liability.

The Treasury Department sets the credit rate on QZABs at a rate estimated to allow issuance of the bonds without discount and without interest cost to the issuer. The maximum term of the bond is determined by the Treasury Department, so that the present value of the obligation to repay the bond is 50 percent of the face value of the bond.

Issuers of QZABs are not required to report issuance of such bonds to the IRS under present law.

Arbitrage restrictions on tax-exempt bonds

To prevent States and local governments from issuing more tax-exempt bonds than is necessary for the activity being financed or from issuing such bonds earlier than needed for the purpose of the borrowing, the income exclusion for interest paid on States and local bonds does not apply to any arbitrage bond.[13] An arbitrage bond is defined as any bond that is part of an issue if any proceeds of the issue are reasonably expected to be used (or intentionally are used) to acquire higher yielding investments or to replace funds that are used to acquire higher yielding investments.[14] In general, arbitrage profits may be earned only during specified periods (e.g., defined "temporary periods" before funds are needed for the purpose of the borrowing) or on specified types of investments (e.g., "reasonably required reserve or replacement funds"). Subject to limited exceptions, profits that are earned during these periods or on such investments must be rebated to the Federal government. Under present law, the arbitrage rules apply to CREBs and Gulf tax credit bonds, but do not apply to QZABs.

Explanation of Provision

The provision extends the present-law provision for two years (through December 31, 2007).

In addition, the provision imposes the arbitrage requirements of section 148 that apply to interest-bearing tax-exempt bonds to QZABs. Principles under section 148 and the regulations thereunder shall apply for purposes of determining the yield restriction and arbitrage rebate requirements applicable to QZABs. For example, for arbitrage purposes, the yield on an issue of QZABs is computed by taking into account all payments of interest, if any, on such bonds, i.e., whether the bonds are issued at par, premium, or discount. However, for purposes of determining yield, the amount of the credit allowed to a taxpayer holding QZABs is not treated as interest, although such credit amount is treated as interest income to the taxpayer.

The provision also imposes new spending requirements for QZABs. An issuer of QZABs must reasonably expect to and actually spend 95 percent or more of the proceeds of such bonds on qualified zone academy property within the five-year period that begins on the date of issuance. To the extent less than 95 percent of the proceeds are used to finance qualified zone academy property during the five-year spending period, bonds will continue to qualify as QZABs if unspent proceeds are used within 90 days from the end of such five-year period to redeem any nonqualified bonds. For these purposes, the amount of nonqualified bonds is to be determined in the same manner as Treasury regulations under section 142. The provision provides that the five-year spending period may be extended by the Secretary if the issuer establishes that the failure to meet the spending requirement is due to reasonable cause and the related purposes for issuing the bonds will continue to proceed with due diligence.

Finally, issuers of QZABs are required to report issuance to the IRS in a manner similar to the information returns required for tax-exempt bonds.

13. Sec. 103(b)(2).
14. Sec. 148.

Effective Date

The provision extending issuance authority is effective for obligations issued after December 31, 2005. The provisions imposing arbitrage restrictions, reporting requirements, and spending requirements apply to obligations issued after the date of enactment with respect to allocations of the annual aggregate bond cap for calendar years after 2005.

[¶5012] Section 108. Above-the-line deduction for certain expenses of elementary and secondary school teachers.

(Code Sec. 62)

[Joint Committee on Taxation Report — JCX-50-06]

Present Law

In general, ordinary and necessary business expenses are deductible (sec. 162). However, in general, unreimbursed employee business expenses are deductible only as an itemized deduction and only to the extent that the individual's total miscellaneous deductions (including employee business expenses) exceed two percent of adjusted gross income. An individual's otherwise allowable itemized deductions may be further limited by the overall limitation on itemized deductions, which reduces itemized deductions for taxpayers with adjusted gross income in excess of $150,500 (for 2006).[15] In addition, miscellaneous itemized deductions are not allowable under the alternative minimum tax.

Certain expenses of eligible educators are allowed an above-the-line deduction. Specifically, for taxable years beginning after December 31, 2001, and prior to January 1, 2006, an above-the-line deduction is allowed for up to $250 annually of expenses paid or incurred by an eligible educator for books, supplies (other than nonathletic supplies for courses of instruction in health or physical education), computer equipment (including related software and services) and other equipment, and supplementary materials used by the eligible educator in the classroom. To be eligible for this deduction, the expenses must be otherwise deductible under 162 as a trade or business expense. A deduction is allowed only to the extent the amount of expenses exceeds the amount excludable from income under section 135 (relating to education savings bonds), 529(c)(1) (relating to qualified tuition programs), and section 530(d)(2) (relating to Coverdell education savings accounts).

An eligible educator is a kindergarten through grade 12 teacher, instructor, counselor, principal, or aide in a school for at least 900 hours during a school year. A school means any school which provides elementary education or secondary education, as determined under State law.

The above-the-line deduction for eligible educators is not allowed for taxable years beginning after December 31, 2005.

Explanation of Provision

The present-law provision is extended for two years, through December 31, 2007.

Effective Date

The provision is effective for expenses paid or incurred in taxable years beginning after December 31, 2005.

15. The adjusted income threshold is $75,250 in the case of a married individual filing a separate return (for 2006). For 2007, the adjusted income threshold is $156,400 ($78,200 for a married individual filing a separate return).

[¶5013] Section 109. Extension and expansion of expensing of brownfields remediation costs.

(Code Sec. 198)

[Joint Committee on Taxation Report — JCX-50-06]

Present Law

Present law allows a deduction for ordinary and necessary expenses paid or incurred in carrying on any trade or business.[16] Treasury regulations provide that the cost of incidental repairs that neither materially add to the value of property nor appreciably prolong its life, but keep it in an ordinarily efficient operating condition, may be deducted currently as a business expense. Section 263(a)(1) limits the scope of section 162 by prohibiting a current deduction for certain capital expenditures. Treasury regulations define "capital expenditures" as amounts paid or incurred to materially add to the value, or substantially prolong the useful life, of property owned by the taxpayer, or to adapt property to a new or different use. Amounts paid for repairs and maintenance do not constitute capital expenditures. The determination of whether an expense is deductible or capitalizable is based on the facts and circumstances of each case.

Taxpayers may elect to treat certain environmental remediation expenditures that would otherwise be chargeable to capital account as deductible in the year paid or incurred.[17] The deduction applies for both regular and alternative minimum tax purposes. The expenditure must be incurred in connection with the abatement or control of hazardous substances at a qualified contaminated site. In general, any expenditure for the acquisition of depreciable property used in connection with the abatement or control of hazardous substances at a qualified contaminated site does not constitute a qualified environmental remediation expenditure. However, depreciation deductions allowable for such property, which would otherwise be allocated to the site under the principles set forth in Commissioner v. Idaho Power Co.[18] and section 263A, are treated as qualified environmental remediation expenditures.

A "qualified contaminated site" (a so-called "brownfield") generally is any property that is held for use in a trade or business, for the production of income, or as inventory and is certified by the appropriate State environmental agency to be an area at or on which there has been a release (or threat of release) or disposal of a hazardous substance. Both urban and rural property may qualify. However, sites that are identified on the national priorities list under the Comprehensive Environmental Response, Compensation, and Liability Act of 1980 ("CERCLA")[19] cannot qualify as targeted areas. Hazardous substances generally are defined by reference to sections 101(14) and 102 of CERCLA, subject to additional limitations applicable to asbestos and similar substances within buildings, certain naturally occurring substances such as radon, and certain other substances released into drinking water supplies due to deterioration through ordinary use. Petroleum products generally are not regarded as hazardous substances for purposes of section 198 (except for purposes of determining qualified environmental remediation expenditures in the "Gulf Opportunity Zone" under section 1400N(g), as described below).[20]

In the case of property to which a qualified environmental remediation expenditure otherwise would have been capitalized, any deduction allowed under section 198 is treated as a depreciation deduction and the property is treated as section 1245 property. Thus, deductions for qualified environmental remediation expenditures are subject to re-

16. Sec. 162.
17. Sec. 198.
18. 418 U.S. 1 (1974).
19. Pub. L. No. 96-510 (1980).
20. Section 101(14) of CERCLA specifically excludes "petroleum, including crude oil or any fraction thereof which is not otherwise specifically listed or designated as a hazardous substance under subparagraphs (A) through (F) of this paragraph," from the definition of "hazardous substance."

capture as ordinary income upon a sale or other disposition of the property. In addition, sections 280B (demolition of structures) and 468 (special rules for mining and solid waste reclamation and closing costs) do not apply to amounts that are treated as expenses under this provision.

Eligible expenditures are those paid or incurred before January 1, 2006.

Under section 1400N(g), the above provisions apply to expenditures paid or incurred to abate contamination at qualified contaminated sites in the Gulf Opportunity Zone (defined as that portion of the Hurricane Katrina Disaster Area determined by the President to warrant individual or individual and public assistance from the Federal government under the Robert T. Stafford Disaster Relief and Emergency Assistance Act by reason of Hurricane Katrina) before January 1, 2008; in addition, within the Gulf Opportunity Zone section 1400N(g) broadens the definition of hazardous substance to include petroleum products (defined by reference to section 4612(a)(3)).

Explanation of Provision

The provision extends for two years the present-law provisions relating to environmental remediation expenditures (through December 31, 2007).

In addition, the provision expands the definition of hazardous substance to include petroleum products. Under the provision, petroleum products are defined by reference to section 4612(a)(3), and thus include crude oil, crude oil condensates and natural gasoline.[21]

Effective Date

The provision applies to expenditures paid or incurred after December 31, 2005, and before January 1, 2008.

[¶5014] Section 110. Tax incentives for investment in the District of Columbia.

(Code Sec. 1400, 1400A, 1400B, 1400C)

[Joint Committee on Taxation Report — JCX-50-06]

Present Law

In general

The Taxpayer Relief Act of 1997 designated certain economically depressed census tracts within the District of Columbia as the District of Columbia Enterprise Zone (the "D.C. Zone"), within which businesses and individual residents are eligible for special tax incentives. The census tracts that compose the D.C. Zone are (1) all census tracts that presently are part of the D.C. enterprise community designated under section 1391 (i.e., portions of Anacostia, Mt. Pleasant, Chinatown, and the easternmost part of the District), and (2) all additional census tracts within the District of Columbia where the poverty rate is not less than 20 percent. The D.C. Zone designation remains in effect for the period from January 1, 1998, through December 31, 2005. In general, the tax incentives available in connection with the D.C. Zone are a 20-percent wage credit, an additional $35,000 of section 179 expensing for qualified zone property, expanded tax-exempt financing for certain zone facilities, and a zero-percent capital gains rate from the sale of certain qualified D.C. zone assets.

21. The present law exceptions for sites on the national priorities list under CERCLA, and for substances with respect to which a removal or remediation is not permitted under section 104 of CERCLA by reason of subsection (a)(3) thereof, would continue to apply to all hazardous substances (including petroleum products).

Wage credit

A 20-percent wage credit is available to employers for the first $15,000 of qualified wages paid to each employee (i.e., a maximum credit of $3,000 with respect to each qualified employee) who (1) is a resident of the D.C. Zone, and (2) performs substantially all employment services within the D.C. Zone in a trade or business of the employer.

Wages paid to a qualified employee who earns more than $15,000 are eligible for the wage credit (although only the first $15,000 of wages is eligible for the credit). The wage credit is available with respect to a qualified full-time or part-time employee (employed for at least 90 days), regardless of the number of other employees who work for the employer. In general, any taxable business carrying out activities in the D.C. Zone may claim the wage credit, regardless of whether the employer meets the definition of a "D.C. Zone business."[22]

An employer's deduction otherwise allowed for wages paid is reduced by the amount of wage credit claimed for that taxable year.[23] Wages are not to be taken into account for purposes of the wage credit if taken into account in determining the employer's work opportunity tax credit under section 51 or the welfare-to-work credit under section 51A.[24] In addition, the $15,000 cap is reduced by any wages taken into account in computing the work opportunity tax credit or the welfare-to-work credit.[25] The wage credit may be used to offset up to 25 percent of alternative minimum tax liability.[26]

Section 179 expensing

In general, a D.C. Zone business is allowed an additional $35,000 of section 179 expensing for qualifying property placed in service by a D.C. Zone business.[27] The section 179 expensing allowed to a taxpayer is phased out by the amount by which 50 percent of the cost of qualified zone property placed in service during the year by the taxpayer exceeds $200,000 ($400,000 for taxable years beginning after 2002 and before 2010). The term "qualified zone property" is defined as depreciable tangible property (including buildings), provided that (1) the property is acquired by the taxpayer (from an unrelated party) after the designation took effect, (2) the original use of the property in the D.C. Zone commences with the taxpayer, and (3) substantially all of the use of the property is in the D.C. Zone in the active conduct of a trade or business by the taxpayer.[28] Special rules are provided in the case of property that is substantially renovated by the taxpayer.

Tax-exempt financing

A qualified D.C. Zone business is permitted to borrow proceeds from tax-exempt qualified enterprise zone facility bonds (as defined in section 1394) issued by the District of Columbia.[29] Such bonds are subject to the District of Columbia's annual private activity bond volume limitation. Generally, qualified enterprise zone facility bonds for the District of Columbia are bonds 95 percent or more of the net proceeds of which are used to finance certain facilities within the D.C. Zone. The aggregate face amount of all outstanding qualified enterprise zone facility bonds per qualified D.C. Zone business

22. However, the wage credit is not available for wages paid in connection with certain business activities described in section 144(c)(6)(B) or certain farming activities. In addition, wages are not eligible for the wage credit if paid to (1) a person who owns more than five percent of the stock (or capital or profits interests) of the employer, (2) certain relatives of the employer, or (3) if the employer is a corporation or partnership, certain relatives of a person who owns more than 50 percent of the business.
23. Sec. 280C(a).
24. Secs. 1400H(a), 1396(c)(3)(A) and 51A(d)(2) .
25. Secs. 1400H(a), 1396(c)(3)(B) and 51A(d)(2).
26. Sec. 38(c)(2).
27. Sec. 1397A.
28. Sec. 1397D.
29. Sec. 1400A.

may not exceed $15 million and may be issued only while the D.C. Zone designation is in effect.

Zero-percent capital gains

A zero-percent capital gains rate applies to capital gains from the sale of certain qualified D.C. Zone assets held for more than five years.[30] In general, a qualified "D.C. Zone asset" means stock or partnership interests held in, or tangible property held by, a D.C. Zone business. For purposes of the zero-percent capital gains rate, the D.C. Enterprise Zone is defined to include all census tracts within the District of Columbia where the poverty rate is not less than 10 percent.

In general, gain eligible for the zero-percent tax rate means gain from the sale or exchange of a qualified D.C. Zone asset that is (1) a capital asset or property used in the trade or business as defined in section 1231(b), and (2) acquired before January 1, 2006. Gain that is attributable to real property, or to intangible assets, qualifies for the zero-percent rate, provided that such real property or intangible asset is an integral part of a qualified D.C. Zone business.[31] However, no gain attributable to periods before January 1, 1998, and after December 31, 2010, is qualified capital gain.

District of Columbia homebuyer tax credit

First-time homebuyers of a principal residence in the District of Columbia are eligible for a nonrefundable tax credit of up to $5,000 of the amount of the purchase price. The $5,000 maximum credit applies both to individuals and married couples. Married individuals filing separately can claim a maximum credit of $2,500 each. The credit phases out for individual taxpayers with adjusted gross income between $70,000 and $90,000 ($110,000-$130,000 for joint filers). For purposes of eligibility, "first-time homebuyer" means any individual if such individual did not have a present ownership interest in a principal residence in the District of Columbia in the one-year period ending on the date of the purchase of the residence to which the credit applies. The credit expired for purchases after December 31, 2005.[32]

Explanation of Provision

The provision extends the designation of the D.C. Zone for two years (through December 31, 2007), thus extending the wage credit and section 179 expensing for two years.

The provision extends the tax-exempt financing authority for two years, applying to bonds issued during the period beginning on January 1, 1998, and ending on December 31, 2007.

The provision extends the zero-percent capital gains rate applicable to capital gains from the sale of certain qualified D.C. Zone assets for two years.

The provision extends the first-time homebuyer credit for two years, through December 31, 2007.

Effective Date

The provision is effective for periods beginning after, bonds issued after, acquisitions after, and property purchased after December 31, 2005.

30. Sec. 1400B.
31. However, sole proprietorships and other taxpayers selling assets directly cannot claim the zero-percent rate on capital gain from the sale of any intangible property (i.e., the integrally related test does not apply).
32. Sec. 1400C(i).

[¶5015] Section 111. Indian employment tax credit.

(Code Sec. 45A)

[Joint Committee on Taxation Report — JCX-50-06]

Present Law

In general, a credit against income tax liability is allowed to employers for the first $20,000 of qualified wages and qualified employee health insurance costs paid or incurred by the employer with respect to certain employees (sec. 45A). The credit is equal to 20 percent of the excess of eligible employee qualified wages and health insurance costs during the current year over the amount of such wages and costs incurred by the employer during 1993. The credit is an incremental credit, such that an employer's current-year qualified wages and qualified employee health insurance costs (up to $20,000 per employee) are eligible for the credit only to the extent that the sum of such costs exceeds the sum of comparable costs paid during 1993. No deduction is allowed for the portion of the wages equal to the amount of the credit.

Qualified wages means wages paid or incurred by an employer for services performed by a qualified employee. A qualified employee means any employee who is an enrolled member of an Indian tribe or the spouse of an enrolled member of an Indian tribe, who performs substantially all of the services within an Indian reservation, and whose principal place of abode while performing such services is on or near the reservation in which the services are performed. An "Indian reservation" is a reservation as defined in section 3(d) of the Indian Financing Act of 1974 or section 4(1) of the Indian Child Welfare Act of 1978. For purposes of the preceding sentence, section 3(d) is applied by treating "former Indian reservations in Oklahoma" as including only lands that are (1) within the jurisdictional area of an Oklahoma Indian tribe as determined by the Secretary of the Interior, and (2) recognized by such Secretary as an area eligible for trust land status under 25 C.F.R. Part 151 (as in effect on August 5, 1997).

An employee is not treated as a qualified employee for any taxable year of the employer if the total amount of wages paid or incurred by the employer with respect to such employee during the taxable year exceeds an amount determined at an annual rate of $30,000 (which after adjusted for inflation after 1993 is currently $35,000). In addition, an employee will not be treated as a qualified employee under certain specific circumstances, such as where the employee is related to the employer (in the case of an individual employer) or to one of the employer's shareholders, partners, or grantors. Similarly, an employee will not be treated as a qualified employee where the employee has more than a 5 percent ownership interest in the employer. Finally, an employee will not be considered a qualified employee to the extent the employee's services relate to gaming activities or are performed in a building housing such activities.

The wage credit is available for wages paid or incurred on or after January 1, 1994, in taxable years that begin before January 1, 2006.

Explanation of Provision

The provision extends for two years the present-law employment credit provision (through taxable years beginning on or before December 31, 2007).

Effective Date

The provision is effective for taxable years beginning after December 31, 2005.

[¶5016] Section 112. Accelerated depreciation for business property on Indian reservations.

(Code Sec. 168)

[Joint Committee on Taxation Report — JCX-50-06]

Present Law

With respect to certain property used in connection with the conduct of a trade or business within an Indian reservation, depreciation deductions under section 168(j) are determined using the following recovery periods:

3-year property	2 years
5-year property	3 years
7-year property	4 years
10-year property	6 years
15-year property	9 years
20-year property	12 years
Nonresidential real property	22 years

"Qualified Indian reservation property" eligible for accelerated depreciation includes property which is (1) used by the taxpayer predominantly in the active conduct of a trade or business within an Indian reservation, (2) not used or located outside the reservation on a regular basis, (3) not acquired (directly or indirectly) by the taxpayer from a person who is related to the taxpayer (within the meaning of section 465(b)(3)(C)), and (4) described in the recovery-period table above. In addition, property is not "qualified Indian reservation property" if it is placed in service for purposes of conducting gaming activities. Certain "qualified infrastructure property" may be eligible for the accelerated depreciation even if located outside an Indian reservation, provided that the purpose of such property is to connect with qualified infrastructure property located within the reservation (e.g., roads, power lines, water systems, railroad spurs, and communications facilities).

An "Indian reservation" means a reservation as defined in section 3(d) of the Indian Financing Act of 1974 or section 4(1) of the Indian Child Welfare Act of 1978. For purposes of the preceding sentence, section 3(d) is applied by treating "former Indian reservations in Oklahoma" as including only lands that are (1) within the jurisdictional area of an Oklahoma Indian tribe as determined by the Secretary of the Interior, and (2) recognized by such Secretary as an area eligible for trust land status under 25 C.F.R. Part 151 (as in effect on August 5, 1997).

The depreciation deduction allowed for regular tax purposes is also allowed for purposes of the alternative minimum tax. The accelerated depreciation for Indian reservation property is available with respect to property placed in service on or after January 1, 1994, and before January 1, 2006.

Explanation of Provision

The provision extends for two years the present-law incentive relating to depreciation of qualified Indian reservation property (to apply to property placed in service through December 31, 2007).

Effective Date

The provision applies to property placed in service after December 31, 2005.

[¶5017] Section 113. Fifteen-year straight-line cost recovery for qualified leasehold improvements and qualified restaurant property.

(Code Sec. 168)

[Joint Committee on Taxation Report — JCX-50-06]

Present Law

In general

A taxpayer generally must capitalize the cost of property used in a trade or business and recover such cost over time through annual deductions for depreciation or amortization. Tangible property generally is depreciated under the modified accelerated cost recovery system ("MACRS"), which determines depreciation by applying specific recovery periods, placed-in-service conventions, and depreciation methods to the cost of various types of depreciable property (sec. 168). The cost of nonresidential real property is recovered using the straight-line method of depreciation and a recovery period of 39 years. Nonresidential real property is subject to the mid-month placed-in-service convention. Under the mid-month convention, the depreciation allowance for the first year property is placed in service is based on the number of months the property was in service, and property placed in service at any time during a month is treated as having been placed in service in the middle of the month.

Depreciation of leasehold improvements

Generally, depreciation allowances for improvements made on leased property are determined under MACRS, even if the MACRS recovery period assigned to the property is longer than the term of the lease. This rule applies regardless of whether the lessor or the lessee places the leasehold improvements in service. If a leasehold improvement constitutes an addition or improvement to nonresidential real property already placed in service, the improvement generally is depreciated using the straight-line method over a 39-year recovery period, beginning in the month the addition or improvement was placed in service. However, exceptions exist for certain qualified leasehold improvements and certain qualified restaurant property.

Qualified leasehold improvement property

Section 168(e)(3)(E)(iv) provides a statutory 15-year recovery period for qualified leasehold improvement property placed in service before January 1, 2006. Qualified leasehold improvement property is recovered using the straight-line method. Leasehold improvements placed in service in 2006 and later are subject to the general rules described above.

Qualified leasehold improvement property is any improvement to an interior portion of a building that is nonresidential real property, provided certain requirements are met. The improvement must be made under or pursuant to a lease either by the lessee (or sublessee), or by the lessor, of that portion of the building to be occupied exclusively by the lessee (or sublessee). The improvement must be placed in service more than three years after the date the building was first placed in service. Qualified leasehold improvement property does not include any improvement for which the expenditure is attributable to the enlargement of the building, any elevator or escalator, any structural component benefiting a common area, or the internal structural framework of the building. However, if a lessor makes an improvement that qualifies as qualified leasehold improvement property, such improvement does not qualify as qualified leasehold improvement property to any subsequent owner of such improvement. An exception to the rule applies in the case of death and certain transfers of property that qualify for non-recognition treatment.

Qualified restaurant property

Section 168(e)(3)(E)(v) provides a statutory 15-year recovery period for qualified restaurant property placed in service before January 1, 2006. For purposes of the provision, qualified restaurant property means any improvement to a building if such improvement is placed in service more than three years after the date such building was first placed in service and more than 50 percent of the building's square footage is devoted to the preparation of, and seating for on-premises consumption of, prepared meals. Qualified restaurant property is recovered using the straight-line method.

Explanation of Provision

The present-law provisions are extended for two years (through December 31, 2007).

Effective Date

The provision applies to property placed in service after December 31, 2005.

[¶5019] Section 115. Parity in application of certain limits to mental health benefits.

(Code Sec. 9812)

[Joint Committee on Taxation Report — JCX-50-06]

Present Law

The Code, the Employee Retirement Income Security Act of 1974 ("ERISA") and the Public Health Service Act ("PHSA") contain provisions under which group health plans that provide both medical and surgical benefits and mental health benefits cannot impose aggregate lifetime or annual dollar limits on mental health benefits that are not imposed on substantially all medical and surgical benefits ("mental health parity requirements"). In the case of a group health plan which provides benefits for mental health, the mental health parity requirements do not affect the terms and conditions (including cost sharing, limits on numbers of visits or days of coverage, and requirements relating to medical necessity) relating to the amount, duration, or scope of mental health benefits under the plan, except as specifically provided in regard to parity in the imposition of aggregate lifetime limits and annual limits.

The Code imposes an excise tax on group health plans which fail to meet the mental health parity requirements. The excise tax is equal to $100 per day during the period of noncompliance and is generally imposed on the employer sponsoring the plan if the plan fails to meet the requirements. The maximum tax that can be imposed during a taxable year cannot exceed the lesser of 10 percent of the employer's group health plan expenses for the prior year or $500,000. No tax is imposed if the Secretary determines that the employer did not know, and in exercising reasonable diligence would not have known, that the failure existed.

The mental health parity requirements do not apply to group health plans of small employers nor do they apply if their application results in an increase in the cost under a group health plan of at least one percent. Further, the mental health parity requirements do not require group health plans to provide mental health benefits.

The Code, ERISA and PHSA mental health parity requirements are scheduled to expire with respect to benefits for services furnished after December 31, 2006.

Explanation of Provision

The provision extends the present-law Code excise tax for failure to comply with the mental health parity requirements through December 31, 2007. It also extends the ERISA and PHSA requirements through December 31, 2007.

Effective Date

The provision is effective on the date of enactment.

[¶5020] Section 116. Corporate donations of scientific property used for research and of computer technology and equipment.

(Code Sec. 170)

[Joint Committee on Taxation Report — JCX-50-06]

Present Law

In the case of a charitable contribution of inventory or other ordinary-income or short-term capital gain property, the amount of the charitable deduction generally is limited to the taxpayer's basis in the property. In the case of a charitable contribution of tangible personal property, the deduction is limited to the taxpayer's basis in such property if the use by the recipient charitable organization is unrelated to the organization's tax-exempt purpose. In cases involving contributions to a private foundation (other than certain private operating foundations), the amount of the deduction is limited to the taxpayer's basis in the property.[39]

Under present law, a taxpayer's deduction for charitable contributions of scientific property used for research and for contributions of computer technology and equipment generally is limited to the taxpayer's basis (typically, cost) in the property. However, certain corporations may claim a deduction in excess of basis for a "qualified research contribution" or a "qualified computer contribution."[40] This enhanced deduction is equal to the lesser of (1) basis plus one-half of the item's appreciation (i.e., basis plus one half of fair market value in excess of basis) or (2) two times basis. The enhanced deduction for qualified computer contributions expired for any contribution made during any taxable year beginning after December 31, 2005.

A qualified research contribution means a charitable contribution of inventory that is tangible personal property. The contribution must be to a qualified educational or scientific organization and be made not later than two years after construction of the property is substantially completed. The original use of the property must be by the donee, and be used substantially for research or experimentation, or for research training, in the U.S. in the physical or biological sciences. The property must be scientific equipment or apparatus, constructed by the taxpayer, and may not be transferred by the donee in exchange for money, other property, or services. The donee must provide the taxpayer with a written statement representing that it will use the property in accordance with the conditions for the deduction. For purposes of the enhanced deduction, property is considered constructed by the taxpayer only if the cost of the parts used in the construction of the property (other than parts manufactured by the taxpayer or a related person) do not exceed 50 percent of the taxpayer's basis in the property.

A qualified computer contribution means a charitable contribution of any computer technology or equipment, which meets standards of functionality and suitability as established by the Secretary of the Treasury. The contribution must be to certain educational organizations or public libraries and made not later than three years after the taxpayer acquired the property or, if the taxpayer constructed the property, not later than the date construction of the property is substantially completed.[41] The original use of the property must be by the donor or the donee,[42] and in the case of the donee, must be used substantially for educational purposes related to the function or purpose of the donee.

39. Sec. 170(e)(1).
40. Secs. 170(e)(4) and 170(e)(6).
41. If the taxpayer constructed the property and reacquired such property, the contribution must be within three years of the date the original construction was substantially completed. Sec. 170(e)(6)(D)(i).
42. This requirement does not apply if the property was reacquired by the manufacturer and contributed. Sec. 170(e)(6)(D)(ii).

The property must fit productively into the donee's education plan. The donee may not transfer the property in exchange for money, other property, or services, except for shipping, installation, and transfer costs. To determine whether property is constructed by the taxpayer, the rules applicable to qualified research contributions apply. Contributions may be made to private foundations under certain conditions.[43]

Explanation of Provision

The provision extends the present-law provision relating to the enhanced deduction for computer technology and equipment for two years to apply to contributions made during any taxable year beginning after December 31, 2005, and before January 1, 2008.

Under the provision, property assembled by the taxpayer, in addition to property constructed by the taxpayer, is eligible for either the enhanced deduction relating to computer technology and equipment or to scientific property used for research. It is not intended that old or used components assembled by the taxpayer into scientific property or computer technology or equipment are eligible for the enhanced deduction.

Effective Date

The provision is effective for taxable years beginning after December 31, 2005.

[¶5021] Section 117. Availability of medical savings accounts.

(Code Sec. 220)

[Joint Committee on Taxation Report — JCX-50-06]

Present Law

Archer medical savings accounts

In general

Within limits, contributions to an Archer medical savings account ("Archer MSA") are deductible in determining adjusted gross income if made by an eligible individual and are excludable from gross income and wages for employment tax purposes if made by the employer of an eligible individual. Earnings on amounts in an Archer MSA are not currently taxable. Distributions from an Archer MSA for medical expenses are not includible in gross income. Distributions not used for medical expenses are includible in gross income. In addition, distributions not used for medical expenses are subject to an additional 15-percent tax unless the distribution is made after age 65, death, or disability.

Eligible individuals

Archer MSAs are available to employees covered under an employer-sponsored high deductible plan of a small employer and self-employed individuals covered under a high deductible health plan. An employer is a small employer if it employed, on average, no more than 50 employees on business days during either the preceding or the second preceding year. An individual is not eligible for an Archer MSA if he or she is covered under any other health plan in addition to the high deductible plan.

Tax treatment of and limits on contributions

Individual contributions to an Archer MSA are deductible (within limits) in determining adjusted gross income (i.e., "above-the-line"). In addition, employer contributions are excludable from gross income and wages for employment tax purposes (within the same limits), except that this exclusion does not apply to contributions made through a

43. Sec. 170(e)(6)(C).

cafeteria plan. In the case of an employee, contributions can be made to an Archer MSA either by the individual or by the individual's employer.

The maximum annual contribution that can be made to an Archer MSA for a year is 65 percent of the deductible under the high deductible plan in the case of individual coverage and 75 percent of the deductible in the case of family coverage.

Definition of high deductible plan

A high deductible plan is a health plan with an annual deductible of at least $1,800 and no more than $2,700 in the case of individual coverage and at least $3,650 and no more than $5,450 in the case of family coverage (for 2006). In addition, the maximum out-of-pocket expenses with respect to allowed costs (including the deductible) must be no more than $3,650 in the case of individual coverage and no more than $6,650 in the case of family coverage (for 2006). A plan does not fail to qualify as a high deductible plan merely because it does not have a deductible for preventive care as required by State law. A plan does not qualify as a high deductible health plan if substantially all of the coverage under the plan is for certain permitted coverage. In the case of a self-insured plan, the plan must in fact be insurance (e.g., there must be appropriate risk shifting) and not merely a reimbursement arrangement.

Cap on taxpayers utilizing Archer MSAs and expiration of pilot program

The number of taxpayers benefiting annually from an Archer MSA contribution is limited to a threshold level (generally 750,000 taxpayers). The number of Archer MSAs established has not exceeded the threshold level.

After 2005, no new contributions may be made to Archer MSAs except by or on behalf of individuals who previously made (or had made on their behalf) Archer MSA contributions and employees who are employed by a participating employer.

Trustees of Archer MSAs are generally required to make reports to the Treasury by August 1 regarding Archer MSAs established by July 1 of that year. If the threshold level is reached in a year, the Secretary is required to make and publish such determination by October 1 of such year.

Health savings accounts

Health savings accounts ("HSAs") were enacted by the Medicare Prescription Drug, Improvement, and Modernization Act of 2003. Like Archer MSAs, an HSA is a tax-exempt trust or custodial account to which tax-deductible contributions may be made by individuals with a high deductible health plan. HSAs provide tax benefits similar to, but more favorable than, those provide by Archer MSAs. HSAs were established on a permanent basis.

Explanation of Provision

The provision extends for two years the present-law Archer MSA provisions (through December 31, 2007).

The report required by Archer MSA trustees to be made on August 1, 2005, or August 1, 2006, (as the case may be) is treated as timely filed if made before the close of the 90-day period beginning on the date of enactment. The determination and publication with respect to calendar year 2005 or 2006 whether the threshold level has been exceeded is treated as timely if made before the close of the 120-day period beginning on the date of enactment. If it is determined that 2005 or 2006 is a cut-off year, the cut-off date is the last date of such 120-day period.

Effective Date

The provision is effective on the date of enactment.

[¶5022] Section 118. Taxable income limit on percentage depletion for oil and natural gas produced from marginal properties.

(Code Sec. 613A)

[Joint Committee on Taxation Report — JCX-50-06]

Present Law

The Code permits taxpayers to recover their investments in oil and gas wells through depletion deductions. Two methods of depletion are currently allowable under the Code: (1) the cost depletion method, and (2) the percentage depletion method. Under the cost depletion method, the taxpayer deducts that portion of the adjusted basis of the depletable property which is equal to the ratio of units sold from that property during the taxable year to the number of units remaining as of the end of taxable year plus the number of units sold during the taxable year. Thus, the amount recovered under cost depletion may never exceed the taxpayer's basis in the property.

The Code generally limits the percentage depletion method for oil and gas properties to independent producers and royalty owners. Generally, under the percentage depletion method, 15 percent of the taxpayer's gross income from an oil- or gas-producing property is allowed as a deduction in each taxable year. The amount deducted generally may not exceed 100 percent of the taxable income from that property in any year. For marginal production, the 100-percent taxable income limitation has been suspended for taxable years beginning after December 31, 1997, and before January 1, 2006.

Marginal production is defined as domestic crude oil and natural gas production from stripper well property or from property substantially all of the production from which during the calendar year is heavy oil. Stripper well property is property from which the average daily production is 15 barrel equivalents or less, determined by dividing the average daily production of domestic crude oil and domestic natural gas from producing wells on the property for the calendar year by the number of wells. Heavy oil is domestic crude oil with a weighted average gravity of 20 degrees API or less (corrected to 60 degrees Fahrenheit).

Explanation of Provision

The provision extends for two years the present-law taxable income limitation suspension provision for marginal production (through taxable years beginning on or before December 31, 2007).

Effective Date

The provision applies to taxable years beginning after December 31, 2005.

[¶5023] Section 119. American Samoa economic development credit.

(Code Sec. 30A)

[Joint Committee on Taxation Report — JCX-50-06]

Present Law

In general

Certain domestic corporations with business operations in the U.S. possessions are eligible for the possession tax credit.[44] This credit offsets the U.S. tax imposed on certain income related to operations in the U.S. possessions.[45] For purposes of the credit, possessions include, among other places, American Samoa. Subject to certain limitations de-

44. Secs. 27(b), 936.
45. Domestic corporations with activities in Puerto Rico are eligible for the section 30A economic activity credit. That credit is calculated under the rules set forth in section 936.

scribed below, the amount of the possession tax credit allowed to any domestic corporation equals the portion of that corporation's U.S. tax that is attributable to the corporation's non-U.S. source taxable income from (1) the active conduct of a trade or business within a U.S. possession, (2) the sale or exchange of substantially all of the assets that were used in such a trade or business, or (3) certain possessions investment.[46] No deduction or foreign tax credit is allowed for any possessions or foreign tax paid or accrued with respect to taxable income that is taken into account in computing the credit under section 936.[47] The section 936 credit expires for taxable years beginning after December 31, 2005.

To qualify for the possession tax credit for a taxable year, a domestic corporation must satisfy two conditions. First, the corporation must derive at least 80 percent of its gross income for the three-year period immediately preceding the close of the taxable year from sources within a possession. Second, the corporation must derive at least 75 percent of its gross income for that same period from the active conduct of a possession business.

The possession tax credit is available only to a corporation that qualifies as an existing credit claimant. The determination of whether a corporation is an existing credit claimant is made separately for each possession. The possession tax credit is computed separately for each possession with respect to which the corporation is an existing credit claimant, and the credit is subject to either an economic activity-based limitation or an income-based limit.

Qualification as existing credit claimant

A corporation is an existing credit claimant with respect to a possession if (1) the corporation was engaged in the active conduct of a trade or business within the possession on October 13, 1995, and (2) the corporation elected the benefits of the possession tax credit in an election in effect for its taxable year that included October 13, 1995.[48] A corporation that adds a substantial new line of business (other than in a qualifying acquisition of all the assets of a trade or business of an existing credit claimant) ceases to be an existing credit claimant as of the close of the taxable year ending before the date on which that new line of business is added.

Economic activity-based limit

Under the economic activity-based limit, the amount of the credit determined under the rules described above may not exceed an amount equal to the sum of (1) 60 percent of the taxpayer's qualified possession wages and allocable employee fringe benefit expenses, (2) 15 percent of depreciation allowances with respect to short-life qualified tangible property, plus 40 percent of depreciation allowances with respect to medium-life qualified tangible property, plus 65 percent of depreciation allowances with respect to long-life qualified tangible property, and (3) in certain cases, a portion of the taxpayer's possession income taxes.

Income-based limit

As an alternative to the economic activity-based limit, a taxpayer may elect to apply a limit equal to the applicable percentage of the credit that would otherwise be allowable with respect to possession business income; the applicable percentage currently is 40 percent.

---

46. Under phase-out rules described below, investment only in Guam, American Samoa, and the Northern Mariana Islands (and not in other possessions) now may give rise to income eligible for the section 936 credit.
47. Sec. 936(c).
48. A corporation will qualify as an existing credit claimant if it acquired all the assets of a trade or business of a corporation that (1) actively conducted that trade or business in a possession on October 13, 1995, and (2) had elected the benefits of the possession tax credit in an election in effect for the taxable year that included October 13, 1995.

Repeal and phase out

In 1996, the section 936 credit was repealed for new claimants for taxable years beginning after 1995 and was phased out for existing credit claimants over a period including taxable years beginning before 2006. The amount of the available credit during the phase-out period generally is reduced by special limitation rules. These phase-out period limitation rules do not apply to the credit available to existing credit claimants for income from activities in Guam, American Samoa, and the Northern Mariana Islands. As described previously, the section 936 credit is repealed for all possessions, including Guam, American Samoa, and the Northern Mariana Islands, for all taxable years beginning after 2005.

Explanation of Provision

Under the provision, a domestic corporation that is an existing credit claimant with respect to American Samoa and that elected the application of section 936 for its last taxable year beginning before January 1, 2006 is allowed, for two taxable years, a credit based on the economic activity-based limitation rules described above. The credit is not part of the Code but is computed based on the rules secs. 30A and 936.

The amount of the credit allowed to a qualifying domestic corporation under the provision is equal to the sum of the amounts used in computing the corporation's economic activity-based limitation (described above in the present law section) with respect to American Samoa, except that no credit is allowed for the amount of any American Samoa income taxes. Thus, for any qualifying corporation the amount of the credit equals the sum of (1) 60 percent of the corporation's qualified American Samoa wages and allocable employee fringe benefit expenses and (2) 15 percent of the corporation's depreciation allowances with respect to short-life qualified American Samoa tangible property, plus 40 percent of the corporation's depreciation allowances with respect to medium-life qualified American Samoa tangible property, plus 65 percent of the corporation's depreciation allowances with respect to long-life qualified American Samoa tangible property.

The present-law section 936(c) rule denying a credit or deduction for any possessions or foreign tax paid with respect to taxable income taken into account in computing the credit under section 936 does not apply with respect to the credit allowed by the provision.

The two-year credit allowed by the provision is intended to provide additional time for the development of a comprehensive, long-term economic policy toward American Samoa. It is expected that in developing a long-term policy, non-tax policy alternatives should be carefully considered. It is expected that long-term policy toward the possessions should take into account the unique circumstances in each possession.

Effective Date

The provision is effective for the first two taxable years December 31, 2005, and before January 1, 2008.

[¶5024] Section 120. Extension of bonus depreciation for certain qualified Gulf Opportunity Zone property.

(Code Sec. 1400N)

[Joint Committee on Taxation Report — JCX-50-06]

Present Law

In general

A taxpayer is allowed to recover, through annual depreciation deductions, the cost of certain property used in a trade or business or for the production of income. The amount of the depreciation deduction allowed with respect to tangible property for a taxable year is determined under the modified accelerated cost recovery system ("MACRS"). Under MACRS, different types of property generally are assigned applicable recovery periods and depreciation methods. The recovery periods applicable to most tangible personal property (generally tangible property other than residential rental property and nonresidential real property) range from 3 to 25 years. The depreciation methods generally applicable to tangible personal property are the 200-percent and 150-percent declining balance methods, switching to the straight-line method for the taxable year in which the depreciation deduction would be maximized.

Gulf Opportunity Zone property

Present law provides an additional first-year depreciation deduction equal to 50 percent of the adjusted basis of qualified Gulf Opportunity Zone[49] property. In order to qualify, property generally must be placed in service on or before December 31, 2007 (December 31, 2008 in the case of nonresidential real property and residential rental property).

The additional first-year depreciation deduction is allowed for both regular tax and alternative minimum tax purposes for the taxable year in which the property is placed in service. The additional first-year depreciation deduction is subject to the general rules regarding whether an item is deductible under section 162 or subject to capitalization under section 263 or section 263A. The basis of the property and the depreciation allowances in the year of purchase and later years are appropriately adjusted to reflect the additional first-year depreciation deduction. In addition, the provision provides that there is no adjustment to the allowable amount of depreciation for purposes of computing a taxpayer's alternative minimum taxable income with respect to property to which the provision applies. A taxpayer is allowed to elect out of the additional first-year depreciation for any class of property for any taxable year.

In order for property to qualify for the additional first-year depreciation deduction, it must meet all of the following requirements. First, the property must be property (1) to which the general rules of the Modified Accelerated Cost Recovery System ("MACRS") apply with an applicable recovery period of 20 years or less, (2) computer software other than computer software covered by section 197, (3) water utility property (as defined in section 168(e)(5)), (4) certain leasehold improvement property, or (5) certain nonresidential real property and residential rental property. Second, substantially all of the use of such property must be in the Gulf Opportunity Zone and in the active conduct of a trade or business by the taxpayer in the Gulf Opportunity Zone. Third, the original use of the property in the Gulf Opportunity Zone must commence with the taxpayer on or after August 28, 2005. (Thus, used property may constitute qualified property so long as it has not previously been used within the Gulf Opportunity Zone. In addition, it is intended that additional capital expenditures incurred to recondition or rebuild property the original use of which in the Gulf Opportunity Zone began with the taxpayer would satisfy the "original use" requirement. See Treasury Regulation 1.48-2 Example 5.) Finally, the property must be acquired by purchase (as defined under section 179(d)) by the taxpayer on or after August 28, 2005 and placed in service on or before December 31, 2007. For qualifying nonresidential real property and residential rental property, the property must be placed in service on or before December 31, 2008, in lieu of December 31, 2007. Property does not qualify if a binding written contract for the acquisition of such property was in effect before August 28, 2005. However, property is not precluded from qualifying for the additional first-year depreciation merely be-

49. The "Gulf Opportunity Zone" is defined as that portion of the Hurricane Katrina Disaster Area determined by the President to warrant individual or individual and public assistance from the Federal government under the Robert T. Stafford Disaster Relief and Emergency Assistance Act by reason of Hurricane Katrina. The term "Hurricane Katrina disaster area" means an area with respect to which a major disaster has been declared by the President before September 14, 2005, under section 401 of the Robert T. Stafford Disaster Relief and Emergency Assistance Act by reason of Hurricane Katrina.

cause a binding written contract to acquire a component of the property is in effect prior to August 28, 2005.

Property that is manufactured, constructed, or produced by the taxpayer for use by the taxpayer qualifies if the taxpayer begins the manufacture, construction, or production of the property on or after August 28, 2005, and the property is placed in service on or before December 31, 2007 (and all other requirements are met). In the case of qualified nonresidential real property and residential rental property, the property must be placed in service on or before December 31, 2008. Property that is manufactured, constructed, or produced for the taxpayer by another person under a contract that is entered into prior to the manufacture, construction, or production of the property is considered to be manufactured, constructed, or produced by the taxpayer.

Under a special rule, property any portion of which is financed with the proceeds of a tax-exempt obligation under section 103 is not eligible for the additional first-year depreciation deduction. Recapture rules apply under the provision if the property ceases to be qualified Gulf Opportunity Zone property.

Explanation of Provision

The provision extends the placed-in-service deadline for specified Gulf Opportunity Zone extension property to qualify for the additional first-year depreciation deduction.[50] Specified Gulf Opportunity Zone extension property is defined as property substantially all the use of which is in one or more specified portions of the Gulf Opportunity Zone and which is either: (1) nonresidential real property or residential rental property which is placed in service by the taxpayer on or before December 31, 2010, or (2) in the case of a taxpayer who places in service a building described in (1), property described in section 168(k)(2)(A)(i)[51] if substantially all the use of such property is in such building and such property is placed in service within 90 days of the date the building is placed in service. However, in the case of nonresidential real property or residential rental property, only the adjusted basis of such property attributable to manufacture, construction, or production before January 1, 2010 ("progress expenditures") is eligible for the additional first-year depreciation.

The specified portions of the Gulf Opportunity Zone are defined as those portions of the Gulf Opportunity Zone which are in a county or parish which is identified by the Secretary of the Treasury (or his delegate) as being a county or parish in which hurricanes occurring in 2005 damaged (in the aggregate) more than 60 percent of the housing units in such county or parish which were occupied (determined according to the 2000 Census.)[52]

Effective Date

The provision applies as if included in section 101 of the Gulf Opportunity Zone Act of 2005[53] ("GOZA"). Section 101 of GOZA is effective for property placed in service on or after August 28, 2005, in taxable years ending on or after such date.

50. The extension of the placed-in-service deadline does not apply for purposes of the increased section 179 expensing limit available to Gulf Opportunity Zone property.
51. Generally, property described in section 168(k)(2)(A)(i) is (1) property to which the general rules of the Modified Accelerated Cost Recovery System ("MACRS") apply with an applicable recovery period of 20 years or less, (2) computer software other than computer software covered by section 197, (3) water utility property (as defined in section 168(e)(5)), or (4) certain leasehold improvement property.
52. The Office of the Federal Coordinator for Gulf Coast Rebuilding at the Department of Homeland Security, in cooperation with the Federal Emergency Management Agency, the Small Business Administration, and the Department of Housing and Urban Development, compiled data to assess the full extent of housing damage due to 2005 Hurricanes Katrina, Rita, and Wilma. The data was published on February 12, 2006 and is available at www.dhs.gov/xlibrary/assets/GulfCoast_HousingDamageEstimates_021206.pdf (last accessed December 5, 2006). It is intended that the Secretary or his delegate will make use of this data in identifying counties and parishes which qualify under the provision.
53. Pub. L. No. 109-135 (2005).

[¶5025] Section 121. Authority for undercover operations.

(Code Sec. 7608)

[Joint Committee on Taxation Report — JCX-50-06]

Present Law

IRS undercover operations are exempt from the otherwise applicable statutory restrictions controlling the use of government funds (which generally provide that all receipts must be deposited in the general fund of the Treasury and all expenses paid out of appropriated funds). In general, the exemption permits the IRS to use proceeds from an undercover operation to pay additional expenses incurred in the undercover operation. The IRS is required to conduct a detailed financial audit of large undercover operations in which the IRS is using proceeds from such operations and to provide an annual audit report to the Congress on all such large undercover operations.

The provision was originally enacted in The Anti-Drug Abuse Act of 1988. The exemption originally expired on December 31, 1989, and was extended by the Comprehensive Crime Control Act of 1990 to December 31, 1991. There followed a gap of approximately four and a half years during which the provision had lapsed. In the Taxpayer Bill of Rights II, the authority to use proceeds from undercover operations was extended for five years, through 2000. The Community Renewal Tax Relief Act of 2000 extended the authority of the IRS to use proceeds from undercover operations for an additional five years, through 2005. The Gulf Opportunity Zone Act of 2005 extended the authority through December 31, 2006.

Explanation of Provision

The provision extends for one year the present-law authority of the IRS to use proceeds from undercover operations to pay additional expenses incurred in conducting undercover operations (through December 31, 2007).

Effective Date

The provision is effective on the date of enactment.

[¶5026] Section 122(a). Disclosures of certain tax return information: disclosures to facilitate combined employment tax reporting.

(Code Sec. 6103)

[Joint Committee on Taxation Report — JCX-50-06]

Present Law

Traditionally, Federal tax forms are filed with the Federal government and State tax forms are filed with individual States. This necessitates duplication of items common to both returns. The Code permits the IRS to disclose taxpayer identity information and signatures to any agency, body, or commission of any State for the purpose of carrying out with such agency, body or commission a combined Federal and State employment tax reporting program approved by the Secretary.[54] The Federal disclosure restrictions, safeguard requirements, and criminal penalties for unauthorized disclosure and unauthorized inspection do not apply with respect to disclosures or inspections made pursuant to this authority. This provision expires after December 31, 2006.

Separately, under section 6103(c), the IRS may disclose a taxpayer's return or return information to such person or persons as the taxpayer may designate in a request for or consent to such disclosure. Pursuant to Treasury regulations, a taxpayer's participation in a combined return filing program between the IRS and a State agency, body or commis-

54. Sec. 6103(d)(5).

sion constitutes a consent to the disclosure by the IRS to the State agency of taxpayer identity information, signature and items of common data contained on the return.[55] No disclosures may be made under this authority unless there are provisions of State law protecting the confidentiality of such items of common data.

Explanation of Provision

The provision extends for one year the present-law authority under section 6103(d)(5) for the combined employment tax reporting program (through December 31, 2007).

Effective Date

The provision applies to disclosures after December 31, 2006.

[¶ 5027] Section 122(b). Disclosures of certain tax return information: disclosures relating to terrorist activities.

(Code Sec. 6103)

[Joint Committee on Taxation Report — JCX-50-06]

Present Law

In general

Section 6103 provides that returns and return information may not be disclosed by the IRS, other Federal employees, State employees, and certain others having access to the information except as provided in the Internal Revenue Code. Section 6103 contains a number of exceptions to this general rule of nondisclosure that authorize disclosure in specifically identified circumstances (including nontax criminal investigations) when certain conditions are satisfied.

Among the disclosures permitted under the Code is disclosure of returns and return information for purposes of investigating terrorist incidents, threats, or activities, and for analyzing intelligence concerning terrorist incidents, threats, or activities. The term "terrorist incident, threat, or activity" is statutorily defined to mean an incident, threat, or activity involving an act of domestic terrorism or international terrorism.[56] In general, returns and taxpayer return information must be obtained pursuant to an ex parte court order. Return information, other than taxpayer return information, generally is available upon a written request meeting specific requirements. The IRS also is permitted to make limited disclosures of such information on its own initiative to the appropriate Federal law enforcement agency. No disclosures may be made under these provisions after December 31, 2006. The procedures applicable to these provisions are described in detail below.

Disclosure of returns and return information — by ex parte court order

Ex parte court orders sought by Federal law enforcement and Federal intelligence agencies

The Code permits, pursuant to an ex parte court order, the disclosure of returns and return information (including taxpayer return information) to certain officers and employees of a Federal law enforcement agency or Federal intelligence agency. These officers and employees are required to be personally and directly engaged in any investigation of, response to, or analysis of intelligence and counterintelligence information concerning any terrorist incident, threat, or activity. These officers and employees are permitted to use this information solely for their use in the investigation, response, or

55. Treas. Reg. sec. 301.6103(c)-1(d)(2).
56. Sec. 6103(b)(11). For this purpose, "domestic terrorism" is defined in 18 U.S.C. Sec. 2331(5) and "international terrorism" is defined in 18 U.S.C. sec. 2331.

analysis, and in any judicial, administrative, or grand jury proceeding, pertaining to any such terrorist incident, threat, or activity.

The Attorney General, Deputy Attorney General, Associate Attorney General, an Assistant Attorney General, or a United States attorney, may authorize the application for the ex parte court order to be submitted to a Federal district court judge or magistrate. The Federal district court judge or magistrate would grant the order if based on the facts submitted he or she determines that: (1) there is reasonable cause to believe, based upon information believed to be reliable, that the return or return information may be relevant to a matter relating to such terrorist incident, threat, or activity; and (2) the return or return information is sought exclusively for the use in a Federal investigation, analysis, or proceeding concerning any terrorist incident, threat, or activity.

Special rule for ex parte court ordered disclosure initiated by the IRS

If the Secretary possesses returns or return information that may be related to a terrorist incident, threat, or activity, the Secretary may on his own initiative, authorize an application for an ex parte court order to permit disclosure to Federal law enforcement. In order to grant the order, the Federal district court judge or magistrate must determine that there is reasonable cause to believe, based upon information believed to be reliable, that the return or return information may be relevant to a matter relating to such terrorist incident, threat, or activity. The information may be disclosed only to the extent necessary to apprise the appropriate Federal law enforcement agency responsible for investigating or responding to a terrorist incident, threat, or activity and for officers and employees of that agency to investigate or respond to such terrorist incident, threat, or activity. Further, use of the information is limited to use in a Federal investigation, analysis, or proceeding concerning a terrorist incident, threat, or activity. Because the Department of Justice represents the Secretary in Federal district court, the Secretary is permitted to disclose returns and return information to the Department of Justice as necessary and solely for the purpose of obtaining the special IRS ex parte court order.

Disclosure of return information other than by ex parte court order

Disclosure by the IRS without a request

The Code permits the IRS to disclose return information, other than taxpayer return information, related to a terrorist incident, threat, or activity to the extent necessary to apprise the head of the appropriate Federal law enforcement agency responsible for investigating or responding to such terrorist incident, threat, or activity. The IRS on its own initiative and without a written request may make this disclosure. The head of the Federal law enforcement agency may disclose information to officers and employees of such agency to the extent necessary to investigate or respond to such terrorist incident, threat, or activity. A taxpayer's identity is not treated as return information supplied by the taxpayer or his or her representative.

Disclosure upon written request of a Federal law enforcement agency

The Code permits the IRS to disclose return information, other than taxpayer return information, to officers and employees of Federal law enforcement upon a written request satisfying certain requirements. The request must: (1) be made by the head of the Federal law enforcement agency (or his delegate) involved in the response to or investigation of terrorist incidents, threats, or activities, and (2) set forth the specific reason or reasons why such disclosure may be relevant to a terrorist incident, threat, or activity. The information is to be disclosed to officers and employees of the Federal law enforcement agency who would be personally and directly involved in the response to or investigation of terrorist incidents, threats, or activities. The information is to be used by such officers and employees solely for such response or investigation.

The Code permits the redisclosure by a Federal law enforcement agency to officers and employees of State and local law enforcement personally and directly engaged in the response to or investigation of the terrorist incident, threat, or activity. The State or local law enforcement agency must be part of an investigative or response team with the Federal law enforcement agency for these disclosures to be made.

Disclosure upon request from the Departments of Justice or Treasury for intelligence analysis of terrorist activity

Upon written request satisfying certain requirements discussed below, the IRS is to disclose return information (other than taxpayer return information) to officers and employees of the Department of Justice, Department of Treasury, and other Federal intelligence agencies, who are personally and directly engaged in the collection or analysis of intelligence and counterintelligence or investigation concerning terrorist incidents, threats, or activities. Use of the information is limited to use by such officers and employees in such investigation, collection, or analysis.

The written request is to set forth the specific reasons why the information to be disclosed is relevant to a terrorist incident, threat, or activity. The request is to be made by an individual who is: (1) an officer or employee of the Department of Justice or the Department of Treasury, (2) appointed by the President with the advice and consent of the Senate, and (3) responsible for the collection, and analysis of intelligence and counterintelligence information concerning terrorist incidents, threats, or activities. The Director of the United States Secret Service also is an authorized requester under the Act.

Explanation of Provision

The provision extends for one year the present-law terrorist activity disclosure provisions (through December 31, 2007).

Effective Date

The provision applies to disclosures after December 31, 2006.

[¶ 5028] Section 122(c). Disclosures of certain tax return information: disclosures relating to student loans.

(Code Sec. 6103)

[Joint Committee on Taxation Report — JCX-50-06]

Present Law

Present law prohibits the disclosure of returns and return information, except to the extent specifically authorized by the Code. An exception is provided for disclosure to the Department of Education (but not to contractors thereof) of a taxpayer's filing status, adjusted gross income and identity information (i.e., name, mailing address, taxpayer identifying number) to establish an appropriate repayment amount for an applicable student loan. The disclosure authority for the income-contingent loan repayment program is scheduled to expire after December 31, 2006.

The Department of Education utilizes contractors for the income-contingent loan verification program. The specific disclosure exception for the program does not permit disclosure of return information to contractors. As a result, the Department of Education obtains return information from the Internal Revenue Service by taxpayer consent (under section 6103(c)), rather than under the specific exception for the income-contingent loan verification program (sec. 6103(l)(13)).

Explanation of Provision

The provision extends for one year the present-law authority to disclose return information for purposes of the income-contingent loan repayment program (through December 31, 2007).

Effective Date

The provision applies to requests made after December 31, 2006.

[¶5029] Section 123. Special rule for elections under expired provisions.

(Code Sec. 41, 280C)

[Joint Committee on Taxation Report — JCX-50-06]

Present Law

Under present law, various elections under provisions of the Code must be made by a certain date and in a certain manner. For example, the election under section 280C(c)(3) of a reduced credit for increasing research expenditures must be made not later than the time for filing a return (including extensions).

Explanation of Provision

The provision provides that, in the case of any taxable year which ends after December 31, 2005 and before the date of enactment of the bill, an election under section 41(c)(4), 280C(c)(3)(C), or any other expired provision of the Code which is extended by the bill is treated as timely if made not later than April 15, 2007, or such other time as the Secretary or his designee provide. The election shall be made in the manner prescribed by the Secretary or his designee.

Effective Date

The provision is effective on the date of enactment.

[¶5031] Section 201. Credit for electricity produced from certain renewable resources.

(Code Sec. 45)

[Joint Committee on Taxation Report — JCX-50-06]

Present Law

In general

An income tax credit is allowed for the production of electricity at qualified facilities using qualified energy resources (sec. 45). Qualified energy resources comprise wind, closed-loop biomass, open-loop biomass, geothermal, energy, solar energy, small irrigation power, municipal solid waste, and qualified hydropower production. Qualified facilities are, generally, facilities that generate electricity using qualified energy resources. To be eligible for the credit, electricity produced from qualified energy resources at qualified facilities must be sold by the taxpayer to an unrelated person. In addition to the electricity production credit, an income tax credit is allowed for the production of refined coal and Indian coal at qualified facilities.

Credit amounts and credit period

In general

The base amount of the credit is 1.5 cents per kilowatt-hour (indexed annually for inflation) of electricity produced. The amount of the credit is 1.9 cents per kilowatt-hour for 2006. A taxpayer may generally claim a credit during the 10-year period commencing with the date the qualified facility is placed in service. The credit is reduced for grants, tax-exempt bonds, subsidized energy financing, and other credits.

The amount of credit a taxpayer may claim is phased out as the market price of electricity (or refined coal in the case of the refined coal production credit) exceeds certain threshold levels. The electricity production credit is reduced over a 3 cent phase-out range to the extent the annual average contract price per kilowatt hour of electricity sold in the prior year from the same qualified energy resource exceeds 8 cents (adjusted for inflation). The refined coal credit is reduced over an $8.75 phase-out range as the reference price of the fuel used as feedstock for the refined coal exceeds the reference price for such fuel in 2002 (adjusted for inflation).

Reduced credit amounts and credit periods

Generally, in the case of open-loop biomass facilities (including agricultural livestock waste nutrient facilities), geothermal energy facilities, solar energy facilities, small irrigation power facilities, landfill gas facilities, and trash combustion facilities, the 10-year credit period is reduced to five years commencing on the date the facility was originally placed in service, for qualified facilities placed in service before August 8, 2005. However, for qualified open-loop biomass facilities (other than a facility described in sec. 45(d)(3)(A)(i) that uses agricultural livestock waste nutrients) placed in service before October 22, 2004, the five-year period commences on January 1, 2005. In the case of a closed-loop biomass facility modified to co-fire with coal, to co-fire with other biomass, or to co-fire with coal and other biomass, the credit period begins no earlier than October 22, 2004.

In the case of open-loop biomass facilities (including agricultural livestock waste nutrient facilities), small irrigation power facilities, landfill gas facilities, trash combustion facilities, and qualified hydropower facilities the otherwise allowable credit amount is 0.75 cent per kilowatt-hour, indexed for inflation measured after 1992 (currently 0.9 cents per kilowatt-hour for 2006).

Credit applicable to refined coal

The amount of the credit for refined coal is $4.375 per ton (also indexed for inflation after 1992 and equaling $5.679 per ton for 2006).

Credit applicable to Indian coal

A credit is available for the sale of Indian coal to an unrelated third part from a qualified facility for a seven-year period beginning on January 1, 2006, and before January 1, 2013. The amount of the credit for Indian coal is $1.50 per ton for the first four years of the seven-year period and $2.00 per ton for the last three years of the seven-year period. Beginning in calendar years after 2006, the credit amounts are indexed annually for inflation using 2005 as the base year.

Other limitations on credit claimants and credit amounts

In general, in order to claim the credit, a taxpayer must own the qualified facility and sell the electricity produced by the facility (or refined coal or Indian coal, with respect to those credits) to an unrelated party. A lessee or operator may claim the credit in lieu of the owner of the qualifying facility in the case of qualifying open-loop biomass facilities and in the case of a closed-loop biomass facilities modified to co-fire with coal, to co-fire with other biomass, or to co-fire with coal and other biomass. In the case of a poultry waste facility, the taxpayer may claim the credit as a lessee or operator of a facility owned by a governmental unit.

For all qualifying facilities, other than closed-loop biomass facilities modified to co-fire with coal, to co-fire with other biomass, or to co-fire with coal and other biomass, the amount of credit a taxpayer may claim is reduced by reason of grants, tax-exempt bonds, subsidized energy financing, and other credits, but the reduction cannot exceed 50 percent of the otherwise allowable credit. In the case of closed-loop biomass facilities modified to co-fire with coal, to co-fire with other biomass, or to co-fire with coal and other biomass, there is no reduction in credit by reason of grants, tax-exempt bonds, subsidized energy financing, and other credits.

The credit for electricity produced from renewable sources is a component of the general business credit (sec. 38(b)(8)). Generally, the general business credit for any taxable year may not exceed the amount by which the taxpayer's net income tax exceeds the greater of the tentative minimum tax or so much of the net regular tax liability as exceeds $25,000. Excess credits may be carried back one year and forward up to 20 years.

A taxpayer's tentative minimum tax is treated as being zero for purposes of determining the tax liability limitation with respect to the section 45 credit for electricity produced from a facility (placed in service after October 22, 2004) during the first four years of production beginning on the date the facility is placed in service.

Qualified facilities

Wind energy facility

A wind energy facility is a facility that uses wind to produce electricity. To be a qualified facility, a wind energy facility must be placed in service after December 31, 1993, and before January 1, 2008.

Closed-loop biomass facility

A closed-loop biomass facility is a facility that uses any organic material from a plant which is planted exclusively for the purpose of being used at a qualifying facility to produce electricity. In addition, a facility can be a closed-loop biomass facility if it is a facility that is modified to use closed-loop biomass to co-fire with coal, with other biomass, or with both coal and other biomass, but only if the modification is approved under the Biomass Power for Rural Development Programs or is part of a pilot project of the Commodity Credit Corporation.

To be a qualified facility, a closed-loop biomass facility must be placed in service after December 31, 1992, and before January 1, 2008. In the case of a facility using closed-loop biomass but also co-firing the closed-loop biomass with coal, other biomass, or coal and other biomass, a qualified facility must be originally placed in service and modified to co-fire the closed-loop biomass at any time before January 1, 2008.

Open-loop biomass (including agricultural livestock waste nutrients) facility

An open-loop biomass facility is a facility that uses open-loop biomass to produce electricity. For purposes of the credit, open-loop biomass is defined as (1) any agricultural livestock waste nutrients or (2) any solid, nonhazardous, cellulosic waste material or any lignin material that is segregated from other waste materials and which is derived from:

- forest-related resources, including mill and harvesting residues, precommercial thinnings, slash, and brush;
- solid wood waste materials, including waste pallets, crates, dunnage, manufacturing and construction wood wastes, landscape or right-of-way tree trimming; or
- agricultural sources, including orchard tree crops, vineyard, grain, legumes, sugar, and other crop by-products or residues.

Agricultural livestock waste nutrients are defined as agricultural livestock manure and litter, including bedding material for the disposition of manure. Wood waste materials do not qualify as open-loop biomass to the extent they are pressure treated, chemically treated, or painted. In addition, municipal solid waste, gas derived from the biodegradation of solid waste, and paper which is commonly recycled do not qualify as open-loop biomass. Open-loop biomass does not include closed-loop biomass or any biomass burned in conjunction with fossil fuel (co-firing) beyond such fossil fuel required for start up and flame stabilization.

In the case of an open-loop biomass facility that uses agricultural livestock waste nutrients, a qualified facility is one that was originally placed in service after October 22, 2004, and before January 1, 2008, and has a nameplate capacity rating which is not less than 150 kilowatts. In the case of any other open-loop biomass facility, a qualified facility is one that was originally placed in service before January 1, 2008.

Geothermal facility

A geothermal facility is a facility that uses geothermal energy to produce electricity. Geothermal energy is energy derived from a geothermal deposit which is a geothermal reservoir consisting of natural heat which is stored in rocks or in an aqueous liquid or vapor (whether or not under pressure). To be a qualified facility, a geothermal facility must be placed in service after October 22, 2004 and before January 1, 2008.

Solar facility

A solar facility is a facility that uses solar energy to produce electricity. To be a qualified facility, a solar facility must be placed in service after October 22, 2004 and before January 1, 2006.

Small irrigation facility

A small irrigation power facility is a facility that generates electric power through an irrigation system canal or ditch without any dam or impoundment of water. The installed capacity of a qualified facility must be not less than 150 kilowatts but less than five megawatts. To be a qualified facility, a small irrigation facility must be originally placed in service after October 22, 2004 and before January 1, 2008.

Landfill gas facility

A landfill gas facility is a facility that uses landfill gas to produce electricity. Landfill gas is defined as methane gas derived from the biodegradation of municipal solid waste. To be a qualified facility, a landfill gas facility must be placed in service after October 22, 2004 and before January 1, 2008.

Trash combustion facility

Trash combustion facilities are facilities that burn municipal solid waste (garbage) to produce steam to drive a turbine for the production of electricity. To be a qualified facility, a trash combustion facility must be placed in service after October 22, 2004 and before January 1, 2008. A qualified trash combustion facility includes a new unit, placed in service after October 22, 2004, that increases electricity production capacity at an existing trash combustion facility. A new unit generally would include a new burner/boiler and turbine. The new unit may share certain common equipment, such as trash handling equipment, with other pre-existing units at the same facility. Electricity produced at a new unit of an existing facility qualifies for the production credit only to the extent of the increased amount of electricity produced at the entire facility.

Hydropower facility

A qualifying hydropower facility is (1) a facility that produced hydroelectric power (a hydroelectric dam) prior to August 8, 2005, at which efficiency improvements or additions to capacity have been made after such date and before January 1, 2009, that enable the taxpayer to produce incremental hydropower or (2) a facility placed in service before August 8, 2005, that did not produce hydroelectric power (a nonhydroelectric dam) on such date, and to which turbines or other electricity generating equipment have been added such date and before January 1, 2009.

At an existing hydroelectric facility, the taxpayer may only claim credit for the production of incremental hydroelectric power. Incremental hydroelectric power for any taxable year is equal to the percentage of average annual hydroelectric power produced at the facility attributable to the efficiency improvement or additions of capacity determined by using the same water flow information used to determine an historic average annual hydroelectric power production baseline for that facility. The Federal Energy Regulatory Commission will certify the baseline power production of the facility and the percentage increase due to the efficiency and capacity improvements.

At a nonhydroelectric dam, the facility must be licensed by the Federal Energy Regulatory Commission and meet all other applicable environmental, licensing, and regulatory requirements and the turbines or other generating devices must be added to the facility after August 8, 2005 and before January 1, 2009. In addition there must not be any enlargement of the diversion structure, or construction or enlargement of a bypass channel, or the impoundment or any withholding of additional water from the natural stream channel.

Refined coal facility

A qualifying refined coal facility is a facility producing refined coal that is placed in service after October 22, 2004 and before January 1, 2009. Refined coal is a qualifying liquid, gaseous, or solid synthetic fuel produced from coal (including lignite) or high-carbon fly ash, including such fuel used as a feedstock. A qualifying fuel is a fuel that when burned emits 20 percent less nitrogen oxides and either SO2 or mercury than the burning of feedstock coal or comparable coal predominantly available in the marketplace as of January 1, 2003, and if the fuel sells at prices at least 50 percent greater than the prices of the feedstock coal or comparable coal. In addition, to be qualified refined coal the fuel must be sold by the taxpayer with the reasonable expectation that it will be used for the primary purpose of producing steam.

Indian coal facility

A qualified Indian coal facility is a facility which is placed in service before January 1, 2009, that produces coal from reserves that on June 14, 2005, were owned by a Federally recognized tribe of Indians or were held in trust by the United States for a tribe or its members.

Summary of credit rate and credit period by facility type

Table 1.—Summary of Section 45 Credit for Electricity Produced from Certain Renewable Resources, for Refined Coal, and for Indian Coal

Eligible electricity production or coal production activity	Credit amount for 2006 (cents per kilowatt-hour; dollars per ton)	Credit period for facilities placed in service on or before August 8, 2005 (years from placed-in-service date)	Credit period facilities placed in service after August 8, 2005 (years from placed-in-service date)
Wind	1.9	10	10
Closed-loop biomass	1.9	10[1]	10[1]
Open-loop biomass (including agricultural livestock waste nutrient facilities)	0.9	5[2]	10
Geothermal	1.9	5	10
Solar	1.9	5	10
Small irrigation power	0.9	5	10
Municipal solid waste (including landfill gas facilities and trash combustion facilities)	0.9	5	10
Qualified hydropower	0.9	N/A	10
Refined Coal	5.679	10	10
Indian Coal	1.50	7[3]	7[3]

[1] In the case of certain co-firing closed-loop facilities, the credit period begins no earlier than October 22, 2004.

[2] For certain facilities placed in service before October 22, 2004, the 5-year credit period commences on January 1, 2005.

[3] For Indian coal, the credit period begins for coal sold after January 1, 2006.

For eligible pre-existing facilities and other facilities placed in service prior to January 1, 2005, the credit period commences on January 1, 2005. In the case of certain co-firing closed-loop facilities, the credit period begins no earlier than October 22, 2004. For Indian coal, the credit period begins for coal sold after January 1, 2006, for facilities placed-in-service before January 1, 2009.

Taxation of cooperatives and their patrons

For Federal income tax purposes, a cooperative generally computes its income as if it were a taxable corporation, with one exception-the cooperative may exclude from its taxable income distributions of patronage dividends. Generally, cooperatives that are subject to the cooperative tax rules of subchapter T of the Code[57] are permitted a deduction for patronage dividends from their taxable income only to the extent of net income that is derived from transactions with patrons who are members of the cooperative.[58] The availability of such deductions from taxable income has the effect of allowing the cooperative to be treated like a conduit with respect to profits derived from transactions with patrons who are members of the cooperative. For taxable years ending on or before August 8, 2005, cooperatives may not pass any portion of the income tax credit for electricity production through to their patrons.

For taxable years ending after August 8, 2005, eligible cooperatives may elect to pass any portion of the credit through to their patrons. An eligible cooperative is defined as a cooperative organization that is owned more than 50 percent by agricultural producers or entities owned by agricultural producers. The credit may be apportioned among patrons

57. Sec. 1381, et seq.
58. Sec. 1382.

eligible to share in patronage dividends on the basis of the quantity or value of business done with or for such patrons for the taxable year. The election must be made on a timely filed return for the taxable year, and once made, is irrevocable for such taxable year. The amount of the credit apportioned to patrons is not included in the organization's credit for the taxable year of the organization. The amount of the credit apportioned to a patron is included in the taxable year the patron with or within which the taxable year of the organization ends. If the amount of the credit for any taxable year is less than the amount of the credit shown on the cooperative's return for such taxable year, an amount equal to the excess of the reduction in the credit over the amount not apportioned to patrons for the taxable year is treated as an increase in the cooperative's tax. The increase is not treated as tax imposed for purposes of determining the amount of any tax credit.

Explanation of Provision

The provision extends through December 31, 2008, the period during which certain facilities may be placed in service as qualified facilities for purposes of the electricity production credit. The placed-in-service date extension applies for all qualified facilities, except for qualified solar, refined coal, and Indian coal facilities.

Effective Date

The provision is effective for facilities placed in service after December 31, 2007.

[¶5032] Section 202. Credit to holders of clean renewable energy bonds.

(Code Sec. 54)

[Joint Committee on Taxation Report — JCX-50-06]

Present Law

Tax exempt bonds

Interest on State and local governmental bonds generally is excluded from gross income for Federal income tax purposes if the proceeds of the bonds are used to finance direct activities of these governmental units or if the bonds are repaid with revenues of the governmental units. Activities that can be financed with these tax-exempt bonds include the financing of electric power facilities (i.e., generation, transmission, distribution, and retailing).

Interest on State or local government bonds to finance activities of private persons ("private activity bonds") is taxable unless a specific exception is contained in the Code (or in a non-Code provision of a revenue Act). The term "private person" generally includes the Federal government and all other individuals and entities other than States or local governments. The Code includes exceptions permitting States or local governments to act as conduits providing tax-exempt financing for certain private activities. In most cases, the aggregate volume of these tax-exempt private activity bonds is restricted by annual aggregate volume limits imposed on bonds issued by issuers within each State. For calendar year 2006, these annual volume limits, which are indexed for inflation, equal $80 per resident of the State, or $246.6 million, if greater.

The tax exemption for State and local bonds also does not apply to any arbitrage bond.[59] An arbitrage bond is defined as any bond that is part of an issue if any proceeds of the issue are reasonably expected to be used (or intentionally are used) to acquire higher yielding investments or to replace funds that are used to acquire higher yielding investments.[60] In general, arbitrage profits may be earned only during specified periods (e.g., defined "temporary periods") before funds are needed for the purpose of the bor-

59. Secs. 103(a) and (b)(2).
60. Sec. 148.

rowing or on specified types of investments (e.g., "reasonably required reserve or replacement funds"). Subject to limited exceptions, investment profits that are earned during these periods or on such investments must be rebated to the Federal government.

An issuer must file with the IRS certain information about the bonds issued by them in order for that bond issue to be tax-exempt.[61] Generally, this information return is required to be filed no later the 15th day of the second month after the close of the calendar quarter in which the bonds were issued.

Clean renewable energy bonds

As an alternative to traditional tax-exempt bonds, States and local governments may issue clean renewable energy bonds ("CREBs"). CREBs are defined as any bond issued by a qualified issuer if, in addition to the requirements discussed below, 95 percent or more of the proceeds of such bonds are used to finance capital expenditures incurred by qualified borrowers for facilities that qualify for the tax credit under section 45 (other than Indian coal production facilities), without regard to the placed-in-service date requirements of that section. The term "qualified issuers" includes (1) governmental bodies (including Indian tribal governments); (2) mutual or cooperative electric companies (described in section 501(c)(12) or section 1381(a)(2)(C), or a not-for-profit electric utility which has received a loan or guarantee under the Rural Electrification Act); and (3) clean energy bond lenders. The term "qualified borrower" includes a governmental body (including an Indian tribal government) and a mutual or cooperative electric company.

In addition, Notice 2006-7 provides that projects that may be financed with CREBs include any facility owned by a qualified borrower that is functionally related and subordinate (as determined under Treas. Reg. sec. 1.103-8(a)(3)) to any qualified facility described in sections 45(d)(1) through (d)(9) (determined without regard to any placed in service date) and owned by such qualified borrower.

Unlike tax-exempt bonds, CREBs are not interest-bearing obligations. Rather, the taxpayer holding CREBs on a credit allowance date is entitled to a tax credit. The amount of the credit is determined by multiplying the bond's credit rate by the face amount on the holder's bond. The credit rate on the bonds is determined by the Secretary and is to be a rate that permits issuance of CREBs without discount and interest cost to the qualified issuer. The credit accrues quarterly and is includible in gross income (as if it were an interest payment on the bond), and can be claimed against regular income tax liability and alternative minimum tax liability.

CREBs are subject to a maximum maturity limitation. The maximum maturity is the term which the Secretary estimates will result in the present value of the obligation to repay the principal on a CREBs being equal to 50 percent of the face amount of such bond. In addition, the Code requires level amortization of CREBs during the period such bonds are outstanding.

CREBs also are subject to the arbitrage requirements of section 148 that apply to traditional tax-exempt bonds. Principles under section 148 and the regulations thereunder apply for purposes of determining the yield restriction and arbitrage rebate requirements applicable to CREBs.

To qualify as CREBs, the qualified issuer must reasonably expect to and actually spend 95 percent or more of the proceeds of such bonds on qualified projects within the five-year period that begins on the date of issuance. To the extent less than 95 percent of the proceeds are used to finance qualified projects during the five-year spending period, bonds will continue to qualify as CREBs if unspent proceeds are used within 90 days from the end of such five-year period to redeem any "nonqualified bonds." The five-year spending period may be extended by the Secretary upon the qualified issuer's

61. Sec. 149(e).

request demonstrating that the failure to satisfy the five-year requirement is due to reasonable cause and the projects will continue to proceed with due diligence.

Issuers of CREBs are required to report issuance to the IRS in a manner similar to the information returns required for tax-exempt bonds. There is a national CREB limitation of $800 million. CREBs must be issued before January 1, 2008. Under present law, no more than $500 million of CREBs authority may be allocated to projects for governmental bodies.

Explanation of Provision

The provision authorizes an additional $400 million of CREBs that may be issued and extends the authority to issue such bonds through December 31, 2008. It is expected that the additional authority will be allocated through a new application process similar to that set forth in Notice 2005-98, 2005-52 I.R.B 1211.

In addition to increasing the national limitation on the amount of CREBs, the provision increases the maximum amount of CREBs that may be allocated to qualified projects of governmental bodies to $750 million.

The provision provides an extension of the CREBs program, but it is expected that Congress will review the efficacy of the program, including the efficacy of imposing limitations on allocations to projects for governmental bodies, before granting additional extensions.

Effective Date

The provision authorizing an additional $400 million of CREBs and extending the authority to issue such bonds through December 31, 2008, is effective for bonds issued after December 31, 2006. The provision increasing the maximum amount of CREBs that may be allocated to qualified projects of governmental bodies is effective for allocations or reallocations after December 31, 2006.

[¶5033] Section 203. Performance standards for sulfur dioxide removal in advanced coal-based generation technology units designed to use subbituminous coal.

(Code Sec. 48A)

[Joint Committee on Taxation Report — JCX-50-06]

Present Law

An investment tax credit is available for investments in certain qualifying advanced coal projects (sec. 48A). The credit amount is 20 percent for investments in qualifying projects that use integrated gasification combined cycle ("IGCC"). The credit amount is 15 percent for investments in qualifying projects that use other advanced coal-based electricity generation technologies.

To qualify, an advanced coal project must be located in the United States and use an advanced coal-based generation technology to power a new electric generation unit or to retrofit or repower an existing unit. An electric generation unit using an advanced coal-based technology must be designed to achieve a 99 percent reduction in sulfur dioxide and a 90 percent reduction in mercury, as well as to limit emissions of nitrous oxide and particulate matter.

The fuel input for a qualifying project, when completed, must use at least 75 percent coal. The project, consisting of one or more electric generation units at one site, must have a nameplate generating capacity of at least 400 megawatts, and the taxpayer must provide evidence that a majority of the output of the project is reasonably expected to be acquired or utilized.

Credits are available only for projects certified by the Secretary of Treasury, in consultation with the Secretary of Energy. Certifications are issued using a competitive bidding process. The Secretary of Treasury must establish a certification program no later than 180 days after August 8, 2005, and each project application must be submitted during the three-year period beginning on the date such certification program is established.

The Secretary of Treasury may allocate $800 million of credits to IGCC projects and $500 million to projects using other advanced coal-based electricity generation technologies. Qualified projects must be economically feasible and use the appropriate clean coal technologies. With respect to IGCC projects, credit-eligible investments include only investments in property associated with the gasification of coal, including any coal handling and gas separation equipment. Thus, investments in equipment that could operate by drawing fuel directly from a natural gas pipeline do not qualify for the credit.

In determining which projects to certify that use IGCC technology, the Secretary must allocate power generation capacity in relatively equal amounts to projects that use bituminous coal, subbituminous coal, and lignite as primary feedstock. In addition, the Secretary must give high priority to projects which include greenhouse gas capture capability, increased by-product utilization, and other benefits.

Explanation of Provision

The provision modifies one of the performance requirements necessary for an electric generation unit to be treated as using advanced coal-based generation technology. Under the provision, the performance requirement relating to the removal of sulfur dioxide is changed so that an electric generation unit designed to use subbituminous coal can meet the standard if it is designed either to remove 99 percent of the sulfur dioxide or to achieve an emission limit of 0.04 pounds of sulfur dioxide per million British thermal units on a 30-day average.

Effective Date

The provision is effective for advanced coal project certification applications submitted after October 2, 2006.

[¶5034] Section 204. Deduction for energy efficient commercial buildings.

(Code Sec. 179D)

[Joint Committee on Taxation Report — JCX-50-06]

Present Law

In general

Code section 179D provides a deduction equal to energy-efficient commercial building property expenditures made by the taxpayer. Energy-efficient commercial building property expenditures is defined as property (1) which is installed on or in any building located in the United States that is within the scope of Standard 90.1-2001 of the American Society of Heating, Refrigerating, and Air Conditioning Engineers and the Illuminating Engineering Society of North America ("ASHRAE/IESNA"), (2) which is installed as part of (i) the interior lighting systems, (ii) the heating, cooling, ventilation, and hot water systems, or (iii) the building envelope, and (3) which is certified as being installed as part of a plan designed to reduce the total annual energy and power costs with respect to the interior lighting systems, heating, cooling, ventilation, and hot water systems of the building by 50 percent or more in comparison to a reference building which meets the minimum requirements of Standard 90.1-2001 (as in effect on April 2, 2003). The deduction is limited to an amount equal to $1.80 per square foot of the property for which such expenditures are made. The deduction is allowed in the year in which the property is placed in service.

Certain certification requirements must be met in order to qualify for the deduction. The Secretary, in consultation with the Secretary of Energy, will promulgate regulations that describe methods of calculating and verifying energy and power costs using qualified computer software based on the provisions of the 2005 California Nonresidential Alternative Calculation Method Approval Manual or, in the case of residential property, the 2005 California Residential Alternative Calculation Method Approval Manual.

The Secretary is required to prescribe procedures for the inspection and testing for compliance of buildings that are comparable, given the difference between commercial and residential buildings, to the requirements in the Mortgage Industry National Accreditation Procedures for Home Energy Rating Systems. Individuals qualified to determine compliance are only those recognized by one or more organizations certified by the Secretary for such purposes.

For energy-efficient commercial building property expenditures made by a public entity, such as public schools, the Secretary is required to promulgate regulations that allow the deduction to be allocated to the person primarily responsible for designing the property in lieu of the public entity.

If a deduction is allowed under this provision, the basis of the property is reduced by the amount of the deduction.

Partial allowance of deduction

In the case of a building that does not meet the overall building requirement of a 50-percent energy savings, a partial deduction is allowed with respect to each separate building system that comprises energy efficient property and which is certified by a qualified professional as meeting or exceeding the applicable system-specific savings targets established by the Secretary of the Treasury. The applicable system-specific savings targets to be established by the Secretary are those that would result in a total annual energy savings with respect to the whole building of 50 percent, if each of the separate systems met the system specific target. The separate building systems are (1) the interior lighting system, (2) the heating, cooling, ventilation and hot water systems, and (3) the building envelope. The maximum allowable deduction is $0.60 per square foot for each separate system.

In the case of system-specific partial deductions, in general no deduction is allowed until the Secretary establishes system-specific targets. However, in the case of lighting system retrofits, until such time as the Secretary issues final regulations, the system-specific energy savings target for the lighting system is deemed to be met by a reduction in Lighting Power Density of 40 percent (50 percent in the case of a warehouse) of the minimum requirements in Table 9.3.1.1 or Table 9.3.1.2 of ASHRAE/IESNA Standard 90.1-2001. Also, in the case of a lighting system that reduces lighting power density by 25 percent, a partial deduction of 30 cents per square foot is allowed. A pro-rated partial deduction is allowed in the case of a lighting system that reduces lighting power density between 25 percent and 40 percent. Certain lighting level and lighting control requirements must also be met in order to qualify for the partial lighting deductions.

The deduction is effective for property placed in service after December 31, 2005 and prior to January 1, 2008.

Explanation of Provision

The provision extends the deduction to property placed in service prior to January 1, 2009.

Effective Date

The provision is effective on the date of enactment.

[¶5035] Section 205. Credit for new energy efficient homes.

(Code Sec. 45L)

[Joint Committee on Taxation Report — JCX-50-06]

Present Law

Code section 45L provides a credit to an eligible contractor for the construction of a qualified new energy-efficient home. To qualify as a new energy-efficient home, the home must be: (1) a dwelling located in the United States, (2) substantially completed after August 8, 2005, and (3) certified in accordance with guidance prescribed by the Secretary to have a projected level of annual heating and cooling energy consumption that meets the standards for either a 30-percent or 50-percent reduction in energy usage, compared to a comparable dwelling constructed in accordance with the standards of chapter 4 of the 2003 International Energy Conservation Code as in effect (including supplements) on August 8, 2005, and any applicable Federal minimum efficiency standards for equipment. With respect to homes that meet the 30-percent standard, one-third of such 30 percent savings must come from the building envelope, and with respect to homes that meet the 50-percent standard, one-fifth of such 50 percent savings must come from the building envelope.

Manufactured homes that conform to Federal manufactured home construction and safety standards are eligible for the credit provided all the criteria for the credit are met. The eligible contractor is the person who constructed the home, or in the case of a manufactured home, the producer of such home.

The credit equals $1,000 in the case of a new home that meets the 30 percent standard and $2,000 in the case of a new home that meets the 50 percent standard. Only manufactured homes are eligible for the $1,000 credit.

In lieu of meeting the standards of chapter 4 of the 2003 International Energy Conservation Code, manufactured homes certified by a method prescribed by the Administrator of the Environmental Protection Agency under the Energy Star Labeled Homes program are eligible for the $1,000 credit provided criteria (1) and (2), above, are met.

The credit is part of the general business credit. No credits attributable to qualified new energy efficient homes can be carried back to any taxable year ending on or before the effective date of the credit.

The credit applies to homes whose construction is substantially completed after December 31, 2005, and which are purchased after December 31, 2005 and prior to January 1, 2008.

Explanation of Provision

The provision extends the credit to homes whose construction is substantially completed after December 31, 2005, and which are purchased after December 31, 2005 and prior to January 1, 2009.

Effective Date

The provision is effective on the date of enactment.

[¶5036] Section 206. Credit for residential energy efficient property.

(Code Sec. 25D)

[Joint Committee on Taxation Report — JCX-50-06]

Present Law

Code section 25D provides a personal tax credit for the purchase of qualified photovoltaic property and qualified solar water heating property that is used exclusively for purposes other than heating swimming pools and hot tubs. The credit is equal to 30 percent of qualifying expenditures, with a maximum credit for each of these systems of property of $2,000. Section 25D also provides a 30 percent credit for the purchase of qualified fuel cell power plants. The credit for any fuel cell may not exceed $500 for each 0.5 kilowatt of capacity.

Qualifying solar water heating property means an expenditure for property to heat water for use in a dwelling unit located in the United States and used as a residence if at least half of the energy used by such property for such purpose is derived from the sun. Qualified photovoltaic property is property that uses solar energy to generate electricity for use in a dwelling unit. A qualified fuel cell power plant is an integrated system comprised of a fuel cell stack assembly and associated balance of plant components that (1) converts a fuel into electricity using electrochemical means, (2) has an electricity-only generation efficiency of greater than 30 percent. The qualified fuel cell power plant must be installed on or in connection with a dwelling unit located in the United States and used by the taxpayer as a principal residence.

The credit is nonrefundable, and the depreciable basis of the property is reduced by the amount of the credit. Expenditures for labor costs allocable to onsite preparation, assembly, or original installation of property eligible for the credit are eligible expenditures.

Certain equipment safety requirements need to be met to qualify for the credit. Special proration rules apply in the case of jointly owned property, condominiums, and tenant-stockholders in cooperative housing corporations. If less than 80 percent of the property is used for nonbusiness purposes, only that portion of expenditures that is used for nonbusiness purposes is taken into account.

The credit applies to property placed in service after December 31, 2005 and prior to January 1, 2008.

Explanation of Provision

The provision extends the credit to property placed in service after December 31, 2005 and prior to January 1, 2009. The provision also clarifies that all property, not just photovoltaic property, that uses solar energy to generate electricity for use in a dwelling unit is qualifying property.

Effective Date

The provision is effective on the date of enactment.

[¶5037] Section 207. Energy credit.

(Code Sec. 48)

[Joint Committee on Taxation Report — JCX-50-06]

Present Law

In general

A nonrefundable, 10-percent business energy credit is allowed for the cost of new property that is equipment (1) that uses solar energy to generate electricity, to heat or cool a structure, or to provide solar process heat, or (2) used to produce, distribute, or use energy derived from a geothermal deposit, but only, in the case of electricity generated by geothermal power, up to the electric transmission stage. Property used to generate energy for the purposes of heating a swimming pool is not eligible solar energy property.

The business energy tax credits are components of the general business credit (sec. 38(b)(1)). The business energy tax credits, when combined with all other components of the general business credit, generally may not exceed for any taxable year the excess of the taxpayer's net income tax over the greater of (1) 25 percent of so much of the net regular tax liability as exceeds $25,000 or (2) the tentative minimum tax. An unused general business credit generally may be carried back one year and carried forward 20 years (sec. 39).

In general, property that is public utility property is not eligible for the credit. This rule is waived in the case of telecommunication companies' purchases of fuel cell and microturbine property.

The credit is nonrefundable. The taxpayer's basis in the property is reduced by the amount of the credit claimed.

Special rules for solar energy property

The credit for solar energy property is increased to 30 percent in the case of periods after December 31, 2005 and prior to January 1, 2008. Additionally, equipment that uses fiber-optic distributed sunlight to illuminate the inside of a structure is solar energy property eligible for the 30-percent credit.

Fuel cells and microturbines

The business energy credit also applies for the purchase of qualified fuel cell power plants, but only for periods after December 31, 2005 and prior to January 1, 2008. The credit rate is 30 percent. A qualified fuel cell power plant is an integrated system composed of a fuel cell stack assembly and associated balance of plant components that (1) converts a fuel into electricity using electrochemical means, (2) has an electricity-only generation efficiency of greater than 30 percent. The credit may not exceed $500 for each 0.5 kilowatt of capacity.

The business energy credit also applies for the purchase of qualifying stationary microturbine power plants, but only for periods after December 31, 2005 and prior to January 1, 2008. The credit is limited to the lesser of 10 percent of the basis of the property or $200 for each kilowatt of capacity.

A qualified stationary microturbine power plant is an integrated system comprised of a gas turbine engine, a combustor, a recuperator or regenerator, a generator or alternator, and associated balance of plant components that converts a fuel into electricity and thermal energy. Such system also includes all secondary components located between the existing infrastructure for fuel delivery and the existing infrastructure for power distribution, including equipment and controls for meeting relevant power standards, such as voltage, frequency and power factors. Such system must have an electricity-only generation efficiency of not less that 26 percent at International Standard Organization conditions and a capacity of less than 2,000 kilowatts.

Additionally, for purposes of the fuel cell and microturbine credits, and only in the case of telecommunications companies, the general present-law section 48 restriction that would otherwise prohibit telecommunication companies from claiming the new credit due to their status as public utilities is waived.

Explanation of Provision

The provision extends the present law credit at current credit rates through December 31, 2008.

Effective Date

The provision is effective on the date of enactment.

[¶5038] Section 208. Special rule for qualified methanol or ethanol fuel.

(Code Sec. 4041)

[Joint Committee on Taxation Report — JCX-50-06]

Present Law

The term "qualified methanol or ethanol fuel" means any liquid at least 85 percent of which consists of methanol, ethanol or other alcohol produced from coal (including peat). Qualified methanol or ethanol fuel is taxed at a reduced rate. Qualified methanol is taxed at 12.35 cents per gallon. Qualified ethanol is taxed at 13.25 cents per gallon. These reduced rates expire after September 30, 2007.

Explanation of Provision

The provision extends the reduced rates for qualified methanol or ethanol fuel through December 31, 2008.

Effective Date

The provision is effective on the date of enactment.

[¶5039] Section 209. Special depreciation allowance for cellulosic biomass ethanol plant property.

(Code Sec. 168)

[Joint Committee on Taxation Report — JCX-50-06]

Present Law

A taxpayer is allowed to recover, through annual depreciation deductions, the cost of certain property used in a trade or business or for the production of income. The amount of the depreciation deduction allowed with respect to tangible property for a taxable year is determined under the modified accelerated cost recovery system ("MACRS"). Under MACRS, different types of property generally are assigned applicable recovery periods and depreciation methods. The recovery periods applicable to most tangible personal property (generally tangible property other than residential rental property and nonresidential real property) range from 3 to 25 years. The depreciation methods generally applicable to tangible personal property are the 200-percent and 150-percent declining balance methods, switching to the straight-line method for the taxable year in which the depreciation deduction would be maximized.

In lieu of depreciation, a taxpayer with a sufficiently small amount of annual investment may elect to deduct (or "expense") such costs (sec. 179). Present law provides that the maximum amount a taxpayer may expense, for taxable years beginning in 2003 through 2009, is $100,000 of the cost of qualifying property placed in service for the taxable year. The $100,000 amount is reduced (but not below zero) by the amount by which the cost of qualifying property placed in service during the taxable year exceeds $400,000. The $100,000 and $400,000 amounts are indexed for inflation for taxable years beginning after 2003 and before 2010. In general, under section 179, qualifying property is defined as depreciable tangible personal property that is purchased for use in the active conduct of a trade or business. Additional section 179 incentives are provided with respect to a qualified property used by a business in the New York Liberty Zone (sec. 1400L(f)), an empowerment zone (sec. 1397A), a renewal community (sec. 1400J), or the Gulf Opportunity Zone (section 1400N). Recapture rules generally apply with respect to property that ceases to be qualified property.

Section 179C provides a temporary election to expense 50 percent of the cost of qualified refinery property. Qualified refinery property generally includes assets, located in the United States, used in the refining of liquid fuels: (1) with respect to the construction of which there is a binding construction contract before January 1, 2008; (2) which are placed in service before January 1, 2012; (3) which increase the output capacity of an existing refinery by at least five percent or increase the percentage of total throughput attributable to qualified fuels (as defined in section 45K(c)) such that it equals or exceeds 25 percent; and (4) which meet all applicable environmental laws in effect when the property is placed in service.

For purposes of section 179C, the term "refinery" refers to facilities the primary purpose of which is the processing of crude oil (whether or not previously refined) or qualified fuels as defined in section 45K(c). The limitation of section 45K(d) requiring domestic production of qualified fuels is not applicable with respect to the definition of refinery under this provision; thus, otherwise qualifying refinery property is eligible even if the primary purpose of the refinery is the processing of oil produced from shale and tar sands outside the United States. The term refinery would include a facility which processes coal or biomass via gas into liquid fuel.

Explanation of Provision

The provision allows an additional first-year depreciation deduction equal to 50 percent of the adjusted basis of qualified cellulosic biomass ethanol plant property. In order to qualify, the property generally must be placed in service before January 1, 2013.

Qualified cellulosic biomass ethanol plant property means property used in the U.S. solely to produce cellulosic biomass ethanol. For this purpose, cellulosic biomass ethanol means ethanol derived from any lignocellulosic or hemicellulosic matter that is available on a renewable or recurring basis. For example, lignocellulosic or hemicellulosic matter that is available on a renewable or recurring basis includes bagasse (from sugar cane), corn stalks, and switchgrass.

The additional first-year depreciation deduction is allowed for both regular tax and alternative minimum tax purposes for the taxable year in which the property is placed in service. The additional first-year depreciation deduction is subject to the general rules regarding whether an item is deductible under section 162 or subject to capitalization under section 263 or section 263A. The basis of the property and the depreciation allowances in the year of purchase and later years are appropriately adjusted to reflect the additional first-year depreciation deduction. In addition, the provision provides that there is no adjustment to the allowable amount of depreciation for purposes of computing a taxpayer's alternative minimum taxable income with respect to property to which the provision applies. A taxpayer is allowed to elect out of the additional first-year depreciation for any class of property for any taxable year.

In order for property to qualify for the additional first-year depreciation deduction, it must meet the following requirements. The original use of the property must commence with the taxpayer on or after the date of enactment of the provision. The property must be acquired by purchase (as defined under section 179(d)) by the taxpayer after the date of enactment and placed in service before January 1, 2013. Property does not qualify if a binding written contract for the acquisition of such property was in effect on or before the date of enactment.

Property that is manufactured, constructed, or produced by the taxpayer for use by the taxpayer qualifies if the taxpayer begins the manufacture, construction, or production of the property after the date of enactment, and the property is placed in service before January 1, 2013 (and all other requirements are met). Property that is manufactured, constructed, or produced for the taxpayer by another person under a contract that is entered into prior to the manufacture, construction, or production of the property is considered to be manufactured, constructed, or produced by the taxpayer.

Property any portion of which is financed with the proceeds of a tax-exempt obligation under section 103 is not eligible for the additional first-year depreciation deduction. Recapture rules apply under the provision if the property ceases to be qualified cellulosic biomass ethanol plant property.

Property with respect to which the taxpayer has elected 50 percent expensing under section 179C is not eligible for the additional first-year depreciation deduction under the provision.

Effective Date

The provision applies to property placed in service after the date of enactment, in taxable years ending after such date.

[¶5041] Section 211. Treatment of coke and coke gas.

(Code Sec. 45K)

[Joint Committee on Taxation Report — JCX-50-06]

Present Law

Certain fuels produced from "non-conventional sources" and sold to unrelated parties are eligible for an income tax credit equal to $3 (generally adjusted for inflation)[67] per barrel or Btu oil barrel equivalent ("non-conventional source fuel credit").[68] Qualified fuels must be produced within the United States.

Qualified fuels include:

- oil produced from shale and tar sands;
- gas produced from geopressured brine, Devonian shale, coal seams, tight formations, or biomass; and
- liquid, gaseous, or solid synthetic fuels produced from coal (including lignite).

Generally, the non-conventional source fuel credit has expired, except for certain biomass gas and synthetic fuels sold before January 1, 2008, and produced at facilities placed in service after December 31, 1992, and before July 1, 1998.

The non-conventional source fuel credit provision also includes a credit for coke or coke gas produced at qualified facilities during a four-year period beginning on the later of January 1, 2006, or the date the facility was placed in service. For purposes of the coke production credit, qualified facilities are facilities placed in service before January

67. The inflation adjustment is generally calculated using 1979 as the base year. Generally, the value of the credit for fuel produced in 2005 was $6.79 per barrel-of-oil equivalent produced, which is approximately $1.20 per thousand cubic feet of natural gas. In the case of fuel sold after 2005, the credit for coke or coke gas is indexed for inflation using 2004 as the base year instead of 1979.

68. Sec. 29 (for tax years ending before 2006); sec. 45K (for tax years ending after 2005).

1, 1993, or after June 30, 1998, and before January 1, 2010. The amount of credit-eligible coke produced at any one facility may not exceed an average barrel-of-oil equivalent of 4,000 barrels per day.

The non-conventional source fuel credit is reduced (but not below zero) over a $6 (inflation-adjusted) phase-out period as the reference price for oil exceeds $23.50 per barrel (also adjusted for inflation). The reference price is the Secretary's estimate of the annual average wellhead price per barrel for all domestic crude oil. The credit did not phase-out for 2005 because the reference price for that year of $50.26 did not exceed the inflation adjusted threshold of $51.35. Beginning with taxable years ending after December 31, 2005, the non-conventional source fuel credit is part of the general business credit (sec. 38).

Explanation of Provision

The provision repeals the phase-out limitation for coke and coke gas otherwise eligible for a credit under section 45K(g). The provision also clarifies that qualifying facilities producing coke and coke gas under section 45K(g) do not include facilities that produce petroleum-based coke or coke gas. The provision does not modify the existing 4,000 barrel-of-oil equivalent per day limitation.

Effective Date

The provision is effective as if included in section 1321 of the Energy Policy Act of 2005.

[¶ 5045] Section 302, 303, 304, 305, 306, 307. FSA and HRA terminations to fund HSAs; Repeal of annual deductible limitation on HSA contributions; Modification of cost-of-living adjustment; Contribution limitation not reduced for part-year coverage; Exception to requirement for employers to make comparable health saving account contributions; One-time distribution from individual retirement plans to fund HSAS.

(Code Sec. 106, 223, 408, 4980G)

[Joint Committee on Taxation Report — JCX-50-06]

Present Law

Health savings accounts

In general

Individuals with a high deductible health plan (and no other health plan other than a plan that provides certain permitted coverage) may establish a health savings account ("HSA"). In general, HSAs provide tax-favored treatment for current medical expenses as well as the ability to save on a tax-favored basis for future medical expenses. In general, HSAs are tax-exempt trusts or custodial accounts created exclusively to pay for the qualified medical expenses of the account holder and his or her spouse and dependents.

Within limits, contributions to an HSA made by or on behalf of an eligible individual are deductible by the individual. Contributions to an HSA are excludable from income and employment taxes if made by the employer. Earnings on amounts in HSAs are not taxable. Distributions from an HSA for qualified medical expenses are not includible in gross income. Distributions from an HSA that are not used for qualified medical expenses are includible in gross income and are subject to an additional tax of 10 percent. The 10-percent additional tax does not apply if the distribution is made after death, disability, or the individual attains the age of Medicare eligibility (i.e., age 65).

Eligible individuals

Eligible individuals for HSAs are individuals who are covered by a high deductible health plan and no other health plan that is not a high deductible health plan and which provides coverage for any benefit which is covered under the high deductible health plan. After an individual has attained age 65 and becomes enrolled in Medicare benefits, contributions cannot be made to an HSA.[69] Eligible individuals do not include individuals who may be claimed as a dependent on another person's tax return.

An individual with other coverage in addition to a high deductible health plan is still eligible for an HSA if such other coverage is certain permitted insurance or permitted coverage. Permitted insurance is: (1) insurance if substantially all of the coverage provided under such insurance relates to (a) liabilities incurred under worker's compensation law, (b) tort liabilities, (c) liabilities relating to ownership or use of property (e.g., auto insurance), or (d) such other similar liabilities as the Secretary of Treasury may prescribe by regulations; (2) insurance for a specified disease or illness; and (3) insurance that provides a fixed payment for hospitalization. Permitted coverage is coverage (whether provided through insurance or otherwise) for accidents, disability, dental care, vision care, or long-term care.

A high deductible health plan is a health plan that, for 2007, has a deductible that is at least $1,100 for self-only coverage or $2,200 for family coverage and that has an out-of-pocket expense limit that is no more than $5,500 in the case of self-only coverage and $11,000 in the case of family coverage.[70] Out-of-pocket expenses include deductibles, co-payments, and other amounts (other than premiums) that the individual must pay for covered benefits under the plan. A plan is not a high deductible health plan if substantially all of the coverage is for permitted coverage or coverage that may be provided by permitted insurance, as described above. A plan does not fail to be a high deductible health plan by reason of failing to have a deductible for preventive care.

Health flexible spending arrangement ("FSAs") and health reimbursement arrangements ("HRAs") are health plans that constitute other coverage under the HSA rules. These arrangements are discussed in more detail, below. An individual who is covered by a high deductible health plan and a health FSA or HRA generally is not eligible to make contributions to an HSA. An individual is eligible to make contributions to an HSA if the health FSA or HRA is: (1) a limited purpose health FSA or HRA; (2) a suspended HRA; (3) a post-deductible health FSA or HRA; or (4) a retirement HRA.[71]

Tax treatment of and limits on contributions

Contributions to an HSA by or on behalf of an eligible individual are deductible (within limits) in determining adjusted gross income (i.e., "above-the-line") of the individual. In addition, employer contributions to HSAs (including salary reduction contributions made through a cafeteria plan) are excludable from gross income and wages for

69. Sec. 223(b)(7), as interpreted by Notice 2004-2, 2004-2 I.R.B. 269, corrected by Announcement 2004-67, 2004-36 I.R.B. 459.

70. The limits are indexed for inflation. For 2006, a high deductible plan is a health plan that has a deductible that is at least $1,050 for self-only coverage or $2,100 for family coverage and that has an out-of-pocket expense limit that is no more than $5,250 in the case of self-only coverage and $10,500 in the case of family coverage. The family coverage limits always will be twice the self-only coverage limits (as indexed for inflation). In the case of the plan using a network of providers, the plan does not fail to be a high deductible health plan (if it would otherwise meet the requirements of a high deductible health plan) solely because the out-of-pocket expense limit for services provided outside of the network exceeds the out-of-pocket expense limits. In addition, such plan's deductible for out-of-network services is not taken into account in determining the annual contribution limit (i.e., the deductible for services within the network is used for such purpose).

71. Rev. Rul. 2004-45, 2004-22 I.R.B. 1. A limited purpose health FSA pays or reimburses benefits for permitted coverage and a limited purpose HRA pays or reimburses benefits for permitted insurance or permitted coverage. A limited purpose health FSA or HRA may also pay or reimburse preventive care benefits. A suspended HRA does not pay medical expense incurred during a suspension period except for preventive care, permitted insurance and permitted coverage. A post-deductible health FSA or HRA does not pay or reimburse any medical expenses incurred before the minimum annual deductible under the HSA rules is satisfied. A retirement HSA pays or reimburses only medical expenses incurred after retirement.

employment tax purposes. In the case of an employee, contributions to an HSA may be made by both the individual and the individual's employer. All contributions are aggregated for purposes of the maximum annual contribution limit. Contributions to Archer MSAs reduce the annual contribution limit for HSAs.

The maximum aggregate annual contribution that can be made to an HSA is the lesser of (1) 100 percent of the annual deductible under the high deductible health plan, or (2) (for 2007) $2,850 in the case of self-only coverage and $5,650 in the case of family coverage.[72] The annual contribution limit is the sum of the limits determined separately for each month, based on the individual's status and health plan coverage as of the first day of the month. The annual contribution limits are increased for individuals who have attained age 55 by the end of the taxable year. In the case of policyholders and covered spouses who are age 55 or older, the HSA annual contribution limit is greater than the otherwise applicable limit by $700 in 2006, $800 in 2007, $900 in 2008, and $1,000 in 2009 and thereafter. As in determining the general annual contribution limit, the increase in the annual contribution limit for individuals who have attained age 55 is also determined on a monthly basis. As previously discussed, contributions, including catch-up contributions, cannot be made once an individual is enrolled in Medicare.

In the case of individuals who are married to each other and either spouse has family coverage, both spouses are treated as having only the family coverage with the lowest annual deductible. The annual contribution limit (without regard to the catch-up contribution amounts) is divided equally between the spouses unless they agree on a different division (after reduction for amounts paid from any Archer MSA of the spouses).

An excise tax applies to contributions in excess of the maximum contribution amount for the HSA. The excise tax generally is equal to six percent of the cumulative amount of excess contributions that are not distributed from the HSA.

Amounts can be rolled over into an HSA from another HSA or from an Archer MSA.

Comparable contributions

If an employer makes contributions to employees' HSAs, the employer must make available comparable contributions on behalf of all employees with comparable coverage during the same period. Contributions are considered comparable if they are either of the same amount or the same percentage of the deductible under the plan. If employer contributions do not satisfy the comparability rule during a period, then the employer is subject to an excise tax equal to 35 percent of the aggregate amount contributed by the employer to HSAs for that period. The comparability rule does not apply to contributions made through a cafeteria plan.

Taxation of distributions

Distributions from an HSA for qualified medical expenses of the individual and his or her spouse or dependents generally are excludable from gross income. In general, amounts in an HSA can be used for qualified medical expenses even if the individual is not currently eligible for contributions to the HSA.

Qualified medical expenses generally are defined as under section 213(d) and include expenses for diagnosis, cure, mitigation, treatment, or prevention of disease. Qualified medical expenses do not include expenses for insurance other than for (1) long-term care insurance, (2) premiums for health coverage during any period of continuation coverage required by Federal law, (3) premiums for health care coverage while an individual is receiving unemployment compensation under Federal or State law, or (4) in the case of an account beneficiary who has attained the age of Medicare eligibility, health insurance premiums for Medicare, other than premiums for Medigap policies. Such qualified

72. These amounts are indexed for inflation. For 2006, the dollar limits are $2,700 in the case of self-only coverage and $5,450 in the case of family coverage.

health insurance premiums include, for example, Medicare Part A and Part B premiums, Medicare HMO premiums, and the employee share of premiums for employer-sponsored health insurance including employer-sponsored retiree health insurance. Whether the expenses are qualified medical expenses is determined as of the time the expenses were incurred.

For purposes of determining the itemized deduction for medical expenses, distributions from an HSA for qualified medical expenses are not treated as expenses paid for medical care under section 213. Distributions from an HSA that are not for qualified medical expenses are includible in gross income. Distributions includible in gross income also are subject to an additional 10-percent tax unless made after death, disability, or the individual attains the age of Medicare eligibility (i.e., age 65).

Reporting requirements

Employer contributions are required to be reported on the employee's Form W-2. Trustees of HSAs may be required to report to the Secretary of the Treasury amounts with respect to contributions, distributions, the return of excess contributions, and other matters as determined appropriate by the Secretary. In addition, the Secretary may require providers of high deductible health plans to make reports to the Secretary and to account beneficiaries as the Secretary determines appropriate.

Health flexible spending arrangements and health reimbursement arrangements

Arrangements commonly used by employers to reimburse medical expenses of their employees (and their spouses and dependents) include health flexible spending arrangements ("FSAs") and health reimbursement accounts ("HRAs"). Health FSAs typically are funded on a salary reduction basis, meaning that employees are given the option to reduce current compensation and instead have the compensation used to reimburse the employee for medical expenses. If the health FSA meets certain requirements, then the compensation that is forgone is not includible in gross income or wages and reimbursements for medical care from the health FSA are excludable from gross income and wages. Health FSAs are subject to the general requirements relating to cafeteria plans, including a requirement that a cafeteria plan generally may not provide deferred compensation.[73] This requirement often is referred to as the "use-it-or-lose-it-rule." Until May of 2005, this requirement was interpreted to mean that amounts available from a health FSA as of the end of a plan year must be forfeited by the employee. In May 2005, the Treasury Department issued a notice that allows a grace period not to exceed two and one-half months immediately following the end of the plan year during which unused amounts may be used.[74] An individual participating in a health FSA that allows reimbursements during a grace period is generally not eligible to make contributions to the HSA until the first month following the end of the grace period even if the individual's health FSA has no unused benefits as of the end of the prior plan year.[75] Health FSAs are subject to certain other requirements, including rules that require that the FSA have certain characteristics similar to insurance.

HRAs operate in a manner similar to health FSAs, in that they are an employer-maintained arrangement that reimburses employees for medical expenses. Some of the rules applicable to HRAs and health FSAs are similar, e.g., the amounts in the arrangements can only be used to reimburse medical expenses and not for other purposes. Some of the rules are different. For example, HRAs cannot be funded on a salary reduction basis and the use-it-or-lose-it rule does not apply. Thus, amounts remaining at the end of the year may be carried forward to be used to reimburse medical expenses in the next year.[76] Re-

73. Sec. 125(d)(2).
74. Notice 2005-42, 2005-23 I.R.B. 1204.
75. Notice 2005-86, 2005-49 I.R.B. 1075.
76. Guidance with respect to HRAs, including the interaction of FSAs and HRAs in the case an individual is covered under both, is provided in Notice 2002-45, 2002-2 C.B. 93.

imbursements for insurance covering medical care expenses are allowable reimbursements under an HRA, but not under a health FSA.

As mentioned above, subject to certain limited exceptions, health FSAs and HRAs constitute other coverage under the HSA rules.

Explanation of Provision

Allow rollovers from health FSAs and HRAs into HSAs for a limited time

The provision allows certain amounts in a health FSA or HRA to be distributed from the health FSA or HRA and contributed through a direct transfer to an HSA without violating the otherwise applicable requirements for such arrangements. The amount that can be distributed from a health FSA or HRA and contributed to an HSA may not exceed an amount equal to the lesser of (1) the balance in the health FSA or HRA as of September 21, 2006 or (2) the balance in the health FSA or HRA as of the date of the distribution. The balance in the health FSA or HRA as of any date is determined on a cash basis (i.e., expenses incurred that have not been reimbursed as of the date the determination is made are not taken into account). Amounts contributed to an HSA under the provision are excludable from gross income and wages for employment tax purposes, are not taken into account in applying the maximum deduction limitation for other HSA contributions, and are not deductible. Contributions must be made directly to the HSA before January 1, 2012. The provision is limited to one distribution with respect to each health FSA or HRA of the individual.

The provision is designed to assist individuals in transferring from another type of health plan to a high deductible health plan. Thus, if an individual for whom a contribution is made under the provision does not remain an eligible individual during the testing period, the amount of the contribution is includible in gross income of the individual. An exception applies if the employee ceases to be an eligible individual by reason of death or disability. The testing period is the period beginning with the month of the contribution and ending on the last day of the 12th month following such month. The amount is includible for the taxable year of the first day during the testing period that the individual is not an eligible individual. A 10-percent additional tax also applies to the amount includible.

A modified comparability rule applies with respect to contributions under the provision. If the employer makes available to any employee the ability to make contributions to the HSA from distributions from a health FSA or HRA under the provision, all employees who are covered under a high deductible plan of the employer must be allowed to make such distributions and contributions. The present-law excise tax applies if this requirement is not met.

For example, suppose the balance in a health FSA as of September 21, 2006, is $2,000 and the balance in the account as January 1, 2008 is $3,000. Under the provision, a health FSA will not be considered to violate applicable rules if, as of January 1, 2008, an amount not to exceed $2,000 is distributed from the health FSA and contributed to an HSA of the individual. The $2,000 distribution would not be includible in income, and the subsequent contribution would not be deductible and would not count against the annual maximum tax deductible contribution that can be made to the HSA. If the individual ceases to be an eligible individual as of June 1, 2008, the $2,000 contribution amount is included in gross income and subject to a 10-percent additional tax. If instead the distribution and contribution are made as of June 30, 2008, when the balance in the health FSA is $1,500, the amount of the distribution and contribution is limited to $1,500.

The present law rule that an individual is not an eligible individual if the individual has coverage under a general purpose health FSA or HRA continues to apply. Thus, for example, if the health FSA or HRA from which the contribution is made is a general purpose health FSA or HRA and the individual remains eligible under such arrangement after the distribution and contribution, the individual is not an eligible individual.

Certain FSA coverage treated as disregarded coverage

The provision provides that, for taxable years beginning after December 31, 2006, in certain cases, coverage under a health flexible spending arrangement ("FSA") during the period immediately following the end of a plan year during which unused benefits or contributions remaining at the end of such plan year may be paid or reimbursed to plan participants for qualified expenses is disregarded coverage. Such coverage is disregarded if (1) the balance in the health FSA at the end of the plan year is zero, or (2) in accordance with rules prescribed by the Secretary of Treasury, the entire remaining balance in the health FSA at the end of the plan year is contributed to an HSA as provided under another provision of the bill.[77]

Thus, for example, if as of December 31, 2006, a participant's health FSA balance is zero, coverage under the health FSA during the period from January 1, 2007, until March 15, 2007 (i.e., the "grace period") is disregarded in determining if tax deductible contributions can be made to an HSA for that period. Similarly, if the entire balance in an individual's health FSA as of December 31, 2006, is distributed and contributed to an HSA (as under another provision of the bill) coverage during the health FSA grace period is disregarded.

It is intended that the Secretary will provide guidance under the provision with respect to the timing of health FSA distributions contributed to an HSA in order to facilitate such rollovers and the establishment of HSAs in connection with high deductible plans. For example, it is intended that the Secretary would provide rules under which coverage is disregarded if, before the end of a year, an individual elects high deductible plan coverage and to contribute any remaining FSA balance to an HSA in accordance with the provision even if the trustee-to-trustee transfer cannot be completed until the following plan year. Similar rules apply for the general provision allowing amounts from a health FSA or HRA to be contributed to an HSA in order to facilitate such contributions at the beginning of an employee's first year of HSA eligibility.

The provision does not modify the permitted health FSA grace period allowed under existing Treasury guidance.

Repeal of annual plan deductible limitation on HSA contribution limitation

The provision modifies the limit on the annual deductible contributions that can be made to an HSA so that the maximum deductible contribution is not limited to the annual deductible under the high deductible health plan. Thus, under the provision, the maximum aggregate annual contribution that can be made to an HSA is $2,850 (for 2007) in the case of self-only coverage and $5,650 (for 2007) in the case of family coverage.

Earlier indexing of cost of living adjustments

Under the provision, in the case of adjustments made for any taxable year beginning after 2007, the Consumer Price Index for a calendar year is determined as of the close of the 12-month period ending on March 31 of the calendar year (rather than August 31 as under present law) for the purpose of making cost-of-living adjustments for the HSA dollar amounts that are indexed for inflation (i.e., the contribution limits and the high-deductible health plan requirements). The provision also requires the Secretary of Treasury to publish the adjusted amounts for a year no later than June 1 of the preceding calendar year.

---

77. The amount that can be contributed is limited to the balance in the health FSA as of September 21, 2006.

Allow full contribution for months preceding month that taxpayer is an eligible individual

In general, the provision allows individuals who become covered under a high deductible plan in a month other than January to make the full deductible HSA contribution for the year. Under the provision, an individual who is an eligible individual during the last month of a taxable year is treated as having been an eligible individual during every month during the taxable year for purposes of computing the amount that may be contributed to the HSA for the year. Thus, such individual is allowed to make contributions for months before the individual was enrolled in a high deductible health plan. For the months preceding the last month of the taxable year that the individual is treated as an eligible individual solely by reason of the provision, the individual is treated as having been enrolled in the same high deductible health plan in which the individual was enrolled during the last month of the taxable year.

If an individual makes contributions under the provision and does not remain an eligible individual during the testing period, the amount of the contributions attributable to months preceding the month in which the individual was an eligible individual which could not have been made but for the provision are includible in gross income. An exception applies if the employee ceases to be an eligible individual by reason of death or disability. The testing period is the period beginning with the last month of the taxable year and ending on the last day of the 12th month following such month. The amount is includible for the taxable year of the first day during the testing period that the individual is not an eligible individual. A 10-percent additional tax also applies to the amount includible.

For example, suppose individual "A" enrolls in high deductible plan "H" in December of 2007 and is otherwise an eligible individual in that month. A was not an eligible individual in any other month in 2007. A may make HSA contributions as if she had been enrolled in plan H for all of 2007. If A ceases to be an eligible individual (e.g., if she ceases to be covered under the high deductible health plan) in June 2008, an amount equal to the HSA deduction attributable to treating A as an eligible individual for January through November 2007 is included in income in 2008. In addition, a 10-percent additional tax applies to the amount includible.

Modify employer comparable contribution requirements for contributions made to nonhighly compensated employees

The provision provides an exception to the comparable contribution requirements which allows employers to make larger HSA contributions for nonhighly compensated employees than for highly compensated employees. Highly compensated employees are defined as under section 414(q) and include any employee who was (1) a five-percent owner at any time during the year or the preceding year; or (2) for the preceding year, (A) had compensation from the employer in excess of $100,000[78] (for 2007) and (B) if elected by the employer, was in the group consisting of the top-20 percent of employees when ranked based on compensation. Nonhighly compensated employees are employees not included in the definition of highly compensated employee under section 414(q).

The comparable contribution rules continue to apply to the contributions made to nonhighly compensated employees so that the employer must make available comparable contributions on behalf of all nonhighly compensated employees with comparable coverage during the same period.

For example, an employer is permitted to make a $1,000 contribution to the HSA of each nonhighly compensated employee for a year without making contributions to the HSA of each highly compensated employee.

78. This amount is indexed for inflation.

One-time rollovers from IRAs into HSAs

The provision allows a one-time contribution to an HSA of amounts distributed from an individual retirement arrangement ("IRA"). The contribution must be made in a direct trustee-to-trustee transfer. Amounts distributed from an IRA under the provision are not includible in income to the extent that the distribution would otherwise be includible in income. In addition, such distributions are not subject to the 10-percent additional tax on early distributions.

In determining the extent to which amounts distributed from the IRA would otherwise be includible in income, the aggregate amount distributed from the IRA is treated as includible in income to the extent of the aggregate amount which would have been includible if all amounts were distributed from all IRAs of the same type (i.e., in the case of a traditional IRA, there is no pro-rata distribution of basis). As under present law, this rule is applied separately to Roth IRAs and other IRAs.

The amount that can be distributed from the IRA and contributed to an HSA is limited to the otherwise maximum deductible contribution amount to the HSA computed on the basis of the type of coverage under the high deductible health plan at the time of the contribution. The amount that can otherwise be contributed to the HSA for the year of the contribution from the IRA is reduced by the amount contributed from the IRA. No deduction is allowed for the amount contributed from an IRA to an HSA.

Under the provision, only one distribution and contribution may be made during the lifetime of the individual, except that if a distribution and contribution are made during a month in which an individual has self-only coverage as of the first day of the month, an additional distribution and contribution may be made during a subsequent month within the taxable year in which the individual has family coverage. The limit applies to the combination of both contributions.

If the individual does not remain an eligible individual during the testing period, the amount of the distribution and contribution is includible in gross income of the individual. An exception applies if the employee ceases to be an eligible individual by reason of death or disability. The testing period is the period beginning with the month of the contribution and ending on the last day of the 12th month following such month. The amount is includible for the taxable year of the first day during the testing period that the individual is not an eligible individual. A 10-percent additional tax also applies to the amount includible.

The provision does not apply to simplified employee pensions ("SEPs") or to SIMPLE retirement accounts.

Effective Date

The provision allowing rollovers from heath FSAs and HRAs into HSAs is effective for distributions and contributions on or after the date of enactment and before January 1, 2012. The provision disregarding certain FSA coverage is effective after the date of enactment with respect to coverage for taxable years beginning after December 31, 2006. The provision repealing the annual plan limitation on the HSA contribution limitation is effective for taxable years beginning after December 31, 2006. The provision relating to cost-of-living adjustments is effective for adjustments made for taxable years beginning after 2007. The provision allowing contributions for months preceding the month that the taxpayer is an eligible individual is effective for taxable years beginning after December 31, 2006. The provision modifying the comparability rule is effective for taxable years beginning after December 31, 2006. The provision allowing one-time rollovers from an IRA into an HSA is effective for taxable years beginning after December 31, 2006.

[¶5052] Section 401. Deduction allowable with respect to income attributable to domestic production activities in Puerto Rico.

(Code Sec. 199)

[Joint Committee on Taxation Report — JCX-50-06]

Present Law

In general

Present law provides a deduction from taxable income (or, in the case of an individual, adjusted gross income) that is equal to a portion of the taxpayer's qualified production activities income. For taxable years beginning after 2009, the deduction is nine percent of such income. For taxable years beginning in 2005 and 2006, the deduction is three percent of income and, for taxable years beginning in 2007, 2008 and 2009, the deduction is six percent of income. For taxpayers subject to the 35-percent corporate income tax rate, the 9-percent deduction effectively reduces the corporate income tax rate to just under 32 percent on qualified production activities income.

Qualified production activities income

In general, "qualified production activities income" is equal to domestic production gross receipts (defined by section 199(c)(4)), reduced by the sum of: (1) the costs of goods sold that are allocable to such receipts; and (2) other expenses, losses, or deductions which are properly allocable to such receipts.

Domestic production gross receipts

"Domestic production gross receipts" generally are gross receipts of a taxpayer that are derived from: (1) any sale, exchange or other disposition, or any lease, rental or license, of qualifying production property[79] that was manufactured, produced, grown or extracted by the taxpayer in whole or in significant part within the United States; (2) any sale, exchange or other disposition, or any lease, rental or license, of qualified film[80] produced by the taxpayer; (3) any sale, exchange or other disposition of electricity, natural gas, or potable water produced by the taxpayer in the United States; (4) construction activities performed in the United States; or (5) engineering or architectural services performed in the United States for construction projects located in the United States.

For purposes of section 199, the United States does not include Puerto Rico or other U.S. possessions.[81]

Wage limitation

For taxable years beginning after May 17, 2006, the amount of the deduction for a taxable year is limited to 50 percent of the wages paid by the taxpayer, and properly allocable to domestic production gross receipts, during the calendar year that ends in such taxable year.[82] Wages paid to bona fide residents of Puerto Rico generally are not included in the wage limitation amount.[83]

---

79. "Qualifying production property" generally includes any tangible personal property, computer software, or sound recordings.
80. "Qualified film" includes any motion picture film or videotape (including live or delayed television programming, but not including certain sexually explicit productions) if 50 percent or more of the total compensation relating to the production of such film (including compensation in the form of residuals and participations) constitutes compensation for services performed in the United States by actors, production personnel, directors, and producers.
81. Sec. 7701(a)(9) ("the term 'United States' when used in a geographical sense includes only the States and the District of Columbia").
82. For purposes of the provision, "wages" include the sum of the amounts of wages as defined in section 3401(a) and elective deferrals that the taxpayer properly reports to the Social Security Administration with respect to the employment of employees of the taxpayer during the calendar year ending during the taxpayer's taxable year. For taxable years beginning before May 18, 2006, the limitation is based upon all wages paid by the taxpayer, rather than only wages properly allocable to domestic production gross receipts.
83. Sec. 3401(a)(8)(C).

Explanation of Provision

The provision amends section 199 of the Code to include Puerto Rico within the definition of the United States for purposes of determining the domestic production gross receipts of eligible taxpayers. Under the provision, a taxpayer is allowed to treat Puerto Rico as part of the United States for purposes of section 199 (thus allowing the taxpayer to take into account its Puerto Rico business activity for purposes of calculating its domestic production gross receipts and qualified production activities income), but only if all of the taxpayer's gross receipts from sources within Puerto Rico are currently taxable for U.S. Federal income tax purposes. Consequently, a controlled foreign corporation is not eligible for the section 199deduction made available by the provision. In addition, any such taxpayer is also allowed to take into account wages paid to bona fide residents of Puerto Rico for purposes of calculating the 50-percent wage limitation.

Effective Date

The provision is effective for the first two taxable years beginning after December 31, 2005, and before January 1, 2008.

[¶ 5053] Section 402, 403. Credit for prior year minimum tax liability made refundable after period of years; returns required in connection with certain options.

(Code Sec. 53, 6039)

[Joint Committee on Taxation Report — JCX-50-06]

Present Law

In general

Present law imposes an alternative minimum tax ("AMT") on an individual taxpayer to the extent the taxpayer's tentative minimum tax liability exceeds his or her regular income tax liability. An individual's tentative minimum tax is the sum of (1) 26 percent of so much of the taxable excess as does not exceed $175,000 ($87,500 in the case of a married individual filing a separate return) and (2) 28 percent of the remaining taxable excess. The taxable excess is the amount by which the alternative minimum taxable income ("AMTI") exceeds an exemption amount.

An individual's AMTI is the taxpayer's taxable income increased by certain preference items and adjusted by determining the tax treatment of certain items in a manner that negates the deferral of income resulting from the regular tax treatment of those items.

The individual AMT attributable to deferral adjustments generates a minimum tax credit that is allowable to the extent the regular tax (reduced by other nonrefundable credits) exceeds the tentative minimum tax in a future taxable year. Unused minimum tax credits are carried forward indefinitely.

AMT treatment of incentive stock options

One of the adjustments in computing AMTI is the tax treatment of the exercise of an incentive stock option. An incentive stock option is an option granted by a corporation in connection with an individual's employment, so long as the option meets certain specified requirements.[84] Under the regular tax, the exercise of an incentive stock option is tax-free if the stock is not disposed of within one year of exercise of the option or within two years of the grant of the option.[85] The individual then computes the long-term capital gain or loss on the sale of the stock using the amount paid for the stock as

84. Sec. 422.
85. Sec. 421.

the cost basis. If the holding period requirements are not satisfied, the individual generally takes into account at the exercise of the option an amount of ordinary income equal to the excess of the fair market value of the stock on the date of exercise over the amount paid for the stock. The cost basis of the stock is increased by the amount taken into account.[86]

Under the individual alternative minimum tax, the exercise of an incentive stock option is treated as the exercise of an option other than an incentive stock option. Under this treatment, generally the individual takes into account as ordinary income for purposes of computing AMTI the excess of the fair market value of the stock at the date of exercise over the amount paid for the stock.[87] When the stock is later sold, for purposes of computing capital gain or loss for purposes of AMTI, the adjusted basis of the stock includes the amount taken into account as AMTI.

The adjustment relating to incentive stock options is a deferral adjustment and therefore generates an AMT credit in the year the stock is sold.[88]

Furnishing of information

Under present law,[89] employers are required to provide to employees information regarding the transfer of stock pursuant to the exercise of an incentive stock option and to transfers of stock under an employee stock purchase plan where the option price is between 85 percent and 100 percent of the value of the stock.[90]

Explanation of Provision

Allowance of credit

Under the provision, an individual's minimum tax credit allowable for any taxable year beginning before January 1, 2013, is not less than the "AMT refundable credit amount". The "AMT refundable credit amount" is the greater of (1) the lesser of $5,000 or the long-term unused minimum tax credit, or (2) 20 percent of the long-term unused minimum tax credit. The long-term unused minimum tax credit for any taxable year means the portion of the minimum tax credit attributable to the adjusted net minimum tax for taxable years before the 3rd taxable year immediately preceding the taxable year (assuming the credits are used on a first-in, first-out basis). In the case of an individual whose adjusted gross income for a taxable year exceeds the threshold amount (within the meaning of section 151(d)(3)(C)), the AMT refundable credit amount is reduced by the applicable percentage (within the meaning of section 151(d)(3)(B)). The additional credit allowable by reason of this provision is refundable.

Example.—Assume in 2010 an individual has an adjusted gross income that results in an applicable percentage of 50 percent under section 151(d)(3)(B), a regular tax of $45,000, a tentative minimum tax of $40,000, no other credits allowable, and a minimum tax credit for the taxable year (before limitation under section 53(c)) of $1.1 million of which $1 million is a long-term unused minimum tax credit.

The AMT refundable credit amount for the taxable year is $100,000 (20 percent of the $1 million long-term unused minimum tax credit reduced by an applicable percentage of 50 percent). The minimum tax credit allowable for the taxable year is $100,000 (the greater of the AMT refundable credit amount or the amount of the credit otherwise

86. If the stock is sold at a loss before the required holding periods are met, the amount taken into account may not exceed the amount realized on the sale over the adjusted basis of the stock. If the stock is sold after the taxable year in which the option was exercised but before the required holding periods are met, the required inclusion is made in the year the stock is sold.
87. If the stock is sold in the same taxable year the option is exercised, no adjustment in computing AMTI is required.
88. If the stock is sold for less than the amount paid for the stock, the loss may not be allowed in full in computing AMTI by reason of the $3,000 limit on the deductibility of net capital losses. Thus, the excess of the regular tax over the tentative minimum tax may not reflect the full amount of the loss.
89. Sec. 6039.
90. Sec. 423(c).

allowable). The $5,000 credit allowable without regard to this provision is nonrefundable and the additional $95,000 of credit allowable by reason of this provision is treated as a refundable credit. Thus, the taxpayer has an overpayment of $55,000 ($45,000 regular tax less $5,000 nonrefundable AMT credit less $95,000 refundable AMT credit). The $55,000 overpayment is allowed as a refund or credit to the taxpayer. The remaining $1 million minimum tax credit is carried forward to future taxable years.

If, in the above example, the adjusted gross income did not exceed the threshold amount under section 151(d)(3)(C), the AMT refundable credit amount for the taxable year would be $200,000, and the overpayment would be $155,000.

Information returns

The provision requires an employer to make an information return with the IRS, in addition to providing information to the employee, regarding the transfer of stock pursuant to exercise of an incentive stock option, and to certain stock transfers regarding employee stock purchase plans.

Effective Date

The provision relating to the minimum tax credit applies to taxable years beginning after the date of enactment.

The provision relating to returns applies to calendar years beginning after the date of enactment.

[¶5055] Section 404. Partial expensing for advanced mine safety equipment.

(Code Sec. 179E)

[Joint Committee on Taxation Report — JCX-50-06]

Present Law

A taxpayer generally must capitalize the cost of property used in a trade or business and recover such cost over time through annual deductions for depreciation or amortization. Tangible property generally is depreciated under the Modified Accelerated Cost Recovery System ("MACRS"), which determines depreciation by applying specific recovery periods, placed-in-service conventions, and depreciation methods to the cost of various types of depreciable property (sec. 168).

Personal property is classified under MACRS based on the property's class life unless a different classification is specifically provided in section 168. The class life applicable for personal property is the asset guideline period (midpoint class life as of January 1, 1986). Based on the property's classification, a recovery period is prescribed under MACRS. In general, there are six classes of recovery periods to which personal property can be assigned. For example, personal property that has a class life of four years or less has a recovery period of three years, whereas personal property with a class life greater than four years but less than 10 years has a recovery period of five years. The class lives and recovery periods for most property are contained in Revenue Procedure 87-56.[91]

In lieu of depreciation, a taxpayer with a sufficiently small amount of annual investment may elect to deduct (or "expense") such costs. Present law provides that the maximum amount a taxpayer may expense, for taxable years beginning in 2003 through 2009, is $100,000 of the cost of qualifying property placed in service for the taxable year. In general, qualifying property is defined as depreciable tangible personal property that is purchased for use in the active conduct of a trade or business. The $100,000

91. 1987-2 C.B. 674 (as clarified and modified by Rev. Proc. 88-22, 1988-1 C.B. 785).

amount is reduced (but not below zero) by the amount by which the cost of qualifying property placed in service during the taxable year exceeds $400,000.

Explanation of Provision

Under the provision, a taxpayer may elect to treat 50 percent of the cost of any qualified advanced mine safety equipment property as a deduction in the taxable year in which the equipment is placed in service.

Advanced mine safety equipment property means any of the following: (1) emergency communication technology or devices used to allow a miner to maintain constant communication with an individual who is not in the mine; (2) electronic identification and location devices that allow individuals not in the mine to track at all times the movements and location of miners working in or at the mine; (3) emergency oxygen-generating, self-rescue devices that provide oxygen for at least 90 minutes; (4) pre-positioned supplies of oxygen providing each miner on a shift the ability to survive for at least 48 hours; and (5) comprehensive atmospheric monitoring systems that monitor the levels of carbon monoxide, methane and oxygen that are present in all areas of the mine and that can detect smoke in the case of a fire in a mine.

To be treated as qualified advanced mine safety equipment property under the provision, the original use of the property must have commenced with the taxpayer, and the taxpayer must have placed the property in service after the date of enactment.

The portion of the cost of any property with respect to which an expensing election under section 179 is made may not be taken into account for purposes of the 50-percent deduction allowed under this provision. For Federal tax purposes, the basis of property is reduced by the portion of its cost that is taken into account for purposes of the 50-percent deduction allowed under the provision.

The provision requires the taxpayer to report information required by the Treasury Secretary with respect to the operation of mines of the taxpayer, in order for the deduction to be allowed for the taxable year.

An election made by the taxpayer under the provision may not be revoked except with the consent of the Secretary.

The provision includes a termination rule providing that it does not apply to property placed in service after December 31, 2008.

Effective Date

The provision applies to costs paid or incurred after the date of enactment, with regard to property placed in service on or before December 31, 2008.

[¶5056] Section 405. Mine rescue team training tax credit.

(Code Sec. 38, 45N, 280C)

[Joint Committee on Taxation Report — JCX-50-06]

Present Law

There is no present law credit for expenditures incurred by a taxpayer to train mine rescue workers. In general, a deduction is allowed for all ordinary and necessary expenses that are paid or incurred by the taxpayer during the taxable year in carrying on any trade or business.[92] A taxpayer that employs individuals as miners in underground mines will generally be permitted to deduct as ordinary and necessary expenses the educational expenditures such taxpayer incurs to train its employees in the principles, proce-

92. Sec. 162(a).

dures, and techniques of mine rescue, as well as the wages paid by the taxpayer for the time its employees were engaged in such training.

Explanation of Provision

Under the provision, a taxpayer which is an eligible employer may claim a credit with respect to each qualified mine rescue team employee equal to the lesser of (1) 20 percent of the amount paid or incurred by the taxpayer during the taxable year with respect to the training program costs of such qualified mine rescue team employee (including wages of the employee while attending the program), or (2) $10,000.[93] For purposes of the provision, "wages" has the meaning given to such term by sec. 3306(b) (determined without regard to any dollar limitation contained in that section). An eligible employer is any taxpayer which employs individuals as miners in underground mines in the United States. No deduction is allowed for the amount of the expenses otherwise deductible which is equal to the amount of the credit.

A qualified mine rescue team employee is any full-time employee of the taxpayer who is a miner eligible for more than six months of a taxable year to serve as a mine rescue team member by virtue of either having completed the initial 20-hour course of instruction prescribed by the Mine Safety and Health Administration's Office of Educational Policy and Development, or receiving at least 40 hours of refresher training in such instruction.

Effective Date

The provision is effective for taxable years beginning after December 31, 2005, and before January 1, 2009.

[¶ 5057] Section 406. Whistleblower reforms.

(Code Sec. 62, 7443A, 7623)

[Joint Committee on Taxation Report — JCX-50-06]

Present Law

The Code authorizes the IRS to pay such sums as deemed necessary for: "(1) detecting underpayments of tax; and (2) detecting and bringing to trial and punishment persons guilty of violating the internal revenue laws or conniving at the same."[94] Amounts are paid based on a percentage of tax, fines, and penalties (but not interest) actually collected based on the information provided. For specific information that caused the investigation and resulted in recovery, the IRS administratively has set the reward in an amount not to exceed 15 percent of the amounts recovered. For information, although not specific, that nonetheless caused the investigation and was of value in the determination of tax liabilities, the reward is not to exceed 10 percent of the amount recovered. For information that caused the investigation, but had no direct relationship to the determination of tax liabilities, the reward is not to exceed one percent of the amount recovered. The reward ceiling is $10 million (for payments made after November 7, 2002), and the reward floor is $100. No reward will be paid if the recovery was so small as to call for payment of less than $100 under the above formulas. Both the ceiling and percentages can be increased with a special agreement. The Code permits the IRS to disclose return information pursuant to a contract for tax administration services.[95]

Explanation of Provision

The provision reforms the reward program for individuals who provide information regarding violations of the tax laws to the Secretary. Generally, the provision establishes

93. The credit is part of the general business credit (sec. 38).
94. Sec. 7623.
95. Sec. 6103(n).

a reward floor of 15 percent of the collected proceeds (including penalties, interest, additions to tax and additional amounts) if the IRS moves forward with an administrative or judicial action based on information brought to the IRS's attention by an individual. The provision caps the available reward at 30 percent of the collected proceeds. The provision permits awards of lesser amounts (but no more than 10 percent) if the action was based principally on allegations (other than information provided by the individual) resulting from a judicial or administrative hearing, government report, hearing, audit, investigation, or from the news media.

The provision requires the Secretary to issue guidance within one year of the date of enactment for the operation of a Whistleblower Office within the IRS to administer the reward program. To the extent possible, it is expected that such guidance will address the recommendations of the Treasury Inspector General for Tax Administration regarding the informant's reward program, including the recommendations to centralize management of the reward program and to reduce the processing time for claims.[96] Under the provision, the Whistleblower Office may seek assistance from the individual providing information or from his or her legal representative, and may reimburse the costs incurred by any legal representative out of the amount of the reward. To the extent the disclosure of returns or return information is required to render such assistance, the disclosure must be pursuant to an IRS tax administration contract. It is expected that such disclosures will be infrequent and will be made only when the assigned task cannot be properly or timely completed without the return information to be disclosed.

The provision also provides an above-the-line deduction for attorneys' fees and costs paid by, or on behalf of, the individual in connection with any award for providing information regarding violations of the tax laws. The amount that may be deducted above-the-line may not exceed the amount includible in the taxpayer's gross income for the taxable year on account of such award (whether by suit or agreement and whether as lump sum or periodic payments).

The provision permits an individual to appeal the amount or a denial of an award determination to the United States Tax Court (the "Tax Court") within 30 days of such determination. Under the provision, Tax Court review of an award determination may be assigned to a special trial judge.

In addition, the provision requires the Secretary to conduct a study and report to Congress on the effectiveness of the whistleblower reward program and any legislative or administrative recommendations regarding the administration of the program.

Effective Date

The provision generally is effective for information provided on or after the date of enactment.

[¶5058] Section 407. Frivolous tax submissions.

(Code Sec. 6320, 6330, 6702, 7122)

[Joint Committee on Taxation Report — JCX-50-06]

Present Law

The Code provides that an individual who files a frivolous income tax return is subject to a penalty of $500 imposed by the IRS (sec. 6702). The Code also permits the Tax Court[97] to impose a penalty of up to $25,000 if a taxpayer has instituted or main-

96. Treasury Inspector General for Tax Administration, The Informants' Rewards Program Needs More Centralized Management Oversight, 2006-30-092 (June 2006).

97. Because in general the Tax Court is the only pre-payment forum available to taxpayers, it deals with most of the frivolous, groundless, or dilatory arguments raised in tax cases.

tained proceedings primarily for delay or if the taxpayer's position in the proceeding is frivolous or groundless (sec. 6673(a)).

Explanation of Provision

The provision modifies the IRS-imposed penalty by increasing the amount of the penalty to up to $5,000 and by applying it to all taxpayers and to all types of Federal taxes.

The provision also modifies present law with respect to certain submissions that raise frivolous arguments or that are intended to delay or impede tax administration. The submissions to which the provision applies are requests for a collection due process hearing, installment agreements, and offers-in-compromise. First, the provision permits the IRS to disregard such requests. Second, the provision permits the IRS to impose a penalty of up to $5,000 for such requests, unless the taxpayer withdraws the request after being given an opportunity to do so.

The provision requires the IRS to publish a list of positions, arguments, requests, and submissions determined to be frivolous for purposes of these provisions.

Effective Date

The provision applies to submissions made and issues raised after the date on which the Secretary first prescribes the required list of frivolous positions.

[¶5059] Section 408. Addition of meningococcal and human papillomavirus vaccines to list of taxable vaccines.

(Code Sec. 4132)

[Joint Committee on Taxation Report — JCX-50-06]

Present Law

A manufacturer's excise tax is imposed at the rate of 75 cents per dose[98] on the following vaccines routinely recommended for administration to children: diphtheria, pertussis, tetanus, measles, mumps, rubella, polio, HIB (haemophilus influenza type B), hepatitis A, hepatitis B, varicella (chicken pox), rotavirus gastroenteritis, streptococcus pneumoniae and trivalent vaccines against influenza. The tax applied to any vaccine that is a combination of vaccine components equals 75 cents times the number of components in the combined vaccine.

Amounts equal to net revenues from this excise tax are deposited in the Vaccine Injury Compensation Trust Fund to finance compensation awards under the Federal Vaccine Injury Compensation Program for individuals who suffer certain injuries following administration of the taxable vaccines. This program provides a Federal "no fault" insurance system substitute for the State-law tort and private liability insurance systems otherwise applicable to vaccine manufacturers. All persons immunized after September 30, 1988, with covered vaccines must pursue compensation under this Federal program before bringing civil tort actions under State law.

Explanation of Provision

The provision adds meningococcal vaccines and human papillomavirus vaccines to the list of taxable vaccines.

Effective Date

The provision is effective for vaccines sold or used on or after the first day of the first month beginning more than four weeks after the date of enactment.

98. Sec. 4131.

In the case of sales on or before the effective date for which delivery is made after such date, the delivery date shall be considered the sale date.

[¶5060] Section 409. Clarification of taxation of certain settlement funds made permanent.

(Code Sec. 468B)

[Joint Committee on Taxation Report — JCX-50-06]

Present Law

The cleanup of hazardous waste sites is sometimes funded by environmental "settlement funds" or escrow accounts. These escrow accounts are established in consent decrees between the Environmental Protection Agency ("EPA") and the settling parties under the jurisdiction of a Federal district court. The EPA uses these accounts to resolve claims against private parties under Comprehensive Environmental Response, Compensation, and Liability Act of 1980 ("CERCLA").

Present law provides that certain settlement funds established in consent decrees for the sole purpose of resolving claims under CERCLA are to be treated as beneficially owned by the United States government and therefore, not subject to Federal income tax.

To qualify the settlement fund must be: (1) established pursuant to a consent decree entered by a judge of a United States District Court; (2) created for the receipt of settlement payments for the sole purpose of resolving claims under CERCLA; (3) controlled (in terms of expenditures of contributions and earnings thereon) by the government or an agency or instrumentality thereof; and (4) upon termination, any remaining funds will be disbursed to such government entity and used in accordance with applicable law. For purposes of the provision, a government entity means the United States, any State of political subdivision thereof, the District of Columbia, any possession of the United States, and any agency or instrumentality of the foregoing.

The provision does not apply to accounts or funds established after December 31, 2010.

Explanation of Provision

The provision permanently extends to funds and accounts established after December 31, 2010, the treatment of certain settlement funds as beneficially owned by the United States government and therefore, not subject to Federal income tax.

Effective Date

The provision is effective as if included in section 201 of the Tax Increase Prevention and Reconciliation Act of 2005.

[¶5061] Section 410. Modification of active business definition under section 355 made permanent.

(Code Sec. 355)

[Joint Committee on Taxation Report — JCX-50-06]

Present Law

A corporation generally is required to recognize gain on the distribution of property (including stock of a subsidiary) to its shareholders as if the corporation had sold such property for its fair market value. In addition, the shareholders receiving the distributed property are ordinarily treated as receiving a dividend of the value of the distribution (to the extent of the distributing corporation's earnings and profits), or capital gain in the case of a stock buyback that significantly reduces the shareholder's interest in the parent corporation.

An exception to these rules applies if the distribution of the stock of a controlled corporation satisfies the requirements of section 355 of the Code. If all the requirements are satisfied, there is no tax to the distributing corporation or to the shareholders on the distribution.

One requirement to qualify for tax-free treatment under section 355 is that both the distributing corporation and the controlled corporation must be engaged immediately after the distribution in the active conduct of a trade or business that has been conducted for at least five years and was not acquired in a taxable transaction during that period (the "active business test").[99] For this purpose, prior to the enactment of the Tax Increase Prevention and Reconciliation Act of 2005, if the distributing or the controlled corporation to which the test was being applied was itself the parent of other subsidiary corporations, the determination whether such parent corporation was considered engaged in the active conduct of a trade or business was made only at that parent corporation level. The test would be satisfied only if (1) that corporation itself was directly engaged in the active conduct of a trade or business, or (2) that corporation was not directly engaged in the active conduct of a trade or business, but substantially all its assets consisted of stock and securities of one or more corporations that it controls that are engaged in the active conduct of a trade or business.[100] Thus, different tests applied, depending upon whether the corporation being tested itself was engaged in the active conduct of a trade or business, or whether it was a holding company holding stock of other corporations that were engaged in the active conduct of a trade or business.

The Tax Increase Prevention and Reconciliation Act of 2005 provided that the active trade or business test is always determined by reference to the relevant affiliated group. For the distributing corporation, the relevant affiliated group consists of the distributing corporation as the common parent and all corporations affiliated with the distributing corporation through stock ownership described in section 1504(a)(1)(B) (regardless of whether the corporations are includible corporations under section 1504(b)), immediately after the distribution. The relevant affiliated group for a controlled corporation is determined in a similar manner (with the controlled corporation as the common parent).

The provision enacted in the Tax Increase Prevention and Reconciliation Act of 2005 applies to distributions after the date of enactment and on or before December 31, 2010, with three exceptions. The provision does not apply to distributions (1) made pursuant to an agreement which is binding on the date of enactment and at all times thereafter, (2) described in a ruling request submitted to the IRS on or before the date of enactment, or (3) described on or before the date of enactment in a public announcement or in a filing with the Securities and Exchange Commission. The distributing corporation may irrevocably elect not to have the exceptions described above apply.

The provision also applies, solely for the purpose of determining whether, after the date of enactment, there is continuing qualification under the requirements of section

99. Sec. 355(b). In determining whether a corporation is engaged in an active trade or business that satisfies the requirement, old IRS guidelines for advance ruling purposes required that the value of the gross assets of the trade or business being relied on must ordinarily constitute at least five percent of the total fair market value of the gross assets of the corporation directly conducting the trade or business. Rev. Proc. 2003-3, sec. 4.01(30), 2003-1 I.R.B. 113. More recently, the IRS suspended this specific rule in connection with its general administrative practice of moving IRS resources away from advance rulings on factual aspects of section 355 transactions in general. Rev. Proc. 2003-48, 2003-29 I.R.B. 86.

100. Section 355(b)(2)(A). The IRS position has been that the statutory "substantially all" test has required that at least 90 percent of the fair market value of the corporation's gross assets consist of stock and securities of a controlled corporation that is engaged in the active conduct of a trade or business. Rev. Proc. 96-30, sec. 4.03(5), 1996-1 C.B. 696; Rev. Proc. 77-37, sec. 3.04, 1977-2 C.B. 568.

355(b)(2)(A) of distributions made before such date, as a result of an acquisition, disposition, or other restructuring after such date on or before December 31, 2010.[101]

Explanation of Provision

The provision deletes the sunset date of December 31, 2010, for all purposes of the provision enacted in the Tax Increase Prevention and Reconciliation Act of 2005. Thus, that provision is made permanent.

Effective Date

The provision is effective as if included in section 202 of the Tax Increase Prevention and Reconciliation Act of 2005.

[¶5062] Section 411. Revision of state veterans limit made permanent.

(Code Sec. 143)

[Joint Committee on Taxation Report — JCX-50-06]

Present Law

Private activity bonds are bonds that nominally are issued by States or local governments, but the proceeds of which are used (directly or indirectly) by a private person and payment of which is derived from funds of such private person. The exclusion from income for State and local bonds does not apply to private activity bonds, unless the bonds are issued for certain permitted purposes ("qualified private activity bonds"). The definition of a qualified private activity bond includes both qualified mortgage bonds and qualified veterans' mortgage bonds.

Qualified mortgage bonds are issued to make mortgage loans to qualified mortgagors for owner-occupied residences. The Code imposes several limitations on qualified mortgage bonds, including income limitations for homebuyers and purchase price limitations for the home financed with bond proceeds. In addition, qualified mortgage bonds generally cannot be used to finance a mortgage for a homebuyer who had an ownership interest in a principal residence in the three years preceding the execution of the mortgage (the "first-time homebuyer" requirement).

Qualified veterans' mortgage bonds are private activity bonds the proceeds of which are used to make mortgage loans to certain veterans. Authority to issue qualified veterans' mortgage bonds is limited to States that had issued such bonds before June 22, 1984. Qualified veterans' mortgage bonds are not subject to the State volume limitations generally applicable to private activity bonds. Instead, annual issuance in each State is subject to a separate State volume limitation. The five States eligible to issue these bonds are Alaska, California, Oregon, Texas, and Wisconsin. Loans financed with qualified veterans' mortgage bonds can be made only with respect to principal residences and can not be made to acquire or replace existing mortgages. Under prior law, mortgage loans made with the proceeds of bonds issued by the five States could be made only to veterans who served on active duty before 1977 and who applied for the financing before the date 30 years after the last date on which such veteran left active service (the "eligibility period"). However, in the case of qualified veterans' mortgage bonds issued by the States of Alaska, Oregon, and Wisconsin, the Tax Increase Prevention and Reconciliation Act of 2005 ("TIPRA") repealed the requirement that veterans receiving loans financed with qualified veterans' mortgage bonds must have served before 1977

---

101. For example, a holding company taxpayer that had distributed a controlled corporation in a spin-off prior to the date of enactment, in which spin-off the taxpayer satisfied the "substantially all" active business stock test of prior law section 355(b)(2)(A) immediately after the distribution, would not be deemed to have failed to satisfy any requirement that it continue that same qualified structure for any period of time after the distribution, solely because of a restructuring that occurred after the date of enactment and before January 1, 2010, and that would satisfy the requirements of new section 355(b)(2)(A).

and reduced the eligibility period to 25 years (rather than 30 years) following release from the military service.

In addition, TIPRA provided new State volume limits for qualified veterans' mortgage bonds issued in the States of Alaska, Oregon and Wisconsin. In 2010, the new annual limit on the total volume of veterans' bonds that can be issued in each of these three States is $25 million. These volume limits are phased-in over the four-year period immediately preceding 2010 by allowing the applicable percentage of the 2010 volume limits. The following table provides those percentages.

Calendar Year:	Applicable Percentage is:
2006	20 percent
2007	40 percent
2008	60 percent
2009	80 percent

The volume limits are zero for 2011 and each year thereafter. Unused allocation cannot be carried forward to subsequent years.

Explanation of Provision

The provision makes permanent TIPRA's changes to the definition of an eligible veteran and the State volume limits for qualified veterans' mortgage bonds issued by the States of Alaska, Oregon, and Wisconsin. The total volume of veterans' bonds that can be issued in each of these three States is $25 million for 2010 and each calendar year thereafter.

Effective Date

The provision is effective as if included in section 203 of TIPRA.

[¶5063] Section 412. Capital gains treatment for certain self-created musical works made permanent.

(Code Sec. 1221)

[Joint Committee on Taxation Report — JCX-50-06]

Present Law

Capital gains

The maximum tax rate on the net capital gain income of an individual is 15 percent for taxable years beginning in 2006. By contrast, the maximum tax rate on an individual's ordinary income is 35 percent. The reduced 15-percent rate generally is available for gain from the sale or exchange of a capital asset for which the taxpayer has satisfied a holding-period requirement. Capital assets generally include all property held by a taxpayer with certain specified exclusions.

An exclusion from the definition of a capital asset applies to inventory property or property held by a taxpayer primarily for sale to customers in the ordinary course of the taxpayer's trade or business.[102] Another exclusion from capital asset status applies to copyrights, literary, musical, or artistic compositions, letters or memoranda, or similar property held by a taxpayer whose personal efforts created the property (or held by a taxpayer whose basis in the property is determined by reference to the basis of the taxpayer whose personal efforts created the property).[103] Under a provision included in the

102. Sec. 1221(a)(1).
103. Sec. 1221(a)(3).

Tax Increase Prevention and Reconciliation Act of 2005 ("TIPRA"),[104] at the election of a taxpayer, the section 1221(a)(1) and (a)(3)exclusions from capital asset status do not apply to musical compositions or copyrights in musical works sold or exchanged before January 1, 2011 by a taxpayer described in section 1221(a)(3).[105] Thus, if a taxpayer who owns musical compositions or copyrights in musical works that the taxpayer created (or if a taxpayer to which the musical compositions or copyrights have been transferred by the works' creator in a substituted basis transaction) elects the application of this provision, gain from a sale of the compositions or copyrights is treated as capital gain, not ordinary income.

Charitable contributions

A taxpayer generally is allowed a deduction for the fair market value of property contributed to a charity. If a taxpayer makes a contribution of property that would have generated ordinary income (or short-term capital gain), the taxpayer's charitable contribution deduction generally is limited to the property's adjusted basis.[106] The determination whether property would have generated ordinary income (or short-term capital gain) is made without regard to new section 1221(b)(3) described above.[107]

Explanation of Provision

The provision makes permanent the availability of the section 1221(b)(3) election to treat certain sales of musical compositions or copyrights in musical works as being sales of capital assets (and therefore as generating capital gain). The provision also makes permanent the accompanying rule limiting to adjusted basis the amount of a charitable contribution deduction allowed for musical compositions or copyrights in musical works to which a taxpayer has elected the application of section 1221(b)(3).

Effective Date

The provision is effective as if included in section 204 of the Tax Increase Prevention and Reconciliation Act of 2005.

[¶5064] Section 413. Reduction in minimum vessel tonnage which qualifies for tonnage tax made permanent.

(Code Sec. 1355)

[Joint Committee on Taxation Report — JCX-50-06]

Present Law

The United States employs a "worldwide" tax system, under which domestic corporations generally are taxed on all income, including income from shipping operations, whether derived in the United States or abroad. In order to mitigate double taxation, a foreign tax credit for income taxes paid to foreign countries is provided to reduce or eliminate the U.S. tax owed on such income, subject to certain limitations.

Generally, the United States taxes foreign corporations only on income that has a sufficient nexus to the United States. Thus, a foreign corporation is generally subject to U.S. tax only on income, including income from shipping operations, which is "effectively connected" with the conduct of a trade or business in the United States (sec. 882). Such "effectively connected income" generally is taxed in the same manner and at the same rates as the income of a U.S. corporation.

The United States imposes a four percent tax on the amount of a foreign corporation's U.S. source gross transportation income (sec. 887). Transportation income includes in-

104. Pub. L. No. 109-222, sec. 204(a) (2006).
105. Sec. 1221(b)(3).
106. Sec. 170(e)(1)(A).
107. Sec. 170(e)(1)(A), as modified by TIPRA, Pub. L. No. 109-222, sec. 204(b) (2006).

come from the use (or hiring or leasing for use) of a vessel and income from services directly related to the use of a vessel. Fifty percent of the transportation income attributable to transportation that either begins or ends (but not both) in the United States is treated as U.S. source gross transportation income. The tax does not apply, however, to U.S. source gross transportation income that is treated as income effectively connected with the conduct of a U.S. trade or business. U.S. source gross transportation income is not treated as effectively connected income unless (1) the taxpayer has a fixed place of business in the United States involved in earning the income, and (2) substantially all the income is attributable to regularly scheduled transportation.

The tax imposed by section 882 or 887 on income from shipping operations may be limited by an applicable U.S. income tax treaty or by an exemption of a foreign corporation's international shipping operations income in instances where a foreign country grants an equivalent exemption (sec. 883).

Notwithstanding the general rules described above, the American Jobs Creation Act of 2004 ("AJCA")[108] generally allows corporations that are qualifying vessel operators[109] to elect a "tonnage tax" in lieu of the corporate income tax on taxable income from certain shipping activities. Accordingly, an electing corporation's gross income does not include its income from qualifying shipping activities (and items of loss, deduction, or credit are disallowed with respect to such excluded income), and electing corporations are only subject to tax on these activities at the maximum corporate income tax rate on their notional shipping income, which is based on the net tonnage of the corporation's qualifying vessels.[110] No deductions are allowed against the notional shipping income of an electing corporation, and no credit is allowed against the notional tax imposed under the tonnage tax regime. In addition, special deferral rules apply to the gain on the sale of a qualifying vessel, if such vessel is replaced during a limited replacement period.

Prior to the enactment of the Tax Increase Prevention and Reconciliation Act of 2005 ("TIPRA"),[111] a "qualifying vessel" was defined as a self-propelled (or a combination of self-propelled and non-self-propelled) United States flag vessel of not less than 10,000 deadweight tons[112] that is used exclusively in the United States foreign trade. TIPRA expands the definition of "qualifying vessel" to include self-propelled (or a combination of self-propelled and non-self-propelled) United States flag vessels of not less than 6,000 deadweight tons used exclusively in the United States foreign trade. The modified definition of TIPRA applies for taxable years beginning after December 31, 2005 and ending before January 1, 2011.

Explanation of Provision

The provision makes permanent the minimum 6,000 deadweight tons threshold.

108. Pub. L. No. 108-357, sec. 248. The tonnage tax regime is effective for taxable years beginning after the date of enactment of AJCA (October 22, 2004).

109. Generally, a qualifying vessel operator is a corporation that (1) operates one or more qualifying vessels and (2) meets certain requirements with respect to its shipping activities.

110. An electing corporation's notional shipping income for the taxable year is the product of the following amounts for each of the qualifying vessels it operates: (1) the daily notional shipping income from the operation of the qualifying vessel, and (2) the number of days during the taxable year that the electing corporation operated such vessel as a qualifying vessel in the United States foreign trade. The daily notional shipping income from the operation of a qualifying vessel is (1) 40 cents for each 100 tons of so much of the net tonnage of the vessel as does not exceed 25,000 net tons, and (2) 20 cents for each 100 tons of so much of the net tonnage of the vessel as exceeds 25,000 net tons. "United States foreign trade" means the transportation of goods or passengers between a place in the United States and a foreign place or between foreign places. The temporary use in the United States domestic trade (i.e., the transportation of goods or passengers between places in the United States) of any qualifying vessel or the temporary ceasing to use a qualifying vessel may be disregarded, under special rules.

111. Pub. L. No. 109-222, sec. 205 (May 17, 2006).

112. Deadweight measures the lifting capacity of a ship expressed in long tons (2,240 lbs.), including cargo, crew, and consumables such as fuel, lube oil, drinking water, and stores. It is the difference between the number of tons of water a vessel displaces without such items on board and the number of tons it displaces when fully loaded.

Effective Date

The provision is effective as if included in section 205 of the Tax Increase Prevention and Reconciliation Act of 2005.

[¶5066] Section 415. Great Lakes domestic shipping to not disqualify vessel from tonnage tax.

(Code Sec. 1355)

[Joint Committee on Taxation Report — JCX-50-06]

Present Law

The United States employs a "worldwide" tax system, under which domestic corporations generally are taxed on all income, including income from shipping operations, whether derived in the United States or abroad. In order to mitigate double taxation, a foreign tax credit for income taxes paid to foreign countries is provided to reduce or eliminate the U.S. tax owed on such income, subject to certain limitations.

Generally, the United States taxes foreign corporations only on income that has a sufficient nexus to the United States. Thus, a foreign corporation is generally subject to U.S. tax only on income, including income from shipping operations, which is "effectively connected" with the conduct of a trade or business in the United States (sec. 882). Such "effectively connected income" generally is taxed in the same manner and at the same rates as the income of a U.S. corporation.

The United States imposes a four percent tax on the amount of a foreign corporation's U.S. source gross transportation income (sec. 887). Transportation income includes income from the use (or hiring or leasing for use) of a vessel and income from services directly related to the use of a vessel. Fifty percent of the transportation income attributable to transportation that either begins or ends (but not both) in the United States is treated as U.S. source gross transportation income. The tax does not apply, however, to U.S. source gross transportation income that is treated as income effectively connected with the conduct of a U.S. trade or business. U.S. source gross transportation income is not treated as effectively connected income unless (1) the taxpayer has a fixed place of business in the United States involved in earning the income, and (2) substantially all the income is attributable to regularly scheduled transportation.

The tax imposed by section 882 or 887 on income from shipping operations may be limited by an applicable U.S. income tax treaty or by an exemption of a foreign corporation's international shipping operations income in instances where a foreign country grants an equivalent exemption (sec. 883).

Notwithstanding the general rules described above, the American Jobs Creation Act of 2004 ("AJCA")[114] generally allows corporations that are qualifying vessel operators[115] to elect a "tonnage tax" in lieu of the corporate income tax on taxable income from certain shipping activities. Accordingly, an electing corporation's gross income does not include its income from qualifying shipping activities (and items of loss, deduction, and credit are disallowed with respect to such excluded income),[116] and electing corporations are only subject to tax on these activities at the maximum corporate income tax rate on their notional shipping income, which is based on the net tonnage of the corporation's

114. Pub. L. No. 108-357, sec. 248. The tonnage tax regime is effective for taxable years beginning after the date of enactment of AJCA (October 22, 2004).

115. Generally, a qualifying vessel operator is a corporation that (1) operates one or more qualifying vessels and (2) meets certain requirements with respect to its shipping activities.

116. Sec. 1357.

qualifying vessels operated in the United States foreign trade.[117] "United States foreign trade" means the transportation of goods or passengers between a place in the United States and a foreign place or between foreign places. No deductions are allowed against the notional shipping income of an electing corporation, and no credit is allowed against the notional tax imposed under the tonnage tax regime. In addition, special deferral rules apply to the gain on the sale of a qualifying vessel, if such vessel is replaced during a limited replacement period.

A "qualifying vessel" is defined as a self-propelled (or a combination of self-propelled and non-self-propelled) United States flag vessel of not less than 6,000 deadweight tons[118] that is used exclusively in the United States foreign trade. Notwithstanding the "exclusively in the United States foreign trade" requirement, the temporary use of any qualifying vessel in the United States domestic trade (i.e., the transportation of goods or passengers between places in the United States) may be disregarded, and treated as the continued use of such vessel in the United States foreign trade, if the electing corporation provides timely notice of such temporary use to the Secretary. However, if a qualifying vessel is operated in the United States domestic trade for more than 30 days during the taxable year, then no usage in the United States domestic trade during such year may be disregarded (and the vessel is thereby disqualified). The Secretary has the authority to prescribe regulations as may be necessary or appropriate to carry out the purposes of the statutory rules relating to the temporary domestic use of vessels.[119]

Explanation of Provision

Under the provision, a corporation for which a tonnage tax election is in effect ("electing corporation") may make a further election with respect to a qualifying vessel used during a taxable year in "qualified zone domestic trade." The term "qualified zone domestic trade" means the transportation of goods or passengers between places in the "qualified zone" if such transportation is in the United States domestic trade. The transportation of goods or passengers between a U.S. port in the qualified zone and a U.S. port outside the qualified zone (in either direction) is United States domestic trade that is not qualified zone domestic trade.

The term "qualified zone" means the Great Lakes Waterway and the St. Lawrence Seaway. This area consists of the deep-draft waterways of Lake Superior, Lake Michigan, Lake Huron (including Lake St. Clair), Lake Eire [*sic,* Erie], and Lake Ontario, connecting deep-draft channels, including the Detroit River, the St. Clair River, the St. Marys River, and the Welland Canal, and the waterway between the port of Sept-Iles, Quebec and Lake Ontario, including all locks, canals, and connecting and contiguous waters that are part of these deep-draft waterways.

Activities in qualified zone domestic trade are not qualifying shipping activities and, therefore, do not qualify for the tonnage tax regime. In the case of a qualifying vessel for which an election under this provision ("qualified zone domestic trade election") is in force, the Secretary is to prescribe rules for the proper allocation of income, expenses, losses, and deductions between the qualified shipping activities and the other activities of such vessel. These rules may include intra-vessel allocation rules that are different

117. An electing corporation's notional shipping income for the taxable year is the product of the following amounts for each of the qualifying vessels it operates: (1) the daily notional shipping income from the operation of the qualifying vessel, and (2) the number of days during the taxable year that the electing corporation operated such vessel as a qualifying vessel in the United States foreign trade. The daily notional shipping income from the operation of a qualifying vessel is (1) 40 cents for each 100 tons of so much of the net tonnage of the vessel as does not exceed 25,000 net tons, and (2) 20 cents for each 100 tons of so much of the net tonnage of the vessel as exceeds 25,000 net tons.

118. Prior to the enactment on May 17, 2006 of Pub. L. No. 109-222, the Tax Increase Prevention and Reconciliation Act of 2005 ("TIPRA"), "qualifying vessel" meant a self-propelled (or a combination of self-propelled and non-self-propelled) United States flag vessel of not less than 10,000 deadweight tons used exclusively in the United States foreign trade. TIPRA changed the threshold to 6,000 deadweight tons, effective for taxable years beginning after December 31, 2005 and ending before January 1, 2011. Section 1283 of this Act permanently extends the 6,000 deadweight tons threshold.

119. Sec. 1355(g).

than the rules pertaining to allocations of items between qualifying vessels and other vessels.

An electing corporation making a qualified zone domestic trade election with respect to a vessel is not required to give notice to the Secretary of the use of such vessel in qualified zone domestic trade, and an otherwise qualifying vessel does not cease to be a qualifying vessel solely due to such use when such election is in effect, even if such use exceeds 30 days during the taxable year. An electing corporation making a qualified zone domestic trade election with respect to a vessel is treated as using such vessel in qualified zone domestic trade during any period of temporary use in the United States domestic trade (other than qualified zone domestic trade) if such electing corporation gives timely notice to the Secretary stating that it temporarily operates or has operated in the United States domestic trade (other than qualified zone domestic trade) a qualifying vessel which had been used in the United States foreign trade or qualified zone domestic trade, and that it intends to resume operating such vessel in the United States foreign trade or qualified zone domestic trade. The period of such permissible temporary use of such vessel in such United States domestic trade continues until the earlier of the date on which the electing corporation abandons its intention to resume operation of the vessel in the United States foreign trade or qualified zone domestic trade, or the electing corporation resumes operation of the vessel in the United States foreign trade or qualified zone domestic trade. However, if a qualifying vessel is operated in the United States domestic trade (other than qualified zone domestic trade) for more than 30 days during the taxable year, then no usage in the United States domestic trade (other than qualified zone domestic trade) during such year may be disregarded (and the vessel is thereby disqualified). Thus, a vessel used for 120 days in the taxable year in qualified zone domestic trade and 180 days in the taxable year in the United States foreign trade is not a qualifying vessel if it is used for over 30 days in the taxable year in the United States domestic trade that is not qualified zone domestic trade.

Under the provision, the Secretary may specify the time, manner and other conditions for making, maintaining, and terminating the qualified zone domestic trade election.

Effective Date

The provision is effective for taxable years beginning after date of enactment.

[¶5067] Section 416. Use of qualified mortgage bonds to finance residences for veterans without regard to first-time homebuyer requirement.

(Code Sec. 143)

[Joint Committee on Taxation Report — JCX-50-06]

Present Law

Private activity bonds are bonds that nominally are issued by States or local governments, but the proceeds of which are used (directly or indirectly) by a private person and payment of which is derived from funds of such private person. The exclusion from income for State and local bonds does not apply to private activity bonds, unless the bonds are issued for certain permitted purposes ("qualified private activity bonds"). The definition of a qualified private activity bond includes both qualified mortgage bonds and qualified veterans' mortgage bonds.

Qualified mortgage bonds are issued to make mortgage loans to qualified mortgagors for owner-occupied residences. The Code imposes several limitations on qualified mortgage bonds, including income limitations for homebuyers and purchase price limitations for the home financed with bond proceeds. In addition, qualified mortgage bonds generally cannot be used to finance a mortgage for a homebuyer who had an ownership interest in a principal residence in the three years preceding the execution of the mortgage (the "first-time homebuyer" requirement).

Qualified veterans' mortgage bonds are private activity bonds the proceeds of which are used to make mortgage loans to certain veterans. Authority to issue qualified veterans' mortgage bonds is limited to States that had issued such bonds before June 22, 1984. Qualified veterans' mortgage bonds are not subject to the State volume limitations generally applicable to private activity bonds. Instead, annual issuance in each State is subject to a separate State volume limitation. The five States eligible to issue these bonds are Alaska, California, Oregon, Texas, and Wisconsin. Loans financed with qualified veterans' mortgage bonds can be made only with respect to principal residences and can not be made to acquire or replace existing mortgages. Under prior law, mortgage loans made with the proceeds of bonds issued by the five States could be made only to veterans who served on active duty before 1977 and who applied for the financing before the date 30 years after the last date on which such veteran left active service (the "eligibility period"). However, in the case of qualified veterans' mortgage bonds issued by the States of Alaska, Oregon, and Wisconsin, the Tax Increase Prevention and Reconciliation Act of 2005 ("TIPRA") repealed the requirement that veterans receiving loans financed with qualified veterans' mortgage bonds must have served before 1977 and reduced the eligibility period to 25 years (rather than 30 years) following release from the military service. In addition, TIPRA provided new State volume limits for qualified veterans' mortgage bonds issued in the States of Alaska, Oregon and Wisconsin, phased-in over a four-year period.

Explanation of Provision

Under the provision, qualified mortgage bonds may be issued to finance mortgages for veterans who served in the active military without regard to the first-time homebuyer requirement. Present-law income and purchase price limitations apply to loans to veterans financed with the proceeds of qualified mortgage bonds. Veterans are eligible for the exception from the first-time homebuyer requirement without regard to the date they last served on active duty or the date they applied for a loan after leaving active duty. However, veterans may only use the exception one time.

Effective Date

The provision applies to bonds issued after the date of enactment and before January 1, 2008.

[¶5068] Section 417. Exclusion of gain from sale of a principal residence by certain employees of the intelligence community.

(Code Sec. 121)

[Joint Committee on Taxation Report — JCX-50-06]

Present Law

Under present law, an individual taxpayer may exclude up to $250,000 ($500,000 if married filing a joint return) of gain realized on the sale or exchange of a principal residence. To be eligible for the exclusion, the taxpayer must have owned and used the residence as a principal residence for at least two of the five years ending on the sale or exchange. A taxpayer who fails to meet these requirements by reason of a change of place of employment, health, or, to the extent provided under regulations, unforeseen circumstances is able to exclude an amount equal to the fraction of the $250,000 ($500,000 if married filing a joint return) that is equal to the fraction of the two years that the ownership and use requirements are met.

Present law also contains special rules relating to members of the uniformed services or the Foreign Service of the United States. An individual may elect to suspend for a maximum of 10 years the five-year test period for ownership and use during certain absences due to service in the uniformed services or the Foreign Service of the United States. The uniformed services include: (1) the Armed Forces (the Army, Navy, Air

Force, Marine Corps, and Coast Guard); (2) the commissioned corps of the National Oceanic and Atmospheric Administration; and (3) the commissioned corps of the Public Health Service. If the election is made, the five-year period ending on the date of the sale or exchange of a principal residence does not include any period up to 10 years during which the taxpayer or the taxpayer's spouse is on qualified official extended duty as a member of the uniformed services or in the Foreign Service of the United States. For these purposes, qualified official extended duty is any period of extended duty while serving at a place of duty at least 50 miles away from the taxpayer's principal residence or under orders compelling residence in government furnished quarters. Extended duty is defined as any period of duty pursuant to a call or order to such duty for a period in excess of 90 days or for an indefinite period. The election may be made with respect to only one property for a suspension period.

Explanation of Provision

Under the provision, specified employees of the intelligence community may elect to suspend the running of the five-year test period during any period in which they are serving on extended duty. The term "employee of the intelligence community" means an employee of the Office of the Director of National Intelligence, the Central Intelligence Agency, the National Security Agency, the Defense Intelligence Agency, the National Geospatial-Intelligence Agency, or the National Reconnaissance Office. The term also includes employment with: (1) any other office within the Department of Defense for the collection of specialized national intelligence through reconnaissance programs; (2) any of the intelligence elements of the Army, the Navy, the Air Force, the Marine Corps, the Federal Bureau of Investigation, the Department of the Treasury, the Department of Energy, and the Coast Guard; (3) the Bureau of Intelligence and Research of the Department of State; and (4) the elements of the Department of Homeland Security concerned with the analyses of foreign intelligence information. To qualify, a specified employee must move from one duty station to another and the new duty station must be located outside of the United States. As under present law, the five-year period may not be extended more than 10 years.

Effective Date

The provision is effective for sales and exchanges after the date of enactment and before January 1, 2011.

[¶5069] Section 418. Sale of property by judicial officers.

(Code Sec. 1043)

[Joint Committee on Taxation Report — JCX-50-06]

Present Law

Present law provides special rules for deferring the recognition of gain on sales of property which are required in order to comply with certain conflict of interest requirements imposed by the Federal government. Certain executive branch Federal employees (and their spouses and minor or dependent children) who are required to divest property in order to comply with conflict of interest requirements may elect to postpone the recognition of resulting gains by investing in certain replacement property within a 60-day period. The basis of the replacement property is reduced by the amount of the gain not recognized. Permitted replacement property is limited to any obligation of the United States or any diversified investment fund approved by regulations issued by the Office of Government Ethics. The rule applies only to sales under certificates of divestiture issued by the President or the Director of the Office of Government Ethics.

Explanation of Provision

The provision extends the provision deferring recognition of gain to a judicial officer who receives a certificate of divestiture from the Judicial Conference of the United States (or its designee) regarding the divestiture of certain property reasonably necessary to comply with conflict of interest rules or the judicial canon. For purposes of this provision, a judicial officer means the Chief Justice of the United States, the Associate Justices of the Supreme Court, and the judges of the United States courts of appeals, United States district courts, including the district courts in Guam, the Northern Mariana Islands, and the Virgin Islands, Court of Appeals for the Federal Circuit, Court of International Trade, Tax Court, Court of Federal Claims, Court of Appeals for Veterans Claims, United States Court of Appeals for the Armed Forces, and any court created by Act of Congress, the judges of which are entitled to hold office during good behavior.

Effective Date

The provision applies to sales after the date of enactment.

[¶5070] Section 419. Premiums for mortgage insurance.

(Code Sec. 163, 6050H)

[Joint Committee on Taxation Report — JCX-50-06]

Present Law

Present law provides that qualified residence interest is deductible notwithstanding the general rule that personal interest is nondeductible (sec. 163(h)).

Qualified residence interest is interest on acquisition indebtedness and home equity indebtedness with respect to a principal and a second residence of the taxpayer. The maximum amount of home equity indebtedness is $100,000. The maximum amount of acquisition indebtedness is $1 million. Acquisition indebtedness means debt that is incurred in acquiring constructing, or substantially improving a qualified residence of the taxpayer, and that is secured by the residence. Home equity indebtedness is debt (other than acquisition indebtedness) that is secured by the taxpayer's principal or second residence, to the extent the aggregate amount of such debt does not exceed the difference between the total acquisition indebtedness with respect to the residence, and the fair market value of the residence.

Explanation of Provision

The provision provides that premiums paid or accrued for qualified mortgage insurance by a taxpayer during the taxable year in connection with acquisition indebtedness on a qualified residence of the taxpayer are treated as interest that is qualified residence interest and thus deductible. The amount allowable as a deduction under the provision is phased out ratably by 10 percent for each $1,000 by which the taxpayer's adjusted gross income exceeds $100,000 ($500 and $50,000, respectively, in the case of a married individual filing a separate return). Thus, the deduction is not allowed if the taxpayer's adjusted gross income exceeds $110,000 ($55,000 in the case of married individual filing a separate return).

For this purpose, qualified mortgage insurance means mortgage insurance provided by the Veterans Administration, the Federal Housing Administration, or the Rural Housing Administration, and private mortgage insurance (defined in section 2 of the Homeowners Protection Act of 1998 as in effect on the date of enactment of the provision).

Amounts paid for qualified mortgage insurance that are properly allocable to periods after the close of the taxable year are treated as paid in the period to which they are allocated. No deduction is allowed for the unamortized balance if the mortgage is paid before its term (except in the case of qualified mortgage insurance provided by the Department of Veterans Affairs or Rural Housing Administration).

The provision does not apply with respect to any mortgage insurance contract issued before January 1, 2007. The provision terminates for any amount paid or accrued after December 21, 2007, or properly allocable to any period after that date.

Reporting rules apply under the provision.

Effective Date

The provision is effective for amounts paid or accrued after December 31, 2006.

[¶5071] Section 420. Modification of refunds for kerosene used in aviation.

(Code Sec. 6427)

[Joint Committee on Taxation Report — JCX-50-06]

Present Law

Nontaxable uses of kerosene

In general, if kerosene on which tax has been imposed is used by any person for a nontaxable use, a refund in an amount equal to the amount of tax imposed may be obtained either by the purchaser, or in specific cases, the registered ultimate vendor of the kerosene.[120] However, the 0.1 cent per gallon representing the Leaking Underground Storage Tank Trust Fund financing rate generally is not refundable, except for exports.[121]

A nontaxable use is any use which is exempt from the tax imposed by section 4041(a)(1)other than by reason of a prior imposition of tax.[122] Nontaxable uses of kerosene include:

- Use on a farm for farming purposes;[123]
- Use in foreign trade or trade between the United States and any of its possessions;[124]
- Use as a fuel in vessels and aircraft owned by the United States or any foreign nation and constituting equipment of the armed forces thereof;[125]
- Exclusive use of a state or local government;[126]
- Export or shipment to a possession of the United States;[127]
- Exclusive use of a nonprofit educational organization;[128]
- Use as a fuel in an aircraft museum for the procurement, care, or exhibition of aircraft of the type used for combat or transport in World War II;[129] and
- Use as a fuel in (a) helicopters engaged in the exploration for or the development or removal of hard minerals, oil, or gas and in timber (including logging) operations if the helicopters neither take off from nor land at a facility eligible for Airport Trust Fund assistance or otherwise use federal aviation services during flights or (b) any air transportation for the purpose of providing emergency medical services (1) by helicopter or (2)

120. Sec. 6427(l).
121. Sec. 6430.
122. Sec. 6427(l)(2).
123. Sec. 4041(f).
124. Sec. 4041(g)(1).
125. Id.
126. Sec. 4041(g)(2).
127. Sec. 4041(g)(3).
128. Sec. 4041(g)(4).
129. Sec. 4041(h).

by a fixed-wing aircraft equipped for and exclusively dedicated on that flight to acute care emergency medical services.[130]

- Off-highway business use.

Since 4041(a) is limited to the delivery into the fuel supply tank of a diesel-powered highway vehicle or train, kerosene delivered into the fuel supply tank of aircraft is a nontaxable use for purposes of section 4041(a).

Claims for refund of kerosene used in aviation

"Commercial aviation" is the use of an aircraft in a business of transporting persons or property for compensation or hire by air, with certain exceptions.[131] All other aviation is noncommercial aviation.

For fuel not removed directly into the wing of an airplane, the Safe, Accountable, Flexible, Efficient, Transportation Equity Act: A Legacy for Users ("SAFETEA") changed the rate of taxation for aviation-grade kerosene from 21.8 cents per gallon to the general kerosene and diesel rate of 24.3 cents per gallon.[132] In order to preserve the aviation rate for fuel actually used in aviation, the 21.8 cent rate of taxation (or as the case may be, the 4.3 cent commercial aviation rate, or the nontaxable use rate) is achieved through a refund when the fuel is used in aviation (a refund of 2.5 cents for taxable noncommercial aviation, 20 cents in the case of commercial aviation, and 24.3 cents for nontaxable uses).[133] These changes became effective on October 1, 2005.

Prior to October 1, 2005, if fuel that was previously taxed was used in noncommercial aviation for a nontaxable use, generally, the ultimate purchaser of such fuel (other than for the exclusive use of a State or local government, or for use on a farm for farming purposes) could claim a refund for the tax that was paid. SAFETEA eliminated the ability of a purchaser to file for a refund with respect to fuel used in noncommercial aviation. Instead, the registered ultimate vendor is the exclusive party entitled to a refund with respect to kerosene used in noncommercial aviation.[134] An ultimate vendor is the person who sells the kerosene to an ultimate purchaser for use in noncommercial aviation. If the fuel was used for a nontaxable use, the vendor may make a claim for 24.3 cents per gallon, otherwise, the vendor is permitted to claim 2.5 cents per gallon for kerosene sold for use in noncommercial aviation.[135]

For commercial aviation, the ultimate purchaser has the option of filing a claim itself, or waiving the right to refund to its ultimate vendor, if the vendor agrees to file on behalf of the purchaser.[136]

A separate special rule also applies to kerosene sold to a State or local government, regardless of whether the kerosene was sold for aviation or other purposes.[137] In general, this rule makes the registered ultimate vendor the appropriate party for filing refund

130. Secs. 4041(l), 4261(f) and (g).
131. "Commercial aviation" does not include aircraft used for skydiving, small aircraft on nonestablished lines or transportation for affiliated group members.
132. Sec. 11161 of Pub. L. No. 109-59 (2005).
133. Sec. 6427(l)(1), (4) and (5).
134. Sec. 6427(l)(5)(B).
135. Sec. 6427(l)(5)(A). Under this provision, of the 24.4 cents of tax imposed on kerosene used in taxable noncommercial aviation, the 0.1 cent for the Leaking Underground Storage Tank Trust Fund financing rate and 21.8 cents of the tax imposed on kerosene cannot be refunded. The limitations of sec. 6427(l)(5)(A) on the amount that cannot be refunded do not apply to uses exempt from tax. However, sec. 6430 prevents a refund of the Leaking Underground Storage Tank Trust Fund financing rate in all cases except export. Sec. 6427(l)(5)(B) requires that all amounts that would have been paid to the ultimate purchaser pursuant to sec. 6427(l)(1) are to paid to the ultimate registered vendor, therefore the ultimate registered vendor is the only claimant for both nontaxable and taxable use of kerosene in noncommercial aviation.
136. Sec. 6427(l)(4)(B).
137. Sec. 6427(l)(6).

claims on behalf of a State or local government. Special rules apply for credit card sales.[138]

Explanation of Provision

In general

The provision allows purchasers that use kerosene for an exempt aviation purpose (other than in the case of a State or local government) to make a claim for refund of the tax that was paid on such fuel or waive their right to claim a refund to their registered ultimate vendors. As a result, under the provision, crop-dusters, air ambulances, aircraft engaged in foreign trade and other exempt users may either make the claim for refund of the 24.3 cents per gallon themselves or waive the right to their vendors.

General noncommercial aviation use (which is entitled to a refund of 2.5 cents-per-gallon) remains an exclusive ultimate vendor rule. The rules for State and local governments also are unchanged.

Special rule for purchases of kerosene used in aviation on a farm for farming purposes

For kerosene used in aviation on a farm for farming purposes that was purchased after December 31, 2004, and before October 1, 2005, the Secretary is to pay to the ultimate purchaser (without interest) an amount equal to the aggregate amount of tax imposed on such fuel, reduced by any payments made to the ultimate vendor of such fuel. Such claims must be filed within 3 months of the date of enactment and may not duplicate claims filed under section 6427(l).

Effective Date

In general, the provision is effective for kerosene sold after September 30, 2005. For kerosene used for an exempt aviation purpose eligible for the waiver rule created by the provision, the ultimate purchaser is treated as having waived the right to payment and as having assigned such right to the ultimate vendor if the vendor meets the requirements of subparagraph (A), (B) or (D) of section 6416(a)(1). The rule of the preceding sentence applies to kerosene sold after September 30, 2005, and before the date of enactment.

The special rule for kerosene used in aviation on a farm for farming purposes is effective on the date of enactment.

[¶5072] Section 421. Regional income tax agencies treated as states for purposes of confidentiality and disclosure requirements.

(Code Sec. 6103)

[Joint Committee on Taxation Report — JCX-50-06]

Present Law

Generally, tax returns and return information ("tax information") is confidential and may not be disclosed unless authorized in the Code. One exception to the general rule of confidentiality is the disclosure of the tax information to States.

Tax information with respect to certain taxes is open to inspection by State agencies, bodies, commissions, or its legal representatives, charged under the laws of the State with tax administration responsibilities.[139] Such inspection is permitted only to the ex-

138. If certain conditions are met, a registered credit card issuer may make the claim for refund in place of the ultimate vendor. If the diesel fuel or kerosene is purchased with a credit card issued to a State but the credit card issuer is not registered with the IRS (or does not meet certain other conditions) the credit card issuer must collect the amount of the tax and the State is the proper claimant.
139. Sec. 6103(d)(1).

tent necessary for State tax administration proposes. The Code requires a written request from the head of the agency, body or commission as a prerequisite for disclosure. State officials who receive this information may redisclose it to the agency's contractors but only for State tax administration purposes.[140]

The term "State" includes the 50 States, the District of Columbia, and certain territories.[141] In addition, cities with populations in excess of 250,000 that impose a tax or income or wages and with which the IRS is entered into an agreement regarding disclosure also are treated as States.[142]

Explanation of Provision

The provision broadens the definition of "State" to include a regional income tax agency administering the tax laws of municipalities which have a collective population in excess of 250,000. Specifically, under the provision, the term "State" includes any governmental entity (1) that is formed and operated by a qualified group of municipalities, and (2) with which the Secretary (in his sole discretion) has entered into an agreement regarding disclosure. The term "qualified group of municipalities" means, with respect to any governmental entity, two or more municipalities: (1) each of which imposes a tax on income or wages, (2) each of which, under the authority of a State statute, administers the laws relating to the imposition of such taxes through such entity, and (3) which collectively have a population in excess of 250,000 (as determined under the most recent decennial United States census data available).

The regional income tax agency is treated as a State for purposes of applying the confidentiality and disclosure provisions for State tax officials, determining the scope of tax administration, applying the rules governing disclosures in judicial and administrative tax proceedings, and applying the safeguard procedures. Because a regional income tax agency administers the laws of its member municipalities, the provision provides that references to State law, State proceedings or State tax returns should be treated as references to the law, proceedings or tax returns of the municipalities which form and operate the regional income tax agency.

Inspection by or disclosure to an entity described above shall be only for the purpose of and to the extent necessary in the administration of the tax laws of the member municipalities in such entity relating to the imposition of a tax on income or wages. Such entity may not redisclose tax information to its member municipalities. This rule does not preclude the entity from disclosing data in a form which cannot be associated with or otherwise identify directly or indirectly a particular taxpayer.[143]

The provision requires that a regional income tax agency conduct on-site reviews every three years of all of its contractors or other agents receiving Federal returns and return information. If the duration of the contract or agreement is less than three years, a review is required at the mid-point of the contract. The purpose of the review is to assess the contractor's efforts to safeguard Federal tax information. This review is intended to cover secure storage, restricting access, computer security, and other safeguards deemed appropriate by the Secretary. Under the provision, the regional income tax agency is required to submit a report of its findings to the IRS and certify annually that such contractors and other agents are in compliance with the requirements to safeguard the confidentiality of Federal tax information. The certification is required to include the name and address of each contractor or other agent with the agency, the duration of the contract, and a description of the contract or agreement with the regional income tax agency.

---

140. Sec. 6103(n).
141. Sec. 6103(b)(5)(A).
142. Sec. 6103(b)(5)(B).
143. By definition "return information" does not include data in a form which cannot be associated with or otherwise identify directly or indirectly a particular taxpayer (sec. 6103(b)(2)).

This provision does not alter or affect in any way the right of the IRS to conduct safeguard reviews of regional income tax agency contractors or other agents. It also does not affect the right of the IRS to approve initially the safeguard language in the contract or agreement and the safeguards in place prior to any disclosures made in connection with such contracts or agreements.

Effective Date

The provision is effective for disclosures made after December 31, 2006.

[¶ 5074] Section 423. Modification of railroad track maintenance credit. (Code Sec. 45G)

[Joint Committee on Taxation Report — JCX-50-06]

Present Law

Present law provides a 50-percent business tax credit for qualified railroad track maintenance expenditures paid or incurred by an eligible taxpayer during the taxable year. The credit is limited to the product of $3,500 times the number of miles of railroad track (1) owned or leased by an eligible taxpayer as of the close of its taxable year, and (2) assigned to the eligible taxpayer by a Class II or Class III railroad that owns or leases such track at the close of the taxable year. Each mile of railroad track may be taken into account only once, either by the owner of such mile or by the owner's assignee, in computing the per-mile limitation. Under the provision, the credit is limited in respect of the total number of miles of track (1) owned or leased by the Class II or Class III railroad and (2) assigned to the Class II or Class III railroad for purposes of the credit.

Qualified railroad track maintenance expenditures are defined as expenditures (whether or not otherwise chargeable to capital account) for maintaining railroad track (including roadbed, bridges, and related track structures) owned or leased as of January 1, 2005, by a Class II or Class III railroad.

An eligible taxpayer means any Class II or Class III railroad, and any person who transports property using the rail facilities of a Class II or Class III railroad or who furnishes railroad-related property or services to a Class II or Class III railroad, but only with respect to miles of railroad track assigned to such person by such railroad under the provision.

The terms Class II or Class III railroad have the meanings given by the Surface Transportation Board.

The provision applies to qualified railroad track maintenance expenditures paid or incurred during taxable years beginning after December 31, 2004, and before January 1, 2008.

Explanation of Provision

The provision modifies the definition of qualified railroad track expenditures, so that the term means gross expenditures (whether or not otherwise chargeable to capital account) for maintaining railroad track (including roadbed, bridges, and related track structures) owned or leased as of January 1, 2005, by a Class II or Class III railroad (determined without regard to any consideration for such expenditures given by the Class II or Class III railroad which made the assignment of such track).

Thus, for example, under the provision, qualified railroad track maintenance expenditures are not reduced by the discount amount in the case of discounted freight shipping rates, the increment in a markup of the price for track materials, or by debt forgiveness or by cash payments made by the Class II or Class III railroad to the assignee as consideration for the expenditures. Consideration received directly or indirectly from persons other that the Class II or Class III railroad, however, does reduce the amount of qualified railroad track maintenance expenditures. No inference is intended under the provision as to whether or not any such consideration is or is not includable in the assignee's income for Federal tax purposes.

Effective Date

The provision is effective for expenditures paid or incurred during taxable years beginning after December 31, 2004, and before January 1, 2008.

[¶5075] Section 424. Modification of excise tax on unrelated business taxable income of charitable remainder trusts.

(Code Sec. 664)

[Joint Committee on Taxation Report — JCX-50-06]

Present Law

A charitable remainder annuity trust is a trust that is required to pay, at least annually, a fixed dollar amount of at least five percent of the initial value of the trust to a noncharity for the life of an individual or for a period of 20 years or less, with the remainder passing to charity. A charitable remainder unitrust is a trust that generally is required to pay, at least annually, a fixed percentage of at least five percent of the fair market value of the trust's assets determined at least annually to a noncharity for the life of an individual or for a period 20 years or less, with the remainder passing to charity.[145]

A trust does not qualify as a charitable remainder annuity trust if the annuity for a year is greater than 50 percent of the initial fair market value of the trust's assets. A trust does not qualify as a charitable remainder unitrust if the percentage of assets that are required to be distributed at least annually is greater than 50 percent. A trust does not qualify as a charitable remainder annuity trust or a charitable remainder unitrust unless the value of the remainder interest in the trust is at least 10 percent of the value of the assets contributed to the trust.

Distributions from a charitable remainder annuity trust or charitable remainder unitrust are treated in the following order as: (1) ordinary income to the extent of the trust's current and previously undistributed ordinary income for the trust's year in which the distribution occurred; (2) capital gains to the extent of the trust's current capital gain and previously undistributed capital gain for the trust's year in which the distribution occurred; (3) other income (e.g., tax-exempt income) to the extent of the trust's current and previously undistributed other income for the trust's year in which the distribution occurred; and (4) corpus.[146]

In general, distributions to the extent they are characterized as income are includible in the income of the beneficiary for the year that the annuity or unitrust amount is required to be distributed even though the annuity or unitrust amount is not distributed until after the close of the trust's taxable year.[147]

Charitable remainder annuity trusts and charitable remainder unitrusts are exempt from Federal income tax for a tax year unless the trust has any unrelated business taxable income for the year. Unrelated business taxable income includes certain debt financed income. A charitable remainder trust that loses exemption from income tax for a taxable year is taxed as a regular complex trust. As such, the trust is allowed a deduc-

145. Sec. 664(d).
146. Sec. 664(b).
147. Treas. Reg. sec. 1.664-1(d)(4).

tion in computing taxable income for amounts required to be distributed in a taxable year, not to exceed the amount of the trust's distributable net income for the year.

Explanation of Provision

The provision imposes a 100-percent excise tax on the unrelated business taxable income of a charitable remainder trust. This replaces the present-law rule that takes away the income tax exemption of a charitable remainder trust for any year in which the trust has any unrelated business taxable income. Consistent with present law, the tax is treated as paid from corpus. The unrelated business taxable income is considered income of the trust for purposes of determining the character of the distribution made to the beneficiary.

Effective Date

The provision is effective for taxable years beginning after December 31, 2006.

[¶ 5076] Section 425. Loans to qualified continuing care facilities made permanent.

(Code Sec. 7872)

[Joint Committee on Taxation Report — JCX-50-06]

Present Law

In general

For calendar years beginning before January 1, 2006, present law provides generally that certain loans that bear interest at a below-market rate are treated as loans bearing interest at the market rate, accompanied by imputed payments characterized in accordance with the substance of the transaction (for example, as a gift, compensation, a dividend, or interest).[148]

An exception to this imputation rule is provided for any calendar year for a below-market loan made by a lender to a qualified continuing care facility pursuant to a continuing care contract, if the lender or the lender's spouse attains age 65 before the close of the calendar year.[149]

The exception applies only to the extent the aggregate outstanding loans by the lender (and spouse) to any qualified continuing care facility do not exceed $163,300 (for 2006).[150]

For this purpose, a continuing care contract means a written contract between an individual and a qualified continuing care facility under which: (1) the individual or the individual's spouse may use a qualified continuing care facility for the life or lives of one or both individuals; (2) the individual or the individual's spouse will first reside in a separate, independent living unit with additional facilities outside such unit for the providing of meals and other personal care and will not require long-term nursing care, and then will be provided long-term and skilled nursing care as the health of the individual or the individual's spouse requires; and (3) no additional substantial payment is required if the individual or the individual's spouse requires increased personal care services or long-term and skilled nursing care.[151]

For this purpose, a qualified continuing care facility means one or more facilities that are designed to provide services under continuing care contracts, and substantially all of the residents of which are covered by continuing care contracts. A facility is not treated

148. Sec. 7872.
149. Sec. 7872(g).
150. Rev. Rul. 2005-75, 2005-49 I.R.B. 1073.
151. Sec. 7872(g)(3).

as a qualified continuing care facility unless substantially all facilities that are used to provide services required to be provided under a continuing care contract are owned or operated by the borrower. For these purposes, a nursing home is not a qualified continuing care facility.[152]

Special rule for calendar years beginning after 2005 and before 2011

The Tax Increase Prevention and Reconciliation Act of 2005 ("TIPRA") includes a provision modifying the exception under section 7872 relating to loans to continuing care facilities. Among other things, the modification eliminates the dollar cap on aggregate outstanding loans.[153]

Under the TIPRA provision, a continuing care contract is a written contract between an individual and a qualified continuing care facility under which: (1) the individual or the individual's spouse may use a qualified continuing care facility for the life or lives of one or both individuals; (2) the individual or the individual's spouse will be provided with housing, as appropriate for the health of such individual or individual's spouse, (i) in an independent living unit (which has additional available facilities outside such unit for the provision of meals and other personal care), and (ii) in an assisted living facility or a nursing facility, as is available in the continuing care facility; and (3) the individual or the individual's spouse will be provided assisted living or nursing care as the health of the individual or the individual's spouse requires, and as is available in the continuing care facility. The Secretary is required to issue guidance that limits the term "continuing care contract" to contracts that provide only facilities, care, and services described in the preceding sentence.[154]

For purposes of defining the terms "continuing care contract" and "qualified continuing care facility," the term "assisted living facility" is intended to mean a facility at which assistance is provided (1) with activities of daily living (such as eating, toileting, transferring, bathing, dressing, and continence) or (2) in cases of cognitive impairment, to protect the health or safety of an individual. The term "nursing facility" is intended to mean a facility that offers care requiring the utilization of licensed nursing staff.

The TIPRA modifications generally are effective for calendar years beginning after December 31, 2005, with respect to loans made before, on, or after such date. The TIPRA modifications do not apply to any calendar year after 2010. Thus, the TIPRA modifications do not apply with respect to interest imputed after December 31, 2010. After such date, the law as in effect prior to enactment applies.

Explanation of Provision

The provision makes permanent the TIPRA modifications to section 7872 regarding below-market loans to qualified continuing care facilities.

Effective Date

The provision is effective as if included in section 209 of the TIPRA.

[¶5077] Section 426. Technical corrections.

(Code Sec. 954)

[Joint Committee on Taxation Report — JCX-50-06]

In general

The bill includes technical corrections to recently enacted tax legislation. Except as otherwise provided, the amendments made by the technical corrections contained in the

152. Sec. 7872(g)(4).
153. Sec. 7872(h).
154. Sec. 7872(h)(2).

bill take effect as if included in the original legislation to which each amendment relates.

Amendment Related to the Tax Increase Prevention and Reconciliation Act of 2005

Look-through treatment and regulatory authority (Act sec. 103(b)).—Under the Act, for taxable years beginning after 2005 and before 2009, dividends, interest (including factoring income which is treated as equivalent to interest under sec. 954(c)(1)(E)), rents, and royalties received by one controlled foreign corporation ("CFC") from a related CFC are not treated as foreign personal holding company income to the extent attributable or properly allocable to non-subpart F income of the payor (the "TIPRA look-through rule"). The Act further provides that the Secretary shall prescribe such regulations as are appropriate to prevent the abuse of the purposes of the rule.

Section 952(b) provides that subpart F income of a CFC does not include any item of income from sources within the United States which is effectively connected with the conduct by such CFC of a trade or business within the United States ("ECI") unless such item is exempt from taxation (or is subject to a reduced rate of tax) pursuant to a tax treaty. Thus, for example, a payment of interest from a CFC all of the income of which is U.S.-source ECI (and therefore not subpart F income) may receive the unintended benefit of the TIPRA look-through rule under the Act, even though the payment may be deductible for U.S. tax purposes.

The provision conforms the TIPRA look-through rule to the rule's purpose of allowing U.S. companies to redeploy their active foreign earnings (i.e., CFC earnings subject to U.S. tax deferral) without an additional tax burden in appropriate circumstances. Under the provision, in order to be excluded from foreign personal holding company income under the TIPRA look-through rule, the dividend, interest, rent, or royalty also must not be attributable or properly allocable to income of the related party payor that is treated as ECI. Thus, for example, a payment of interest made by a CFC does not qualify under the TIPRA look-through rule to the extent that the interest payment is allocated to the CFC's ECI. This is the case even if the interest payment creates or increases a net operating loss of the CFC. The rule applies to dividends, notwithstanding that dividends are not deductible.

The provision clarifies the authority of the Secretary to issue regulations under the TIPRA look-through rule, as amended by this provision. It is intended that the Secretary will prescribe regulations that are necessary or appropriate to carry out the amended TIPRA look-through rule, including, but not limited to, regulations that prevent the inappropriate use of the amended TIPRA look-through rule to strip income from the U.S. income tax base. Regulations issued pursuant to this authority may, for example, include regulations that prevent the application of the amended TIPRA look-through rule to interest deemed to arise under certain related party factoring arrangements pursuant to section 864(d), or under other transactions the net effect of which is the deduction of a payment, accrual, or loss for U.S. tax purposes without a corresponding inclusion in the subpart F income of the CFC income recipient, where such inclusion would have resulted in the absence of the amended TIPRA look-through rule.

Amendment related to the American Jobs Creation Act of 2004

Modification of effective date of exception from interest suspension rules for certain listed and reportable transactions (Act sec. 903).—Section 903 of the American Jobs Creation Act of 2004 ("AJCA"), as modified by section 303 of the Gulf Opportunity Zone Act of 2005, provides that the Secretary of the Treasury may permit interest suspension where taxpayers have acted reasonably and in good faith. For provisions that are included in the Code, section 7701(a)(11) provides that the term "Secretary of the Treasury" means the Secretary in his nondelegable capacity, and the term "Secretary" means the Secretary or his delegate. However, section 903 of AJCA (as modified) is not included in the Code. To clarify that the Secretary may delegate authority under section 903 of AJCA (as modified), the provision adds the words "or the Secretary's delegate" following the reference to the Secretary of the Treasury.

[¶5079] Section 403 (Div. C, Title IV). Withdrawal of certain Federal land and interests in Federal land from location, entry, and patent under the mining laws and disposition under the mineral and geothermal leasing laws.

(Code Sec. None)

[Joint Committee on Taxation Report — JCX-50-06]

Present Law

Gain from the sale or exchange of land held more than one year generally is treated as long-term capital gain. Generally, the net capital gain of an individual is subject to a maximum tax rate of 15 percent. The net capital gain of a corporation is subject to tax at the same rate as ordinary income.

Explanation of Provision

In general

The provision provides a 25-percent exclusion from gross income of long-term capital gain from the conservation sale of a qualifying mineral or geothermal interest.[172] The conservation sale must be made to an eligible entity that intends that the acquired property be used for qualified conservation purposes in perpetuity.[173]

Qualifying interests

A qualifying mineral or geothermal interest means an interest in any mineral or geothermal deposit located on eligible Federal land which constitutes a taxpayer's entire interest in such deposit. Eligible Federal land means (1) Bureau of Land Management land and any Federally-owned minerals located south of the Blackfeet Indian Reservation and East of the Lewis and Clark national Forest to the Eastern edge of R. 8 W., beginning in T. 29 N. down to and including T. 19 N. and all of T. 18 N., R. 7 W, (2) the Forest Service land and any Federally-owned minerals located in the Rocky Mountain Division of the Lewis and Clark national Forest, including the approximately 356,111 acres of land made unavailable for leasing by the August 28, 1997, Record of Decision for the Lewis and Clark National Forest Oil and Gas Leasing Environmental Impact Statement and that is located form T. 31 N. to T. 16 N. and R. 13 W. to R. 7 W., and (3) the Forest Service land and any Federally-owned minerals located within the Badger Two Medicine area of the Flathead National Forest, including the land located in T. 29 N. from the Western edge of R. 16 W. to the Eastern edge of R. 13 W. and the land located in T. 28 N., Rs 13 and 14 W. All such land is as generally depicted on the map entitled "Rocky Mountain Front Mineral Withdrawal Area" and dated December 31, 2006. The map shall be on file and available for inspection in the Office of the Chief of the Forest Service.

An interest in property is not the entire interest of the taxpayer if such interest was divided in an attempt to avoid the requirement that the taxpayer sell the taxpayer's entire interest in the property. An interest may be considered the taxpayer's entire interest notwithstanding that the taxpayer retains an interest in other deposits, even if the other de-

172. In a non tax-related provision, the provision also provides that, subject to valid existing rights, eligible Federal land (including any interest in eligible Federal land) is withdrawn from: (1) all forms of location, entry, and patent under the mining laws; and (2) disposition under all laws relating to mineral and geothermal leasing.

173. The exclusion is mandatory if all of the requirements of the provision are satisfied, and a taxpayer need not file an election to take advantage of the exclusion. A taxpayer who transfers qualifying property to a qualified organization may opt out of the 25-percent exclusion by choosing not to satisfy one or more of the provision's requirements without having to file a formal election with the Secretary, such as by failing to obtain the requisite letter of intent from the qualified organization.

posits are contiguous with the sold deposit and were acquired by the taxpayer along with such deposit in a single conveyance. It is intended that the partial interest rules contained in Treasury Regulations section 1.170A-7(a)(2)(i) and generally applicable to charitable contributions of partial interests be applied similarly for purposes of this provision.

Conservation sales

A conservation sale is a sale (excluding a transfer made by order of condemnation or eminent domain) to an eligible entity, defined as a Federal, State, or local government, or an agency or department thereof or a section 501(c)(3) organization that is organized and operated primarily to meet a qualified conservation purpose. In addition, to be a conservation sale, the organization acquiring the property interest must provide the taxpayer with a written letter stating that the acquisition will serve one or more qualified conservation purposes, that the use of the deposits will be exclusively for conservation purposes, and that such use will continue in the event of a subsequent transfer of the acquired interest. A qualified conservation purpose is: (1) the preservation of land areas for outdoor recreation by, or the education of, the general public; (2) the protection of a relatively natural habitat of fish, wildlife, or plants, or similar ecosystem; or (3) the preservation of open space (including farmland and forest land) where the preservation is for the scenic enjoyment of the general public or pursuant to a clearly delineated Federal, State, or local governmental conservation policy and will yield a significant public benefit. Use of property is not considered to be exclusively for conservation purposes unless the conservation purpose is protected in perpetuity and no surface mining is permitted with respect to the property (sec. 170(h)(5)).

Protection of conservation purposes

The provision provides for the imposition of penalty excise taxes if an eligible entity fails to take steps consistent with the protection of conservation purposes. If ownership or possession of the property is transferred by a qualified organization, then: (1) a 20-percent excise tax applies to the fair market value of the property, and (2) any realized gain or income is subject to an additional excise tax imposed at the highest income tax rate applicable to C corporations. In the case of a transfer by an eligible entity to another eligible entity, the excise tax does not apply if the transferee provides the transferor at the time of the transfer a letter of intent (as described above). In the case of a transfer by an eligible entity to a transferee that is not an eligible entity, the excise tax does not apply if it is established to the satisfaction of the Secretary that the transfer is exclusively for conservation purposes (as provided in section 170(h)(5)) and the transferee provides the transferor a letter of intent (as described above) at the time of the transfer. Once a transfer has been subject to the excise tax, the excise tax may not apply to any subsequent transfers. The provision provides that the Secretary may require such reporting as may be necessary or appropriate to further the purpose that any conservation use be in perpetuity.

Effective Date

The provision is effective for sales occurring on or after the date of enactment.

¶ 6000. Act Section Cross Reference Table

Act §	Code §	Topic	Generally effective date	Analysis ¶	Com Rep ¶
101(a)	222(e)	Above-the-line deduction for higher-education expenses is retroactively extended from 2005 through 2007	Tax years beginning after Dec. 31, 2005 and before Jan. 1, 2008	102	5001
101(b)(1)	222(b)(2)(B)	Above-the-line deduction for higher-education expenses is retroactively extended from 2005 through 2007	Tax years beginning after Dec. 31, 2005 and before Jan. 1, 2008	102	5001
102(a)	45D(f)(1)(D)	$3.5 billion new markets tax credit limitation is extended to include 2008	Date of enactment	1001	5002
102(b)	45D(i)(6)	New markets tax credit regs are to ensure that non-metropolitan counties receive a proportional allocation of qualified equity investments	Date of enactment	1002	5002
103(a)	164(b)(5)(I)	Election to claim itemized deduction for state and local general sales taxes is retroactively extended from 2005 through 2007	Tax years beginning after Dec. 31, 2005 and before Jan. 1, 2008	101	5003
104(a)(1)	41(h)(1)(B)	Research credit is extended retroactively to amounts paid or incurred after Dec. 31, 2005 and before Jan. 1, 2008	Amounts paid or incurred after Dec. 31, 2005	201	5004
104(a)(2)	45C(b)(1)(D)	Research credit is extended retroactively to amounts paid or incurred after Dec. 31, 2005 and before Jan. 1, 2008	Amounts paid or incurred after Dec. 31, 2005	201	5004
104(b)(1)	41(c)(4)(A)	Rates for the elective alternative incremental research credit are increased	Tax years ending after Dec. 31, 2006	202	5004
104(c)(1)	41(c)(5)	Alternative simplified credit can be elected for qualified research expenses	Tax years ending after Dec. 31, 2006	203	5004

Act §	Code §	Topic	Generally effective date	Analysis ¶	Com Rep ¶
104(c)(2)	41(c)(4)	Alternative simplified credit can be elected for qualified research expenses	Tax years ending after Dec. 31, 2006	203	5004
105(a)	51(c)(4)(B)	Work opportunity credit is retroactively restored to Jan. 1, 2006 and is extended two years to Dec. 31, 2007 for most targeted groups	Individuals who begin work for the employer after Dec. 31, 2005 and before Jan. 1, 2008	801	5005
105(a)	51A(f)	Welfare-to-work credit is retroactively restored to Jan. 1, 2006 and, after Dec. 31, 2006, is consolidated with the work opportunity credit	Individuals who begin work for the employer after Dec. 31, 2005 and before Jan. 1, 2008	805	5005
105(b)	51(d)(4)	The "family low-income requirement" is eliminated for the work opportunity credit group consisting of "qualified ex-felons"	Individuals who begin work for the employer after Dec. 31, 2006 and before Jan. 1, 2008	804	5005
105(c)	51(d)(8)(A)(i)	Maximum age of a "qualified food stamp recipient" is increased from 24 to 39 for purposes of the work opportunity credit	Individuals who begin work for the employer after Dec. 31, 2006 and before Jan. 1, 2008	803	5005
105(d)	51(d)(12)(A)(ii)(II)	Deadline for submitting paperwork for certification of employees under the work opportunity credit is extended to 28 days after the beginning of work	Individuals who begin work for the employer after Dec. 31, 2006 and before Jan. 1, 2008	802	5005
105(e)(1)	51(d)(1)(I)	Welfare-to-work credit is retroactively restored to Jan. 1, 2006 and, after Dec. 31, 2006, is consolidated with the work opportunity credit	Individuals who begin work for the employer after Dec. 31, 2006 and before Jan. 1, 2008	805	5005

Act §	Code §	Topic	Generally effective date	Analysis ¶	Com Rep ¶
105(e)(2)	51(d)(10)	Welfare-to-work credit is retroactively restored to Jan. 1, 2006 and, after Dec. 31, 2006, is consolidated with the work opportunity credit	Individuals who begin work for the employer after Dec. 31, 2006 and before Jan. 1, 2008	805	5005
105(e)(3)	51(e)	Welfare-to-work credit is retroactively restored to Jan. 1, 2006 and, after Dec. 31, 2006, is consolidated with the work opportunity credit	Individuals who begin work for the employer after Dec. 31, 2006 and before Jan. 1, 2008	805	5005
105(e)(4)(A)	51A	Welfare-to-work credit is retroactively restored to Jan. 1, 2006 and, after Dec. 31, 2006, is consolidated with the work opportunity credit	Individuals who begin work for the employer after Dec. 31, 2006 and before Jan. 1, 2008	805	5005
106(a)	32(c)(2)(B)(vi)(II)	Election to include combat pay as earned income for purposes of the earned income credit (EIC) is extended through 2007	Tax years beginning after Dec. 31, 2006	106	5010
107(a)	1397E(e)(1)	Permitted issuance of qualified zone academy bonds of up to $400 million per year is extended retroactively through Dec. 31, 2007	Obligations issued after Dec. 31, 2005 and before Jan. 1, 2008	1003	5011
107(b)(1)(A)	1397E(d)(1)(E)	Qualified zone academy bond issuers must meet new expenditure, arbitrage, and reporting requirements	Obligations issued after date of enactment	1004	5011
107(b)(1)(B)	1397E(h)	Qualified zone academy bond issuers must meet new expenditure, arbitrage, and reporting requirements	Obligations issued after date of enactment	1004	5011
107(b)(1)(B)	1397E(f)	Qualified zone academy bond issuers must meet new expenditure, arbitrage, and reporting requirements	Obligations issued after date of enactment	1004	5011

Act §	Code §	Topic	Generally effective date	Analysis ¶	Com Rep ¶
107(b)(1)(B)	1397E(g)	Qualified zone academy bond issuers must meet new expenditure, arbitrage, and reporting requirements	Obligations issued after date of enactment	1004	5011
108(a)	62(a)(2)(D)	Up-to-$250 above-the-line deduction for teachers' out-of-pocket classroom-related expenses is retroactively extended for two years through 2007	Expenses paid or incurred in tax years beginning after Dec. 31, 2005 and before Jan. 1, 2008	103	5012
109(a)	198(h)	Election to expense qualified environmental remediation costs is retroactively restored and is extended for two years to apply to expenditures paid or incurred after Dec. 31, 2005 and before Jan. 1, 2008	Expenditures paid or incurred after Dec. 31, 2005 and before Jan. 1, 2008	505	5013
109(b)	198(d)(1)	Definition of hazardous substances for purposes of expensing election for environmental remediation costs is expanded to include petroleum products	Expenditures paid or incurred after Dec. 31, 2005	506	5013
110(a)(1)	1400(f)(1)	DC Enterprise Zone and enterprise community designations are retroactively extended for two years through Dec. 31, 2007	Periods beginning after Dec. 31, 2005 and ending before Jan. 1, 2008	1103	5014
110(a)(1)	1400(f)(2)	DC Enterprise Zone and enterprise community designations are retroactively extended for two years through Dec. 31, 2007	Periods beginning after Dec. 31, 2005 and ending before Jan. 1, 2008	1103	5014
110(b)(1)	1400A(b)	Higher tax-exempt enterprise zone facility bond limit for DC Zone bonds is retroactively extended to apply to bonds issued after Dec. 31, 2005 and before Jan. 1, 2008	Bonds issued after Dec. 31, 2005 and before Jan. 1, 2008	1104	5014

Act §	Code §	Topic	Generally effective date	Analysis ¶	Com Rep ¶
110(c)(1)	1400B(b)(2)(A)(i)	Zero percent capital gains rate for DC Zone assets is retroactively extended for two years to apply to assets acquired before Jan. 1, 2008 and includes gain attributable to periods before Jan. 1, 2013	Acquisitions after Dec. 31, 2005 and before Jan. 1, 2008	1102	5014
110(c)(1)	1400B(b)(3)(A)	Zero percent capital gains rate for DC Zone assets is retroactively extended for two years to apply to assets acquired before Jan. 1, 2008 and includes gain attributable to periods before Jan. 1, 2013	Acquisitions after Dec. 31, 2005 and before Jan. 1, 2008	1102	5014
110(c)(1)	1400B(b)(4)(A)(i)	Zero percent capital gains rate for DC Zone assets is retroactively extended for two years to apply to assets acquired before Jan. 1, 2008 and includes gain attributable to periods before Jan. 1, 2013	Acquisitions after Dec. 31, 2005 and before Jan. 1, 2008	1102	5014
110(c)(1)	1400B(b)(4)(B)(i)(I)	Zero percent capital gains rate for DC Zone assets is retroactively extended for two years to apply to assets acquired before Jan. 1, 2008 and includes gain attributable to periods before Jan. 1, 2013	Acquisitions after Dec. 31, 2005 and before Jan. 1, 2008	1102	5014
110(c)(2)(A)(i)	1400B(e)(2)	Zero percent capital gains rate for DC Zone assets is retroactively extended for two years to apply to assets acquired before Jan. 1, 2008 and includes gain attributable to periods before Jan. 1, 2013	Date of enactment	1102	5014

Act §	Code §	Topic	Generally effective date	Analysis ¶	Com Rep ¶
110(c)(2)(B)	1400B(g)(2)	Zero percent capital gains rate for DC Zone assets is retroactively extended for two years to apply to assets acquired before Jan. 1, 2008 and includes gain attributable to periods before Jan. 1, 2013	Date of enactment	1102	5014
110(d)(1)	1400C(i)	DC homebuyer credit is retroactively extended for two years to apply to property bought before Jan. 1, 2008	Property bought after Dec. 31, 2005 and before Jan. 1, 2008	1101	5014
111(a)	45A(f)	Indian employment credit is extended retroactively for tax years beginning after Dec. 31, 2005 and before Jan. 1, 2008	Tax years beginning after Dec. 31, 2005 and before Jan. 1, 2008	807	5015
112(a)	168(j)(8)	Depreciation tax breaks for Indian reservation property are extended retroactively to property placed in service after Dec. 31, 2005 and before Jan. 1, 2008	Property placed in service after Dec. 31, 2005 and before Jan. 1, 2008	510	5016
113(a)	168(e)(3)(E)(iv)	Placed-in-service deadline for the treatment of "qualified leasehold improvement property" as 15-year MACRS property is retroactively restored to Jan. 1, 2006 and is extended for two years to Dec. 31, 2007	Property placed in service after Dec. 31, 2005 and before Jan. 1, 2008	502	5017
113(a)	168(e)(3)(E)(v)	Placed-in-service deadline for the treatment of "qualified restaurant property" as 15-year MACRS property is retroactively restored to Jan. 1, 2006 and is extended for two years to Dec. 31, 2007	Property placed in service after Dec. 31, 2005 and before Jan. 1, 2008	503	5017
115(a)	9812(f)(3)	Mental health parity requirements extended through 2007	Date of enactment	402	5019

Act §	Code §	Topic	Generally effective date	Analysis ¶	Com Rep ¶
116(a)(1)	170(e)(6)(G)	Enhanced deduction for qualified computer contributions by corporations is retroactively extended for two years through 2007	Contributions made in tax years beginning after Dec. 31, 2005, and before Jan. 1, 2008	602	5020
116(b)(1)(A)	170(e)(4)(B)(ii)	Property assembled by donor qualifies for enhanced deduction for qualified research contributions and qualified computer contributions	Tax years beginning after Dec. 31, 2005	603	5020
116(b)(1)(B)	170(e)(4)(B)(iii)	Property assembled by donor qualifies for enhanced deduction for qualified research contributions and qualified computer contributions	Tax years beginning after Dec. 31, 2005	603	5020
116(b)(2)(A)	170(e)(6)(B)(ii)	Property assembled by donor qualifies for enhanced deduction for qualified research contributions and qualified computer contributions	Tax years beginning after Dec. 31, 2005	603	5020
116(b)(2)(B)	170(e)(6)(D)	Property assembled by donor qualifies for enhanced deduction for qualified research contributions and qualified computer contributions	Tax years beginning after Dec. 31, 2005	603	5020
117(a)	220(i)(2)	Archer MSA program is extended through 2007—trustees' reports for 2005 and 2006 will be timely if made within 90 days of date of enactment	Date of enactment	307	5021
118(a)	613A(c)(6)(H)	Suspension of taxable income limitation on percentage depletion from marginal oil and gas wells is retroactively extended for two years to include tax years beginning before Jan. 1, 2008	Tax years beginning after Dec. 31, 2005 and before Jan. 1, 2008	507	5022
119	30A	Possessions tax credit for American Samoa retroactively extended through 2007 for existing claimants	Tax years beginning after Dec. 31, 2005 and before Jan. 1, 2008	1303	5023

Act §	Code §	Topic	Generally effective date	Analysis ¶	Com Rep ¶
120(a)	1400N(d)(6)	Placed-in-service deadline for "qualified Gulf Opportunity Zone property" is for some purposes extended to Dec. 31, 2010 (and to as much as 90 days beyond) for certain property used in highly damaged portions of the GO Zone	Tax years beginning after Aug. 27, 2005	504	5024
120(b)	1400N(e)(2)	Placed-in-service deadline for "qualified Gulf Opportunity Zone property" is for some purposes extended to Dec. 31, 2010 (and to as much as 90 days beyond) for certain property used in highly damaged portions of the GO Zone	Tax years beginning after Aug. 27, 2005	504	5024
121	7608(c)(6)	IRS's authority to churn income earned from undercover operations is extended through 2007	Date of enactment	1412	5025
122(a)(1)	6103(d)(5)(B)	IRS's authority to disclose taxpayer identity information to facilitate combined federal/state employment tax reporting is extended for one year through Dec. 31, 2007	Disclosures after Dec. 31, 2006 and before Jan. 1, 2008	1403	5026
122(b)(1)	6103(i)(3)(C)(iv)	IRS's authority to disclose tax information in terrorism and national security investigations is extended for one year through Dec. 31, 2007	Disclosures after Dec. 31, 2006 and before Jan. 1, 2008	1405	5027
122(b)(1)	6103(i)(7)(E)	IRS's authority to disclose tax information in terrorism and national security investigations is extended for one year through Dec. 31, 2007	Disclosures after Dec. 31, 2006 and before Jan. 1, 2008	1405	5027
122(c)(1)	6103(l)(13)(D)	IRS's authority to disclose requested return information to the Dept. of Education to monitor income-contingent student loan repayments is extended for one year for requests made through Dec. 31, 2007	Requests made after Dec. 31, 2006 and before Jan. 1, 2008	1404	5028

Act §	Code §	Topic	Generally effective date	Analysis ¶	Com Rep ¶
123(a)	280C(c)(3)(C)	Taxpayers with a tax year ending after 2005 have until Apr. 15, 2007 to make elections under expired provisions that are retroactively extended by the 2006 Tax Relief and Health Care Act	Tax years ending after Dec. 31, 2005 and before date of enactment	701	5029
123(a)	41(c)(4)	Taxpayers with a tax year ending after 2005 have until Apr. 15, 2007 to make elections under expired provisions that are retroactively extended by the 2006 Tax Relief and Health Care Act	Tax years ending after Dec. 31, 2005 and before date of enactment	701	5029
123(b)	None	Taxpayers with a tax year ending after 2005 have until Apr. 15, 2007 to make elections under expired provisions that are retroactively extended by the 2006 Tax Relief and Health Care Act	Tax years ending after Dec. 31, 2005 and before date of enactment	701	5029
201	45(d)(1)	Placed-in-service date is extended for one year through Dec. 31, 2008 for certain qualified facilities for purposes of the credit for electricity produced from renewable resources	Facilities placed in service after Dec. 31, 2007	903	5031
201	45(d)(2)(A)	Placed-in-service date is extended for one year through Dec. 31, 2008 for certain qualified facilities for purposes of the credit for electricity produced from renewable resources	Facilities placed in service after Dec. 31, 2007	903	5031
201	45(d)(3)(A)	Placed-in-service date is extended for one year through Dec. 31, 2008 for certain qualified facilities for purposes of the credit for electricity produced from renewable resources	Facilities placed in service after Dec. 31, 2007	903	5031

Act §	Code §	Topic	Generally effective date	Analysis ¶	Com Rep ¶
201	45(d)(4)	Placed-in-service date is extended for one year through Dec. 31, 2008 for certain qualified facilities for purposes of the credit for electricity produced from renewable resources	Facilities placed in service after Dec. 31, 2007	903	5031
201	45(d)(5)	Placed-in-service date is extended for one year through Dec. 31, 2008 for certain qualified facilities for purposes of the credit for electricity produced from renewable resources	Facilities placed in service after Dec. 31, 2007	903	5031
201	45(d)(6)	Placed-in-service date is extended for one year through Dec. 31, 2008 for certain qualified facilities for purposes of the credit for electricity produced from renewable resources	Facilities placed in service after Dec. 31, 2007	903	5031
201	45(d)(7)	Placed-in-service date is extended for one year through Dec. 31, 2008 for certain qualified facilities for purposes of the credit for electricity produced from renewable resources	Facilities placed in service after Dec. 31, 2007	903	5031
201	45(d)(9)	Placed-in-service date is extended for one year through Dec. 31, 2008 for certain qualified facilities for purposes of the credit for electricity produced from renewable resources	Facilities placed in service after Dec. 31, 2007	903	5031
202(a)(1)	54(f)(1)	National CREB limitation raised to $1.2 billion; amount allocable to governmental borrowers raised to $750 million; termination date for issuance of CREBs extended through end of 2008	Bonds issued after Dec. 31, 2006	906	5032

Act §	Code §	Topic	Generally effective date	Analysis ¶	Com Rep ¶
202(a)(2)	54(f)(2)	National CREB limitation raised to $1.2 billion; amount allocable to governmental borrowers raised to $750 million; termination date for issuance of CREBs extended through end of 2008	Allocations or reallocations made after Dec. 31, 2006	906	5032
202(a)(3)	54(m)	National CREB limitation raised to $1.2 billion; amount allocable to governmental borrowers raised to $750 million; termination date for issuance of CREBs extended through end of 2008	Bonds issued after Dec. 31, 2006	906	5032
203(a)	48A(f)(1)	An alternative low-sulfur standard is met for advanced coal-based generation technology units using subbituminous coal where an emission level of 0.04 pounds or less of SO_2 per million Btu is achieved	Applications for certification submitted after Oct. 2, 2006	905	5033
204	179D(h)	Deduction for energy efficient commercial building property is extended for one year through Dec. 31, 2008	Date of enactment	501	5034
205	45L(g)	Energy efficient home credit for eligible contractors is extended through 2008	Qualified new energy efficient homes acquired after Dec. 31, 2007 and before Jan. 1, 2009	901	5035
206(a)	25D(g)	Residential energy efficient property credit is extended for one year, through 2008; solar energy property qualifying for credit is clarified	Date of enactment	105	5036
206(b)(1)	25D(a)(1)	Residential energy efficient property credit is extended for one year, through 2008; solar energy property qualifying for credit is clarified	Date of enactment	105	5036

Act §	Code §	Topic	Generally effective date	Analysis ¶	Com Rep ¶
206(b)(1)	25D(b)(1)(A)	Residential energy efficient property credit is extended for one year, through 2008; solar energy property qualifying for credit is clarified	Date of enactment	105	5036
206(b)(1)	25D(e)(4)(A)(i)	Residential energy efficient property credit is extended for one year, through 2008; solar energy property qualifying for credit is clarified	Date of enactment	105	5036
206(b)(2)	25D(d)(2)	Residential energy efficient property credit is extended for one year, through 2008; solar energy property qualifying for credit is clarified	Date of enactment	105	5036
207(1)	48(a)(2)(A)(i)(II)	Increase in business energy tax credit for solar energy property from 10% to 30% is extended through Dec. 31, 2008, as are the 30% credit for qualified fuel cell propertyand the 10% credit for qualified microturbine property	Periods after Dec. 31, 2007 and before Jan. 1, 2009	902	5037
207(1)	48(a)(3)(A)(ii)	Increase in business energy tax credit for solar energy property from 10% to 30% is extended through Dec. 31, 2008, as are the 30% credit for qualified fuel cell propertyand the 10% credit for qualified microturbine property	Periods after Dec. 31, 2007 and before Jan. 1, 2009	902	5037
207(2)	48(c)(1)(E)	Increase in business energy tax credit for solar energy property from 10% to 30% is extended through Dec. 31, 2008, as are the 30% credit for qualified fuel cell propertyand the 10% credit for qualified microturbine property	Periods after Dec. 31, 2007 and before Jan. 1, 2009	902	5037

Act §	Code §	Topic	Generally effective date	Analysis ¶	Com Rep ¶
207(2)	48(c)(2)(E)	Increase in business energy tax credit for solar energy property from 10% to 30% is extended through Dec. 31, 2008, as are the 30% credit for qualified fuel cell propertyand the 10% credit for qualified microturbine property	Periods after Dec. 31, 2007 and before Jan. 1, 2009	902	5037
208(a)	4041(b)(2)(D)	Reduced retail excise tax rates for qualified methanol and qualified ethanol fuels (scheduled to terminate after Sept. 30, 2007) are extended through Dec. 31, 2008	Date of enactment	1501	5038
208(b)	4041(b)(2)(C)(ii)	Reduced retail excise tax rates for qualified methanol and qualified ethanol fuels (scheduled to terminate after Sept. 30, 2007) are extended through Dec. 31, 2008	Date of enactment	1501	5038
209(a)	168(l)	50% bonus depreciation and AMT relief are allowed for "qualified cellulosic biomass ethanol plant property" purchased after date of enactment and placed in service before Jan. 1, 2013	Property purchased after date of enactment and placed in service before Jan. 1, 2013	508	5039
211(a)	45K(g)(2)	Nonconventional source production credit for coke and coke gas is not subject to the phase-out limitation, and the credit does not apply to a facility producing coke or coke gas from petroleum-based products	Fuel produced and sold after Dec. 31, 2005	904	5041
211(b)	45K(g)(1)	Nonconventional source production credit for coke and coke gas is not subject to the phase-out limitation, and the credit does not apply to a facility producing coke or coke gas from petroleum-based products	Fuel produced and sold after Dec. 31, 2005	904	5041

Act §	Code §	Topic	Generally effective date	Analysis ¶	Com Rep ¶
302(a)	106(e)	One-time rollovers from health FSAs and HRAs into HSAs permitted through 2011	For distributions on or after date of enactment	302	5045
302(b)	223(c)(1)(B)(iii)	One-time rollovers from health FSAs and HRAs into HSAs permitted through 2011	For distributions on or after date of enactment	302	5045
303(a)	223(b)(2)	Limit on HSA contributions is no longer restricted by health plan's annual deductible	For tax years beginning after Dec. 31, 2006	303	5045
304	223(g)(1)	Cost-of-living adjustment for HSA and HDHP dollar amounts is modified—tax years beginning after 2007	For adjustments made for tax years beginning after 2007	305	5045
305(a)	223(b)(8)	Individuals who establish health savings accounts mid-year can contribute the full-year amount	Tax years beginning after Dec. 31, 2006	306	5045
306(a)	4980G(d)	Employers can make larger HSA contributions for nonhighly compensated employees than for highly compensated employees, without violating comparability rule	Tax years beginning after Dec. 31, 2006	304	5045
307(a)	408(d)(9)	Eligible individuals may elect one-time tax-free rollover of IRA distribution into an HSA	Tax years beginning after Dec. 31, 2006	301	5045
307(b)	223(b)(4)(C)	Eligible individuals may elect one-time tax-free rollover of IRA distribution into an HSA	Tax years beginning after Dec. 31, 2006	301	5045
401(a)	199(d)(8)	Domestic production activities deduction extended retroactively to production activities in Puerto Rico for first two tax years beginning after 2005	First two tax years beginning after Dec. 31, 2005 and before Jan. 1, 2008	1302	5052
402(a)	53(e)	Portion of minimum tax credit attributable to years before the third immediately preceding tax year is made refundable	Tax years beginning after date of enactment and before Jan. 1, 2013	1201	5053

Act §	Code §	Topic	Generally effective date	Analysis ¶	Com Rep ¶
402(b)(1)	6211(b)(4)(A)	AMT refundable credit may result in negative amount of tax in deficiency computation	Tax years beginning after date of enactment	1202	5053
403(a)	6039(a)	Corporations must report to IRS transfers of stock from exercises of incentive stock options or purchases from employee stock purchase plans	Calendar years beginning after date of enactment	401	5053
403(a)(Div. C, Title IV)	None	25% of qualifying gain from conservation sales of qualifying mineral or geothermal interests excluded from gross income	Sales on or after date of enactment	1606	5079
403(b)	6039(b)	Corporations must report to IRS transfers of stock from exercises of incentive stock options or purchases from employee stock purchase plans	Calendar years beginning after date of enactment	401	5053
403(b)(2)(Div. C, Title IV)	None	25% of qualifying gain from conservation sales of qualifying mineral or geothermal interests excluded from gross income	Sales on or after date of enactment	1606	5079
403(c)(1)	6724(d)(1)(B)(xix)	Corporations must report to IRS transfers of stock from exercises of incentive stock options or purchases from employee stock purchase plans	Calendar years beginning after date of enactment	401	5053
403(c)(Div. C, Title IV)	61	25% of qualifying gain from conservation sales of qualifying mineral or geothermal interests excluded from gross income	Sales on or after date of enactment	1606	5079
404(a)	179E	Taxpayers can elect to expense 50% of the cost of "qualified advanced mine safety equipment property" placed in service after date of enactment and before Jan. 1, 2009	Costs paid or incurred after date of enactment	509	5055

Act §	Code §	Topic	Generally effective date	Analysis ¶	Com Rep ¶
404(b)(1)	263(a)(1)(L)	Taxpayers can elect to expense 50% of the cost of "qualified advanced mine safety equipment property" placed in service after date of enactment and before Jan. 1, 2009	Costs paid or incurred after date of enactment	509	5055
404(b)(2)	312(k)(3)(B)	Taxpayers can elect to expense 50% of the cost of "qualified advanced mine safety equipment property" placed in service after date of enactment and before Jan. 1, 2009	Costs paid or incurred after date of enactment	509	5055
404(b)(3)	1245(a)(2)(C)	Taxpayers can elect to expense 50% of the cost of "qualified advanced mine safety equipment property" placed in service after date of enactment and before Jan. 1, 2009	Costs paid or incurred after date of enactment	509	5055
404(b)(3)	1245(a)(3)(C)	Taxpayers can elect to expense 50% of the cost of "qualified advanced mine safety equipment property" placed in service after date of enactment and before Jan. 1, 2009	Costs paid or incurred after date of enactment	509	5055
405(a)	45N	A 20% credit is available for amounts paid or incurred in tax years beginning after Dec. 31, 2005 and before Jan. 1, 2009 for training mine rescue teams	Tax years beginning after Dec. 31, 2005 and before Jan. 1, 2009	806	5056
405(b)	38(b)(31)	A 20% credit is available for amounts paid or incurred in tax years beginning after Dec. 31, 2005 and before Jan. 1, 2009 for training mine rescue teams	Tax years beginning after Dec. 31, 2005 and before Jan. 1, 2009	806	5056

Act §	Code §	Topic	Generally effective date	Analysis ¶	Com Rep ¶
405(c)	280C(e)	A 20% credit is available for amounts paid or incurred in tax years beginning after Dec. 31, 2005 and before Jan. 1, 2009 for training mine rescue teams	Tax years beginning after Dec. 31, 2005 and before Jan. 1, 2009	806	5056
406(a)(1)(B)	7623(a)	Whistleblower rewards are increased, to maximum of 30% (up from 15%) of collected proceeds, interest, penalties, and additional amounts	Information provided on or after date of enactment	1409	5057
406(a)(1)(C)	7623(a)	Whistleblower rewards are increased, to maximum of 30% (up from 15%) of collected proceeds, interest, penalties, and additional amounts	Information provided on or after date of enactment	1409	5057
406(a)(1)(D)	7623(b)	Whistleblower rewards are increased, to maximum of 30% (up from 15%) of collected proceeds, interest, penalties, and additional amounts	Information provided on or after date of enactment	1409	5057
406(a)(2)(A)	7443A(b)(5)	Whistleblower rewards are increased, to maximum of 30% (up from 15%) of collected proceeds, interest, penalties, and additional amounts	Information provided on or after date of enactment	1409	5057
406(a)(3)	62(a)(21)	Above-the-line deduction is allowed for attorneys' fees and court costs relating to whistleblower rewards	Information provided on or after date of enactment	1410	5057
406(b)	7623	IRS Whistleblower Office is established to administer whistleblower reward program	Date of enactment	1411	5057
406(c)	7623	IRS Whistleblower Office is established to administer whistleblower reward program	Date of enactment	1411	5057
407(a)	6702	Penalty for frivolous submissions upped to $5,000, extended to other submissions	Submissions made and issues raised after IRS prescribes a list of frivolous positions	1407	5058

Act §	Code §	Topic	Generally effective date	Analysis ¶	Com Rep ¶
407(b)(1)	6330(g)	Frivolous submissions are subject to IRS dismissal	Submissions made and issues raised after IRS prescribes a list of frivolous positions	1408	5058
407(b)(2)	6330(c)(4)	Frivolous submissions are subject to IRS dismissal	Submissions made and issues raised after IRS prescribes a list of frivolous positions	1408	5058
407(b)(3)	6330(b)(1)	Frivolous submissions are subject to IRS dismissal	Submissions made and issues raised after IRS prescribes a list of frivolous positions	1408	5058
407(c)(1)	6320(b)(1)	Frivolous submissions are subject to IRS dismissal	Submissions made and issues raised after IRS prescribes a list of frivolous positions	1408	5058
407(c)(2)	6320(c)	Frivolous submissions are subject to IRS dismissal	Submissions made and issues raised after IRS prescribes a list of frivolous positions	1408	5058
407(d)	7122(f)	Frivolous submissions are subject to IRS dismissal	Submissions made and issues raised after IRS prescribes a list of frivolous positions	1408	5058
408(a)	4132(a)(1)(O)	Meningococcal vaccine and human papillomavirus vaccine is subject to 75 cents per dose manufacturers excise tax	Sales and uses on or after first day of first month beginning more than four weeks after date of enactment	1503	5059

Act §	Code §	Topic	Generally effective date	Analysis ¶	Com Rep ¶
408(a)(Div. C, Title IV)	6015(e)(1)	Tax Court has jurisdiction to review IRS's denial of equitable innocent spouse relief from joint liability even if no deficiency was asserted against the requestor of relief	Liability for taxes arising or remaining unpaid on or after date of enactment	1401	None
408(b)	4132(a)(1)(P)	Meningococcal vaccine and human papillomavirus vaccine is subject to 75 cents per dose manufacturers excise tax	Sales and uses on or after first day of first month beginning more than four weeks after date of enactment	1503	5059
408(b)(1)(Div. C, Title IV)	6015(e)(1)(A)(i)(II)	Tax Court has jurisdiction to review IRS's denial of equitable innocent spouse relief from joint liability even if no deficiency was asserted against the requestor of relief	Liability for taxes arising or remaining unpaid on or after date of enactment	1401	None
408(b)(2)(Div. C, Title IV)	6015(e)(1)(B)(i)	Tax Court has jurisdiction to review IRS's denial of equitable innocent spouse relief from joint liability even if no deficiency was asserted against the requestor of relief	Liability for taxes arising or remaining unpaid on or after date of enactment	1401	None
408(b)(3)(Div. C, Title IV)	6015(e)(1)(B)(ii)	Tax Court has jurisdiction to review IRS's denial of equitable innocent spouse relief from joint liability even if no deficiency was asserted against the requestor of relief	Liability for taxes arising or remaining unpaid on or after date of enactment	1401	None
408(b)(4)(Div. C, Title IV)	6015(e)(4)	Tax Court has jurisdiction to review IRS's denial of equitable innocent spouse relief from joint liability even if no deficiency was asserted against the requestor of relief	Liability for taxes arising or remaining unpaid on or after date of enactment	1401	None

Act §	Code §	Topic	Generally effective date	Analysis ¶	Com Rep ¶
408(b)(5)(Div. C, Title IV)	6015(e)(5)	Tax Court has jurisdiction to review IRS's denial of equitable innocent spouse relief from joint liability even if no deficiency was asserted against the requestor of relief	Liability for taxes arising or remaining unpaid on or after date of enactment	1401	None
408(b)(6)(Div. C, Title IV)	6015(g)(2)	Tax Court has jurisdiction to review IRS's denial of equitable innocent spouse relief from joint liability even if no deficiency was asserted against the requestor of relief	Liability for taxes arising or remaining unpaid on or after date of enactment	1401	None
408(b)(7)(Div. C, Title IV)	6015(h)(2)	Tax Court has jurisdiction to review IRS's denial of equitable innocent spouse relief from joint liability even if no deficiency was asserted against the requestor of relief	Liability for taxes arising or remaining unpaid on or after date of enactment	1401	None
409(a)	468B(g)(3)	Federal tax exemption for settlement funds and escrow accounts established for the sole purpose of resolving CERCLA claims is made permanent	Accounts and funds established after May 17, 2006	1605	5060
410(a)	355(b)(3)(A)	Code Sec. 355 active trade or business test that treats members of a separate affiliated group as one corporation made permanent	Distributions after May 17, 2006	1602	5061
410(a)	355(b)(3)(D)	Code Sec. 355 active trade or business test that treats members of a separate affiliated group as one corporation made permanent	Distributions after May 17, 2006	1602	5061
411(a)	143(l)(3)(B)	$25 million volume limits on qualified veterans' mortgage bonds issued by Alaska, Oregon, and Wisconsin won't sunset after 2010	Allocations of state volume limit after Apr. 5, 2006	1604	5062

Act §	Code §	Topic	Generally effective date	Analysis ¶	Com Rep ¶
412(a)	1221(b)(3)	Capital gain treatment for certain self-created musical works, originally set to expire Dec. 31, 2010, is made permanent	Sales and exchanges in tax years beginning after May 17, 2006	1601	5063
413(a)	1355(a)(4)	6,000 ton weight minimum for qualifying vessels in alternative tonnage tax regime made permanent	Tax years beginning after Dec 31, 2005	1608	5064
415	1355(g)	Great Lakes domestic shipping excepted from general rules on temporary domestic use of vessels for tonnage tax purposes	Tax years beginning after date of enactment	1609	5066
416(a)	143(d)(2)(D)	Qualified mortgage bonds can be used to finance mortgages for veterans without regard to first-time homebuyer requirement	Bonds issued after date of enactment, and before Jan. 1, 2008	1603	5067
417(a)	121(d)(9)(A)	Up to ten-year suspension of the five-year period for determining whether the principal residence gain exclusion applies is extended to apply to sales or exchanges by employees of the intelligence community before Jan. 1, 2011	Sales or exchanges after date of enactment and before Jan. 1, 2011	107	5068
417(b)	121(d)(9)(C)(iv)	Up to ten-year suspension of the five-year period for determining whether the principal residence gain exclusion applies is extended to apply to sales or exchanges by employees of the intelligence community before Jan. 1, 2011	Sales or exchanges after date of enactment and before Jan. 1, 2011	107	5068

Act §	Code §	Topic	Generally effective date	Analysis ¶	Com Rep ¶
417(c)	121(d)(9)(C)(vi)	Up to ten-year suspension of the five-year period for determining whether the principal residence gain exclusion applies is extended to apply to sales or exchanges by employees of the intelligence community before Jan. 1, 2011	Sales or exchanges after date of enactment and before Jan. 1, 2011	107	5068
418(a)(1)	1043(b)(1)	Federal judges can defer gain on conflict-of-interest sales	Sales after date of enactment	109	5069
418(a)(2)	1043(b)(2)	Federal judges can defer gain on conflict-of-interest sales	Sales after date of enactment	109	5069
418(a)(3)	1043(b)(5)(B)	Federal judges can defer gain on conflict-of-interest sales	Sales after date of enactment	109	5069
418(b)	1043(b)(6)	Federal judges can defer gain on conflict-of-interest sales	Sales after date of enactment	109	5069
419(a)	163(h)(3)(E)	Deduction is allowed for mortgage insurance premiums paid or incurred with respect to qualified residences in 2007, subject to phaseout based on AGI	Amounts paid or accrued after Dec. 31, 2006	104	5070
419(b)	163(h)(4)(E)	Deduction is allowed for mortgage insurance premiums paid or incurred with respect to qualified residences in 2007, subject to phaseout based on AGI	Amounts paid or accrued after Dec. 31, 2006 and before Jan. 1, 2008, for mortgage contracts issued after Dec. 31, 2006	104	5070

Act §	Code §	Topic	Generally effective date	Analysis ¶	Com Rep ¶
419(b)	163(h)(4)(F)	Deduction is allowed for mortgage insurance premiums paid or incurred with respect to qualified residences in 2007, subject to phaseout based on AGI	Amounts paid or accrued after Dec. 31, 2006 and before Jan. 1, 2008, for mortgage contracts issued after Dec. 31, 2006	104	5070
419(c)	6050H(h)	Deduction is allowed for mortgage insurance premiums paid or incurred with respect to qualified residences in 2007, subject to phaseout based on AGI	Amounts paid or accrued after Dec. 31, 2006 and before Jan. 1, 2008, for mortgage contracts issued after Dec. 31, 2006	104	5070
420(a)	6427(l)(4)	Ultimate purchaser of kerosene for exempt aviation use (other than state and local government) may claim excise tax refund itself, for fuel sold after Sept. 30, 2005	For kerosene sold after Sept. 30, 2005	1502	5071
420(b)(1)	6427(l)(5)	Ultimate purchaser of kerosene for exempt aviation use (other than state and local government) may claim excise tax refund itself, for fuel sold after Sept. 30, 2005	For kerosene sold after Sept. 30, 2005	1502	5071
421(a)	6103(b)(5)	Regional income tax agencies are treated as States for purposes of confidentiality and disclosure of returns and return information	Disclosures made after Dec. 31, 2006	1406	5072
421(b)	6103(d)(6)	Regional income tax agencies are treated as States for purposes of confidentiality and disclosure of returns and return information	Disclosures made after Dec. 31, 2006	1406	5072

Act §	Code §	Topic	Generally effective date	Analysis ¶	Com Rep ¶
423(a)	45G(d)	Qualified railroad track maintenance expenditures for purposes of the railroad track maintenance credit means "gross" expenditures; definition of expenditures is further modified	Tax years beginning after Dec. 31, 2004	1607	5074
424(a)	664(c)	Rules for taxing charitable remainder trusts' UBTI are modified	Tax years beginning after 2006	601	5075
425(a)	7872(h)(4)	Temporary TIPRA amendments that eliminated the dollar cap on below market loans to qualified continuing care facilities, and that eased other rules, are made permanent	Calendar years beginning after 2005 for loans made at any time	108	5076
426(a)(1)	954(c)(6)(A)	Look-through rule doesn't apply to dividends, interest, rents and royalties received from a CFC which are effectively connected with a U.S. trade or business for tax years beginning before 2009	Tax years of foreign corporations beginning after Dec. 31, 2005 and before Jan. 1, 2009 and tax years of U.S. shareholders with or within which such tax years of foreign corporations end	1301	5077
426(b)	6404(g)(2)	IRS's authority to exercise reasonable cause exception from continuation of interest on reportable avoidance transactions and listed transactions, is clarified	For interest accruing on, before, or after Oct. 3, 2004	1402	5077

¶ 6001. Code Section Cross Reference Table

Code §	Act §	Topic	Generally effective date	Analysis ¶	Com Rep ¶
25D(a)(1)	206(b)(1)	Residential energy efficient property credit is extended for one year, through 2008; solar energy property qualifying for credit is clarified	Date of enactment	105	5036
25D(b)(1)(A)	206(b)(1)	Residential energy efficient property credit is extended for one year, through 2008; solar energy property qualifying for credit is clarified	Date of enactment	105	5036
25D(d)(2)	206(b)(2)	Residential energy efficient property credit is extended for one year, through 2008; solar energy property qualifying for credit is clarified	Date of enactment	105	5036
25D(e)(4)(A)(i)	206(b)(1)	Residential energy efficient property credit is extended for one year, through 2008; solar energy property qualifying for credit is clarified	Date of enactment	105	5036
25D(g)	206(a)	Residential energy efficient property credit is extended for one year, through 2008; solar energy property qualifying for credit is clarified	Date of enactment	105	5036
30A	119	Possessions tax credit for American Samoa retroactively extended through 2007 for existing claimants	Tax years beginning after Dec. 31, 2005 and before Jan. 1, 2008	1303	5023
32(c)(2)(B)(vi)(II)	106(a)	Election to include combat pay as earned income for purposes of the earned income credit (EIC) is extended through 2007	Tax years beginning after Dec. 31, 2006	106	5010

Code §	Act §	Topic	Generally effective date	Analysis ¶	Com Rep ¶
38(b)(31)	405(b)	A 20% credit is available for amounts paid or incurred in tax years beginning after Dec. 31, 2005 and before Jan. 1, 2009 for training mine rescue teams	Tax years beginning after Dec. 31, 2005 and before Jan. 1, 2009	806	5056
41(c)(4)	104(c)(2)	Alternative simplified credit can be elected for qualified research expenses	Tax years ending after Dec. 31, 2006	203	5004
41(c)(4)	123(a)	Taxpayers with a tax year ending after 2005 have until Apr. 15, 2007 to make elections under expired provisions that are retroactively extended by the 2006 Tax Relief and Health Care Act	Tax years ending after Dec. 31, 2005 and before date of enactment	701	5029
41(c)(4)(A)	104(b)(1)	Rates for the elective alternative incremental research credit are increased	Tax years ending after Dec. 31, 2006	202	5004
41(c)(5)	104(c)(1)	Alternative simplified credit can be elected for qualified research expenses	Tax years ending after Dec. 31, 2006	203	5004
41(h)(1)(B)	104(a)(1)	Research credit is extended retroactively to amounts paid or incurred after Dec. 31, 2005 and before Jan. 1, 2008	Amounts paid or incurred after Dec. 31, 2005	201	5004
45(d)(1)	201	Placed-in-service date is extended for one year through Dec. 31, 2008 for certain qualified facilities for purposes of the credit for electricity produced from renewable resources	Facilities placed in service after Dec. 31, 2007	903	5031
45(d)(2)(A)	201	Placed-in-service date is extended for one year through Dec. 31, 2008 for certain qualified facilities for purposes of the credit for electricity produced from renewable resources	Facilities placed in service after Dec. 31, 2007	903	5031

Code §	Act §	Topic	Generally effective date	Analysis ¶	Com Rep ¶
45(d)(3)(A)	201	Placed-in-service date is extended for one year through Dec. 31, 2008 for certain qualified facilities for purposes of the credit for electricity produced from renewable resources	Facilities placed in service after Dec. 31, 2007	903	5031
45(d)(4)	201	Placed-in-service date is extended for one year through Dec. 31, 2008 for certain qualified facilities for purposes of the credit for electricity produced from renewable resources	Facilities placed in service after Dec. 31, 2007	903	5031
45(d)(5)	201	Placed-in-service date is extended for one year through Dec. 31, 2008 for certain qualified facilities for purposes of the credit for electricity produced from renewable resources	Facilities placed in service after Dec. 31, 2007	903	5031
45(d)(6)	201	Placed-in-service date is extended for one year through Dec. 31, 2008 for certain qualified facilities for purposes of the credit for electricity produced from renewable resources	Facilities placed in service after Dec. 31, 2007	903	5031
45(d)(7)	201	Placed-in-service date is extended for one year through Dec. 31, 2008 for certain qualified facilities for purposes of the credit for electricity produced from renewable resources	Facilities placed in service after Dec. 31, 2007	903	5031
45(d)(9)	201	Placed-in-service date is extended for one year through Dec. 31, 2008 for certain qualified facilities for purposes of the credit for electricity produced from renewable resources	Facilities placed in service after Dec. 31, 2007	903	5031

Code §	Act §	Topic	Generally effective date	Analysis ¶	Com Rep ¶
45A(f)	111(a)	Indian employment credit is extended retroactively for tax years beginning after Dec. 31, 2005 and before Jan. 1, 2008	Tax years beginning after Dec. 31, 2005 and before Jan. 1, 2008	807	5015
45C(b)(1)(D)	104(a)(2)	Research credit is extended retroactively to amounts paid or incurred after Dec. 31, 2005 and before Jan. 1, 2008	Amounts paid or incurred after Dec. 31, 2005	201	5004
45D(f)(1)(D)	102(a)	$3.5 billion new markets tax credit limitation is extended to include 2008	Date of enactment	1001	5002
45D(i)(6)	102(b)	New markets tax credit regs are to ensure that non-metropolitan counties receive a proportional allocation of qualified equity investments	Date of enactment	1002	5002
45G(d)	423(a)	Qualified railroad track maintenance expenditures for purposes of the railroad track maintenance credit means "gross" expenditures; definition of expenditures is further modified	Tax years beginning after Dec. 31, 2004	1607	5074
45K(g)(1)	211(b)	Nonconventional source production credit for coke and coke gas is not subject to the phase-out limitation, and the credit does not apply to a facility producing coke or coke gas from petroleum-based products	Fuel produced and sold after Dec. 31, 2005	904	5041
45K(g)(2)	211(a)	Nonconventional source production credit for coke and coke gas is not subject to the phase-out limitation, and the credit does not apply to a facility producing coke or coke gas from petroleum-based products	Fuel produced and sold after Dec. 31, 2005	904	5041

Code §	Act §	Topic	Generally effective date	Analysis ¶	Com Rep ¶
45L(g)	205	Energy efficient home credit for eligible contractors is extended through 2008	Qualified new energy efficient homes acquired after Dec. 31, 2007 and before Jan. 1, 2009	901	5035
45N	405(a)	A 20% credit is available for amounts paid or incurred in tax years beginning after Dec. 31, 2005 and before Jan. 1, 2009 for training mine rescue teams	Tax years beginning after Dec. 31, 2005 and before Jan. 1, 2009	806	5056
48(a)(2)(A)(i)(II)	207(1)	Increase in business energy tax credit for solar energy property from 10% to 30% is extended through Dec. 31, 2008, as are the 30% credit for qualified fuel cell propertyand the 10% credit for qualified microturbine property	Periods after Dec. 31, 2007 and before Jan. 1, 2009	902	5037
48(a)(3)(A)(ii)	207(1)	Increase in business energy tax credit for solar energy property from 10% to 30% is extended through Dec. 31, 2008, as are the 30% credit for qualified fuel cell propertyand the 10% credit for qualified microturbine property	Periods after Dec. 31, 2007 and before Jan. 1, 2009	902	5037
48(c)(1)(E)	207(2)	Increase in business energy tax credit for solar energy property from 10% to 30% is extended through Dec. 31, 2008, as are the 30% credit for qualified fuel cell propertyand the 10% credit for qualified microturbine property	Periods after Dec. 31, 2007 and before Jan. 1, 2009	902	5037

Code §	Act §	Topic	Generally effective date	Analysis ¶	Com Rep ¶
48(c)(2)(E)	207(2)	Increase in business energy tax credit for solar energy property from 10% to 30% is extended through Dec. 31, 2008, as are the 30% credit for qualified fuel cell propertyand the 10% credit for qualified microturbine property	Periods after Dec. 31, 2007 and before Jan. 1, 2009	902	5037
48A(f)(1)	203(a)	An alternative low-sulfur standard is met for advanced coal-based generation technology units using subbituminous coal where an emission level of 0.04 pounds or less of SO_2 per million Btu is achieved	Applications for certification submitted after Oct. 2, 2006	905	5033
51(c)(4)(B)	105(a)	Work opportunity credit is retroactively restored to Jan. 1, 2006 and is extended two years to Dec. 31, 2007 for most targeted groups	Individuals who begin work for the employer after Dec. 31, 2005 and before Jan. 1, 2008	801	5005
51(d)(1)(I)	105(e)(1)	Welfare-to-work credit is retroactively restored to Jan. 1, 2006 and, after Dec. 31, 2006, is consolidated with the work opportunity credit	Individuals who begin work for the employer after Dec. 31, 2006 and before Jan. 1, 2008	805	5005
51(d)(4)	105(b)	The "family low-income requirement" is eliminated for the work opportunity credit group consisting of "qualified ex-felons"	Individuals who begin work for the employer after Dec. 31, 2006 and before Jan. 1, 2008	804	5005
51(d)(8)(A)(i)	105(c)	Maximum age of a "qualified food stamp recipient" is increased from 24 to 39 for purposes of the work opportunity credit	Individuals who begin work for the employer after Dec. 31, 2006 and before Jan. 1, 2008	803	5005

Code §	Act §	Topic	Generally effective date	Analysis ¶	Com Rep ¶
1(d)(10)	105(e)(2)	Welfare-to-work credit is retroactively restored to Jan. 1, 2006 and, after Dec. 31, 2006, is consolidated with the work opportunity credit	Individuals who begin work for the employer after Dec. 31, 2006 and before Jan. 1, 2008	805	5005
1(d)(12)(A)(ii)(II)	105(d)	Deadline for submitting paperwork for certification of employees under the work opportunity credit is extended to 28 days after the beginning of work	Individuals who begin work for the employer after Dec. 31, 2006 and before Jan. 1, 2008	802	5005
51(e)	105(e)(3)	Welfare-to-work credit is retroactively restored to Jan. 1, 2006 and, after Dec. 31, 2006, is consolidated with the work opportunity credit	Individuals who begin work for the employer after Dec. 31, 2006 and before Jan. 1, 2008	805	5005
51A	105(e)(4)(A)	Welfare-to-work credit is retroactively restored to Jan. 1, 2006 and, after Dec. 31, 2006, is consolidated with the work opportunity credit	Individuals who begin work for the employer after Dec. 31, 2006 and before Jan. 1, 2008	805	5005
51A(f)	105(a)	Welfare-to-work credit is retroactively restored to Jan. 1, 2006 and, after Dec. 31, 2006, is consolidated with the work opportunity credit	Individuals who begin work for the employer after Dec. 31, 2005 and before Jan. 1, 2008	805	5005
53(e)	402(a)	Portion of minimum tax credit attributable to years before the third immediately preceding tax year is made refundable	Tax years beginning after date of enactment and before Jan. 1, 2013	1201	5053

Code §	Act §	Topic	Generally effective date	Analysis ¶	Com Rep ¶
54(f)(1)	202(a)(1)	National CREB limitation raised to $1.2 billion; amount allocable to governmental borrowers raised to $750 million; termination date for issuance of CREBs extended through end of 2008	Bonds issued after Dec. 31, 2006	906	5032
54(f)(2)	202(a)(2)	National CREB limitation raised to $1.2 billion; amount allocable to governmental borrowers raised to $750 million; termination date for issuance of CREBs extended through end of 2008	Allocations or reallocations made after Dec. 31, 2006	906	5032
54(m)	202(a)(3)	National CREB limitation raised to $1.2 billion; amount allocable to governmental borrowers raised to $750 million; termination date for issuance of CREBs extended through end of 2008	Bonds issued after Dec. 31, 2006	906	5032
61	403(c)(Div. C, Title IV)	25% of qualifying gain from conservation sales of qualifying mineral or geothermal interests excluded from gross income	Sales on or after date of enactment	1606	5079
62(a)(2)(D)	108(a)	Up-to-$250 above-the-line deduction for teachers' out-of-pocket classroom-related expenses is retroactively extended for two years through 2007	Expenses paid or incurred in tax years beginning after Dec. 31, 2005 and before Jan. 1, 2008	103	5012
62(a)(21)	406(a)(3)	Above-the-line deduction is allowed for attorneys' fees and court costs relating to whistleblower rewards	Information provided on or after date of enactment	1410	5057
106(e)	302(a)	One-time rollovers from health FSAs and HRAs into HSAs permitted through 2011	For distributions on or after date of enactment	302	5045

Code §	Act §	Topic	Generally effective date	Analysis ¶	Com Rep ¶
121(d)(9)(A)	417(a)	Up to ten-year suspension of the five-year period for determining whether the principal residence gain exclusion applies is extended to apply to sales or exchanges by employees of the intelligence community before Jan. 1, 2011	Sales or exchanges after date of enactment and before Jan. 1, 2011	107	5068
121(d)(9)(C)(iv)	417(b)	Up to ten-year suspension of the five-year period for determining whether the principal residence gain exclusion applies is extended to apply to sales or exchanges by employees of the intelligence community before Jan. 1, 2011	Sales or exchanges after date of enactment and before Jan. 1, 2011	107	5068
121(d)(9)(C)(vi)	417(c)	Up to ten-year suspension of the five-year period for determining whether the principal residence gain exclusion applies is extended to apply to sales or exchanges by employees of the intelligence community before Jan. 1, 2011	Sales or exchanges after date of enactment and before Jan. 1, 2011	107	5068
143(d)(2)(D)	416(a)	Qualified mortgage bonds can be used to finance mortgages for veterans without regard to first-time homebuyer requirement	Bonds issued after date of enactment, and before Jan. 1, 2008	1603	5067
143(l)(3)(B)	411(a)	$25 million volume limits on qualified veterans' mortgage bonds issued by Alaska, Oregon, and Wisconsin won't sunset after 2010	Allocations of state volume limit after Apr. 5, 2006	1604	5062

Code §	Act §	Topic	Generally effective date	Analysis ¶	Com Rep ¶
163(h)(3)(E)	419(a)	Deduction is allowed for mortgage insurance premiums paid or incurred with respect to qualified residences in 2007, subject to phaseout based on AGI	Amounts paid or accrued after Dec. 31, 2006 and before Jan. 1, 2008, for mortgage contracts issued after Dec. 31, 2006	104	5070
163(h)(4)(E)	419(b)	Deduction is allowed for mortgage insurance premiums paid or incurred with respect to qualified residences in 2007, subject to phaseout based on AGI	Amounts paid or accrued after Dec. 31, 2006 and before Jan. 1, 2008, for mortgage contracts issued after Dec. 31, 2006	104	5070
163(h)(4)(F)	419(b)	Deduction is allowed for mortgage insurance premiums paid or incurred with respect to qualified residences in 2007, subject to phaseout based on AGI	Amounts paid or accrued after Dec. 31, 2006 and before Jan. 1, 2008, for mortgage contracts issued after Dec. 31, 2006	104	5070
164(b)(5)(I)	103(a)	Election to claim itemized deduction for state and local general sales taxes is retroactively extended from 2005 through 2007	Tax years beginning after Dec. 31, 2005 and before Jan. 1, 2008	101	5003
168(e)(3)(E)(iv)	113(a)	Placed-in-service deadline for the treatment of "qualified leasehold improvement property" as 15-year MACRS property is retroactively restored to Jan. 1, 2006 and is extended for two years to Dec. 31, 2007	Property placed in service after Dec. 31, 2005 and before Jan. 1, 2008	502	5017

Code §	Act §	Topic	Generally effective date	Analysis ¶	Com Rep ¶
168(e)(3)(E)(v)	113(a)	Placed-in-service deadline for the treatment of "qualified restaurant property" as 15-year MACRS property is retroactively restored to Jan. 1, 2006 and is extended for two years to Dec. 31, 2007	Property placed in service after Dec. 31, 2005 and before Jan. 1, 2008	503	5017
168(j)(8)	112(a)	Depreciation tax breaks for Indian reservation property are extended retroactively to property placed in service after Dec. 31, 2005 and before Jan. 1, 2008	Property placed in service after Dec. 31, 2005 and before Jan. 1, 2008	510	5016
168(l)	209(a)	50% bonus depreciation and AMT relief are allowed for "qualified cellulosic biomass ethanol plant property" purchased after date of enactment and placed in service before Jan. 1, 2013	Property purchased after date of enactment and placed in service before Jan. 1, 2013	508	5039
170(e)(4)(B)(ii)	116(b)(1)(A)	Property assembled by donor qualifies for enhanced deduction for qualified research contributions and qualified computer contributions	Tax years beginning after Dec. 31, 2005	603	5020
170(e)(4)(B)(iii)	116(b)(1)(B)	Property assembled by donor qualifies for enhanced deduction for qualified research contributions and qualified computer contributions	Tax years beginning after Dec. 31, 2005	603	5020
170(e)(6)(B)(ii)	116(b)(2)(A)	Property assembled by donor qualifies for enhanced deduction for qualified research contributions and qualified computer contributions	Tax years beginning after Dec. 31, 2005	603	5020
170(e)(6)(D)	116(b)(2)(B)	Property assembled by donor qualifies for enhanced deduction for qualified research contributions and qualified computer contributions	Tax years beginning after Dec. 31, 2005	603	5020

Code §	Act §	Topic	Generally effective date	Analysis ¶	Com Rep ¶
170(e)(6)(G)	116(a)(1)	Enhanced deduction for qualified computer contributions by corporations is retroactively extended for two years through 2007	Contributions made in tax years beginning after Dec. 31, 2005, and before Jan. 1, 2008	602	5020
179D(h)	204	Deduction for energy efficient commercial building property is extended for one year through Dec. 31, 2008	Date of enactment	501	5034
179E	404(a)	Taxpayers can elect to expense 50% of the cost of "qualified advanced mine safety equipment property" placed in service after date of enactment and before Jan. 1, 2009	Costs paid or incurred after date of enactment	509	5055
198(d)(1)	109(b)	Definition of hazardous substances for purposes of expensing election for environmental remediation costs is expanded to include petroleum products	Expenditures paid or incurred after Dec. 31, 2005	506	5013
198(h)	109(a)	Election to expense qualified environmental remediation costs is retroactively restored and is extended for two years to apply to expenditures paid or incurred after Dec. 31, 2005 and before Jan. 1, 2008	Expenditures paid or incurred after Dec. 31, 2005 and before Jan. 1, 2008	505	5013
199(d)(8)	401(a)	Domestic production activities deduction extended retroactively to production activities in Puerto Rico for first two tax years beginning after 2005	First two tax years beginning after Dec. 31, 2005 and before Jan. 1, 2008	1302	5052
220(i)(2)	117(a)	Archer MSA program is extended through 2007—trustees' reports for 2005 and 2006 will be timely if made within 90 days of date of enactment	Date of enactment	307	5021

Code §	Act §	Topic	Generally effective date	Analysis ¶	Com Rep ¶
22(b)(2)(B)	101(b)(1)	Above-the-line deduction for higher-education expenses is retroactively extended from 2005 through 2007	Tax years beginning after Dec. 31, 2005 and before Jan. 1, 2008	102	5001
22(e)	101(a)	Above-the-line deduction for higher-education expenses is retroactively extended from 2005 through 2007	Tax years beginning after Dec. 31, 2005 and before Jan. 1, 2008	102	5001
23(b)(2)	303(a)	Limit on HSA contributions is no longer restricted by health plan's annual deductible	For tax years beginning after Dec. 31, 2006	303	5045
23(b)(4)(C)	307(b)	Eligible individuals may elect one-time tax-free rollover of IRA distribution into an HSA	Tax years beginning after Dec. 31, 2006	301	5045
23(b)(8)	305(a)	Individuals who establish health savings accounts mid-year can contribute the full-year amount	Tax years beginning after Dec. 31, 2006	306	5045
23(c)(1)(B)(iii)	302(b)	One-time rollovers from health FSAs and HRAs into HSAs permitted through 2011	For distributions on or after date of enactment	302	5045
23(g)(1)	304	Cost-of-living adjustment for HSA and HDHP dollar amounts is modified—tax years beginning after 2007	For adjustments made for tax years beginning after 2007	305	5045
263(a)(1)(L)	404(b)(1)	Taxpayers can elect to expense 50% of the cost of "qualified advanced mine safety equipment property" placed in service after date of enactment and before Jan. 1, 2009	Costs paid or incurred after date of enactment	509	5055
280C(c)(3)(C)	123(a)	Taxpayers with a tax year ending after 2005 have until Apr. 15, 2007 to make elections under expired provisions that are retroactively extended by the 2006 Tax Relief and Health Care Act	Tax years ending after Dec. 31, 2005 and before date of enactment	701	5029

Code §	Act §	Topic	Generally effective date	Analysis ¶	Com Rep ¶
280C(e)	405(c)	A 20% credit is available for amounts paid or incurred in tax years beginning after Dec. 31, 2005 and before Jan. 1, 2009 for training mine rescue teams	Tax years beginning after Dec. 31, 2005 and before Jan. 1, 2009	806	5056
312(k)(3)(B)	404(b)(2)	Taxpayers can elect to expense 50% of the cost of "qualified advanced mine safety equipment property" placed in service after date of enactment and before Jan. 1, 2009	Costs paid or incurred after date of enactment	509	5055
355(b)(3)(A)	410(a)	Code Sec. 355 active trade or business test that treats members of a separate affiliated group as one corporation made permanent	Distributions after May 17, 2006	1602	5061
355(b)(3)(D)	410(a)	Code Sec. 355 active trade or business test that treats members of a separate affiliated group as one corporation made permanent	Distributions after May 17, 2006	1602	5061
408(d)(9)	307(a)	Eligible individuals may elect one-time tax-free rollover of IRA distribution into an HSA	Tax years beginning after Dec. 31, 2006	301	5045
468B(g)(3)	409(a)	Federal tax exemption for settlement funds and escrow accounts established for the sole purpose of resolving CERCLA claims is made permanent	Accounts and funds established after May 17, 2006	1605	5060
613A(c)(6)(H)	118(a)	Suspension of taxable income limitation on percentage depletion from marginal oil and gas wells is retroactively extended for two years to include tax years beginning before Jan. 1, 2008	Tax years beginning after Dec. 31, 2005 and before Jan. 1, 2008	507	5022
664(c)	424(a)	Rules for taxing charitable remainder trusts' UBTI are modified	Tax years beginning after 2006	601	5075

Code §	Act §	Topic	Generally effective date	Analysis ¶	Com Rep ¶
954(c)(6)(A)	426(a)(1)	Look-through rule doesn't apply to dividends, interest, rents and royalties received from a CFC which are effectively connected with a U.S. trade or business for tax years beginning before 2009	Tax years of foreign corporations beginning after Dec. 31, 2005 and before Jan. 1, 2009 and tax years of U.S. shareholders with or within which such tax years of foreign corporations end	1301	5077
1043(b)(1)	418(a)(1)	Federal judges can defer gain on conflict-of-interest sales	Sales after date of enactment	109	5069
1043(b)(2)	418(a)(2)	Federal judges can defer gain on conflict-of-interest sales	Sales after date of enactment	109	5069
1043(b)(5)(B)	418(a)(3)	Federal judges can defer gain on conflict-of-interest sales	Sales after date of enactment	109	5069
1043(b)(6)	418(b)	Federal judges can defer gain on conflict-of-interest sales	Sales after date of enactment	109	5069
1221(b)(3)	412(a)	Capital gain treatment for certain self-created musical works, originally set to expire Dec. 31, 2010, is made permanent	Sales and exchanges in tax years beginning after May 17, 2006	1601	5063
1245(a)(2)(C)	404(b)(3)	Taxpayers can elect to expense 50% of the cost of "qualified advanced mine safety equipment property" placed in service after date of enactment and before Jan. 1, 2009	Costs paid or incurred after date of enactment	509	5055
1245(a)(3)(C)	404(b)(3)	Taxpayers can elect to expense 50% of the cost of "qualified advanced mine safety equipment property" placed in service after date of enactment and before Jan. 1, 2009	Costs paid or incurred after date of enactment	509	5055

Code §	Act §	Topic	Generally effective date	Analysis ¶	Com Rep ¶
1355(a)(4)	413(a)	6,000 ton weight minimum for qualifying vessels in alternative tonnage tax regime made permanent	Tax years beginning after Dec 31, 2005	1608	5064
1355(g)	415	Great Lakes domestic shipping excepted from general rules on temporary domestic use of vessels for tonnage tax purposes	Tax years beginning after date of enactment	1609	5066
1397E(d)(1)(E)	107(b)(1)(A)	Qualified zone academy bond issuers must meet new expenditure, arbitrage, and reporting requirements	Obligations issued after date of enactment	1004	5011
1397E(e)(1)	107(a)	Permitted issuance of qualified zone academy bonds of up to $400 million per year is extended retroactively through Dec. 31, 2007	Obligations issued after Dec. 31, 2005 and before Jan. 1, 2008	1003	5011
1397E(f)	107(b)(1)(B)	Qualified zone academy bond issuers must meet new expenditure, arbitrage, and reporting requirements	Obligations issued after date of enactment	1004	5011
1397E(g)	107(b)(1)(B)	Qualified zone academy bond issuers must meet new expenditure, arbitrage, and reporting requirements	Obligations issued after date of enactment	1004	5011
1397E(h)	107(b)(1)(B)	Qualified zone academy bond issuers must meet new expenditure, arbitrage, and reporting requirements	Obligations issued after date of enactment	1004	5011
1400(f)(1)	110(a)(1)	DC Enterprise Zone and enterprise community designations are retroactively extended for two years through Dec. 31, 2007	Periods beginning after Dec. 31, 2005 and ending before Jan. 1, 2008	1103	5014
1400(f)(2)	110(a)(1)	DC Enterprise Zone and enterprise community designations are retroactively extended for two years through Dec. 31, 2007	Periods beginning after Dec. 31, 2005 and ending before Jan. 1, 2008	1103	5014

Code §	Act §	Topic	Generally effective date	Analysis ¶	Com Rep ¶
400A(b)	110(b)(1)	Higher tax-exempt enterprise zone facility bond limit for DC Zone bonds is retroactively extended to apply to bonds issued after Dec. 31, 2005 and before Jan. 1, 2008	Bonds issued after Dec. 31, 2005 and before Jan. 1, 2008	1104	5014
1400B(b)(2)(A)(i)	110(c)(1)	Zero percent capital gains rate for DC Zone assets is retroactively extended for two years to apply to assets acquired before Jan. 1, 2008 and includes gain attributable to periods before Jan. 1, 2013	Acquisitions after Dec. 31, 2005 and before Jan. 1, 2008	1102	5014
1400B(b)(3)(A)	110(c)(1)	Zero percent capital gains rate for DC Zone assets is retroactively extended for two years to apply to assets acquired before Jan. 1, 2008 and includes gain attributable to periods before Jan. 1, 2013	Acquisitions after Dec. 31, 2005 and before Jan. 1, 2008	1102	5014
1400B(b)(4)(A)(i)	110(c)(1)	Zero percent capital gains rate for DC Zone assets is retroactively extended for two years to apply to assets acquired before Jan. 1, 2008 and includes gain attributable to periods before Jan. 1, 2013	Acquisitions after Dec. 31, 2005 and before Jan. 1, 2008	1102	5014
1400B(b)(4)(B)(i)(I)	110(c)(1)	Zero percent capital gains rate for DC Zone assets is retroactively extended for two years to apply to assets acquired before Jan. 1, 2008 and includes gain attributable to periods before Jan. 1, 2013	Acquisitions after Dec. 31, 2005 and before Jan. 1, 2008	1102	5014

Code §	Act §	Topic	Generally effective date	Analysis ¶	Com Rep ¶
1400B(e)(2)	110(c)(2)(A)(i)	Zero percent capital gains rate for DC Zone assets is retroactively extended for two years to apply to assets acquired before Jan. 1, 2008 and includes gain attributable to periods before Jan. 1, 2013	Date of enactment	1102	5014
1400B(g)(2)	110(c)(2)(B)	Zero percent capital gains rate for DC Zone assets is retroactively extended for two years to apply to assets acquired before Jan. 1, 2008 and includes gain attributable to periods before Jan. 1, 2013	Date of enactment	1102	5014
1400C(i)	110(d)(1)	DC homebuyer credit is retroactively extended for two years to apply to property bought before Jan. 1, 2008	Property bought after Dec. 31, 2005 and before Jan. 1, 2008	1101	5014
1400N(d)(6)	120(a)	Placed-in-service deadline for "qualified Gulf Opportunity Zone property" is for some purposes extended to Dec. 31, 2010 (and to as much as 90 days beyond) for certain property used in highly damaged portions of the GO Zone	Tax years beginning after Aug. 27, 2005	504	5024
1400N(e)(2)	120(b)	Placed-in-service deadline for "qualified Gulf Opportunity Zone property" is for some purposes extended to Dec. 31, 2010 (and to as much as 90 days beyond) for certain property used in highly damaged portions of the GO Zone	Tax years beginning after Aug. 27, 2005	504	5024
4041(b)(2)(C)(ii)	208(b)	Reduced retail excise tax rates for qualified methanol and qualified ethanol fuels (scheduled to terminate after Sept. 30, 2007) are extended through Dec. 31, 2008	Date of enactment	1501	5038

Code §	Act §	Topic	Generally effective date	Analysis ¶	Com Rep ¶
4041(b)(2)(D)	208(a)	Reduced retail excise tax rates for qualified methanol and qualified ethanol fuels (scheduled to terminate after Sept. 30, 2007) are extended through Dec. 31, 2008	Date of enactment	1501	5038
4132(a)(1)(O)	408(a)	Meningococcal vaccine and human papillomavirus vaccine is subject to 75 cents per dose manufacturers excise tax	Sales and uses on or after first day of first month beginning more than four weeks after date of enactment	1503	5059
4132(a)(1)(P)	408(b)	Meningococcal vaccine and human papillomavirus vaccine is subject to 75 cents per dose manufacturers excise tax	Sales and uses on or after first day of first month beginning more than four weeks after date of enactment	1503	5059
4980G(d)	306(a)	Employers can make larger HSA contributions for nonhighly compensated employees than for highly compensated employees, without violating comparability rule	Tax years beginning after Dec. 31, 2006	304	5045
6015(e)(1)	408(a)(Div. C, Title IV)	Tax Court has jurisdiction to review IRS's denial of equitable innocent spouse relief from joint liability even if no deficiency was asserted against the requestor of relief	Liability for taxes arising or remaining unpaid on or after date of enactment	1401	None
6015(e)(1)(A)(i)(II)	408(b)(1)(Div. C, Title IV)	Tax Court has jurisdiction to review IRS's denial of equitable innocent spouse relief from joint liability even if no deficiency was asserted against the requestor of relief	Liability for taxes arising or remaining unpaid on or after date of enactment	1401	None

Code §	Act §	Topic	Generally effective date	Analysis ¶	Com Re ¶
6015(e)(1)(B)(i)	408(b)(2)(Div. C, Title IV)	Tax Court has jurisdiction to review IRS's denial of equitable innocent spouse relief from joint liability even if no deficiency was asserted against the requestor of relief	Liability for taxes arising or remaining unpaid on or after date of enactment	1401	None
6015(e)(1)(B)(ii)	408(b)(3)(Div. C, Title IV)	Tax Court has jurisdiction to review IRS's denial of equitable innocent spouse relief from joint liability even if no deficiency was asserted against the requestor of relief	Liability for taxes arising or remaining unpaid on or after date of enactment	1401	None
6015(e)(4)	408(b)(4)(Div. C, Title IV)	Tax Court has jurisdiction to review IRS's denial of equitable innocent spouse relief from joint liability even if no deficiency was asserted against the requestor of relief	Liability for taxes arising or remaining unpaid on or after date of enactment	1401	None
6015(e)(5)	408(b)(5)(Div. C, Title IV)	Tax Court has jurisdiction to review IRS's denial of equitable innocent spouse relief from joint liability even if no deficiency was asserted against the requestor of relief	Liability for taxes arising or remaining unpaid on or after date of enactment	1401	None
6015(g)(2)	408(b)(6)(Div. C, Title IV)	Tax Court has jurisdiction to review IRS's denial of equitable innocent spouse relief from joint liability even if no deficiency was asserted against the requestor of relief	Liability for taxes arising or remaining unpaid on or after date of enactment	1401	None
6015(h)(2)	408(b)(7)(Div. C, Title IV)	Tax Court has jurisdiction to review IRS's denial of equitable innocent spouse relief from joint liability even if no deficiency was asserted against the requestor of relief	Liability for taxes arising or remaining unpaid on or after date of enactment	1401	None

Code §	Act §	Topic	Generally effective date	Analysis ¶	Com Rep ¶
6039(a)	403(a)	Corporations must report to IRS transfers of stock from exercises of incentive stock options or purchases from employee stock purchase plans	Calendar years beginning after date of enactment	401	5053
6039(b)	403(b)	Corporations must report to IRS transfers of stock from exercises of incentive stock options or purchases from employee stock purchase plans	Calendar years beginning after date of enactment	401	5053
6050H(h)	419(c)	Deduction is allowed for mortgage insurance premiums paid or incurred with respect to qualified residences in 2007, subject to phaseout based on AGI	Amounts paid or accrued after Dec. 31, 2006	104	5070
6103(b)(5)	421(a)	Regional income tax agencies are treated as States for purposes of confidentiality and disclosure of returns and return information	Disclosures made after Dec. 31, 2006	1406	5072
6103(d)(5)(B)	122(a)(1)	IRS's authority to disclose taxpayer identity information to facilitate combined federal/state employment tax reporting is extended for one year through Dec. 31, 2007	Disclosures after Dec. 31, 2006 and before Jan. 1, 2008	1403	5026
6103(d)(6)	421(b)	Regional income tax agencies are treated as States for purposes of confidentiality and disclosure of returns and return information	Disclosures made after Dec. 31, 2006	1406	5072
6103(i)(3)(C)(iv)	122(b)(1)	IRS's authority to disclose tax information in terrorism and national security investigations is extended for one year through Dec. 31, 2007	Disclosures after Dec. 31, 2006 and before Jan. 1, 2008	1405	5027
6103(i)(7)(E)	122(b)(1)	IRS's authority to disclose tax information in terrorism and national security investigations is extended for one year through Dec. 31, 2007	Disclosures after Dec. 31, 2006 and before Jan. 1, 2008	1405	5027

Code §	Act §	Topic	Generally effective date	Analysis ¶	Com Rep ¶
6103(l)(13)(D)	122(c)(1)	IRS's authority to disclose requested return information to the Dept. of Education to monitor income-contingent student loan repayments is extended for one year for requests made through Dec. 31, 2007	Requests made after Dec. 31, 2006 and before Jan. 1, 2008	1404	5028
6211(b)(4)(A)	402(b)(1)	AMT refundable credit may result in negative amount of tax in deficiency computation	Tax years beginning after date of enactment	1202	5053
6320(b)(1)	407(c)(1)	Frivolous submissions are subject to IRS dismissal	Submissions made and issues raised after IRS prescribes a list of frivolous positions	1408	5058
6320(c)	407(c)(2)	Frivolous submissions are subject to IRS dismissal	Submissions made and issues raised after IRS prescribes a list of frivolous positions	1408	5058
6330(b)(1)	407(b)(3)	Frivolous submissions are subject to IRS dismissal	Submissions made and issues raised after IRS prescribes a list of frivolous positions	1408	5058
6330(c)(4)	407(b)(2)	Frivolous submissions are subject to IRS dismissal	Submissions made and issues raised after IRS prescribes a list of frivolous positions	1408	5058
6330(g)	407(b)(1)	Frivolous submissions are subject to IRS dismissal	Submissions made and issues raised after IRS prescribes a list of frivolous positions	1408	5058

Code §	Act §	Topic	Generally effective date	Analysis ¶	Com Rep ¶
6404(g)(2)	426(b)	IRS's authority to exercise reasonable cause exception from continuation of interest on reportable avoidance transactions and listed transactions, is clarified	For interest accruing on, before, or after Oct. 3, 2004	1402	5077
6427(l)(4)	420(a)	Ultimate purchaser of kerosene for exempt aviation use (other than state and local government) may claim excise tax refund itself, for fuel sold after Sept. 30, 2005	For kerosene sold after Sept. 30, 2005	1502	5071
6427(l)(5)	420(b)(1)	Ultimate purchaser of kerosene for exempt aviation use (other than state and local government) may claim excise tax refund itself, for fuel sold after Sept. 30, 2005	For kerosene sold after Sept. 30, 2005	1502	5071
6702	407(a)	Penalty for frivolous submissions upped to $5,000, extended to other submissions	Submissions made and issues raised after IRS prescribes a list of frivolous positions	1407	5058
6724(d)(1)(B)(xix)	403(c)(1)	Corporations must report to IRS transfers of stock from exercises of incentive stock options or purchases from employee stock purchase plans	Calendar years beginning after date of enactment	401	5053
7122(f)	407(d)	Frivolous submissions are subject to IRS dismissal	Submissions made and issues raised after IRS prescribes a list of frivolous positions	1408	5058
7443A(b)(5)	406(a)(2)(A)	Whistleblower rewards are increased, to maximum of 30% (up from 15%) of collected proceeds, interest, penalties, and additional amounts	Information provided on or after date of enactment	1409	5057

Code §	Act §	Topic	Generally effective date	Analysis ¶	Com Rep ¶
7608(c)(6)	121	IRS's authority to churn income earned from undercover operations is extended through 2007	Date of enactment	1412	5025
7623	406(b)	IRS Whistleblower Office is established to administer whistleblower reward program	Date of enactment	1411	5057
7623	406(c)	IRS Whistleblower Office is established to administer whistleblower reward program	Date of enactment	1411	5057
7623(a)	406(a)(1)(B)	Whistleblower rewards are increased, to maximum of 30% (up from 15%) of collected proceeds, interest, penalties, and additional amounts	Information provided on or after date of enactment	1409	5057
7623(a)	406(a)(1)(C)	Whistleblower rewards are increased, to maximum of 30% (up from 15%) of collected proceeds, interest, penalties, and additional amounts	Information provided on or after date of enactment	1409	5057
7623(b)	406(a)(1)(D)	Whistleblower rewards are increased, to maximum of 30% (up from 15%) of collected proceeds, interest, penalties, and additional amounts	Information provided on or after date of enactment	1409	5057
7872(h)(4)	425(a)	Temporary TIPRA amendments that eliminated the dollar cap on below market loans to qualified continuing care facilities, and that eased other rules, are made permanent	Calendar years beginning after 2005 for loans made at any time	108	5076
9812(f)(3)	115(a)	Mental health parity requirements extended through 2007	Date of enactment	402	5019
None	123(b)	Taxpayers with a tax year ending after 2005 have until Apr. 15, 2007 to make elections under expired provisions that are retroactively extended by the 2006 Tax Relief and Health Care Act	Tax years ending after Dec. 31, 2005 and before date of enactment	701	5029

Code §	Act §	Topic	Generally effective date	Analysis ¶	Com Rep ¶
None	403(a)(Div. C, Title IV)	25% of qualifying gain from conservation sales of qualifying mineral or geothermal interests excluded from gross income	Sales on or after date of enactment	1606	5079
None	403(b)(2)(Div. C, Title IV)	25% of qualifying gain from conservation sales of qualifying mineral or geothermal interests excluded from gross income	Sales on or after date of enactment	1606	5079

¶ 6002. Code Sections Amended by Act

Code Sec.	Act Sec.	Code Sec.	Act Sec.
25D(a)(1)	206(b)(1)	45L(g)	205
25D(b)(1)(A)	206(b)(1)	45N	405(a)
25D(d)(2)	206(b)(2)(A)	48	207(1)
25D(d)(2)	206(b)(2)(B)	48	207(2)
25D(e)(4)(A)(i)	206(b)(1)	48A(f)(1)	203(a)
25D(g)	206(a)	51(c)(4)(B)	105(a)
32(c)(2)(B)(vi)(II)	106(a)	51(d)(1)(G)	105(e)(1)
38(b)(29)	405(b)	51(d)(1)(H)	105(e)(1)
38(b)(30)	405(b)	51(d)(1)(I)	105(e)(1)
38(b)(31)	405(b)	51(d)(4)(A)	105(b)
41(c)(4)(A)	104(b)(1)(A)	51(d)(4)(B)	105(b)
41(c)(4)(A)	104(b)(1)(B)	51(d)(4)(C)	105(b)
41(c)(4)(A)	104(b)(1)(C)	51(d)(8)(A)(i)	105(c)
41(c)(5)	104(c)(1)	51(d)(10)	105(e)(2)
41(c)(6)	104(c)(1)	51(d)(11)	105(e)(2)
41(c)(7)	104(c)(1)	51(d)(12)	105(e)(2)
41(h)(1)(B)	104(a)(1)	51(d)(12)(A)(ii)(II)	105(d)
45(d)	201	51(d)(13)	105(e)(2)
45A(f)	111(a)	51(e)	105(e)(3)
45C(b)(1)(D)	104(a)(2)	51A(f)	105(a)
45D(f)(1)(D)	102(a)	53(e)	402(a)
45D(i)(4)	102(b)	54(f)(1)	202(a)(1)
45D(i)(5)	102(b)	54(f)(2)	202(a)(2)
45D(i)(6)	102(b)	54(l)(3)(B)	107(b)(2)
45G(d)	423(a)(1)	54(m)	202(a)(3)
45G(d)	423(a)(2)	62(a)(2)(D)	108(a)
45K(g)(1)	211(b)	62(a)(21)	406(a)(3)
45K(g)(2)(D)	211(a)	106(e)	302(a)

Code Sec.	Act Sec.	Code Sec.	Act Sec.
121(d)(9)	417(d)	199(d)(8)	401(a)
121(d)(9)(A)	417(a)	199(d)(9)	401(a)
121(d)(9)(C)(iv)	417(b)	220	117(c)
121(d)(9)(C)(v)	417(b)	220(i)(2)	117(a)
121(d)(9)(C)(vi)	417(c)	220(i)(3)(B)	117(a)
143(d)(2)(B)	416(a)	220(j)(2)	117(b)(1)(A)
143(d)(2)(C)	416(a)	220(j)(2)	117(b)(1)(B)
143(d)(2)(D)	416(a)	220(j)(4)(A)	117(b)(2)
143(l)(3)(B)	411(a)	222(b)(2)(B)	101(b)(1)
148	414(a)	222(b)(2)(B)	101(b)(2)
163(h)(3)(E)	419(a)	222(e)	101(a)
163(h)(4)(E)	419(b)	223(b)(2)(A)	303(a)(1)
163(h)(4)(F)	419(b)	223(b)(2)(B)	303(a)(2)
164(b)(5)(I)	103(a)	223(b)(4)(A)	307(b)
168(e)(3)(E)(iv)	113(a)	223(b)(4)(B)	307(b)
168(e)(3)(E)(v)	113(a)	223(b)(4)(C)	307(b)
168(j)(8)	112(a)	223(b)(8)	305(a)
168(l)	209(a)	223(c)(1)(B)(i)	302(b)
170(e)(4)(B)(ii)	116(b)(1)(A)	223(c)(1)(B)(ii)	302(b)
170(e)(4)(B)(iii)	116(b)(1)(B)	223(c)(1)(B)(iii)	302(b)
170(e)(6)(B)(ii)	116(b)(2)(A)	223(d)(1)(A)(ii)(I)	303(b)
170(e)(6)(D)	116(b)(2)(B)	223(g)(1)	304
170(e)(6)(G)	116(a)(1)	263(a)(1)(J)	404(b)(1)
179D(h)	204	263(a)(1)(K)	404(b)(1)
179E	404(a)	263(a)(1)(L)	404(b)(1)
198(d)(1)(A)	109(b)	280C	123
198(d)(1)(B)	109(b)	280C(e)	405(c)
198(d)(1)(C)	109(b)	312(k)(3)(B)	404(b)(2)
198(h)	109(a)	355(b)(3)(A)	410(a)

Code Sec.	Act Sec.	Code Sec.	Act Sec.
355(b)(3)(D)	410(a)	1397E(k)	107(b)(1)(B)
408(d)(9)	307(a)	1397E(l)	107(b)(1)(B)
468B(g)(3)	409(a)	1400(f)	110(a)(1)
613A(c)(6)(H)	118(a)	1400A(b)	110(b)(1)
664(c)	424(a)	1400B(b)	110(c)(1)
936	119	1400B(e)(2)	110(c)(2)(A)(i)
954(c)(6)(A)	426(a)(1)(A)	1400B(e)(2)	110(c)(2)(A)(ii)
954(c)(6)(A)	426(a)(1)(B)	1400B(g)(2)	110(c)(2)(B)
1043(b)(1)(A)	418(a)(1)(A)	1400C(i)	110(d)(1)
1043(b)(1)(B)	418(a)(1)(B)	1400F(d)	110(c)(2)(C)
1043(b)(2)(A)	418(a)(2)(A)	1400N(d)(6)	120(a)
1043(b)(2)(B)	418(a)(2)(B)	1400N(e)(2)	120(b)
1043(b)(5)(B)	418(a)(3)	1400N(l)(7)(B)(ii)	107(b)(2)
1043(b)(6)	418(b)	4041	420(d)
1221(b)(3)	412(a)	4041(b)(2)(B)	208(c)
1245(a)(2)(C)	404(b)(3)	4041(b)(2)(C)(ii)	208(b)
1245(a)(3)(C)	404(b)(3)	4041(b)(2)(D)	208(a)
1355(a)(4)	413(a)	4081	420(d)
1355(g)	415(a)	4082(d)(2)(B)	420(b)(2)
1355(h)	415(a)	4132(a)(1)(O)	408(a)
1397E(d)(1)(C)(iii)	107(b)(1)(A)	4132(a)(1)(P)	408(b)
1397E(d)(1)(D)	107(b)(1)(A)	4980G(d)	306(a)
1397E(d)(1)(E)	107(b)(1)(A)	5388(c)(3)	422(a)
1397E(e)(1)	107(a)	5754(c)(1)	401(f)(2)(B)
1397E(f)	107(b)(1)(B)	5761(c)	401(f)(2)(A)
1397E(g)	107(b)(1)(B)	5761(d)	401(f)(1)
1397E(h)	107(b)(1)(B)	5761(e)	401(f)(1)
1397E(i)	107(b)(1)(B)	5761(f)	401(f)(1)
1397E(j)	107(b)(1)(B)	6015(e)(1)	408(a)

Code Sec.	Act Sec.	Code Sec.	Act Sec.
6015(e)(1)(A)(i)(II)	408(b)(1)	6330(c)(4)(B)	407(b)(2)(D)
6015(e)(1)(B)(i)	408(b)(2)(A)	6330(c)(4)(B)	407(b)(2)(B)
6015(e)(1)(B)(i)	408(b)(2)(B)	6330(g)	407(b)(1)
6015(e)(1)(B)(ii)	408(b)(3)	6404	426(b)(1)
6015(e)(4)	408(b)(4)	6420	420(d)
6015(e)(5)	408(b)(5)	6427	420(d)
6015(g)(2)	408(b)(6)	6427(i)(4)(A)	420(b)(3)(A)
6015(h)(2)	408(b)(7)	6427(i)(4)(A)	420(b)(3)(B)
6039	403(c)(3)	6427(l)(1)	420(b)(4)
6039(a)	403(a)	6427(l)(4)	420(a)
6039(a)	403(c)	6427(l)(5)	420(b)(1)
6039(b)	403(b)	6427(l)(5)	420(b)(1)
6039(c)	403(b)	6702	407(a)
6039(d)	403(b)	6724(d)(1)(B)(xix)	403(c)(1)
6050H(h)	419(c)	6724(d)(1)(B)(xvii)	403(c)(1)
6103(b)(5)	421(a)	6724(d)(1)(B)(xviii)	403(c)(1)
6103(d)(5)(B)	122(a)(1)	6724(d)(2)(B)	403(c)(2)
6103(d)(6)	421(b)	7122(f)	407(d)
6103(i)(3)(C)(iv)	122(b)(1)	7443A(b)(5)	406(a)(2)(A)
6103(i)(7)(E)	122(b)(1)	7443A(b)(6)	406(a)(2)(A)
6103(l)(13)(D)	122(c)(1)	7443A(b)(7)	406(a)(2)(A)
6211(b)(4)(A)	402(b)(1)	7443A(c)	406(a)(2)(B)
6320(b)(1)	407(c)(1)	7608(c)(6)	121
6320(c)	407(c)(2)	7623	406(a)(1)(C)
6330(b)(1)	407(b)(3)	7623	406(b)
6330(c)(4)	407(b)(2)(C)	7623	406(c)
6330(c)(4)(A)	407(b)(2)(A)	7623(a)	406(a)(1)(A)
6330(c)(4)(A)(i)	407(b)(2)(A)	7623(a)(1)	406(a)(1)(B)
6330(c)(4)(A)(ii)	407(b)(2)(B)	7623(b)	406(a)(1)(D)

Code Sec.	Act Sec.	Code Sec.	Act Sec.
7652(f)(1)	114(a)	9704(j)	211(a)
7872(h)(4)	425(a)	9705(b)	212(a)(1)(C)
9014(2)	210(b)	9705(b)(1)	212(a)(1)(A)
9502(d)(2)	420(b)(5)(A)	9705(b)(2)	212(a)(1)(B)
9502(d)(3)	420(b)(5)(B)	9706(h)	212(a)(3)
9503(c)(7)	420(b)(6)(B)	9707(a)	213(b)(1)
9503(c)(7)(A)	420(b)(6)(A)	9711(c)	211(b)
9503(c)(7)(B)	420(b)(6)(A)	9712(a)(3)	212(b)(1)
9508(c)	210(a)(1)	9712(a)(4)	212(b)(1)
9508(c)	210(a)(2)	9712(d)(1)	212(b)(2)(A)
9701(c)(8)	211(d)	9712(d)(2)(B)	212(b)(2)(B)(i)
9702(b)	213(a)	9712(d)(3)	212(b)(2)(B)(ii)
9704(d)	212(a)(2)(A)	9712(d)(4)	211(c)
9704(e)(1)	212(a)(2)(B)(i)	9721	213(b)(2)
9704(e)(3)(A)	212(a)(2)(B)(ii)	9812(f)(3)	115(a)
9704(f)(2)(C)	212(a)(2)(C)		

¶ 6003. Act Sections Amending Code

Act Sec.	Code Sec.	Act Sec.	Code Sec.
101(a)	222(e)	107(b)(1)(B)	1397E(g)
101(b)(1)	222(b)(2)(B)	107(b)(1)(B)	1397E(h)
101(b)(2)	222(b)(2)(B)	107(b)(1)(B)	1397E(i)
102(a)	45D(f)(1)(D)	107(b)(1)(B)	1397E(j)
102(b)	45D(i)(4)	107(b)(1)(B)	1397E(k)
102(b)	45D(i)(5)	107(b)(1)(B)	1397E(l)
102(b)	45D(i)(6)	107(b)(2)	54(l)(3)(B)
103(a)	164(b)(5)(I)	107(b)(2)	1400N(l)(7)(B)(ii)
104(a)(1)	41(h)(1)(B)	108(a)	62(a)(2)(D)
104(a)(2)	45C(b)(1)(D)	109(a)	198(h)
104(b)(1)(A)	41(c)(4)(A)	109(b)	198(d)(1)(A)
104(b)(1)(B)	41(c)(4)(A)	109(b)	198(d)(1)(B)
104(b)(1)(C)	41(c)(4)(A)	109(b)	198(d)(1)(C)
104(c)(1)	41(c)(5)	110(a)(1)	1400(f)
104(c)(1)	41(c)(6)	110(b)(1)	1400A(b)
104(c)(1)	41(c)(7)	110(c)(1)	1400B(b)
105(a)	51(c)(4)(B)	110(c)(2)(A)(i)	1400B(e)(2)
105(a)	51A(f)	110(c)(2)(A)(ii)	1400B(e)(2)
105(b)	51(d)(4)(A)	110(c)(2)(B)	1400B(g)(2)
105(b)	51(d)(4)(B)	110(c)(2)(C)	1400F(d)
105(b)	51(d)(4)(C)	110(d)(1)	1400C(i)
105(c)	51(d)(8)(A)(i)	111(a)	45A(f)
105(d)	51(d)(12)(A)(ii)(II)	112(a)	168(j)(8)
105(e)(1)	51(d)(1)(G)	113(a)	168(e)(3)(E)(iv)
105(e)(1)	51(d)(1)(H)	113(a)	168(e)(3)(E)(v)
105(e)(1)	51(d)(1)(I)	114(a)	7652(f)(1)
105(e)(2)	51(d)(10)	115(a)	9812(f)(3)
105(e)(2)	51(d)(11)	116(a)(1)	170(e)(6)(G)
105(e)(2)	51(d)(12)	116(b)(1)(A)	170(e)(4)(B)(ii)
105(e)(2)	51(d)(13)	116(b)(1)(B)	170(e)(4)(B)(iii)
105(e)(3)	51(e)	116(b)(2)(A)	170(e)(6)(B)(ii)
106(a)	32(c)(2)(B)(vi)(II)	116(b)(2)(B)	170(e)(6)(D)
107(a)	1397E(e)(1)	117(a)	220(i)(2)
107(b)(1)(A)	1397E(d)(1)(C)(iii)	117(a)	220(i)(3)(B)
107(b)(1)(A)	1397E(d)(1)(D)	117(b)(1)(A)	220(j)(2)
107(b)(1)(A)	1397E(d)(1)(E)	117(b)(1)(B)	220(j)(2)
107(b)(1)(B)	1397E(f)	117(b)(2)	220(j)(4)(A)

Act Sec.	Code Sec.	Act Sec.	Code Sec.
117(c)	220	212(a)(1)(A)	9705(b)(1)
118(a)	613A(c)(6)(H)	212(a)(1)(B)	9705(b)(2)
119	936	212(a)(1)(C)	9705(b)
120(a)	1400N(d)(6)	212(a)(2)(A)	9704(d)
120(b)	1400N(e)(2)	212(a)(2)(B)(i)	9704(e)(1)
121	7608(c)(6)	212(a)(2)(B)(ii)	9704(e)(3)(A)
122(a)(1)	6103(d)(5)(B)	212(a)(2)(C)	9704(f)(2)(C)
122(b)(1)	6103(i)(3)(C)(iv)	212(a)(3)	9706(h)
122(b)(1)	6103(i)(7)(E)	212(b)(1)	9712(a)(3)
122(c)(1)	6103(l)(13)(D)	212(b)(1)	9712(a)(4)
123	280C	212(b)(2)(A)	9712(d)(1)
201	45(d)	212(b)(2)(B)(i)	9712(d)(2)(B)
202(a)(1)	54(f)(1)	212(b)(2)(B)(ii)	9712(d)(3)
202(a)(2)	54(f)(2)	213(a)	9702(b)
202(a)(3)	54(m)	213(b)(1)	9707(a)
203(a)	48A(f)(1)	213(b)(2)	9721
204	179D(h)	302(a)	106(e)
205	45L(g)	302(b)	223(c)(1)(B)(i)
206(a)	25D(g)	302(b)	223(c)(1)(B)(ii)
206(b)(1)	25D(a)(1)	302(b)	223(c)(1)(B)(iii)
206(b)(1)	25D(b)(1)(A)	303(a)(1)	223(b)(2)(A)
206(b)(1)	25D(e)(4)(A)(i)	303(a)(2)	223(b)(2)(B)
206(b)(2)(A)	25D(d)(2)	303(b)	223(d)(1)(A)(ii)(I)
206(b)(2)(B)	25D(d)(2)	304	223(g)(1)
207(1)	48	305(a)	223(b)(8)
207(2)	48	306(a)	4980G(d)
208(a)	4041(b)(2)(D)	307(a)	408(d)(9)
208(b)	4041(b)(2)(C)(ii)	307(b)	223(b)(4)(A)
208(c)	4041(b)(2)(B)	307(b)	223(b)(4)(B)
209(a)	168(l)	307(b)	223(b)(4)(C)
210(a)(1)	9508(c)	401(a)	199(d)(8)
210(a)(2)	9508(c)	401(a)	199(d)(9)
210(b)	9014(2)	401(f)(1)	5761(d)
211(a)	45K(g)(2)(D)	401(f)(1)	5761(e)
211(a)	9704(j)	401(f)(1)	5761(f)
211(b)	45K(g)(1)	401(f)(2)(A)	5761(c)
211(b)	9711(c)	401(f)(2)(B)	5754(c)(1)
211(c)	9712(d)(4)	402(a)	53(e)
211(d)	9701(c)(8)	402(b)(1)	6211(b)(4)(A)

Act Sec.	Code Sec.	Act Sec.	Code Sec.
403(a)	6039(a)	407(b)(2)(C)	6330(c)(4)
403(b)	6039(b)	407(b)(2)(D)	6330(c)(4)(B)
403(b)	6039(c)	407(b)(3)	6330(b)(1)
403(b)	6039(d)	407(c)(1)	6320(b)(1)
403(c)	6039(a)	407(c)(2)	6320(c)
403(c)(1)	6724(d)(1)(B)(xvii)	407(d)	7122(f)
403(c)(1)	6724(d)(1)(B)(xviii)	408(a)	4132(a)(1)(O)
403(c)(1)	6724(d)(1)(B)(xix)	408(a)	6015(e)(1)
403(c)(2)	6724(d)(2)(B)	408(b)	4132(a)(1)(P)
403(c)(3)	6039	408(b)(1)	6015(e)(1)(A)(i)(II)
404(a)	179E	408(b)(2)(A)	6015(e)(1)(B)(i)
404(b)(1)	263(a)(1)(J)	408(b)(2)(B)	6015(e)(1)(B)(i)
404(b)(1)	263(a)(1)(K)	408(b)(3)	6015(e)(1)(B)(ii)
404(b)(1)	263(a)(1)(L)	408(b)(4)	6015(e)(4)
404(b)(2)	312(k)(3)(B)	408(b)(5)	6015(e)(5)
404(b)(3)	1245(a)(2)(C)	408(b)(6)	6015(g)(2)
404(b)(3)	1245(a)(3)(C)	408(b)(7)	6015(h)(2)
405(a)	45N	409(a)	468B(g)(3)
405(b)	38(b)(29)	410(a)	355(b)(3)(A)
405(b)	38(b)(30)	410(a)	355(b)(3)(D)
405(b)	38(b)(31)	411(a)	143(l)(3)(B)
405(c)	280C(e)	412(a)	1221(b)(3)
406(a)(1)(A)	7623(a)	413(a)	1355(a)(4)
406(a)(1)(B)	7623(a)(1)	414(a)	148
406(a)(1)(C)	7623	415(a)	1355(g)
406(a)(1)(D)	7623(b)	415(a)	1355(h)
406(a)(2)(A)	7443A(b)(5)	416(a)	143(d)(2)(B)
406(a)(2)(A)	7443A(b)(6)	416(a)	143(d)(2)(C)
406(a)(2)(A)	7443A(b)(7)	416(a)	143(d)(2)(D)
406(a)(2)(B)	7443A(c)	417(a)	121(d)(9)(A)
406(a)(3)	62(a)(21)	417(b)	121(d)(9)(C)(iv)
406(b)	7623	417(b)	121(d)(9)(C)(v)
406(c)	7623	417(c)	121(d)(9)(C)(vi)
407(a)	6702	417(d)	121(d)(9)
407(b)(1)	6330(g)	418(a)(1)(A)	1043(b)(1)(A)
407(b)(2)(A)	6330(c)(4)(A)	418(a)(1)(B)	1043(b)(1)(B)
407(b)(2)(A)	6330(c)(4)(A)(i)	418(a)(2)(A)	1043(b)(2)(A)
407(b)(2)(B)	6330(c)(4)(A)(ii)	418(a)(2)(B)	1043(b)(2)(B)
407(b)(2)(B)	6330(c)(4)(B)	418(a)(3)	1043(b)(5)(B)

Act Sec.	Code Sec.	Act Sec.	Code Sec.
418(b)	1043(b)(6)	420(b)(6)(B)	9503(c)(7)
419(a)	163(h)(3)(E)	420(d)	4041
419(b)	163(h)(4)(E)	420(d)	4081
419(b)	163(h)(4)(F)	420(d)	6420
419(c)	6050H(h)	420(d)	6427
420(a)	6427(l)(4)	421(a)	6103(b)(5)
420(b)(1)	6427(l)(5)	421(b)	6103(d)(6)
420(b)(1)	6427(l)(5)	422(a)	5388(c)(3)
420(b)(2)	4082(d)(2)(B)	423(a)(1)	45G(d)
420(b)(3)(A)	6427(i)(4)(A)	423(a)(2)	45G(d)
420(b)(3)(B)	6427(i)(4)(A)	424(a)	664(c)
420(b)(4)	6427(l)(1)	425(a)	7872(h)(4)
420(b)(5)(A)	9502(d)(2)	426(a)(1)(A)	954(c)(6)(A)
420(b)(5)(B)	9502(d)(3)	426(a)(1)(B)	954(c)(6)(A)
420(b)(6)(A)	9503(c)(7)(A)	426(b)(1)	6404
420(b)(6)(A)	9503(c)(7)(B)		

¶ 6004. FTC 2nd ¶s Affected by Act

FTC 2d ¶	Analysis ¶	FTC 2d ¶	Analysis ¶	FTC 2d ¶	Analysis ¶
A-2601	1410	J-2901	108	L-16458	905
A-2611.2	103	J-2917	108	L-16481 *et seq.*	906
A-4224.1	106	J-2988	108	L-16494	906
A-4258	1101	J-2990	108	L-17704	904
A-4471	102	J-2991	108	L-17710	904
A-4781	105	J-3182	1604	L-17771	903
A-4782	105	J-3182.1	1603, 1604	L-17771.1	903
A-4785	105	J-3187	1603	L-17771.2	903
A-8220	508	J-3363	1103, 1104	L-17771.3	903
A-8801	1201	J-3396.4	1103	L-17771.4	903
C-5039	601	J-3396.5	1103	L-17771.5	903
F-4803	1602	J-3401	1004	L-17771.6	903
F-10304	509	K-3221	603	L-17775	801
G-2791	1605	K-3241	602, 603	L-17776	805
H-1325.46	402	K-3251	601	L-17777	805
H-1342.2	307	K-4510 *et seq.*	101	L-17778	805
H-1343.3	307	K-5470.1 *et seq.*	104	L-17783	805
H-1344.3	307	L-3171	501	L-17783.2	805
H-1346	307	L-4325 *et seq.*	1302	L-17784.1	802
H-1349.1	302	L-4339	1302	L-17785.2	804
H-1350	302	L-4385 *et seq.*	1302	L-17786.1	803
H-1350 *et seq.*	301	L-5601	509	L-17786.3	801
H-1350.3	302	L-6150.7	505	L-17835	805
H-1350.4A	302	L-6164	506	L-17835 *et seq.*	805
H-1350.7	303, 306	L-6339.1	1405	L-17836	805
H-1350.8	301	L-8208	502, 503	L-17840	805
H-1350.9	302	L-8208.1	502	L-17842	805
H-1350.14	305	L-8208.2	503	L-17856	805
H-1350.19	302, 304	L-8210	502, 503	L-17927	1001
H-2417.2	302	L-8806	510	L-17941	901
H-2461	302	L-8917	502, 503	L-17942	901
H-12253.1	301	L-9337.7	504	L-18051	1607
I-3805	109	L-9403	502, 503	N-2729	507
I-3806	109	L-9997	504	O-1502	1303
I-4521	107	L-15201	806	O-1504	1303
I-4528.1	107	L-15209	806	O-1510	1303
I-4528.2	107	L-15300	201, 701	O-1513	1303
I-4557	107	L-15301	203	O-1513.1	1303
I-4557.1	107	L-15302.1	202, 203,	O-1517	1303
I-4563	107		701	O-1518	1303
I-4563.1	107	L-15308	701	O-1519	1303
I-6601	1601	L-15500	201	O-1605.1	1303
I-8751	1102	L-15614	201	O-2447.2	1301
I-8752	1102	L-15641	1103	O-11554	1608, 1609
I-8753	1102	L-15645.7	1004	O-11557	1609
I-8754	1102	L-15645.12	1003, 1004	S-2609	1403
I-8755	1102	L-15671	807	S-3207	401
I-8756	1102	L-16401	902	S-6201	1406
I-8762	1103	L-16402	902	S-6339.1	1405
I-10106	509	L-16436.1	902	S-6342.1	1405
I-10204	509	L-16437.1	902	S-6344.1	1405

FTC 2d ¶	Analysis ¶	FTC 2d ¶	Analysis ¶	FTC 2d ¶	Analysis ¶
S-6344.2	1405	U-2148	1401	V-1815	401
S-6356.1	1404	U-2148.1	1401	V-1816	401
T-1031	1409, 1411	U-2149	1401	V-8550	1401
T-1036	1409	U-2151	1401	W-1564.2E	1502
T-1182.1	1412	U-2152	1401	W-1725	1501
T-1505	1202	V-1401.1	1402	W-2952	1503
T-3414	1401				

¶ 6005. USTR ¶ s Affected by Act

USTR ¶	Analysis ¶	USTR ¶	Analysis ¶	USTR ¶	Analysis ¶
25D4	105	1214.14	107	10,434	109
324.05	106	1254.05	302	12,214.45	1601
384	806	1434.012	1603	12,454.01	509
384.02	806	1434.019	1603, 1604	12,454.05	509
414	201, 701	1484	1004	13,554	1608, 1609
414.01	202, 203,	1634.052	104	13,97E4	1004
	701	1644.03	101	13,97E4.01	1003, 1004
454.09	903	1684.01	502, 503,	14,004.01	1103
454.10	903		510	14,00A4	1103, 1104
454.11	903	1684.02	502, 503	14,00B4	1102, 1103
454.12	903	1684.03	502, 503	14,00B4.01	1102
454.13	903	1704.42	602, 603	14,00C4	1101
454.14	903	179D4	501	14,00N4.021	504
454.15	903	1984	505, 506	14,00N4.025	504
45A4	807	1994 *et seq.*	1302	40,414	1501
45C4	201	2204.02	307	41,314	1503
45D4	1001	2224.01	102	49,80G4	302, 304
45G4	1607	2234	301, 302	60,154	1401
45K4	904	2234.02	302, 306	60,154.03	1401
45K4.02	904	2234.03	301, 303,	60,154.04	1401
45L4	901		305	60,394	401
484	902	2234.05	302	61,034.01	1404
48A4	905	2634	509	61,034.06	1405
514	801, 802,	280C4	701	61,034.07	1403, 1406
	803, 804	3124.04	509	62,114	1202
51A4	805	3554.02	1602	64,044	1402
534	1201	4084.03	301	64,274	1502
544 *et seq.*	906	468B4	1605	67,224	401
564.01	508	514A	805	76,084	1412
624	1410	6134.009	507	76,234	1409, 1411
624.02	103	613A4	507	78,724.02	108
1054.01	302	6644	601	78,724.201	108
1214	107	9314.06	1303	98,124	402
1214.08	107	9544.02	1301		

¶ 6006. Tax Desk ¶ s Affected by Act

TaxDesk ¶	Analysis ¶	TaxDesk ¶	Analysis ¶	TaxDesk ¶	Analysis ¶
133,044	302	289,100	302	384,003	202, 203, 701
133,045.2	302	289,101 *et seq.*	301	384,018	201
143,003.1	301	289,104	302	384,019	701
155,001	108	289,104.5	302	384,039	807
155,020	108	289,107	303, 306	384,711	1001
155,056	108	289,108	301	384,756	1003, 1004
155,058	108	289,109	302	384,757	1004
155,059	108	289,117	302, 304	384,801 *et seq.*	906
158,013	1004	307,800 *et seq.*	1302	384,810	906
171,023	509	307,803	1302	394,500	1303
223,103	509	308,101	501	394,501	1303
223,105	509	314,501 *et seq.*	104	394,503	1303
225,701	107	326,019 *et seq.*	101	394,505	1303
225,708.2	107	331,629	601	394,507	1303
225,737	107	331,721	603	394,510	1303
225,737.1	107	331,741	602, 603	394,515	1303
225,743	107	352,001	102	394,519	1303
225,743.1	107	380,500	806	396,001	904
237,426.1	1602	380,501	1607	396,107	905
245,556	1102	380,509	806	444,043	1409, 1411
246,552	1102	380,700	801, 805	560,702	1410
246,553	1102	380,700.1	805	560,706.1	103
246,554	1102	380,701	805	568,801	1101
246,555	1102	380,707	805	569,025.1	106
246,560	1102, 1103	380,708	802	569,561	105
252,501	1601	380,712	804	569,562	105
256,201	509	380,716	803	569,565	105
266,208	502, 503	380,718	801	569,571	901
266,208.1	502	381,300	805	569,572	901
266,208.2	503	381,300 *et seq.*	805	570,950	1401
266,211	502, 503	381,301	805	644,602	1608, 1609
267,007	510	381,305	805	644,606	1609
267,018	502, 503	381,307	805	651,030	601
267,503	502, 503	381,311	805	691,501	1201
268,601	504	381,315	805	696,513	508
268,801	505, 506	381,600	902	812,016	401
269,332	504	381,601	902	822,501	1202
271,001	507	381,602	902	852,006.1	1402
288,101	307	384,001	201, 203, 701	861,035	401
288,105	307				
289,000	302				

¶ 6007. Pension Analysis ¶s Affected by Act

PCA ¶	Analysis ¶
¶ 10,641.7	303

¶ 6008. Pension Explanations ¶ s Affected by Act

PE ¶	Analysis ¶	PE ¶	Analysis ¶	PE ¶	Analysis ¶
98,124	402	223-4.02	302	2234.03	301
105-4.01	302	223-4.03	303, 305	4084.03	301
125-4.05	302	223-4.05	302	4980G-4	302, 304
223-4	302	2234 *et seq.*	301	ER712-4	402

¶ 6009. Estate Planning Analysis ¶ s Affected by Act

EPTC/EPA ¶	Analysis ¶	EPTC/EPA ¶	Analysis ¶
41,502	601	85,640	601

¶ 6010
Current and Prospective Effective Dates

Arranged in Code section order, this table shows the topic related to a change to each specified Code section made by a Tax Act passed by the 107th, 108th, or the 109th Congress, the current and/or prospective effective date of that change, and the Complete Analysis ¶ in which the topic is or has been analyzed.

Code	Topic	Effective Date	Complete Analysis ¶
1(g)(2)(A)	Unearned income of children under age 18 (instead of under age 14) is subject to kiddie tax	Tax years beginning after Dec. 31, 2005	¶ 204 Tax Increase Prevention and Reconciliation Act of 2005
1(g)(2)(C)	Unearned income of children under age 18 (instead of under age 14) is subject to kiddie tax	Tax years beginning after Dec. 31, 2005	¶ 204 Tax Increase Prevention and Reconciliation Act of 2005
1(g)(4)(C)	Distributions from certain qualified disability trusts are excepted from kiddie tax	Tax years beginning after Dec. 31, 2005	¶ 205 Tax Increase Prevention and Reconciliation Act of 2005
1(h)(1)(B)	5% and 15% tax rates on adjusted net capital gain are extended for two years	Tax years beginning after Dec. 31, 2008 and before Jan. 1, 2011	¶ 101 Tax Increase Prevention and Reconciliation Act of 2005
1(h)(1)(B)	Post-2007 0% tax rate on adjusted net capital gains is extended for two years	Tax years beginning after Dec. 31, 2008 and before Jan. 1, 2011	¶ 102 Tax Increase Prevention and Reconciliation Act of 2005
1(h)(1)(B)	5% tax rate on adjusted net capital gains is reduced to 0% for tax years beginning in 2008	Tax years beginning after 2007, and beginning before Jan. 1, 2009	¶ 102 Jobs and Growth Tax Relief Reconciliation Act of 2003
1(h)(1)(C)	5% and 15% tax rates on adjusted net capital gain are extended for two years	Tax years beginning after Dec. 31, 2008 and before Jan. 1, 2011	¶ 101 Tax Increase Prevention and Reconciliation Act of 2005
1(h)(1)(D)(i)	5% and 15% adjusted capital gains rates on noncorporate taxpayers' qualified dividend income are extended for two years	Tax years beginning after Dec. 31, 2008 and before Jan. 1, 2011	¶ 107 Tax Increase Prevention and Reconciliation Act of 2005

Code	Topic	Effective Date	Complete Analysis ¶
1(h)(3)(B)	5% and 15% adjusted capital gains rates on noncorporate taxpayers' qualified dividend income are extended for two years	Tax years beginning after Dec. 31, 2008 and before Jan. 1, 2011	¶ 107 Tax Increase Prevention and Reconciliation Act of 2005
1(h)(11)	5% and 15% adjusted capital gains rates on noncorporate taxpayers' qualified dividend income are extended for two years	Tax years beginning after Dec. 31, 2008 and before Jan. 1, 2011	¶ 107 Tax Increase Prevention and Reconciliation Act of 2005
1(h)(11)(D)(ii)	Long-term capital loss treatment for losses of individuals, trusts, and estates on stock to the extent extraordinary dividends were taxed as capital gains is extended for two years	Tax years beginning after Dec. 31, 2008 and before Jan. 1, 2011	¶ 108 Tax Increase Prevention and Reconciliation Act of 2005
23(b)(4)	Nonrefundable personal credits may offset AMT through 2006 (instead of 2005)	Tax years beginning after Dec. 31, 2005 and before Jan. 1, 2007	¶ 202 Tax Increase Prevention and Reconciliation Act of 2005
23(b)(4)	Carryover rules for personal credits are redrafted to cover years in which credits are and years in which they aren't allowed against AMT	Tax years beginning after Dec. 31, 2005	¶ 601 Gulf Opportunity Zone and Katrina Emergency Tax Relief Acts of 2005
23(c)	Carryover rules for personal credits are redrafted to cover years in which credits are and years in which they aren't allowed against AMT	Tax years beginning after Dec. 31, 2005	¶ 601 Gulf Opportunity Zone and Katrina Emergency Tax Relief Acts of 2005
23(c)	Individuals will be allowed 30% credit for photovoltaic, solar hot water, and fuel cell property installed in their home in 2006 and 2007, subject to dollar limits	Property placed in service after Dec. 31, 2005 and before Jan. 1, 2008	¶ 104 Tax Provisions of the Energy and Transportation Acts of 2005

Code	Topic	Effective Date	Complete Analysis ¶
24(b)(3)	Nonrefundable personal credits may offset AMT through 2006 (instead of 2005)	Tax years beginning after Dec. 31, 2005 and before Jan. 1, 2007	¶ 202 Tax Increase Prevention and Reconciliation Act of 2005
24(b)(3)	Carryover rules for personal credits are redrafted to cover years in which credits are and years in which they aren't allowed against AMT	Tax years beginning after Dec. 31, 2005	¶ 601 Gulf Opportunity Zone and Katrina Emergency Tax Relief Acts of 2005
24(d)(1)	Carryover rules for personal credits are redrafted to cover years in which credits are and years in which they aren't allowed against AMT	Tax years beginning after Dec. 31, 2005	¶ 601 Gulf Opportunity Zone and Katrina Emergency Tax Relief Acts of 2005
25(e)(1)(C)	Nonrefundable personal credits may offset AMT through 2006 (instead of 2005)	Tax years beginning after Dec. 31, 2005 and before Jan. 1, 2007	¶ 202 Tax Increase Prevention and Reconciliation Act of 2005
25(e)(1)(C)	Carryover rules for personal credits are redrafted to cover years in which credits are and years in which they aren't allowed against AMT	Tax years beginning after Dec. 31, 2005	¶ 601 Gulf Opportunity Zone and Katrina Emergency Tax Relief Acts of 2005
25(e)(1)(C)	Individuals will be allowed 30% credit for photovoltaic, solar hot water, and fuel cell property installed in their home in 2006 and 2007, subject to dollar limits	Property placed in service after Dec. 31, 2005 and before Jan. 1, 2008	¶ 104 Tax Provisions of the Energy and Transportation Acts of 2005
25B(b)	Income limits on the saver's credit will be indexed for inflation after 2006	Tax years beginning after 2006	¶ 2204 Pension Protection Act of 2006
25B(h)	Saver's credit is made permanent	Aug. 17, 2006	¶ 2203 Pension Protection Act of 2006

Code	Topic	Effective Date	Complete Analysis ¶
25B(g)	Nonrefundable personal credits may offset AMT through 2006 (instead of 2005)	Tax years beginning after Dec. 31, 2005 and before Jan. 1, 2007	¶ 202 Tax Increase Prevention and Reconciliation Act of 2005
25B(g)	Carryover rules for personal credits are redrafted to cover years in which credits are and years in which they aren't allowed against AMT	Tax years beginning after Dec. 31, 2005	¶ 601 Gulf Opportunity Zone and Katrina Emergency Tax Relief Acts of 2005
25C	Individuals will be allowed personal credit up to $500 lifetime limit for energy efficient improvements to principal residence in 2006 and 2007	Property placed in service after Dec. 31, 2005 and before Jan. 1, 2008	¶ 103 Tax Provisions of the Energy and Transportation Acts of 2005
25D	Individuals will be allowed 30% credit for photovoltaic, solar hot water, and fuel cell property installed in their home in 2006 and 2007, subject to dollar limits	Property placed in service after Dec. 31, 2005 and before Jan. 1, 2008	¶ 104 Tax Provisions of the Energy and Transportation Acts of 2005
25D(a)(1)	Residential energy efficient property credit is extended for one year, through 2008; solar energy property qualifying for credit is clarified	Date of enactment of the 2006 Tax Relief and Health Care Act	¶ 105 Tax Provisions of the Tax Relief and Health Care Act of 2006
25D(b)(1)	Dollar limits on residential energy efficient property credit aren't reduced by carryovers from prior years	Property placed in service after Dec. 31, 2005	¶ 604 Gulf Opportunity Zone and Katrina Emergency Tax Relief Acts of 2005
25D(b)(1)(A)	Residential energy efficient property credit is extended for one year, through 2008; solar energy property qualifying for credit is clarified	Date of enactment of the 2006 Tax Relief and Health Care Act	¶ 105 Tax Provisions of the Tax Relief and Health Care Act of 2006

Code	Topic	Effective Date	Complete Analysis ¶
25D(c)	Carryover rules for personal credits are redrafted to cover years in which credits are and years in which they aren't allowed against AMT	Tax years beginning after Dec. 31, 2005	¶ 601 Gulf Opportunity Zone and Katrina Emergency Tax Relief Acts of 2005
25D(c)(2)	Nonrefundable personal credits may offset AMT through 2006 (instead of 2005)	Tax years beginning after Dec. 31, 2005 and before Jan. 1, 2007	¶ 202 Tax Increase Prevention and Reconciliation Act of 2005
25D(d)(2)	Residential energy efficient property credit is extended for one year, through 2008; solar energy property qualifying for credit is clarified	Date of enactment of the 2006 Tax Relief and Health Care Act	¶ 105 Tax Provisions of the Tax Relief and Health Care Act of 2006
25D(e)(4)	Joint occupancy rule for credit for residential energy efficient property is revised	Property placed in service after Dec. 31, 2005	¶ 605 Gulf Opportunity Zone and Katrina Emergency Tax Relief Acts of 2005
25D(e)(4)(A)(i)	Residential energy efficient property credit is extended for one year, through 2008; solar energy property qualifying for credit is clarified	Date of enactment of the 2006 Tax Relief and Health Care Act	¶ 105 Tax Provisions of the Tax Relief and Health Care Act of 2006
25D(g)	Residential energy efficient property credit is extended for one year, through 2008; solar energy property qualifying for credit is clarified	Date of enactment of the 2006 Tax Relief and Health Care Act	¶ 105 Tax Provisions of the Tax Relief and Health Care Act of 2006
26(a)(2)	Nonrefundable personal credits may offset AMT through 2006 (instead of 2005)	Tax years beginning after Dec. 31, 2005 and before Jan. 1, 2007	¶ 202 Tax Increase Prevention and Reconciliation Act of 2005
29	Nonconventional fuel production credit will be an elective general business credit for tax years ending after Dec. 31, 2005	Tax years ending after Dec. 31, 2005	¶ 301 Tax Provisions of the Energy and Transportation Acts of 2005

Code	Topic	Effective Date	Complete Analysis ¶
29(c)(2)(A)	Nonconventional fuel production credit will be an elective general business credit for tax years ending after Dec. 31, 2005	Tax years ending after Dec. 31, 2005	¶ 301 Tax Provisions of the Energy and Transportation Acts of 2005
29(e)	Nonconventional fuel production credit will be an elective general business credit for tax years ending after Dec. 31, 2005	Tax years ending after Dec. 31, 2005	¶ 301 Tax Provisions of the Energy and Transportation Acts of 2005
29(h)	Nonconventional fuel credit will be available for coke and coke gas fuel produced and sold after Dec. 31, 2005	Fuel produced and sold after Dec. 31, 2005, in tax years ending after Dec. 31, 2005	¶ 302 Tax Provisions of the Energy and Transportation Acts of 2005
30(b)(3)(A)	Nonconventional fuel production credit will be an elective general business credit for tax years ending after Dec. 31, 2005	Tax years ending after Dec. 31, 2005	¶ 301 Tax Provisions of the Energy and Transportation Acts of 2005
30A	Possessions tax credit for American Samoa retroactively extended through 2007 for existing claimants	Tax years beginning after Dec. 31, 2005 and before Jan. 1, 2008	¶ 1303 Tax Provisions of the Tax Relief and Health Care Act of 2006
30B	Alternative motor vehicle credit for fuel cell, hybrid, lean burn technology and alternative fuel vehicles	Property placed in service after Dec. 31, 2005 in tax years ending after that date	¶ 201 Tax Provisions of the Energy and Transportation Acts of 2005
30B(b)	New qualified fuel cell motor vehicle credit	Property placed in service after Dec. 31, 2005 in tax years ending after that date	¶ 202 Tax Provisions of the Energy and Transportation Acts of 2005
30B(c)	New advanced lean burn technology motor vehicle credit	Property placed in service after Dec. 31, 2005	¶ 203 Tax Provisions of the Energy and Transportation Acts of 2005
30B(d)	New qualified hybrid motor vehicle credit	Property placed in service after Dec. 31, 2005 in tax years ending after that date	¶ 204 Tax Provisions of the Energy and Transportation Acts of 2005

Code	Topic	Effective Date	Complete Analysis ¶
30B(e)	New qualified alternative fuel motor vehicle credit	Property placed in service after Dec. 31, 2005 in tax years ending after that date	¶ 205 Tax Provisions of the Energy and Transportation Acts of 2005
30B(h)(6)	Treatment of alternative motor vehicle credit is clarified where vehicle is sold to a tax-exempt entity effective for property placed in service after Dec. 31, 2005	Property placed in service after Dec. 31, 2005	¶ 607 Gulf Opportunity Zone and Katrina Emergency Tax Relief Acts of 2005
30C	Credit provided for qualified alternative fuel vehicle refueling property	Property placed in service after Dec. 31, 2005	¶ 206 Tax Provisions of the Energy and Transportation Acts of 2005
30C(e)(2)	Application of business credit limitations to credits for alternative fuel vehicle refueling property sold to exempt entities clarified	Property placed in service after Dec. 31, 2005	¶ 609 Gulf Opportunity Zone and Katrina Emergency Tax Relief Acts of 2005
32(c)(2)(B)(vi)(II)	Election to include combat pay as earned income for purposes of the earned income credit (EIC) is extended through 2007	Tax years beginning after Dec. 31, 2006	¶ 106 Tax Provisions of the Tax Relief and Health Care Act of 2006
32(c)(2)(B)(vi)(II)	Election to include combat pay as earned income for purposes of the earned income credit (EIC) is extended through 2006	Tax years beginning after Dec. 31, 2005	¶ 603 Gulf Opportunity Zone and Katrina Emergency Tax Relief Acts of 2005
38(b)	Qualified employers receive credit for providing lodging to employees affected by Hurricane Katrina	Lodging furnished beginning Jan. 1, 2006	¶ 128 Gulf Opportunity Zone and Katrina Emergency Tax Relief Acts of 2005
38(b)	Credit provided for qualified alternative fuel vehicle refueling property	Property placed in service after Dec. 31, 2005	¶ 206 Tax Provisions of the Energy and Transportation Acts of 2005

Code	Topic	Effective Date	Complete Analysis ¶
38(b)(22)	Nonconventional fuel production credit will be an elective general business credit for tax years ending after Dec. 31, 2005	Tax years ending after Dec. 31, 2005	¶ 301 Tax Provisions of the Energy and Transportation Acts of 2005
38(b)(23)	New energy efficient home credit of $2,000 ($1,000 for certain homes) is available to eligible contractors for qualified new energy efficient homes acquired after Dec. 31, 2005 and before Jan. 1, 2008	Qualified new energy efficient homes acquired after Dec. 31, 2005 and before Jan. 1, 2008	¶ 102 Tax Provisions of the Energy and Transportation Acts of 2005
38(b)(24)	Business tax credit will be allowed for manufacturers of energy efficient dishwashers, clothes washers, and refrigerators in 2006 and 2007	Appliances produced after Dec. 31, 2005	¶ 105 Tax Provisions of the Energy and Transportation Acts of 2005
38(b)(31)	A 20% credit is available for amounts paid or incurred in tax years beginning after Dec. 31, 2005 and before Jan. 1, 2009 for training mine rescue teams	Tax years beginning after Dec. 31, 2005 and before Jan. 1, 2009	¶ 806 Tax Provisions of the Tax Relief and Health Care Act of 2006
40A(f)	Income tax credit and excise tax credits and payments will be provided for renewable diesel fuel sold or used after Dec. 31, 2005 and before Jan. 1, 2009	Fuel sold or used after Dec. 31, 2005	¶ 309 Tax Provisions of the Energy and Transportation Acts of 2005
41(c)(4)	Alternative simplified credit can be elected for qualified research expenses	Tax years ending after Dec. 31, 2006	¶ 203 Tax Provisions of the Tax Relief and Health Care Act of 2006

Code	Topic	Effective Date	Complete Analysis ¶
41(c)(4)	Taxpayers with a tax year ending after 2005 have until Apr. 15, 2007 to make elections under expired provisions that are retroactively extended by the 2006 Tax Relief and Health Care Act	Tax years ending after Dec. 31, 2005 and before date of enactment of the 2006 Tax Relief and Health Care Act	¶ 701 Tax Provisions of the Tax Relief and Health Care Act of 2006
41(c)(4)(A)	Rates for the elective alternative incremental research credit are increased	Tax years ending after Dec. 31, 2006	¶ 202 Tax Provisions of the Tax Relief and Health Care Act of 2006
41(c)(5)	Alternative simplified credit can be elected for qualified research expenses	Tax years ending after Dec. 31, 2006	¶ 203 Tax Provisions of the Tax Relief and Health Care Act of 2006
41(h)(1)(B)	Research credit is extended retroactively to amounts paid or incurred after Dec. 31, 2005 and before Jan. 1, 2008	Amounts paid or incurred after Dec. 31, 2005	¶ 201 Tax Provisions of the Tax Relief and Health Care Act of 2006
45(d)(1)	Placed-in-service date is extended for one year through Dec. 31, 2008 for certain qualified facilities for purposes of the credit for electricity produced from renewable resources	Facilities placed in service after Dec. 31, 2007	¶ 903 Tax Provisions of the Tax Relief and Health Care Act of 2006
45(d)(2)(A)	Placed-in-service date is extended for one year through Dec. 31, 2008 for certain qualified facilities for purposes of the credit for electricity produced from renewable resources	Facilities placed in service after Dec. 31, 2007	¶ 903 Tax Provisions of the Tax Relief and Health Care Act of 2006

Code	Topic	Effective Date	Complete Analysis ¶
45(d)(3)(A)	Placed-in-service date is extended for one year through Dec. 31, 2008 for certain qualified facilities for purposes of the credit for electricity produced from renewable resources	Facilities placed in service after Dec. 31, 2007	¶ 903 Tax Provisions of the Tax Relief and Health Care Act of 2006
45(d)(4)	Placed-in-service date is extended for one year through Dec. 31, 2008 for certain qualified facilities for purposes of the credit for electricity produced from renewable resources	Facilities placed in service after Dec. 31, 2007	¶ 903 Tax Provisions of the Tax Relief and Health Care Act of 2006
45(d)(5)	Placed-in-service date is extended for one year through Dec. 31, 2008 for certain qualified facilities for purposes of the credit for electricity produced from renewable resources	Facilities placed in service after Dec. 31, 2007	¶ 903 Tax Provisions of the Tax Relief and Health Care Act of 2006
45(d)(6)	Placed-in-service date is extended for one year through Dec. 31, 2008 for certain qualified facilities for purposes of the credit for electricity produced from renewable resources	Facilities placed in service after Dec. 31, 2007	¶ 903 Tax Provisions of the Tax Relief and Health Care Act of 2006
45(d)(7)	Placed-in-service date is extended for one year through Dec. 31, 2008 for certain qualified facilities for purposes of the credit for electricity produced from renewable resources	Facilities placed in service after Dec. 31, 2007	¶ 903 Tax Provisions of the Tax Relief and Health Care Act of 2006

Code	Topic	Effective Date	Complete Analysis ¶
45(d)(9)	Placed-in-service date is extended for one year through Dec. 31, 2008 for certain qualified facilities for purposes of the credit for electricity produced from renewable resources	Facilities placed in service after Dec. 31, 2007	¶ 903 Tax Provisions of the Tax Relief and Health Care Act of 2006
45A(f)	Indian employment credit is extended retroactively for tax years beginning after Dec. 31, 2005 and before Jan. 1, 2008	Tax years beginning after Dec. 31, 2005 and before Jan. 1, 2008	¶ 807 Tax Provisions of the Tax Relief and Health Care Act of 2006
45C(b)(1)(D)	Research credit is extended retroactively to amounts paid or incurred after Dec. 31, 2005 and before Jan. 1, 2008	Amounts paid or incurred after Dec. 31, 2005	¶ 201 Tax Provisions of the Tax Relief and Health Care Act of 2006
45D(f)(1)(D)	$3.5 billion new markets tax credit limitation is extended to include 2008	Date of enactment of the 2006 Tax Relief and Health Care Act	¶ 1001 Tax Provisions of the Tax Relief and Health Care Act of 2006
45D(i)(6)	New markets tax credit regs are to ensure that non-metropolitan counties receive a proportional allocation of qualified equity investments	Date of enactment of the 2006 Tax Relief and Health Care Act	¶ 1002 Tax Provisions of the Tax Relief and Health Care Act of 2006
45K(a)	Election requirement is eliminated for the nonconventional source production credit	Tax credits determined under the '86 Code for tax years ending after Dec. 31, 2005	¶ 610 Gulf Opportunity Zone and Katrina Emergency Tax Relief Acts of 2005
45K(a)	Nonconventional fuel production credit will be an elective general business credit for tax years ending after Dec. 31, 2005	Tax years ending after Dec. 31, 2005	¶ 301 Tax Provisions of the Energy and Transportation Acts of 2005

Code	Topic	Effective Date	Complete Analysis ¶
45K(b)(6)	Nonconventional fuel production credit will be an elective general business credit for tax years ending after Dec. 31, 2005	Tax years ending after Dec. 31, 2005	¶ 301 Tax Provisions of the Energy and Transportation Acts of 2005
45K(g)(1)	Nonconventional source production credit for coke and coke gas is not subject to the phase-out limitation, and the credit does not apply to a facility producing coke or coke gas from petroleum-based products	Fuel sold after Dec. 31, 2005	¶ 904 Tax Provisions of the Tax Relief and Health Care Act of 2006
45K(g)(2)	Nonconventional source production credit for coke and coke gas is not subject to the phase-out limitation, and the credit does not apply to a facility producing coke or coke gas from petroleum-based products	Fuel sold after Dec. 31, 2005	¶ 904 Tax Provisions of the Tax Relief and Health Care Act of 2006
45L	New energy efficient home credit of $2,000 ($1,000 for certain homes) is available to eligible contractors for qualified new energy efficient homes acquired after Dec. 31, 2005 and before Jan. 1, 2008	Qualified new energy efficient homes acquired after Dec. 31, 2005 and before Jan. 1, 2008	¶ 102 Tax Provisions of the Energy and Transportation Acts of 2005
45L(g)	Energy efficient home credit for eligible contractors is extended through 2008	Qualified new energy efficient homes acquired after Dec. 31, 2007 and before Jan. 1, 2009	¶ 901 Tax Provisions of the Tax Relief and Health Care Act of 2006

Code	Topic	Effective Date	Complete Analysis ¶
45M	Business tax credit will be allowed for manufacturers of energy efficient dishwashers, clothes washers, and refrigerators in 2006 and 2007	Appliances produced after Dec. 31, 2005	¶ 105 Tax Provisions of the Energy and Transportation Acts of 2005
45N	A 20% credit is available for amounts paid or incurred in tax years beginning after Dec. 31, 2005 and before Jan. 1, 2009 for training mine rescue teams	Tax years beginning after Dec. 31, 2005 and before Jan. 1, 2009	¶ 806 Tax Provisions of the Tax Relief and Health Care Act of 2006
48(a)(1)	10% energy credit will be allowed for qualified microturbine property in periods after Dec. 31, 2005 and before Jan. 1, 2008	Periods after Dec. 31, 2005, in tax years ending after Dec. 31, 2005	¶ 324 Tax Provisions of the Energy and Transportation Acts of 2005
48(a)(1)	30% energy credit will be allowed for qualified fuel cell property for periods after Dec. 31, 2005 and before Jan. 1, 2008	Periods after Dec. 31, 2005, in tax years ending after Dec. 31, 2005	¶ 323 Tax Provisions of the Energy and Transportation Acts of 2005
48(a)(2)(A)	10% energy credit will be allowed for qualified microturbine property in periods after Dec. 31, 2005 and before Jan. 1, 2008	Periods after Dec. 31, 2005, in tax years ending after Dec. 31, 2005	¶ 324 Tax Provisions of the Energy and Transportation Acts of 2005
48(a)(2)(A)	30% energy credit will be allowed for qualified fuel cell property for periods after Dec. 31, 2005 and before Jan. 1, 2008	Periods after Dec. 31, 2005, in tax years ending after Dec. 31, 2005	¶ 323 Tax Provisions of the Energy and Transportation Acts of 2005
48(a)(2)(A)	Energy credit for solar energy property will increase from 10% to 30% for property placed in service after Dec. 31, 2005 and before Jan. 1, 2008	Periods after Dec. 31, 2005, in tax years ending after Dec. 31, 2005	¶ 322 Tax Provisions of the Energy and Transportation Acts of 2005

Code	Topic	Effective Date	Complete Analysis
48(a)(2)(A)(i)(II)	Increase in business energy tax credit for solar energy property from 10% to 30% is extended through Dec. 31, 2008, as are the 30% credit for qualified fuel cell property and the 10% credit for qualified microturbine property	Periods after Dec. 31, 2007 and before Jan. 1, 2009	¶ 902 Tax Provisio of the Tax Relief and Health Care A of 2006
48(a)(3)(A)(i)	Energy credit for solar energy property will increase from 10% to 30% for property placed in service after Dec. 31, 2005 and before Jan. 1, 2008	Periods after Dec. 31, 2005, in tax years ending after Dec. 31, 2005	¶ 322 Tax Provisio of the Energy and Transportation Acts of 2005
48(a)(3)(A)(ii)	Increase in business energy tax credit for solar energy property from 10% to 30% is extended through Dec. 31, 2008, as are the 30% credit for qualified fuel cell property and the 10% credit for qualified microturbine property	Periods after Dec. 31, 2007 and before Jan. 1, 2009	¶ 902 Tax Provisio of the Tax Relief and Health Care A of 2006
48(a)(3)(A)(ii)	Energy credit for solar energy property will increase from 10% to 30% for property placed in service after Dec. 31, 2005 and before Jan. 1, 2008	Periods after Dec. 31, 2005, in tax years ending after Dec. 31, 2005	¶ 322 Tax Provisio of the Energy and Transportation Acts of 2005
48(a)(3)(A)(iii)	10% energy credit will be allowed for qualified microturbine property in periods after Dec. 31, 2005 and before Jan. 1, 2008	Periods after Dec. 31, 2005, in tax years ending after Dec. 31, 2005	¶ 324 Tax Provisio of the Energy and Transportation Acts of 2005

Code	Topic	Effective Date	Complete Analysis ¶
48(a)(3)(A)(iii)	30% energy credit will be allowed for qualified fuel cell property for periods after Dec. 31, 2005 and before Jan. 1, 2008	Periods after Dec. 31, 2005, in tax years ending after Dec. 31, 2005	¶ 323 Tax Provisions of the Energy and Transportation Acts of 2005
48(c)	10% energy credit will be allowed for qualified microturbine property in periods after Dec. 31, 2005 and before Jan. 1, 2008	Periods after Dec. 31, 2005, in tax years ending after Dec. 31, 2005	¶ 324 Tax Provisions of the Energy and Transportation Acts of 2005
48(c)	30% energy credit will be allowed for qualified fuel cell property for periods after Dec. 31, 2005 and before Jan. 1, 2008	Periods after Dec. 31, 2005, in tax years ending after Dec. 31, 2005	¶ 323 Tax Provisions of the Energy and Transportation Acts of 2005
48(c)(1)(E)	Increase in business energy tax credit for solar energy property from 10% to 30% is extended through Dec. 31, 2008, as are the 30% credit for qualified fuel cell property and the 10% credit for qualified microturbine property	Periods after Dec. 31, 2007 and before Jan. 1, 2009	¶ 902 Tax Provisions of the Tax Relief and Health Care Act of 2006
48(c)(2)(E)	Increase in business energy tax credit for solar energy property from 10% to 30% is extended through Dec. 31, 2008, as are the 30% credit for qualified fuel cell property and the 10% credit for qualified microturbine property	Periods after Dec. 31, 2007 and before Jan. 1, 2009	¶ 902 Tax Provisions of the Tax Relief and Health Care Act of 2006

Code	Topic	Effective Date	Complete Analysis ¶
48A(f)(1)	An alternative low-sulfur standard is met for advanced coal-based generation technology units using subbituminous coal where an emission level of 0.04 pounds or less of SO2 per million Btu is achieved	Applications for certification submitted after Oct. 2, 2006	¶ 905 Tax Provisions of the Tax Relief and Health Care Act of 2006
51(c)(4)(B)	Work opportunity credit is retroactively restored to Jan. 1, 2006 and is extended two years to Dec. 31, 2007 for most targeted groups	Individuals who begin work for the employer after Dec. 31, 2005 and before Jan. 1, 2008	¶ 801 Tax Provisions of the Tax Relief and Health Care Act of 2006
51(d)(1)(I)	Welfare-to-work credit is retroactively restored to Jan. 1, 2006 and, after Dec. 31, 2006, is consolidated with the work opportunity credit	Individuals who begin work for the employer after Dec. 31, 2005 (after Dec. 31, 2006 for credit consolidation and post-consolidation rules) and before Jan. 1, 2008	¶ 805 Tax Provisions of the Tax Relief and Health Care Act of 2006
51(d)(4)	The "family low-income requirement" is eliminated for the work opportunity credit group consisting of "qualified ex-felons"	Individuals who begin work for the employer after Dec. 31, 2006 and before Jan. 1, 2008	¶ 804 Tax Provisions of the Tax Relief and Health Care Act of 2006
51(d)(8)(A)(i)	Maximum age of a "qualified food stamp recipient" is increased from 24 to 39 for purposes of the work opportunity credit	Individuals who begin work for the employer after Dec. 31, 2006 and before Jan. 1, 2008	¶ 803 Tax Provisions of the Tax Relief and Health Care Act of 2006
51(d)(10)	Welfare-to-work credit is retroactively restored to Jan. 1, 2006 and, after Dec. 31, 2006, is consolidated with the work opportunity credit	Individuals who begin work for the employer after Dec. 31, 2005 (after Dec. 31, 2006 for credit consolidation and post-consolidation rules) and before Jan. 1, 2008	¶ 805 Tax Provisions of the Tax Relief and Health Care Act of 2006

Code	Topic	Effective Date	Complete Analysis ¶
51(d)(12)(A)(ii)(II)	Deadline for submitting paperwork for certification of employees under the work opportunity credit is extended to 28 days after the beginning of work	Individuals who begin work for the employer after Dec. 31, 2006 and before Jan. 1, 2008	¶ 802 Tax Provisions of the Tax Relief and Health Care Act of 2006
51(e)	Welfare-to-work credit is retroactively restored to Jan. 1, 2006 and, after Dec. 31, 2006, is consolidated with the work opportunity credit	Individuals who begin work for the employer after Dec. 31, 2005 (after Dec. 31, 2006 for credit consolidation and post-consolidation rules) and before Jan. 1, 2008	¶ 805 Tax Provisions of the Tax Relief and Health Care Act of 2006
51A	Welfare-to-work credit is retroactively restored to Jan. 1, 2006 and, after Dec. 31, 2006, is consolidated with the work opportunity credit	Individuals who begin work for the employer after Dec. 31, 2005 (after Dec. 31, 2006 for credit consolidation and post-consolidation rules) and before Jan. 1, 2008	¶ 805 Tax Provisions of the Tax Relief and Health Care Act of 2006
51A(f)	Welfare-to-work credit is retroactively restored to Jan. 1, 2006 and, after Dec. 31, 2006, is consolidated with the work opportunity credit	Individuals who begin work for the employer after Dec. 31, 2005 (after Dec. 31, 2006 for credit consolidation and post-consolidation rules) and before Jan. 1, 2008	¶ 805 Tax Provisions of the Tax Relief and Health Care Act of 2006
53(d)(1)(B)(iii)	Nonconventional fuel production credit will be an elective general business credit for tax years ending after Dec. 31, 2005	Credits determined under IRC of 1986 for tax years ending after Dec. 31, 2005	¶ 301 Tax Provisions of the Energy and Transportation Acts of 2005
53(e)	Portion of minimum tax credit attributable to years before the third immediately preceding tax year is made refundable	Tax years beginning after and before Jan. 1, 2013	¶ 1201 Tax Provisions of the Tax Relief and Health Care Act of 2006
54	Nonrefundable tax credit will be allowed to holders of clean renewable energy bonds issued after 2005	Bonds issued after Dec. 31, 2005	¶ 601 Tax Provisions of the Energy and Transportation Acts of 2005

Code	Topic	Effective Date	Complete Analysis ¶
54(c)(2)	Louisiana, Mississippi, and Alabama are authorized to issue Gulf tax credit bonds	Bonds issued after Dec. 31, 2005 and before Jan. 1, 2007	¶ 148 Gulf Opportunity Zone and Katrina Emergency Tax Relief Acts of 2005
54(f)(1)	National CREB limitation raised to $1.2 billion; amount allocable to governmental borrowers raised to $750 million; termination date for issuance of CREBs extended through end of 2008	Bonds issued, and allocations or reallocations made after, Dec. 31, 2006	¶ 906 Tax Provisions of the Tax Relief and Health Care Act of 2006
54(f)(2)	National CREB limitation raised to $1.2 billion; amount allocable to governmental borrowers raised to $750 million; termination date for issuance of CREBs extended through end of 2008	Bonds issued, and allocations or reallocations made after, Dec. 31, 2006	¶ 906 Tax Provisions of the Tax Relief and Health Care Act of 2006
54(l)(5)	Clean renewable energy bond (CREB) credit rule treating the credit as a payment for estimated tax penalty purposes is repealed	Bonds issued after Dec. 31, 2005	¶ 613 Gulf Opportunity Zone and Katrina Emergency Tax Relief Acts of 2005
54(m)	National CREB limitation raised to $1.2 billion; amount allocable to governmental borrowers raised to $750 million; termination date for issuance of CREBs extended through end of 2008	Bonds issued, and allocations or reallocations made after, Dec. 31, 2006	¶ 906 Tax Provisions of the Tax Relief and Health Care Act of 2006
55(b)(3)(B)	5% (0% in 2008) and 15% maximum AMT rates on adjusted net capital gain are extended for two years	Tax years beginning after Dec. 31, 2008 and before Jan. 1, 2011	¶ 103 Tax Increase Prevention and Reconciliation Act of 2005

Code	Topic	Effective Date	Complete Analysis ¶
55(b)(3)(C)	5% (0% in 2008) and 15% maximum AMT rates on adjusted net capital gain are extended for two years	Tax years beginning after Dec. 31, 2008 and before Jan. 1, 2011	¶ 103 Tax Increase Prevention and Reconciliation Act of 2005
55(c)(3)	Nonconventional fuel production credit will be an elective general business credit for tax years ending after Dec. 31, 2005	Credits determined under IRC of 1986 for tax years ending after Dec. 31, 2005	¶ 301 Tax Provisions of the Energy and Transportation Acts of 2005
55(d)(1)(A)	AMT exemption amounts for 2006 are increased to $42,500 (from $33,750) for unmarrieds, to $62,550 (from $45,000) for joint filers, and to $31,275 (from $22,500) for marrieds filing separately	Tax years beginning in 2006	¶ 201 Tax Increase Prevention and Reconciliation Act of 2005
55(d)(1)(B)	AMT exemption amounts for 2006 are increased to $42,500 (from $33,750) for unmarrieds, to $62,550 (from $45,000) for joint filers, and to $31,275 (from $22,500) for marrieds filing separately	Tax years beginning in 2006	¶ 201 Tax Increase Prevention and Reconciliation Act of 2005
57(a)(7)	7% AMT preference percentage for excluded gain on sale of qualified small business stock is extended for two years	Tax years beginning after Dec. 31, 2008 and before Jan. 1, 2011	¶ 104 Tax Increase Prevention and Reconciliation Act of 2005
61	25% of qualifying gain from conservation sales of qualifying mineral or geothermal interests excluded from gross income	Sales on or after date of enactment of the 2006 Tax Relief and Health Care Act	¶ 1606 Tax Provisions of the Tax Relief and Health Care Act of 2006

Code	Topic	Effective Date	Complete Analysis ¶
62(a)(2)(D)	Up-to-$250 above-the-line deduction for teachers' out-of-pocket classroom-related expenses is retroactively extended for two years through 2007	Expenses paid or incurred in tax years beginning after Dec. 31, 2005 and before Jan. 1, 2008	¶ 103 Tax Provisions of the Tax Relief and Health Care Act of 2006
62(a)(21)	Above-the-line deduction is allowed for attorneys' fees and court costs relating to whistleblower rewards	Information provided on or after date of enactment of the 2006 Tax Relief and Health Care Act	¶ 1410 Tax Provisions of the Tax Relief and Health Care Act of 2006
68(f)	Limitation on itemized deductions will phase-out starting in 2006 and be eliminated after 2009	Tax years beginning after Dec. 31, 2005	¶ 105 Economic Growth and Tax Relief Reconciliation Act of 2001
68(g)	Limitation on itemized deductions will phase-out starting in 2006 and be eliminated after 2009	Tax years beginning after Dec. 31, 2005	¶ 105 Economic Growth and Tax Relief Reconciliation Act of 2001
72(e)(11)	Qualified long-term care insurance can be provided as a rider to an annuity contract after 2009	After Dec. 31, 2009	¶ 2402 Pension Protection Act of 2006
72(t)(10)	Waiver of 10% early withdrawal tax for distributions made to public safety employees who have separated from service after age 50	Distributions made after Aug. 17, 2006	¶ 1110 Pension Protection Act of 2006
101(j)	Income tax treatment of proceeds from employer-owned life insurance modified; new compliance procedures added	Life insurance contracts issued after Aug. 17, 2006	¶ 2401 Pension Protection Act of 2006
106(e)	One-time rollovers from health FSAs and HRAs into HSAs permitted through 2011	For distributions on or after date of enactment of the 2006 Tax Relief and Health Care Act	¶ 302 Tax Provisions of the Tax Relief and Health Care Act of 2006

Code	Topic	Effective Date	Complete Analysis ¶
119	Value of lodging provided to employees and their families is excluded from employee's income for employees affected by Hurricane Katrina	Lodging furnished beginning Jan. 1, 2006	¶ 106 Gulf Opportunity Zone and Katrina Emergency Tax Relief Acts of 2005
121(d)(9)	Extension of the $250,000 exclusion of gain from the sale of a decedent's principal residence to sales by estates, heirs of decedents, and qualified revocable trusts—estates of decedents dying after Dec. 31, 2009	Estates of decedents dying after Dec. 31, 2009	¶ 331 Economic Growth and Tax Relief Reconciliation Act of 2001
121(d)(9)(A)	Up to ten-year suspension of the five-year period for determining whether the principal residence gain exclusion applies is extended to apply to sales or exchanges by employees of the intelligence community before Jan. 1, 2011	Sales or exchanges after date of enactment of the 2006 Tax Relief and Health Care Act and before Jan. 1, 2011	¶ 107 Tax Provisions of the Tax Relief and Health Care Act of 2006
121(d)(9)(C)(iv)	Up to ten-year suspension of the five-year period for determining whether the principal residence gain exclusion applies is extended to apply to sales or exchanges by employees of the intelligence community before Jan. 1, 2011	Sales or exchanges after date of enactment of the 2006 Tax Relief and Health Care Act and before Jan. 1, 2011	¶ 107 Tax Provisions of the Tax Relief and Health Care Act of 2006

Code	Topic	Effective Date	Complete Analysis ¶
121(d)(9)(C)(vi)	Up to ten-year suspension of the five-year period for determining whether the principal residence gain exclusion applies is extended to apply to sales or exchanges by employees of the intelligence community before Jan. 1, 2011	Sales or exchanges after date of enactment of the 2006 Tax Relief and Health Care Act and before Jan. 1, 2011	¶ 107 Tax Provisions of the Tax Relief and Health Care Act of 2006
142(f)(1)	Exempt facility bond "local furnishing" requirements are relaxed for certain Alaska hydroelectric facilities	Aug. 17, 2006	¶ 2403 Pension Protection Act of 2006
142(f)(1)	Exempt facility bond "local furnishing" requirements are relaxed for certain Alaska hydroelectric facilities	Aug. 17, 2006	¶ 2403 Pension Protection Act of 2006
142(f)(3)	Exempt facility bond "local furnishing" requirements are relaxed for certain Alaska hydroelectric facilities	Aug. 17, 2006	¶ 2403 Pension Protection Act of 2006
143(d)(2)(D)	Qualified mortgage bonds can be used to finance mortgages for veterans without regard to first-time homebuyer requirement	Bonds issued after date of enactment of the 2006 Tax Relief and Health Care Act, and before Jan. 1, 2008	¶ 1603 Tax Provisions of the Tax Relief and Health Care Act of 2006
143(l)(3)(B)	New $25 million volume limits on qualified veterans' mortgage bonds issued by Alaska, Oregon, and Wisconsin will be phased in from 2006 to 2009; issuance will terminate after 2010	Allocations of state volume limit after Apr. 5, 2006	¶ 903 Tax Increase Prevention and Reconciliation Act of 2005

Code	Topic	Effective Date	Complete Analysis ¶
143(l)(3)(B)(iv)	$25 million volume limits on qualified veterans' mortgage bonds issued by Alaska, Oregon, and Wisconsin won't sunset after 2010	Allocations of state volume limit after Apr. 5, 2006	¶ 1604 Tax Provisions of the Tax Relief and Health Care Act of 2006
143(l)(4)	Loans financed with veterans' mortgage bonds issued by Alaska, Oregon, and Wisconsin made available to post-1976 veterans for 25 years after leaving active service	Bonds issued on or after May 17, 2006	¶ 904 Tax Increase Prevention and Reconciliation Act of 2005
144(a)(4)(F)	Allowance of additional $10 million capital expenditures (i.e., $20 million total maximum) for small issue bonds generally is accelerated to bonds issued after 2006 (instead of Sept. 30, 2009)	May 17, 2006 for bonds issued after Dec. 31, 2006	¶ 901 Tax Increase Prevention and Reconciliation Act of 2005
144(a)(4)(F)	Allowance of additional $10 million capital expenditures for small issue bonds issued after Sept. 30, 2009 won't be limited to facilities financed with urban development action grants	Bonds issued after Sept. 30, 2009	¶ 1307 American Jobs Creation Act of 2004
144(a)(4)(G)	Allowance of additional $10 million capital expenditures (i.e., $20 million total maximum) for small issue bonds generally is accelerated to bonds issued after 2006 (instead of Sept. 30, 2009)	May 17, 2006 for bonds issued after Dec. 31, 2006	¶ 901 Tax Increase Prevention and Reconciliation Act of 2005

Code	Topic	Effective Date	Complete Analysis ¶
144(a)(4)(G)	Allowance of additional $10 million capital expenditures for small issue bonds issued after Sept. 30, 2009 won't be limited to facilities financed with urban development action grants	Bonds issued after Sept. 30, 2009	¶ 1307 American Jobs Creation Act of 2004
148(f)(4)(D)(ii)	Pooled financing bonds must meet requirements relating to loan origination, written loan commitments, and redemptions, and are counted in applying small issuer exception to arbitrage rebate requirements	Bonds issued after May 17, 2006	¶ 902 Tax Increase Prevention and Reconciliation Act of 2005
149(f)(1)	Pooled financing bonds must meet requirements relating to loan origination, written loan commitments, and redemptions, and are counted in applying small issuer exception to arbitrage rebate requirements	Bonds issued after May 17, 2006	¶ 902 Tax Increase Prevention and Reconciliation Act of 2005
149(f)(2)(A)	Pooled financing bonds must meet requirements relating to loan origination, written loan commitments, and redemptions, and are counted in applying small issuer exception to arbitrage rebate requirements	Bonds issued after May 17, 2006	¶ 902 Tax Increase Prevention and Reconciliation Act of 2005

Code	Topic	Effective Date	Complete Analysis ¶
149(f)(4)	Pooled financing bonds must meet requirements relating to loan origination, written loan commitments, and redemptions, and are counted in applying small issuer exception to arbitrage rebate requirements	Bonds issued after May 17, 2006	¶ 902 Tax Increase Prevention and Reconciliation Act of 2005
149(f)(5)	Pooled financing bonds must meet requirements relating to loan origination, written loan commitments, and redemptions, and are counted in applying small issuer exception to arbitrage rebate requirements	Bonds issued after May 17, 2006	¶ 902 Tax Increase Prevention and Reconciliation Act of 2005
151(d)(3)(E)	Full personal exemption will be restored—phaseout will be gradually reduced after 2005 and completely eliminated after 2009	Tax years beginning after Dec. 31, 2005	¶ 104 Economic Growth and Tax Relief Reconciliation Act of 2001
151(d)(3)(F)	Full personal exemption will be restored—phaseout will be gradually reduced after 2005 and completely eliminated after 2009	Tax years beginning after Dec. 31, 2005	¶ 104 Economic Growth and Tax Relief Reconciliation Act of 2001
163(d)(4)(B)	Exclusion of qualified dividend income from investment income for investment interest deduction limit purposes (unless taxpayer elects to include it) is extended for two years	Tax years beginning after Dec. 31, 2008 and before Jan. 1, 2011	¶ 109 Tax Increase Prevention and Reconciliation Act of 2005

Code	Topic	Effective Date	Complete Analysis ¶
163(h)(3)(E)	Deduction is allowed, for taxpayers with AGI not exceeding $109,000, for mortgage insurance premiums paid or incurred with respect to qualified residences in 2007	Amounts paid or accrued after Dec. 31, 2006 and before Jan. 1, 2008, for mortgage contracts issued after Dec. 31, 2006	¶ 104 Tax Provisions of the Tax Relief and Health Care Act of 2006
163(h)(4)(E)	Deduction is allowed, for taxpayers with AGI not exceeding $109,000, for mortgage insurance premiums paid or incurred with respect to qualified residences in 2007	Amounts paid or accrued after Dec. 31, 2006 and before Jan. 1, 2008, for mortgage contracts issued after Dec. 31, 2006	¶ 104 Tax Provisions of the Tax Relief and Health Care Act of 2006
163(h)(4)(F)	Deduction is allowed, for taxpayers with AGI not exceeding $109,000, for mortgage insurance premiums paid or incurred with respect to qualified residences in 2007	Amounts paid or accrued after Dec. 31, 2006 and before Jan. 1, 2008, for mortgage contracts issued after Dec. 31, 2006	¶ 104 Tax Provisions of the Tax Relief and Health Care Act of 2006
163(j)(8)	Earnings-stripping rules are applied to corporate partners	Tax years beginning on or after May 17, 2006	¶ 503 Tax Increase Prevention and Reconciliation Act of 2005
163(j)(9)(D)	Earnings-stripping rules are applied to corporate partners	Tax years beginning on or after May 17, 2006	¶ 503 Tax Increase Prevention and Reconciliation Act of 2005
164(b)(5)(I)	Election to claim itemized deduction for state and local general sales taxes is retroactively extended from 2005 through 2007	Tax years beginning after Dec. 31, 2005 and before Jan. 1, 2008	¶ 101 Tax Provisions of the Tax Relief and Health Care Act of 2006

Code	Topic	Effective Date	Complete Analysis ¶
167(g)(8)	Five-year amortization election for expenses of creating or acquiring musical compositions or music copyrights for property placed in service in tax years beginning after Dec. 31, 2005, and before Jan. 1, 2011	Expenses paid or incurred for property placed in service in tax years beginning after Dec. 31, 2005, and before Jan. 1, 2011	¶ 405 Tax Increase Prevention and Reconciliation Act of 2005
167(h)(5)	Major integrated oil companies must use 5-year amortization for geological and geophysical expenditures	Amounts paid or incurred after May 17, 2006	¶ 404 Tax Increase Prevention and Reconciliation Act of 2005
168(e)(3)(E)(iv)	Placed-in-service deadline for the treatment of "qualified leasehold improvement property" as 15-year MACRS property is retroactively restored to Jan. 1, 2006 and is extended for two years to Dec. 31, 2007	Property placed in service after Dec 31, 2005 and before Jan. 1, 2008	¶ 502 Tax Provisions of the Tax Relief and Health Care Act of 2006
168(e)(3)(E)(v)	Placed-in-service deadline for the treatment of "qualified restaurant property" as 15-year MACRS property is retroactively restored to Jan. 1, 2006 and is extended for two years to Dec. 31, 2007	Property placed in service after Dec 31, 2005 and before Jan. 1, 2008	¶ 503 Tax Provisions of the Tax Relief and Health Care Act of 2006
168(j)(8)	Depreciation tax breaks for Indian reservation property are extended retroactively to property placed in service after Dec. 31, 2005 and before Jan. 1, 2008	Property placed in service after Dec. 31, 2005 and before Jan. 1, 2008	¶ 510 Tax Provisions of the Tax Relief and Health Care Act of 2006

Code	Topic	Effective Date	Complete Analysis ¶
168(l)	50% bonus depreciation and AMT relief are allowed for "qualified cellulosic biomass ethanol plant property" purchased after and placed in service before Jan. 1, 2013	Property purchased after date of enactment of the 2006 Tax Relief and Health Care Act and placed in service before Jan. 1, 2013	¶ 508 Tax Provisions of the Tax Relief and Health Care Act of 2006
170(b)(1)(E)	Individuals' qualified conservation contributions before 2008 are deductible up to 50% (100% for farmers and ranchers) of contribution base; 15-year carryover is allowed	Contributions made in tax years beginning after Dec. 31, 2005, and before Jan. 1, 2008	¶ 1511 Pension Protection Act of 2006
170(b)(2)	Qualified conservation contributions by corporate farmers and ranchers are deductible up to 100% of taxable income; 15-year carryover is allowed	Contributions made in tax years beginning after Dec. 31, 2005 and before Jan. 1, 2008	¶ 1512 Pension Protection Act of 2006
170(d)(2)	Qualified conservation contributions by corporate farmers and ranchers are deductible up to 100% of taxable income; 15-year carryover is allowed	Contributions made in tax years beginning after Dec. 31, 2005 and before Jan. 1, 2008	¶ 1512 Pension Protection Act of 2006
170(e)(1)	Capital asset treatment for charitable contributions of creative property is determined after 2009 without regard to the modified-carryover-basis-at-death rules	Estates of decedents dying after Dec. 31, 2009	¶ 330 Economic Growth and Tax Relief Reconciliation Act of 2001
170(e)(1)(A)	Capital gain treatment is permitted for certain self-created musical works sold or exchanged before Jan. 1, 2011	Sales and exchanges in tax years beginning after May 17, 2006 and before Jan. 1, 2011	¶ 208 Tax Increase Prevention and Reconciliation Act of 2005

Code	Topic	Effective Date	Complete Analysis ¶
170(e)(1)(B)(i)(II)	Deduction for charitable contributions of tangible personal property exceeding $5,000 must be reduced or recaptured if donee sells property within three years of contribution	Contributions after Sept. 1, 2006	¶ 1505 Pension Protection Act of 2006
170(e)(1)(B)(iv)	Deductions are limited for charitable contributions of taxidermy property	For contributions made after July 25, 2006	¶ 1515 Pension Protection Act of 2006
170(e)(3)(C)(iv)	Above-basis deduction for charitable contributions of apparently wholesome food inventory is retroactively extended through end of 2007	Contributions made after Dec. 31, 2005 and before Jan. 1, 2008	¶ 1504 Pension Protection Act of 2006
170(e)(3)(D)(iv)	Corporate above-basis charitable deduction for book inventory contributions to schools is retroactively extended through end of 2007	Contributions made after Dec. 31, 2005 and before Jan. 1, 2008	¶ 1503 Pension Protection Act of 2006
170(e)(4)(B)(ii)	Property assembled by donor qualifies for enhanced deduction for qualified research contributions and qualified computer contributions	Tax years beginning after Dec. 31, 2005	¶ 603 Tax Provisions of the Tax Relief and Health Care Act of 2006
170(e)(4)(B)(iii)	Property assembled by donor qualifies for enhanced deduction for qualified research contributions and qualified computer contributions	Tax years beginning after Dec. 31, 2005	¶ 603 Tax Provisions of the Tax Relief and Health Care Act of 2006

Code	Topic	Effective Date	Complete Analysis ¶
170(e)(6)(B)(ii)	Property assembled by donor qualifies for enhanced deduction for qualified research contributions and qualified computer contributions	Tax years beginning after Dec. 31, 2005	¶ 603 Tax Provisions of the Tax Relief and Health Care Act of 2006
170(e)(6)(D)	Property assembled by donor qualifies for enhanced deduction for qualified research contributions and qualified computer contributions	Tax years beginning after Dec. 31, 2005	¶ 603 Tax Provisions of the Tax Relief and Health Care Act of 2006
170(e)(6)(G)	Enhanced deduction for qualified computer contributions by corporations is retroactively extended for two years through 2007	Contributions made in tax years beginning after Dec. 31, 2005, and before Jan. 1, 2008	¶ 602 Tax Provisions of the Tax Relief and Health Care Act of 2006
170(e)(7)	Deduction for charitable contributions of tangible personal property exceeding $5,000 must be reduced or recaptured if donee sells property within three years of contribution	Contributions after Sept. 1, 2006	¶ 1505 Pension Protection Act of 2006
170(f)(11)(E)	Qualified appraiser is defined for charitable deduction purposes	For appraisals prepared for returns or submissions filed after Aug. 17, 2006	¶ 1507 Pension Protection Act of 2006
170(f)(13)	Taxpayers claiming qualified conservation contribution in excess of $10,000 for building exterior in historic district must pay $500 fee to IRS	Contributions made 180 days after Aug. 17, 2006	¶ 1509 Pension Protection Act of 2006

Code	Topic	Effective Date	Complete Analysis ¶
170(f)(14)	Qualified conservation contribution is disallowed for structure or land area in registered historic district; deduction for qualified conservation contributions is reduced by rehabilitation credit	Contributions made after Aug. 17, 2006	¶ 1510 Pension Protection Act of 2006
170(f)(15)	Deductions are limited for charitable contributions of taxidermy property	For contributions made after July 25, 2006	¶ 1515 Pension Protection Act of 2006
170(f)(16)	Deductions for charitable contributions of clothing and household items are limited	For contributions made after Aug. 17, 2006	¶ 1502 Pension Protection Act of 2006
170(f)(17)	Donor recordkeeping requirements are toughened for charitable monetary contributions	Contributions made in tax years beginning after Aug. 17, 2006	¶ 1501 Pension Protection Act of 2006
170(f)(18)	Charitable deduction isn't allowed for contributions to donor advised funds of certain sponsoring organizations; deductible contributions require additional substantiation	Contributions made after the date that is 180 days after Aug. 17, 2006	¶ 1514 Pension Protection Act of 2006
170(h)(4)(B)	New requirements are added for contributions of easements on building exteriors located in registered historic districts	Contributions made after July 25, 2006	¶ 1508 Pension Protection Act of 2006

Code	Topic	Effective Date	Complete Analysis ¶
170(h)(4)(C)	Qualified conservation contribution is disallowed for structure or land area in registered historic district; deduction for qualified conservation contributions is reduced by rehabilitation credit	Contributions made after Aug. 17, 2006	¶ 1510 Pension Protection Act of 2006
170(o)	Charitable deduction for fractional interest gifts of tangible personal property is limited; later fractional contributions must be valued consistently with initial one	Contributions, bequests, and gifts made after Aug. 17, 2006	¶ 1513 Pension Protection Act of 2006
172(b)(1)(I)	Election to extend carryback period for 2003, 2004, and 2005 NOLs to five years (from two years) for companies that, before 2008, invest in electric transmission equipment or pollution control facilities	Elections made in tax years ending after Dec. 31, 2005 and before 2009	¶ 326 Tax Provisions of the Energy and Transportation Acts of 2005
172(b)(1)(I)(i)	Five-year carryback election for electric utility company NOLs applies to NOLs for 2003, 2004, and 2005; election is made for 2006, 2007, or 2008	Elections made for tax years ending after Dec. 31, 2005 and before 2009	¶ 1804 Gulf Opportunity Zone and Katrina Emergency Tax Relief Acts of 2005
172(b)(1)(I)(ii)(I)	Five-year carryback election for electric utility company NOLs applies to NOLs for 2003, 2004, and 2005; election is made for 2006, 2007, or 2008	Elections made for tax years ending after Dec. 31, 2005 and before 2009	¶ 1804 Gulf Opportunity Zone and Katrina Emergency Tax Relief Acts of 2005

Code	Topic	Effective Date	Complete Analysis ¶
172(b)(1)(I)(iv)(II)	Five-year carryback election for electric utility company NOLs applies to NOLs for 2003, 2004, and 2005; election is made for 2006, 2007, or 2008	Elections made for tax years ending after Dec. 31, 2005 and before 2009	¶ 1804 Gulf Opportunity Zone and Katrina Emergency Tax Relief Acts of 2005
179(b)(1)	The $100,000 Code Sec. 179 expense election limit, $400,000 phaseout threshold, and inflation adjustments are extended for two years to tax years beginning before Jan. 1, 2010	Tax years beginning after 2007 and before 2010	¶ 401 Tax Increase Prevention and Reconciliation Act of 2005
179(b)(2)	The $100,000 Code Sec. 179 expense election limit, $400,000 phaseout threshold, and inflation adjustments are extended for two years to tax years beginning before Jan. 1, 2010	Tax years beginning after 2007 and before 2010	¶ 401 Tax Increase Prevention and Reconciliation Act of 2005
179(b)(5)(A)	The $100,000 Code Sec. 179 expense election limit, $400,000 phaseout threshold, and inflation adjustments are extended for two years to tax years beginning before Jan. 1, 2010	Tax years beginning after 2007 and before 2010	¶ 401 Tax Increase Prevention and Reconciliation Act of 2005
179(c)(2)	Right to revoke or change the Code Sec. 179 expense election without IRS consent is extended for two years to tax years beginning before Jan. 1, 2010	Tax years beginning after 2007 and before 2010	¶ 402 Tax Increase Prevention and Reconciliation Act of 2005

Code	Topic	Effective Date	Complete Analysis ¶
179(d)(1)(A)(ii)	Inclusion of off-the-shelf computer software as "section 179 property" eligible for the expensing election is extended for two years to tax years beginning before Jan. 1, 2010	Tax years beginning after 2007 and before 2010	¶ 403 Tax Increase Prevention and Reconciliation Act of 2005
179D	Deduction will be allowed for costs of energy efficient commercial building property placed in service after Dec. 31, 2005 and before Jan. 1, 2008	Property placed in service after Dec. 31, 2005 and before Jan. 1, 2008	¶ 101 Tax Provisions of the Energy and Transportation Acts of 2005
179D(h)	Deduction for energy efficient commercial building property is extended for one year through Dec. 31, 2008	Date of enactment of the 2006 Tax Relief and Health Care Act	¶ 501 Tax Provisions of the Tax Relief and Health Care Act of 2006
179E	Taxpayers can elect to expense 50% of the cost of "qualified advanced mine safety equipment property" placed in service after and before Jan. 1, 2009	Costs paid or incurred after date of enactment of the 2006 Tax Relief and Health Care Act	¶ 509 Tax Provisions of the Tax Relief and Health Care Act of 2006
196(c)(13)	New energy efficient home credit of $2,000 ($1,000 for certain homes) is available to eligible contractors for qualified new energy efficient homes acquired after Dec. 31, 2005 and before Jan. 1, 2008	Qualified new energy efficient homes acquired after Dec. 31, 2005 and before Jan. 1, 2008	¶ 102 Tax Provisions of the Energy and Transportation Acts of 2005
198(d)(1)	Definition of hazardous substances for purposes of expensing election for environmental remediation costs is expanded to include petroleum products	Expenditures paid or incurred after Dec. 31, 2005	¶ 506 Tax Provisions of the Tax Relief and Health Care Act of 2006

Code	Topic	Effective Date	Complete Analysis ¶
198(h)	Election to expense qualified environmental remediation costs is retroactively restored and is extended for two years to apply to expenditures paid or incurred after Dec. 31, 2005 and before Jan. 1, 2008	Expenditures paid or incurred after Dec. 31, 2005 and before Jan. 1, 2008	¶ 505 Tax Provisions of the Tax Relief and Health Care Act of 2006
199(b)(2)(B)	Only wages allocable to domestic production gross receipts may be taken into account in determining 50%-of-W-2-wages limitation on U.S. production activities deduction	Tax years beginning after May 17, 2006	¶ 301 Tax Increase Prevention and Reconciliation Act of 2005
199(d)(1)(A)(iii)	Special rule for computing a partner's or S corporation shareholder's W-2 wages for purposes of the 50%-of-W-2-wages limitation on U.S. production activities deduction is repealed	Tax years beginning after May 17, 2006	¶ 302 Tax Increase Prevention and Reconciliation Act of 2005
199(d)(8)	Domestic production activities deduction extended retroactively to production activities in Puerto Rico for first two tax years beginning after 2005	First two tax years beginning after Dec. 31, 2005 and before Jan. 1, 2008	¶ 1302 Tax Provisions of the Tax Relief and Health Care Act of 2006
219(b)(5)(C)	Additional IRA deductions allowed to participants in certain 401(k) plans of bankrupt employer where crimes triggered the bankruptcy	Tax years beginning after Dec. 31, 2006	¶ 104 Pension Protection Act of 2006
219(g)(8)	AGI limitations on traditional IRA and Roth IRA contributions will be indexed for inflation after 2006	Tax years beginning after 2006	¶ 106 Pension Protection Act of 2006

Code	Topic	Effective Date	Complete Analysis ¶
220(i)(2)	Archer MSA program is extended through 2007—trustees' reports for 2005 and 2006 will be timely if made within 90 days of	Date of enactment of the 2006 Tax Relief and Health Care Act	¶ 307 Tax Provisions of the Tax Relief and Health Care Act of 2006
222(b)(2)(B)	Above-the-line deduction for higher-education expenses is retroactively extended from 2005 through 2007	Tax years beginning after Dec. 31, 2005 and before Jan. 1, 2008	¶ 102 Tax Provisions of the Tax Relief and Health Care Act of 2006
222(e)	Above-the-line deduction for higher-education expenses is retroactively extended from 2005 through 2007	Tax years beginning after Dec. 31, 2005 and before Jan. 1, 2008	¶ 102 Tax Provisions of the Tax Relief and Health Care Act of 2006
223(b)(2)	Deductible limitation on HSA contributions modified	For tax years beginning after Dec. 31, 2006	¶ 303 Tax Provisions of the Tax Relief and Health Care Act of 2006
223(b)(4)(C)	Eligible individuals may elect one-time tax-free rollover of IRA distribution into an HSA	Tax years beginning after Dec. 31, 2006	¶ 301 Tax Provisions of the Tax Relief and Health Care Act of 2006
223(b)(8)	Individuals who establish health savings accounts mid-year can contribute the full-year amount	Tax years beginning after Dec. 31, 2006	¶ 306 Tax Provisions of the Tax Relief and Health Care Act of 2006
223(c)(1)(B)(iii)	One-time rollovers from health FSAs and HRAs into HSAs permitted through 2011	For distributions on or after date of enactment of the 2006 Tax Relief and Health Care Act	¶ 302 Tax Provisions of the Tax Relief and Health Care Act of 2006
223(g)(1)	Cost-of-living adjustment for HSA and HDHP dollar amounts is modified—tax years beginning after 2007	For adjustments made for tax years beginning after 2007	¶ 305 Tax Provisions of the Tax Relief and Health Care Act of 2006

Code	Topic	Effective Date	Complete Analysis ¶
263(a)(1)(K)	Deduction will be allowed for costs of energy efficient commercial building property placed in service after Dec. 31, 2005 and before Jan. 1, 2008	Property placed in service after Dec. 31, 2005 and before Jan. 1, 2008	¶ 101 Tax Provisions of the Energy and Transportation Acts of 2005
263(a)(1)(L)	Taxpayers can elect to expense 50% of the cost of "qualified advanced mine safety equipment property" placed in service after and before Jan. 1, 2009	Costs paid or incurred after date of enactment of the 2006 Tax Relief and Health Care Act	¶ 509 Tax Provisions of the Tax Relief and Health Care Act of 2006
280C(a)	Qualified employers receive credit for providing lodging to employees affected by Hurricane Katrina	Lodging furnished beginning Jan. 1, 2006	¶ 128 Gulf Opportunity Zone and Katrina Emergency Tax Relief Acts of 2005
280C(c)(3)(C)	Taxpayers with a tax year ending after 2005 have until Apr. 15, 2007 to make elections under expired provisions that are retroactively extended by the 2006 Tax Relief and Health Care Act	Tax years ending after Dec. 31, 2005 and before date of enactment of the 2006 Tax Relief and Health Care Act	¶ 701 Tax Provisions of the Tax Relief and Health Care Act of 2006
280C(e)	A 20% credit is available for amounts paid or incurred in tax years beginning after Dec. 31, 2005 and before Jan. 1, 2009 for training mine rescue teams	Tax years beginning after Dec. 31, 2005 and before Jan. 1, 2009	¶ 806 Tax Provisions of the Tax Relief and Health Care Act of 2006
306(a)(1)(D)	Qualified dividend income treatment for ordinary income on disposition of Code Sec. 306 stock extended for two years	Tax years beginning after Dec. 31, 2008 and before Jan. 1, 2011	¶ 113 Tax Increase Prevention and Reconciliation Act of 2005
312(k)(3)(B)	Taxpayers can elect to expense 50% of the cost of "qualified advanced mine safety equipment property" placed in service after and before Jan. 1, 2009	Costs paid or incurred after date of enactment of the 2006 Tax Relief and Health Care Act	¶ 509 Tax Provisions of the Tax Relief and Health Care Act of 2006

Code	Topic	Effective Date	Complete Analysis ¶
312(k)(3)(B)	Deduction will be allowed for costs of energy efficient commercial building property placed in service after Dec. 31, 2005 and before Jan. 1, 2008	Property placed in service after Dec. 31, 2005 and before Jan. 1, 2008	¶ 101 Tax Provisions of the Energy and Transportation Acts of 2005
341	Repeal of collapsible corporation provisions is extended two years	Tax years beginning after Dec. 31, 2008 and before Jan. 1, 2011	¶ 505 Tax Increase Prevention and Reconciliation Act of 2005
355(b)(3)	Code Section 355 definition of active conduct of a trade or business made less restrictive for certain controlled groups—pre-Jan. 1, 2011 distributions	Distributions made after May 17, 2006 and before Jan. 1, 2011	¶ 501 Tax Increase Prevention and Reconciliation Act of 2005
355(b)(3)(A)	Code Sec. 355 active trade or business test that treats members of a separate affiliated group as one corporation made permanent	Distributions after May 17, 2006	¶ 1602 Tax Provisions of the Tax Relief and Health Care Act of 2006
355(b)(3)(D)	Code Sec. 355 active trade or business test that treats members of a separate affiliated group as one corporation made permanent	Distributions after May 17, 2006	¶ 1602 Tax Provisions of the Tax Relief and Health Care Act of 2006
355(g)	Distribution can't qualify as a Code Sec. 355 corporate division if the distributing corporation or the controlled corporation is a disqualified investment corporation	Distributions after May 17, 2006	¶ 502 Tax Increase Prevention and Reconciliation Act of 2005
401(a)(5)(G)	Exemption from nondiscrimination and minimum participation rules extended to all government plans	Any year beginning after Aug. 17, 2006	¶ 1402 Pension Protection Act of 2006

Code	Topic	Effective Date	Complete Analysis ¶
401(a)(26)(G)	Exemption from nondiscrimination and minimum participation rules extended to all government plans	Any year beginning after Aug. 17, 2006	¶ 1402 Pension Protection Act of 2006
401(a)(35)	Diversification rights established for participants in defined contribution plans	For plan years beginning after Dec. 31, 2006	¶ 1302 Pension Protection Act of 2006
401(a)(36)	Qualified "pension plans" can allow distributions to 62-year-old working employees	For distributions made in plan years beginning after Dec. 31, 2006	¶ 1107 Pension Protection Act of 2006
401(k)(3)(G)	Exemption from nondiscrimination and minimum participation rules extended to all government plans	Any year beginning after Aug. 17, 2006	¶ 1402 Pension Protection Act of 2006
401(k)(13)	Automatic contribution arrangements for 401(k) plans	Plan years beginning after Dec. 31, 2007	¶ 401 Pension Protection Act of 2006
401(m)(12)	Automatic contribution arrangements for 401(k) plans	Plan years beginning after Dec. 31, 2007	¶ 401 Pension Protection Act of 2006
402(c)(2)(A)	Nontaxable distributions from a qualified plan or a 403(b) annuity may be directly rolled over tax-free to either another qualified plan or 403(b) annuity if the separate accounting requirements are met	Tax years beginning after Dec. 31, 2006	¶ 1101 Pension Protection Act of 2006
402(c)(11)(A)	Nonspouse beneficiaries can roll over into IRAs, distributions from qualified plans, tax-sheltered annuities, and government plans	Distributions made after Dec. 31, 2006	¶ 102 Pension Protection Act of 2006
402(f)	Notice and consent period for qualified plan distributions extended from 90 to 180 days	Years beginning after 2006	¶ 903 Pension Protection Act of 2006

Code	Topic	Effective Date	Complete Analysis ¶
402(g)(7)(A)(ii)	$15,000 cumulative limit on catch-up contributions made to a 403(b) annuity plan must be reduced by designated Roth contributions made to the plan in earlier years	Tax years beginning after Dec. 31, 2005	¶ 1805 Gulf Opportunity Zone and Katrina Emergency Tax Relief Acts of 2005
402(l)	Distributions of up to $3,000 from governmental plans to pay for the health or long-term care insurance of public safety officers are excluded from income	Distributions in tax years beginning after Dec. 31, 2006	¶ 1401 Pension Protection Act of 2006
402A	401(k) and 403(b) plans may treat post-2005 elective deferrals as after-tax Roth IRA-type contributions	Tax years beginning after Dec. 31, 2005	¶ 417 Economic Growth and Tax Relief Reconciliation Act of 2001
403(a)	Distributions of up to $3,000 from governmental plans to pay for the health or long-term care insurance of public safety officers are excluded from income	Distributions in tax years beginning after Dec. 31, 2006	¶ 1401 Pension Protection Act of 2006
403(a)(4)(B)	Nonspouse beneficiaries can roll over into IRAs, distributions from qualified plans, tax-sheltered annuities, and government plans	Distributions made after Dec. 31, 2006	¶ 102 Pension Protection Act of 2006
403(b)	Distributions of up to $3,000 from governmental plans to pay for the health or long-term care insurance of public safety officers are excluded from income	Distributions in tax years beginning after Dec. 31, 2006	¶ 1401 Pension Protection Act of 2006

Code	Topic	Effective Date	Complete Analysis ¶
403(b)(8)(B)	Nonspouse beneficiaries can roll over into IRAs, distributions from qualified plans, tax-sheltered annuities, and government plans	Distributions made after Dec. 31, 2006	¶ 102 Pension Protection Act of 2006
404(a)(1)(A)	Defined benefit plan deduction limits increased with separate limits set for single-employer and multiemployer plans	For years beginning after Dec. 31, 2007	¶ 510 Pension Protection Act of 2006
404(a)(1)(D)	Defined benefit plan deduction limits increased with separate limits set for single-employer and multiemployer plans	For years beginning after Dec. 31, 2007	¶ 510 Pension Protection Act of 2006
404(a)(7)(C)(iii)	Defined benefit plan deduction limits increased with separate limits set for single-employer and multiemployer plans	Contributions for tax years beginning after Dec. 31, 2005	¶ 510 Pension Protection Act of 2006
404(a)(7)(C)(iv)	Defined benefit plan deduction limits increased with separate limits set for single-employer and multiemployer plans	For years beginning after Dec. 31, 2007	¶ 510 Pension Protection Act of 2006
404(a)(7)(C)(v)	Defined benefit plan deduction limits increased with separate limits set for single-employer and multiemployer plans	Contributions for tax years beginning after Dec. 31, 2007	¶ 510 Pension Protection Act of 2006
404(o)	Defined benefit plan deduction limits increased with separate limits set for single-employer and multiemployer plans	For years beginning after Dec. 31, 2007	¶ 510 Pension Protection Act of 2006

Code	Topic	Effective Date	Complete Analysis ¶
408(d)(8)	IRA distributions donated to charity in 2006 and 2007 may be tax-free up to $100,000 for each year	For IRA distributions made during 2006 and 2007	¶ 101 Pension Protection Act of 2006
408(d)(9)	Eligible individuals may elect one-time tax-free rollover of IRA distribution into an HSA	Tax years beginning after Dec. 31, 2006	¶ 301 Tax Provisions of the Tax Relief and Health Care Act of 2006
408A(c)(3)(B)	Rollovers to Roth IRAs from qualified plans, 403(b) annuities, and governmental section 457 plans will be permitted after 2007 if AGI-based limit is met, but tax must be paid on otherwise tax-deferred distributions	For distributions made after Dec. 31, 2007	¶ 103 Pension Protection Act of 2006
408A(c)(3)(B)	AGI limit on conversion of non-Roth IRAs to Roth IRAs is eliminated; income from conversion can be deferred and spread over two years—after 2009	For tax years beginning after Dec. 31, 2009	¶ 203 Tax Increase Prevention and Reconciliation Act of 2005
408A(c)(3)(C)	AGI limitations on traditional IRA and Roth IRA contributions will be indexed for inflation after 2006	Tax years beginning after 2006	¶ 106 Pension Protection Act of 2006
408A(d)(3)	Rollovers to Roth IRAs from qualified plans, 403(b) annuities, and governmental section 457 plans will be permitted after 2007 if AGI-based limit is met, but tax must be paid on otherwise tax-deferred distributions	For distributions made after Dec. 31, 2007	¶ 103 Pension Protection Act of 2006

Code	Topic	Effective Date	Complete Analysis ¶
408A(d)(3)(A)(iii)	AGI limit on conversion of non-Roth IRAs to Roth IRAs is eliminated; income from conversion can be deferred and spread over two years—after 2009	For tax years beginning after Dec. 31, 2009	¶ 203 Tax Increase Prevention and Reconciliation Act of 2005
408A(d)(3)(E)(i)	AGI limit on conversion of non-Roth IRAs to Roth IRAs is eliminated; income from conversion can be deferred and spread over two years—after 2009	For tax years beginning after Dec. 31, 2009	¶ 203 Tax Increase Prevention and Reconciliation Act of 2005
408A(e)	Rollovers to Roth IRAs from qualified plans, 403(b) annuities, and governmental section 457 plans will be permitted after 2007 if AGI-based limit is met, but tax must be paid on otherwise tax-deferred distributions	For distributions made after Dec. 31, 2007	¶ 103 Pension Protection Act of 2006
409A(b)(3)	Funding of nonqualified deferred compensation plan by sponsor of underfunded or terminated single-employer defined benefit plan triggers income, interest, and 20% penalty to "covered employees"	Transfers or other reservation of assets after Aug. 17, 2006	¶ 511 Pension Protection Act of 2006
409A(b)(3)	Funding of nonqualified deferred compensation plan by sponsor of underfunded or terminated single-employer defined benefit plan triggers income, interest, and 20% penalty to "covered employees"	Transfers or other reservation of assets after Aug. 17, 2006	¶ 511 Pension Protection Act of 2006

Code	Topic	Effective Date	Complete Analysis ¶
409A(b)(4)	Funding of nonqualified deferred compensation plan by sponsor of underfunded or terminated single-employer defined benefit plan triggers income, interest, and 20% penalty to "covered employees"	Transfers or other reservation of assets after Aug. 17, 2006	¶ 511 Pension Protection Act of 2006
411(a)	Faster vesting schedule applies to all employer contributions to defined contribution plans	For contributions made for plan years beginning after Dec. 31, 2006	¶ 1301 Pension Protection Act of 2006
411(a)(11)	Notice and consent period for qualified plan distributions extended from 90 to 180 days	Years beginning after 2006	¶ 903 Pension Protection Act of 2006
411(a)(11)	Plan distribution consent notice must describe consequences of participant's failure to defer receipt of distribution	Years beginning after 2006	¶ 905 Pension Protection Act of 2006
411(a)(13)	New rules established retroactively for creation of cash balance and other hybrid "applicable defined benefit plans"	Distributions made after Aug. 17, 2006 for periods beginning on or after June 29, 2005	¶ 201 Pension Protection Act of 2006
411(b)(5)	New rules established retroactively for creation of cash balance and other hybrid "applicable defined benefit plans"	Distributions made after Aug. 17, 2006 for periods beginning on or after June 29, 2005	¶ 201 Pension Protection Act of 2006
412(a)	Minimum funding rules revised for defined benefit plans	Plan years beginning after Dec. 31, 2007	¶ 501 Pension Protection Act of 2006
412(b)	Minimum funding rules revised for defined benefit plans	Plan years beginning after Dec. 31, 2007	¶ 501 Pension Protection Act of 2006

Code	Topic	Effective Date	Complete Analysis ¶
412(b)(3)	Details of special funding rules for multiemployer plans in critical status	For plan years beginning after 2007	¶ 607 Pension Protection Act of 2006
412(b)(5)(B)(ii)(II)	Rules for determining permissible range of interest rates in calculating current funding liability are extended through plan years beginning in 2007	Aug. 17, 2006	¶ 503 Pension Protection Act of 2006
412(c)	Rules revised for obtaining a minimum funding waiver	Plan years beginning after Dec. 31, 2007	¶ 509 Pension Protection Act of 2006
412(d)	Minimum funding rules revised for defined benefit plans	Plan years beginning after Dec. 31, 2007	¶ 501 Pension Protection Act of 2006
412(d)(3)	Rules revised for obtaining a minimum funding waiver	Plan years beginning after Dec. 31, 2007	¶ 509 Pension Protection Act of 2006
412(e)	Minimum funding rules revised for defined benefit plans	Plan years beginning after Dec. 31, 2007	¶ 501 Pension Protection Act of 2006
412(l)(7)(C)(i)(IV)	Rules for determining permissible range of interest rates in calculating current funding liability are extended through plan years beginning in 2007	Aug. 17, 2006	¶ 503 Pension Protection Act of 2006
414(d)	Other provisions	Aug. 17, 2006	¶ 2404 Pension Protection Act of 2006
414(f)(6)	Plans can elect to revoke election not to be treated as multiemployer plan (which will establish multiemployer plan status), and tax-exempt organizations can elect multiemployer plan status—before Aug. 18, 2007	Aug. 17, 2006	¶ 706 Pension Protection Act of 2006
414(h)(2)	Other provisions	For any year beginning on or after Aug. 17, 2006	¶ 2404 Pension Protection Act of 2006

Code	Topic	Effective Date	Complete Analysis ¶
414(w)	Automatic contribution arrangements for 401(k) plans	Plan years beginning after Dec. 31, 2007	¶ 401 Pension Protection Act of 2006
414(x)	Special rules established for treatment of defined benefit plans combined with 401(k) plans—after 2009	Plan years beginning after Dec. 31, 2009	¶ 402 Pension Protection Act of 2006
415(b)(2)	Other provisions	For any year beginning on or after Aug. 17, 2006	¶ 2404 Pension Protection Act of 2006
415(b)(2)(E)(ii)	Amendment of interest rate assumptions that may be used for applying benefit limits to lump-sum distributions made under defined benefit plans	For distributions made after 2005	¶ 1103 Pension Protection Act of 2006
415(b)(3)	Active participation restriction eliminated from "average compensation for high three years" definition when determining annual benefit limit	Years beginning after Dec. 31, 2005	¶ 1106 Pension Protection Act of 2006
415(b)(10)	Other provisions	For any year beginning on or after Aug. 17, 2006	¶ 2404 Pension Protection Act of 2006
415(b)(11)	Other provisions	For years beginning after 2006	¶ 2404 Pension Protection Act of 2006
417(a)(1)(A)(ii)	Plans subject to survivor annuity requirement will have to provide "qualified optional survivor annuity" form of benefit after 2007	For plan years beginning after Dec. 31, 2007	¶ 1105 Pension Protection Act of 2006
417(a)(3)(A)(i)	Plans subject to survivor annuity requirement will have to provide "qualified optional survivor annuity" form of benefit after 2007	For plan years beginning after Dec. 31, 2007	¶ 1105 Pension Protection Act of 2006

ode	Topic	Effective Date	Complete Analysis ¶
17(a)(6)	Notice and consent period for election to waive Qualified Joint and Survivor Annuity extended from 90 to 180 days	Years beginning after 2006	¶ 904 Pension Protection Act of 2006
17(e)(3)	Interest rate and mortality table to be used for calculating the lump-sum present value of a participant's accrued benefit under the cash-out rules	For plan years beginning after Dec. 31, 2007	¶ 1104 Pension Protection Act of 2006
17(g)	Plans subject to survivor annuity requirement will have to provide "qualified optional survivor annuity" form of benefit after 2007	For plan years beginning after Dec. 31, 2007	¶ 1105 Pension Protection Act of 2006
18E(d)(1)	Multiemployer plan sponsors must make advance determinations of impending insolvencies over a five-year period, instead of a three-year period	For determinations made in plan years beginning after 2007	¶ 705 Pension Protection Act of 2006
19A(c)(6)	Deductions permitted for contributions to fund a reserve for medical benefits for future years through a bona fide association	Tax years beginning after Dec. 31, 2006	¶ 2001 Pension Protection Act of 2006
20(a)	Multiemployer plans may transfer excess pension assets to retiree health accounts	Transfers made in tax years beginning after Dec. 31, 2006	¶ 2003 Pension Protection Act of 2006
20(e)(2)	Rules on transfer of excess pension assets to retiree health accounts are integrated with new funding rules	Plan years beginning after 2007	¶ 2004 Pension Protection Act of 2006

Code	Topic	Effective Date	Complete Analysis ¶
420(e)(4)	Rules on transfer of excess pension assets to retiree health accounts are integrated with new funding rules	Plan years beginning after 2007	¶ 2004 Pension Protection Act of 2006
420(e)(5)	Multiemployer plans may transfer excess pension assets to retiree health accounts	Transfers made in tax years beginning after Dec. 31, 2006	¶ 2003 Pension Protection Act of 2006
420(f)	Single-employer plans can use excess pension assets to fund future retiree health benefits; rules established for funding collectively bargained retiree health benefits	For transfers made after Aug. 17, 2006	¶ 2002 Pension Protection Act of 2006
430(a)	New funding standards for single-employer defined benefit plans gear minimum required contribution to "target normal cost" and "funding shortfall," upgrade valuation and actuarial standards, and add strict rules for "at-risk" plans	Plan years beginning after Dec. 31, 2007	¶ 502 Pension Protection Act of 2006
430(b)	New funding standards for single-employer defined benefit plans gear minimum required contribution to "target normal cost" and "funding shortfall," upgrade valuation and actuarial standards, and add strict rules for "at-risk" plans	Plan years beginning after Dec. 31, 2007	¶ 502 Pension Protection Act of 2006

Code	Topic	Effective Date	Complete Analysis ¶
430(c)	New funding standards for single-employer defined benefit plans gear minimum required contribution to "target normal cost" and "funding shortfall," upgrade valuation and actuarial standards, and add strict rules for "at-risk" plans	Plan years beginning after Dec. 31, 2007	¶ 502 Pension Protection Act of 2006
430(d)	New funding standards for single-employer defined benefit plans gear minimum required contribution to "target normal cost" and "funding shortfall," upgrade valuation and actuarial standards, and add strict rules for "at-risk" plans	Plan years beginning after Dec. 31, 2007	¶ 502 Pension Protection Act of 2006
430(e)	New funding standards for single-employer defined benefit plans gear minimum required contribution to "target normal cost" and "funding shortfall," upgrade valuation and actuarial standards, and add strict rules for "at-risk" plans	Plan years beginning after Dec. 31, 2007	¶ 502 Pension Protection Act of 2006
430(f)	New funding standards for single-employer defined benefit plans gear minimum required contribution to "target normal cost" and "funding shortfall," upgrade valuation and actuarial standards, and add strict rules for "at-risk" plans	Plan years beginning after Dec. 31, 2007	¶ 502 Pension Protection Act of 2006

Code	Topic	Effective Date	Complete Analysis ¶
430(g)	New funding standards for single-employer defined benefit plans gear minimum required contribution to "target normal cost" and "funding shortfall," upgrade valuation and actuarial standards, and add strict rules for "at-risk" plans	Plan years beginning after Dec. 31, 2007	¶ 502 Pension Protection Act of 2006
430(h)	New funding standards for single-employer defined benefit plans gear minimum required contribution to "target normal cost" and "funding shortfall," upgrade valuation and actuarial standards, and add strict rules for "at-risk" plans	Plan years beginning after Dec. 31, 2007	¶ 502 Pension Protection Act of 2006
430(i)	New funding standards for single-employer defined benefit plans gear minimum required contribution to "target normal cost" and "funding shortfall," upgrade valuation and actuarial standards, and add strict rules for "at-risk" plans	Plan years beginning after Dec. 31, 2007	¶ 502 Pension Protection Act of 2006
430(j)	Quarterly installments of minimum contributions to underfunded single-employer DB plans are required under new funding standards; liens imposed where unpaid contributions exceed $1 million.	Plan years beginning after Dec. 31, 2007	¶ 506 Pension Protection Act of 2006

Code	Topic	Effective Date	Complete Analysis ¶
430(k)	Quarterly installments of minimum contributions to underfunded single-employer DB plans are required under new funding standards; liens imposed where unpaid contributions exceed $1 million	Plan years beginning after Dec. 31, 2007	¶ 506 Pension Protection Act of 2006
430(l)	Quarterly installments of minimum contributions to underfunded single-employer DB plans are required under new funding standards; liens imposed where unpaid contributions exceed $1 million	Plan years beginning after Dec. 31, 2007	¶ 506 Pension Protection Act of 2006
431(a)	Rules on minimum funding standards for multiemployer plans relocated and modified	Plan years beginning after 2007	¶ 601 Pension Protection Act of 2006
431(b)	Rules on minimum funding standards for multiemployer plans relocated and modified	Plan years beginning after 2007	¶ 601 Pension Protection Act of 2006
431(c)	Special rules for charges and credits to multiemployer plans' funding standard accounts	Plan years beginning after 2007	¶ 603 Pension Protection Act of 2006
431(c)(5)	New full funding limitation rules to apply to multiemployer plan funding standard accounts	Plan years beginning after 2007	¶ 602 Pension Protection Act of 2006
431(c)(6)	New full funding limitation rules to apply to multiemployer plan funding standard accounts	Plan years beginning after 2007	¶ 602 Pension Protection Act of 2006

Code	Topic	Effective Date	Complete Analysis
431(d)	Extension of amortization periods for multiemployer plans	Plan years beginning after 2007	¶ 604 Pension Protection Act of 2006
432(a)	Overview of special funding rules for multiemployer plans in endangered or critical status; annual certification by plan actuary; notice requirements	For plan years beginning after 2007	¶ 605 Pension Protection Act of 2006
432(b)(1)	Special funding rules for multiemployer plans in endangered status	For plan years beginning after 2007	¶ 606 Pension Protection Act of 2006
432(b)(2)	Details of special funding rules for multiemployer plans in critical status	For plan years beginning after 2007	¶ 607 Pension Protection Act of 2006
432(b)(3)(A)	Overview of special funding rules for multiemployer plans in endangered or critical status; annual certification by plan actuary; notice requirements	For plan years beginning after 2007	¶ 605 Pension Protection Act of 2006
432(b)(3)(B)	Overview of special funding rules for multiemployer plans in endangered or critical status; annual certification by plan actuary; notice requirements	For plan years beginning after 2007	¶ 605 Pension Protection Act of 2006
432(b)(3)(C)	Overview of special funding rules for multiemployer plans in endangered or critical status; annual certification by plan actuary; notice requirements	For plan years beginning after 2007	¶ 605 Pension Protection Act of 2006
432(c)	Special funding rules for multiemployer plans in endangered status	For plan years beginning after 2007	¶ 606 Pension Protection Act of 2006
432(d)	Special funding rules for multiemployer plans in endangered status	For plan years beginning after 2007	¶ 606 Pension Protection Act of 2006

Code	Topic	Effective Date	Complete Analysis ¶
432(e)	Details of special funding rules for multiemployer plans in critical status	For plan years beginning after 2007	¶ 607 Pension Protection Act of 2006
432(f)	Details of special funding rules for multiemployer plans in critical status	For plan years beginning after 2007	¶ 607 Pension Protection Act of 2006
432(g)	Details of special funding rules for multiemployer plans in critical status	For plan years beginning after 2007	¶ 607 Pension Protection Act of 2006
432(g)	Special funding rules for multiemployer plans in endangered status	For plan years beginning after 2007	¶ 606 Pension Protection Act of 2006
432(h)	Details of special funding rules for multiemployer plans in critical status	For plan years beginning after 2007	¶ 607 Pension Protection Act of 2006
432(h)	Special funding rules for multiemployer plans in endangered status	For plan years beginning after 2007	¶ 606 Pension Protection Act of 2006
432(i)(1)	Details of special funding rules for multiemployer plans in critical status	For plan years beginning after 2007	¶ 607 Pension Protection Act of 2006
432(i)(2)	Special funding rules for multiemployer plans in endangered status	For plan years beginning after 2007	¶ 606 Pension Protection Act of 2006
432(i)(3)	Special funding rules for multiemployer plans in endangered status	For plan years beginning after 2007	¶ 606 Pension Protection Act of 2006
432(i)(4)	Special funding rules for multiemployer plans in endangered status	For plan years beginning after 2007	¶ 606 Pension Protection Act of 2006
432(i)(5)	Details of special funding rules for multiemployer plans in critical status	For plan years beginning after 2007	¶ 607 Pension Protection Act of 2006
432(i)(7)	Details of special funding rules for multiemployer plans in critical status	For plan years beginning after 2007	¶ 607 Pension Protection Act of 2006

Code	Topic	Effective Date	Complete Analysis ¶
432(i)(8)	Overview of special funding rules for multiemployer plans in endangered or critical status; annual certification by plan actuary; notice requirements	For plan years beginning after 2007	¶ 605 Pension Protection Act of 2006
432(i)(10)	Details of special funding rules for multiemployer plans in critical status	For plan years beginning after 2007	¶ 607 Pension Protection Act of 2006
436	Funding-based limits imposed on benefits and benefit accruals under single-employer plans	Plan years beginning after Dec. 31, 2007	¶ 1102 Pension Protection Act of 2006
457(a)	Distributions of up to $3,000 from governmental plans to pay for the health or long-term care insurance of public safety officers are excluded from income	Distributions in tax years beginning after Dec. 31, 2006	¶ 1401 Pension Protection Act of 2006
457(e)(11)(D)	Certain voluntary early retirement incentive plans maintained by educational entities are exempt from the section 457 deferred compensation rules, and are treated like welfare plans under ERISA	For tax years ending after Aug. 17, 2006	¶ 1406 Pension Protection Act of 2006
457(e)(16)(B)	Nonspouse beneficiaries can roll over into IRAs, distributions from qualified plans, tax-sheltered annuities, and government plans	Distributions made after Dec. 31, 2006	¶ 102 Pension Protection Act of 2006

Code	Topic	Effective Date	Complete Analysis ¶
457(f)(2)(F)	Certain employment retention plans maintained by educational entities are exempt from the section 457 deferred compensation rules, and are treated like welfare plans under ERISA	For tax years ending after Aug. 17, 2006	¶ 1407 Pension Protection Act of 2006
457(f)(4)	Certain employment retention plans maintained by educational entities are exempt from the section 457 deferred compensation rules, and are treated like welfare plans under ERISA	For tax years ending after Aug. 17, 2006	¶ 1407 Pension Protection Act of 2006
468A(b)	Nuclear decommissioning fund rules will be modified for tax years beginning after Dec. 31, 2005	Tax years beginning after Dec. 31, 2005	¶ 802 Tax Provisions of the Energy and Transportation Acts of 2005
468A(d)(1)	Nuclear decommissioning fund rules will be modified for tax years beginning after Dec. 31, 2005	Tax years beginning after Dec. 31, 2005	¶ 802 Tax Provisions of the Energy and Transportation Acts of 2005
468A(d)(2)(A)	Nuclear decommissioning fund rules will be modified for tax years beginning after Dec. 31, 2005	Tax years beginning after Dec. 31, 2005	¶ 802 Tax Provisions of the Energy and Transportation Acts of 2005
468A(e)(2)	Nuclear decommissioning fund rules will be modified for tax years beginning after Dec. 31, 2005	Tax years beginning after Dec. 31, 2005	¶ 802 Tax Provisions of the Energy and Transportation Acts of 2005
468A(f)	Nuclear decommissioning fund rules will be modified for tax years beginning after Dec. 31, 2005	Tax years beginning after Dec. 31, 2005	¶ 802 Tax Provisions of the Energy and Transportation Acts of 2005

Code	Topic	Effective Date	Complete Analysis ¶
468B(g)	Certain CERCLA environmental settlement funds established before Jan. 1, 2011 are treated as not subject to federal income tax	Accounts and funds established after May 17, 2006	¶ 303 Tax Increase Prevention and Reconciliation Act of 2005
468B(g)(3)	Federal tax exemption for settlement funds and escrow accounts established for the sole purpose of resolving CERCLA claims is made permanent	Accounts and funds established after May 17, 2006	¶ 1605 Tax Provisions of the Tax Relief and Health Care Act of 2006
501(c)(21)(C)	"Aggregate limit" on payments from black lung disability trusts for accident or health benefits is eliminated	For tax years beginning after Dec. 31, 2006	¶ 2005 Pension Protection Act of 2006
501(q)	Credit counseling organizations must meet consumer protection requirements to qualify as tax-exempt	Tax years beginning after Aug. 17, 2006 (one year later for existing organizations)	¶ 1904 Pension Protection Act of 2006
501(q)(4)(B)	Debt management plan services are an unrelated trade or business, if organization is not a tax-exempt credit counseling organization	Tax years beginning after Aug. 17, 2006 (one year later for existing organizations)	¶ 1903 Pension Protection Act of 2006
508(f)	Sponsoring organizations must notify IRS of any donor advised fund they maintain or intend to maintain	For organizations applying for tax-exempt status after Aug. 17, 2006	¶ 1607 Pension Protection Act of 2006
509	Stricter accountability required for exception from private foundation status for Type III supporting organizations; certain gifts to supporting organizations barred	Aug. 17, 2006	¶ 1613 Pension Protection Act of 2006

ode	Topic	Effective Date	Complete Analysis ¶
)9	Stricter accountability required for exception from private foundation status for Type III supporting organizations; certain gifts to supporting organizations barred	Aug. 17, 2006	¶ 1613 Pension Protection Act of 2006
09(a)(3)(B)	Stricter accountability required for exception from private foundation status for Type III supporting organizations; certain gifts to supporting organizations barred	Aug. 17, 2006	¶ 1613 Pension Protection Act of 2006
09(e)	Codification of rule that gross investment income of private foundations includes annuities, income from notional principal contracts, and other substantially similar income	Tax years beginning after Aug. 17, 2006	¶ 1609 Pension Protection Act of 2006
09(f)	Stricter accountability required for exception from private foundation status for Type III supporting organizations; certain gifts to supporting organizations barred	Aug. 17, 2006	¶ 1613 Pension Protection Act of 2006
512(b)(13)(E)	Specified payments made by a controlled entity to its tax-exempt parent in 2006 or 2007 are included in UBTI to the extent they exceed fair market value	For payments received or accrued after Dec. 31, 2005 and before Jan. 1, 2008, under a binding written contract in effect on Aug. 17, 2006	¶ 1902 Pension Protection Act of 2006

Code	Topic	Effective Date	Complete Analysis ¶
513(j)	Debt management plan services are an unrelated trade or business, if organization is not a tax-exempt credit counseling organization	Tax years beginning after Aug. 17, 2006 (one year later for existing organizations)	¶ 1903 Pension Protection Act of 2006
514(c)(9)(C)	Other provisions	Aug. 17, 2006	¶ 2404 Pension Protection Act of 2006
529	2001 EGTRRA changes to qualified tuition program rules are made permanent	Aug. 17, 2006	¶ 2201 Pension Protection Act of 2006
529(f)	IRS is given broad regulatory authority to prevent abuse of qualified tuition programs	Aug. 17, 2006	¶ 2202 Pension Protection Act of 2006
531	15% accumulated earnings tax rate and 15% personal holding company tax rate are extended two years	Tax years beginning after Dec. 31, 2008 and before Jan. 1, 2011	¶ 504 Tax Increase Prevention and Reconciliation Act of 2005
541	15% accumulated earnings tax rate and 15% personal holding company tax rate are extended two years	Tax years beginning after Dec. 31, 2008 and before Jan. 1, 2011	¶ 504 Tax Increase Prevention and Reconciliation Act of 2005
545(b)(2)	Individuals' qualified conservation contributions before 2008 are deductible up to 50% (100% for farmers and ranchers) of contribution base; 15-year carryover is allowed	Contributions made in tax years beginning after Dec. 31, 2005, and before Jan. 1, 2008	¶ 1511 Pension Protection Act of 2006
584(c)	Passthrough of qualified dividend income by common trust funds is extended for two years	Tax years beginning after Dec. 31, 2008 and before Jan. 1, 2011	¶ 111 Tax Increase Prevention and Reconciliation Act of 2005

Code	Topic	Effective Date	Complete Analysis ¶
613A(c)(6)(H)	Suspension of taxable income limitation on percentage depletion from marginal oil and gas wells is retroactively extended for two years to include tax years beginning before Jan. 1, 2008	Tax years beginning after Dec. 31, 2005 and before Jan. 1, 2008	¶ 507 Tax Provisions of the Tax Relief and Health Care Act of 2006
664(c)	Rules for taxing charitable remainder trusts' UBTI are modified	Tax years beginning after Dec. 31, 2006	¶ 601 Tax Provisions of the Tax Relief and Health Care Act of 2006
664(g)(3)(E)	Qualified employer securities transferred by charitable remainder trust to ESOP must be allocated to participants based on fair market value when allocated	Aug. 17, 2006	¶ 1303 Pension Protection Act of 2006
684(a)	Gain recognition rule for transfers of appreciated property to non-grantor foreign trusts and foreign estates will be extended to transfers at death to nonresident aliens after 2009	For transfers after Dec. 31, 2009	¶ 313 Economic Growth and Tax Relief Reconciliation Act of 2001
684(b)	Gain recognition rule for transfers of appreciated property to non-grantor foreign trusts and foreign estates will be extended to transfers at death to nonresident aliens after 2009	For transfers after Dec. 31, 2009	¶ 313 Economic Growth and Tax Relief Reconciliation Act of 2001
691(c)(4)	5% and 15% adjusted capital gains rates on noncorporate taxpayers' qualified dividend income are extended for two years	Tax years beginning after Dec. 31, 2008 and before Jan. 1, 2011	¶ 107 Tax Increase Prevention and Reconciliation Act of 2005

Code	Topic	Effective Date	Complete Analysis ¶
702(a)(5)	Passthrough of qualified dividend income by partnerships is extended for two years	Tax years beginning after Dec. 31, 2008 and before Jan. 1, 2011	¶ 112 Tax Increase Prevention and Reconciliation Act of 2005
772(a)(10)	Nonconventional fuel production credit will be an elective general business credit for tax years ending after Dec. 31, 2005	Credits determined under IRC of 1986 for tax years ending after Dec. 31, 2005	¶ 301 Tax Provisions of the Energy and Transportation Acts of 2005
772(d)(5)	Nonconventional fuel production credit will be an elective general business credit for tax years ending after Dec. 31, 2005	Credits determined under IRC of 1986 for tax years ending after Dec. 31, 2005	¶ 301 Tax Provisions of the Energy and Transportation Acts of 2005
848(e)(6)	Qualified long-term care insurance can be provided as a rider to an annuity contract after 2009	Tax years beginning after 2009	¶ 2402 Pension Protection Act of 2006
852(b)(3)(E)	Qualified investment entity FIRPTA exclusion is amended	Tax years of qualified investment entities beginning after Dec. 31, 2005	¶ 603 Tax Increase Prevention and Reconciliation Act of 2005
854(a)	Passthrough of qualified dividend income by RICs and REITs is extended for two years	Tax years beginning after Dec. 31, 2008 and before Jan. 1, 2011	¶ 110 Tax Increase Prevention and Reconciliation Act of 2005
854(b)(1)(B)	Passthrough of qualified dividend income by RICs and REITs is extended for two years	Tax years beginning after Dec. 31, 2008 and before Jan. 1, 2011	¶ 110 Tax Increase Prevention and Reconciliation Act of 2005
854(b)(1)(C)	Passthrough of qualified dividend income by RICs and REITs is extended for two years	Tax years beginning after Dec. 31, 2008 and before Jan. 1, 2011	¶ 110 Tax Increase Prevention and Reconciliation Act of 2005
854(b)(2)	Passthrough of qualified dividend income by RICs and REITs is extended for two years	Tax years beginning after Dec. 31, 2008 and before Jan. 1, 2011	¶ 110 Tax Increase Prevention and Reconciliation Act of 2005

Code	Topic	Effective Date	Complete Analysis ¶
854(b)(5)	Passthrough of qualified dividend income by RICs and REITs is extended for two years	Tax years beginning after Dec. 31, 2008 and before Jan. 1, 2011	¶ 110 Tax Increase Prevention and Reconciliation Act of 2005
857(c)(2)	Passthrough of qualified dividend income by RICs and REITs is extended for two years	Tax years beginning after Dec. 31, 2008 and before Jan. 1, 2011	¶ 110 Tax Increase Prevention and Reconciliation Act of 2005
864(f)	Election to allocate interest and certain other expenses on worldwide basis will be available after 2008	Tax years beginning after Dec. 31, 2008	¶ 731 American Jobs Creation Act of 2004
864(f)	Election will be available after 2008 to treat bank and financial holding companies as includible corporations if worldwide interest allocation election is made	Tax years beginning after Dec. 31, 2008	¶ 732 American Jobs Creation Act of 2004
871(k)(2)(E)	Qualified investment entity FIRPTA exclusion is amended	Tax years of qualified investment entities beginning after Dec. 31, 2005	¶ 603 Tax Increase Prevention and Reconciliation Act of 2005
897(h)(1)	Qualified investment entity FIRPTA exclusion is amended	Tax years of qualified investment entities beginning after Dec. 31, 2005	¶ 603 Tax Increase Prevention and Reconciliation Act of 2005
897(h)(4)(A)(ii)	Qualified investment entity FIRPTA exclusion is amended	Tax years of qualified investment entities beginning after Dec. 31, 2005	¶ 603 Tax Increase Prevention and Reconciliation Act of 2005
897(h)(5)	Certain wash sales of interests in domestically controlled qualified investment entities result in gain recognition under FIRPTA	Tax years beginning after Dec. 31, 2005	¶ 604 Tax Increase Prevention and Reconciliation Act of 2005
904(d)(1)	Reduction of foreign tax credit baskets from nine to two for tax years starting after 2006	For tax years beginning after Dec. 31, 2006	¶ 720 American Jobs Creation Act of 2004

Code	Topic	Effective Date	Complete Analysis ¶
904(d)(2)(A)	Reduction of foreign tax credit baskets from nine to two for tax years starting after 2006	For tax years beginning after Dec. 31, 2006	¶ 720 American Jobs Creation Act of 2004
904(d)(2)(B)(v)	Reduction of foreign tax credit baskets from nine to two for tax years starting after 2006	For tax years beginning after Dec. 31, 2006	¶ 720 American Jobs Creation Act of 2004
904(d)(2)(C)	Reduction of foreign tax credit baskets from nine to two for tax years starting after 2006	For tax years beginning after Dec. 31, 2006	¶ 720 American Jobs Creation Act of 2004
904(d)(2)(H)	Reduction of foreign tax credit baskets from nine to two for tax years starting after 2006	For tax years beginning after Dec. 31, 2006	¶ 720 American Jobs Creation Act of 2004
904(d)(2)(K)	Reduction of foreign tax credit baskets from nine to two for tax years starting after 2006	For tax years beginning after Dec. 31, 2006	¶ 720 American Jobs Creation Act of 2004
904(d)(3)	Reduction of foreign tax credit baskets from nine to two for tax years starting after 2006	For tax years beginning after Dec. 31, 2006	¶ 720 American Jobs Creation Act of 2004
904(g)	Recharacterization of overall domestic loss for tax years after 2006	For U.S. source losses in tax years beginning after Dec 31, 2006	¶ 728 American Jobs Creation Act of 2004
904(g)(2)	Definition of overall domestic loss modified effective 2007	For losses in tax years beginning after Dec 31, 2006	¶ 1113 Gulf Opportunity Zone and Katrina Emergency Tax Relief Acts of 2005
904(h)	Nonrefundable personal credits may offset AMT through 2006 (instead of 2005)	Tax years beginning after Dec. 31, 2005 and before Jan. 1, 2007	¶ 202 Tax Increase Prevention and Reconciliation Act of 2005
904(i)	Carryover rules for personal credits are redrafted to cover years in which credits are and years in which they aren't allowed against AMT	Tax years beginning after Dec. 31, 2005	¶ 601 Gulf Opportunity Zone and Katrina Emergency Tax Relief Acts of 2005

Code	Topic	Effective Date	Complete Analysis ¶
911(b)(2)(D)(ii)	Foreign earned income exclusion amended	Tax years beginning after Dec. 31, 2005	¶ 206 Tax Increase Prevention and Reconciliation Act of 2005
911(c)(1)(A)	Foreign earned income exclusion amended	Tax years beginning after Dec. 31, 2005	¶ 206 Tax Increase Prevention and Reconciliation Act of 2005
911(c)(1)(B)(i)	Foreign earned income exclusion amended	Tax years beginning after Dec. 31, 2005	¶ 206 Tax Increase Prevention and Reconciliation Act of 2005
911(c)(2)	Foreign earned income exclusion amended	Tax years beginning after Dec. 31, 2005	¶ 206 Tax Increase Prevention and Reconciliation Act of 2005
911(f)	Foreign earned income exclusion amended	Tax years beginning after Dec. 31, 2005	¶ 206 Tax Increase Prevention and Reconciliation Act of 2005
953(e)(10)	Exceptions under Subpart F for active banking, financing and insurance income expiring in 2007 extended through tax years beginning before 2009	May 17, 2006	¶ 601 Tax Increase Prevention and Reconciliation Act of 2005
954(c)(6)	Payments between related controlled foreign corporations under foreign personal holding company income rules subject to look-through treatment for tax years beginning before 2009	Tax years of foreign corporations beginning after Dec. 31, 2005 and before Jan. 1, 2009 and tax years of U.S. shareholders with or within which such tax years of foreign corporations end	¶ 602 Tax Increase Prevention and Reconciliation Act of 2005
954(c)(6)(A)	Look-through rule doesn't apply to dividends, interest, rents and royalties received from a CFC which are effectively connected with a U.S. trade or business for tax years beginning before 2009	Tax years of foreign corporations beginning after Dec. 31, 2005 and before Jan. 1, 2009 and tax years of U.S. shareholders with or within which such tax years of foreign corporations end	¶ 1301 Tax Provisions of the Tax Relief and Health Care Act of 2006

Code	Topic	Effective Date	Complete Analysis ¶
954(h)(9)	Exceptions under Subpart F for active banking, financing and insurance income expiring in 2007 extended through tax years beginning before 2009	May 17, 2006	¶ 601 Tax Increase Prevention and Reconciliation Act of 2005
1014(f)	Step-up basis and step-down basis will end and modified carryover basis rules will apply for property acquired from a deceased individual after Dec. 31, 2009	Estates of decedents dying after Dec. 31, 2009 for property acquired from a decedent dying after Dec. 31, 2009	¶ 326 Economic Growth and Tax Relief Reconciliation Act of 2001
1016(a)	Credit provided for qualified alternative fuel vehicle refueling property	Property placed in service after Dec. 31, 2005	¶ 206 Tax Provisions of the Energy and Transportation Acts of 2005
1016(a)(32)	Deduction will be allowed for costs of energy efficient commercial building property placed in service after Dec. 31, 2005 and before Jan. 1, 2008	Property placed in service after Dec. 31, 2005 and before Jan. 1, 2008	¶ 101 Tax Provisions of the Energy and Transportation Acts of 2005
1016(a)(33)	New energy efficient home credit of $2,000 ($1,000 for certain homes) is available to eligible contractors for qualified new energy efficient homes acquired after Dec. 31, 2005 and before Jan. 1, 2008	Qualified new energy efficient homes acquired after Dec. 31, 2005 and before Jan. 1, 2008	¶ 102 Tax Provisions of the Energy and Transportation Acts of 2005
1016(a)(34)	Individuals will be allowed personal credit up to $500 lifetime limit for energy efficient improvements to principal residence in 2006 and 2007	Property placed in service after Dec. 31, 2005 and before Jan. 1, 2008	¶ 103 Tax Provisions of the Energy and Transportation Acts of 2005

Code	Topic	Effective Date	Complete Analysis ¶
1016(a)(35)	Individuals will be allowed 30% credit for photovoltaic, solar hot water, and fuel cell property installed in their home in 2006 and 2007, subject to dollar limits	Property placed in service after Dec. 31, 2005 and before Jan. 1, 2008	¶ 104 Tax Provisions of the Energy and Transportation Acts of 2005
1022	Step-up basis and step-down basis will end and modified carryover basis rules will apply for property acquired from a deceased individual after Dec. 31, 2009	Estates of decedents dying after Dec. 31, 2009 for property acquired from a decedent dying after Dec. 31, 2009	¶ 326 Economic Growth and Tax Relief Reconciliation Act of 2001
1022(g)	Liabilities in excess of the basis of property acquired from a decedent or an estate will be excluded from gain and basis after Dec. 31, 2009	Estates of decedents dying after Dec. 31, 2009	¶ 327 Economic Growth and Tax Relief Reconciliation Act of 2001
1035(a)	Qualified long-term care insurance can be provided as a rider to an annuity contract after 2009	Tax years beginning after 2009	¶ 2402 Pension Protection Act of 2006
1035(a)(4)	Qualified long-term care insurance can be provided as a rider to an annuity contract after 2009	Tax years beginning after 2009	¶ 2402 Pension Protection Act of 2006
1035(b)(2)	Qualified long-term care insurance can be provided as a rider to an annuity contract after 2009	Tax years beginning after 2009	¶ 2402 Pension Protection Act of 2006
1035(b)(3)	Qualified long-term care insurance can be provided as a rider to an annuity contract after 2009	Tax years beginning after 2009	¶ 2402 Pension Protection Act of 2006

Code	Topic	Effective Date	Complete Analysis ¶
1040	Beginning in 2010, an estate or trust will recognize gain if it distributes appreciated property to satisfy a pecuniary bequest, but only to the extent the property has appreciated between the dates of death and of distribution	Estates of decedents dying after Dec. 31, 2009	¶ 328 Economic Growth and Tax Relief Reconciliation Act of 2001
1043(b)(1)	Federal judges can defer gain on conflict-of-interest sales	Sales after date of enactment of the 2006 Tax Relief and Health Care Act	¶ 109 Tax Provisions of the Tax Relief and Health Care Act of 2006
1043(b)(2)	Federal judges can defer gain on conflict-of-interest sales	Sales after date of enactment of the 2006 Tax Relief and Health Care Act	¶ 109 Tax Provisions of the Tax Relief and Health Care Act of 2006
1043(b)(5)(B)	Federal judges can defer gain on conflict-of-interest sales	Sales after date of enactment of the 2006 Tax Relief and Health Care Act	¶ 109 Tax Provisions of the Tax Relief and Health Care Act of 2006
1043(b)(6)	Federal judges can defer gain on conflict-of-interest sales	Sales after date of enactment of the 2006 Tax Relief and Health Care Act	¶ 109 Tax Provisions of the Tax Relief and Health Care Act of 2006
1081	Repeal of nonrecognition treatment for SEC ordered transactions under Public Utility Act of '35 effective Feb. 8, 2006	Feb. 8, 2006	¶ 904 Gulf Opportunity Zone and Katrina Emergency Tax Relief Acts of 2005
1082	Repeal of nonrecognition treatment for SEC ordered transactions under Public Utility Act of '35 effective Feb. 8, 2006	Feb. 8, 2006	¶ 904 Gulf Opportunity Zone and Katrina Emergency Tax Relief Acts of 2005
1083	Repeal of nonrecognition treatment for SEC ordered transactions under Public Utility Act of '35 effective Feb. 8, 2006	Feb. 8, 2006	¶ 904 Gulf Opportunity Zone and Katrina Emergency Tax Relief Acts of 2005

Code	Topic	Effective Date	Complete Analysis ¶
1221(a)(3)(C)	Capital gain treatment for inherited artwork or similar property will not be disallowed after 2009 solely because heir to property takes decedent's carryover basis	Estates of decedents dying after Dec. 31, 2009	¶ 329 Economic Growth and Tax Relief Reconciliation Act of 2001
1221(b)(3)	Capital gain treatment for certain self-created musical works, originally set to expire Dec. 31, 2010, is made permanent	Sales and exchanges in tax years beginning after May 17, 2006	¶ 1601 Tax Provisions of the Tax Relief and Health Care Act of 2006
1221(b)(3)	Capital gain treatment is permitted for certain self-created musical works sold or exchanged before Jan. 1, 2011	Sales and exchanges in tax years beginning after May 17, 2006 and before Jan. 1, 2011	¶ 208 Tax Increase Prevention and Reconciliation Act of 2005
1245(a)	Deduction will be allowed for costs of energy efficient commercial building property placed in service after Dec. 31, 2005 and before Jan. 1, 2008	Property placed in service after Dec. 31, 2005 and before Jan. 1, 2008	¶ 101 Tax Provisions of the Energy and Transportation Acts of 2005
1245(a)(2)(C)	Taxpayers can elect to expense 50% of the cost of "qualified advanced mine safety equipment property" placed in service after and before Jan. 1, 2009	Costs paid or incurred after date of enactment of the 2006 Tax Relief and Health Care Act	¶ 509 Tax Provisions of the Tax Relief and Health Care Act of 2006
1245(a)(3)(C)	Taxpayers can elect to expense 50% of the cost of "qualified advanced mine safety equipment property" placed in service after and before Jan. 1, 2009	Costs paid or incurred after date of enactment of the 2006 Tax Relief and Health Care Act	¶ 509 Tax Provisions of the Tax Relief and Health Care Act of 2006
1246(e)	Basis reduction for foreign investment company stock acquired from decedent repealed after 2009	Estates of decedents dying after 2009	¶ 312 Economic Growth and Tax Relief Reconciliation Act of 2001

Code	Topic	Effective Date	Complete Analysis ¶
1250(b)(3)	No recapture of additional depreciation for energy efficient commercial building property deduction	Property placed in service after Dec. 31, 2005	¶ 703 Gulf Opportunity Zone and Katrina Emergency Tax Relief Acts of 2005
1250(b)(3)	Deduction will be allowed for costs of energy efficient commercial building property placed in service after Dec. 31, 2005 and before Jan. 1, 2008	Property placed in service after Dec. 31, 2005 and before Jan. 1, 2008	¶ 101 Tax Provisions of the Energy and Transportation Acts of 2005
1355(a)(4)	6,000 ton weight minimum for qualifying vessels in alternative tonnage tax regime made permanent	Tax years beginning after Dec 31, 2005	¶ 1608 Tax Provisions of the Tax Relief and Health Care Act of 2006
1355(a)(4)	Weight limit for qualifying vessels in alternative tonnage tax regime lowered for 2006 through 2010	Tax years beginning after Dec. 31, 2005	¶ 305 Tax Increase Prevention and Reconciliation Act of 2005
1355(g)	Great Lakes domestic shipping excepted from general rules on temporary domestic use of vessels for tonnage tax purposes	Tax years beginning after date of enactment of the 2006 Tax Relief and Health Care Act	¶ 1609 Tax Provisions of the Tax Relief and Health Care Act of 2006
1367(a)(2)	S corporation's charitable contribution of property reduces shareholder's basis only by contributed property's basis for tax years beginning in 2006 and 2007	Contributions made in tax years beginning after Dec. 31, 2005	¶ 1506 Pension Protection Act of 2006
1397E(c)	Changes to qualified zone academy bond credit and overpayment refund rules to account for CREB credit, are made effective for tax years beginning after 2005	For tax years beginning after 2005	¶ 620 Gulf Opportunity Zone and Katrina Emergency Tax Relief Acts of 2005

Code	Topic	Effective Date	Complete Analysis ¶
1397E(c)(2)	Nonrefundable tax credit will be allowed to holders of clean renewable energy bonds issued after 2005	Bonds issued after Dec. 31, 2005	¶ 601 Tax Provisions of the Energy and Transportation Acts of 2005
1397E(d)(1)(E)	Qualified zone academy bond issuers must meet new expenditure, arbitrage, and reporting requirements	Obligations issued after date of enactment of the 2006 Tax Relief and Health Care Act	¶ 1004 Tax Provisions of the Tax Relief and Health Care Act of 2006
1397E(e)(1)	Permitted issuance of qualified zone academy bonds of up to $400 million per year is extended retroactively through Dec. 31, 2007	Obligations issued after Dec. 31, 2005 and before Jan. 1, 2008	¶ 1003 Tax Provisions of the Tax Relief and Health Care Act of 2006
1397E(f)	Qualified zone academy bond issuers must meet new expenditure, arbitrage, and reporting requirements	Obligations issued after date of enactment of the 2006 Tax Relief and Health Care Act	¶ 1004 Tax Provisions of the Tax Relief and Health Care Act of 2006
1397E(g)	Qualified zone academy bond issuers must meet new expenditure, arbitrage, and reporting requirements	Obligations issued after date of enactment of the 2006 Tax Relief and Health Care Act	¶ 1004 Tax Provisions of the Tax Relief and Health Care Act of 2006
1397E(h)	Qualified zone academy bond issuers must meet new expenditure, arbitrage, and reporting requirements	Obligations issued after date of enactment of the 2006 Tax Relief and Health Care Act	¶ 1004 Tax Provisions of the Tax Relief and Health Care Act of 2006
1397E(h)	Changes to qualified zone academy bond credit and overpayment refund rules to account for CREB credit, are made effective for tax years beginning after 2005	For tax years beginning after 2005	¶ 620 Gulf Opportunity Zone and Katrina Emergency Tax Relief Acts of 2005

Code	Topic	Effective Date	Complete Analysis ¶
1397E(h)	Credit for holders of qualified zone academy bonds issued after 2005 to be treated as regular tax credit for all tax purposes (rather than just for purposes of procedure and administration rules)	Bonds issued after Dec. 31, 2005	¶ 804 Tax Provisions of the Energy and Transportation Acts of 2005
1400(f)(1)	DC Enterprise Zone and enterprise community designations are retroactively extended for two years through Dec. 31, 2007	Periods beginning after Dec. 31, 2005 and ending before Jan. 1, 2008	¶ 1103 Tax Provisions of the Tax Relief and Health Care Act of 2006
1400(f)(2)	DC Enterprise Zone and enterprise community designations are retroactively extended for two years through Dec. 31, 2007	Periods beginning after Dec. 31, 2005 and ending before Jan. 1, 2008	¶ 1103 Tax Provisions of the Tax Relief and Health Care Act of 2006
1400A(b)	Higher tax-exempt enterprise zone facility bond limit for DC Zone bonds is retroactively extended to apply to bonds issued after Dec. 31, 2005 and before Jan. 1, 2008	Bonds issued after Dec. 31, 2005 and before Jan. 1, 2008	¶ 1104 Tax Provisions of the Tax Relief and Health Care Act of 2006
1400B(b)(2)(A)(i)	Zero percent capital gains rate for DC Zone assets is retroactively extended for two years to apply to assets acquired before Jan. 1, 2008 and includes gain attributable to periods before Jan. 1, 2013	Acquisitions after Dec. 31, 2005 and before Jan. 1, 2008	¶ 1102 Tax Provisions of the Tax Relief and Health Care Act of 2006

Code	Topic	Effective Date	Complete Analysis ¶
1400B(b)(3)(A)	Zero percent capital gains rate for DC Zone assets is retroactively extended for two years to apply to assets acquired before Jan. 1, 2008 and includes gain attributable to periods before Jan. 1, 2013	Acquisitions after Dec. 31, 2005 and before Jan. 1, 2008	¶ 1102 Tax Provisions of the Tax Relief and Health Care Act of 2006
1400B(b)(4)(A)(i)	Zero percent capital gains rate for DC Zone assets is retroactively extended for two years to apply to assets acquired before Jan. 1, 2008 and includes gain attributable to periods before Jan. 1, 2013	Acquisitions after Dec. 31, 2005 and before Jan. 1, 2008	¶ 1102 Tax Provisions of the Tax Relief and Health Care Act of 2006
1400B(b)(4)(B)(i)(I)	Zero percent capital gains rate for DC Zone assets is retroactively extended for two years to apply to assets acquired before Jan. 1, 2008 and includes gain attributable to periods before Jan. 1, 2013	Acquisitions after Dec. 31, 2005 and before Jan. 1, 2008	¶ 1102 Tax Provisions of the Tax Relief and Health Care Act of 2006
1400B(e)(2)	Zero percent capital gains rate for DC Zone assets is retroactively extended for two years to apply to assets acquired before Jan. 1, 2008 and includes gain attributable to periods before Jan. 1, 2013	Acquisitions after Dec. 31, 2005 and before Jan. 1, 2008	¶ 1102 Tax Provisions of the Tax Relief and Health Care Act of 2006

Code	Topic	Effective Date	Complete Analysis ¶
1400B(g)(2)	Zero percent capital gains rate for DC Zone assets is retroactively extended for two years to apply to assets acquired before Jan. 1, 2008 and includes gain attributable to periods before Jan. 1, 2013	Acquisitions after Dec. 31, 2005 and before Jan. 1, 2008	¶ 1102 Tax Provisions of the Tax Relief and Health Care Act of 2006
1400C(d)	Nonrefundable personal credits may offset AMT through 2006 (instead of 2005)	Tax years beginning after Dec. 31, 2005 and before Jan. 1, 2007	¶ 202 Tax Increase Prevention and Reconciliation Act of 2005
1400C(d)	Carryover rules for personal credits are redrafted to cover years in which credits are and years in which they aren't allowed against AMT	Tax years beginning after Dec. 31, 2005	¶ 601 Gulf Opportunity Zone and Katrina Emergency Tax Relief Acts of 2005
1400C(d)	Individuals will be allowed 30% credit for photovoltaic, solar hot water, and fuel cell property installed in their home in 2006 and 2007, subject to dollar limits	Property placed in service after Dec. 31, 2005 and before Jan. 1, 2008	¶ 104 Tax Provisions of the Energy and Transportation Acts of 2005
1400C(i)	DC homebuyer credit is retroactively extended for two years to apply to property bought before Jan. 1, 2008	Property bought after Dec. 31, 2005 and before Jan. 1, 2008	¶ 1101 Tax Provisions of the Tax Relief and Health Care Act of 2006
1400N(c)	Additional allocations of low-income housing credit dollar amounts are available in the Gulf Opportunity Zone for calendar years 2006, 2007, and 2008	Calendar years 2006, 2007, and 2008	¶ 127 Gulf Opportunity Zone and Katrina Emergency Tax Relief Acts of 2005
1400N(l)	Louisiana, Mississippi, and Alabama are authorized to issue Gulf tax credit bonds	Bonds issued after Dec. 31, 2005 and before Jan. 1, 2007	¶ 148 Gulf Opportunity Zone and Katrina Emergency Tax Relief Acts of 2005

Code	Topic	Effective Date	Complete Analysis ¶
1400P(a)	Value of lodging provided to employees and their families is excluded from employee's income for employees affected by Hurricane Katrina	Lodging furnished beginning Jan. 1, 2006	¶ 106 Gulf Opportunity Zone and Katrina Emergency Tax Relief Acts of 2005
1400P(b)	Qualified employers receive credit for providing lodging to employees affected by Hurricane Katrina	Lodging furnished beginning Jan. 1, 2006	¶ 128 Gulf Opportunity Zone and Katrina Emergency Tax Relief Acts of 2005
1400P(c)	Qualified employers receive credit for providing lodging to employees affected by Hurricane Katrina	Lodging furnished beginning Jan. 1, 2006	¶ 128 Gulf Opportunity Zone and Katrina Emergency Tax Relief Acts of 2005
1400P(c)	Value of lodging provided to employees and their families is excluded from employee's income for employees affected by Hurricane Katrina	Lodging furnished beginning Jan. 1, 2006	¶ 106 Gulf Opportunity Zone and Katrina Emergency Tax Relief Acts of 2005
1400P(d)	Qualified employers receive credit for providing lodging to employees affected by Hurricane Katrina	Lodging furnished beginning Jan. 1, 2006	¶ 128 Gulf Opportunity Zone and Katrina Emergency Tax Relief Acts of 2005
1400P(d)	Value of lodging provided to employees and their families is excluded from employee's income for employees affected by Hurricane Katrina	Lodging furnished beginning Jan. 1, 2006	¶ 106 Gulf Opportunity Zone and Katrina Emergency Tax Relief Acts of 2005
1400P(e)	Qualified employers receive credit for providing lodging to employees affected by Hurricane Katrina	Lodging furnished beginning Jan. 1, 2006	¶ 128 Gulf Opportunity Zone and Katrina Emergency Tax Relief Acts of 2005
1445(b)(8)	Certain wash sales of interests in domestically controlled qualified investment entities result in gain recognition under FIRPTA	Tax years beginning after Dec. 31, 2005	¶ 604 Tax Increase Prevention and Reconciliation Act of 2005

Code	Topic	Effective Date	Complete Analysis ¶
1445(e)(1)	15% withholding rate that IRS may impose on USRPI gains passed through to foreign persons by U.S. partnerships, trusts or estates is extended for two years	Tax years beginning after Dec. 31, 2008 and before Jan. 1, 2011	¶ 105 Tax Increase Prevention and Reconciliation Act of 2005
1445(e)(6)	Qualified investment entity FIRPTA exclusion is amended	Tax years of qualified investment entities beginning after Dec. 31, 2005	¶ 603 Tax Increase Prevention and Reconciliation Act of 2005
2055(e)(5)	Charitable deduction isn't allowed for contributions to donor advised funds of certain sponsoring organizations; deductible contributions require additional substantiation	Contributions made after the date that is 180 days after Aug. 17, 2006	¶ 1514 Pension Protection Act of 2006
2055(g)	Charitable deduction for fractional interest gifts of tangible personal property is limited; later fractional contributions must be valued consistently with initial one	Contributions, bequests, and gifts made after Aug. 17, 2006	¶ 1513 Pension Protection Act of 2006
2210	Estate tax will be repealed after 2009	For estates of decedents dying after Dec. 31, 2009	¶ 306 Economic Growth and Tax Relief Reconciliation Act of 2001
2502(a)	Top gift tax rate will be reduced to the top individual income tax rate of 35% on the repeal of the estate tax after 2009	For gifts made after Dec. 31, 2009	¶ 308 Economic Growth and Tax Relief Reconciliation Act of 2001
2511	Transfers to non-grantor trusts will be treated as gifts after 2009	For gifts made after Dec. 31, 2009	¶ 310 Economic Growth and Tax Relief Reconciliation Act of 2001
2511(c)	Provision governing transfers to non-grantor trusts after 2009 clarified; these transfers will be treated as transfers of property by gift	For gifts made after Dec. 31, 2009	¶ 702 Job Creation and Worker Assistance Act of 2002

Code	Topic	Effective Date	Complete Analysis ¶
2522(c)(5)	Charitable deduction isn't allowed for contributions to donor advised funds of certain sponsoring organizations; deductible contributions require additional substantiation	Contributions made after the date that is 180 days after Aug. 17, 2006	¶ 1514 Pension Protection Act of 2006
2522(e)	Charitable deduction for fractional interest gifts of tangible personal property is limited; later fractional contributions must be valued consistently with initial one	Contributions, bequests, and gifts made after Aug. 17, 2006	¶ 1513 Pension Protection Act of 2006
2664	Generation-skipping transfer (GST) tax will be repealed after 2009	For GSTs made after Dec. 31, 2009	¶ 307 Economic Growth and Tax Relief Reconciliation Act of 2001
3401	Tax-exempt employers of proctors for college entrance and placement exams can qualify for Section 530 relief without meeting consistency requirement	Remuneration for services performed after Dec. 31, 2006	¶ 1905 Pension Protection Act of 2006
3402(t)	Government entities will have to report and withhold income tax on certain payments made after 2010	For payments made after Dec. 31, 2010	¶ 802 Tax Increase Prevention and Reconciliation Act of 2005
4041(a)(2)(B)	Retail excise fuels tax imposed on alternative fuels, retail tax on LPG, LNG and CNG modified, for sale or use after Sept. 30, 2006	Sale or use for any period after Sept. 30, 2006	¶ 702 Tax Provisions of the Energy and Transportation Acts of 2005
4041(a)(2)(B)	Retail excise fuels tax imposed on alternative fuels, retail tax on LPG, LNG and CNG modified, for sale or use after Sept. 30, 2006	Sale or use for any period after Sept. 30, 2006	¶ 702 Tax Provisions of the Energy and Transportation Acts of 2005

Code	Topic	Effective Date	Complete Analysis ¶
4041(a)(3)(A)	Retail excise fuels tax imposed on alternative fuels, retail tax on LPG, LNG and CNG modified, for sale or use after Sept. 30, 2006	Sale or use for any period after Sept. 30, 2006	¶ 702 Tax Provisions of the Energy and Transportation Acts of 2005
4041(a)(3)(C)	Retail excise fuels tax imposed on alternative fuels, retail tax on LPG, LNG and CNG modified, for sale or use after Sept. 30, 2006	Sale or use for any period after Sept. 30, 2006	¶ 702 Tax Provisions of the Energy and Transportation Acts of 2005
4041(b)(2)(C)(ii)	Reduced retail excise tax rates for qualified methanol and qualified ethanol fuels (scheduled to terminate after Sept. 30, 2007) are extended through Dec. 31, 2008	Date of enactment of the 2006 Tax Relief and Health Care Act	¶ 1501 Tax Provisions of the Tax Relief and Health Care Act of 2006
4041(b)(2)(D)	Reduced retail excise tax rates for qualified methanol and qualified ethanol fuels (scheduled to terminate after Sept. 30, 2007) are extended through Dec. 31, 2008	Date of enactment of the 2006 Tax Relief and Health Care Act	¶ 1501 Tax Provisions of the Tax Relief and Health Care Act of 2006
4041(g)(5)	Qualified blood collector organizations will be exempted from certain fuel, retail, manufacturers, communications, and highway use excise taxes after 2006	Jan. 1, 2007	¶ 1907 Pension Protection Act of 2006
4081(a)(2)(D)	Diesel-water fuel emulsions taxed at reduced removal-at-terminal excise tax rate (19.7¢ per gallon, instead of 24.3¢), on removals after 2005	Jan. 1, 2006	¶ 704 Tax Provisions of the Energy and Transportation Acts of 2005

ode	Topic	Effective Date	Complete Analysis ¶
081(c)	Diesel-water fuel emulsions taxed at reduced removal-at-terminal excise tax rate (19.7¢ per gallon, instead of 24.3¢), on removals after 2005	Jan. 1, 2006	¶ 704 Tax Provisions of the Energy and Transportation Acts of 2005
101(a)(1)	Retail excise fuels tax imposed on alternative fuels, retail tax on LPG, LNG and CNG modified, for sale or use after Sept. 30, 2006	Sale or use for any period after Sept. 30, 2006	¶ 702 Tax Provisions of the Energy and Transportation Acts of 2005
101(a)(4)	Refunds of excise taxes on post-2005 credit card sales of fuel to certain tax-exempt persons to be made to the credit card issuers	Sales after Dec. 31, 2005	¶ 710 Tax Provisions of the Energy and Transportation Acts of 2005
101(d)	Terminal operators and carriers must use electronic format after 2005 for monthly returns reporting at least 25 receipts and disbursements	Jan. 1, 2006	¶ 1206 American Jobs Creation Act of 2004
132(a)(1)(O)	Meningococcal vaccine and human papillomavirus vaccine is subject to 75 cents per dose manufacturers excise tax	Sales and uses on or after first day of first month beginning more than four weeks after date of enactment of the 2006 Tax Relief and Health Care Act	¶ 1503 Tax Provisions of the Tax Relief and Health Care Act of 2006
132(a)(1)(P)	Meningococcal vaccine and human papillomavirus vaccine is subject to 75 cents per dose manufacturers excise tax	Sales and uses on or after first day of first month beginning more than four weeks after date of enactment of the 2006 Tax Relief and Health Care Act	¶ 1503 Tax Provisions of the Tax Relief and Health Care Act of 2006

Code	Topic	Effective Date	Complete Analysis ¶
4221(a)	Qualified blood collector organizations will be exempted from certain fuel, retail, manufacturers, communications, and highway use excise taxes after 2006	Jan. 1, 2007	¶ 1907 Pension Protection Act of 2006
4221(a)(6)	Qualified blood collector organizations will be exempted from certain fuel, retail, manufacturers, communications, and highway use excise taxes after 2006	Jan. 1, 2007	¶ 1907 Pension Protection Act of 2006
4253(k)	Qualified blood collector organizations will be exempted from certain fuel, retail, manufacturers, communications, and highway use excise taxes after 2006	Jan. 1, 2007	¶ 1907 Pension Protection Act of 2006
4253(k)	Qualified blood collector organizations will be exempted from certain fuel, retail, manufacturers, communications, and highway use excise taxes after 2006	Jan. 1, 2007	¶ 1907 Pension Protection Act of 2006
4483(h)	Qualified blood collector organizations will be exempted from certain fuel, retail, manufacturers, communications, and highway use excise taxes after 2006	Taxable periods beginning after June 30, 2007	¶ 1907 Pension Protection Act of 2006
4611(f)	5¢-per-barrel Oil Spill Liability Trust Fund tax on crude oil and petroleum products will be reinstated starting Apr. 1, 2006	Apr. 1, 2006	¶ 725 Tax Provisions of the Energy and Transportation Acts of 2005

Code	Topic	Effective Date	Complete Analysis ¶
4940(c)(2)	Codification of rule that gross investment income of private foundations includes annuities, income from notional principal contracts, and other substantially similar income	Tax years beginning after Aug. 17, 2006	¶ 1609 Pension Protection Act of 2006
4940(c)(4)(A)	Excise tax on private foundation's net investment income applies to capital gains from appreciation, including gains on assets used for exempt purposes—rules similar to the like-kind exchange rules apply—carrybacks of losses not allowed	Tax years beginning after Aug. 17, 2006	¶ 1610 Pension Protection Act of 2006
4940(c)(4)(C)	Excise tax on private foundation's net investment income applies to capital gains from appreciation, including gains on assets used for exempt purposes—rules similar to the like-kind exchange rules apply—carrybacks of losses not allowed	Tax years beginning after Aug. 17, 2006	¶ 1610 Pension Protection Act of 2006
4940(c)(4)(D)	Excise tax on private foundation's net investment income applies to capital gains from appreciation, including gains on assets used for exempt purposes—rules similar to the like-kind exchange rules apply—carrybacks of losses not allowed	Tax years beginning after Aug. 17, 2006	¶ 1610 Pension Protection Act of 2006

Code	Topic	Effective Date	Complete Analysis
4941(a)(1)	Penalty excise taxes on private foundations and public charities are increased	For tax years beginning after Aug. 17, 2006	¶ 1901 Pension Protection Act of 2006
4941(a)(2)	Penalty excise taxes on private foundations and public charities are increased	For tax years beginning after Aug. 17, 2006	¶ 1901 Pension Protection Act of 2006
4941(c)(2)	Penalty excise taxes on private foundations and public charities are increased	For tax years beginning after Aug. 17, 2006	¶ 1901 Pension Protection Act of 2006
4942(a)	Penalty excise taxes on private foundations and public charities are increased	For tax years beginning after Aug. 17, 2006	¶ 1901 Pension Protection Act of 2006
4942(g)(4)	Distributions by nonoperating private foundations to certain supporting organizations are not qualifying distributions	Distributions and expenditures after Aug. 17, 2006	¶ 1608 Pension Protection Act of 2006
4943(a)(1)	Penalty excise taxes on private foundations and public charities are increased	For tax years beginning after Aug. 17, 2006	¶ 1901 Pension Protection Act of 2006
4943(e)	Tax on excess business holdings extended to donor advised funds	Tax years beginning after Aug. 17, 2006	¶ 1603 Pension Protection Act of 2006
4943(f)	Excess business holdings rules applied to supporting organizations	Tax years beginning after Aug. 17, 2006	¶ 1612 Pension Protection Act of 2006
4944(a)	Penalty excise taxes on private foundations and public charities are increased	For tax years beginning after Aug. 17, 2006	¶ 1901 Pension Protection Act of 2006
4944(d)(2)	Penalty excise taxes on private foundations and public charities are increased	For tax years beginning after Aug. 17, 2006	¶ 1901 Pension Protection Act of 2006

Code	Topic	Effective Date	Complete Analysis ¶
4945(a)	Penalty excise taxes on private foundations and public charities are increased	For tax years beginning after Aug. 17, 2006	¶ 1901 Pension Protection Act of 2006
4945(c)(2)	Penalty excise taxes on private foundations and public charities are increased	For tax years beginning after Aug. 17, 2006	¶ 1901 Pension Protection Act of 2006
4945(d)(4)	Distributions by nonoperating private foundations to certain supporting organizations are not qualifying distributions	Distributions and expenditures after Aug. 17, 2006	¶ 1608 Pension Protection Act of 2006
4947(a)(2)	Split-interest trusts subject to private foundation restrictions after 2009 if charitable deduction claimed under Code Sec. 642(c)	For deductions for tax years beginning after 2009	¶ 311 Economic Growth and Tax Relief Reconciliation Act of 2001
4958(c)(2)	Certain distributions from donor advised funds to donors, donor advisors, or related persons are automatically treated as excess benefit transactions	For transactions occurring after Aug. 17, 2006	¶ 1605 Pension Protection Act of 2006
4958(c)(3)	Special rules for excess benefit transactions are enacted for Code Sec. 509(a)(3) supporting organizations	Transactions occurring after Aug. 17, 2006	¶ 1611 Pension Protection Act of 2006
4958(d)(2)	Penalty excise taxes on private foundations and public charities are increased	For tax years beginning after Aug. 17, 2006	¶ 1901 Pension Protection Act of 2006
4958(f)(1)(D)	Special rules for excess benefit transactions are enacted for Code Sec. 509(a)(3) supporting organizations	Transactions occurring after Aug. 17, 2006	¶ 1611 Pension Protection Act of 2006

Code	Topic	Effective Date	Complete Analysis ¶
4958(f)(1)(E)	Donors and donor advisors are "disqualified persons" for donor advised funds, and investment advisors are "disqualified persons" for sponsoring organizations, for excess benefit transaction tax purposes	For transactions occurring after Aug. 17, 2006	¶ 1604 Pension Protection Act of 2006
4958(f)(1)(F)	Donors and donor advisors are "disqualified persons" for donor advised funds, and investment advisors are "disqualified persons" for sponsoring organizations, for excess benefit transaction tax purposes	For transactions occurring after Aug. 17, 2006	¶ 1604 Pension Protection Act of 2006
4958(f)(6)	Certain distributions from donor advised funds to donors, donor advisors, or related persons are automatically treated as excess benefit transactions	For transactions occurring after Aug. 17, 2006	¶ 1605 Pension Protection Act of 2006
4958(f)(7)	Donors and donor advisors are "disqualified persons" for donor advised funds, and investment advisors are "disqualified persons" for sponsoring organizations, for excess benefit transaction tax purposes	For transactions occurring after Aug. 17, 2006	¶ 1604 Pension Protection Act of 2006

Code	Topic	Effective Date	Complete Analysis ¶
4958(f)(8)	Donors and donor advisors are "disqualified persons" for donor advised funds, and investment advisors are "disqualified persons" for sponsoring organizations, for excess benefit transaction tax purposes	For transactions occurring after Aug. 17, 2006	¶ 1604 Pension Protection Act of 2006
4965	Excise tax is imposed on tax-exempt entities that are parties to prohibited tax shelter transactions, and on entity managers who knowingly approve prohibited tax shelter transactions	Tax years ending after May 17, 2006	¶ 701 Tax Increase Prevention and Reconciliation Act of 2005
4966	New taxes imposed on taxable distributions from donor advised funds	Tax years beginning after Aug. 17, 2006	¶ 1601 Pension Protection Act of 2006
4967	New taxes imposed on prohibited benefits received by a donor, donor advisor or related person from a donor advised fund	Tax years beginning after Aug. 17, 2006	¶ 1602 Pension Protection Act of 2006
4971(a)	Excise tax on failure to meet minimum funding standards integrated with new funding rules	Plan years beginning after 2007	¶ 505 Pension Protection Act of 2006
4971(b)	Excise tax on failure to meet minimum funding standards integrated with new funding rules	Plan years beginning after 2007	¶ 505 Pension Protection Act of 2006
4971(c)(4)	Excise tax on failure to meet minimum funding standards integrated with new funding rules	Plan years beginning after 2007	¶ 505 Pension Protection Act of 2006
4971(g)	New excise tax scheme applies to multiemployer plans in critical or endangered status	For plan years beginning 2007	¶ 608 Pension Protection Act of 2006

Code	Topic	Effective Date	Complete Analysis ¶
4972(c)(6)(A)	Defined benefit plan deduction limits increased with separate limits set for single-employer and multiemployer plans	Contributions for tax years beginning after Dec. 31, 2005	¶ 510 Pension Protection Act of 2006
4975(d)(17)	Investment advice may be provided under 401(k) plans and IRAs, despite conflicts of interest; employers are exempt from fiduciary liability	For investment advice provided by a fiduciary for a fee or other compensation after Dec. 31, 2006	¶ 801 Pension Protection Act of 2006
4975(d)(18)	Block trades are exempt from prohibited transaction rules	For transactions occurring after Aug. 17, 2006	¶ 1203 Pension Protection Act of 2006
4975(d)(19)	Transactions made through regulated electronic communication trading systems are exempt from the prohibited transaction rules	For transactions occurring after Aug. 17, 2006	¶ 1204 Pension Protection Act of 2006
4975(d)(20)	Certain transactions between plans and service providers are exempt from prohibited transaction rules if made for adequate consideration	For transactions occurring after Aug. 17, 2006	¶ 1201 Pension Protection Act of 2006
4975(d)(21)	Certain foreign exchange transactions are exempt from prohibited transaction rules	For transactions occurring after Aug. 17, 2006	¶ 1202 Pension Protection Act of 2006
4975(d)(22)	Securities cross trades are exempt from prohibited transaction rules	For transactions occurring after Aug. 17, 2006	¶ 1205 Pension Protection Act of 2006
4975(d)(23)	Certain otherwise prohibited transactions involving securities and commodities that are corrected within 14 days are exempt from the prohibited transaction rules	Prohibited transactions discovered, or that should have been discovered, after Aug. 17, 2006	¶ 1206 Pension Protection Act of 2006

Code	Topic	Effective Date	Complete Analysis ¶
4975(f)(8)	Investment advice may be provided under 401(k) plans and IRAs, despite conflicts of interest; employers are exempt from fiduciary liability	For investment advice provided by a fiduciary for a fee or other compensation after Dec. 31, 2006	¶ 801 Pension Protection Act of 2006
4975(f)(9)	Block trades are exempt from prohibited transaction rules	For transactions occurring after Aug. 17, 2006	¶ 1203 Pension Protection Act of 2006
4975(f)(10)	Certain transactions between plans and service providers are exempt from prohibited transaction rules if made for adequate consideration	For transactions occurring after Aug. 17, 2006	¶ 1201 Pension Protection Act of 2006
4975(f)(11)	Certain otherwise prohibited transactions involving securities and commodities that are corrected within 14 days are exempt from the prohibited transaction rules	Prohibited transactions discovered, or that should have been discovered, after Aug. 17, 2006	¶ 1206 Pension Protection Act of 2006
4979(f)	Automatic contribution arrangements for 401(k) plans	Plan years beginning after Dec. 31, 2007	¶ 401 Pension Protection Act of 2006
4980F(e)(1)	Pension plans will have to provide additional information in annual reports but not send summary annual reports; multiemployer plans will have to provide new summary reports to employers and unions, and give plan information to participants or employers upon request	For plan years beginning after Dec. 31, 2007	¶ 901 Pension Protection Act of 2006

Code	Topic	Effective Date	Complete Analysis ¶
4980G(d)	Employers can make larger HSA contributions to nonhighly compensated employees than highly compensated employees without violating comparability rule	Tax years beginning after Dec. 31, 2006	¶ 304 Tax Provisions of the Tax Relief and Health Care Act of 2006
6011(g)	Taxable parties to a prohibited tax shelter transaction must disclose that tax shelter status to any tax-exempt entity that is a party to the transaction	Disclosures the due date for which is after May 17, 2006	¶ 703 Tax Increase Prevention and Reconciliation Act of 2005
6015(e)(1)	Tax Court has jurisdiction to review IRS's denial of equitable innocent spouse relief from joint liability even if no deficiency was asserted against the requestor of relief	Liability for taxes arising or remaining unpaid on or after date of enactment of the 2006 Tax Relief and Health Care Act	¶ 1401 Tax Provisions of the Tax Relief and Health Care Act of 2006
6015(e)(1)(A)(i)(II)	Tax Court has jurisdiction to review IRS's denial of equitable innocent spouse relief from joint liability even if no deficiency was asserted against the requestor of relief	Liability for taxes arising or remaining unpaid on or after date of enactment of the 2006 Tax Relief and Health Care Act	¶ 1401 Tax Provisions of the Tax Relief and Health Care Act of 2006
6015(e)(1)(B)(i)	Tax Court has jurisdiction to review IRS's denial of equitable innocent spouse relief from joint liability even if no deficiency was asserted against the requestor of relief	Liability for taxes arising or remaining unpaid on or after date of enactment of the 2006 Tax Relief and Health Care Act	¶ 1401 Tax Provisions of the Tax Relief and Health Care Act of 2006
6015(e)(1)(B)(ii)	Tax Court has jurisdiction to review IRS's denial of equitable innocent spouse relief from joint liability even if no deficiency was asserted against the requestor of relief	Liability for taxes arising or remaining unpaid on or after date of enactment of the 2006 Tax Relief and Health Care Act	¶ 1401 Tax Provisions of the Tax Relief and Health Care Act of 2006

Code	Topic	Effective Date	Complete Analysis ¶
6015(e)(4)	Tax Court has jurisdiction to review IRS's denial of equitable innocent spouse relief from joint liability even if no deficiency was asserted against the requestor of relief	Liability for taxes arising or remaining unpaid on or after date of enactment of the 2006 Tax Relief and Health Care Act	¶ 1401 Tax Provisions of the Tax Relief and Health Care Act of 2006
6015(e)(5)	Tax Court has jurisdiction to review IRS's denial of equitable innocent spouse relief from joint liability even if no deficiency was asserted against the requestor of relief	Liability for taxes arising or remaining unpaid on or after date of enactment of the 2006 Tax Relief and Health Care Act	¶ 1401 Tax Provisions of the Tax Relief and Health Care Act of 2006
6015(g)(2)	Tax Court has jurisdiction to review IRS's denial of equitable innocent spouse relief from joint liability even if no deficiency was asserted against the requestor of relief	Liability for taxes arising or remaining unpaid on or after date of enactment of the 2006 Tax Relief and Health Care Act	¶ 1401 Tax Provisions of the Tax Relief and Health Care Act of 2006
6015(h)(2)	Tax Court has jurisdiction to review IRS's denial of equitable innocent spouse relief from joint liability even if no deficiency was asserted against the requestor of relief	Liability for taxes arising or remaining unpaid on or after date of enactment of the 2006 Tax Relief and Health Care Act	¶ 1401 Tax Provisions of the Tax Relief and Health Care Act of 2006
6018	"Large transfers" (generally over $1.3 million) at death will have to be reported to IRS when estate tax repealed after 2009	For estates of decedents dying after Dec. 31, 2009	¶ 332 Economic Growth and Tax Relief Reconciliation Act of 2001
6019(b)	Donors will be required to provide donees with information about property reported on gift tax returns after 2009	For transfers after 2009	¶ 333 Economic Growth and Tax Relief Reconciliation Act of 2001
6033(a)(2)	Tax-exempt entities must disclose participation in prohibited tax shelter transactions to IRS	Disclosures the due date for which is after May 17, 2006	¶ 702 Tax Increase Prevention and Reconciliation Act of 2005

Code	Topic	Effective Date	Complete Analysis ¶
6033(a)(3)(B)	Code Sec. 509(a)(3) supporting organizations must file annual information returns containing specific information	Returns filed for tax years ending after Aug. 17, 2006	¶ 1614 Pension Protection Act of 2006
6033(h)	Information returns of parent tax-exempt organizations must include information about transactions with controlled entities	Returns due after Aug. 17, 2006	¶ 1803 Pension Protection Act of 2006
6033(i)	Exempt organizations not required to file annual information returns because normal annual gross receipts are $25,000 or less must file annual notices with IRS	Notices and returns for annual periods beginning after 2006	¶ 1804 Pension Protection Act of 2006
6033(j)	Exempt organization status can be revoked for failing to file annual information returns or notices for three consecutive years	Returns and notices for annual periods beginning after 2006	¶ 1801 Pension Protection Act of 2006
6033(j)	Exempt organization status can be revoked for failing to file annual information returns or notices for three consecutive years	Returns and notices for annual periods beginning after 2006	¶ 1801 Pension Protection Act of 2006
6033(j)	Exempt organizations not required to file annual information returns because normal annual gross receipts are $25,000 or less must file annual notices with IRS	Notices and returns for annual periods beginning after 2006	¶ 1804 Pension Protection Act of 2006
6033(j)	Exempt organization status can be revoked for failing to file annual information returns or notices for three consecutive years	Returns and notices for annual periods beginning after 2006	¶ 1801 Pension Protection Act of 2006

Code	Topic	Effective Date	Complete Analysis ¶
6033(k)	Sponsoring organizations must disclose information about donor advised funds on information returns	For returns filed for tax years ending after Aug. 17, 2006	¶ 1606 Pension Protection Act of 2006
6033(l)	Code Sec. 509(a)(3) supporting organizations must file annual information returns containing specific information	Returns filed for tax years ending after Aug. 17, 2006	¶ 1614 Pension Protection Act of 2006
6034	Split-interest trusts must file annual information returns under Code Sec. 6034 even if they must currently distribute all net income	Returns for tax years beginning after Dec. 31, 2006	¶ 1806 Pension Protection Act of 2006
6039(a)	Corporations must report to IRS transfers of stock from exercises of incentive stock options or purchases from employee stock purchase plans	Calendar years beginning after date of enactment of the 2006 Tax Relief and Health Care Act	¶ 401 Tax Provisions of the Tax Relief and Health Care Act of 2006
6039(b)	Corporations must report to IRS transfers of stock from exercises of incentive stock options or purchases from employee stock purchase plans	Calendar years beginning after date of enactment of the 2006 Tax Relief and Health Care Act	¶ 401 Tax Provisions of the Tax Relief and Health Care Act of 2006
6039I	Income tax treatment of proceeds from employer-owned life insurance modified; new compliance procedures added	Life insurance contracts issued after Aug. 17, 2006	¶ 2401 Pension Protection Act of 2006
6049(b)(2)(B)	Tax-exempt interest is subject to information reporting in the same manner as interest paid on taxable obligations	Interest paid after Dec. 31, 2005	¶ 801 Tax Increase Prevention and Reconciliation Act of 2005

Code	Topic	Effective Date	Complete Analysis ¶
6049(d)(8)	Nonrefundable tax credit will be allowed to holders of clean renewable energy bonds issued after 2005	Bonds issued after Dec. 31, 2005	¶ 601 Tax Provisions of the Energy and Transportation Acts of 2005
6049(d)(8)(A)	Louisiana, Mississippi, and Alabama are authorized to issue Gulf tax credit bonds	Bonds issued after Dec. 31, 2005 and before Jan. 1, 2007	¶ 148 Gulf Opportunity Zone and Katrina Emergency Tax Relief Acts of 2005
6050H(h)	Deduction is allowed, for taxpayers with AGI not exceeding $109,000, for mortgage insurance premiums paid or incurred with respect to qualified residences in 2007	Amounts paid or accrued after Dec. 31, 2006	¶ 104 Tax Provisions of the Tax Relief and Health Care Act of 2006
6050L(a)(1)	Charitable donees must report disposition within three years of receipt of charitable deduction property	Returns filed after Sept. 1, 2006	¶ 1802 Pension Protection Act of 2006
6050U	Qualified long-term care insurance can be provided as a rider to an annuity contract after 2009	For charges made after Dec. 31, 2009	¶ 2402 Pension Protection Act of 2006
6050V	Certain exempt organizations that acquire interests in life insurance contracts within two years after Aug. 17, 2006 must file information returns—penalties imposed for failure to comply	For acquisitions of contracts after Aug. 17, 2006	¶ 1805 Pension Protection Act of 2006
6075(a)	"Large transfers" (generally over $1.3 million) at death will have to be reported to IRS when estate tax repealed after 2009	For estates of decedents dying after Dec. 31, 2009	¶ 332 Economic Growth and Tax Relief Reconciliation Act of 2001

Code	Topic	Effective Date	Complete Analysis ¶
6103(a)(2)	Limits on disclosure of returns and return information apply to information disclosed to appropriate state officers under Code Sec. 6104(c)	Aug. 17, 2006, but not for requests made before Aug. 17, 2006	¶ 1703 Pension Protection Act of 2006
6103(b)(5)	Regional income tax agencies are treated as States for purposes of confidentiality and disclosure of returns and return information	Disclosures made after Dec. 31, 2006	¶ 1406 Tax Provisions of the Tax Relief and Health Care Act of 2006
6103(d)(5)(B)	IRS's authority to disclose taxpayer identity information to facilitate combined federal/ state employment tax reporting is extended for one year through Dec. 31, 2007	Disclosures after Dec. 31, 2006 and before Jan. 1, 2008	¶ 1403 Tax Provisions of the Tax Relief and Health Care Act of 2006
6103(d)(5)(B)	IRS's authority to disclose taxpayer identity information to facilitate combined federal/ state employment tax reporting is extended for one year through Dec. 31, 2006	Disclosures after Dec. 31, 2005 and before Jan. 1, 2007	¶ 1701 Gulf Opportunity Zone and Katrina Emergency Tax Relief Acts of 2005
6103(d)(6)	Regional income tax agencies are treated as States for purposes of confidentiality and disclosure of returns and return information	Disclosures made after Dec. 31, 2006	¶ 1406 Tax Provisions of the Tax Relief and Health Care Act of 2006
6103(i)(3)(C)(iv)	IRS's authority to disclose tax information in terrorism and national security investigations is extended for one year through Dec. 31, 2007	Disclosures after Dec. 31, 2006 and before Jan. 1, 2008	¶ 1405 Tax Provisions of the Tax Relief and Health Care Act of 2006

Code	Topic	Effective Date	Complete Analysis ¶
6103(i)(3)(C)(iv)	IRS's authority to disclose tax information in terrorism and national security investigations is extended for one year through Dec. 31, 2006	Disclosures after Dec. 31, 2005 and before Jan. 1, 2007	¶ 1703 Gulf Opportunity Zone and Katrina Emergency Tax Relief Acts of 2005
6103(i)(7)(E)	IRS's authority to disclose tax information in terrorism and national security investigations is extended for one year through Dec. 31, 2007	Disclosures after Dec. 31, 2006 and before Jan. 1, 2008	¶ 1405 Tax Provisions of the Tax Relief and Health Care Act of 2006
6103(i)(7)(E)	IRS's authority to disclose tax information in terrorism and national security investigations is extended for one year through Dec. 31, 2006	Disclosures after Dec. 31, 2005 and before Jan. 1, 2007	¶ 1703 Gulf Opportunity Zone and Katrina Emergency Tax Relief Acts of 2005
6103(l)(13)(D)	IRS's authority to disclose requested return information to the Dept. of Education to monitor income-contingent student loan repayments is extended for one year for requests made through Dec. 31, 2007	Requests made after Dec. 31, 2006 and before Jan. 1, 2008	¶ 1404 Tax Provisions of the Tax Relief and Health Care Act of 2006
6103(l)(13)(D)	IRS's authority to disclose return information to the Dept. of Education to monitor income-contingent student loan repayments is extended for one year for requests made through Dec. 31, 2006	Requests for disclosure made after Dec. 31, 2005 and before Jan. 1, 2007	¶ 1702 Gulf Opportunity Zone and Katrina Emergency Tax Relief Acts of 2005

Code	Topic	Effective Date	Complete Analysis ¶
6103(p)(3)(A)	Recordkeeping and reporting requirements apply to IRS's disclosure to appropriate state officers of tax-exempt organizations' returns and return information	Aug. 17, 2006, but not for requests made before Aug. 17, 2006	¶ 1704 Pension Protection Act of 2006
6103(p)(4)	Safeguards apply to IRS's disclosure of tax-exempt organizations' returns to appropriate state officers	Aug. 17, 2006, but not for requests made before Aug. 17, 2006	¶ 1705 Pension Protection Act of 2006
6103(p)(4)(F)	Safeguards apply to IRS's disclosure of tax-exempt organizations' returns to appropriate state officers	Aug. 17, 2006, but not for requests made before Aug. 17, 2006	¶ 1705 Pension Protection Act of 2006
6103(p)(4)(F)(i)	Safeguards apply to IRS's disclosure of tax-exempt organizations' returns to appropriate state officers	Aug. 17, 2006, but not for requests made before Aug. 17, 2006	¶ 1705 Pension Protection Act of 2006
6104(b)	Information about non-charitable beneficiaries of split-interest trusts is not available for public inspection	Returns for tax years beginning after Dec. 31, 2006	¶ 1808 Pension Protection Act of 2006
6104(c)(2)	IRS can disclose to appropriate state officers tax-exempt status applications and proposed determinations regarding Code Sec. 501(c)(3) organizations	Aug. 17, 2006, but not for requests made before Aug. 17, 2006	¶ 1702 Pension Protection Act of 2006
6104(c)(3)	IRS can disclose to appropriate state officers returns and return information of certain non-Code Sec. 501(c)(1) or non-Code Sec. 501(c)(3) organizations	Aug. 17, 2006, but not for requests made before Aug. 17, 2006	¶ 1709 Pension Protection Act of 2006

Code	Topic	Effective Date	Complete Analysis ¶
6104(c)(4)	Returns of certain tax-exempt organizations can be disclosed in civil administrative and judicial proceedings related to the enforcement of state laws	Aug. 17, 2006, but not for requests made before Aug. 17, 2006	¶ 1710 Pension Protection Act of 2006
6104(c)(5)	Disclosure of returns and return information relating to tax exempt organizations is prohibited if disclosure seriously impairs federal tax administration	Aug. 17, 2006, but not for requests made before Aug. 17, 2006	¶ 1711 Pension Protection Act of 2006
6104(c)(6)(A)	IRS can disclose to appropriate state officers returns and return information of certain non-Code Sec. 501(c)(1) or non-Code Sec. 501(c)(3) organizations	Aug. 17, 2006, but not for requests made before Aug. 17, 2006	¶ 1709 Pension Protection Act of 2006
6104(c)(6)(A)	IRS can disclose to appropriate state officers tax-exempt status applications and proposed determinations regarding Code Sec. 501(c)(3) organizations	Aug. 17, 2006, but not for requests made before Aug. 17, 2006	¶ 1702 Pension Protection Act of 2006
6104(c)(6)(A)	Returns of certain tax-exempt organizations can be disclosed in civil administrative and judicial proceedings related to the enforcement of state laws	Aug. 17, 2006, but not for requests made before Aug. 17, 2006	¶ 1710 Pension Protection Act of 2006
6104(c)(6)(B)	IRS can disclose to appropriate state officers returns and return information of certain non-Code Sec. 501(c)(1) or non-Code Sec. 501(c)(3) organizations	Aug. 17, 2006, but not for requests made before Aug. 17, 2006	¶ 1709 Pension Protection Act of 2006

Code	Topic	Effective Date	Complete Analysis ¶
6104(c)(6)(B)	IRS can disclose to appropriate state officers tax-exempt status applications and proposed determinations regarding Code Sec. 501(c)(3) organizations	Aug. 17, 2006, but not for requests made before Aug. 17, 2006	¶ 1702 Pension Protection Act of 2006
6104(d)(1)(A)(ii)	Code Sec. 501(c)(3) organizations must make available for public inspection copies of their annual unrelated business income tax (UBIT) returns	Returns filed after Aug. 17, 2006	¶ 1701 Pension Protection Act of 2006
6206	Refunds of excise taxes on post-2005 credit card sales of fuel to certain tax-exempt persons to be made to the credit card issuers	Sales after Dec. 31, 2005	¶ 710 Tax Provisions of the Energy and Transportation Acts of 2005
6211(b)(4)(A)	AMT refundable credit may result in negative amount of tax in deficiency computation	Tax years beginning after date of enactment of the 2006 Tax Relief and Health Care Act	¶ 1202 Tax Provisions of the Tax Relief and Health Care Act of 2006
6214(b)	Tax Court authority to apply equitable recoupment doctrine is codified	Tax Court actions or proceedings for which a decision has not become final as of Aug. 17, 2006	¶ 2103 Pension Protection Act of 2006
6320(b)(1)	Frivolous submissions are subject to IRS dismissal	Submissions made and issues raised after IRS prescribes a list of frivolous positions	¶ 1408 Tax Provisions of the Tax Relief and Health Care Act of 2006
6320(c)	Frivolous submissions are subject to IRS dismissal	Submissions made and issues raised after IRS prescribes a list of frivolous positions	¶ 1408 Tax Provisions of the Tax Relief and Health Care Act of 2006
6330(b)(1)	Frivolous submissions are subject to IRS dismissal	Submissions made and issues raised after IRS prescribes a list of frivolous positions	¶ 1408 Tax Provisions of the Tax Relief and Health Care Act of 2006
6330(c)(4)	Frivolous submissions are subject to IRS dismissal	Submissions made and issues raised after IRS prescribes a list of frivolous positions	¶ 1408 Tax Provisions of the Tax Relief and Health Care Act of 2006

Code	Topic	Effective Date	Complete Analysis ¶
6330(d)(1)	Tax Court has sole jurisdiction over all Collection Due Process appeals	Determinations after the date which is 60 days after Aug. 17, 2006	¶ 2102 Pension Protection Act of 2006
6330(g)	Frivolous submissions are subject to IRS dismissal	Submissions made and issues raised after IRS prescribes a list of frivolous positions	¶ 1408 Tax Provisions of the Tax Relief and Health Care Act of 2006
6401(b)(1)	Changes to qualified zone academy bond credit and overpayment refund rules to account for CREB credit, are made effective for tax years beginning after 2005	For tax years beginning after 2005	¶ 620 Gulf Opportunity Zone and Katrina Emergency Tax Relief Acts of 2005
6401(b)(1)	Nonrefundable tax credit will be allowed to holders of clean renewable energy bonds issued after 2005	Bonds issued after Dec. 31, 2005	¶ 601 Tax Provisions of the Energy and Transportation Acts of 2005
6416(a)(4)	Refunds of excise taxes on post-2005 credit card sales of fuel to certain tax-exempt persons to be made to the credit card issuers	Sales after Dec. 31, 2005	¶ 710 Tax Provisions of the Energy and Transportation Acts of 2005
6416(b)(2)	Qualified blood collector organizations will be exempted from certain fuel, retail, manufacturers, communications, and highway use excise taxes after 2006	Jan. 1, 2007	¶ 1907 Pension Protection Act of 2006
6416(b)(2)	Refunds of excise taxes on post-2005 credit card sales of fuel to certain tax-exempt persons to be made to the credit card issuers	Sales after Dec. 31, 2005	¶ 710 Tax Provisions of the Energy and Transportation Acts of 2005

Code	Topic	Effective Date	Complete Analysis ¶
6416(b)(2)(E)	Qualified blood collector organizations will be exempted from certain fuel, retail, manufacturers, communications, and highway use excise taxes after 2006	Jan. 1, 2007	¶ 1907 Pension Protection Act of 2006
6416(b)(4)(B)(iii)	Qualified blood collector organizations will be exempted from certain fuel, retail, manufacturers, communications, and highway use excise taxes after 2006	Jan. 1, 2007	¶ 1907 Pension Protection Act of 2006
6421(c)	Qualified blood collector organizations will be exempted from certain fuel, retail, manufacturers, communications, and highway use excise taxes after 2006	Jan. 1, 2007	¶ 1907 Pension Protection Act of 2006
6426(a)	Excise tax credit or refund permitted for alternative fuels and alternative fuel mixtures, for sale or use after Sept. 30, 2006	Sale or use for any period after Sept. 30, 2006	¶ 709 Tax Provisions of the Energy and Transportation Acts of 2005
6426(d)	Excise tax credit or refund permitted for alternative fuels and alternative fuel mixtures, for sale or use after Sept. 30, 2006	Sale or use for any period after Sept. 30, 2006	¶ 709 Tax Provisions of the Energy and Transportation Acts of 2005
6426(d)(2)(F)	Excise tax credit or refund permitted for alternative fuels and alternative fuel mixtures, for sale or use after Sept. 30, 2006	Sale or use for any period after Sept. 30, 2006	¶ 709 Tax Provisions of the Energy and Transportation Acts of 2005
6426(e)	Excise tax credit or refund permitted for alternative fuels and alternative fuel mixtures, for sale or use after Sept. 30, 2006	Sale or use for any period after Sept. 30, 2006	¶ 709 Tax Provisions of the Energy and Transportation Acts of 2005

Code	Topic	Effective Date	Complete Analysis ¶
6427(e)(1)	Excise tax credit or refund permitted for alternative fuels and alternative fuel mixtures, for sale or use after Sept. 30, 2006	Sale or use for any period after Sept. 30, 2006	¶ 709 Tax Provisions of the Energy and Transportation Acts of 2005
6427(e)(2)	Excise tax credit or refund permitted for alternative fuels and alternative fuel mixtures, for sale or use after Sept. 30, 2006	Sale or use for any period after Sept. 30, 2006	¶ 709 Tax Provisions of the Energy and Transportation Acts of 2005
6427(e)(4)	Excise tax credit or refund permitted for alternative fuels and alternative fuel mixtures, for sale or use after Sept. 30, 2006	Sale or use for any period after Sept. 30, 2006	¶ 709 Tax Provisions of the Energy and Transportation Acts of 2005
6427(e)(5)(C)	Excise tax credit or refund permitted for alternative fuels and alternative fuel mixtures, for sale or use after Sept. 30, 2006	Sale or use for any period after Sept. 30, 2006	¶ 709 Tax Provisions of the Energy and Transportation Acts of 2005
6427(e)(5)(D)	Excise tax credit or refund permitted for alternative fuels and alternative fuel mixtures, for sale or use after Sept. 30, 2006	Sale or use for any period after Sept. 30, 2006	¶ 709 Tax Provisions of the Energy and Transportation Acts of 2005
6427(i)(1)	Diesel-water fuel emulsions taxed at reduced removal-at-terminal excise tax rate (19.7¢ per gallon, instead of 24.3¢), on removals after 2005	Jan. 1, 2006	¶ 704 Tax Provisions of the Energy and Transportation Acts of 2005
6427(i)(2)	Diesel-water fuel emulsions taxed at reduced removal-at-terminal excise tax rate (19.7¢ per gallon, instead of 24.3¢), on removals after 2005	Jan. 1, 2006	¶ 704 Tax Provisions of the Energy and Transportation Acts of 2005

Code	Topic	Effective Date	Complete Analysis ¶
6427(l)(6)	Refunds of excise taxes on post-2005 credit card sales of fuel to certain tax-exempt persons to be made to the credit card issuers	Sales after Dec. 31, 2005	¶ 710 Tax Provisions of the Energy and Transportation Acts of 2005
6427(m)	Diesel-water fuel emulsions taxed at reduced removal-at-terminal excise tax rate (19.7¢ per gallon, instead of 24.3¢), on removals after 2005	Jan. 1, 2006	¶ 704 Tax Provisions of the Energy and Transportation Acts of 2005
6501(m)	Credit provided for qualified alternative fuel vehicle refueling property	Property placed in service after Dec. 31, 2005	¶ 206 Tax Provisions of the Energy and Transportation Acts of 2005
6652(c)	$100 per day penalties imposed where exempt organizations fail to make required disclosures to IRS relating to prohibited tax shelter transactions	Disclosures the due date for which is after May 17, 2006	¶ 704 Tax Increase Prevention and Reconciliation Act of 2005
6652(c)(1)(E)	Exempt organizations not required to file annual information returns because normal annual gross receipts are $25,000 or less must file annual notices with IRS	Notices and returns for annual periods beginning after 2006	¶ 1804 Pension Protection Act of 2006
6652(c)(2)	Penalty on split interest trusts for failing to file a Code Sec. 6034 return is doubled for smaller trusts and increased ten-fold for larger trusts; penalty may be imposed without prior IRS written demand	Returns for tax years beginning after Dec. 31, 2006	¶ 1807 Pension Protection Act of 2006

Code	Topic	Effective Date	Complete Analysis ¶
6655	Percentages and due dates of otherwise required estimated tax payments due from corporations are changed for some installment due dates in 2006, and 2010 to 2013	May 17, 2006	¶ 803 Tax Increase Prevention and Reconciliation Act of 2005
6662(e)(1)(A)	Substantial and gross valuation penalty tests changed to 150%/200% from 200%/400% for income taxes and to 65%/40% from 50%/25% for estate and gift taxes	Returns filed after Aug. 17, 2006	¶ 2301 Pension Protection Act of 2006
6662(g)	Substantial and gross valuation penalty tests changed to 150%/200% from 200%/400% for income taxes and to 65%/40% from 50%/25% for estate and gift taxes	Returns filed after Aug. 17, 2006	¶ 2301 Pension Protection Act of 2006
6662(h)(2)(A)	Substantial and gross valuation penalty tests changed to 150%/200% from 200%/400% for income taxes and to 65%/40% from 50%/25% for estate and gift taxes	Returns filed after Aug. 17, 2006	¶ 2301 Pension Protection Act of 2006
6662(h)(2)(C)	Substantial and gross valuation penalty tests changed to 150%/200% from 200%/400% for income taxes and to 65%/40% from 50%/25% for estate and gift taxes	Returns filed after Aug. 17, 2006	¶ 2301 Pension Protection Act of 2006
6664(c)(2)	Substantial and gross valuation penalty tests changed to 150%/200% from 200%/400% for income taxes and to 65%/40% from 50%/25% for estate and gift taxes	Returns filed after Aug. 17, 2006	¶ 2301 Pension Protection Act of 2006

Code	Topic	Effective Date	Complete Analysis ¶
6664(c)(3)	Substantial and gross valuation penalty tests changed to 150%/200% from 200%/400% for income taxes and to 65%/40% from 50%/25% for estate and gift taxes	Returns filed after Aug. 17, 2006	¶ 2301 Pension Protection Act of 2006
6675(a)	Refunds of excise taxes on post-2005 credit card sales of fuel to certain tax-exempt persons to be made to the credit card issuers	Sales after Dec. 31, 2005	¶ 710 Tax Provisions of the Energy and Transportation Acts of 2005
6675(b)(1)	Refunds of excise taxes on post-2005 credit card sales of fuel to certain tax-exempt persons to be made to the credit card issuers	Sales after Dec. 31, 2005	¶ 710 Tax Provisions of the Energy and Transportation Acts of 2005
6695A	Penalty imposed for valuation misstatements attributable to incorrect appraisals	Appraisals prepared for returns or submissions filed after Aug. 17, 2006	¶ 2302 Pension Protection Act of 2006
6696	Penalty imposed for valuation misstatements attributable to incorrect appraisals	Appraisals prepared for returns or submissions filed after Aug. 17, 2006	¶ 2302 Pension Protection Act of 2006
6702	Penalty for frivolous submissions upped to $5,000, extended to other submissions	Submissions made and issues raised after IRS prescribes a list of frivolous positions	¶ 1407 Tax Provisions of the Tax Relief and Health Care Act of 2006
6716	"Large transfers" (generally over $1.3 million) at death will have to be reported to IRS when estate tax repealed after 2009	For estates of decedents dying after Dec. 31, 2009	¶ 332 Economic Growth and Tax Relief Reconciliation Act of 2001
6716	Donors will be required to provide donees with information about property reported on gift tax returns after 2009	For transfers after 2009	¶ 333 Economic Growth and Tax Relief Reconciliation Act of 2001

Code	Topic	Effective Date	Complete Analysis ¶
6720B	Deduction for charitable contributions of tangible personal property exceeding $5,000 must be reduced or recaptured if donee sells property within three years of contribution	Identifications made after Aug. 17, 2006	¶ 1505 Pension Protection Act of 2006
6721(e)(2)(D)	Certain exempt organizations that acquire interests in life insurance contracts within two years after Aug. 17, 2006 must file information returns—penalties imposed for failure to comply	For acquisitions of contracts after Aug. 17, 2006	¶ 1805 Pension Protection Act of 2006
6724(d)	Qualified long-term care insurance can be provided as a rider to an annuity contract after 2009	After Dec. 31, 2009	¶ 2402 Pension Protection Act of 2006
6724(d)(1)(B)(xiv)	Certain exempt organizations that acquire interests in life insurance contracts within two years after Aug. 17, 2006 must file information returns—penalties imposed for failure to comply	For acquisitions of contracts after Aug. 17, 2006	¶ 1805 Pension Protection Act of 2006
6724(d)(1)(B)(xix)	Corporations must report to IRS transfers of stock from exercises of incentive stock options or purchases from employee stock purchase plans	Calendar years beginning after date of enactment of the 2006 Tax Relief and Health Care Act	¶ 401 Tax Provisions of the Tax Relief and Health Care Act of 2006
7122(c)	Partial payments are required with submissions of offers in compromise; offers are deemed accepted if not rejected within a certain period	Offers in compromise submitted on and after the date that is 60 days after May 17, 2006	¶ 804 Tax Increase Prevention and Reconciliation Act of 2005

Code	Topic	Effective Date	Complete Analysis ¶
7122(c)(3)(C)	Partial payments are required with submissions of offers in compromise; offers are deemed accepted if not rejected within a certain period	Offers in compromise submitted on and after the date that is 60 days after May 17, 2006	¶ 804 Tax Increase Prevention and Reconciliation Act of 2005
7122(f)	Frivolous submissions are subject to IRS dismissal	Submissions made and issues raised after IRS prescribes a list of frivolous positions	¶ 1408 Tax Provisions of the Tax Relief and Health Care Act of 2006
7122(f)	Partial payments are required with submissions of offers in compromise; offers are deemed accepted if not rejected within a certain period	Offers in compromise submitted on and after the date that is 60 days after May 17, 2006	¶ 804 Tax Increase Prevention and Reconciliation Act of 2005
7213(a)(2)	Unauthorized disclosure of tax-exempt organization's returns and return information acquired under Code Sec. 6104(c) is subject to criminal penalties	Aug. 17, 2006, but not for requests made before Aug. 17, 2006	¶ 1708 Pension Protection Act of 2006
7213A(a)(2)	Unauthorized inspection of tax-exempt organization's returns and return information acquired under Code Sec. 6104(c) is subject to criminal penalties	Aug. 17, 2006, but not for requests made before Aug. 17, 2006	¶ 1706 Pension Protection Act of 2006
7428(b)(4)	Exempt organization status can be revoked for failing to file annual information returns or notices for three consecutive years	Returns and notices for annual periods beginning after 2006	¶ 1801 Pension Protection Act of 2006
7431(a)(2)	Tax-exempt organizations can sue for damages for unauthorized disclosure or inspection of the organization's returns and return information	Aug. 17, 2006, but not for requests made before Aug. 17, 2006	¶ 1707 Pension Protection Act of 2006

Code	Topic	Effective Date	Complete Analysis ¶
7443A(b)(5)	Whistleblower rewards are increased, to maximum of 30% (up from 15%) of collected proceeds, interest, penalties, and additional amounts	Information provided on or after date of enactment of the 2006 Tax Relief and Health Care Act	¶ 1409 Tax Provisions of the Tax Relief and Health Care Act of 2006
7443A(b)(5)	Tax Court special trial judges may hear and decide any small case employment tax proceeding	Any small case employment tax proceeding for which a decision is not final before Aug. 17, 2006	¶ 2104 Pension Protection Act of 2006
7443A(c)	Tax Court special trial judges may hear and decide any small case employment tax proceeding	Any small case employment tax proceeding for which a decision is not final before Aug. 17, 2006	¶ 2104 Pension Protection Act of 2006
7443B	Retired special trial judges of the Tax Court can be recalled for judicial duty for certain periods	Aug. 17, 2006	¶ 2106 Pension Protection Act of 2006
7451	Tax Court authorization to impose a petition filing fee is broadened to cover any Tax Court petition	Aug. 17, 2006	¶ 2101 Pension Protection Act of 2006
7475(b)	Tax Court may use the annual registration fee on Tax Court practitioners to provide services to pro se taxpayers	Aug. 17, 2006	¶ 2105 Pension Protection Act of 2006
7518(g)(6)(A)	15% maximum tax rate on individuals' nonqualifying withdrawals from Merchant Marine capital gain accounts of capital construction funds (CCFs) is extended for two years	Tax years beginning after Dec. 31, 2008 and before Jan. 1, 2011	¶ 106 Tax Increase Prevention and Reconciliation Act of 2005

Code	Topic	Effective Date	Complete Analysis ¶
7608(c)(6)	IRS's authority to churn income earned from undercover operations is extended through 2007	Date of enactment of the 2006 Tax Relief and Health Care Act	¶ 1412 Tax Provisions of the Tax Relief and Health Care Act of 2006
7623	IRS Whistleblower Office is established to administer whistleblower reward program	Date of enactment of the 2006 Tax Relief and Health Care Act	¶ 1411 Tax Provisions of the Tax Relief and Health Care Act of 2006
7623(a)	Whistleblower rewards are increased, to maximum of 30% (up from 15%) of collected proceeds, interest, penalties, and additional amounts	Information provided on or after date of enactment of the 2006 Tax Relief and Health Care Act	¶ 1409 Tax Provisions of the Tax Relief and Health Care Act of 2006
7623(a)	Whistleblower rewards are increased, to maximum of 30% (up from 15%) of collected proceeds, interest, penalties, and additional amounts	Information provided on or after date of enactment of the 2006 Tax Relief and Health Care Act	¶ 1409 Tax Provisions of the Tax Relief and Health Care Act of 2006
7623(b)	Whistleblower rewards are increased, to maximum of 30% (up from 15%) of collected proceeds, interest, penalties, and additional amounts	Information provided on or after date of enactment of the 2006 Tax Relief and Health Care Act	¶ 1409 Tax Provisions of the Tax Relief and Health Care Act of 2006
7701(a)(47)	Definition of "executor" that applies for estate tax purposes will apply for tax purposes generally, after 2009.	Estates of decedents dying after Dec. 31, 2009	¶ 606 Economic Growth and Tax Relief Reconciliation Act of 2001
7701(a)(49)	Qualified blood collector organizations will be exempted from certain fuel, retail, manufacturers, communications, and highway use excise taxes after 2006	Jan. 1, 2007	¶ 1907 Pension Protection Act of 2006

Code	Topic	Effective Date	Complete Analysis ¶
7701(o)	Definition of convention or association of churches does not preclude individual members	Aug. 17, 2006	¶ 1906 Pension Protection Act of 2006
7702B(e)	Qualified long-term care insurance can be provided as a rider to an annuity contract after 2009	After Dec. 31, 2009	¶ 2402 Pension Protection Act of 2006
7872(g)(6)	Dollar cap on below-market loans made to qualified continuing care facilities temporarily eliminated, and other rules temporarily eased, for years 2006 through 2010	Calendar years beginning after Dec. 31, 2005	¶ 207 Tax Increase Prevention and Reconciliation Act of 2005
7872(h)	Dollar cap on below-market loans made to qualified continuing care facilities temporarily eliminated, and other rules temporarily eased, for years 2006 through 2010	Calendar years beginning after Dec. 31, 2005	¶ 207 Tax Increase Prevention and Reconciliation Act of 2005
7872(h)(4)	Temporary TIPRA amendments that eliminated the dollar cap on below market loans to qualified continuing care facilities, and that eased other rules, are made permanent	Calendar years beginning after Dec. 31, 2005	¶ 108 Tax Provisions of the Tax Relief and Health Care Act of 2006
9812(f)(3)	Mental health parity requirements extended through 2007	Date of enactment of the 2006 Tax Relief and Health Care Act	¶ 402 Tax Provisions of the Tax Relief and Health Care Act of 2006
None	Taxpayers with a tax year ending after 2005 have until Apr. 15, 2007 to make elections under expired provisions that are retroactively extended by the 2006 Tax Relief and Health Care Act	Tax years ending after Dec. 31, 2005 and before date of enactment of the 2006 Tax Relief and Health Care Act	¶ 701 Tax Provisions of the Tax Relief and Health Care Act of 2006

Code	Topic	Effective Date	Complete Analysis ¶
None	25% of qualifying gain from conservation sales of qualifying mineral or geothermal interests excluded from gross income	Sales on or after date of enactment of the 2006 Tax Relief and Health Care Act	¶ 1606 Tax Provisions of the Tax Relief and Health Care Act of 2006
None	25% of qualifying gain from conservation sales of qualifying mineral or geothermal interests excluded from gross income	Sales on or after date of enactment of the 2006 Tax Relief and Health Care Act	¶ 1606 Tax Provisions of the Tax Relief and Health Care Act of 2006
None	EPCRS to remain under IRS control, and focus more on small employer plans	Aug. 17, 2006	¶ 808 Pension Protection Act of 2006
None	One-participant plans with assets of $250,000 or less won't have to file annual returns	Jan. 1, 2007	¶ 908 Pension Protection Act of 2006
None	New simplified annual return filing requirements after 2006 for retirement plans with fewer than 25 employees	Plan years beginning after 2006	¶ 907 Pension Protection Act of 2006
None	Extended amendment period and anti-cutback relief provided for plan changes made to comply with 2006 Pension Act provisions	Aug. 17, 2006	¶ 807 Pension Protection Act of 2006
None	Other provisions	Aug. 17, 2006	¶ 2404 Pension Protection Act of 2006
None	Other provisions	Aug. 17, 2006	¶ 2404 Pension Protection Act of 2006
None	Transitional relief from additional funding requirements for certain bus companies is modified	Plan years beginning after Dec. 31, 2005	¶ 513 Pension Protection Act of 2006
None	Other provisions	Aug. 17, 2006	¶ 2404 Pension Protection Act of 2006

Code	Topic	Effective Date	Complete Analysis ¶
None	Transitional rule for multiemployer plans with a PBGC funding agreement in place before June 30, 2005	Aug. 17, 2006	¶ 609 Pension Protection Act of 2006
None	Extension of amortization periods for multiemployer plans	Plan years beginning after 2007	¶ 604 Pension Protection Act of 2006
None	Exemption from underfunding excise taxes provided to special fishery employer pension plans	Aug. 17, 2006	¶ 610 Pension Protection Act of 2006
None	DOL, IRS, and PBGC to study the effect of the 2006 Pension Act on the operation and funding of multiemployer defined benefit plans	Aug. 17, 2006	¶ 612 Pension Protection Act of 2006
None	Details of special funding rules for multiemployer plans in critical status	For plan years beginning after 2007	¶ 607 Pension Protection Act of 2006
None	New excise tax scheme applies to multiemployer plans in critical or endangered status	For plan years beginning after 2007	¶ 608 Pension Protection Act of 2006
None	Overview of special funding rules for multiemployer plans in endangered or critical status; annual certification by plan actuary; notice requirements	For plan years beginning after 2007	¶ 605 Pension Protection Act of 2006
None	Special funding rules for multiemployer plans in endangered status	For plan years beginning after 2007	¶ 606 Pension Protection Act of 2006
None	DOL, IRS, and PBGC to study the effect of the 2006 Pension Act on the operation and funding of multiemployer defined benefit plans	Aug. 17, 2006	¶ 612 Pension Protection Act of 2006

Code	Topic	Effective Date	Complete Analysis ¶
None	Details of special funding rules for multiemployer plans in critical status	For plan years beginning after 2007	¶ 607 Pension Protection Act of 2006
None	New excise tax scheme applies to multiemployer plans in critical or endangered status	For plan years beginning after 2007	¶ 608 Pension Protection Act of 2006
None	Overview of special funding rules for multiemployer plans in endangered or critical status; annual certification by plan actuary; notice requirements	For plan years beginning after 2007	¶ 605 Pension Protection Act of 2006
None	Special funding rules for multiemployer plans in endangered status	For plan years beginning after 2007	¶ 606 Pension Protection Act of 2006
None	Rules for determining permissible range of interest rates in calculating current funding liability are extended through plan years beginning in 2007	Aug. 17, 2006	¶ 503 Pension Protection Act of 2006
None	Commercial passenger airlines' single-employer pension plans may either cease future benefit accruals and amortize plan liability over 17 years, or amortize their shortfall over 10 years	Plan years ending after Aug. 17, 2006	¶ 512 Pension Protection Act of 2006
None	Investment advice may be provided under 401(k) plans and IRAs, despite conflicts of interest; employers are exempt from fiduciary liability	For investment advice provided by a fiduciary for a fee or other compensation after Dec. 31, 2006	¶ 801 Pension Protection Act of 2006

Code	Topic	Effective Date	Complete Analysis ¶
None	Investment advice may be provided under 401(k) plans and IRAs, despite conflicts of interest; employers are exempt from fiduciary liability	For investment advice provided by a fiduciary for a fee or other compensation after Dec. 31, 2006	¶ 801 Pension Protection Act of 2006
None	Defined contribution plan fiduciaries are not subject to the "safest available annuity standard" when choosing an annuity provider for pension benefit distributions	Aug. 17, 2006	¶ 802 Pension Protection Act of 2006
None	New rules established retroactively for creation of cash balance and other hybrid "applicable defined benefit plans"	Distributions made after Aug. 17, 2006 for periods beginning on or after June 29, 2005	¶ 201 Pension Protection Act of 2006
None	New rules established retroactively for creation of cash balance and other hybrid "applicable defined benefit plans"	Distributions made after Aug. 17, 2006 for periods beginning on or after June 29, 2005	¶ 201 Pension Protection Act of 2006
None	New rules established retroactively for creation of cash balance and other hybrid "applicable defined benefit plans"	Distributions made after Aug. 17, 2006 for periods beginning on or after June 29, 2005	¶ 201 Pension Protection Act of 2006
None	IRS must issue regs applying 2006 Pension Act's applicable defined benefit plan conversion provisions to situations involving mergers and acquisitions	Within 12 months after Aug. 17, 2006	¶ 202 Pension Protection Act of 2006
None	IRA and pension provisions enacted in EGTRRA made "permanent"	Aug. 17, 2006	¶ 301 Pension Protection Act of 2006

Code	Topic	Effective Date	Complete Analysis ¶
None	Governmental plans' reasonable good faith interpretation of RMD rules is enough	Aug. 17, 2006	¶ 1404 Pension Protection Act of 2006
None	Individuals who elected to receive pre-'97 distributions of "applicable amounts" from TEO 457 plans cannot be excluded from participation	Aug. 17, 2006	¶ 1403 Pension Protection Act of 2006
None	IRS directed to issue regs extending to beneficiaries the rules governing hardship withdrawals from 401(k) plans, 403(b) annuities, 457 plans, and nonqualified deferred compensation plans	Within 180 days after Aug. 17, 2006	¶ 1108 Pension Protection Act of 2006
None	IRS to provide for direct payment of tax refunds to IRAs	Tax years beginning after Dec. 31, 2006	¶ 105 Pension Protection Act of 2006
None	Other provisions	Aug. 17, 2006	¶ 2404 Pension Protection Act of 2006
None	Repeal of collapsible corporation provisions is extended two years	Tax years beginning after Dec. 31, 2008 and before Jan. 1, 2011	¶ 505 Tax Increase Prevention and Reconciliation Act of 2005
None	15% accumulated earnings tax rate and 15% personal holding company tax rate are extended two years	Tax years beginning after Dec. 31, 2008 and before Jan. 1, 2011	¶ 504 Tax Increase Prevention and Reconciliation Act of 2005
None	15% maximum tax rate on individuals' nonqualifying withdrawals from Merchant Marine capital gain accounts of capital construction funds (CCFs) is extended for two years	Tax years beginning after Dec. 31, 2008 and before Jan. 1, 2011	¶ 106 Tax Increase Prevention and Reconciliation Act of 2005

Code	Topic	Effective Date	Complete Analysis ¶
None	15% withholding rate that IRS may impose on USRPI gains passed through to foreign persons by U.S. partnerships, trusts or estates is extended for two years	Tax years beginning after Dec. 31, 2008 and before Jan. 1, 2011	¶ 105 Tax Increase Prevention and Reconciliation Act of 2005
None	5% (0% in 2008) and 15% maximum AMT rates on adjusted net capital gain are extended for two years	Tax years beginning after Dec. 31, 2008 and before Jan. 1, 2011	¶ 103 Tax Increase Prevention and Reconciliation Act of 2005
None	5% and 15% adjusted capital gains rates on noncorporate taxpayers' qualified dividend income are extended for two years	Tax years beginning after Dec. 31, 2008 and before Jan. 1, 2011	¶ 107 Tax Increase Prevention and Reconciliation Act of 2005
None	5% and 15% tax rates on adjusted net capital gain are extended for two years	Tax years beginning after Dec. 31, 2008 and before Jan. 1, 2011	¶ 101 Tax Increase Prevention and Reconciliation Act of 2005
None	7% AMT preference percentage for excluded gain on sale of qualified small business stock is extended for two years	Tax years beginning after Dec. 31, 2008 and before Jan. 1, 2011	¶ 104 Tax Increase Prevention and Reconciliation Act of 2005
None	Exclusion of qualified dividend income from investment income for investment interest deduction limit purposes (unless taxpayer elects to include it) is extended for two years	Tax years beginning after Dec. 31, 2008 and before Jan. 1, 2011	¶ 109 Tax Increase Prevention and Reconciliation Act of 2005
None	Long-term capital loss treatment for losses of individuals, trusts, and estates on stock to the extent extraordinary dividends were taxed as capital gains is extended for two years	Tax years beginning after Dec. 31, 2008 and before Jan. 1, 2011	¶ 108 Tax Increase Prevention and Reconciliation Act of 2005

Code	Topic	Effective Date	Complete Analysis ¶
None	Passthrough of qualified dividend income by RICs and REITs is extended for two years	Tax years beginning after Dec. 31, 2008 and before Jan. 1, 2011	¶ 110 Tax Increase Prevention and Reconciliation Act of 2005
None	Passthrough of qualified dividend income by common trust funds is extended for two years	Tax years beginning after Dec. 31, 2008 and before Jan. 1, 2011	¶ 111 Tax Increase Prevention and Reconciliation Act of 2005
None	Passthrough of qualified dividend income by partnerships is extended for two years	Tax years beginning after Dec. 31, 2008 and before Jan. 1, 2011	¶ 112 Tax Increase Prevention and Reconciliation Act of 2005
None	Post-2007 0% tax rate on adjusted net capital gains is extended for two years	Tax years beginning after Dec. 31, 2008 and before Jan. 1, 2011	¶ 102 Tax Increase Prevention and Reconciliation Act of 2005
None	Qualified dividend income treatment for ordinary income on disposition of Code Sec. 306 stock extended for two years	Tax years beginning after Dec. 31, 2008 and before Jan. 1, 2011	¶ 113 Tax Increase Prevention and Reconciliation Act of 2005
None	FSC and ETI binding contract transition rules repealed	Tax years beginning after May 17, 2006	¶ 304 Tax Increase Prevention and Reconciliation Act of 2005
None	Carryover rules for personal credits are redrafted to cover years in which credits are and years in which they aren't allowed against AMT	Tax years beginning after Dec. 31, 2005	¶ 601 Gulf Opportunity Zone and Katrina Emergency Tax Relief Acts of 2005
None	Carryover rules for personal credits are redrafted to cover years in which credits are and years in which they aren't allowed against AMT	Tax years beginning after Dec. 31, 2005	¶ 601 Gulf Opportunity Zone and Katrina Emergency Tax Relief Acts of 2005

Code	Topic	Effective Date	Complete Analysis ¶
None	EGTRRA sunset applicability—10% bracket income levels increase to $7,000 (from $6,000) for singles and marrieds-filing-separate, and to $14,000 (from $12,000) for joint filers, for 2005-2007; 10% income levels adjusted for inflation, annually, for 2004-2010	Tax years beginning after Dec. 31, 2010	¶ 106 Working Families Tax Relief Act of 2004
None	EGTRRA sunset applicability—15% bracket for joint filers increased to twice the single bracket for 2005-2007 to eliminate marriage penalty	Tax years beginning after Dec. 31, 2010	¶ 104 Working Families Tax Relief Act of 2004
None	EGTRRA sunset applicability—Basic standard deduction for joint filers, for 2005 through 2008, increased to 200% of amount for unmarrieds, eliminating marriage penalty	Tax years beginning after Dec. 31, 2010	¶ 105 Working Families Tax Relief Act of 2004
None	EGTRRA sunset applicability—Child tax credit increased to $1,000 per child for 2005 and thereafter	Tax years beginning after Dec. 31, 2010	¶ 201 Working Families Tax Relief Act of 2004
None	EGTRRA sunset applicability—Combat pay counts as earned income in determining refundable child tax credit	Tax years beginning after Dec. 31, 2010	¶ 203 Working Families Tax Relief Act of 2004

Code	Topic	Effective Date	Complete Analysis ¶
None	EGTRRA sunset applicability—Increase in the refundable child tax credit to 15% (from 10%) of earned income in excess of threshold amount accelerated to 2004 (from 2005)	Tax years beginning after Dec. 31, 2010	¶ 202 Working Families Tax Relief Act of 2004
None	EGTRRA sunset applicability—AMT exemption amount of $40,250 for unmarrieds, $58,000 for joint filers, continued for 2005	Tax years beginning after Dec. 31, 2010	¶ 101 Working Families Tax Relief Act of 2004
None	EGTRRA sunset applicability—Taxpayers may elect to treat combat pay as earned income for purposes of earned income credit before 2006	Tax years beginning after Dec. 31, 2010	¶ 213 Working Families Tax Relief Act of 2004
None	2001 EGTRRA sunset of reduction of tax rates for top four brackets	Tax years beginning after Dec. 31, 2010	¶ 202 Jobs and Growth Tax Relief Reconciliation Act of 2003
None	Sunset of reduction of 10%/8% and 20%/18% maximum AMT rates on adjusted net capital gains to 5% (0% in 2008) and 15%	Tax years beginning after Dec. 31, 2008	¶ 103 Jobs and Growth Tax Relief Reconciliation Act of 2003
None	Sunset of reduction of 10%/8% and 20%/18% tax rates on adjusted net capital gain to 5% and 15% for most net capital gain taken into account after May 5, 2003	Tax years beginning after Dec. 31, 2008	¶ 101 Jobs and Growth Tax Relief Reconciliation Act of 2003
None	Sunset of reduction of 5% tax rate on adjusted net capital gains to 0% for tax years beginning in 2008	Tax years beginning after Dec. 31, 2008	¶ 102 Jobs and Growth Tax Relief Reconciliation Act of 2003

Code	Topic	Effective Date	Complete Analysis ¶
None	Sunset of reduction of AMT preference for excluded gain on sale of qualified small business stock from 28% (or 42%) to 7% for stock disposed of after May 5, 2003	Tax years beginning after Dec. 31, 2008	¶ 104 Jobs and Growth Tax Relief Reconciliation Act of 2003
None	Sunset of reduction of accumulated earnings tax and personal holding company tax rates to 15%	Tax years beginning after Dec. 31, 2008	¶ 401 Jobs and Growth Tax Relief Reconciliation Act of 2003
None	Sunset of repeal of collapsible corporation rules	Tax years beginning after Dec. 31, 2008	¶ 403 Jobs and Growth Tax Relief Reconciliation Act of 2003
None	Sunset of individual's treatment of loss on stock as long-term capital loss to the extent extraordinary dividends were taxed as capital gains	Tax years beginning after Dec. 31, 2008	¶ 108 Jobs and Growth Tax Relief Reconciliation Act of 2003
None	Sunset of reduction in maximum tax rate on individuals' nonqualifying withdrawals from Merchant Marine capital gain accounts of capital construction funds (CCFs)	Tax years beginning after Dec. 31, 2008	¶ 106 Jobs and Growth Tax Relief Reconciliation Act of 2003
None	Sunset of taxation of noncorporate taxpayers' qualified dividend income at favorable adjusted net capital gains rates, rather than ordinary income rates	Tax years beginning after Dec. 31, 2008	¶ 107 Jobs and Growth Tax Relief Reconciliation Act of 2003
None	Sunset of treatment of ordinary income on disposition of Code Sec. 306 stock as qualified dividend income	Tax years beginning after Dec. 31, 2008	¶ 113 Jobs and Growth Tax Relief Reconciliation Act of 2003

Code	Topic	Effective Date	Complete Analysis ¶
None	Sunset of pass through of qualified dividend income by RICs and REITs	Tax years beginning after Dec. 31, 2008	¶ 110 Jobs and Growth Tax Relief Reconciliation Act of 2003
None	Sunset of pass through of qualified dividend income by common trust funds	Tax years beginning after Dec. 31, 2008	¶ 111 Jobs and Growth Tax Relief Reconciliation Act of 2003
None	Sunset of pass through of qualified dividend income by partnerships	Tax years beginning after Dec. 31, 2008	¶ 112 Jobs and Growth Tax Relief Reconciliation Act of 2003
None	Sunset of exclusion of qualified dividend income from investment income for purposes of investment interest deduction limit	Tax years beginning after Dec. 31, 2008	¶ 109 Jobs and Growth Tax Relief Reconciliation Act of 2003
None	Sunset of reduction in withholding rate that IRS may impose on USRPI gains passed through to foreign persons by U.S. partnerships, trusts or estates	Tax years beginning after Dec. 31, 2008	¶ 105 Jobs and Growth Tax Relief Reconciliation Act of 2003
None	2001 Act provisions sunset and won't apply to tax, plan, or limitation years beginning after Dec. 31, 2010; Estate, gift and transfer tax provisions sunset and won't apply to estates of decedents dying, gifts made, or generation skipping transfers, after Dec. 31, 2010	Tax, plan, or limitation years beginning after Dec. 31, 2010, or, in the case of Title V of the 2001 Act relating to estate, gift, and generation skipping transfer taxes, estates of decedents dying, gifts made, or generation skipping transfers, after Dec. 31, 2010	¶ 701 Economic Growth and Tax Relief Reconciliation Act of 2001

INDEX

References are to paragraph numbers